Diversity and Affirmative Action in Public Service

ASPA Classics

Conceived and sponsored by the American Society for Public Administration (ASPA), the ASPA Classics series will publish volumes on topics that have been, and continue to be, central to the contemporary development of public administration. The ASPA Classics are intended for classroom use, and may be quite suitable for libraries and general reference collections. Drawing from the *Public Administration Review (PAR)* and other journals related to the ASPA sections, each volume in the series is edited by a scholar who is charged with presenting a thorough and balanced perspective on an enduring issue. These journals now represent some six decades of collective wisdom. Yet, many of the writings collected in the ASPA Classics might not otherwise easily come to the attention of future public managers. Given the explosion in research and writing on all aspects of public administration in recent decades, these ASPA Classics anthologies should point readers to definitive or groundbreaking authors whose voices should not be lost in the cacophony of the newest administrative technique or invention.

Public servants carry out their responsibilities in a complex, multi-dimensional environment. The mission of ASPA Classics is to provide the reader with a historical and first hand view of the development of the topic at hand. As such, each ASPA Classics volume presents the most enduring scholarship, often in complete, or nearly complete, original form on the given topic. Each volume will be devoted to a specific continuing concern to the administration of all public sector programs. Early volumes in the series address public sector performance, public service as commitment, and diversity and affirmative action in public service. Future volumes will include equally important dialogues on classic ideas as enduring ideas, reinventing government, public budgeting, and public service ethics.

The volume editors are to be commended for volunteering for the substantial task of compiling and editing these unique collections of articles which might not otherwise be readily available to scholars, teachers, and students.

Books in This Series

Diversity and Affirmative Action in Public Service

edited by

Walter D. Broadnax

American University

Routledge
Taylor & Francis Group
New York London

An ASPA Classics Volume

First published 2000 by Westview Press

Published 2019 by Routledge
52 Vanderbilt Avenue, New York, NY 10017
2 Park Square, Milton Park, Abingdon, Oxon OX14 4RN

First issued in hardback 2019

Routledge is an imprint of the Taylor & Francis Group, an informa business

Library of Congress Cataloging-in-Publication Data
   Diversity and affirmative action in public service/edited by Walter D. Broadnax.
      p. cm.—(ASPA classics)
   Includes bibliographical references and index.
   ISBN 0-8133-6691-7 (hc.)—ISBN 0-8133-6690-9 (pbk.)
   1. Diversity in the workplace.   2. Affirmative action programs.   3. Civil service—Minority employment.   I. Broadnax, Walter D.   II. Series.
HF5549.5.M5 D55 1999
331.13'3'0973—dc21   99-048881

ISBN 13: 978-0-367-31542-9 (hbk)
ISBN 13: 978-0-8133-6690-6 (pbk)

CONTENTS

ILLUSTRATIONS

Tables

Figures

INTRODUCTION

As readers examine this volume, they will discover that there are five sections and the subject matter ranges from a discussion of representative bureaucracy and equal employment opportunity to aging and disabilities as an important aspect of diversity and affirmative action in the United States. Each section provides a somewhat different perspective on the subject of differences, particularly differences found in a public service context. However, the themes of equal opportunity, diversity, and affirmative action run through each chapter and take on their own nuance in relation to the overall theme—strategies for inclusion of those seeking greater entry or access to active participation in the American public service.

The study of public administration is a relatively young enterprise, having only emerged within the political science literature near the turn of the century.[1] The literature began to develop and accumulate until in 1939 the *Public Administration Review (PAR)* was founded. Since that time the field has continued to grow and develop. However, when one looks closely at the many and varied contributions published in this important journal, one finds that a quite small number of articles have been devoted to race, ethnicity, gender, or differences in general. This fact begs the question: Should one be surprised by the relatively small number of scholarly products presented in this particular forum between 1939 and 1999? Well, probably not, because we must remember that it has only been roughly forty years since segregation was declared illegal.[2] Therefore, on the one hand, it only makes sense that the number of contributions might be smaller for this specific domain. On the other hand, the subject of race and differences has captured a substantial amount of our national psychic energy. And yet, it seems to occupy such a small part of the scholarly materials produced between the inception of *PAR* and now. One hint as to why may be found in the number of minorities pursuing scholarship in this policy and management arena as well as the discomfort the subject often causes, still, in polite society within our country today.

Diversity, race, and gender are words that elicit for most Americans images of struggle, strife, and even violence. Whether we are talking about the antebellum South or the desegregation of Central High School in Little Rock, Arkansas, ending discrimination has been a long and difficult struggle, and too often that struggle has been etched with violence. However, it was out of a violent period in our history that the subject of African Americans in public service emerged as a serious topic of discussion and scholarship.

As Americans sat in front of their television sets in 1957 watching the mobs trying to deny black children seats in an all-white school, many began to realize that something needed to be done to prevent these kinds of eruptions from occurring on a regular basis. But even with the anxiety created by the desegregation of our schools in the 1950s and early 1960s, not until the Watts riots of 1964, the Detroit riots of 1967, and the riots that followed Dr. Martin Luther King's assassination in 1968 was there a rallying cry demanding that something must be done.

The desire to make America more inclusive took on new meaning during the late 1960s and early 1970s. The idea that society was pulling itself apart was widely accepted. Between what came to be called the Civil Rights Movement and the war in Vietnam, our streets were too often filled with rioters, looters, and other forms of dissident behavior. But public action was required to do something about the situation. In Little Rock, we saw the police and then the National Guard facilitating the desegregation of Central High School, and public sector intervention was required to quell riots in Los Angeles, Detroit, Washington, D.C., and numerous other cities across the land. With each intervention, it became increasingly clear that in order for our public service to be fully effective as well as perceived as being fair, it would have to include people of color —that is, it would have to diversify.

As the literature in this volume indicates, the earlier discussions of equal employment and affirmative action were primarily about African Americans. However, over time, we see the prominent addition of women to the discussion (1972) and other groups as well. What had been a fairly tightly focused analysis and debate increasingly became more complex, now including gender, disabilities, sexual orientation, and ethnicity, thus more broadly defining discrimination than ever before. But in all of these cases, one of the challenges was how to increase the number of blacks and others in public sector (public service) jobs. If the government was going to lead the way, then the government must itself become more diverse. This was particularly true if it was going to incorporate the private sector in the initiative and begin to monitor its results.

The early debate focused on whether blacks had some special or particular claim to public sector employment or whether they had any particular claim to employment in any sector beyond merit (employment test scores, university degrees, experience, etc.). The selection of articles for this volume reflects this debate and the struggle that early on was between notions of diversity, fairness, inclusiveness, equal employment opportunity, and affirmative action. Yes, there were some issues that needed to be addressed regarding discrimination, but beyond ceasing to discriminate, what was the government's responsibility, and how could discrimination regarding a particular group be resolved affirmatively without tramping upon those all important individual rights? We will see here that these were the challenges then (forty years ago), and they are the challenges now.

As one tries to ascertain where we have been and where we may be going regarding affirmative action, one sees that the courts have progressively begun to attack the scope of acceptable federal as well as state affirmative action programs. In *Adarand v. Pena,* the Supreme Court applied to federal actions the standard already binding on states and localities: Programs must serve a "compelling" interest and must be "narrowly tailored." Furthermore, the court has indicated that even when a compelling interest is found, race-based methods are permitted only after race-neutral methods are considered and found wanting. With *Podberesky v. Kirwan,* the Fourth U.S. Circuit Court of Appeals struck down a University of Maryland scholarship program restricted to African Americans, and in 1997 the Fifth Circuit rejected an admissions procedure at the University of Texas Law School that divided applicants into two groups—first, blacks and Mexican-Americans, and second, all others—and then applied different admission standards to the two groups. In *Hopwood v. Texas,* the court held that the law school's interest in diversity did not constitute a "compelling state interest" and that the school could not take race into account in any form in its admission process.[3]

At first blush, the record might appear to be one in which affirmative action, particularly where applied to achieve diversity, is quickly losing its appeal as well as its social, political, and legal currency. If this is true, the seeds for the demise of affirmative action may have been sewn long ago. Looking at the various contributions to this volume, we find that save for Levine, Lovell, Nigro, Herbert, Dorn, and Hunt the support for affirmative action is generally articulated in a somewhat guarded, if not negative, fashion. And even where there is strong support for particular initiatives, one finds a degree of guardedness in the overall position. The guardedness to some extent may be explained by the following quotation from William A. Galston: "The history of the affirmative action debate confirms that we can neither avoid nor fully erase the tension between equal opportunity and personal liberty."[4]

Galston's admonition effectively sums up the tensions that the reader will discover between and among various of the offerings included here. Moreover, these tensions are representative of the stresses and strains found in the literature on this subject, regardless of the particular academic or professional domain. Therefore, we should not be surprised to find these pressures and fissures when examining diversity and affirmative action in the public service.

Turning to the overall structure of the book, it was necessary, from my point of view, to include several symposia in their entirety. The thought of selecting one or two pieces from each symposium certainly presented itself as a reasonable approach. However, the decision to include the full treatment of each symposium selected was made to give the reader a fuller flavor of the tensions at play during the time in which the articles were generated. Rather than look much more broadly and well beyond the major currents found within the field of public administration, these selected pieces provide a rather clear picture of what the issues were and are. In addition, they provide insights regarding those ideas upon which the debate turned, and turns today.

As articulated earlier, this collection of essays will provide the reader with a lucid picture of where we have been and to some extent where we might be headed in terms of affirmative action and diversity in the public service. Only in the Stillman piece (presented later in this volume) do we see clearly the anxiety and even pessimism about whether there is some hope of changing the attitudes and behaviors of those who currently dominate the system. According to Stillman, the notions of integration, diversification, equality, and power sharing were and would probably remain anathema to those already in charge—white males.

Although race and gender represent only two of the five sections in this book, arguably they are the dominant themes cross-cutting this enterprise, and they undergird the discussions of representative bureaucracy, aging, and disability as well as diversity. Said differently, the "beef" here is found in the discussions of race and gender and how they inform those more collateral discussions related to equal employment opportunity and affirmative action.

The foregoing discussion provides insights into the early concerns, challenges, and opportunities regarding equal employment opportunity and affirmative action. We see that many of the central concerns and tensions evinced in the late 1960s and early 1970s remain important to the discussion and debate today. Always, it seems that the challenge has been one of trying to open up the public service so that it could become more inclusive, where minorities believe that the process as well as the outcome are fair and where the majority or those not benefiting directly from such affirmative efforts feel that they are not being unduly disadvantaged by the process or the outcome. The goal, while worthwhile, has remained somewhat elusive because of our inability to satisfy the concerns of the many who would not become direct beneficiaries of such actions. It is also fair to point out that although there are problems that must be overcome in the aging and disabilities arena, they do not seem to be quite as challenging for the agents of change as are those concerns related more specifically to race and gender.

Given the context and forces that produced early efforts to diversify the public service, it is important for us to look at least briefly at the context that seems to be emerging today. Earlier in this introduction, the evolution of the court's position on affirmative action and diversity was sketched out. As one examines that sketch, it is relatively clear that an anti-affirmative action posture is emerging in the courts, even in the face of discrimination or continued discrimination. It appears that there is an increasingly strong desire to limit as much as possible the use of affirmative action mechanisms in the effort to diversify the public service. This is also the case for other institutions and organizations, such as public colleges and universities, which in many instances are dedicated to the preparation of individuals for the public service. The drive to limit is spreading.

From a more socio-political point of view, the nation is having to address the existence of skinheads, who subscribe openly to Nazism and racial and religious hatred.

Such groups have been connected to various firebombings, beatings, and harassment of individuals across the country. The state of Wyoming, partially in response to the death of an openly gay college student who died at the hands of members of a particular hate group, is attempting to pass major hate crimes legislation.

On yet another front, Conservative Citizens Councils (CCCs) are asserting themselves in the name of white power and the need for whites to have organizations willing to very aggressively defend the rights and privileges of white citizens. This group has evolved out of the old White Citizen Councils, which were formed in response to the Civil Rights Movement in the south. It appears that the goals of these two groups are very much the same; however, the current CCCs are much more tactful and mindful of the media than their predecessor organizations ever were. The goal is to turn the nation away from the matter of diversity (some of the CCCs might say mongrelization) in America. The argument being made by these groups is that whites built this country. Therefore, it is their country over which to hold dominion and they should and will decide what is the proper role and place in society for people of color, gays, women, and so on. But again, the overriding concerns seem to focus on racial differences, although there remains substantial amounts of religious and other forms of bigotry.

Again the question may be asked, is this debate and all of its attendant tensions about merit, efficiency, and economy, or is it in essence a struggle that revolves around race? Although it may be somewhat unpopular to say so, most serious-thinking Americans realize that this debate is primarily about race and the use of various mechanisms designed to change the racial mix within our institutions and organizations. In 1954 we were discussing integration at "all deliberate speed," and in 1999 we are discussing inclusiveness within the society and its institutions based mostly on one criterion—merit. Again, merit as defined in fairly narrow kinds of ways, for example, test scores, IQ scores, employment examinations, entrance examinations, and so on.[5] The point here is that merit, if more broadly defined, could become an instrument for greater inclusion rather than an instrument of exclusion. Exclusion effectively lowers minority influence in our commerce, governance, and daily national life.[6]

When you examine where we are and from whence we have come, there is an important constant that is rarely discussed. That constant is that the more progress that is made (verifiable progress), the more tension that seems to be produced in reaction to the successes realized and experienced. The model seems to hold, except when applied to the United States military. Here the goal of critical mass seems to have been reached. There are now enough minorities and women emerging in leadership roles that the institution seems to have seriously evolved such that these changes are now somewhat securely embedded in the overall military organizational fabric. However, in far many other places, the traditional response has all too often been: "We have our minority person (token), and there is no need to look further—we have done it. Now, on with the show."

As Lichtenberg and Luban point out, fairness is an important value too.[7] It is in my view an important thing to remember when discussing affirmative action and diversity or equal employment opportunity. The goal should be to change in a direction that takes us away from discrimination and what becomes virtually single race dominance and exclusivity in the conduct of public affairs. This is an important goal and should not be lost sight of in the swirling debate.

Before closing this introduction, it is very important to observe that in the 1960s and 1970s, there were few people of color contributing to *PAR* and to the public administration literature, broadly defined. There were also very few women. Today there are many more women (not enough, but many more), and to a lesser extent there are more analysts and practitioners who are people of color—more, but still not yet enough to begin to tip the scales toward substantial change in what is being discussed and how it is being discussed within our field.

Where symposia are included, look to them for a bit of depth in regard to a particular aspect of the larger subject of diversity and affirmative action in the public service. As mentioned earlier, they are there to make the picture as clear as possible.

Again, the reader will find the articles included here useful in terms of gaining an historical perspective and an understanding of the enduring nature of the challenges we continue to face regarding equal employment opportunities for all in America's public service.

Notes

1. Two of the seminal works often cited regarding the emergence of public administration as an academic enterprise in the United States are: Woodrow Wilson, "The Study of Administration," *Political Science Quarterly*, June 1887, and Frank J. Goodnow, *Politics and Administration* (New York: Mcmillan, 1900).

2. The Supreme Court decision *Brown v. Topeka Board of Education*, 1954, was the landmark case that declared that separate but equal no longer would be the law of the land. Prior to this court ruling, African Americans, women, and other minorities were relatively invisible in many aspects of mainstream society, including the academy.

3. See William A. Galston, "Affirmative Action Status Report: Evidence and Options," *Report from the Institute for Philosophy and Public Policy: Special Issue*, Winter/Spring 1997.

4. Ibid., p. 9.

5. The famous 1971 *Griggs v. Duke Power* originally challenged examination processes and procedures that effectively barred African American workers from hiring and promotion opportunities. Therefore, there is uneasiness in certain quarters of society when merit becomes narrowly defined as one's score on an examination that may have little relevance to the job or position in question.

6. The *Hopwood v. Texas* decision and the passage of the California Civil Rights Initiative have both been credited with a precipitous decline in university enrollments at the University of Texas and the University of California.

7. See Judith Lichtenberg and David Luben, "The Merits of Merit," *Report from the Institute for Philosophy and Public Policy: Special Issue*, Winter/Spring 1997.

Part One

Representative Bureaucracy and Equal Employment Opportunity

The first section of this book begins with a selection of essays that discuss the concepts of representative bureaucracy and equal employment opportunity. Each of the authors wrestles with the notions of merit, equity, and efficiency within the practice and to a lesser extent, the study of American public administration. As you read each of these pieces, it will become clear that to some degree all of the writers perceive that the level of inclusiveness found in public sector occupations and organizations rests below what many in society found to be acceptable.

Frederickson's essay leads off this section by indicating that in American public administration, the watchwords have traditionally been efficiency (getting the most service for the available dollar) and economy (providing an agreed-upon level of service for the fewest possible dollars). For several decades, issues of equity and justice were not central to public servants or to public administration theorists. To remedy what he views as inadequate in both thought and practice, Frederickson develops a theory of social equity and puts it forward as the third pillar for public administration. He argues that social equity should hold the same status as the values of economy and efficiency in public administration. After exploring the theoretical and philosophical developments of equity, his article reviews the role of the courts and the law in developing social equity. The essay makes clear that historically speaking, the courts have been the venue of last resort for issues of inequality, disparate treatment, and the unequal provision of services. The author also highlights the importance of employment law in mitigating inequalities occurring in both the public and private sectors. Ultimately, Frederickson suggests that public servants are tasked to balance the needs of efficiency and economy along with the demands of fairness and equality.

In his article on social equity in public service, McGregor explores the conflict found in the two social equity doctrines often debated in public affairs. He points out that each of the camps, the equity camp and the merit camp, claims to be consistent with principles of justice and democracy, and each criticizes the other for undermining those principles. The essay explores the effects of this conflict and the potential impact of its possible resolution on civil service employment in the United States. The author, primarily concerned with the politics of the struggle to define social equity in the public service, begins by analyzing the history of civil service and the development of the merit concept. He then takes a close look at federal policy toward resolving problems of modern social equity. It is this analysis that enables McGregor to conclude that it is the courts, and not the executive nor the legislative branches of government, that have been the driving force behind social equity. The Supreme Court's decision in *Griggs v. Duke Power* substantiates this point because it determined the establishment of the Doctrine of Job Relatedness—which stipulates that employers can no longer measure and rank applicants in the abstract, but only with regard to their ability to perform a given job. It was through this vehicle that the forceful use of the consent decree to mandate certain hiring targets with firm timetables in place first surfaced as a remedy. The essay's inclusion of tables charting the progress (much of which has been driven by the courts) made by minorities and women into higher-level jobs (within civilian federal employment between 1965 and 1971) clearly makes his point. Finally, the author suggests that there are many ways to measure the excellence desired in the public service and that the social equity doctrine requires that the basis for judging people be pluralistic.

Nachmias and Rosenbloom in their piece acknowledge that the concept of representative bureaucracy is unclear and ambiguous. They point out that the usefulness of such terminology is limited by the tendency to fail to specify the exact meaning of "representation." The authors set out to overcome some of this ambiguity by suggesting a new way of measuring integration within bureaucracies and other organizational structures. The measure, called the Measure of Variation, quantifies the degree of integration within the organizational unit as a whole. The strength of this measure lies in its sensitivity to the degree of social integration in different organizations and organizational levels. Their essay offers a point-in-time perspective of the variance found in the degree of integration in the General Schedule (GS) work forces of federal agencies in 1970, as well as a finding that the degree of integration in the GS is inversely associated with grade level (i.e., the higher the grade level, the less integration). By embracing a more empirically based approach to the issue of equal employment opportunity, the authors hope to avoid much of the confusion and debate as to whether a particular organization had a representative work force or not. Using their measuring scheme, it could be accurately measured.

Looking at the first of Lewis's two articles, we see that he focuses on the progress made toward racial and sexual equality in the federal civil service during the 1980s. Using published data on the federal workforce in GS and GS-equivalent (white-collar) pay systems, Lewis examines the impact of the Reagan administration's policies on progress toward racial and sexual equality. Despite Reagan's rejection of the statistical evidence of what constituted continued patterns of discrimination and his strong rhetoric and posture against affirmative action, Lewis concludes that women and minorities continued to make progress toward greater representation in the workforce and more equal job rewards, such as salary, throughout the decade between 1976 and 1986. In his second article, he examines entry levels and advancement rates during the first eight years of the federal careers of white and minority males and females who entered civil service shortly after finishing school between 1973 and 1982. After reviewing the data, he concludes that white males were doing much better than women and minorities at the critical early stage of their careers. During the time frame evaluated, white males entered more desirable occupations through higher grades and experienced greater upward mobility in the first few years of their careers. The author indicates that the level and type of education were found to be the most significant factors with regard to initial career placement. Interestingly, where these two factors were comparable, there was little difference in the initial placement of white males, minorities, and women. The advancement patterns studied indicated that among those entering the GS shortly after school (e.g., within three years), race did not play a major role. The findings were less compelling for employees who waited at least four years after school before entering the GS.

The last contribution selected for this section focusing on representation and equal employment opportunity spotlights the United States military and its progress to date in dealing successfully with race within the ranks.

Stillman begins his 1974 article on racial unrest in the military by discussing two of the numerous racially motivated incidents occurring during the late 1960s and early 1970s. After describing the incidents, he turns his focus to the Department of Defense's (DOD's) attempts to deal with racial unrest, particularly as related to the distribution of nonwhite personnel within the various grades and ranks in the department, off-based housing, and the military system of justice. Stillman boldly provides some predictions about expected trends regarding black-white relationships within the U.S. armed forces. He proffers that although he believes that there will be continued pressure on the military to make positive steps toward achieving equality of opportunity for minorities in the military, ultimately, he is not very optimistic about blacks' chances of being able to rise through the ranks successfully and to take on greater responsibilities. He believes this is particularly true with respect to those positions that have been traditionally dominated and controlled by white males. Overall, the author found it difficult to quantify the experiences of blacks in the armed services and also seemed to be resigned to an acceptance of the status quo, that is, those in control will maintain that control.

Frederickson begins the section with a very optimistic piece and Stillman ends it with a rather pessimistic assessment of how successful the military establishment would be in its efforts to further integrate, create a representative workforce, and make equal employment opportunity a meaningful concept therein.

The issues and conflicts raised in this section are still being debated and discussed. The issues of merit, equity, representation, and equal employment opportunity: How will we recognize them when we see them and how do we get from here to there without pulling the society apart? The authors then and now provide the reader with a good sense of what was on the table and to a great extent remains on the table today.

1

PUBLIC ADMINISTRATION AND SOCIAL EQUITY

H. George Frederickson

In 1968 a theory of social equity was developed and put forward as the "third pillar" for public administration, with the same status as economy and efficiency as values or principles to which public administration should adhere. Considerable progress has been made in social equity in the past 20 years. Theoretically, the works of Rawls and Rae and associates provide a language and a road map for understanding the complexity of the subject. The courts were especially supportive of principles of social equity in the later years of Chief Justice Earl Warren and during the years of Chief Justice Warren Burger. The present period, marked by the leadership of William Rehnquist, evidences a significant drawing back from the earlier commitment to equity. The decisions of state courts, based upon state constitutions and the common law, hold considerable promise for advancing social equity principles. Scholarly research demonstrates the belief of the American people in fairness, justice, and equality and their recognition of the complexity of the subject and their ambivalence toward competing claims for equality. Research on public administration finds that bureaucratic decision rules and the processes of policy implementation tend to favor principles of social equity.

It was 1968. Inequality and injustice, especially based on race, was pervasive. A government built on a Constitution claiming the equal protection of the laws had failed in that promise. Public administrators, those who daily operate the government, were not without responsibility. Both in theory and practice public administration had, beginning in the 1940s, emphasized concepts of decision making,

Source: *Public Administration Review* 50 (March/April 1990): 228–237.

systems analysis, operations research or management science, and rationality. In running the government the administrator's job was to be efficient (getting the most service possible for available dollars) or economical (providing an agreed-upon level of services for the fewest possible dollars). It should be no surprise, therefore, that issues of inequity and injustice were not central to public servants or to public administration theorists.

To remedy what seemed a glaring inadequacy in both thought and practice, I developed a theory of social equity and put it forward as the "third pillar" for public administration, holding the same status as economy and efficiency as values or principles to which public administration should adhere. The initial reasoning went this way:

> To say that a service may be well managed and that a service may be efficient and economical, still begs these questions: Well managed for whom? Efficient for whom? Economical for whom? We have generally assumed in public administration a convenient oneness with the public. We have not focused our attention or concern to the issue of variations in social and economic conditions. It is of great convenience, both theoretically and practically, to assume that citizen A is the same as citizen B and that they both receive public services in equal measure. This assumption may be convenient, but it is obviously both illogical and empirically inaccurate.[1]

Social equity began as a challenge to the adequacy of concepts of efficiency and economy as guides for public administration. In time social equity took on a broader meaning.

> Social equity is a phrase that comprehends an array of value preferences, organizational design preferences, and management style preferences. Social equity emphasizes equality in government services. Social equity emphasizes responsibility for decisions and program implementation for public managers. Social equity emphasizes change in public management. Social equity emphasizes responsiveness to the needs of citizens rather than the needs of public organizations. Social equity emphasizes an approach to the study of and education for public administration that is interdisciplinary, applied, problem solving in character, and sound theoretically.[2]

The development of the concept of social equity was followed by a considerable literature both pro and con. Philosophically the views ranged from social equity as providing the proper normative basis for a new public administration on the one hand to social equity as an attempt by some to "steal popular sovereignty" on the other.[3] Researchers, especially in the public policy fields, began to analyze variations in the distribution of public service by income, race, and neighborhood, and eventually by gender. The concept of equity was included in the first adopted Principles for the American Society for Public Administration (ASPA), which later became the Code of Ethics. In 1981, the *ASPA Professional Standards and Ethics Workbook and Study Guide for Public Administrators,* in the section on professional ethics, listed as the first two Principles to be the pursuit of equality, which is to say citizen A being equal to citizen B, and equity, which is to say adjusting shares so that citizen A is made equal with citizen B.[4]

In the past 20 years the phrase social equity has taken its place as a descriptor for variables in the analytic constructs of researchers in the field, as a concept in the philosophy of public administration, and as a guide for ethical behavior for public servants. With the passage of 20 years and the attendant advantages of hindsight, some stock taking is called for, and the Golden Anniversary of the *Public Administration Review* is an appropriate occasion for this reflection.

This review of the place of social equity in public administration begins, as it should, with philosophical and theoretical developments. That is followed by a consideration of the especially important relationship between social equity and the law and what has transpired in the last generation. Following that, developments in analysis and research are reviewed.

Philosophical and Theoretical Developments

Public administration, it has been said, is the marriage of the arts and sciences of government to the arts and sciences of management.[5] Efficiency and economy are primarily theories of management while social equity is primarily a theory of government. In the early years of modern American public administration the marriage, particularly in the conceptions of Woodrow Wilson, was balanced.[6] Theories of business efficiency were routinely mixed with theories of democratic government, the argument being that a government can and should be efficient and fair. However, by the 1950s the marriage was dominated by management theories and issues, having begged questions of equity and fairness. Even though it was and is generally agreed that public administration is part of the political process, there was little interest in developing specifics regarding the ends to which politics and public administration could be put.

In the early years it was also the conventional wisdom that public administration was neutral and only marginally involved in policy making. Under those conditions it is possible to ignore social equity. Now the theology holds that public administration is a part or form of politics, that it often exercises leadership in the policy process, and that neutrality is next to impossible. If that is the case, then it is not logically possible to dismiss social equity as a suggested guide for administrative action, equal to economy and efficiency.

Initial attempts to return to the marriage questions of equity and fairness were simplistic and superficial. Willbern, in his splendid review of the early literature on social equity and the so-called new public administration, observed that critics were "not very precise in defining the goals or values toward which administration and knowledge must be arrived."[7] He concluded that:

> Those who wanted to challenge the "system" and the "establishment" on grounds of
> social equity have met with a good many rebuffs and even evidence of backlash. But

it would probably be a great mistake to dismiss these essays as an expression of a passing mood, an articulation of the particular times in which they were written. On intellectual, analytical grounds, there is something of value and consequence here, a real addition to our faulty and inadequate understanding of human behavior in administrative situations.[8]

So the task was clear, social equity needed flesh on its bones if it was to be taken seriously as a third pillar for public administration. The process was begun with a symposium on "Social Equity and Public Administration," which appeared in the *Public Administration Review* in 1974. In an especially important way, that symposium is illustrative of theory building in public administration.

First, the subject is parsed, in this case, into considerations of social equity: (1) as the basis for a just, democratic society; (2) as influencing the behavior of organization man; (3) as the legal basis for distributing public services; (4) as the practical basis for distributing public services; (5) as operationalized in compound federalism; and, (6) as a challenge for research and analysis.[9]

Second, the subject having been taken apart, good theory building suggests putting it back together. Looking back, it is now clear that considerable progress has been made in thinking about, understanding, and applying various parts of the subject. But it has yet to be put back together.

Third is the arduous task of definition. In this case, it was appropriate to turn to the theories of distributive justice for definition. The phrase social equity and the word equality were essentially without definition in the field. As Rae and his associates have said: "Equality is the simplest and most abstract of notions, yet the practices of the world are irremediably concrete and complex. How, imaginably, could the former govern the latter?"[10] Yet, social equity was advanced in the 1960s and 1970s as an essential third pillar of public administration.

When ideas such as social equity or the public interest or liberty are suggested as guides for public action, the most compelling definitions are often the most abstract. And so it was in this case. The initial attempts to define social equity as it applies to public administration were fastened to John Rawls' *A Theory of Justice.*[11] The Rawlsian construct as an ideal type addresses the distribution of rights, duties, and advantages in a just society. Justice, to Rawls, is fairness. To achieve fairness the first principle is that each person is guaranteed equal basic liberties consistent with an extensive system of liberty for all. The second principle calls for social and economic inequalities to be managed so that they are of greatest benefit to the least advantaged (the difference principle); it seeks to make offices and positions open to all under conditions of *fair* equality of opportunity.

For much of the last two decades perspectives on Rawlsian justice have occupied the intellectual high ground of concern for social equity. While philosophical and scholarly interest in Rawlsian theory has been strong, and certainly the objectives of fairness through justice are compatible with the social equity perspective on public administration, the theory has thus far been of limited use in the busy world of government.

This analysis turns, then, to a more descriptive theory for both greater definition and more likely applicability to the theories and practices of public administration. Following Douglas Rae and associates, a rudimentary language and a road map are set forth for the notion of equality, with attendant definitions and examples.[12] I label this the Compound Theory of Social Equity. This Compound Theory serves as the basis for later considerations of legal and research perspectives on social equity in public administration.

Simple Individual Equalities

Individual equality consists of one class of equals, and one relationship of equality holds among them. The best examples would be one person-one vote and the price mechanism of the market, which offers a Big Mac or a Whopper at a specific price to whomever wishes to buy. The Golden Rule or Immanuel Kant's Categorical Imperative are formulas for individual equalities.

Segmented Equality

Any complex society with a division of labor tends to practice segmented equality. Farmers have a different system of taxation than do business owners, and both differ from wage earners. In segmented equality, one assumes that equality exists within the category (e.g., farmers) and that inequality exists between the segments. All forms of hierarchy use the concept of segmented equality. All five-star generals are equal to each other as are all privates first-class. Equal pay for equal work is segmented equality. Segmented equality is, in fact, systematic or structured inequality. Segmented equality is critically important for public policy and administration because virtually every public service is delivered on a segmented basis and always by segmented hierarchies.

Block Equalities

Both simple individual and segmented equalities are in fact individual equalities. Block equalities, on the other hand, call for equality *between* groups or subclasses. The railroad accommodations for Blacks and whites could be separate, so long as they were equal in *Plessy* v. *Ferguson* (1889).[13] *Brown* v. *Board of Education* (1954)[14] later concluded that separation by race meant inequality; therefore, the U.S. Supreme Court required school services to be based upon simple individual equality rather than block equality, using race to define blocks. The claims for comparable worth systems of pay for women are, interestingly, block egalitarianism mixed with equal pay for equal work, which is segmented equality.

The Domain of Equality

How does one decide what is to be distributed equally? The domain of equality marks off the goods, services, or benefits being distributed. If schools and fire protection are to be provided, why not golf courses or recreational facilities? Domains of equality can be narrowly or broadly defined, and they can have to do with *allocations* based on a public agency's resources or they can be based on *claims*—claimants' demands for equality. Domains of equality constantly shift, aggregate, and disaggregate. Certain domains are largely controlled by the market such as jobs, wages, and investments, while others are controlled primarily by government. It is often the case that the governmental domain seeks equality to correct inequalities resulting from the market or from previous governmental policies. Unemployment compensation, Aid to Families with Dependent Children, college tuition grants, and food stamps are all kinds of governmental compensatory inequality to offset other inequalities outside of the governmental domain of allocation but within a broader domain of claims.

Domains can also be intergenerational, as in the determination of whether present taxpayers or their children pay for the federal debt built up by current deficits.

Equalities of Opportunity

Equalities of opportunity are divided into *prospect* and *means* opportunity. Two people have equal opportunity for a job if each has the same probability for attaining the job under conditions of prospect equality of opportunity. Two people have equal opportunity for a job if each has the same talents or qualifications for the job under conditions of means-equal opportunity. Examples of pure prospect equality of opportunity are few, but the draft lottery for the Vietnam War is very close. In means equality of opportunity, *equal rules,* such as Intelligent Quotient (I.Q.) tests, Standard Achievement Test (SAT) scores, equal starting and finishing points for footraces, and so forth define opportunity. "The purpose and effect of these equal means is not equal prospect of success, but legitimately unequal prospects of success."[15] Aristotle's notion that equals are to be treated equally would constitute means-based equality of opportunity.

In any given society not all talent can be equally developed. Following John Schaar: "Every society has a set of values, and these are arranged in a more or less tidy hierarchy. . . . The equality of opportunity formula must be revised to read: equality of opportunity for all to develop those talents which are highly valued by a given people at a given time."[16] How else, for example, can one explain the status of rock musicians in popular culture?

The Value of Equality

The value of equality begins with the concept of *lot equality* in which shares are identical (similar housing, one vote, etc.) or equal. The advantage of lot equality is that only the individual can judge what pleases or displeases him or her. Lots can also be easily measured and distributed, and they imply nothing about equal well-being. The problem, of course, is that lot equality is insensitive to significant variations in need. To remedy this, Rae and associates suggest a "person equality" in which there is nonarbitrary rule-based distribution of shares based on nonneutral judgments about individuals' needs. A threatened person may require more protection (and police officials may so decide) merely to make that person equal to the nonthreatened person. The same can be said for the crippled as against the healthy child, the mentally retarded as against the bright. Person-regarding equality is often practiced in public administration to "make the rules humane."

It is clear that any universal scope for equality is both impossible and undesirable. Rather than a simple piece of rhetoric or a slogan, the Compound Theory of Social Equity is a complex of definitions and concepts. Equality then changes from one thing to many things—equalities. If public administration is to be inclined toward social equity, at least this level of explication of the subject is required. In the policy process, any justification of policy choices claiming to enhance social equity needs to be analyzed in terms of such questions as: (1) Is this equality individual, segmented, or block? (2) Is this equality direct, or is it means-equal opportunity or prospect-equal opportunity? (3) What forms of social equity can be advanced so as to improve the lot of the least advantaged, yet sustain democratic government and a viable market economy? The Compound Theory of Social Equity would serve as the language of the framework for attempts in both theory building and practice, and it would serve to answer these questions.

Social Equity and the Law

Marshall Dimock made this dicta famous: "public administration is the law in action." It should be no surprise, then, that the most significant developments in social equity have their genesis in the law. "Local, state and national legislators—and their counterparts in the executive branches—too often have ignored, abdicated or traded away their responsibilities. . . . By default, then, if for no other reason, the courts would often have the final say."[17] The courts are the last resort for those claiming unequal treatment in either the protection of the law or the provision of service. Elected officials—both legislators and executives—are naturally inclined to the views and interests of the majority. Appointed officials—the public administrators—have until recent years been primarily concerned with efficiency and economy, although effectiveness was also an early concern, as noted by Dwight Waldo in *The Administrative State.*[18]

Employment

The most important legal influences resulting in more equitable government are in the field of employment, both public and nonpublic. The legal (not to mention administrative) questions are: who ought to be entitled to a job, what are the criteria, and how ought they to be applied?

The Civil Rights Act of 1964 as amended and the Equal Employment Act of 1972 were designed to guarantee equal access to public and private employment. This was done by a combination of block equalities (whereby persons in different racial categories could be compared and, if found subject to different treatment, a finding of violation of law would be made) and a means-equal opportunities logic (whereby fair measurements of talent, skill, and ability would determine who gets jobs). The landmark case was *Griggs* v. *Duke Power,* in which the U.S. Supreme Court held that job qualifications that were not relevant to a specific job and that on their face favored whites over Blacks were a violation of the law.[19] The Court clearly rejected the idea of prospect equality, but because it upheld the idea of equality by blocks or, to use the words of the law, "protected groups," a strong social equity signal was sent. Race-consciousness as an affirmative action was to be based upon equality between Blacks and whites both in the work cohort and between the work cohort and the labor market—a kind of double application of equality.

John Nalbandian, in a recent review of case law on affirmative action in employment, observed that cases subsequent to *Griggs* have systematically limited "affirmative action tightly within the scope of the problem it was supposed to solve." The case law has sought to limit negative effects, such as unwanted inequality befalling nonminorities as a result of these programs.[20] *The University of California Regents* v. *Bakke* was the most celebrated example of judicial support for block equality to bring Blacks up to an enrollment level equal to whites, while at the same time protecting a nonminority claimant who would likely have qualified for admissions in the absence of a protected class.[21]

The affirmative action laws, and the Court's interpretations of them, have had a significant effect on equalizing employment opportunities, first between minorities and nonminorities and more recently by gender.[22] Nalbandian predicts, however, that the values of social equity may decline in a shift toward a new balance in employment practices, giving greater emphasis to efficiency.[23]

Contracting

In the 1977 Public Works Employment Act the national government established a minority-business-enterprise 10-percent setaside, requiring that 10 percent of all public works contracts be reserved for firms owned by minorities. The 10-percent setaside was tested and affirmed in *Fullilove* v. *Klutznik* (1980). U.S. Supreme Court Justice Thurgood Marshall, for the majority, said:

> It is indisputable that Congress' articulated purpose for enacting the set-aside provision was to remedy the present effects of past racial discrimination. . . .
>
> Today, by upholding this race-conscious remedy, the Court accords Congress the authority to undertake the task of moving our society toward a state of meaningful

equality of opportunity, not an abstract version of equality in which the effects of past discrimination would be forever frozen into our social fabric.[24]

For the minority, Potter Stewart argued:

> On its face, the minority business enterprise provision at issue in this case denies the equal protection of the law. . . . The fourteenth Amendment was adopted to ensure . . . that the law would honor no preference based on lineage.[25]

Clearly, in this case, Marshall and Stewart use different domains and diverge on the issue of what is to be equal. To Marshall, block equality is essential, while to Stewart individual equality is required. Finally, as to employment (in this case contracting) opportunities, Marshall prefers it to be prospect equality while Stewart wants it to be means equality.

In a 1989 affirmation of the 10-percent set-aside provisions of the 1977 Federal Public Works Employment Act, the U.S. Supreme Court struck down a 30-percent setaside for minority construction firms on contracts with the city of Richmond, Virginia. This was immediately regarded as a significant setback for the affirmative action programs of 33 states and over 200 municipalities. The *Richmond* decision reasoned that the 14th Amendment was violated by the set-aside because it denied *whites* equal protection of the law.[26] No doubt the set-aside provision has enhanced social equity. It is clear, however, that the law has used inequality to achieve equality.

Government Service

In 1968 Andrew Hawkins, a Black handyman living in a neighborhood called the Promised Land, an all-Black section of Shaw, Mississippi, gathered significant data to show that municipal services such as paved streets, sewers, and gutters were unequally distributed. Because these services were available in the white section of Shaw, Hawkins charged that he and his class were deprived of the 14th Amendment guarantee of equal protection of the law. The U.S. District Court disagreed, saying that such a distribution had to do with issues of "municipal administration" that were "resolved at the ballot box."[27] On appeal, the decision of the District Court was overturned by the U.S. Court of Appeals, in part based on this amicus curiae brief from the Harvard-MIT (Massachusetts Institute of Technology) Joint Center for Urban Studies:

> . . . invidious discrimination in the qualitative and quantitative rendition of basic governmental services violates an unyielding principle . . . that a trial court may not permit a defendant local government to rebut substantial statistical evidence of discrimination on the basis of race by entering a general disclaimer of illicit motive or by a loose and undocumented plea of administrative convenience. No such defense can be accepted as an adequate rebuttal of a prima facie case established by uncontroverted statistical evidence of an overwhelming disparity in the level and kind of

public services rendered to citizens who differ neither in terms of desire nor need, but only in the color of their skin.[28]

While the appellate court ruled in Hawkins' favor, it construed the issue of equal protection so narrowly as to all but preclude significant court intervention in service allocation decisions where *intent* to discriminate cannot be conclusively demonstrated.

Desegregation of public schools following *Brown* v. *Board of Education* has resulted in varied and creative ways to define and achieve equality. Busing is a means of achieving at least the appearance of block equality. Busing has, however, been primarily from the inner city out. Magnet schools are an attempt to equalize the racial mix via busing in the other direction. Building schools at the margins of primarily white and primarily Black (or Hispanic) neighborhoods preserves the concept of the neighborhood school while achieving integration. The major problem has been jurisdictional or to use the language of equality, domain. The familiar inner city, primarily non-white school district surrounded by suburban, primarily white school districts significantly limits the possible equalizing effects of *Brown* v. *Board of Education.* This is especially the case when wealth and tax base follow white movement to the suburbs. State courts have in many places interpreted the equality clauses of state constitutions to bring about greater equality. Beginning with *Serrano* v. *Priest* in California, state equalization formulas for school funding have in many states required the augmentation of funding in poor districts.[29] Ordinarily this is done on a dollar-per-student basis. This procedure broadens the domain of the issue to the state, and it is also a simple formula for individual equality. It does, of course, bring about this equality by race-based inequality.

From the point of view of competing concepts of equality, the Kansas City Missouri School District desegregation cases may be the most interesting. After *Brown* v. *Board of Education* determined that separate but equal schooling was in fact unequal and unconstitutional, two questions remained. Was it sufficient for school districts and state departments of education to stop segregating? Or, was it necessary to repair the damage done by a century of racially separate school systems? In *United States* v. *Jefferson City Board of Education* the Court of Appeals declared that school officials: "have an affirmative duty under the Fourteenth Amendment to bring about an integrated unitary school system in which there are no Negro schools and no white schools—just schools. . . . In fulfilling this duty it is not enough for school authorities to offer Negro children the opportunity to attend formerly all-white schools. The necessity of overcoming the effects of the dual school system in this circuit requires integration of faculties, facilities and activities as well as students."[30]

Later in *Swann* v. *Charlotte-Mecklenburg Board of Education* the U.S. Supreme Court stated that "the objective today remains to eliminate from the public schools all vestiges of state imposed segregation."[31]

Two conditions pertain in Kansas City, Missouri. First is a dual housing market resulting from an interaction between private and governmental parties in the real estate industry, resulting in racially segregated residential areas. This has resulted in racially segregated schools roughly mirroring the segregated neighborhoods. Originally segregated all-Black schools are now schools of mostly Black students and teachers. The 11 suburban school districts surrounding Kansas City have almost all white students and teachers.

In *Jenkins* v. *Missouri* in 1984 the trial court under Judge Clark found the Kansas City Missouri School District and the State of Missouri liable for the unconstitutional segregation of the public schools.[32] The problem, of course, was the remedy. It is one thing to identify inequality; it is another to achieve equality. The School District tried and failed to secure passage of tax levies and bond issues to comply with Judge Clark's order.

Following the *Liddell* and *Griffin* cases, Judge Clark ordered both tax increases and bond issuances to cover the remedies sought in 1986.[33] The court also held that 75 percent of the cost of the plan was allocated to the State of Missouri for funding. The appellate court sustained all of Judge Clark's remedies with the exception of a 1.5-percent surcharge on incomes earned in Kansas City by nonresidents and instructed the state and the district to proceed with the remedies.[34]

If the majority of the citizens had turned down bond issues and had refused higher taxation to enable the school district to meet its desegregation objectives, how could the judge justify imposing those taxes as a matter of law? He said,

> A majority has no right to deny others the constitutional guarantees to which they are entitled. This court, having found that vestiges of unconstitutional discrimination still exist in the KCMSD is not so callous as to accept the proposition that it is helpless to enforce a remedy to correct the past violations. . . . The court must weigh the constitutional rights of the taxpayers against the constitutional rights of the plaintiff students in this case. The court is of the opinion that the balance is clearly in favor of the students who are helpless without the aid of this court.[35]

From an equality point of view, there are several examples of competing views of fairness. *First,* with the individual definition of equality, each vote is equal to each other vote, and the majority wins in a representative democracy. The court here clearly said that a majority cannot vote away the constitutional rights of a minority to equal schooling. *Second* is the dimension of time or inter-generational equality. The century of inequality in schools for Black children was to be remedied by a period of inequality toward nonminorities to correct for the past. *Third* is the question of domain. To what extent should the issue be confined to one school district? Because schools are constitutionally established in the State of Missouri, Judge Clark concluded that the funding solutions for desegregation were ultimately the responsibility of the state. Indeed, Arthur A. Bensen II, an attorney for the plaintiff, argued persuasively that it was fully within the authority of Judge

Clark not only to impose either state or areawide financing to solve school desegregation but also to reorganize the school districts to eliminate the vestiges of prior
discrimination.[36] The judge chose not to go that far.

Many more examples of equality can be traced to the courts, including equalizing funding for male and female student athletes in schools and colleges.

An especially interesting and relevant interpretation of the relationship between social equity and law as they have to do with public administration is provided by Charles M. Harr and Daniel W. Fessler. They suggest that the basis for
equality in the law is less likely to be found in the United States Constitution and
federal statutes and more likely to be found in state constitutions and statutes.
"Recognizing the growing practical difficulties in relying on the equal protection
clause, we assert the existence—the convincing and determinative presence—of a
common law doctrine, *the duty to serve,* as an avenue of appeal that predates the
federal Constitution."[37] More than 700 years before the Constitution, judge-made
law in the England of Henry III held "that, at a fundamental level of social organization, all persons similarly situated in terms of need have an enforceable claim of
equal, adequate and nondiscriminatory access to essential services; in addition
this doctrine makes such legal access largely a governmental responsibility."[38] All
monopolies—states, districts, utilities—are in the common law "clothed with a
public interest" and obligated to the "doctrine of equal service."[39] If Harr and
Fessler are right and if the state-based school funding equalization cases are illustrative, social equity will emerge at the grass roots rather than be imposed by the
federal courts.

Social Equity and Analysis

Consequent with the development of theories of distributive justice and the law
of equality has been the emergence of policy analysis. Over the past 25 years many
of America's major universities have established schools of public policy that specialize in the interdisciplinary study of policy issues. In addition, many existing
schools and departments of public administration have started to emphasize the
policy analysis perspective. Virtually every policy field—health care, transportation, law enforcement, fire protection, housing, education, natural resources and
the environment, national defense, is now the subject of regular review and
analysis. Generalized scholarly journals as well as journals specializing in some
policy fields are now available, and virtually every issue has articles dealing with
some form of equity.[40]

Both the ideological and methodological perspectives in policy analysis have
been dominated by economics. Although governments are not markets, market-
model applications are widely used in policy analysis. The logic is simple. If, in
economic theory, both individuals and firms maximize their utilities, their citizens and government bureaus do the same. This perspective has been especially
compatible with popular contemporary governmental ideas such as deregulation,

privatization, school vouchers, public-private partnerships, cut-back management, and the minimalist or so-called "night watchman" view of American government. While the economic model has been a powerful influence on policy analysis, it has been tempered, especially in recent years, by use of measures of both general and individual well-being that are more compatible with governmental goals. Long-standing and powerful governmental concepts, such as justice, fairness, individual rights, and equality, are now being measured and used in analysis. Broad collective measures, the so-called social indicators such as unemployment and homelessness, are now more often used in policy analysis. Measurements of variations in the distribution of public services by age, race, gender, income, and the like are relatively routine. Social equity concepts are used not only as theory or as legal standards but as measures or variables in research. The problem, of course, in social equity analysis, as in the use of social equity in law or theory, is the compound character of equality.

At the level of the individual, data and findings are now available that map, in at least a rudimentary way, personal views and preferences regarding equality. Jennifer Hochschild has determined that people have contradictory views of equality.[41] These contradictory views are not determined so much by income level or political ideology as by more subtle distinctions. People have varied opinions about equality depending on what domain of life is being considered and how equality is being defined. Using three different domains, *social* (including home, family, school, and community), *economic* (including jobs, wages, taxes, and wealth), and *political* (including voting, representation, and law), and using two conceptions of equality first, equal shares and equal procedures, and second, differentiation (a combination of segmented equality and means-based equality of opportunity) Hochschild's findings are as follows.

In the social domain people hold strongly to norms of equal shares and equal procedures. Equal treatment of children, one spouse, equal sacrifice for the family, and equal treatment in the neighborhood mark the general views of the poor, the middle class, and the rich. In schools, equal or fair procedures are important to just determination of grades. In schools, families tend to move somewhat away from strict individual equality toward a differentiation based upon investment, such as the handicapped child's needing more, an example of Rawlsian justice. And there is evidence of a differentiation of investment for the more gifted or those with greater potential. People are not, however, equally happy with the egalitarian character of social life. If they feel they have some control over their fate and are able to act on the principles of equality, they are more happy. If not, they are bitter and unhappy.

These same people endorse differentiation or means-based equality in the economic domain. People, in other words, want an equal chance to become unequal. Productivity should be rewarded, the poor feeling this would produce more equal incomes, the rich believing it would result in less equal incomes. Private property is deeply supported. Accumulated wealth is not generally opposed by poor or rich, and both strongly oppose inheritance taxes. And both partially abandon their different views when it comes to poverty, feeling that "something should be done."

In the political domain these people are egalitarian again. Political and civil rights should be distributed equally to all. "They want tax and social welfare policies mainly to take from the rich and give to the poor and middle classes. Their vision of utopia always includes more equality. . . ."[42] There is deep resentment over perceived unfairness resulting from loopholes in the graduated income tax because it treats people unequally. Many people endorse tuition subsidies for the poor, housing subsidies, and even a national health insurance.

Yet, with all of this, Hochschild found ambivalence. People recognize that their views are sometimes inconsistent or that they are confused. And there is some helplessness and anger over whom to blame for inequality or how to make things better.

As the different domains of people's lives best explain how they feel about equality, they also generally conform to the compound conception of social equity set out in Section II. Both in the theoretical model and in people's outlooks, equality splits into equalities depending on domains, dimensions of time, jurisdictions, abilities, effort, and luck.

Field research on the distribution of local government service is filled with implications for social equity and public administration. Much of this research tests the "underclass hypothesis." If one accepts that hypothesis, it follows that the distribution of libraries, parks, fire protection, water, sewers, policy protection, and education services follows power, wealth, and racial variations. The findings of research on municipal services generally indicate that the underclass hypothesis does not hold.[43] Fixed services such as parks and libraries exhibit "unpatterned inequalities" that are not correlated with power, wealth, or race. These inequalities are more a function of the age of the neighborhood and the condition of housing. Mobile services such as police and fire protection tend to be distributed relatively equally, and such variation as can be determined is not associated with race or wealth. On the burden side, evidence indicates that property tax assessments are unequal in the direction of lower proportionate assessments for minorities and the poor and higher proportionate assessments for the rich and the white.[44]

Both interdistrict and intradistrict school funding variations have tended, on the other hand, to confirm the under-class hypothesis. In the past 20 years, primarily as a result of court cases, more than half of the states have undertaken school-finance reforms designed to equalize funding between schools within districts or between districts. When compared to nonschool-finance reform states, the reform states now evidence greater equity in per-student funding.[45]

Why has the underclass hypothesis not been demonstrated in field research, except in the case of schools? Robert Lineberry and others argue persuasively that urban and state bureaucracies, following patterned decision rules or service delivery rules, have distributed public services in such a way as to ameliorate the effects of poverty and race. The effects of municipal reform, including city managers, merit-based bureaucracies, at-large elections, non-partisan elections, and the like, have strengthened the public services at the local level. The public services are routinized, patterned, incremental, and predictable, following understood or accepted decision rules or service delivery rules. Police and fire rules require decentralization and wide discretion in deployment of staff and equipment. Social services tend to respond to stated demands. Each service has some basis for its service delivery rules.[46]

What is most significant here is that it is bureaucracy, professional public administration, particularly in larger cities, that distributes public services either generally equally or in the direction of those especially in need. The point is that public administration understands and practices social equity. Social equity is understood or given, in the same way as efficiency or economy, in general public administration practice.

What explains school funding inequities? School bureaucracies have virtually no control over interdistrict funding levels. What explains Shaw, Mississippi, and other glaring examples of race-based service inequity? Often it is the lack of a genuinely professional public service.

Conclusions

This article first reviewed the suggestion made in 1968 that social equity should be the third pillar for the theory and practice of public administration. Theoretical, legal, and analytical developments of the last 20 years were then assessed.

While the more abstract theories of distributive justice were found to be intellectually challenging, the theories that hold the most promise for both empirical verification and practical application to social equity and public administration are those that dissect the subject and illuminate the complexity of equality as an idea and a guide. That theory, coupled with the methodological tools of policy analysts, facilitates examination of the distribution of burdens and benefits so as to make informed decisions that are fair. Legally, equality issues probably reached their zenith in the latter stages of the Warren Court. Both the Burger and Rehnquist Courts have narrowed the emphasis on affirmative action, equity in service distribution, and the like.

For social equity to be a standard for policy judgment and public action, analysis must move from equality to equalities and equity to equities. A compound theory of social equity which details alternative and sometimes competing forms of equality will serve to better inform the practice of public administration. It will always be the task of public servants to balance the needs for efficiency, economy, and social equity—but there can be no balance if public servants understand only the complexities of economy and efficiency but cannot plumb the details of fairness and equality.

A nascent theory is presented here. A fully developed compound theory of social equity and public administration is the theoretical and research objective.

Such a theory needs to be parsed by policy field and informed by the effects of federalism. It must define, if not predict, the effects of alternative policies, organizational structures, and management styles on the equity of public programs.

It is a great irony of these times that all of this has occurred during a period referred to as the "age of the new individualism" or the "age of narcissism."[47] The dominant political ethos of the last 12 years has been pro-business and anti-government, anti-tax, anti-welfare, and particularly anti-bureaucracy. This ideological consensus seems to indicate that the majority share this ethos. In addition, this has been a lengthy period of sustained economic growth. Yet, under the surface of majoritarian consensus, one sees a significant adjustment of the workforce from primary production to information and service at net lower wages, a sharp increase in two-worker families, a profound discontinuity in income and ability to acquire housing, transportation, and food, an increase in homelessness, and an increase in poverty.[48] Thus, while social equity has undergone development as a theory—and while public administrators have, following a social equity ethic, ameliorated the effects of inequality—still inequality has increased as a fact.[49]

Most important in these conclusions is the research which indicates that public administration tends to practice social equity. This is no surprise to those who are in public management at the local level. Public administrators solve problems, ameliorate inequalities, exercise judgment in service allocation matters, and use discretion in the application of generalized policy. Fairness and equity have always been common-sense guides for action. Some are concerned that this seems to put bureaucracy in a political role.[50] No doubt exists that public administration is a form of politics. The issue is, what theories and beliefs guide public administrators' actions? As it has evolved in the last 20 years, social equity has served to order the understanding of public administration and to inform the judgment necessary to be both effective and fair.

Notes

1. H. George Frederickson, *The New Public Administration* (University: The University of Alabama Press, 1980), p. 37.

2. *Ibid.*, p. 6.

3. George Berkeley, *The Administrative Revolution: Notes on the Passing of Organization Man* (Englewood Cliffs, NJ: Prentice-Hall, 1971); Victor Thompson, *Without Sympathy or Enthusiasm* (Tuscaloosa, AL: The University of Alabama Press, 1975).

4. Herman Mertins, Jr., and Patrick J. Hennigan, eds. *ASPA Professional Standards and Ethics Workbook and Study Guide for Public Administration* (Washington: The American Society for Public Administration, 1981), pp. 22–23.

5. Dwight Waldo, *The Administrative State* (San Francisco: The Ronald Press, 1948).

6. Woodrow Wilson, "The Study of Administration," *Political Science Quarterly,* vol. 56 (December 1941: originally copyrighted in 1887).

7. York Willbern, "Is the New Public Administration Still with Us?" *Public Administration Review,* vol. 33 (July/August 1973), p. 376.

8. *Ibid.*, p. 378.

9. David K. Hart, "Social Equity, Justice and the Equitable Administrator"; Michael M. Harmon, "Social Equity and Organization Man: Motivation and Organizational Democracy"; Eugene B. McGregor, Jr., "Social Equity and the Public Service"; Steven R. Chitwood, "Social Equity and Social Service Productivity"; David O. Porter and Teddie Wood Porter, "Social Equity and Fiscal Federalism"; Orion J. White, Jr., and Bruce L. Gates, "Statistical Theory and Equity in the Delivery of Social Services," vol. 34, *Public Administration Review* (January/February 1974), pp. 3–51.

10. Douglas Rae and Associates, *Equalities* (Cambridge, MA: Harvard University Press, 1981), p. 3.

11. John A. Rawls, *A Theory of Justice* (Cambridge, MA: Harvard University Press, 1971).

12. Much of what appears in the following page is taken from Rae and Associates, *Equalities* (Cambridge, MA: Harvard University Press, 1981).

13. *Plessy* v. *Ferguson*, 163 U.S. 537 (1896).

14. *Brown* v. *Board of Education of Topeka* (I) 3/4/47 U.S. 483 (1954).

15. Rae, *op. cit.*, p. 66.

16. John Scharr, "Equality of Opportunity and Beyond," in *NOMOS IX: Equality*, J. Rowland Pennock and John W. Chapman, eds. (New York: Atherton Press, 1967), p. 231. See also Scharr, "Some Ways of Thinking About Equality," *Journal of Politics*, vol. 26 (November 1964), pp. 867–895.

17. Charles M. Haar and Daniel W. Fessler, *Fairness and Justice: Law in the Service of Equality* (New York: Simon and Schuster, 1986), p. 18.

18. Waldo, *op. cit.*

19. *Griggs* v. *Duke Power Company*, 401 U.S. 424 (1971). The U.S. Supreme Court in 1989 stepped considerably back from the Duke Power requirement that employees must demonstrate that the hiring requirements do not discriminate. In *Wards Grove Packing* v. *Antonio*, in a five-to-four decision, the U.S. Supreme Court now requires a plaintiff to prove employment discrimination. See *The New York Times* (June 7, 1989), pp. 1 and 11. *Wards Grove Packing* v. *Antonio*, Doc. No. 87-1387, 5 June 1989.

20. John Nalbandian, "The U.S. Supreme Court's 'Consensus' on Affirmative Action," vol. 49, *Public Administration Review* (January/February 1989), pp. 38–45.

21. *University of California Regents* v. *Bakke*, 438 U.S. 265 (1978).

22. Patricia W. Ingraham and David H. Rosenbloom, "The New Public Personnel and the New Public Service," vol. 49, *Public Administration Review* (March/April 1989), pp. 116–125.

23. Nalbandian, *op. cit.*, p. 44.

24. *Fullilove* v. *Klutznik*, 448 U.S. 448 (1980).

25. *Idem.*

26. From *The New York Times* (January 24, 1989), pp. 1 and 12. See *City of Richmond* v. *Crosan*, 98 LE2d 976, 108 SCt 1010 (1989).

27. *Hawkins* v. *Town of Shaw*, 303 F. Supp. 1162, 1171 (N.D. MISS. 1969).

28. Haar and Fessler, *op. cit.*, p. 14.

29. *John Serrano, Jr., et al.* v. *Ivy Baker Priest*, 5 Cal. 3d584. See also Richard Lehane, *The Quest for Justice: The Politics of School Finance Reform* (New York: Longman, 1978).

30. *Green* v. *School Board*, 391 U.S. 430, 437–38 (1968).

31. *Swann* v. *Charlotte-Mecklenburg Board of Education*, 402 U.S. 1 (1971).

32. *Jenkins* v. *Missouri*, 593 F. Supp. 1485 (W.D. MO 1984).

33. *Liddell v. State of Missouri*, 731 F. 2D 1294, 1323 (8 Cir. 1984) and *Griffin v. School Board of Prince Edward County*. 377 U.S. 218, 233, 84 S. Cp. 1226, 1234, 12 L. Ed. 2d256 (1964).

34. *Jenkins v. State of Missouri*, 855 Fed. R. 8th Circuit 1297–1319.

35. *Jenkins v. State of Missouri*, 672 F. Supp. 412.

36. Arthur A. Bensen II, "The Liability of Missouri Suburban School Districts for the Unconstitutional Segregation of Neighboring Urban School Districts, University of Missouri at Kansas *City Law Review*, vol. 53 (Spring 1985), pp. 349–375. Bensen's argument was counter to case law based on *Milliken* v. *Bradley*, 418 U.S. 717 (1974), in which the U.S. Supreme Court found that jurisdictional boundaries are not barriers to effective segregation, except desegregation under certain conditions. Bensen claims that the Kansas City case satisfies those conditions.

37. Haar and Fessler, *op. cit.*, p. 43.

38. *Ibid.*, p. 21.

39. *Idem.*

40. See especially, the *Policy Studies Journal*, the *Policy Studies Review*, and the *Journal of Policy Analysis and Management*.

41. Jennifer L. Hochschild, *What's Fair? American Beliefs About Distributive Justice* (Cambridge, MA: Harvard University Press, 1981). Much of this page summarizes *What's Fair?*

42. *Ibid.*, p. 181.

43. See Robert L. Lineberry, *Equality and Urban Policy: The Distribution of Municipal Services* (Beverly Hills, CA: SAGE Publications, 1977) for a thorough review of the literature as well as a full presentation of the "decision rules" hypothesis.

44. *Idem.*

45. Leanna Stiefel and Robert Berne, "The Equity Effects of State School Finance Reform: A Methodological Critique and New Evidence," *Policy Sciences*, vol. 13 (February 1981), pp. 75–98.

46. Lineberry, *op. cit.*, and Bryan D. Jones, Saadia R. Greenberg, Clifford Kaufman, and Joseph Drew, "Service Delivery Rules and the Distribution of Local Government Services: Three Detroit Bureaucracies," *Journal of Politics*, vol. 40 (May 1978), pp. 333–368.

47. Christopher Lasch, *The Culture of Narcissism: American Life in an Age of Diminishing Expectations* (New York: Norton, 1978).

48. Frank Levy, *Dollars and Dreams: The Changing American Income Distribution* (New York: Russell Sage Foundation, 1987).

49. William Julius Wilson. *The Truly Disadvantaged: The Inner City, the Underclass and Public Policy* (Chicago: The University of Chicago Press, 1987).

50. Rodney E. Hero, "The Urban Service Delivery Literature: Some Questions and Considerations," *Polity*, vol. 18 (Summer 1986), pp. 659–677.

2

SOCIAL EQUITY AND THE PUBLIC SERVICE

Eugene B. McGregor Jr.

Social equity doctrines in public affairs are popularly regarded as the enemy of merit principles. The equity camp defends popular (i.e., reasonably equal) distribution of opportunity and reward, and the merit camp connotes elitism and competitive excellence.[1] Each side claims to be consistent with principles of justice and democracy, and criticizes the other for undermining the same principles. The debate is not new in politics and public administration,[2] and the schism between democratic "Jeffersonianism" and aristocratic "Hamiltonianism" is sometimes exploited to shore up respective arguments.[3] In this round of the struggle, however, it appears that proponents of social equity are the plaintiffs and may carry the day. And the sounds of battle have been getting louder. Schools, particularly, are being scrutinized in terms of the extent to which degrees and tests are used as sorting devices to provide equal opportunity for their students and graduates.[4] Government, particularly public administration which comprises so much of government, is now under close reexamination in terms of both structure and control[5] and the professional philosophy of its practitioners.[6] Predictably, the battle has arrived in the front yard of the public service,[7] and it is the purpose of this essay to explore the effects of the conflict and its possible resolution on public administration.

This essay is limited to a discussion of the implications of the clash between "social equity" and "merit" for civil service employment in the United States. Not given treatment in this analysis are the important and related questions of "citizen participation"—justifications and strategies for involving average citizens in policy making—and the "representative bureaucracy" arguments which find that

Source: *Public Administration Review* 34 (January/February 1974): 18–29.

bureaucracies perform more satisfactorily by having on the payroll adequate representations of the major social and functional interest of a society.[8] The sole concern of this essay is with the politics of the struggle to define social equity in the public services of the United States.

What is particularly significant about the recent debates over equity and merit is that civil service history offers few clues about the scope of the present problem. Merit originally meant, under the Pendleton Act of 1883 and Hatch Acts of 1939 and 1940, that religion and partisan politics ought to be eliminated as a basis for determining employment and promotion in all but the top jobs of the appointive civil service. The American definition of merit did not, except in the minds of hopeful Presidents, establish a mandate for competitive excellence in which only the brightest minds and the best trained workers and professionals were sought out and hired on a competitive basis. True, there were registers established for certain kinds of jobs and "rules of three" (or four, or five) would govern appointments at the federal, state, and local levels of government.[9] But the original merit principle seems to have been largely a minimum competence principle which provided enormous opportunities to use merit public employment as a tool of public policy. Veterans preference policies are the oldest examples of an application of the social equity ethic. Once a candidate was certified as at least minimally competent, the fact of having been a veteran could be included in the determination of employment eligibility.

However, it has only been since the Ramspeck Act of 1940, which prohibited discrimination in federal employment because of race, creed, or color, that one can find the beginning of an evolving federal policy toward modern social equity problems. And the real impetus toward social equity in the public service has come, ironically enough, not from the Executive or Legislative Branches, but from the courts. Two separate legal developments have become important: One is a subtle change in the "doctrine of privilege" and the second is the precedent established by the Supreme Court's decision in *Griggs* v. *Duke Power*.

The Doctrine of Substantial Interest

The rights of citizens employed and seeking employment in the public service have until the 1960s been defined under what Arch Dotson has called "the doctrine of privilege."[10] Public office, under this doctrine, was not a right but a privilege held at the pleasure of a government which could impose on its employees restrictions deemed necessary to protect its sovereignty. Limitations on the "rights" of employees to bargain collectively, to enjoy ordinary political freedom and to have the protections of due process and judicial review were justified, since an employee had no right to civil service employment in the first place. As Dotson pouts out, however, the judicial conclusion about the rights of public employees was derived from the Holmesian premise that "the petitioner may have a constitutional right to talk politics, but he has no constitutional right to be a policeman" (*McAuliffe* v. *New Bedford,* 155 Mass. 216, 220 (1892)):

From the assertion that there exists no constitutional right *to* public employment, it is also inferred that there can be no constitutional right *in* public employment. The progression is that, since there are no fundamental claims in employment, employment is maintained by the state as a privilege. And since employment is a privilege, then it may be regulated summarily by the government grantor. The whole argument, however, depends upon the first step: that since there is no right *to*, there can be no right *in* public employment.[11]

More recent judgments by the Supreme Court have found that the conclusion does not follow from the Holmesian premise, and a new doctrine, which David H. Rosenbloom calls the "doctrine of substantial interest," has evolved.[12] This new doctrine presently accepts the original premise that there is no constitutional right to public employment, but rejects the conclusion that there are therefore no rights which cannot be abridged while employed. The doctrine requires that "whenever there is a substantial interest, other than employment by the state, involved in the discharge of a public employee, he can be removed neither on arbitrary grounds nor without a procedure calculated to determine whether legitimate grounds do exist" (*Birnbaum* v. *Trussell*, 371 F. 2d 672, 678 [1966]). Thus, the political and civil liberties of civil servants are coming to be redefined and protected under due processes and judicial review. Individual equality for blacks and whites, men and women alike, is now formally acknowledged in public service grievance procedures affecting those who are already in government employment.

What has not changed under the doctrine of substantial interest, however, is the idea that public employment is a privilege. Government is not obligated to guarantee *individual* equality of access to civil service positions or individual due process in the competition for jobs.[13] Under *Griggs* v. *Duke Power Co.*, 401 U.S., 424,433 (March 8, 1971), however, the Supreme Court has moved to establish *social* equality of access to civil service positions. The basis for the court's decision was not the doctrine of substantial interest, but Title VII of the Civil Rights Act of 1964.

Griggs v. *Duke Power Co.*

The case of Griggs and the Duke Power Company of Draper, North Carolina, was a classic example of social inequity under the 1964 Civil Rights Act. Common laborers were required to have a high school diploma and perform satisfactorily on two aptitude tests in order to enter low-skill occupations in company divisions other than the "labor division." While the company merit qualifications were not found to be motivated by discriminatory purpose, the clear effect of the selection policy was to concentrate Negroes in the lower-paid labor division. Furthermore, the employment practice could not be proven to be either job related (one did not need a high school diploma to be a good janitor) or an accurate predictor of job performance. Thus unlawful discrimination was found to exist and ordered to be corrected.

The Supreme Court, in reversing the Court of Appeals for the 4th Circuit, was clear in its position that standards of merit were not being disallowed to provide employment for the unqualified. Chief Justice Burger's opinion summarizes the court's position:

> Nothing in the Act (1964 Civil Rights Act) precludes the use of testing or measuring procedures; obviously they are useful. What Congress has forbidden is giving these devices and mechanisms controlling force unless they are demonstrably a reasonable measure of job performance. Congress has not commanded that the less qualified be preferred over the better qualified simply because of minority origins. Far from disparaging job qualifications as such, Congress has made such qualifications the controlling factor, so that race, religion, nationality and sex become irrelevant. What Congress has commanded is that *any* tests used must measure the person for the job and not the person in the abstract.

What the court did establish was a two-step procedure for determining whether unlawful, and thus correctable, discrimination exists. The plaintiff must show that the employment practice has a differential effect on people on a basis of either race, sex, religion, or national origin. But once discrimination is demonstrated, the burden of proof shifts to the employer to prove the validity of his employment practices. In neither step is the presence or absence of an invidious intent on the part of the employer relevant to the case. Parenthetically, where de facto discrimination cannot be shown the question of validity never arises, regardless of the relevance or irrelevance of employee selection procedures to the work people do.

The Doctrine of Job Relatedness

While *Griggs* looms as the landmark case in the legal definition of social equity, the Supreme Court did not say precisely what constituted valid recruitment, selection, and promotion procedures. It did legitimize what we refer to here as the "job relatedness doctrine." Employers may *not* measure and rank applicants in the abstract, but only with regard to their ability to perform a given job. Just what sorts of employment practices the doctrine does permit is seen in the growing body of law arising from increasing numbers of conflicts over social equity.

Table 2.1 summarizes 22 court contests similar to Griggs. In each, minority group plaintiffs charged that discriminatory employment practices were found in the recruitment, selection, and promotion practices of public sector employers. Most commonly cited by the plaintiffs were the discriminatory use of aptitude tests and educational degrees. In all but one case (*Douglas* v. *Hampton*) the plaintiff established the discriminatory impact of the selection procedures. In only four cases (two of which are on appeal) did the courts find in favor of the defendants.

The conclusions to be drawn from such a summary are tentative, but several things seem clear. One is that where selection practices are shown to have a differential effect for minorities (cases regarding sex are not shown here[14]), the courts

TABLE 2.1 Court Cases on Public Sector Racial Discrimination

Case	Year of Highest Court Decision	Highest Court	Defendant Jurisdiction	Administrative/ Personnel Sector	Issues
1. Johnson v. Louisiana State Employment Service[2]	1968	W.D. La.	State of Louisiana	Employment service workers	EEOC conciliation agreement involving an application for employment in the SES.
2. Arrington v. MBTA[1]	1969	D. Mass	Massachusetts Bay Transportation Authority	Drivers and toll collectors	Selection procedures using the GATB test, preliminary injunction.
3. Penn v. Stumpf [2]	1970	N.D. Calif.	Oakland, Calif.	Police	Selection.
4. Strain v. Philpot	1971	M.D. Ala.	Alabama Cooperative Extension Service	Agricultural extension service workers	Recruitment, selection procedures, rule-of-three, educational requirements and hiring quota, and classification.
5. Morrow v. Crisler[4]	1971	S.D. Miss.	State of Mississippi	Highway Patrol	Recruitment and selection procedures including Otis Quick Scoring Mental Test, segregated departments and facilities
6. Allen v. City of Mobile[1]	1971	5th Cir.	Mobile, Alabama	Police	Selection procedures, classification promotion tests.
7. Western Addition Community Organization v. Alioto	1971	N.D. Calif.	San Francisco, Calif.	Firemen	Selection procedures, preliminary injunction.
8. Coffey v. Brady	1971	M.C. Fla.	Jacksonville, Florida	Firemen	Selection procedures including job analysis, affirmative action plan, and hiring quota.
9. U.S. v. Frazer	1972	M.D. Ala.	State of Alabama	State workers hired under federal grant	Violation of non-discrimination clause in federal grant regulations.
10. NAACP v. Allen	1972	M.D. Ala.	State of Alabama	Police	Recruitment and selection procedures including hiring quotas.
11. Castro v. Beecher[5]	1971 and 1972 (multiple cases)	1st Cir.	Boston, Massachusetts	Police	Selection procedures including height requirement, hiring quota.[5]
12. Baker v. Columbus Municipal Separate School District	1972	5th Cir.	Columbus, Mississippi	Teacher	Selection procedures including the NTE test and hiring quota.
13. Hogue v. Bach	1972	D. Colo.	Denver, Colorado	Police	Recruitment and selection procedures, preliminary injunction.

(continues)

TABLE 2.1 *(continued)*

Case	Year of Highest Court Decision	Highest Court	Defendant Jurisdiction	Administrative/Personnel Sector	Issues
14. NAACP v. Imperial Irrigation District	1972	S.D. Calif.	Imperial Irrigation District, Calif.	Irrigation workers	Selection procedures including Bennett mechanical comprehension test, primary mental ability test, affirmative action plan, and hiring quota.
15. Carter v. Gallagher[3]	1973	8th Cir.	Minneapolis, Minnesota	Firemen	Selection procedures including educational requirement, age, arrest and conviction records, examinations, hiring quota, and affirmative action plan.
16. U.S. v. City of Montgomery	1972	N.D. Ala.	Montgomery, Alabama	Water, sewer, and personnel workers	Selection procedures, classification, seniority, affirmative action plan.
17. Commonwealth v. O'Neil (in progress)	1972	3rd Cir.[4]	Philadelphia, Penna.	Police	Selection procedures including hiring quota, preliminary injunction.
18. Chance v. Board of Examiners	1972	2nd Cir.	New York City	School principals	Promotion test, preliminary injunction.
19. Armstead v. Starkville Municipal Separate School District	1972	5th Cir.	Starkville, Miss.	Teachers	Selection procedures including the GRE test, educational requirement, and hiring quota.
20. Douglas v. Hampton[1] (on appeal)	1972	D.D.C.[4]	U.S. Civil Service Commission and U.S. Department of Housing and Urban Development Washington, D.C.	Urban interns who took FSEE	FSEE as a selection device.
21. Davis v. Washington[1] (on appeal)	1972 (multiple cases)	D.D.C.[4]	Washington, D.C.	Police	Selection test.
22. Bennett v. Gravelle[2]	1972	Md.	Washington Suburban Sanitary Commission, Maryland	Former employees of WSSC	Educational requirements, hiring quota, back pay.

SOURCE: Adopted from *Judicial Mandates for Affirmative Action* (Washington, D.C.: National Civil Service League, February 1972).

1 The case was decided in favor of the defendant.
2 Settled out of court either in favor of plaintiffs or as a conciliation agreement which ascribes no guilt to either party.
3 Writ of Certiorari denied.
4 Case either still in progress or on appeal as of the time of manuscript completion.
5 The first circuit court upheld the defendant's use of a high school diploma, swimming test, and height requirements as selection devices (reversing the district court) and upheld the district court's order that a new test be developed. A hiring procedure was defined by the circuit court as compensatory relief for minorities who failed the old, invalid entrance exam.

do not hesitate to enjoin or change those practices which do not clear rational or empirical validity. Second, aptitude tests and educational degrees appear to be the most vulnerable selection devices for policemen, firemen, and other occupational sectors where administrative and scientific skill is not an initial job requirement. Where such exams and degrees are used, often a pass-fail standard is applied such that once a candidate has crossed the exam hurdle, other job-related criteria are used to determine eligibility for appointment.

Third, with the exception of cases involving teachers and school principals, the courts have not provided clear guidelines for cases of discrimination involving the better-paid administrative, professional, and technical (APT) occupations. In many respects, these occupations are the current frontier in the fight against racial and sex discrimination for several reasons. One is that government at all levels accounts for two-fifths of all the jobs at the APT level in society. A second is that the stakes are higher in terms of salary and benefits, prestige, and power held by people in these jobs. A third is that discrimination can take on a more subtle character because the jobs are often less precisely defined.

The shifting mix of the federal workforce provides some clues about the problems of social equity in the public service. As Table 2.2 shows, the total federal civilian workforce has grown very little over the past decade—less than 18 per cent (or less than 2 per cent per year on an average). The growth of white collar employment, as indicated by the increase in employment on the General Schedule, was nearly twice as great as total employment. Furthermore, the per cent increase from 1960 to 1971 has risen increasingly as the General Schedule rank increases. Indeed, the "supergrade" stratum shows a sizable 167 per cent increase over the 11-year span.

One conclusion is inescapable, in spite of the crude imputations made from diverse data sources. Over time, the federal portion of the public service is best characterized as a manpower mix which has shifted in the direction of high-level, white collar employment. This high-level of APT employment is seen in the per cent increase of the grades above GS-12 which have expanded over twice as much as the grades GS-11 and below. Thus, the battle-ground on which social equity is to be fought would appear to have shifted to a grade level presently above the direct reach of the courts' recent decisions. (The implications of the doctrine of job-relatedness will be dealt with later.)

Interestingly, the highest stratum—the supergrade ranks—show a substantial vacancy rate. There exist more hiring "authorities" than people actually employed, either as part of the General Schedule or under Public Law 80-313 (under which highly skilled scientific and technical professionals can be hired).[15] The real significance in this vacancy rate is not that the new hiring of minorities and women can begin immediately. Somehow money must be appropriated and programs funded before such hiring can occur. Equally clear, however, is that limitations on the numbers of people in these positions are not due to the failure of the Congress to authorize a generous enough manpower ceiling, but to patterns of budgetary politics and manpower allocations.

TABLE 2.2 Composition of the Federal White Collar, Civilian Workforce, 1960–1971

	1960 N	1960 %	1962 N	1962 %	1964 N	1964 %	1966 N	1966 %	1968 N	1968 %	1970 N	1970 %	1971 N	1971 %	Percent Inc. 1960–71
General Schedule[1] Employment (1,000)	972	40.0*	1,058	42.2*	1,090	43.4*	1,189	43.2*	1,302	43.7*	1,285	43.9	1,298	45.4*	33.5
Total federal civilian Workforce (1,000)	2,430	–	2,505	–	2,510	–	2,750	–	2,980	–	2,928	–	2,860	–	17.7
GS-16-18[1] (N rounded to nearest 1,000; imputed real number in parenthesis)	2 (1944)	0.2	2 (2116)	0.2	3 (3270)	0.3	4 (3567)	0.3	5 (5208)	0.3	N.A.		5 (4855)	6.4	+167.1
GS-12-15[1] (N in 1,000)	129	13.3	161	15.2	194	17.8	214	18.0	250	19.2	N.A.		291[2]	22.4	+125.6
GS-9-11[1] (N in 1,000)	200	20.6	225	21.3	258	23.7	272	22.9	294	22.6	N.A.		304[2]	23.4	+52.0
GS-5-8[1] (N in 1,000)	275	28.3	298	28.2	301	27.6	321	27.0	355	27.3	N.A.		386[2]	29.9	+40.4
GS-1-4[1] (N in 1,000)	366	37.7	371	35.1	335	30.7	378	31.8	398	30.6	N.A.		312[2]	24.0	−14.8
Totals for GS (N = 1,000) employees[4]	972	100.1	1058	100.0	1090	100.1	1189	100.0	1302	100.1	1285	–	1298	100.1	33.5
Number of GS supergrade authorities[3]	1576	–	3019	–	4282	–	4958	–	5318	–	5766	–	5804	–	+268.3
Number of Supergrade authorities: both GS and P.S. 80-313[3]	2606	–	4320	–	5583	–	6292	–	6652	–	7010	–	7048	–	+170.4
Imputed Supergrade vacancy rate (GS)= authorities − employees authorities	none		903	29.9	1012	23.6	1391	28.0	110	8.4	–		612	16.4	–

*Percent of total federal civilian workforce.

[1] U.S. Civil Service Commission, "Grade Trend of Federal Civilian Employment under the General Schedule: 1964–1968" (SM 32-68), p. 7. Data reported are for June 30 of each year; size of N is imputed from percentages given and rounded to the nearest thousand.

[2] U.S. Civil Service Commission, "Pay Structure of the Federal Civil Service" (Bureau of Manpower Information Systems, Manpower Statistics Division, June 30, 1971, SM33-71), p. 20.

[3] U.S. Civil Service Commission, "Executive Manpower in the Federal Service" (Bureau of Executive Manpower, January 1972); note that the numbers reported are authorities rather than the numbers of people actually occupying a position.

[4] Totals may not agree perfectly because of rounding.

Trends for Minorities and Women

Comparisons of the progress minorities and women have made can yield conflicting conclusions. As Tables 2.3 and 2.4 show, a happy picture emerges if one looks at the direction of the trends. Over time, minorities and women are measurably increasing their percentage of the higher-level jobs. Particularly encouraging are the increases on the General Schedule at the level of GS-12 and above where minorities have more than tripled their numbers since 1965 and women have made more modest gains. (Indeed, at the level of "supergrade," women seem to have lost ground.)

At any one time, however, the numbers are not as encouraging. The drop in the proportion of minorities and women employed as the GS level rises is too dramatic to ignore. Minorities seem to have fared better then women. While minorities constituted nearly 15 per cent of the General Schedule in 1970 and held 4.5 per cent of the jobs ranked as GS-12 to GS-18, women constituted over twice the proportion of the General Schedule (i.e., 33.2 per cent) and held 5.1 per cent of the jobs ranked GS-12 to GS-18.

Furthermore, any gains and losses which minorities and women make in absolute numbers must be compared with the overall growth or decline of the stratum. For instance, if minorities double their numbers in a high-level occupational stratum over a period of time while the stratum size also doubles, then minorities have made no proportionate gains. Similarly, if the number of minorities in a low grade level decreases and the total number of people in that grade also decreases by the same proportion, then by that test minorities have made no collective gains.

An examination of Tables 3 and 4 reveals sketchy patterns. Minorities, whose progress has been tracked over a longer period of time, appear to have definitely increased their proportionate share of jobs above GS-12, although they have also increased their share of jobs at all levels because of an over-all increase in their share of the General Schedule. Women, over a much shorter period of time, show more ambiguous results. They gained very slightly in the middle grades (i.e., GS-5 to 15) from 1969 to 1970 and markedly decreased their proportion of grades 1–4. Yet they also show an absolute decline on the number of "supergrades."

Clearly, whatever progress minorities and women have made so far will have to be more than matched for the remainder of the 1970s for any significant progress to be reported over the next six years. Until that time, however, the judgments of the federal courts need to be borne in mind by manpower managers as a parameter within which personnel recruitment and selection must occur.

The Unresolved Problem

Thus we come to the central question: Can the public service have both excellence and equity? It would certainly seem that the two values are not incompatible. Essentially, the notion of social equity embraces the idea that the public service

TABLE 2.3   Civilian Federal Employment of Minorities,* 1965 to 1971

	1965 N	1965 %	1967 N	1967 %	1969 N	1969 %	1970 N	1970 %	1971 N	1971 %	
Minorities: All pay plans[1] (N = 1,000)	367	16.0	497	18.9	500	19.2	505	19.6	503	19.5	Percent of all federal civilian workforce on June 30
Total General Schedule[1]	127	11.3	174	13.7	182	14.1	189	14.7	199	15.2	Percent of total General Schedule on June 30
(N = 1,000) GS 1–4[1]	75	22.2	93	25.2	83	26.8	82	28.0	82	28.3	Percent of stratum on June 30
(N = 1,000) GS 5–8[1]	36	11.7	62	15.0	61	16.7	67	17.8	74	18.9	Percent of stratum on June 30
(N = 1,000) GS 9–11[1]	12	4.7	20	6.8	25	7.9	26	8.3	28	8.9	Percent of stratum on June 30
(N = 1,000) GS 12–18[1]	4	1.7	8	3.3	12	4.0	13	4.5	15	4.9	Percent of stratum on June 30
Minorities GS 12–15[2]	–		–		11,455	N.A.	13,202	N.A.	15,088	4.9	Percent of stratum on November 30, 1971
Minorities GS 16–18[2]	–		–		97	1.4 (N.A.)	130	1.9 (N.A.)	161	2.3 (2.8)	Imputed percent of total authorities[3] (Percent of total paid stratum Nov. 30, 1971)

*Minorities are defined as Negroes, Spanish-surnamed Americans, American Indians, and Orientals.

[1] *Statistical Abstract of the United States*, note the totals are as of December 31 of each year and exclude CIA, NSA, and part-time postal employees.
[2] U.S., *Minority Group Employment in the Federal Government* (November 1971), p. 3, and imputed from Civil Service Commission.

TABLE 2.4 Civilian Federal Employment of Women: 1965 to 1971

	1965 N	1965 %	1967 N	1967 %	1969 N	1969 %	1970 N	1970 %	1971 N	1971 %	
Female paid civilian employment (N = 1,000)[1]	590	25	730	27	730	27	714	27	703	27	Percent of total civilian employment
Total General Schedule employment (N = 1,000)[2]	N.A.		N.A.		665	33.4	657	33.2	N.A.		Percent of schedule as of Oct.31
GS 1-4[2] (N = 1,000)	N.A.		N.S.		262	77.0	247	68.7	N.A.		Percent of stratum as of Oct. 31
GS 5-8[2] (N = 1,000)	N.A.		N.A.		320	32.9	323	34.9	N.A.		Percent of stratum as of Oct. 31
GS 9-11[2] (N = 1,000)	N.A.		N.A.		64	18.1	67	18.5	N.A.		Percent of stratum as of Oct. 31
GS 12-15[2] (N = 1,000)	N.A.		N.A.		16	5.2	17	5.4	N.A.		Percent of stratum as of Oct. 31
GS 16-18[2]	N.A.		N.A.		156	1.6	141	1.6	N.A.		Percent of stratum as of Oct. 31

[1] Statistical Abstract of the United States.

[2] U.S. Civil Service Commission, Study of Employment of Women in the Federal Government in 1970 (Manpower Statistics Division, December 1971, SM 62-06), p. 17.

abandon a prejudgment of people because of ascriptive characteristics[16]—race and sex being two—which have no known (i.e., empirically verified) relationship to excellence on the job. A corollary theme is the elimination of the correlates of these prejudgments, such as tests and degrees, in cases where there is no known or rationally valid relationship between these credentials and job performance. In essence, the prescription for public administration seems to be to provide equal opportunity for each person to contribute the greatest excellence he can.

This position is not tantamount to eliminating tests, grades, and diplomas altogether from selection and promotion processes. In some cases, *they are* useful ranking devices, and in many cases they can be used most profitably as initial, pass-fail, screening devices. Personal interviews, letters of reference, a person's work history, and a sample of a person's work can be far more valid indicators of an ability to do a job than the possession of high test scores and academic credentials. A high school diploma and general mental aptitude test are probably not necessary to the successful performance of janitorial services. Neither is a Ph.D. necessary to the attainment of excellence in jobs where high-level research and teaching are not job requirements. Such credentials may be edifying, helping one structure leisure time, and contributing to job mobility, but their possession does not, in the examples cited, *ipso facto* contribute to excellence on the job.[17]

How, then, can the goals of social equity be achieved in the public service without sacrificing excellence? While not a complete answer to the question,[18] a major step toward reconciling the two values is to recognize and protect the many varieties of excellence found in the public service. In essence, the social equity doctrine requires a pluralistic basis for judging people rather than a monolithic one.[19] Once the field of endeavor is identified, however, a *relevant* standard of excellence can be applied to the recruitment, selection, and promotion of people, whether the occupation is law, accounting, nursing, engineering, or economics. Clearly many fields such as public administration are only beginning to define and apply standards of excellence throughout the discipline. The lack of clear consensus about excellence does not invalidate the quest, nor does it imply an absence of standards. The lack of consensus can even help guarantee a healthy pluralism of competing excellences.

One vehicle for enhancing the twin guardianship of equity and excellence may well be the unionization of public employees. Collective bargaining has been regarded with some suspicion by scholars, politicians, and public administrators alike. Unwarranted attacks on the public treasury, invasion of management prerogatives, protection of mediocrity, and holding public services hostage to illegal strikes and slowdowns are often seen as the pernicious consequences of unionization. Such an outlook bodes ill for the future of public service management, for the growth trend of unions is already clear. The Civil Service Commission finds that as of November 1972, 55 per cent of federal Executive Branch employees (excluding the Postal Service) were represented by unions holding exclusive recognition rights. This percentage refers not to union membership but to numbers of employees covered by union recognition.[20]

Furthermore, increasing numbers of white collar workers are covered by exclusive recognition. In November 1972, 46 per cent of General Schedule (or equivalent) employees were covered, whereas 42 per cent were covered only one year earlier. Substantial union increases are reported in the professional occupations, with the government employees' associations (AFGE, NAGE, NFFE), NAIRE (Internal Revenue), NEA (teachers), ANA (nurses), and AFTE (technical engineers) reporting the largest gains from 1971 to 1972.[21]

A more optimistic outlook on public sector labor relations sees increasingly professionalized employee organizations as useful in solving problems of equity and excellence. For one thing, unions and associations can be used to establish within the major occupational groups standards of, say, good nursing, good economic analysis, good engineering, or good management. Second, these guilds can provide an organized basis for ensuring that acceptable numbers of minorities and women find employment and protection in the public service. Third, unionization may also provide a pluralistic way to answer the inevitable question: Are good nurses worth more or less than good engineers? In the absence of any absolute scale of human worth, the last question would seem best resolved by a reasonably fair bargaining process in which the claims of the different groups can be arbitrated equitably.

However, unionization is not likely to solve for public managers the problem of defining the tasks which must be completed in order to accomplish organizational objectives. Thus, collective bargaining provides only a limited answer to the problems of equity and excellence which have meaning only when it is known what people do for work. For only when it is known what people do can one determine the standard of excellence to be applied and whether social inequity exists because people have been judged in the abstract rather than in terms of their capacity to do a job.

It is clear from the preceding examination of the dynamics of the public personnel system that equity and excellence are beginning to converge. The courts are playing a major role in this convergence because access to public employment is a basic issue, not only between the races but between the social classes. It is also increasingly clear that persons in public employment, as they move up the career ladder, have power in the policy process. Thus, the increased access to public service on the grounds of properly defined excellence mixed with a concern for equal access bodes well, not only for convergence, but for a more equal distribution of power to minorities in the policy process. Frederick Mosher's accurate portrayal of the public service as a rather loose collection of semi-autonomous public "occupations" that attempt to define within the occupation a conception of excellence is being softened by the courts.[22] The autonomy and self-definition of excellence on the part of public service occupations, particularly in fields such as police and fire protection, are changing rather dramatically. The regrettable fact is that the courts have been the prime change agents while "public administrators" and particularly civil service agencies have not been active advocates for equity. Public administrators have more often than not been party to the over-definition of excellence, the unnecessary upgrading of occupational standards for entrance, the use of merit principles to protect incumbent bureaucrats from the "unqualified," and the general preoccupation with credentialling the public service. Perhaps recent actions of the courts will cause public administrators to recognize and respect the efficacy of the social equity ethic and become a more dynamic force for the balance of merit and equity principles.

Interestingly, the advocate of excellence and the proponent of social equity appear to be allies. Both find it essential to discover what public servants actually do for work and how people come to be educated, recruited, selected, and promoted in the work they do. Rarely have two so disparate concerns found such common ground.

Notes

1. A prophetic statement on the clash of values can be found in John W. Gardner, *Excellence: Can We Be Equal and Excellent Too?* (New York: Harper and Row, 1961).

2. A classic political analysis of "aristocratic" and "democratic" criticisms of mass society can be found in William Kornhauser, *The Politics of Mass Society* (New York: The Free Press of Glencoe, 1959).

3. See John Franklin Campbell, *The Foreign Affairs Fudge Factory* (New York: Basic Books, 1971). pp. 46–49, 61–63. Those who think that Jefferson, in defending equality, was sacrificing excellence should read his letter to John Adams (October 28, 1813); Adrienne Kock and William Peden (eds.), *The Life and Selected Writings of Thomas Jefferson* (New York: Random House, 1944), pp. 632–634.

4. Christopher Jencks, *Inequality: A Reassessment of the Effect of Family and Schooling in America* (New York: Basic Books, 1972).

5. "Curriculum Essays on Citizens, Politics, and Administration in Urban Neighborhoods," *Public Administration Review*, Vol. 32, Special Issue (October 1972).

6. Frank Marini (ed.), *Toward a New Public Administration* (Scranton, Pa: Chandler Publishing Company, 1971), especially H. George Frederickson, "Toward a New Public Administration," pp. 309–331.

7. The National Civil Service League has been one of the most vigorous protagonists on the side of social equity; I am indebted to Jean J. Couturier for his insight into many of the major problems. Recent issues of NCSL's *Good Government* show the dimensions of the problem, particularly: Robert H. Dick, "Public Employment and the Disadvantaged: A Close, Hard Look at Testing." Vol 87 (Winter 1969), pp. 1–8; E. Richard Larson, "Discriminatory Selection Devices in Public Employment Systems," Vol. 88 (Winter 1971), p. 107; Jean J. Couturies, "Court Attacks on Testing: Death Knell or Salvation for Civil Service Systems" (Winter 1971), pp. 10–12, and "Governments Can Be the Employers of First Resort" (Summer 1970); William H. Brown III. "Moving Against Job Bias in State and Local Governments," Vol 89 (Winter 1972, pp. 10, 14 and 15. Also, see the policy statement on equal employment opportunity on p. 9.

8. Paul P. Van Riper, *History of the United States Civil Service* (Evanston: Row, Peterson and Co., 1958), pp. 7, 549–559; W. Lloyd Warner, *et al., The American Federal Executive*

(New Haven: Yale University Press, 1963); Samuel Krislov, *The Negro in Federal Employment* (Minneapolis: University of Minnesota Press, 1967), pp. 46–65; and V. Subramaniam, "Representative Bureaucracy: A Reassessment," *American Political Science Review,* Vol. 61 (December 1967), pp. 1010–1019.

9. Van Riper, *op. cit.,* pp. 104–107. The methods used by state and local government in selecting candidates for appointment can be found in Jacob J. Rutstein, "Survey of Current Personnel Systems in State and Local Governments," *Good Government,* Vol 87 (Spring 1971).

10. Arch Dotson, "The Emerging Doctrine of Privilege in Public Employment," *Public Administration Review,* Vol. 15 (Spring 1955), pp. 77–78.

11. *Ibid.,* p. 87.

12. David H. Rosenbloom, *Federal Service and the Constitution: The Development of the Public Employment Relationship* (Ithaca: Cornell University Press, 1971), pp. 17, 169–197.

13. *Ibid.,* especially Chapter 5, "Equality of Access to Civil Service Positions."

14. For court cases involving women, see *Judicial Mandates for Affirmative Action, op. cit.,* pp. 34–36.

15. See "Executive Manpower in the Federal Service" (Washington D.C.: U.S. Civil Service Commission, Bureau of Executive Manpower, January 1972), pp. 2–4.

16. We avoid here the important problem of whether being "color conscious" or "color blind" enhances social equity as a related but separate question. A useful and short discussion of the problem is to be found in Harold Fleming. "The 'Affirmative Action' Debate," *City* (Summer 1972), pp. 28–31.

17. This philosophy is certainly reflected in the National Civil Service League's, "A Model Public Personnel Administration Law" (November 1970). For a discussion of the law, see Jean J. Couturier, "Model Public Personnel Administration Law: Two Views—Pro," and Harold E. Forbes, "Two Views—Con," *Public Personnel Review* (October 1971), pp. 202–214. Some preliminary empirical work already indicates that in the federal service graduate work beyond the bachelor's level does not have a measurable, independent effect on upward mobility of officials who eventually attain the rank of GS-15 and above. Seniority was found to be a far more important explanatory variable, and, indeed, protracted graduate work sometimes was associated with *slower* upward mobility, seemingly because time spent on an advanced degree was time not spent accumulating seniority, Eugene B. McGregor, Jr., "Social Equity and the Public Service," paper delivered at the 1973 National Conference on Public Administration, Los Angeles, April 1–4.

18. An excellent statement on the slippery definitions of "merit" can be found in Frederick C. Mosher, *Democracy and the Public Service* (New York: Oxford University Press, 1968), Chapter 7.

19. See Gardner, *op. cit.,* pp. 151–159.

20. U.S. Civil Service Commission, "Analysis of Data and Report on Union Recognition in the Federal Service" (Office of Labor-Management Relations, Bulletin No. 711–27, April 13, 1973), p. 1.

21. *Ibid,* pp. 5–12.

22. Mosher, *op. cit.*

3

MEASURING BUREAUCRATIC REPRESENTATION AND INTEGRATION

David Nachmias and David H. Rosenbloom

The concept of representative bureaucracy has now occupied an important place in the literature of public administration and political science for some three decades. It has been used as an explanatory tool in discussions concerning political and economic development and the historical and/or contemporary development of national civil services, including those of the United States (Van Riper, 1958), Great Britain (Kingsley, 1944), India (Subramaniam, 1967), the U.S.S.R. (Fainsod, 1963), and ancient China (Menzel, 1963). The concept has also occupied an important place in studies concerning civil rights and equal employment opportunity (Krislov, 1967). Moreover, in recent years the creation of a "representative bureaucracy" has become a major objective of federal personnel policy (Rosenbloom, 1970; 1973). Despite its widespread use—or perhaps because of it—however, the concept of representative bureaucracy is unclear at several points. The purpose of this article is to overcome some of this ambiguity by suggesting a new way of measuring integration (in the sense of socially, ethnically, and/or racially mixed) in bureaucracies and other forms of organizations. This measure complements existing techniques used to assess bureaucratic representativeness and makes it possible to deal with facets of the concept that previously defied empirical research.

Foremost among the limitations found in the use of the concept of representative bureaucracy has been a tendency to fail to specify the exact sense in which the

Source: *Public Administration Review* 33 (November/December 1973): 590–597.

term "representation" is being used. Indeed, it was not until Mosher (1968) addressed the concept that a clear distinction between *passive* (variously called sociological or reflective) representation and *active* representation was introduced. The former, ". . . concerns the source of origin of individuals and the degree to which, collectively, they mirror the total society," whereas the latter refers to the situation in which ". . . an individual (or administrator) is expected to press for the interests and desires of those whom he is presumed to represent, whether they be the whole people or some segment of the people" (pp. 11–13). Most earlier discussions of representative bureaucracy not only had the defect of failing to make clear the sense in which bureaucracies were or were not representative, but also tended to assume that passive representation almost automatically and inevitably begets active representation. Such an assumption, however, as Mosher (1968) has pointed out, would seem to be highly unrealistic in the absence of empirical investigation.

The link between passive and active representation, and a better understanding of what the latter entails, are, of course, crucial to expanding the utility of the concept of representative bureaucracy. Developing more sophisticated approaches concerning the more limited aspect of passive representation would nevertheless be useful at this time, especially in view of the increasing use of "affirmative action" techniques for the hiring and promotion of members of minority groups in public personnel systems.

Assessing Bureaucratic Representativeness

Perhaps the most common approach of determining the degree of bureaucratic representativeness, in the passive sense, has been to compare the proportion of all members of a political community who fall into a specific social category, such as race, ethnicity, class, or religion, to the proportion of all civil servants who also fall into the same category. This was recently done by Hellriegel and Short (1972), who presented such data as are partially summarized in Table 3.1. The implication of this approach is, of course, the normative assumption that a group *ought* to have the same proportional representation in the civil service as it has in the society as a whole. Indeed, as Subramaniam (1967) has pointed out, under a literal reading of this approach representative bureaucracy ". . . would mean a civil service in which *every* economic class, caste, region or religion in a country is represented in exact proportion to its numbers in the population" (p. 1010).

Given the above assumption, a somewhat more sophisticated approach would be to follow Subramaniam (1967) in dividing a group's proportion in the civil service by its proportion in the whole society. This provides a single summary figure where 1.0 symbolizes "perfect" proportional representation, more than 1.0 designates a degree of "over-representation" of a specific group, and less than 1.0 indicates "under-representation." Using this approach with regard to the data presented in Table 3.1, for example, we would obtain the indicies of representa-

TABLE 3.1   Black Population and Federal Employment as Percent of Total Population and Federal Employment, 1940–1970

Year	Black Federal Employment Percent	Total Population in U.S. Percent
1940	4.2	9.8
1950	9.3	10.0
1960	11.7	10.6
1970	15.0	11.2

SOURCE: Don Hellriegel and Larry Short, "Equal Employment Opportunity in the Federal Government: A Comparative Analysis," *Public Administration Review*, Vol. XXXII (November/December 1972), Table 1, p. 854.

tion presented in Table 3.2. The obvious utility of this approach is that it facilitates comparison, both with regard to different time periods and different nations. Thus Subramaniam (1967) was able to make a useful comparison between over-representation of the middle class in the United States and Indian national civil services, finding that in the former it was on the order of 1.35, whereas in the latter it approached 10.

Even the more sophisticated version of the above approach of assessing bureaucratic representativeness has serious limitations, however. First, the index is based on a normative assumption which ignores a number of relevant factors, including the geographical distribution of both social groups and government offices, the distribution of social groups in the *working age* population, and differentiated images with regard to the desirability of working in public bureaucracies and in connection with obtaining the educational and occupational prerequisites required to do so. Secondly, and perhaps more importantly, although the approach does give us an idea of how well various *groups* are passively represented in a bureaucracy, *it does not indicate how well integrated the bureaucracy itself is.* In other words, the proportional approach does not provide much useful informa-

TABLE 3.2   Index of Black Representation in Federal Employment, 1940–1970*

Year	Index of Representation
1940	.42
1950	.93
1960	1.10
1970	1.33

*The index of representation is the percent of all federal employees who are black/the percent of the total population of the U.S. that is black.

tion concerning the degree to which the work force of an organization is socially mixed. Such information is, however, of crucial importance from the perspectives of civil rights, equality, and equal employment opportunity programs. What, for example, can be said if we are confronted with the following data? "In General Schedule positions in the Department of the Interior the index of representation for blacks is .4, for Spanish-surnamed Americans it is .8, for American Indians it is 42.3, and for all other employees it is .9; whereas in the General Schedule positions of the Justice Department the respective figures are .9, 1.2, .3, and 1.0." Obviously, while one can say something about the representation of various groups within these agencies, one cannot say much concerning the different degrees of integration found within the agencies as whole units. Furthermore, one can say virtually nothing about the latter that would be useful in further empirical analysis. What is needed is a supplementary measure which would provide useful information concerning the degree of integration within the organizational unit as a whole (e.g., the agency, office, bureau, national bureaucracy). Such a measure is introduced in the next section.

Measuring Integration

The greater the number of differences among a group of elements, the more mixed is the group as a whole, and therefore the more variation there is to be found within it. Likewise, the smaller the number of differences, the less mixed is the group and the less variation there is within it. For example, there can be no racial differences in an all caucasian group; but, in a racially mixed group, there will always be a smaller or larger number of racial differences among individuals. The amount of differences will depend on the composition of a given group. Thus, one could base a measure of variation on the total number of differences in the specified social characteristics of a group. Such a measure depends on the total number of differences and on a meaningful transformation of this total into an index.

In order to find the total number of differences in a group, the differences between each social characteristic and every other social characteristic are counted and summed. For example, in a group of eight whites and six blacks, each of the eight whites will differ in race from each of the six blacks, thereby making a total of 48 racial differences. In a group of eight whites and three blacks, each of the eight whites differs from each of the three blacks, producing 24 differences. In a group of f whites and no blacks, the obvious result of no differences is obtained by multiplying f by zero. The procedure for determining the total number of actual differences can be expressed in the following equation:

$$\text{Total Observed Differences} = \rightarrow f_i f_j, \, i \neq j$$

where f = the number of ith social characteristics

For example, in a group of seven whites, five blacks, and three Orientals, there would be: $(7 \times 5) + (7 \times 3) + (5 \times 3) = 71$ differences.

The total of observed differences is meaningful only in relation to some well-defined criterion. The number of observed differences may be related to different criteria for different purposes. Relating the observed differences to the maximum number of possible differences, within the same unit, has the effect of controlling for the number of specified social characteristics in that unit. The maximum number of differences occurs when all the frequencies of individual attributes in the group are equal. Thus, the expected maximum can be computed by equalizing the frequencies and then finding the number of differences that would be observed if all frequencies were equal. In symbols:

$$\text{Maximum Possible Differences} = \frac{n(n-1)}{2}$$

$$\left(\frac{f}{n}\right)^2$$

where n = the number of social characteristics
    f = total frequency

In the previous example of eight whites and six blacks, the maximum number of racial differences in a group of 14 is 7 (whites) $\times$ 7 (blacks) = 49. The relative amount of variation may be measured by the ratio between the observed number of differences and the expected maximum, i.e.,

$$\text{Measure of Variation} = \frac{\text{Total Observed Differences}}{\text{Maximum Possible Differences}}$$

Symbolically, the measure of variation can be expressed in the following equation:

$$MV = \rightarrow f_i f_j \qquad i \neq j/$$

$$\frac{n(n-1)}{2}$$

$$\left(\frac{f}{n}\right)^2$$

For nine whites and three blacks the measure of variation is:

$$MV = \frac{27}{36} = .75$$

Among the 15 members of the three racial groups mentioned above, the mean number of members is five. Multiplying each "5" by every other "5" and summing these products, we find the maximum number of differences to be 75. The observed differences, as already calculated, equal 71. Hence,

$$MV = \frac{71}{75} = .94$$

The measure of variation will always vary between zero and one. If the numerator is zero, the measure will likewise be zero and will indicate the complete absence of variation. In the event of an equal division of observed frequencies of attributes, the numerator and denominator will be identical, and the measure will be 1.00, reflecting maximum integration. Intermediate degrees of integration will take on intermediate values. In closing this section it might be appropriate to mention that the reader can find other attempts to deal with integration in a statistical way in Blalock (1960), Clelland (1966), Roseboom (1966), Martin and Gray (1971), and especially Muller (1970), upon which the measure introduced here leans.

Application

The measure of variation has several important applications with regard to the concept of representative bureaucracy. It is a sensitive measure which enables one to compare the degree of social integration in different organizations and organizational levels. In Table 3.3, which is presented for illustrative purposes, selected federal agencies are ranked according to the degree of integration in their General Schedule workforces. The table contains information that clearly indicates the utility of the measure. Although the Equal Employment Opportunity Commission, which has a very large minority group member component, is the most integrated of the agencies, as might be expected, the Government Printing Office, which has had something of a "ghetto-agency" image, is, in fact, also highly integrated, at least in terms of its General Schedule work force. Similarly, despite its traditional "WASP" image, the General Schedule component of the State Department is relatively well integrated. Agencies responsible for broad social programs, such as Labor, HEW, and HUD, turn out to be well integrated, as expected, perhaps, but so do agencies such as the Civil Service Commission and the Veterans Administration which have not enjoyed favorable images with regard to civil rights and equal employment opportunity in the past (Rosenbloom, 1970, pp. 51–52; Krislov, 1967, pp. 125–126, 130–131). On the other hand, the Department of Transportation, which has made significant efforts to hire and promote minority group employees to the supergrades, has an overall low level of integration. It is interesting to note further that if an agency were proportionally representative of the social composition of the society as a whole, its measure of variation would be about .30. Thus, more than half of the agencies in Table 3.3 are more inte-

TABLE 3.3   The Social Integration of the General Schedule Work Forces of
Selected Federal Agencies, 1970 (in percent)

Agency	Black	Spanish Surnamed	American-Indian	Oriental	Other	Total	Measure of Variation
EEOC	49.9	9.5	.8	.9	38.9	748	.71
Government Printing Office	53.6	.4	.2	.3	45.6	1,548	.63
State	31.5	2.2	.3	.9	65.1	5,810	.60
Labor	25.7	1.7	.4	.5	71.7	10,535	.52
GSA	24.1	1.6	.2	1.0	73.2	18,931	.51
HEW	21.3	1.5	2.4	.7	74.1	94,502	.51
CSC	23.0	2.3	.2	.7	73.8	5,216	.50
VA	22.0	1.8	.2	1.0	75.1	115,997	.48
HUD	18.6	1.5	.3	.7	78.9	14,721	.43
Interior	4.0	1.7	12.7	.8	80.9	50,725	.41
Post Office	17.9	.6	.1	.6	80.7	2,775	.40
Small Business Administration	11.6	5.4	.4	.5	82.0	4,272	.39
Commerce	14.5	.6	.1	.8	84.0	29,115	.34
Treasury	12.3	1.5	.1	.7	85.4	82,318	.32
GAO	13.6	.6	.1	.4	85.3	4,598	.32
Justice	9.6	2.4	.1	.4	87.5	36,947	.28
Army	8.7	2.2	.2	1.0	87.9	237,914	.27
Defense (Entire)	7.8	2.4	.2	1.0	88.7	600,044	.26
Navy	8.0	1.3	.2	1.3	89.3	158,986	.25
Air Force	4.6	4.3	.3	.7	90.1	151,217	.23
Agriculture	5.5	1.3	.3	.5	92.3	81,437	.18
Transportation	5.4	1.1	.3	.5	92.8	58,690	.17
NASA	2.7	.6	.1	.6	96.0	27,278	.10

SOURCE: U.S., Civil Service Commission, *Minority Group Employment in the Federal Government*, November 30, 1970.

grated, in terms of their social composition, than is the society at large. This suggests that the social composition of agencies may be an important factor with regard to the link between passive and active representation and, therefore, to policy-making procedures and outputs as well. While these findings are interesting in themselves, it should be emphasized that the great benefit of using the measure of variation to approach questions of this nature is that it provides a single summary figure, which can, in turn, be used in further analysis.

Another useful application of the measure of variation is to employ it in ascertaining the degree of integration found in specific personnel grades or grade groupings. This has been done, again for illustrative purposes, in Table 3.4, which shows the degree of integration in each of the 18 General Schedule grades. Not

TABLE 3.4   Racial and Ethnic Integration in General Schedule Grades in the
Federal Service, 1970

Grade	Measure of Variation
All Grades	.32
1	.71
2	.63
3	.57
4	.50
5	.44
6	.38
7	.31
8	.29
9	.23
10	.14
11	.16
12	.12
13	.10
14	.09
15	.08
16	.06
17	.07
18	.05

surprisingly for those familiar with the federal personnel system and equal employment opportunity in general, the table indicates that the degree of social integration in General Schedule grades is highest in the lower grades and lowest in the higher grades. The nature of this inverse relationship is such that there are only two grades (11 and 17) which are more integrated than the next lowest grade. Grades 1–6 are more integrated and grades 7–18 less integrated than is the General Schedule work force as a whole. For the practitioner, this would probably suggest that in the future equal employment opportunity efforts should be concentrated on grades 7 and above, precisely where past EEO programs have been weakest (Rosenbloom, 1970; 1973).

A third application of the measure of variation demonstrates that its utility is not confined to the realm of description. We have found that: (1) there is considerable variance in the degree of integration in the General Schedule work forces of federal agencies; and (2) the degree of integration in General Schedule grades is inversely associated with grade level. These findings raise the question of whether the different degrees of social integration in agencies is related to the distribution of *positions* within agency General Schedule grade structures. In other words, can one talk in terms of a relative positional influence within agencies which affects social integration? For example, given the inverse relationship between social integration and grade level, we would expect an agency that has three-fourths of all its employees in the lower half of the General Schedule to be considerably more integrated than one in which three-fourths of all employees were in grades GS 10–18. In order to assess the relationship between the distribution of positions within the General Schedule grade structures of agencies and the degree of integration in these agencies, we first used the measure of variation to ascertain the degree of inequality between the number of positions in the General Schedule grade groupings of 1–9 and 10–18 within individual agencies. The results of this procedure are presented in Table 3.5. Subsequently, the measure of variation thus obtained was correlated with agency integration levels (as presented in Table 3.3). As can be readily seen in Table 3.5, there is not very much variation in the distribution of positions between the upper and lower grades. Nor is there a significant relationship between this distribution and levels of social integration in agencies ($r = -14$). Thus, *in general,* whether an agency is well integrated or not does not appear to be related to the distribution of positions within its General Schedule grade structure. On the other hand, using the measure of variation in this way

TABLE 3.5   Distribution of Position in Agencies by Grades Group

Agency	Grades GS 1–9	Grades GS 10–18	Measure of Variation
State	3,691	2,119	.93
Treasury	51,345	30,973	.93
Defense (entire)	397,978	202,066	.89
Army	161,250	76,664	.87
Navy	102,754	56,232	.91
Air Force	103,141	48,076	.87
Justice	23,162	13,785	.94
Post Office	1,154	1,621	.97
Interior	30,153	20,572	.96
Agriculture	53,396	28,041	.90
Commerce	16,202	12,913	.98
Labor	4,928	5,607	.99
HEW	67,571	26,931	.82
HUD	6,993	7,728	.99
DOT	20,829	37,861	.97
CSC	3,271	1,945	.93
EEOC	384	364	.99
GAO	2,197	2,401	.99
GSA	13,371	5,560	.83
GPO	1,331	217	.48
NASA	7,978	19,300	.82
Small Business Administration	2,161	2,111	.99
VA	92,516	23,481	.65

does enable the researcher to identify those agencies, such as the Government Printing Office and the Veterans Administration, which do have a relatively heavy concentration of positions in one part of their grade structures. Such an identification is useful in itself, and if coupled with further analysis, might help make it possible to adopt general equal employment opportunity procedures to the particular needs of such agencies.

Conclusion

The measure of variation discussed in this essay is a useful analytic tool which can be employed in studying several facets of bureaucratic representation. It should be used in conjunction with other tools, such as Subramaniam's "representational ratio," in order to provide a more complete and meaningful picture of the extent to which the work forces or memberships or organizations are socially integrated. Using the two measures to supplement each other makes it possible to learn something about both the position of individual groups in organizations and the social composition of the organizations themselves. The measure of variation, however, is not limited to descriptive use alone and for that reason it can have significant applications in the further exploration of the concept of representative bureaucracy.

As noted earlier, one of the major problems confronting anyone who attempts to deal with the concept of representative bureaucracy lies in discerning the relationship between passive and active representation. Mosher (1967) identified several variables that are likely to affect this relationship. Among them were: the length of time in the organization, the nature and strength of the organization's socialization process, the nature of the position, the length and content of preparatory education, and the strength of associations beyond the agency (p. 13). It is reasonable to assume that an organization's social composition and the degree to which it is integrated also tends to determine the link between passive and active representation. Whether civil servants conceive of themselves as being representatives of the social groups in which they have their origins, or think that representation of such groups should be a part of their role, is likely to be partially dependent on the extent to which members of their groups and members of other, and perhaps competing groups are found within an organization. In the absence of research on this question, we cannot know precisely how different levels of integration would affect the relationship between passive and active representation. It might be the case, however, as was argued by some participants in a panel discussion on "Pluralism, Representation, and Bureaucracy" (C. Payne Lucas, Mark Galanter, and James Guyot) at the American Society for Public Administration's National Conference in 1971, that the lower the degree of integration in an agency, the less likely are its minority group employees (assuming they are also a minority within the agency itself) to conceive of themselves as active representatives of their social groups. Perhaps under empirical analysis it would be possible to find a critical point at which the translation from purely passive representation to active representation as well becomes particularly commonplace and strong. The measure of variation, by providing a single summary figure measuring the degree of integration of the composition of work forces, is an appropriate tool for attacking these questions.

Another aspect of the concept of representative bureaucracy that could be usefully studied with the aid of the measure of variation is one addressed by Krislov (1967): ". . . the wider the range of talents, types, and regional and family contacts found in a bureaucracy, the more likely it is to be able to fulfill its functions, with respect to both internal efficiency and social setting" (p. 64). Many complex questions immediately come to mind. For example, are morale and efficiency related to integration? What effect, if any, does the degree of integration of public agencies have on the general public's image of and support for them? Do the policy-making processes and outputs of well-integrated agencies seem to be better suited to the needs of the community as a whole than those of less well-integrated agencies? The measure of variation alone cannot, of course, supply answers to such questions, but by giving us a way of measuring the integration in agencies as whole units, it does enable us to address them far more satisfactorily.

The measure of variation also has considerable importance from the point of view of equal employment opportunity, as is suggested by the foregoing applications. It could, for example, be a useful aid in studying such phenomena as racial and ethnic "tipping," i.e., the tendency of bureaucracies and agencies to become rapidly less integrated and more dominated, in terms of social composition, by members of minority groups after their proportion reaches a certain point. For instance, Krislov (1967) has observed that it has been the experience of the Patent Office that ". . . after the percentage of Negro employees goes over 50, white workers withdraw more and more from the employment by requesting a transfer or leaving the agency" (p. 132). But, is this generally true in other agencies as well? Is the "tipping" point related to agency size and location? Would there be a similar tendency if the percentage of blacks were 25, that of Spanish-surnamed employees were 25, and that of Indians were 5? Using the measure of variation in investigating such questions might not only increase our knowledge regarding their answers, but might also make it possible to find the point or points at which stable integration could be maximized in practice.

In sum, the measure introduced in this essay is an analytic tool of considerable promise for future research in the general area of representative bureaucracy. It enables the research to complement existing measures in an effort to gain a better understanding of the nature of the social composition of organizational units, subunits, and levels. It could be used as an aid in investigating several major questions pertaining to the concept of representative bureaucracy, including those involving the crucial link between passive and active representation. The measure also has widespread utility with regard to equal employment opportunity, including the identification of EEO problem areas and advances, and the investigation of racial and/or ethnic tipping. In short, the measure could be of considerable descriptive and analytic use to both those interested in theoretical and practical research concerning the social composition of organizations.

References

H. M. Blalock, *Social Statistics* (New York: McGraw-Hill, 1960).

R. C. Clelland, *et al., Basic Statistics with Business Application* (New York: Wiley, 1966).

Merle Fainsod, "Bureaucracy and Modernization: The Russian and Soviet Case," in J. La Palombara (ed.), *Bureaucracy and Political Development* (Princeton, N.J.: Princeton University Press, 1963).

D. Hellriegel and L. Short, "Equal Opportunity in the Federal Government: A Comparative Analysis," *Public Administration Review*, Vol. 32 (November/December 1972), pp. 851–858.

J. Donald Kingsley, *Representative Bureaucracy* (Yellow Springs, Ohio: Antioch Press, 1944).

Samuel Krislov, *The Negro in Federal Employment* (Minneapolis: University of Minnesota Press, 1967).

J. D. Martin and L. Gray, "Measurement of Relative Variation: Sociological Examples," *American Sociological Review*, Vol. 36 (June 1971), pp. 496–502.

Johanna Menzel (ed.), *The Chinese Civil Service* (Boston: D. C. Heath, 1963).

Frederick C. Mosher, *Democracy and the Public Service* (New York: Oxford University Press, 1968).

John H. Muller, *et al., Statistical Reasoning in Sociology* (New York: Houghton Mifflin, 1970).

W. W. Roseboom, *Foundations of the Theory of Prediction* (Homewood, Ill.: Dorsey, 1966).

D. H. Rosenbloom, "The Civil Service Commission's Decision to Authorize the Use of Goals and Time-tables in the Federal Equal Employment Opportunity Program," *Western Political Quarterly* (June 1973).

D. H. Rosenbloom, *The Civil Service Commission's Role in the Federal Equal Employment Opportunity Program, 1965–1970* (Washington D.C.: U. S. Civil Service Commission, 1970).

V. Subramaniam, "Representative Bureaucracy: A Reassessment," *American Political Science Review*, Vol. 61 (December 1967), pp. 1010–1019.

Paul P. Van Riper, *History of the United States Civil Service* (Evanston, Ill.: Row Peterson, 1958).

4

PROGRESS TOWARD RACIAL AND SEXUAL EQUALITY IN THE FEDERAL CIVIL SERVICE?

Gregory B. Lewis

This paper addresses two questions. First, has the federal civil service made progress toward racial and sexual equality in the past decade? Second, has progress slowed during the Reagan Administration? The paper examines changes in total employment, employment at upper grade levels, average grade levels, average salaries, and unexplained salary gaps since 1976 for ten groups—Asian, Native American, Hispanic, black non-Hispanic, and white non-Hispanic men and women. The good news is that women and minorities have made progress relative to white males on all measures, and that progress has continued under Reagan. The bad news is that progress remains slow.

In addition to being one of the largest employers in the country, the federal civil service acts as a symbol of this nation's commitment to racial and sexual equality. Its treatment of women and minorities therefore deserves steady scrutiny, especially since most studies indicate that it is far from a model employer. White males hold the vast majority of high-paying, policy-making positions in the federal civil service. They also earn far more than women and minorities at all education and experience levels. In an effort to increase representation and approach pay equality, federal policy has slowly shifted from strategies for eliminating discrimination to affirmative action to abolish inequality of opportunity to the use of numerical goals and timetables.

Source: *Public Administration Review* 48 (May/June 1988): 700–707.

These goals and timetables have never been popular with the general public (Rosenbloom, 1984) nor with elected or administrative officials (Daley, 1984), however. The election of Ronald Reagan gave goals and timetables a strong opponent in the White House. The Justice Department, which for nearly 20 years before 1981 had sided with women and minorities in court battles, began to join lawsuits on the side of white males charging reverse discrimination. Reagan's Justice Department has argued forcefully against affirmative action plans for state and local governments and private employers, and it has even refused to submit its own goals and timetables to the Equal Employment Opportunity Commission (EEOC). The EEOC, in turn, "has quietly abandoned the use of hiring goals and timetables in settlements with private employers accused of race and sex discrimination" ("EEOC Abandons," 1986), and it has dropped "broad complaints against large companies . . . in favor of more tightly focused cases involving specific persons" (Williams, 1985). The Reagan Administration's rejection of statistical evidence of patterns of discrimination convinces many critics that the federal government has taken a giant step backwards in its treatment of women and minorities on personnel issues. To date, however, little empirical evidence has been reported on whether presidential opposition to affirmative action has slowed progress toward racial and sexual equality. This paper attempts to fill this gap, exploring whether the federal personnel system has made progress in the past decade and whether the rate of progress has slowed since Reagan's election.

What measures best gauge progress? Political scientists and students of public administration have concentrated on the issue of achieving a representative bureaucracy, one that reflects the diversity of the American public and, perhaps, ensures consideration of female and minority perspectives on public policies (Krislov, 1974). Therefore, they have tracked the number of women and minorities in the federal workforce, sometimes with an emphasis on employment by grade, occupation, or agency (e.g., Hellriegel and Short, 1972; Gibson and Yeager, 1975; Kranz, 1977; Rose and Chia, 1978; Guyot, 1979; Rosenbloom, 1980; Kellough and Kay, 1986). Sociologists and, especially, economists have focused more on whether racial and sexual differences in federal salaries result from real differences in qualifications or discriminatory treatment by employers (Corazzini, 1972; Long, 1976; Smith, 1976; Eccles, 1976; Rodgers, 1977; Borjas, 1979, 1983; Taylor, 1979; Taylor and Kim, 1980; Grandjean, 1981; Killingsworth and Reimers, 1983; Abowd and Killingsworth, 1985). They distinguish between total salary differences and the "unexplained" salary differences that remain between white males and other groups after the effects of differing qualifications are controlled. Several papers have questioned whether the "cost" of being black or Hispanic has increased or decreased in the U.S. economy generally, that is, whether the unexplained salary gap has grown or shrunk (Poston, Alvarez, and Tienda, 1976; Gwaltney and Long, 1978; Cotton, 1985).

Data

This paper reports on changes between 1976 and 1986 in both representativeness and salary differences for Asian, Native American, Hispanic, black non-Hispanic, and white non-Hispanic men and women. The analysis of representativeness uses published data on the federal workforce in General Schedule (GS), GS-equivalent (white-collar) pay systems, and the Senior Executive Service taken from the Central Personnel Data File (CPDF). Data as of November 30, 1976, and September 30 of 1980 and 1986 allow comparison of employment changes under Reagan to those of the previous four years. To compensate for the differences between four-year and six-year changes, Tables 1 and 2 report average annual changes for the 1976–1980 and 1980–1986 periods. Unfortunately, the U.S. Office of Personnel Management (OPM) reported figures for full-time employees for 1976 and 1980 but included part-time and intermittent workers in the 1986 figures. Analysis of a one percent sample of federal personnel records for 1986 suggests that only about 85% of GS employees work full-time; thus, the change in definition creates problems of comparability for 1986 total employment. The definition change has minimal impact at the GS-13 level and above, however, since about 97% of those employees work full-time.

Analysis of salary gaps relies on one percent samples of full-time, permanent employees in these pay systems. This sample also comes from the CPDF, but includes information on earnings, education, age, federal experience, and other characteristics of about 12,000 employees annually. This sample covers salaries as of April 1976, 1981, and 1986. Note that the salary analysis uses April 1981 as the dividing line between Carter and Reagan, whereas the representation analysis uses September 1980. Neither point is exactly correct, but each is within four months of January 20, 1981.

Progress Toward Representativeness

Between 1976 and 1986, the white male share of General Schedule-type employment dropped from 50.2% to 41.8% (Table 4.1). All other groups increased their representation, though not equally. Women's share of federal white-collar jobs rose 6.5%, as women in each group made larger gains than men in the same group. Black women showed the greatest increase in the number of jobs held, filling an additional 2.8% of federal jobs by 1986. Asian women nearly tripled their representation. White and Hispanic women also showed substantial numerical increases. Among men, Hispanics and Asians made much larger gains than Blacks.

Representation of white males fell somewhat faster under Carter than Reagan (annual averages of −.9% and −.8%, respectively). Gainers differed somewhat between the two periods. Blacks and Hispanics combined increased their representation at average annual rates of .66% under Carter and .36% under Reagan.

Gregory B. Lewis

TABLE 4.1   Percentages of White Collar Employment

	As a Percentage of GS Workforce			Total Change	Average Annual Change	
	1976	1980	1986	1976–86	1976–80	1980–86
Men:						
White Non-Hispanics	50.18%	46.60%	41.77%	−8.41%	−.90%	−.80%
Black Non-Hispanics	4.55	4.93	4.86	.31	.10	−.01
Hispanics	1.54	2.01	2.31	.77	.12	.05
American Indians and Alaskan Natives	.49	.63	.60	.11	.04	−.01
Asians and Pacific Islanders	.65	.72	1.40	.75	.02	.11
All[a]	57.42	54.88	50.94	−6.48	−.64	−.66
Women:						
White Non-Hispanics	32.15	32.69	33.68	1.53	.14	.16
Black Non-Hispanics	8.23	9.54	11.00	2.77	.33	.24
Hispanics	1.07	1.54	2.22	1.15	.12	.11
American Indians and Alaskan Natives	.69	.77	.88	.19	.02	.02
Asians and Pacific Islanders	.44	.58	1.28	.84	.04	.12
All[a]	42.58	45.12	49.06	6.48	.64	.66
Men and Women Combined[a]						
White Non-Hispanic	82.33	79.29	75.45	−6.68	−.76	−.64
Black Non-Hispanic	12.78	14.46	15.86	2.90	.42	.20
Hispanic	2.61	3.55	4.53	1.92	.24	.16
American Indians and Alaskan Natives	1.18	1.40	1.48	.30	.06	.01
Asians and Pacific Islanders	1.10	1.30	2.68	1.58	.05	.23

[a] Individual elements may not sum to subtotals nor subtotals to totals due to rounding.

SOURCE: U.S. Civil Service Commission, *Federal Civilian Workforce Statistics: Equal Employment Opportunity Statistics: November 1976*, Pamphlet SM70-76B, pp. 2–3; U.S. Office of Personnel Management, "OPM Fact Sheet: Minorities and Women in Federal Employment" (for September 1981); U.S. Office of Personnel Management, *Federal Civilian Workforce Statistics: Affirmative Employment Statistics: September 30, 1986*, Table 2.

Black and Native American males actually comprised a smaller percentage of GS personnel in 1984 than in 1980. Asians, on the other hand, raised their share of federal jobs more than four times as rapidly under Reagan as under Carter (annual average rates of .23% and .05%, respectively). Some slowdown in the growth rate of black women was probably inevitable, given their large share of jobs, but it is surprising that Republican efforts to woo Hispanic votes are not reflected in more Hispanic employment growth.

Gains in employment can be rather hollow, however, if women and minorities only fill clerical jobs and policy-making positions are reserved for white males.

TABLE 4.2   Employment at GS-13 and Above

	As a Percentage of GS Workforce at GS-13 and Above			Total Change	Average Annual Change	
	1976	*1980*	*1986*	*1976–86*	*1976–80*	*1980–86*
Men:						
White Non-Hispanics	89.03%	84.95%	78.95%	−10.08%	−1.02%	−1.00%
Black Non-Hispanics	3.09	3.69	3.67	.58	.15	.00
Hispanics	1.05	1.54	1.87	.82	.12	.06
American Indians and Alaskan Natives	.34	.45	.52	.18	.03	.01
Asians and Pacific Islanders	1.04	1.17	2.00	.96	.03	.14
All[a]	94.56	91.81	87.00	−7.56	−.69	−.80
Women:						
White Non-Hispanics	4.61	6.63	10.46	5.85	.50	.64
Black Non-Hispanics	.63	1.16	1.74	1.11	.13	.10
Hispanics	.07	.17	.30	.23	.02	.02
American Indians and Alaskan Natives	.02	.04	.09	.07	.01	.01
Asians and Pacific Islanders	.11	.19	.41	.30	.02	.04
All[a]	5.44	8.19	13.00	7.56	.69	.80
Men and Women Combined:[a]						
White Non-Hispanic	93.64	91.58	89.41	−4.23	−.52	−.36
Black Non-Hispanic	3.72	4.85	5.41	1.69	.28	.09
Hispanic	1.12	1.71	2.17	1.05	.15	.08
American Indians and Alaskan Natives	.37	.49	.61	.24	.03	.02
Asians and Pacific Islanders	1.15	1.36	2.41	1.26	.05	.18

[a] Individual elements may not sum to subtotals nor subtotals to totals due to rounding.

SOURCE: U.S. Civil Service Commission, *Federal Civilian Workforce Statistics: Equal Employment Opportunity Statistics: November 1976,* Pamphlet SM70-76B, pp. 2–3; U.S. Office of Personnel Management, "OPM Fact Sheet: Minorities and Women in Federal Employment" (for September 1981); U.S. Office of Personnel Management, *Federal Civilian Workforce Statistics: Affirmative Employment Statistics: September 30, 1986,* Table 2.

Table 4.2 shows that white males still held 79% of positions at GS-13 and above in 1986, but that is down from 89% in 1976. Although still quite low, women's share more than doubled (from 5.44% to 13.00%). Minority men's percentage rose by nearly half (from 5.52% to 8.06%). White women were the biggest gainers at the management level, accounting for more than half the white male decline (5.85% versus −10.08%). Black women showed the second-highest numerical increase (taking an additional 1.11% of GS-13+ jobs) and nearly tripled their share. Asian males also showed substantial increases, and remained the only group besides white males to have greater representation at top levels (2.00%) than in the federal workforce as a whole (1.40%).

Diversification of the managerial and policy-making workforce progressed at a similar pace under Carter and Reagan, but the gainers differed under the two Administrations. The white male share of positions at GS-13 and above declined at an average annual rate of 1.02% under Carter and 1.00% under Reagan. Blacks and Hispanics made more rapid gains under Carter, but white women and Asians did better under Reagan.

Salary Differences

White males earn substantially more than all other groups except Asian males, whose average salaries were somewhat higher than those of white males in 1976 and were 5.7% below them in 1986 (Table 4.3, based on one percent samples). Other minority males earn about one-quarter less than white males, and women earn about 35% to 45% less. Nonetheless, all groups except Asian males narrowed the gap over the 1976–86 period. One way to measure the change is with a weighted average of the salary differences.[1] Here, the weighted averages show that the average employee who was not a white male earned 38.2% less than the average white male in 1976, 37.3% less in 1981, and 35.4% less in 1986. Thus, the

TABLE 4.3   Differences Between Average Salaries

	Percent Difference from White Male Mean Salary			*Change*		
	1976	*1980*	*1986*	*1976–86*	*1976–80*	*1980–86*
Men						
Black Non-Hispanics	−26.4	−24.4	−25.8	.6	2.0	−1.4
Hispanics	−28.0	−25.3	−22.9	5.1	2.7	2.4
American Indians and						
Alaskan Natives	−21.4	−21.2	−16.6	4.8	.2	4.6
Asians and Pacific Islanders	1.7	−2.0	−5.7	−7.4	−3.7	−3.7
Women						
White Non-Hispanics	−40.1	−39.4	−36.7	3.4	.7	2.7
Black Non-Hispanics	−43.5	−42.3	−41.3	2.2	1.2	1.0
Hispanics	−44.6	−43.7	−43.2	1.4	.9	.5
American Indians and						
Alaskan Natives	−51.5	−49.7	−46.4	5.1	1.8	3.3
Asians and Pacific Islanders	−34.1	−34.6	−33.3	.8	−.5	1.3
Weighted Average	−38.2	−37.3	−35.4	2.8	.9	1.9

SOURCE: U.S. Office of Personnel Management, *Central Personnel Data File,* one percent sample.

salary gap shrank by 0.9 percentage points from 1976 to 1981 and by 1.9 from 1981 to 1986, further evidence that progress toward equality has not slowed under Reagan.

Differences in average salaries are not indicators of differences in pay for equally qualified workers of different races and sexes, since the typical white male in the federal government is older, more experienced, and better educated than the average member of all other groups except Asian males. Likewise, trends in average salaries need not reflect changes in the treatment of women and minorities if the qualifications of different groups are also changing. Some commentators have argued that discrimination against women has declined but that average salaries have not reflected that because of the influx of younger, less experienced women into the workforce, which depresses women's average salary. If, on the other hand, the qualifications of women and minorities are rising faster than those of white males in the federal government, then shrinking average salary gaps might not reflect changes in federal treatment of women and minorities (Lewis, 1987).

Methodology

A better measure is the "unexplained" salary difference, the gap that remains after controlling the effects of education, experience, age, and other characteristics. The unexplained salary difference is found by regressing annual salary on a variety of factors that human capital economists and sociologists have found to influence earnings. The dependent variable is the natural logarithm of salary rather than the dollar amount, based on theoretical work by Mincer (1973) and empirical verification by Heckman and Polachek (1974) showing that this is the superior specification. Thus, the regression coefficients indicate the proportional change in salary from a one-unit increase in the independent variable. For instance, a coefficient of .012 for veterans' preference would suggest that veterans earn 1.2% more than comparable nonveterans.

Education and work experience develop skills that increase a worker's value on the job, a conclusion supported by a multitude of studies showing that wages and salaries rise steadily with both. Work experience includes both time with the federal government (which this data set records) and time with previous employers (which it does not). Age serves as a proxy for previous experience in this model. With both years of federal experience and years of education also in the model, age implicitly reflects the number of years between leaving school and entering federal employment, that is, the number of years of potential nonfederal experience. Since salaries rise faster earlier than later in one's career, the model includes the squared values of both age and experience to capture their tapering effect on pay.

Although virtually all studies show that education raises salary levels, the exact specification of the relationship between them remains controversial. Most studies posit a linear relationship, on the implicit assumption that each additional year of education has equal value. Others argue that much of education's effect is due to credentialing and that a college diploma gives a special boost to one's compensation. Further, specialized fields of knowledge prepare one for different jobs and should also affect pay (Reed and Miller, 1970; Lewis, 1986). To capture all these effects, the model includes years of education, that value squared, and 22 dummy variables indicating the major field of study of the most recent degree earned (for college graduates only). In addition, dummy variables control for the effects of veterans' preference, physical handicaps, and region of the country.

The model also includes nine dummy variables for sex and minority group status. White males are the reference group. Thus, the coefficient for each sex-minority variable indicates the proportional salary difference between members of that group and white males of the same age, length of federal service, education, major field of study, type of veterans' preference, handicap status, and geographical location. These coefficients are the unexplained salary differences.

Separate regressions are run for 1976, 1981, and 1986 to measure the size of the unexplained salary gap. Deciding the statistical significance of changes in those gaps requires pooling observations from two years. To detect changes between 1976 and 1986, for instance, the samples from those two years are combined and a new regression is run with twice as many variables as the original equations. One new variable, YEAR86, is coded 1 for observations from 1986 and 0 for observations from 1976. A second set of variables is then created by multiplying YEAR86 times the original set of variables. AGE86, for instance, has the value 0 for all 1976 observations and the same value as AGE for all 1986 observations. Thus, the regression coefficient for AGE86 is the difference between the coefficient on AGE in the 1976 regression and the coefficient on AGE in the 1986 regression. The AGE86 coefficient matches the one obtained by subtracting the 1976 from the 1986 AGE coefficient, but this technique produces a t-statistic that allows a test of the statistical significance of the difference.

Critique of the Model

Clearly, the model has many weaknesses if it is expected to identify racial and sexual discrimination by the federal personnel system. First, it does not measure many important individual characteristics, such as intelligence, personality, drive, etc. Second, it does not measure the quality of education or federal experience obtained. Third, the proxy for previous experience is more accurate for white males than for blacks, who experience more unemployment, or for women, many of whom spend several years outside the labor force raising children. Studies using more complete data sets demonstrate that such time out of the labor force depresses a worker's earnings (Corcoran, 1978; Mincer and Polachek, 1978). Fourth, employees may make individual decisions that hurt their careers, such as moving to further their spouses' careers (Mincer, 1978) or turning down promotional opportunities to preserve time for family responsibilities (Hoffman and Reed, 1981).

Findings

The regression results are not reported fully in the interests of space, but they largely confirm the hypothesized effects. The model explains 60% to 70% of the variation in salaries for each year. Salaries rise with age and federal experience, but at declining rates. Each additional year of schooling actually has an increasing impact on salary—the coefficient on years of education is negative but that on years squared is positive. In addition, coefficients on almost all college fields of study are positive. In 1976, returns were greatest for study of the health professions, engineering, computers, communications, and architecture, all of which paid at least 15% more than mere years of education would predict. In 1976, earnings in Washington, DC, were 13.5% higher than those of similar employees stationed outside the United States and about 10% higher than most of the rest of the country. In contrast to earlier studies (Taylor, 1979; Lewis and Emmett, 1984), nonhandicapped veterans were found to earn 3.2% more than comparable nonveterans in 1976. The physically handicapped received 8% less than the nonhandicapped, all else equal.

Table 4.4 presents only the coefficients for the sex-minority groups, which show the unexplained salary differences and the changes in those unexplained

TABLE 4.4   Regression Results

	Unexplained Salary Differential			*Change*		
	1976	*1981*	*1986*	*1976–86*	*1976–81*	*1981–86*
Males						
Asians	−.046c	−.044c	−.059b	−.013	.003	−.016
Native Americans	−.103b	−.115c	−.072b	.034	−.012	.045
Hispanics	−.179a	−.137c	−.130a	.049c	.042c	.006
Black Non-Hispanics	−.210a	−.191a	−.167a	.043b	.019	.024c
Females						
Asians	−.232a	−.220a	−.208a	.024	.012	.012
White Non-Hispanics	−.245a	−.246a	−.206a	.039a	.000	.039a
Black Non-Hispanics	−.297a	−.306a	−.279a	.018	−.009	.026c
Hispanics	−.279a	−.271a	−.233a	.046c	.009	.037
Native Americans	−.342a	−.343a	−.272a	.073c	−.001	.074c

a Significant at .0001, one-tailed test.
b Significant at .01, one-tailed test.
c Significant at .05, one-tailed test.

differences over time. These coefficients indicate that black males, whose average salaries were 26.4% lower than white males' (Table 4.3), were underpaid by 21.0% ($-.210$) relative to white males, given their qualifications (Table 4.4). Asian males suffered the smallest unexplained salary difference (4.6% in 1976), while Native American females bore the largest (34.2%). In each year, the smallest unexplained difference for women is bigger than the largest gap for men. These unexplained gaps are smaller than the gross differences in Table 4.3 for all groups except Asian males. In general, they are about two-thirds as large, suggesting that age, experience, and education explain perhaps one-third of the salary differences between white males and others.

Unexplained salary differences seem to have fallen for almost all groups between 1976 and 1986. The drop was most dramatic for Hispanic males, whose salary disadvantage shrank from 17.9% to 13.0%, a decline that was statistically significant at the .0001 level and that narrowed the gap by more than one-fourth. Shrinkage was also noticeable and statistically significant for black males and Native American, white, and Hispanic females. Coefficients on the 1976–1986 changes are also positive for Native American males and Asian and black females, but they are statistically insignificant.

These coefficients suggest greater salary progress by women and minorities under Reagan than Carter. Between 1976 and 1981, only Hispanic males made statistically significant salary gains relative to white males, and coefficients for the other eight groups are equally split between positive and negative. Between 1981 and 1986, eight of the nine coefficients are positive, and four are statistically significant, suggesting that the salary gap between white males and other comparably qualified employees was smaller in 1986 than at the end of Carter's term.

Comparison of Tables 4.3 and 4.4 indicates that unexplained salary differences closed more than gross ones for six of the nine groups between 1976 and 1986. For white females, for instance, the average salary gap shrank 3.4 percentage points, whereas the unexplained salary difference fell 3.9 percentage points. This suggests that the salary gains of the past decade are not illusory; indeed, they may be stronger than they appear on the surface.

Conclusion

Women and minorities made progress toward greater representation and more equal job rewards throughout the 1976–86 period. The pace was not rapid. It will take another 30 years at this rate before women and minorities fill half the positions at GS-13 and above, and unexplained salary differences will still remain, but progress does appear to be steady. Despite Reagan rhetoric and actions against affirmative action, progress seems to have continued at the same rate since his election as during the previous few years. Diversification of the GS workforce (measured as the decline in the white male share of employment) has slowed somewhat under Reagan, but this broad representativeness no longer appears to be a major problem. Representation in the upper levels of the hierarchy and salary differences *are* major problems, and on these fronts progress continues at a similar pace under Reagan as under Carter.

Perhaps this justifies Reagan's pride in his civil rights enforcement and is a sign that affirmative action is neither needed nor effective. Or it may result from the declining real pay in the federal sector under Reagan, and it may indicate that white male federal employees are more successful than others in obtaining non-federal jobs. Alternatively, it may be further evidence that policy changes at the top may have minimal impact on outcomes. Rosenbloom (1980) and Kellough and Kay (1986) find that the implementation of goals and time-tables in the federal government had no impact on employment of blacks and minimal impact on employment of women. Employment of both groups continued to rise at about the same rates as before. Sigelman and Dometrius (1986) show that changing the racial composition of a workforce is a slow process with fairly steady dynamics. Change in the federal personnel system depends upon millions of individual decisions on hiring, promotion, transfer, and quitting. Even dramatic changes in hiring practices may take years to alter the face of the federal workforce. Bureaucratic resistance slows change further. Stein (1987) notes that only 9% of the city personnel directors she surveyed, reported that federal officials had deemphasized goals and timetables or expressed a desire to abrogate affirmative action plans or consent decrees, and 16% felt that federal officials wanted stronger affirmative action efforts.

Will Reagan policy changes eventually slow progress toward racial and sexual equality, or does that process reflect deep social changes rather than presidential policy initiatives? The latter hypothesis offers more hope that the progress is real and will continue. But it also suggests that changes will be slow and perhaps as impervious to alteration by activist presidents as by conservative ones.

Notes

This research was sponsored by the U.S. Equal Employment Opportunity Commission, Public Sector Programs division. I am grateful to the U.S. Office of Personnel Management for providing statistical data from the Central Personnel Data File for this analysis and to the Carl Vinson Institute of Government and the University of Georgia Faculty Research Fund for partial funding of this research. Lana Stein contributed several helpful insights on a previous draft of this paper. An earlier version was presented at the annual meeting of the American Society for Public Administration, Boston, March 29, 1987.

1. In this case, the weights are the groups' percentages of the nonwhite-male workforce in 1984 (e.g., for black males, 4.83%/(100% − 43.04%) = 8.48%). These weights are multiplied times the salary difference in each year (e.g., for black males in 1976, 8.48% × −26.4% = 2.239%), and the results for all groups are then summed for each year.

References

John M. Abowd and Mark R. Killingsworth, "Employment, Wages, and Earnings of His-panics in the Federal and Nonfederal Sectors: Methodological Issues and their Empiri-cal Consequences," in George J. Borjas and Marta Tienda, eds., *Hispanics in the U.S. Economy* (Orlando: Academic Press, Inc., 1985).

George J. Borjas, "Discrimination in HEW: Is the Doctor Sick or Are the Patients Healthy?" *The Journal of Law and Economics,* vol. 21 (April 1978), pp. 97–110.

George J. Borjas, "The Measurement of Race and Gender Wage Differentials: Evidence from the Public Sector," *Industrial and Labor Relations Review,* vol. 37 (October 1983), pp. 79–91.

Arthur J. Corazzini, "Equality of Employment Opportunity in the Federal White-Collar Civil Service," *Journal of Human Resources,* vol. 7 (Fall 1972), pp. 424–445.

Mary Corcoran, "The Structure of Female Wages," *American Economic Review,* vol. 68 (May 1978), pp. 165–170.

Jeremiah Cotton, "More on the 'Cost' of Being a Black or Mexican American Male Worker," *Social Science Quarterly,* vol. 66 (December 1985), pp. 867–885.

Dennis Daley, "Political and Occupational Barriers to the Implementation of Affirmative Action: Administrative, Executive, and Legislative Attitudes toward Representative Bu-reaucracy," *Review of Public Personnel Administration,* vol. 4 (Summer 1984), pp. 16–30.

Mary Eisner Eccles, "Race, Sex, and Government Jobs: A Study of Affirmative Action Pro-grams in Federal Agencies" (PhD dissertation, Harvard University, 1976).

"EEOC Abandons Hiring Goals, Timetables," *Public Administration Times,* vol. 9 (March 1, 1986), p. 1.

Frank K. Gibson and Samuel Yeager, "Trends in the Federal Employment of Blacks," *Pub-lic Personnel Management,* vol. 4 (May–June 1975), pp. 189–195.

Burke D. Grandjean, "History and Career in a Bureaucratic Labor Market," *American Journal of Sociology,* vol. 86 (March 1981), pp. 1057–1092.

James F. Guyot, "Arithmetic and Inference in Ethnic Analysis: EEO in the Federal Service," *Public Administration Review,* vol. 39 (March/April 1979), pp. 194–197.

James Gwaltney and James Long, "The Relative Earnings of Blacks and Other Minorities," *Industrial and Labor Relations Review,* vol. 31 (April 1978), pp. 336–346.

James Heckman and Solomon Polachek, "Empirical Evidence on the Functional Form of the Earnings-Schooling Relationship," *Journal of the American Statistical Association,* vol. 69 (June 1974), pp. 350–354.

Don Hellriegel and Larry Short, "EEO in the Federal Government: A Comparative Analy-sis," *Public Administration Review,* vol. 32 (November/December 1972), pp. 851–858.

Carl Hoffman and John Shelton Reed, "Sex Discrimination? The XYZ Affair," *The Public Interest,* vol. 62 (Winter 1981), pp. 21–39.

James E. Kellough and Susan Ann Kay, "Affirmative Action in the Federal Bureaucracy: An Impact Analysis," *Review of Public Personnel Administration,* vol. 6 (Spring 1986), pp. 1–13.

Mark R. Killingsworth and Cordelia W. Reimers, "Race, Ranking, Promotions, and Pay at a Federal Facility: A Logit Analysis," *Industrial and Labor Relations Review,* vol. 37 (Oc-tober 1983), pp. 92–107.

Harry Kranz, "How Representative Is the Federal Service?" *Public Personnel Management,* vol. 1 (July/August 1973), pp. 242–255.

Samuel Krislov, *Representative Bureaucracy* (Englewood Cliffs, NJ: Prentice-Hall, Inc., 1974).

Gregory B. Lewis, "Race, Sex, and Supervisory Authority in Federal White-Collar Employment," *Public Administration Review,* vol. 46 (January/February 1986), pp. 25–30.

Gregory B. Lewis, "Changing Patterns of Sexual Discrimination in Federal Employment," *Review of Public Personnel Administration,* vol. 7 (Spring 1987), pp. 1–13.

Gregory B. Lewis and Mark A. Emmett, "Who Pays for Veterans' Preference?" *Administration and Society,* vol. 16 (November 1984), pp. 328–345.

James E. Long, "Employment Discrimination in the Federal Sector," *Journal of Human Resources,* vol. 11 (Winter 1976), pp. 86–97.

Jacob Mincer, *Schooling, Age, and Earnings* (New York: Columbia University Press, 1973).

Jacob Mincer, "Family Migration Decisions," *Journal of Political Economy,* vol. 86 (October 1978), pp. 749–773.

Jacob Mincer and Solomon Polachek, "Women's Earnings Reexamined," *Journal of Human Resources,* vol. 13 (Winter 1978), pp. 118–134.

Dudley L. Posten, David Alvarez, and Marta Tienda, "Earnings Differences Between Anglo and Mexican American Workers in 1960 and 1970: Changes in the 'Cost' of Being a Mexican American," *Social Science Quarterly,* vol. 57 (December 1976), pp. 618–631.

Charles S. Rodgers, "The Internal Allocation of Labor in a Federal Agency" (PhD dissertation, Brandeis University, 1977).

Winfield H. Rose and Tiang Ping Chia, "Impact of the Equal Employment Opportunity Act of 1972 on Black Employment in the Federal Service: A Preliminary Analysis," *Public Administration Review,* vol. 38 (May/June 1978), pp. 245–251.

David H. Rosenbloom, "The Federal Affirmative Action Policy," in David Nachmias, ed., *The Practice of Policy Evaluation* (New York: St. Martin's Press, 1980).

David H. Rosenbloom, "The Declining Salience of Affirmative Action in Federal Personnel Management," *Review of Public Personnel Administration,* vol. 4 (Summer 1984), pp. 31–40.

Lee Sigelman and Nelson C. Dometrius, "Organizational Regeneration and Political Change: A Model with Applications to Affirmative Action," *American Journal of Political Science,* vol. 30 (February 1986), pp. 79–107.

Sharon P. Smith, "Government Wage Differentials by Sex," *Journal of Human Resources,* vol. 11 (Spring 1976), pp. 185–199.

Lana Stein, "Merit Systems and Political Influence: The Case of Local Government," *Public Administration Review,* vol. 47 (May/June 1987), pp. 263–271.

Patricia A. Taylor, "Income Inequality in the Federal Civilian Government," *American Sociological Review,* vol. 44 (June 1979), pp. 468–479.

Patricia A. Taylor and Sung-Soon Kim, "Asian-Americans in the Federal Civil Service 1977," *California Sociologist,* vol. 3 (Winter 1980), pp. 1–16.

Juan Williams, "EEOC Shifting Its Anti-Bias Policy: Agency to Pursue Individual Remedies, Fewer Class Actions," *Washington Post* (February 13, 1985), p. A1.

5

FROM CIVIL RIGHTS TO VALUING DIFFERENCES

Walter D. Broadnax

The United States has been racially, ethnically, sexually, religiously, and philosophically diverse since its earliest beginnings. As the early Europeans and Africans began arriving, they were met by native Americans who had established various cultures and communities across the land. Many of these cultures were internally quite complex, and there was substantial diversity within the overall native American population itself. There were Iroquois, Sioux, Cherokee, Seminoles, Blackfeet, Navajos, Apaches, and numerous other groups and tribes.

Our history is one of the many stresses and strains between different groups over time. There have been wars fought that sprang from those differences. We have moved forward but, at times, it has been with great difficulty. Now, it is late in the 20th century, and we must once again find the resolve and the resources to cope positively with societal change. It is widely known that women, minorities, and immigrants will constitute a much larger proportion of the work force by the year 2000. Moreover, it is reported that

> ... white native born men are no longer a majority in the American workplace. Today, more than half the work force is comprised of women, people of color, and immigrants.[1]

Given our history, these facts indicate that we could be facing one of the greatest challenges in the life of the republic. Can we find appropriate means to help us value and manage diversity in the work place successfully?

Source: *The Bureaucrat* (Winter 1991–1992): 9–13.

The New York state government experience is an example where we find tremendous variety in language, culture, race, religion, ethnicity, sexual orientation, politics, and philosophy. New York is a veritable cauldron of differences; thus, it faces some difficult challenges in the years ahead as the state tries where necessary to reconcile and implement policies derived from concepts such as civil rights, human rights, affirmative action, equal opportunity, desegregation, and now, diversity.[2] If we look at New York state government from several different perspectives, as it wrestles with various ideas and prescriptions for valuing and managing diversity, there are some lessons and experiences that may be useful for others, including public policy and management professionals.

Equal Opportunity and Affirmative Action

As in other parts of the country, the road from civil rights to valuing diversity has been long and sometimes very difficult to travel in New York. In many ways, New York's struggles with regard to equal employment opportunity (EEO) and affirmative action (AA) are no different than those same struggles taking place in other states across this country.

However, New Yorkers pride themselves on being innovative and out front in the human rights, equal opportunity, and affirmative action debate. It remains a debate because there are still disagreements about what equal opportunity and affirmative action mean and how they should best be implemented. There are often even more complex disputes and wrangling about how these policies should be approached within the context of the state's human rights law, which predates both.

To the extent that procedures and protections are still needed to facilitate minority entrance to the work force, their existence often limits our ability to focus on the more promising messages embedded in notions of valuing and managing diversity. Many white males in New York view affirmative action and equal opportunity as ways to cheat them out of what is rightfully theirs. On the other hand, many minorities view the emerging focus on diversity as a means to dilute and even derail equal opportunity and affirmative action initiatives and programs.

Initiatives

In 1988, the Governor's Executive Committee on Affirmative Action, which I chaired, met to discuss the status of various gubernatorial equal opportunity and affirmative action initiatives. The entire meeting was devoted to how state government could best respond to all of the competing demands from various groups, e.g., homosexuals, African-Americans, women, native Americans, Hispanics, Chinese, Jews, white women, African-American women, etc. How could we promote the interest of one group without being accused of subverting the interests of another group?

During this same meeting, we also discussed anticipated worker shortages and how this might increase opportunities for all groups. The participants were initially attracted to this notion, but the natural tendency to worry about who is possibly winning and who is possibly going to be the loser prevailed and the discussion returned to how to ensure equal opportunity and affirmative action related results.

Reactions

The meeting described above presaged the difficulties we would have later on as we began developing the state's first work force plan. Various groups were afraid that human resource strategies laid out in the plan did not explicitly address the need for a continuing emphasis on EEO/AA processes and procedures. Rather, many of the strategies developed within the work force plan were based on notions related to increased diversity in the work place. But, even though representatives of the different interests really wanted to embrace and value diversity, it just did not seem to be as compelling as those concepts which promoted inclusion first.

What the New York experience seems to indicate is that even though people want to value diversity and embrace it as an approach to managing differences in the work force, they are afraid that the gates to good jobs and upward mobility will not be opened without strong policies, procedures, and controls. Most minority group members are suspicious of any discussion that suggests that white males will easily change their attitudes, beliefs, and actions toward them. Therefore, it will be important for people to begin to see that diversity is being valued and that managers are becoming interested in managing differences before equal opportunity programs and affirmative action procedures can be supplanted successfully by other means and methods for bringing all people successfully into the New York state work force.

Value Added Through Diversity

During the late 1960s and 70s, the idea that public bureaucracies might be able to perform their missions better if those who worked within them were more representative of the society at large received a good deal of attention. Moreover, there were some who believed that there was something intrinsically valuable about the perspectives that would be rendered in the policymaking and decision processes by the inclusion of minorities and women.[3] Embedded in the concept of representativeness was the notion of value added to state government by the potentially positive influence women and minorities might have on the policy and decisionmaking processes of government. Either implicitly or explicitly, the belief was that including those who are different will enrich and strengthen what government is as well as what government does.

It is difficult for some people to believe that there could be any value in differences. Recently, it has become chic to point to Japan's success as an industrial power and explain that success by calling attention to her relatively homogeneous population. When this subject arises, rarely does anyone proceed to explain and substantiate this bit of conjecture. Rather, there is usually a pause in the exchange and the conversation or presentation continues. The implication seems to be that we all understand and agree with the notion that sameness (homogeneous populations) produces better products more efficiently.

New York state is many things to many people but it could never be referred to as homogeneous. In fact, it was estimated that in 1980, 16 percent of the state's labor force, 37 percent of its physicians, and 20 percent of its nurses were foreign born.[4]

The state has the largest Jewish population in the world outside of Israel and the largest African-American population in the United States. Putatively, there are over 50 different languages represented within the student body of the City University of New York. The streets of Manhattan are teeming with differences.

Oath of Allegiance

Any state as diverse as New York must constantly search for ways to include people in the processes of business and government. The benefits to be gained from this inclusion can be seen in some very practical and concrete outcomes that have been achieved through the value added derived from diversity. For example, the state had struggled for years with the refusal of native Americans to take an oath of allegiance to the United States. This created a very big problem in that the oath was required in the civil service law covering state employment and the state education law which covered teachers and others under the jurisdiction of the education commissioner. Many attempts had been made over the years to find a solution to this problem so that native Americans would no longer be disadvantaged in the hiring process and officials could be satisfied that they did not wish to undermine the government.

In 1989, the first native American was hired in the affirmative action office of the New York State Department of Civil Service. There was all of the expected discomfort with this action in many parts of the department, but the leadership believed that in order for the state to become seriously inclusionary with regard to native Americans, it would be necessary to create a focus for those interests within the Civil Service Department by hiring a native American. Over the course of several months, this one individual was able to generate support within his own department and find allies within the Department of Education and the state legislature. He worked tirelessly to build rapport and understanding between himself and others across various agencies and units of government. Through this process, he was able to bring the commissioners of Education and Civil Service together around a piece of legislation which established an alternative oath of office for native Americans. This legislation removed a significant legal obstacle to native American employment by the state of New York.

Tangible and Intangible Benefits

In this situation, the value added came in tangible ways, such as the new legislation and revised regulations regarding the oath of office but there were also certain intangible benefits. One such benefit was that nonminorities were able to experience a point of view, a culture, a policy perspective that, in many ways, differed substantially from their own. These differences and the feelings they sometimes generated, often helped them to understand some of the reactions they may have gotten themselves from traditional minorities. Differences, when accepted as legitimate, can keep us from becoming smug. Creating a situation where everyone is considered with dignity and treated with respect empowers more people in the work place. More people empowered translates into a more powerful work place.

Education and Human Resource Development Needs

In the 60s and 70s, many government managers were being exposed to sensitivity training. The objective then was to help white managers deal with what appeared to be a rapidly increasing minority presence in the workplace. Quickly added to the mix was the increasing presence of women, especially in professional and managerial roles. There are many stories about sensitivity training where participants felt things got out of hand. However, the objective was usually an audible and sound one—to help people cope successfully with change.

The Supreme Court decision in *Brown vs. The Topeka Board of Education* had only recently stated that separate but equal was a fantasy and, therefore, public facilities, schools, colleges and universities, and public transportation would have to be desegregated. The decision was handed down in 1954, but it was not until the 1960s that we saw desegregation beginning to unfold seriously. As desegregation accelerated, many people were being asked to shift from a situation where it was legal and common practice to keep minorities out to one where they were being told they should work together in peace and harmony. Something more than saying that it was a good idea was needed.

New Challenges

Today, public managers and government officials face yet another education and development challenge spawned by societal, and to some extent, global change. Some managers, within the space of a 30-year career, have come from a situation where they rarely saw minorities in positions of respect and authority in the workplace, to one where there are large numbers of minority and women technicians, professionals, and managers.

Columbia University's School of Business is developing a comprehensive "Managing Diversity" course. The program, which is being produced by psychologist and diversity consultant, Dr. Anna Duran, is designed for executives and managers who are faced with increasing cultural diversity in their organizations and it will examine the best methods for incorporating approaches to cultural diversity into routine management activities.[5]

Looking closely at recent training efforts, we can find themes and strains that remind us of experiences from the old sensitivity training workshops. A vignette from a training workshop run by Terrance Simmons reveals the following insights.

> The 13 senior-level Unisys managers sitting in a Norcross, Georgia, training center look uneasy. As part of a day-long diversity management workshop, they have just been instructed to compile a list of negative and positive stereotypes that are normally associated with various groups—including blacks, Hispanics, women, and white males . . .

The consultant running the seminar politely asks that the participants be as candid as possible. Just jot down things you have heard or that you have seen. After working for 10 minutes, the group which has been divided into three teams, reads their list aloud.

Although several positive stereotypes were listed for white males—they were labeled leaders and decisionmakers—the group appears disturbed that a number of negative stereotypes were listed for the other groups. For example, women were viewed as pushy, bitchy, and too emotional. Hispanics were seen as lazy, emotional, and unskilled. African-Americans described as uneducated, slow workers, and militant. When asked, almost all managers in modern organizations will say they are not racists or sexists.

The purpose of the exercise is to allow managers safely to recognize and admit, to themselves and their peers, that they really do still harbor some biases against minorities and women. Once this happens, we have made a quantum leap ahead because it becomes obvious that those biases are adversely affecting their ability to manage a diverse workforce productively.[6]

Training

It appears that objectives of the 60s and 70s are similar to those of the 90s and education and training are fundamentally important to reaching them. The National Association of State Personnel Executives has recognized this need for training and education related to diversity. As a result, each semiannual and annual conference has devoted a substantial proportion of the program to providing educational and training opportunities in this area for the state's chief personnel and human resources executives. Regretfully, New York state, like almost every other state, provides too few seminars, workshops, lectures, or experientially-based training and educational programs focusing on cultural diversity for its managers and executives. This can be partially explained by an increasingly difficult financial situation.

Because New York state's human resources system is driven by the fact that its workforce is 97 percent unionized and a civil service approach that requires examinations for most entry-level jobs as well as promotions, diversification of the workforce has been relatively slow. Moreover, training those from minority groups so that they might be able to meet the standards set for most jobs has been cumbersome at best, although some progress has been made over the last few years.

For example, the Civil Service Employees' Association negotiated with the state for the creation of the Civil Service Employees' Advancement Program (CSEAP). This program has helped hundreds of female employees move out of clerical positions and into managerial and professional positions through on-the-job training opportunities. There have also been some smaller successes with transitional programs such as the School-to-Work Bridge Program which provides experiential opportunities for minorities as they are leaving high school or college, thus improving their performance on examinations required for appointment.

Again, the New York experience is one of successes as well as obstacles yet to be overcome, but one where there is an increasing awareness that much remains to be done in order successfully to diversify its workforce. In areas such as mental health, mental retardation and developmental disabilities, and correctional services, here is a rapidly increasing population of minority clients and a situation that is quickly escalating into one that will demand a more diversified workforce.

What Managers Must Understand

As was discussed earlier in this essay, managers sometimes may need help finding out what the problem is before they can be expected to solve it. The process of discovering what the problem is and where it comes from is what many would call education. Education is cognitive but it is also very much affective or emotional in character as well. Black is not necessarily black and white is not necessarily white until people are able to understand such factual information in terms that are useful to them in a personalized way. For example, the fact that white males are no longer in the majority within the workforce is factually true. But, this may mean something different for each individual.

The challenge is to help managers and those they manage to come to value differences. This means that both those who manage and those who are managed must receive assistance in learning what the objectives of the organization are in regard to diversity and then they must receive skills training that will help them achieve those organizational goals. As is true for any organization, the commitment must begin at the top and it must be sustained from the top.

Typically, excellent managers have developed outstanding human resource management skills. They have learned how to create situations for getting the best out of each individual within his or her organization. Yes, this is much more difficult than proceeding as though everyone was the same or as though everyone could become the same. It means that each organization and each leader within his or her organization must take seriously the fact that the world is changing and come to understand that these changes do not have to mitigate against individual aspirations or ambitions. However, if managers are going to take organizational goals related to diversity seriously, they must be treated like all other goals that are important to top management. There must be rewards for those who do well. The behaviors desired must be reinforced.

In a very practical sense, we see organizations like XEROX, where David T. Kearns, the former chairman and chief executive officer (currently deputy secretary of the Department of Education), was able to diversify his corporation culturally. He took it seriously and those working with him were compelled to take it seriously as well.[7] If the person at the top is only paying lip service to the value of diversity, everyone will know it because they will be able to see it. The work place will not have changed.

Tragically, in managing diversity, there are many who still ask what is it that women and minorities want. Complete success would be when there is no need to ask this question because it would be understood that they basically want what we all want and that those wants are tempered and shaped by individual differences and desires. A more conceivable indicator of success would be the existence of increasingly visible public and private organizations across the land where the inclusion of differences was the rule, rather than the exception. Once differences are included, we can then work toward valuing those differences.

Conclusion

Valuing differences has not been something that has come easily in the United States. We have struggled with a host of concepts, notions, and approaches to dealing with differences; they range from legalized perpetual servitude to America the melting pot. But each time we have seriously reached for a solution we have made incremental progress. Today, it seems that the stage may be set for us to take a major step toward valuing diversity by fully embracing the notion of including differences. Once organizations have reached a critical mass in terms of having brought people from different backgrounds and experiences into the working environment, the most important ingredient necessary for learning to value diversity will be in place. The sine qua non of any meaningful discussion of diversity is the successful inclusion of differences.

Notes

1. Loden, Marilyn and Ronnie Hoffman Loeser, "Working Diversity: Managing the Differences," *The Bureaucrat*, Spring 1991, p. 21.

2. See *Public Service Through the State Government Workforce: Meeting the Challenge of Change.* Task Force on the New York State Public Workforce in the 21st Century. Nelson A. Rockefeller Institute, February 1989, and New York State Department of Civil Service Work Force Plan 1989: Preparing Today's Work Force for Tomorrow, Spring 1989.

3. See Broadnax, Walter D., "Role Orientations of Minority and Nonminority Urban Administrators: Forces for Convergence and Divergence." Dissertation, 1975.

4. New York State Department of Civil Service, New York State Workforce Plan 1990: Building a State Workforce in the 1990s, Spring 1990.

5. Thompson, Kevin D., "Back to School," *Black Enterprise,* November 1990, p. 57.

6. Ibid., p. 56.

7. Thomas, R. Roosevelt, "From Affirmative Action to Affirming Diversity," *Harvard Business Review,* March–April 1990, p. 115.

6

EQUAL EMPLOYMENT OPPORTUNITY AND THE EARLY CAREER IN FEDERAL EMPLOYMENT

Gregory B. Lewis

Abstract

Using a one percent sample of federal personnel records, this article examines entry levels and advancement rates during the first eight years of the federal career for white and minority males and females who entered the civil service shortly after leaving school. Once educational levels and major fields of study are controlled for, the four groups have remarkably similar entry levels, suggesting that race and gender have little direct impact on placement levels. Men do have markedly higher early advancement rates than women, however, pulling ahead of comparable women at the rate of better than one-tenth of a grade per year. The implications for equal employment opportunity policy are discussed.

Introduction

In a recent symposium on the future of affirmative action, the participants unanimously declared its prognosis to be bleak. Affirmative action has never gained strong support from the public (Rosenbloom, 1984), from elected or administrative officials (Daley, 1984), or even from public personnel administrators (Davis and West, 1984). Responsible officials were judged unlikely to continue devoting major political capital to a program that generates so much controversy while

Source: *Review of Public Personnel Administration* 6 (Summer 1986): 1–18.

delivering such limited results, particularly during a period emphasizing retrenchment rather than the rights of the disadvantaged (Rosenbloom, 1984; Thompson, 1984). The author expects to see declining enforcement efforts and fewer attempts to improve the credentials of women and minorities. Rather than seeking to establish a more representative bureaucracy, I predict that the country will be satisfied with establishing a goal of race- and sex-neutral treatment of employees.

In this hostile environment, it is more important than ever to focus equal employment efforts on practices that have a real impact on earnings inequality and in which changes can be clearly justified. Federal practices during the early career may be crucial in achieving equality because the course of an employee's career is basically set at that time. The training and career ladders associated with those first jobs largely determine the employee's opportunity for development (Spilerman, 1977). Early advancement patterns may be crucial in deciding one's career ceiling, as employees passed over for early promotions appear less likely to be considered for later ones (Rosenbaum, 1979). If women and minorities are placed lower or receive fewer early promotions than comparably qualified white males, the pattern of inequality may well continue throughout their careers.

One percent sample of federal personnel records is used to examine the critical early period of the federal career, from initial placement through the first eight years of federal work experience. It focuses on employees who entered the General Schedule between April 1973 and April 1982, the earliest and latest years for which one percent samples of the Central Personnel Data File (CPDF), could be obtained. The General Schedule was chosen for analysis because all GS positions are classified into one of 18 grades. These grades indicate the difficulty and responsibility of the work and are the primary determinants of salaries. Grades simplify the study of entry levels because grades, as opposed to salaries, have reasonably constant meanings over time. Advancements simplify the study at entry levels because higher grades mean both greater responsibilities and larger salaries. The article begins with a review of previous studies of earnings inequality in the federal service. Then, it examines the impact of race and sex on entry grade, initial occupation, and early advancement of employees who enter federal service within three years of leaving school. These people are the ones most clearly at an early stage in their careers and whose successes are least affected by experience with different employers. The succeeding section compares findings for this group with results for more experienced employees.

Previous Research

Much remains to be done to accomplish the goal of race- and sex-neutral treatment of federal employees. Average salaries and grade levels of white males remain far higher than those of women and most minorities. Some of the difference can be explained by the higher average qualifications of white males, who tend to be better educated and to have worked longer for the federal government than white women, blacks, Hispanics, and Native Americans. Still, a variety of studies show that even when education, federal experience, age, veterans' preference, occupation, and location are taken into account, men still earn substantially more than women and whites earn more than minorities, except perhaps Orientals (Corazzini, 1972; Long, 1976; Smith, 1976; Eccles, 1976; Rodgers, 1977; Borjas, 1978 and 1983; Taylor, 1979; Taylor and Kim, 1980; Grandjean, 1981; Killingsworth and Reimers, 1983).

Although this line of research suggests strongly that the federal personnel system treats white males better than other groups, few of these studies have taken the additional step of focusing on particular personnel actions or phases of the federal career to establish at what stages the unequal treatment arises. Two dissertations do concentrate on two important career phases—entry levels and promotions. Rodgers (1977) surveyed 259 HEW employees working in the Boston region in July 1976 and found that men had entered federal service one grade higher than comparable women, using a model that controlled for age, years of previous experience, and whether the employee had no college, some college, or a college diploma. He also found that men tended to advance 0.4 grade further than comparable women over the course of their careers, in a model controlling for years of federal service, entry grade, and whether the employee had a college diploma or worked in a professional occupation. In his sample, race did not have a significant impact on either entry or promotion.

Eccles (1976), using a one percent sample of federal personnel records, found that for a person with average characteristics entering federal white-collar employment in 1974, a white man would start 1.1 grades higher than a white woman if both entered nonclerical positions, and 0.5 grade higher if both entered clerical positions. She also reported that a white male with average characteristics had a 68 percent chance of entering a nonclerical position, while a white female with the same characteristics had only a 23 percent chance of doing so. Eccles did indicate, however, that comparable white men and women had similar advancement rates between 1968 and 1973. A white man with average characteristics was expected to progress 0.84 grade if he was a nonclerical employee and 0.80 if a clerical employee. For a white woman with the same characteristics, the expected advancement was 0.77 or 0.68 grade. Similarly, the white male advantage over minorities was much higher for entry levels than advancement rates.

Thus, the studies find problems in both placement and advancement; initial placement patterns are apparently a cause for greater concern than subsequent upward mobility. These studies focus on the impact of federal practices, but both have weaknesses for an evaluation of the civil service today. The most obvious is that their data are rather old. Eccles examines placement ten years ago, while Rodgers considers the entry levels of employees who may have been working 20 or more years when he surveyed them in 1976. Second, Rodgers studied one agency in one region, which may or may not have been representative of the federal service as a whole. Third, Eccles suffered from a serious data deficiency in that the Central Personnel Data File (the basis for both her work and the current paper) contains no information on work experience prior to entering federal service. Though researchers typically finesse this problem by using age or some estimate of "potential" experience (age minus estimated age on completing school), researchers with very detailed data sets have shown that the amount of "real" work experience is crucial in determining salary (Mincer and Polachek, 1974; Corcoran, 1978). A model using age or potential experience will treat a man who has spent ten years in the labor market and a woman who has spent ten years raising children as having equal experience, even though homemaking has been shown to develop far fewer marketable skills. Since age or "potential" experience will be a key variable in entry level, it is difficult to be sure that men and women are being compared realistically.

To avoid the problem caused by poor data on prior experience, the bulk of the current analysis is performed on a sample limited to those who began federal service within three years of leaving school. This ensures that we are examining employees early in their careers and not including people moving into the federal service after working for years in the private sector, the military, or the home. It should also minimize the divergence of male-female career patterns outside the federal service, since most of the men and women entering federal employment within three years of school probably began paid employment shortly after leaving school.

Employees with Little Prior Experience

Table 6.1 presents the initial grades of employees in the sample who entered federal service within three years of leaving school. Women enter primarily through the lowest grades. Nearly two-thirds of the women, over half the minority males, and only one-quarter of the white men take positions at the GS-1 to GS-3 levels. Nearly 30 percent of the white males enter at GS-7 or higher levels, but fewer than 10 percent of the remainder do so. With an average entry grade of 5.2, white men entered 1.5 grades higher than minority males, 1.6 grades higher than white females, and 2.0 grades higher than minority females in the sample.

White males also entered through the most desirable occupations. Positions in professional and administrative series mean not only higher entry grades, but career ladders that involve two-grade promotions from the GS-5 to GS-11 levels. Employees in technical, clerical, and other occupations generally advance one grade at a time. Nearly half of the white males enter through these professional/administrative positions, compared to about 20 percent of the minority males and 10 percent of the females. Approximately three-quarters of the women enter through clerical series, as opposed to well under half of the men.

White men in the sample advanced furthest, an average of 3.6 grades by 1982. This means a gain of an additional 0.3 grade on minority men, 1.3 grades on

TABLE 6.1   Average Entry Levels and Advancement Rates for Employees
Entering Civil Service Within Three Years of Leaving School

	Minority Females	*White Females*	*Minority Males*	*White Males*
Entry Grade				
GS1–GS3 (percent)	72.0	61.4	57.7	25.4
GS4–GS6 (percent)	22.0	29.5	31.5	45.8
GS7–GS9 (percent)	4.4	7.8	7.2	22.0
GS 10 & above (percent)	1.6	1.3	3.6	6.8
Mean Entry Grade	3.19	3.58	3.69	5.21
Entry Occupation				
Professional	4.4	8.2	9.8	29.7
Administrative	4.1	4.8	9.0	13.0
Technical	8.2	12.6	26.2	26.1
Clerical	78.4	71.7	41.8	21.0
Other	5.0	2.7	13.1	10.2
Grades Advanced by 1982 (mean)	2.16	2.26	3.34	3.61
Sample Sizes				
Entry	322	1067	111	64
Advancement	152	480	41	303

SOURCE: Computed by author from one percent sample, U.S. Office of Personnel Management, Central Personnel Data File April 1973–April 1982.

white women, and 1.4 grades on minority women. The male-female difference arose partly because the men entered somewhat earlier, but even on a year-by-year basis, the men were rising faster.

Initial Placement

Clearly, then, men are entering higher and advancing faster than women during the first few years of the federal career. A number of factors could explain this pattern, the most important probably is education. A bachelor's degree or extensive experience is a prerequisite for professional and administrative positions, and further education qualifies one for higher entry grades. Indeed, a model regressing entry grade on years of education alone explains 60 percent of the variance in entry grades for this sample. White males, with an average of 15.3 years of schooling, have nearly two more years of formal education than white females and minority males and females, who average 13.5, 13.6, and 13.2 years, respectively. Viewed from a different angle, 65 percent of the white men in the sample held bachelor's degrees or better, compared to 26 percent of the white females, 30 percent of the minority males, and 18 percent of the minority females.

Reed and Miller (1970) have shown that college graduates' fields of study have a major impact on their salaries. As many federal positions require a specialized educational background, it appears likely that field of study might also prove important in entry grades. When six dummy variables indicating general areas of academic concentration were added to a regression model that only included years of education, the model's explanatory power rose from 60 to 68 percent.

Four additional factors were considered. First, although the variation in "potential" experience was severely limited in this sample, it can still be expected to increase entry levels. "Potential" experience was estimated by subtracting age at leaving school from age upon entering federal employment.

Second, veterans' preference has been criticized as one of the major causes of sexual inequality in federal employment (Fleming and Shanor, 1977). Veterans and the spouses and mothers of deceased or severely disabled veterans are given five- or ten-point bonuses on civil service examinations. The high scores on these examinations are 100 in the absence of these bonuses but veterans can score as high as 110; applicants with scores below 90 were rarely hired in the 1970s; and over 95 percent of the employees entitled to veterans' preference are men. Consequently, veteran males might well be obtaining the most desirable positions and forcing equally qualified nonveteran women to accept lower level entry positions.

The expected positive impact of veterans' preference on salaries has not been demonstrated empirically (see Smith, 1976; Taylor, 1979; Grandjean, 1981; Lewis and Emmert, 1984). Indeed, veterans are frequently found to be earning less than similar nonveterans. Taylor (1979) has hypothesized that veterans enter above their appropriate level due to preference but fall behind thereafter because they lack the qualifications to advance. Lewis and Emmert (1984) find some evidence that veterans are falling behind once inside the service but no evidence of an initial advantage. Veterans' preference is entered into this model in the form of a dummy variable coded 1 for those entitled to preference and 0 otherwise. Standard understandings of how preference works suggest that the coefficient should be positive.

Third, gender and race are entered into the equation through the use of dummy variables. Separate variables are created for white females, minority males, and minority females. The coefficients on these variables indicate the difference between the expected grades for members of these groups and the expected grades of white males with the same educational levels, fields of study, potential experience, and eligibility for veterans' preference.

Fourth, the possibility that placement patterns changed from year to year was investigated through the use of several time variables. Entry year was added to one regression to see if there was a general upward or downward trend in entry grades over time. Interactions between entry year, race, and gender were added to a second equation to see if the gap between white males and other groups was widening or narrowing. In a third equation, dummy variables were included for each entry year to allow for the possibility that expected entry grades might be lower in certain years, such as during recessions or federal hiring freezes. In none of the regressions did the time variables add significantly to the model, suggesting that the placement process was quite stable over the period studied. Consequently, the time variables are not included in any of the results reported below.

Adding potential experience, veterans' preference, race, and gender to the regression analysis contributed minimally to the explanatory power of the model, raising the R^2 only from .68 to .69. The results of this regression analysis are presented in the first column of Table 6.2. The variables have been coded so that the intercept terms represent the expected entry level of a white male high school graduate with no further education or work experience—at an expected grade of 2.42. In general, each additional year of education is associated with an entry grade that is higher by half a grade (0.50). The positive coefficients on the major fields of study indicate that a college degree in any except the residual field is correlated with a higher entry grade than would be expected from the increased years of education alone. As might be expected, the bonuses are largest in law and engineering, 4.37 and 1.59 grades, respectively. Entry grades also tend to be higher for those with more potential experience, at a rate of about one-sixth of a grade (0.17) for each additional year outside of school, all else equal.

Once these factors are taken into account, race, gender, and veterans' preference have little impact on entry levels. The results indicate that white women in the sample are entering 0.08 grade lower than white men in the sample with the same educational and experience backgrounds, but that difference is not statistically significant at even the 0.20 level. The expected difference between white and minority males (0.17 grade) is also statistically insignificant. Note that with a sample size of over 2100, even small effects generally attain statistical significance. Its absence here is surprising, especially since white males entered more than 1.5 grades higher than both these groups, on average. The difference in expected entry grades between white males and minority females is statistically significant, but it is still only 0.29 grade, which is far less than the 2.02 grade difference between the average entry levels for these two groups, indicating that most of the difference can be explained by reasonably legitimate factors.

The boost federal new hires obtain from veterans' preference appears small (0.10 grade) and is statistically insignificant. Even when it is dropped from the model, the difference between white males and females remains insignificant. The boost due to major fields of study is important, however. When majors are dropped from the model, the expected difference between white males and minority females rises to one-half of a grade, and both white females and minority males fall a statistically significant one-quarter of a grade behind white males. Since white males comprise the bulk of those in the most remunerative majors, especially law and engineering, discrimination might be affecting the government's valuation of those fields of study.

TABLE 6.2   Entry and Advancement Models for Employees Entering Civil Service Within Three Years of Leaving School

	Entry Grade	Professional/ Administrative Placement	ADVANCEMENT	
			Interaction with Years of Service	Interaction with Years of Service Squared
White Female	−.08	−.39*	−.15***	—
Minority Female	−.29**	−.59	−.11**	—
Minority Male	−.17	−.15	−.00	—
Years of Education	.50***	1.05***	−.09**	.002**
Major Field of Study				
Biology, Agriculture, and Health Professions	.97***	1.55**	.53**	−.010**
Business and Management	.82**	2.10***	1.01***	−.014***
Engineering, Mathematics, and Physical Sciences	1.59***	2.79***	.89***	−.013***
Law	4.37***	1.24	1.08***	−.026***
Social Sciences	.36**	1.01**	.95**	−.014***
Other	.06	.61	.92***	−.013***
Potential Experience	.17***	.11	−.09**	.001*
Veterans' Preference	.10	−.38	.59*	−.011*
Intercept	2.42***	−5.60***	1.01***	−.058***
R^2	.69	.54	.78	
N	2146	2130	976	

***significant at .0001 level
**significant at .01 level
*significant at .05 level

Entry Occupation

Essentially the same model was applied to placement into professional and administrative occupations, which not only offer higher entry levels but allow employees to "skip" grades as they move up the hierarchy. Because the dependent variable in this case is binary (the employee either did or did not obtain a professional/administrative occupation), regression analysis was rejected in favor of logit analysis, which fits the pattern of error terms better. In logit analysis, the dependent variable is the natural logarithm of the odds ratio, in this case, the ratio of the probability of obtaining a professional/administrative position to the probability of not obtaining such a position. Coefficients are more difficult to interpret in logit analysis than in regression analysis, because they indicate the expected proportional change in the odds ratio and have to be translated back into probabilities to be very meaningful. (For a fuller discussion, see Neter and Wasserman, 1974:329–335.)

The results presented in the second column of Table 6.2 indicate that the same factors that explain entry level also explain occupational placement, accounting for 54 percent of the variance in this case. In general the findings are about the same. Increased education is extremely important in determining the level at which one enters. Potential experience has a positive but insignificant coefficient, and being eligible for veterans's preference does not improve one's odds of placement into a professional/administrative occupation.

Again there are negative coefficients on each of the race/sex variables, but this time only that for white females is statistically significant. And the effects suggested by these coefficients are quite small. For a new hire with three years of college, for instance, the probability of a professional/administrative placement ranges between 5 and 8 percent for the four groups. For those with an MBA, the range is 90 to 94 percent. Only among recent college graduates is there any appreciable variation. A minority female with a bachelor's degree in the social sciences has a 27 percent chance of a professional or administrative placement, while a white male with the same degree has a 40 percent chance. For those with engineering degrees, the comparable figures are 69 and 80 percent. In other words, the sexual differential in placements into these more desirable occupations is statistically significant, but not very substantial.

Advancement Rates

If race and gender appear to have little direct effect on placement beyond their impact on education, do they influence advancement patterns in the early career? The dependent variable to be explained in this case is the number of grades advanced between entry and April 1982, a period of one to eight years depending upon one's entry date. (Employees who entered after April 1981 or who were not employed continuously from entry through 1982 were dropped from the sample, leaving 977 cases.) The key factor here should be federal experience, since the longer the person has been employed, the further he or she is likely to have advanced. Prior research has demonstrated that promotion chances are highest in the first years of employment and decline steadily thereafter. The relationship between federal experience and advancement is curvilinear; that is, the expected advancement in each year of the career is positive, but is somewhat smaller than in the previous year. The best way to deal with this pattern statistically is to include both federal experience and federal experience squared in the model. The coefficient on experience will be positive, indicating that more experienced employees have generally advanced more than those with less experience, but the coefficient on experience squared will be negative, showing that most employees' progress slows later in their careers.

The same factors that influence entry grades may also affect advancement rates, but it is unreasonable to expect an engineering degree, for instance, to have the same impact on advancement over a one-year as over a six-year period. Consequently, all the independent variables in the entry grade model (including the intercept term) are included in the advancement model as interaction terms with both years of federal experience and years of federal experience squared. Thus, their coefficients should be interpreted as the effect of that factor (e.g., an engineering degree) per year of federal service. Table 6.2 displays the interactions with federal experience in the third column and the interactions with federal experience squared in the fourth column. In general, the coefficients in the third and fourth columns have opposing signs, indicating that the advantage or disadvantage associated with the variable (per year of federal service) declines as the career progresses. Interestingly, virtually all the coefficients in this model were statistically significant, except the interactions between the race/sex terms and federal experience squared. This suggests that the impact of gender on annual advancement rates does not decline over the first eight years of federal service. To simplify the presentation, these three interaction terms were dropped from the regression equation reported in Table 6.2.

The intercept interaction terms represent a white male high school graduate, who is expected to advance by nearly one grade during his second year of service and less during each succeeding year. The negative coefficient on potential experience in the third column suggests that those with prior experience advance less rapidly, probably because they are entering the civil service at a higher level, somewhat closer to their career ceiling. The positive coefficients on the major fields of study in the third column indicate that employees with college diplomas move up faster than high school graduates. This is partly due to their greater likelihood of entering professional or administrative occupations, in which it is common to "skip" grades in the early promotions. However, even when entry grade and occupation were controlled for in a separate regression (through a series of dummy variables for each of the nine lowest grades and for entry through a professional/administrative position), college graduates appeared to be advancing faster than high school graduates entering at the same level. College graduates seem to be impressing their superiors more, probably due either to greater abilities or to the credential.

Surprisingly, veterans appear to be climbing more rapidly than nonveterans with the same characteristics. This is in spite of the lack of formal preference that veterans enjoy at entry, and runs counter to Taylor's hypothesis that preference causes veterans to enter above their qualifications and then fall behind.

How do race and gender affect advancement rates? Note first that the model detects no difference between the career patterns of white and minority males. The entry disadvantages of minority males are small and statistically insignificant.

The difference in advancement rates is too small to be reported. Men and women do differ, however. The women are falling behind at a rate of .11 to .15 grades per year. By the end of eight years, women are expected to have fallen 1.2 grades behind similarly educated men.

Because these patterns are rather complex, Figure 6.1 illustrates the expected career paths of inexperienced, nonveteran high school and college graduates (the latter have degrees in the social sciences). The difference between high school and college graduates is dramatic. The white male college graduate's expected entry grade is 2.4 grades higher than the high school graduate's and the gap widens steadily, to 6.7 grades after eight years. Over the course of eight years, the model expects the white male college graduate to advance 8.7 grades while the white male high school graduate rises only 4.4 grades. In addition, the trend suggests that the high school graduate has just about reached his career peak by his eighth year, but the college graduate can expect to keep climbing for another four years.

The figure shows that sex is a more important factor than race in early career success, though neither is nearly as important as education. White and minority male patterns are nearly indistinguishable. The white and minority female paths resemble each other closely. While the male and female curves begin at nearly the same point, however, they diverge noticeably. For both high school and college graduates, women's careers rise slower and peak earlier than men's.

Thus, the findings are reasonably good for employees who enter the civil service shortly after school. Race, gender, and veterans' preference play little direct role in entry, though all may influence how much education a job applicant has received. Race also has little impact on early advancement rates, and the more rapid progress of veterans is not due to formal preference. Only the effect of gender on advancement is troublesome.

More Experienced Employees

Do these reassuring findings hold up for the two-thirds of new civil service employees who have waited four or more years after school to enter federal service? For the sample of these more experienced employees, entry grade gaps were even larger than for the employees entering shortly after school. Mean grades for males were 6.6 for whites and 5.1 for minorities, about 1.5 grades higher than those of their less experienced counterparts. The average entry grades of 3.9 and 3.5 for white and minority women, however, were only about one-third of a grade higher than those of the less experienced women. The percentages of experienced employees obtaining professional/administrative occupations did not differ markedly from those for less experienced employees. Experienced employees did show less advancement than the less experienced group, however, with averages ranging from 2.3 grades for white males to 1.2 grades for minority males.

How much of this difference can be explained by differing characteristics? The entry grade model from Table 6.2 was repeated on the sample of employees with

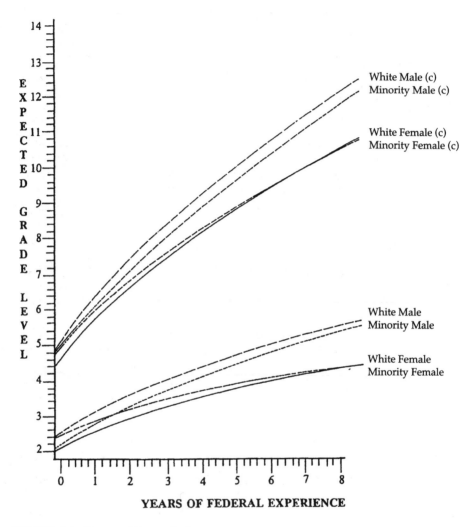

FIGURE 6.1   Expected Career Paths

four or more years between leaving school and entering civil service.[1] This time the grade gap between white males and comparably educated and experienced employees is 1.7 grades with white females, 1.8 grades with minority females, and 0.6 grade with minority males. These unexplained gaps are, respectively, only 65 percent as high as the overall gap of 2.67 grades between white males and females, 58 percent as high as the gap of 3.11 grades between white males and minority females, and 45 percent of the gap of 1.42 grades between white and minority males. In other words, education and experience appear to explain one-third to one-half of the grade differentials between white males and other groups.

Veterans' preference does not explain the gap. Veterans comprise half of the male new hires and 5 percent of the females, but they are actually entering half a grade *lower* than would be predicted from their other characteristics. This suggests that the preferential treatment veterans receive is not enough to overcome the disadvantages they suffer from lower socioeconomic backgrounds and the limited relevance of military experience for civilian employment.

The key problem with this analysis is that "potential" experience is almost certainly not comparable for men and women. Virtually all of the men's time outside of school and federal service will have been spent in other jobs. Most of the women will have devoted much of their time to homemaking and childraising, activities which produce fewer marketable skills. In addition, the higher unemployment rates of minorities and discrimination in the private sector may also mean that minority males may have less, or less valuable, prior experience than white males with the same "potential" experience. To see how important this factor was in determining entry grades, the model was run again with new interaction terms created by multiplying years of education and the two potential experience variables times the race and gender variables. There were no statistically significant differences in the returns on education of white men and either white or minority women. The minority men actually obtained significantly higher returns on their educations. White male potential experience was clearly valued most highly, however. White women received almost no return on potential experience, minority women fared somewhat better, and minority males obtained about four-fifths as great a return on their potential experience as did white males. This pattern could be consistent with equal treatment of work experience for all groups, but it could also represent discrimination. Once the impact of potential experience is accounted for, however, there was no residual advantage to being a white male. This strengthens the conclusion from the initial analysis that male-female differences result primarily from lower educational attainments of women and from lower valuations of women's time outside school and federal employment.

The white male advantage in receiving a professional/administrative placement was stronger for the more experienced group, though still not dramatic. Part, but not all, of the advantage revolves around different valuations of an employee's "potential" experience.

Analysis of advancement patterns, using essentially the same model as that displayed in Table 6.2, reveals a pattern similar to that found for the employees entering shortly after school, though the impact of most variables is weaker. (It should be noted that veterans' preference appears to have no impact on advancement for employees in this group.) As in that case, white males are moving up the federal hierarchy most rapidly. When entry grade is also taken into account, white males are moving ahead of employees with comparable educations, experience, and starting points at the rate of 0.10 to 0.15 grades per year.

Conclusion

The first few years of a federal career are critical in determining an employee's success in the federal service. Initial placement determines not only starting salary but the training provided and the most likely routes for career development. Professional and administrative positions generally provide longer career ladders and the opportunity to skip grades on the upward climb. Clerical occupations may limit both the speed and extent of advancement.

White males are doing much better than women and minorities in this crucial early phase of the federal career. They enter through higher grades and more desirable occupations and they move up further in the first few years. If, as claimed by many authors, the future of affirmative action is bleak, then we may have to depend only on equal employment opportunity efforts to diminish these gaps between white males and others in the early career. How close are we to achieving the EEO goal in entry and early promotions? How much further can EEO alone carry us?

The good news is that the federal personnel system is very close to achieving EEO at entry. Level and type of education is by far the most important factor in initial placement, at least for employees entering the General Schedule within three years of school. This study finds no appreciable differences in initial grades of similarly educated entrants of different races or genders. This conclusion is weaker for employees who waited at least four years after school before entering the General Schedule. Weaknesses in the data set prevent a firm decision on whether discrimination or real differences in work experience cause the racial and sexual grade differentials.

The bad news on entry levels is that little more can be achieved without affirmative action efforts. If educational level is a legitimate indicator of job skills and abilities, then the gap between the average entry grades of white males and other employees can be narrowed only by raising the educational levels of women and minority new hires or by allowing women and minorities to enter at higher grades than similarly educated white males. One problem with trying to raise the relative educational levels of female new hires is that a large percentage of entry jobs are clerical positions, which primarily attract female applicants without college degrees. Unless more men can be drawn into these occupations, the General Schedule will be appealing to far more high school-educated women than high school-educated men. These less-educated entrants will necessarily pull down the average grade of women, unless there is a radical revaluation of clerical work as a result of the comparable worth movement.

The results for advancement patterns are more troublesome than those for entry levels. Race appears to play little role here, at least among those entering the General Schedule shortly after school, but sex is apparently an important factor.

Women are falling behind white men at a rate of one-tenth of a grade or more per year during the early career. Research reported elsewhere finds male-female promotion chances to be quite similar over the bulk of the career (Lewis, 1984), with women probably having the advantage in the middle and late career, so the problem may be limited. Still, early advancement has a longer-lasting impact on salaries than does later advancement, and the salary gains lost early are lost forever.

What can be done to eliminate this differential? A variety of EEO and affirmative action efforts could be considered. Perhaps more training of first-line supervisors is necessary to sensitize them to sexism or racism in their promotion decisions. One unconscious way this may show itself is in a fear that women are more likely than men to quit their jobs, leading them to see early promotions of women as riskier. Later in the career, women who prove their employment stability may be catching up to the levels they should have obtained earlier. If this is indeed happening, this research finds little support for the supervisors' fears, as the women's quit rates are only marginally higher than the men's.

Institutional factors may also create barriers to women's advancement. First, two-grade promotions are generally limited to professional and administrative occupations, where men predominate. Perhaps this policy should be reconsidered. Second, Chertos (1985) finds that promotions in New York state government frequently involve geographical moves, and married women are often unable to re-locate. This pattern probably holds true in the General Schedule as well. She suggests that more effort be made to promote women without requiring them to move. Third, career paths out of clerical positions may be quite limited. This suggests the need for more upward mobility programs or "bridging" occupations, which allow employees to obtain the training and experience necessary to move out of dead-end jobs into professional or administrative occupations. On the other hand, we may also need further research into the possibility that women are consciously choosing to forego advancement opportunities. Hoffman and Reed (1981) report that in one large corporation they studied, women were as likely to be offered promotions as men, but were far more likely to turn them down, largely for family reasons. This seems an improbable explanation in the General Schedule but might be occurring on a limited basis.

In sum, entry levels and early advancement rates demonstrate greater race- and sex-neutrality than many would expect. While this suggests that equal employment opportunity is within our grasp, it also implies that a representative bureaucracy cannot be achieved without substantial affirmative action efforts.

Notes

I would like to thank Frank Thompson, Glen Cain, Roy Bahl, Larry Schroeder and David Rosenbloom for helpful comments on earlier drafts of this paper. I am grateful to the U. S. Office of Personnel Management for providing access to statistical data from the Central Personnel Data File (CPDF) for the analysis presented in this paper. The original version of this research appeared in Lewis (1984).

1. Potential experience squared was added to the model to capture the curvilinear effect of experience.

References

Borjas, G. J. (1978). "Discrimination in HEW? Is the Doctor Sick or Are the Patients Healthy?" *The Journal of Law and Economics* 21 (April): 97–110.

———— (1983). "The Measurement of Race and Gender Wage Differentials: Evidence from the Public Sector." *Industrial and Labor Relations Review* 37 (October): 79–91.

Chertos, C. H. (1985). "Inequality in Promotions: Research and Strategies for Change." Paper presented at the American Society for Public Administration Conference, Indianapolis.

Corazzini, A. J. (1972). "Equality of Employment Opportunity in the Federal White-Collar Civil Service." *Journal of Human Resources* 7 (Fall): 424–445.

Corcoran, M. (1978). "The Structure of Female Wages." *American Economic Review* 68 (May): 165–170.

Daley, D. (1984). "Political and Occupational Barriers to the Implementation of Affirmative Action: Administrative, Executive, and Legislative Attitudes Toward Representative Bureaucracy." *Review of Public Personnel Administration* 4 (Summer): 4–15.

Davis, C. E. and J. P. West. (1984) "Implementing Public Programs: Equal Employment Opportunity. Affirmative Action, and Administrative Policy Options." *Review of Public Personnel.*

Eccles, M. E. (1976). "Race, Sex, and Government Jobs: A Study of Affirmative Action Programs in Federal Agencies." Ph.D. dissertation. Cambridge, MA: Harvard University.

Fleming, J. H. and C. A. Shanor (1977). "Veteran's Preference in Public Employment: Unconstitutional Gender Discrimination." *Emory Law Review* 26 (Winter): 13–64.

Grandjean, B. D. (1981). "History and Career in a Bureaucratic Labor Market." *American Journal of Sociology* 86 (March): 1057–1092.

Hoffman C. and J. S. Reed. (1981). "Sex Discrimination? The XYZ Affair." *Public Interest* 62 (Winter): 21–39.

Killingsworth, M. R. and C. W. Reimers. (1983). "Race, Ranking, Promotions, and Pay at a Federal Facility: A Logit (W) Analysis." *Industrial and Labor Relations Review 37* (October): 92–107.

Lewis, G. B. (1984). "Men and Women in Federal Employment: Placements, Promotions, and Occupations." Ph.D. dissertation. Syracuse, N.Y.: Syracuse University.

Long, J. E. (1976). "Employment Discrimination in the Federal Sector." *Journal of Human Resources* 11 (Winter): 86–97.

Mincer, J. and S. Polachek. (1974). "Family Investments in Human Capital: Earnings of Women." *Journal of Political Economy* 82 (March/April): S76–S108.

Reed, R. H. and H. P. Miller. (1970). "Some Determinants of the Variation in Earnings for College Men." *Journal of Human Resources* 5 (Spring): 177–190.

Rodgers, C. S. (1977). "The Internal Allocation of Labor in a Federal Agency." Ph.D. dissertation. Waltham, MA: Brandeis University.

Rosenbaum, J. E. (1979). "Tournament Mobility: Career Patterns in a Corporation." *Administrative Science Quarterly* 24 (June): 220–241.

Rosenbloom, D. H. (1984). "The Declining Salience of Affirmative Action in Federal Personnel Management." *Review of Public Personnel Administration* 4 (Summer): 31–40.

Smith, S. P. (1976). "Government Wage Differentials by Sex." *Journal of Human Resources* 11 (Spring): 185–199.

Spilerman, S. (1977). "Careers, Labor Market Structure, and Socioeconomic Achievement." *American Journal of Sociology* 83 (November): 551–593.

Taylor, P. A. (1979). "Income Inequality in the Federal Civilian Government." *American Sociological Review* 44 (June): 468–479.

_____ and S. Kim. (1980). "Asian-Americans in the Federal Civil Service 1977." *California Sociologist* 3 (Winter): 1–16.

Thompson, F. J. (1984). "Deregulation at the EEOC: Prospects and Implications." *Review of Public Personnel Administration* 4 (Summer): 41–56.

7

RACIAL UNREST IN THE MILITARY

The Challenge and the Response

Richard Stillman II

Much like the wider American society, the U.S. armed forces witnessed numerous racial incidents in the late 1960s within its ranks. How has the Department of Defense sought to cope with its crisis on the racial front? The article outlines several major efforts undertaken by DOD within the last two years to deal with racial turmoil, particularly in the special problem areas related to the distribution of non-white service personnel, off-base housing, and the military system of justice. The author points up several possible future trends regarding military race relations, trends that are sometimes contradictory and not always optimistic.

Like the American society in general, the U.S. armed forces were rocked in the late 1960s and early 1970s by numerous racial incidents at overseas bases such as Tiensha and Longbinh, South Vietnam; Heidelburg, Germany; Rota, Spain; and on stateside assignments such as Camp Pendleton, California; Great Lakes Naval Base, Illinois; Fort Bragg, North Carolina; Laredo Air Force Base, Texas; Fort Knox, Kentucky; Kaneohe Marine Air Station, Honolulu; and Camp Lejeune, North Carolina, as well as aboard ships at sea: U.S.S. *Constellation*, U.S.S. *Kitty Hawk*, and the fleet oiler, *Hassayampa*. While the intensity and causes of the racial disturbances varied from place to place, the July 20, 1969, Marine Corps Camp Lejeune incident and the October 12, 1972, outbreak aboard the U.S.S. *Kitty Hawk* were two of the most severe conflicts and present something of a classic pattern of racial unrest in the U.S. armed forces.

Source: *Public Administration Review* 34 (May/June 1974): 221–229.

The Camp Lejeune Incident

Camp Lejeune is one of the largest Marine Corps training and command facilities, consisting of approximately 109,047 acres in central North Carolina and housing approximately 42,000 military personnel. In 1969 14 per cent of its troops were black, but the number ran upwards to 25 per cent non-white in certain combat battalions. On the evening of July 20, 1969, several units of the 2nd Marine Division were celebrating at an NCO Club prior to their deployment to the Sixth Fleet in Spain. By 9 p.m. there were approximately 150 black soldiers along with 100 white marines in the clubroom. Minor incidents that night had created a feeling of tension between blacks and whites, particularly when a black marine attempted to cut into a white dancing with a black woman marine. At one point, the club manager called the regimental commander to warn of the increasing tensions, but no action was taken. At about 10:30 p.m., when soldiers began leaving the clubroom, a white enlisted man burst into the room "extremely bloody" and exclaimed loudly that he had been assaulted by a group of black marines. From then on until 11 p.m., fights broke out around the area which left 15 marines injured and one, Corporal Edward E. Blankston, a thrice-wounded Vietnam veteran, dead of massive head injuries.

While the drinking and competition for women at the party had sparked the immediate outbreak of the disturbance, as a Special House Subcommittee that investigated the Lejeune incident later pointed out, the new awareness of black identity and the striving for self-determination on the part of young blacks means that "the new black man has absolutely no desire to lose his identity."[1] Thus racial slurs, as those that were allegedly uttered in the Lejeune NCO Club, easily led to provoking trouble between blacks and whites. Another major factor that precipitated the incident, according to the Special House Subcommittee, was the general breakdown in communications, leadership, and discipline—particularly at the junior officer and senior NCO levels. "There was some tendency," said the report, "to shy away from leadership and disciplinary problems when race was a consideration. On occasion, it was overreaction, to a fear of being labeled a racist or being charged with discrimination." Finally, the Subcommittee further cited the general laxity of security around the Lejeune Base as fostering the disturbance, despite the repeated earlier warnings of the impending trouble that night.

The U.S.S. Kitty Hawk Incident

On October 10, 1972, the attack carrier, U.S.S. *Kitty Hawk,* after a week's leave at the naval base, Subic Bay, Philippines, returned to the combat zone to conduct air operations against North Vietnam. On board were 348 officers and 4,135 enlisted men; of these, five officers and 297 enlisted personnel were black. At 7 p.m. on October 12, 1972, a ship's investigator called a black sailor into his office for questioning concerning the youth's participation in a fight that had occurred the previous week at the Subic Bay enlisted men's club. The young man was accompanied by nine other black sailors who according to later testimony were "belligerent, loud, and used abusive language." After the interrogation, the youths left and within minutes two white mess cooks were assaulted. By 8 p.m. a large number of black sailors congregated in one of the two enlisted men's mess areas. The Marine Security Force was alerted and arrived on the scene, provoking a major confrontation when one marine, according to some reports, drew his revolver on the sailors. At this point the ship's executive officer arrived and asked the marines to leave and succeeded temporarily in calming the dissent group. Nevertheless, despite his efforts and those of the ship's commanding officer, trouble shortly spread throughout the lower decks of the carrier. According to the Congressional Subcommittee Report that later studied this incident:

> The XO, after going below, became aware that small groups, ranging from 5 to 25 blacks, were marauding about the ship attacking whites, pulling many sleeping sailors from their berths and beating them with their fists and chains, dogging wrenches, metal pipes, fire extinguisher nozzles and broom handles. While engaged in this behavior, many were heard to shout, "Kill the son-of-a-bitch! Kill the white trash! Kill, kill, kill."[2]

It was not until 2:30 a.m. that the CO and XO succeeded in restoring order and disarming the hostile groups. A total of 47 men, mostly whites, were treated for injuries that night and 26 sailors, all blacks, were charged with offenses under the Uniform Code of Military Justice.

According to the Special House Subcommittee on Disciplinary Problems in the U.S. Navy that later conducted a two-month study of this incident (as well as the disturbance that occurred abroad the U.S.S. *Constellation* a month later), "Those young blacks, who enter the service from the ghetto with a complete black awareness, probably for the first time find themselves immersed in a predominantly white society which, in civilian life, they had come to mistrust." This "mistrust" has "resulted in a tendency on the part of black sailors to polarize" and thus "a grievance of one black, real or fancied, becomes the grievance of many." Further, the investigators noted "laxity" and "permissiveness" in the U.S. Navy, particularly at the middle-management level. They cited as evidence of this: "The poor personal grooming of the crew, the poor standards of cleanliness, . . . the failure to take corrective action when corrective action was warranted, and the failure to demand an immediate response to lawful orders." The congressional probe also criticized the inadequate planning and use of the Marine Security Forces as well as faulty training and counseling of new Navy recruits relative to their duties and responsibilities while in uniform.

The Military Reactions to the Problems of Racial Unrest Since the Late 1960s

What has been the Pentagon's response to the problems of racial conflict in its ranks? Several steps have been taken to deal with racial tensions in the U.S. armed forces since the late 1960s:

First, there has been a concerted effort to encourage the opportunities for cultural diversity and racial pride among minority groups. On September 3, 1969, General Leonard F. Chapman, then Marine Corps Commandant, issued a message granting permission for the Afro haircut to be worn if neatly trimmed, and allowing blacks to give the "black power clenched-fist salute as long as it did not suggest direct defiance to duly constituted authority." Shortly after General Chapman's directive, the Army, Navy, and Air Force issued similar statements allowing blacks greater cultural diversity within their respective services. Soul music, soul food, ethnic literature, and cosmetics have been increasingly provided at military PX's, commissaries, and service clubs, and sales for these items have totaled over $4 million during the last two years—reflecting their general demand among minority groups in uniform.

Second, steps have been taken throughout the armed services to promote faster communications of grievances on the part of GIs. Some units have set up "hot lines" and "watch committees" for the rapid communication of grievances between black NCOs and senior staff officers, and other units have established human relations committees, human rights officers, and sensitivity training sessions for promoting better racial understanding throughout various command echelons. Other military commanders, such as Major General William Ryan at Camp Lejeune, have issued direct orders banning all racial slurs and have prepared special pamphlets for unit leaders on ways of coping with racial problems in their commands.

Third, the Department of Defense has made a sustained effort to increase the percentage of blacks at senior officer levels. In 1968 there was only one black general, the Air Force's General Benjamin O. Davis, Jr. Today there are 11 blacks at general or flag rank and the recent appointment of a black general, Frederic Davison, as Commander of U.S. Army Forces in Europe is a very apparent symbolic step that emphasizes the military commitment to racial equality at senior command assignments. In another effort to increase Negro representation, the Chief of Naval Operations, Admiral Elmo A. Zumwalt, promised last year to begin a program of increasing the percentages of blacks in the Navy to an overall figure of 12 per cent by 1976. This year 12 per cent of the Navy's enlisted recruits and a similar percentage of incoming U.S. Naval Academy midshipmen were black.

Fourth, in still another endeavor by the Department of Defense to deal with its racial problems, on May 11, 1972, former Secretary of Defense Melvin Laird dedicated the Defense Race Relations Institute at Patrick Air Force Base in Florida. The new Institute, with 44 civilian and military faculty members, is designed to train 1,400 instructors annually for the armed forces in six-week training sessions (with 100 students per session). These instructors in turn are expected both to teach and train others to teach in the required 18-hour course in race relations for all personnel in uniform (a yearly six-hour refresher course in the subject is also required for servicemen). The Navy and Marine Corps have set up their own "executive seminars" on race relations for senior officers with Command duties. As

L. Howard Bennett, former Deputy Assistant Secretary of Defense for Equal Opportunity, predicted: "We will have some 2.5 million Americans in the military undergoing repeated study of how to solve racial problems. This must have some impact on the civilian society because there has never before been a widespread systematic educational attack on America's most pressing problems."[3]

Fifth, in May 1971 the Department of Defense announced that future Army, Navy, and Air Force annual officer efficiency reports would include ratings on an individual's racial attitudes and commitment to equal treatment for minorities in uniform. In the Army, blacks must now be represented on all promotion boards.

Finally, both senior civilian and uniformed Pentagon officials in recent months have repeatedly underscored their commitment to the ideals of racial equality and equal opportunity in the U.S. armed forces. As former Defense Secretary Melvin Laird emphasized last year: "The Department of Defense is committed to the goal of making military and civilian service in the Department a model of equal opportunity for all."[4] Or as Marine Corps Commandant General Robert E. Cushman stressed somewhat more bluntly: "Equal treatment for all Marines and civilian personnel must be carried out vigorously and conscientiously at all times. Those individuals who cannot or will not abide by this principle should seek other employment."[5]

Other Problems on the Racial Front

On-base racial tension has not been the only source of friction between the military and minority groups in recent years. Other issues have been the targets for protest by minority groups both inside and outside the armed services. Both the NAACP's *The Search for Military Justice* (April 1971) and the Congressional Black Caucus Report on *Racism in the Military* (May 1972) were especially critical of three areas of military policy toward non-white soldiers—the distribution of black servicemen, the off-base housing situation, and the military system of justice.[6]

In terms of the distribution of black servicemen, both the NAACP Report and the Congressional Black Caucus Study cited the significant imbalance of black NCOs in the "combat arms and supply branches" as opposed to the "technical specialities." Both reports pointed to 1971 Defense Department figures that showed black NCOs with 19–24 months of service occupied 36 per cent of the Infantry units and 20.8 per cent of the service and supply units, while only 1.1 per cent were found in technical or allied fields, 5.5 per cent in communications and intelligence sections, and 3.6 per cent in medical and dental units. The implication drawn from these figures was that such imbalances have led to a higher number of blacks serving in front line combat units in Vietnam, as well as a slightly higher combat fatality rate for non-whites compared to white soldiers.

Second, both the NAACP and Congressional Black Caucus studies commented that housing "without question is the most pervasive problem confronting the Negro soldier." "At every installation we visited, black soldiers of all ranks

mentioned housing as a major grievance." The dilemma of finding suitable housing for non-white soldiers and their families is indeed a difficult one, for the average military base can normally house only one-half of military families, and the
rest are then required to seek adequate housing in nearby communities. As both
reports emphasized, this frequently means that non-whites must confront the de
facto segregated housing patterns that exist in many civilian communities surrounding military bases, and end up renting or buying homes in neighborhoods
that are the most dilapidated, expensive, and distant from their assigned military
units.

Third, the issue of the military system of justice was raised both by the NAACP
and Congressional Black Caucus studies. Both reports tended to center their criticism on the major effect of the military judicial system—namely, that a higher
percentage of non-whites, in comparison to white soldiers, are receiving judicial
punishments. DOD statistics were again cited by these two reports to show that in
1971 between 25–33 per cent of those GIs who received Article 15 punishments
(punishments imposed by commanding officers outside the regular military
court system) were non-white, and approximately half held in military prisons
for "pre-trial confinements" were black. Air Force figures for 1972 indicated that
28.9 per cent of those discharged under less than honorable conditions were Negroes and that between 33 to 63 per cent serving terms in military prisons for various judicial punishments were black.

DOD's Response

The Department of Defense is currently in the process of responding in separate
ways to each of these major complaints by minority groups:

Black Distribution: The Defense Department is undertaking a careful review of its
Armed Forces Qualification Test (AFQT), which at present serves as the basis for
assigning NCOs to service occupational specialities. It has been discovered that
among NCOs with 19–24 months of service, about 23 per cent of whites had scores
of 30 or below on the AFQT, while 72 per cent of black recruits in 1971 fell into the
same category. A higher percentage of lower AFQT scoring individuals are assigned
to "soft core fields" (such as infantry, administration, or supply units) while the
"hard core areas" (technical occupations) traditionally attract the higher scoring
NCOs. The present selection system based upon the AFQT scores helps to explain
the apparent imbalance of nonwhites serving in the combat arms branches. DOD
manpower specialists are presently wrestling with dilemma of finding an equitable
yet impartial means of allocating individuals to service occupations.

Off-Base Housing: Since the late 1960s the Pentagon has undertaken a rather
elaborate, systematic census of "open housing" areas around its military bases
and has sought to place those rental units whose owners have signed "open housing pledges" on "approved lists" in local base housing offices. Certain landlords
refusing to agree to non-discriminatory policies of the armed services have been

placed on "off-limits lists" to military personnel. DOD has put significant efforts into making its open housing program a workable one; however, judging from the recent criticism by both NAACP and Black Congressional Caucus, the program at least so far has only been partially successful and it, too, like the AFQT, is now currently under review by the Pentagon.[7]

Military Justice: Due to the recent criticism of the NAACP and Black Congressional Caucus studies, former Secretary of Defense Melvin Laird on April 5, 1972, appointed a special Department of Defense Task Force on the Administration of Military Justice, composed of 13 high-ranking military and civilian experts in this field. This senior-level DOD task force was charged with the responsibility: "To make such recommendations to the Secretary of Defense as may be deemed appropriate to eliminate existing deficiencies and/or enhance the opportunity for equal justice for every American serviceman and servicewoman."[8] With this task force's investigation, new reforms in the Uniform Code of Military Justice as well as the general system of dispensing military justice are expected to be forthcoming in the not too distant future.

Trends in Military Race Relations

How will the new and important changes that have occurred within the military during the last four years affect the armed forces? Will the new reforms succeed in providing a climate for harmonious black-white relations? Or will the basic tensions and root causes of the racial tension remain unresolved? In short, what is the future trend in military race relations?

At this point, permit the author to make some educated prognostications about the future shape of black-white relations in the military:

1. *While the problems between blacks and whites in uniform will persist, the intensity of racial unrest will decline in the armed forces—largely due to reasons beyond the military's control.* The withdrawal from Vietnam and the decline of social tensions on the home front plus the general reductions in troop strength have served and will continue to serve as the primary factors in reducing racial unrest in the armed services. While the reforms in the military may have a marginal effect on the general climate of race relations, the return to a peacetime military plus the Nixon Administration's decision to move toward an all-volunteer army in 1973 will have a major impact on quieting racial tensions in ranks. A good case can be made, although with certain exceptions, that short-term draftees between the ages of 18 to 22 during the Vietnam Conflict were largely responsible for many of the racial incidents that occurred in the late 1960s and early 1970s.

As the composition of the military increasingly is made up of more mature, professional careerists in an all-volunteer army, who serve by choice rather than chance, issues involving racial tensions will become less frequent and severe, though this is not to say that problems between races will suddenly disappear. Thorny questions of off-base housing and the distribution of non-whites within the military will remain. Also, scattered flare-ups of racial troubles can be expected here and there, particularly on bases with a large concentration of troops where the competition for women or blatant off-base racial discrimination is especially apparent.

2. *External pressures on the military to "do something" about racial issues will increase, even though the internal racial problems may in fact decline.* The rapid rise in the numbers of black congressmen (from four to 13 within the last decade) will exert a much greater pressure on the armed services to "do something" for nonwhite servicemen. Congressmen in search of good issues that appeal to their local voters will find the U.S. armed forces an appropriate target, since it represents in the abstract "the establishment." Indeed, the Black Congressional Caucus Report on *Racism in the Military* may be only the first in a series of such congressional investigations designed to win support and notoriety for its authors in their home constituencies. Similarly, minority civil rights organizations, eager to find issues to sustain their strength, will find it to their advantage to use the military as a whipping boy for their grievances against the system. This is not to argue that all their complaints will not be justified. To the contrary, especially in terms of individual soldiers' problems in adjusting to military life, congressmen can and will prove helpful in remedying personal injustices.

3. *Pressed from the outside, the Pentagon will continue to experiment with piecemeal reforms in race relations. Certain experiments will prove worthwhile; others will be deemed failures.* Motivated by outside criticism and out of their own self-interest, senior Pentagon military and civilian officials will undoubtedly continue to search for equality of treatment and opportunity for servicemen and will continue to search for suitable methods of presenting the armed forces in a favorable light as a "model employer" before the general public. In the coming years the emphasis will probably be placed upon insuring a fair color distribution throughout the armed forces plus a search for an effective grievance system for handling racial complaints within the military system. Perhaps the Inspector General's Office will be "beefed up," or perhaps a military ombudsman will be established patterned on the Swedish or West German model in order to provide a faster response to "racial" grievances. Also the new Defense Race Relations Institute will play a prominent role in educating soldiers in their responsibilities toward minorities. However, in other areas such as off-post housing, the armed forces may have to abandon its experiments in forcing integration in civilian communities due to local political pressures or the enormous complexities of equitable enforcement of such a program throughout the United States.

4. *Experimentation with new ways of coping with internal racial problems will continue to contradict traditional military principles and may serve to loosen the authoritarian hierarchy of the military.* In responding to its racial problems, the armed services have violated many of their long-standing and cherished principles. For instance, wider cultural diversity contradicts the rule of military uniformity; the sanctity of the chain of command is jeopardized with the establishment

of new channels of communication through human rights committees, human relations officers, of sensitivity training sessions; the unquestioned impartiality of military justice is now being questioned; the traditional non-involvement of the military in civilian affairs is being abandoned in favor of the concept of encouraging local commanders to deal forcefully with off-base housing discrimination; the merit system for promotions, assignments, etc., is being altered by an increasing concern for the "fair" proportion and distribution of minority groups within the armed services.

Many of these changes will impose new and perhaps unforeseen organizational arrangements within the military establishment—perhaps, some will argue, a "freer" sort of hierarchical structure and maybe a more "humanistic" one as well, though new problems will in turn present themselves. For example, what source of authority will a soldier feel he should obey when diverse channels of communication are available between subordinates and superiors? In short, who will command and who will obey if the chain of command becomes increasingly ambiguous and vague? Also, what new patterns of civil-military relations will emerge if local commanders are given freedom to venture willy-nilly into the thorny political thickets of off-post discriminatory habits? Indeed, should Americans allow the military to shed their traditional restraints when it comes to involvement in civilian affairs? And what will replace the merit system as a basis for promotions within the military, if it is decided that the merit concept must be abandoned? Quotas for minorities? Political appointments to officer posts, as was the case in the 18th and 19th centuries before the establishment of a professionalized military?

5. *Military professionalism will be redefined to include a greater respect for minority rights and privileges—though this also will raise new issues and dilemmas.* The traditional West Point virtues of "Duty, Honor, Country" in recent years have been redefined and enlarged to include a concern and respect for the problems of racial minorities. The Defense Race Relations Institute, plus the newly established officer efficiency ratings based in part on an individual's racial attitudes, serve to reinforce this broadening of professional responsibility as well as the recognition for effectively dealing with racial matters as they arise within command situations. A wider sense of professional responsibility in this area can in turn serve as the best means of internal check on the military in its handling of racial issues at all echelons of command. Nevertheless, the widening of professional ethical concerns also entails an immensely difficult task of establishing the appropriate standards, procedures, and means of enforcement. For in practice, what does the term "equal treatment" really imply? Does it mean equal proportions of minorities in all segments of military life—to take the extreme case? Or is it defined by a seemingly contradictory idea of "color blindness" in respect to all professional decisions?

Perhaps one can argue that "equal treatment" really is the professional's "spirit" or "frame of mind" by which he arrives at decisions. But taking this track can only lead to more complicated issues of how can a "spirit" or "frame of mind" be formalized into concrete rules and enforceable procedures—seemingly the lifeblood of military routine. Translating the concept of "equal treatment" into practical terms of operating criterion, standards, and procedures will be a serious issue for the U.S. armed services in the years ahead.

6. *The overall proportion of non-white representation in the armed services will grow, but internal distribution will remain uneven largely due to factors beyond the military's control.* Compared to many civilian professions, statistics place the armed forces in a favorable position in providing career opportunities for Negroes. While blacks make up approximately two per cent of America's practicing physicians, one per cent of lawyers, and less than one per cent of engineers, they are currently 2.3 per cent of the officer ranks and 12.1 per cent of the enlisted personnel in the armed forces. Over the last two decades the percentages of blacks in uniform have steadily risen. Between 1949 and 1972 the percentages of black officers rose in the Navy from 0 to .8 per cent, in the Marines from 0 to 1.3 per cent, in the Air Force from .6 to 1.7 per cent, and in the Army from 1.8 to 4.2 per cent. The enlisted ranks have experienced a similar increase during the last 20 years: the Navy from 4.7 to 5.7 per cent, Marines from 2.1 to 12.3 per cent, Air Force from 5.1 to 12.5 per cent, and the Army from 12.4 to 15.6 per cent.

There is no reason to doubt that this trend will probably continue and perhaps even accelerate during the coming decade. The reason for this expected increase is due to various factors—one of the most important being the excellent image of the armed services within the Negro community as a place for employment and opportunity for advancement. This conclusion is supported by the William Brink and Louis Harris survey of a representative cross-section of 1,059 Negroes who were asked the question: "How would you rate the Army, Navy, Marine Corps, Air Force as a place for a young man to serve?" On the average, between 50 to 60 per cent rated the services either "excellent" or "very good," while less than 5 per cent saw it as a "poor place."[9] Moreover, during the last decade the percentages of non-white volunteer and reenlistment rates in the armed forces have consistently been higher than white percentages. During the mid 1970s one can expect with the elimination of the draft and the introduction of an all volunteer army with significantly more attractive pay scales in all grades that there will continue an upward trend of non-white participation in the armed services (ironically, it may be very well have been the forced induction of middleclass whites by means of the draft during the last decade that kept the military racially balanced).

Yet, despite the probable overall growth in minority representation in the armed forces, the distribution of blacks within the military, at least for the near future, will tend to reflect a significant imbalance—particularly noticeable among the senior staff and service school positions throughout the Navy, as well as within the senior NCO and skilled NCO ranks. The lack of black representation in these areas of the modern meritocratic military is largely, but not altogether, the result of educational and cultural disadvantages that nonwhites face in the larger civilian society, and despite intensive military efforts to remedy this imbalance, improvements are unlikely to occur quickly.

The National Guard also presents a picture of racial imbalance, with only 1.24 per cent colored in the Army Guard and .76 per cent in the Air Guard. Despite the repeated strong criticisms of the Guard's racial imbalance by both the Gessell Committee Report (1964) and the U.S. Commission on Civil Disorders (1968), this situation probably will remain unchanged due to the complexity of factors related to the Guard's local autonomy plus its generally poor image within the black community.[10]

7. *While increasing cultural diversity will be apparent in the armed services, the minority officers and enlisted men who rise to the top ranks now and in future years will tend to be those lifetime careerists who most closely emulate the central professional ideals and values of the service.* "Afro haircuts," "clenched-fist salutes," "soul music," and "soul food" reflect the increasing cultural diversity and tolerance within the ranks of the armed services. As one young black Army officer wrote recently in the pages of the *Military Review:* "The black officer of today defines integration as the acceptance of the individual as he is with his own distinct cultural background, standards, morals, habits, and tastes."[11] Such a statement by an active duty officer in a leading military journal would have been considered unthinkable, indeed revolutionary, only a few years ago. Nevertheless, the successful officers, white or non-white, who in the coming years win the promotions up the professional career ladder, will tend to be those who, as in the past, continue to pursue career lines closest to the ideals of their respective branches of the armed services. This means, in short, following the established professional route to the top by attending the right service schools, holding the appropriate command and staff assignments, having the necessary "time-in-grade," "keeping one's nose clean," and being recognized by military contemporaries as a competent professional soldier.[12]

Reflection upon the service careers of General Benjamin O. Davis, Jr., and Rear Admiral Samuel Gravely, the first black Air Force general and Navy admiral, only confirms the importance of non-Caucasians following the approved path to the top. Davis and Gravely's careers also point out that the making of a modern American general or admiral is a long, complex process that requires 20 to 25 years, at the very least. The generation it takes to produce a qualified senior officer or NCO should serve as an indication that no sudden increase of non-whites in senior positions is possible and that the declining military strength in America's post-Vietnam armed services will undoubtedly stiffen the competition among all races for the diminishing number of "senior slots."

8. *In the near future, perhaps the greatest source of minority frustration in the military will be spawned by the Pentagon's own recruitment efforts which tend to raise unwarranted expectations about the opportunities available in the armed services for minorities.* In their zeal to present the services as a "model employer" and attract young recruits into an all-volunteer armed forces, the Pentagon runs a great risk of "overselling" themselves, particularly to minorities. Current recruitment literature promising "easy promotions," "choice of job assignments," "ample training opportunities," and "world travel" are all eye-catching appeals, but they also serve to raise

unreasonable expectations about the opportunities available in the armed services. Many minority recruits frequently enter services expecting more benefits and fewer responsibilities than exist in reality. As historian Crane Brinton reminds us, nothing spawns revolutions faster than "rising expectations" which are unfulfilled by existing institutions. Indeed, the racial unrest at Camp Lejeune and aboard the *Kitty Hawk* was precipitated in large part by new black recruits, fresh from the central city ghetto, who were thrust suddenly into a confusing and frustrating world of a disciplined, predominantly white, military society. Realistic recruiting information and careful counseling and training sessions for young recruits that truthfully outline the nature of military life would go a long way toward keeping youthful aspirations and ideals about military service within reasonable bounds.

Similarly, senior military and civilian Defense Department officials should exercise caution regarding statements about what the Pentagon is doing or going to do for minorities in uniform. For example, Admiral Elmo Zumwalt promised to raise the total percentage of non-whites in the Navy to 12 per cent by 1976.[13] In light of the Navy's record at prior attempts to increase nonwhite representation significantly, such optimistic statements have little foundation in reality and only can serve to raise unwarranted hopes among minority groups.

9. *The impact upon the individual Negro due to his involvement in the armed services is significant, but just what the tangible effect is, as measured in quantifiable terms, yet remains to be discovered.* Commentators during the last decade have made several optimistic predictions about the Negro's important involvement in the armed forces.[14] Some contend that the strong black representation in Vietnam has given minorities new status and prestige at home. Others believe that that nonwhite involvement in an integrated military has served to raise minorities' educational achievement and social aspirations. Still others view the military as a route for social mobility for deprived groups in the American society. Whether or not such encouraging forecasts are indeed correct is difficult to assess largely because the nature of the assertions do not readily lend themselves to quantifiable verification. Yet, intuitively knowledgeable observers are aware that the experience of the black in the U.S. armed forces has been and will continue to be important for his own personal self-development and generally beneficial for racial minorities as a whole. Yet, just what the specific impact of military life upon minorities has been remains to be ascertained. Perhaps only future historians will know the answer to this question.

Conclusion

When Sammy Davis Jr., returned from Vietnam after entertaining American troops there early in 1972, he said in a press interview:

> It's just 152% better. I mean the effort they are making on black and white relationships. They're bending some rules these days; they're regarding men as individuals.

For example? Well, when I was in the Army I was on a post where a colored guy couldn't get his hair cut. Now you can. There are a thousand little things like that that make things better now.[15]

Davis' comments on the racial advances of the armed forces since he served as a private first-class in World War II reflect the enormous changes that have occurred within the last 30 years. Sammy Davis and his generation saw the armed services as predominantly segregated in most branches and phases of its activities. Non-whites were excluded altogether from Army Aviation, Army Engineers, and the Marine Corps for most of World War II.[16] As Davis commented, "a colored guy couldn't get his haircut" on certain posts.

President Truman's Executive Order 9981, signed July 26, 1948, required "that there shall be equality of treatment in the Armed Services without regard to race, color, religion or national origin."[17] Truman's order ushered in a new era of black-white relationships in the armed forces—an official policy based upon "color blindness" rather than "the color bar." Until the early 1960s the thoroughness with which the military had integrated their ranks drew repeated praise from various outside observers.[18]

The Vietnam and post-Vietnam era, however, has witnessed another shift in military racial policies. New national moods and styles, widespread racial unrest within the ranks, and hostility toward the armed forces as expressed by civil rights and other activist groups has forced the Pentagon to become increasingly "color conscious." Today Department of Defense manpower planners and policy makers are asking questions relative to whether there is an appropriate balance of minorities in the ranks. Is there an appropriate balance at the junior and senior levels? In various occupational categories? Are the middle-level and senior commanders aware of "color" problems and do they know how to cope with them when they arise? Do soldiers have opportunities to reflect their own cultural diversity? Does the military system of justice give non-whites "a fair shake"? Do communities bordering on military installations practice "equal treatment" for all soldiers?

The answers to these questions are indeed complex and are not readily solved by single stroke-of-the-pen solutions. Pentagon manpower specialists expect to grapple with them for some time to come.

Notes

1. Committee on Armed Services, House of Representatives, *Inquiry into the Disturbances at Marine Corps Base, Camp Lejeune, North Carolina,. on July 20, 1969* (Washington, D.C.: U.S. Government Printing Office, December 15, 1969), p. 5056.

2. Committee on Armed Services, House of Representatives, *Report by the Special Subcommittee on Disciplinary Problems in the U.S. Nary* (Washington, D.C.: U.S. Government Printing Office, January 1973), p. 17675.

3. *New York Times,* March 6, 1971, p. 1.

4. *Commanders Digest,* May 18, 1972, p. 1.

5. *New York Times,* August 1, 1972, p. 9.

6. NAACP, *The Search for Military Justice* (New York: NAACP, 1971), and The Congressional Black Caucus, *Racism in the Military: A New System for Rewards and Punishments* (Washington, D.C.: Congressional Black Caucus Office, May 15, 1972).

7. For a good account of the difficulties in implementing the Pentagon's equal housing program, read David Sutton, "The Military Mission Against Off-Base Discrimination," in Charles C. Moskos, Jr. (ed.), *Public Opinion and the Military Establishment* (Beverly Hills: Sage Publications, 1971), pp. 149–184. Also refer to Richard Stillman, *Integration of the Negro in the U.S. Armed Forces* (New York: Praeger Publisher, 1968), pp. 90–95.

8. "Charter of the Task Force on the Administration of Military Justice in the Armed Forces," Office of the Secretary of Defense, April 5, 1972, p. 2.

9. William Brink and Louis Harris, *Black and White: A Study of U.S. Racial Attitudes Today* (New York: Simon and Schuster, 1967), pp. 270–272.

10. For a highly critical assessment of the National Guard's racial imbalance, read William A. McWhirter, "The National Guard—Awake or Asleep?" *Life,* October 27, 1967, pp. 83–98.

11. Captain Julius T. Crouch, "The Black Junior Officer in Today's Army," *Military Review* (May 1972), pp. 61–72.

12. Morris Janowitz's *The Professional Soldier: A Social and Political Portrait* (Glencoe: Free Press, 1960) has a good discussion of professional values and ideals of the military. Also refer to Samuel P. Huntington, *The Soldier and the State: The Theory and Politics of Civil-Military Relations* (Cambridge: Harvard University Press, 1957); and Frederick C. Mosher, *Democracy and the Public Service* (New York: Oxford University Press, 1968).

13. *New York Times,* April 1, 1971, p. 29.

14. Several of these views have appeared in: Charles C. Moskos, Jr., "Racial Integration in the Armed Forces," *American Journal of Sociology* (September 1967), pp. 132–148; Gene Grove, "The Army and the Negro," *New York Times Magazine,* July 24, 1966, p. 43; Whitney M. Young, Jr., "When the Negroes in Vietnam Come Home," *Harpers* (June 1967), pp. 63–69; and Sol Stern, "When the Black GI Comes Home," *New York Times Magazine,* March 24, 1968, pp. 26+.

15. *New York Times,* February 24, 1972, p. 45. Also see Sammy Davis, Jr., "Why I Went to the Troops," *Ebony* (June 1972), pp. 144–148.

16. For a most thorough treatment of military racial policies during World War II, read: Ulysses G. Lee, *The United States Army in World War Two: Special Studies: The Employment of Negro Troops* (Washington, D.C.: U.S. Government Printing Office, 1966).

17. For a discussion of the events leading up to Truman's Executive Order, read Stillman, *op. cit.,* pp. 32–42, or Richard Dalfiume, *Desegregation of the U.S. Armed Forces* (Columbia: University of Missouri Press, 1969), pp. 148–174. For an interesting account of the part social scientists played in desegregation efforts, read Leo Bogart (ed.), *Social Research and the Desegregation of the U.S. Army: Two Original Field Reports* (Chicago: Markham Publishing, 1969).

18. For example of this viewpoint, see Lee Nichols, *Breakthrough on the Color Front* (New York: Random House, 1954).

Part Two

Affirmative Action

This section on affirmative action captures much of what has been and remains the central points of conflict where the implementation of affirmative action programs is concerned. Again, we see that the courts have played a major role in prodding and pushing employers forward on the equal employment opportunity front. However, we see that there has been some evolution in the courts' posture in 1989, particularly as compared to the discussion and theme we find running through the mini-symposium in 1974.

Wrestling with the notion of individual rights and trying to balance those rights with the attempt to consciously transform the racial mix of various organizations has become increasingly difficult, and as the court has evolved, the difficulty has increased.

Nalbandian, in his 1989 review of the Supreme Court's work on affirmative action, finds that the legal reasoning that underpins the court's analysis in discrimination cases is supported by three values: social equity, efficiency, and individual rights. According to the author, the High Court is constantly attempting to determine the appropriate balance between these competing interests. Beyond this tension, there seems to exist a working consensus within the Court that the review of race-conscious affirmative action requires a two-pronged analysis. The first prong examines the justification for taking race into consideration, while the second focuses on the content of the affirmative action itself, with attention to the consequences for nonminority employees. Nalbandian goes on to speculate that affirmative action is not dead, but that the debate is shifting from an emphasis on social equity to a complementary expression of social equity and individual rights and that the legitimacy of affirmative action over time depends on greater weight being given to efficiency in judicial review, public policy forums, and broadly defined management practices. The author's speculation also considers the future configuration of the U.S. Supreme Court, the Court's respect for precedent, and the technical nature of personnel administration.

In his introduction to the mini-symposium on affirmative action in public employment, Nigro suggests that affirmative action is a helpful but ambiguous concept. Although ambiguity guarantees the courts room to maneuver and to innovate in changing circumstances, it may also be counterproductive and lead to unfulfilled expectations, mistrust, and conflict. In the first article, Lovell identifies and clarifies three key issues that arise when implementing affirmative action policies. First, she focuses on the distinction between affirmative action and nondiscrimination. She points out that affirmative action requires more than passive nondiscrimination by an organization—it requires the definition of objectives for redressing employment imbalances and the implementation of plans for reaching those objectives. Goal setting, action plans, and evaluation are the tools required to operationalize affirmative action. Second, the author explains why preferential hiring and setting of numerical targets ("quotas") are necessary. Moreover, numerical objectives provide the only feasible mechanism for defining with any clarity whether established targets are being reached. They provide a means to measure and evaluate progress made. Finally, Lovell addresses why she believes traditional standards of quality must be reexamined.

According to a former executive director of the U.S. Civil Service Commission, equal employment opportunity stops with the act of merely preventing overt discrimination in the competitive process and often touches only superficially on issues involved in making equal opportunity a practical reality. Rosen identifies the necessary components of a successful Equal Employment Opportunity (EEO) program and discusses why affirmative action is the logical next step in establishing nondiscrimination in employment policies. EEO programs must include an efficient means for employees and applicants to surface individual grievances related to equal opportunity. Strong outreach to those groups previously locked out of the mainstream and a reexamination of jobs and ways to attract new participants into the workforce must also be incorporated into the process. Finally, and perhaps the most contentious issue, the use of goals and timetables can be an effective management technique; however, getting buy-in from lower level managers can be difficult. In addition, it should be expected that there will be some problems along the way that will require resolution. There should also be an awareness that if abused, goals and timetables may lead to selection processes dependent on factors other than merit, and once this happens, EEO policies are undermined and management loses credibility.

Levine acknowledges the rhetoric and conflict surrounding affirmative action and focuses on the use of numerical targets to increase minority group representation in public organizations. His findings indicate that the increased pressure on organizations to hire minorities has resulted in a number of practices that enable agencies to adhere to affirmative action targets by lumping minorities into certain areas while "protecting" the larger organization from increased minority group representation. These practices are commonly referred to as "tokenism." The author also reminds the reader that aggregate statistics do not reveal patterns of differential hiring practices or tokenism. Therefore, efforts to evaluate the impact of affirmative action programs must look beyond statistics and focus on emerging differences in patterns among six areas: (1) inter- and intra-organizational mobility, (2) educational and work experience leverage, (3) awards and training and career development opportunities, (4) authority and responsibility, (5) organizational experience, and (6) participation in policy making. His article is quite valuable in that it attempts to take readers beyond simple numeric quantification, beyond what is often referred to as "bean counting," to a place where they come to understand what the numbers alone can't tell them about employment trends.

We hear from a director of personnel about the hiring of minorities in a Sacramento, California, fire department. Danielson flatly states that without operationalizing affirmative action through "selective action recruiting," validation of the fire department's qualifying tests, and attempts to restructure jobs, they would never reach population parity before the year 2000. He also acknowledges that the accelerated hiring of minorities is the only way to achieve affirmative action goals and timetables. His final thoughts indicate a belief that these devices should be used as a "catch up device" only until an occupation becomes representative of the community's population. We hear from another public administrator in the following article (also published as part of the 1974 mini-symposium on affirmative action), which details the National Civil Service League's proposals aimed at achieving equal employment opportunity. The proposals include the following: (1) special programs and selective certification should be used when there is a job-related factor that may improve performance in a particular job while also increasing minority representation, (2) qualifying tests should be rated on a "pass-fail" basis, and (3) a proven valid selection process, that is, a process that is open, representative, and nondiscriminatory, should be developed.

To close the chapter on affirmative action, it is appropriate to touch on several of the salient concluding observations made by Lloyd Nigro, editor of the mini-symposium on affirmative action in public employment. The overall message of the symposium is that effective public administration in a democratic society relies heavily on the existence of genuinely representative bureaucracies. This is primarily because representative public organizations are more likely to assure higher levels of responsiveness and responsibility than could possibly be derived from the simple use of external controls on administrative action. Affirmative action programs provide a means of achieving increasingly representative bureaucracies. In other words, affirmative action programs operationalize equal employment opportunity and make the concept useful. Nigro concludes with the realization that federal agencies must continue with their proactive hiring practices because it has been proven over time that opening up the door is simply not enough to guarantee equal opportunity.

The challenge that Nigro makes to us in 1974 is the challenge that confronts us today. How do we create equal employment opportunity that is observable and that the involved parties accept as generally fair and productive?

8

THE U.S. SUPREME COURT'S "CONSENSUS" ON AFFIRMATIVE ACTION

John Naibandian

Eighteen years have passed since the U.S. Supreme Court's landmark decision in Griggs *v.* Duke Power Company. *Since that time the Court has reviewed numerous cases, and it is now possible to describe the "consensus" that the Court has reached in the way it approaches affirmative action cases. Following a review of the Court's two-part analytical approach to affirmative action, this article analyzes the Court's deliberations with respect to the competing values of individual rights, social equity, and efficiency. The future of affirmative action is examined in terms of the influence of the Court's configuration, its respect for precedent, and the way in which the value of social equity has penetrated public personnel policy and practices.*

Twenty-five years ago Congress passed the Civil Rights Act of 1964, and 18 years ago the U.S. Supreme Court provided its first significant review in *Griggs* v. *Duke Power Company.*[1] Since *Griggs*, the Court has considered several employment discrimination cases, and it finally appears possible to identify the conditions under which a public employer can consider race in personnel actions.

This article delineates those conditions by examining the analytical approach employed by the Court in deliberating employment discrimination cases. It then discusses conflicting values debated in these cases, and in the last part it speculates on the future of affirmative action.

Source: *Public Administration Review* 49 (January/February 1989): 38–45.

111

Factors Impeding Consensus

For a number of years, the Court has confronted different issues which complicated an early answer to the question, "Under what conditions can a public employer take race into consideration in employment decisions?" On the statutory side, unanticipated issues and ambiguities resulting from legislative compromise dictated evolutionary development of the law.[2] These complicating factors are outlined before describing the Court's approach to employment discrimination cases.

First, varied statutory and constitutional issues suggest different standards of judicial review. The analysis in this article focuses on Title VII of the Civil Rights Act of 1964 as amended by the Equal Employment Act of 1972 and the Equal Protection Clause of the 14th Amendment to the United States Constitution. Cases involving claims against *private employers* have been litigated under Title VII which prohibits discrimination in employment based on race, color, religion, gender, or national origin. A case may be filed against a *public employer* under Title VII and/or as a constitutional claim under the Equal Protection Clause of the 14th Amendment. That clause says that no state shall "deny to any person within its jurisdiction the equal protection of the laws." Over the years, the Court has narrowed the differences in its approach to statutory versus constitutional issues.

Second, while administrators commonly use the term "affirmative action," the Court has struggled to sort out the legal distinctions between "color blind" personnel practices, consideration of race as one among several factors in personnel decisions, and focus on race as the major factor in employment decisions. Further confounding these distinctions are the legal differences between the vehicles of affirmative action: voluntary plans, provisions included in consent decrees, and court orders.

A third factor obscuring clear cut conclusions about the use of race consciousness in personnel actions arises from differences between the assumptions about discrimination contained in Title VII and litigation subsequently confronted. When amending Title VII in 1972, Congress acknowledged its prior naivete: "In 1964, employment discrimination tended to be viewed as a series of isolated and distinguishable events, for the most part due to ill-will on the part of some identifiable individual or organization . . . Experience has shown this view to be false."[3] Unfortunately, the Court has had to confront cases involving systemic, yet, in some cases, unintentional discrimination where individual victims are not easily identifiable.

Growing out of these assumptions about discrimination as a fourth factor— the essentially remedial nature of Title VII and the challenge of voluntary affirmative action. The law was designed to compensate individuals who had suffered discrimination. The letter of the law did not envision the possibility of employers taking voluntary steps to overcome racial imbalances in their work force without formally having been found guilty of discrimination. Yet, starting with *Steelwork-*

ers v. *Weber*[4] the Court observed that precluding voluntary affirmative action would run contrary to the spirit of the law.

Finally, an appeal to legislative intent to answer questions of law frequently justifies conflicting positions. This is notably true with regard to Section 706(g) of Title VII, which some justices argue was intended to permit court ordered relief only for identifiable victims of discrimination. While Chief Justice Rehnquist, a strong supporter of this interpretation, claims that the language itself is clear in 706(g), he acknowledges that the legislative history "may be fairly apportioned among both sides."[5]

Each of these factors has challenged the Court's ability definitively to interpret employment discrimination law. Further, legal debate will continue over unresolved points of law like the difference in the meaning of "strict scrutiny," standards of review in Title VII versus 14th Amendment cases, and constitutional standards of review in gender versus race-based affirmative action. Nevertheless, case law has developed since 1971, and it is possible now to generalize at least about the *reasoning* employed by the Court when analyzing employment discrimination cases.

The Court's Two-Part Analytical Approach

Something like a working consensus appears present within the Court that review of race-conscious affirmative action requires a two-part analysis. The first part examines the justification for taking race into consideration. The second focuses on the content of the affirmative action with particular attention to the consequences for nonminority employees.

Justification for Race-Consciousness

Justification for taking affirmative action ranges from overcoming imbalances in "traditionally segregated job categories"[6] to remediating the effects of intentional discrimination.[7] While the Court has not yet agreed fully on what constitutes sufficient justification, *the more impact the affirmative action has on nonminorities, the more justification is required.* For example, the Court determined that "societal discrimination" did not constitute justification for a race-conscious layoff provision—even though contained in a collective bargaining agreement. According to the Court, an inference of *employer* discrimination would have been required.[8]

The most stringent requirement for a public employer is demonstrating a "compelling government purpose" for the use of racial classifications in employment decisions. A lesser standard would be an "important government purpose." But in many ways the Court's argument over standards of justification are rendered moot with Justice O'Connor's observation that "The Court is in agreement that, whatever the formulation [of a level of scrutiny like 'compelling' versus 'important'] employed, remedying past or present racial discrimination by a state actor is a sufficiently weighty state interest to warrant the remedial use of a carefully constructed affirmative action program."[9]

Many administrators do not realize that an inference of employer discrimination may be drawn from a conspicuous racial imbalance in segments of the employer's work force compared to segments of a relevant labor market.[10] Wherever a strong *inference* of employment discrimination can be found, at least a "firm" basis exists for affirmative action.[11]

Means-Ends Analysis

The second half of the Court's reasoning concentrates on the substance of the race-conscious plan or relief. The Court is concerned with limiting affirmative action tightly within the scope of the problem that it is supposed to solve. Regardless of whether a Title VII or 14th Amendment claim, the Court's primary concern in evaluating the scope of affirmative action is with the burden placed on innocent nonminorities.[12]

While the Court has approved benefits to nonvictim minorities,[13] it prefers remedies which provide "make-whole relief " to identifiable victims. With make-whole relief, victims receive what they would have gotten had they not been discriminated against, and nonvictim minorities do not benefit from a racial preference. But even in cases involving make-whole relief, the Court is inclined to review the impact on nonminorities. For example, in *Teamsters* the Court granted make-whole relief but remanded the case to the District Court to determine the actual victims of discrimination. The Supreme Court said: "The District Court will again be faced with the delicate task of adjusting the remedial interests of the discriminatees and the legitimate expectations of other employees innocent of any wrongdoing."[14]

While the Court has acknowledged that innocent third parties may have to bear some of the burden in race-conscious relief,[15] it is more likely to approve where the burden is diffuse and not borne by particular individuals. In *United States* v. *Paradise*, Justice Powell expressed his standard for judging the impact on third parties. He wrote: "Unlike layoff requirements, the promotion requirement at issue in this case does not 'impose the entire burden of achieving racial equality on particular individuals,' and it does not disrupt seriously the lives of innocent individuals."[16]

In addition to this guidance, in *Paradise* Justice Powell succinctly summarized four additional criteria used by the Court to assess whether or not race-conscious relief is narrowly tailored to the problem it is supposed to solve. They are: "(i) the efficacy of alternative remedies; (ii) the planned duration of the remedy; (iii) the relationship between the percentage of minority workers to be employed and the percentage of minority group members in the relevant population or work force; and (iv) the availability of waiver provisions if the hiring plan could not be met."[17]

Paradise illustrates the applicability of Justice Powell's five criteria. The District Court had found the Alabama Department of Public Safety guilty of intentional discrimination and recalcitrant in complying with the terms of subsequent decrees, including development of a valid promotion testing procedure. Frustrated with the delays, the District Court ordered a one-for-one promotion quota which the United States, supporting the Department of Public Safety, claimed violated the Equal Protection Clause of the 14th Amendment.

With the exception of Justice Stevens, who concurred in the judgment supporting the quota but who would have granted broader discretion to the District Court because the case involved intentional discrimination by a governmental body, the Court utilized its two-pronged analysis. The Court unanimously agreed that the District Court had rightly based its enforcement order on a compelling interest in eradicating the Department of Public Safety's "pervasive, systematic, and obstinate discriminatory" exclusion of blacks.[18] The Court's disagreement centered on the nature of the remedy, with Justices Brennan, Blackmun, Marshall, and Powell concluding that it was narrowly tailored and Justices O'Connor, Scalia, and White and Chief Justice Rehnquist finding the opposite.

Justice Brennan writing for a plurality reasoned that (1) no alternatives to the quota were brought to the District Court; (2) the one-for-one requirement was flexible in several ways including: a waiver provision if no qualified minorities were available; promotion only when the Department determined the need for additional supervisory personnel; duration contingent upon the Department's development of a valid promotion procedure; and anticipation of the quota as a onetime occurrence by the District Court; (3) while the one-for-one rate failed to correspond to the 1 to 3 ratio of blacks to whites in the relevant work force, it was appropriate considering the Department's past discrimination and delays in implementing the necessary promotion procedure; and (4) the requirement did not impose an unacceptable burden on innocent nonminorities.

Justice O'Connor's dissenting opinion, joined by Chief Justice Rehnquist and Justices Scalia and White, reiterated the view she expressed in *Sheet Metal Workers* where she argued strongly against quotas—and reluctantly endorsed goals— in court ordered remedies and reluctantly endorsed goals—because of their impact on innocent nonminorities.[19] In *Paradise* she reiterated that conclusion, focusing on what she called the Court's "standardless" view of a "narrowly tailored" remedy for the discrimination which had occurred. She fundamentally objected to the District Court's failure to entertain alternative remedies more specifically targeted at the goal of inducing the Department of Public Safety to develop a valid promotion procedure. She argued that consideration of alternatives is the least action required by the "narrowly tailored" standard.[20] Second, she objected to the one- for-one ratio arguing that it far exceeded the 25 percent minority trooper force eligible for promotion and, therefore, was arbitrary.

The two-part analysis is illustrated as well in *Johnson* v. *Transportation Agency*,[21] the other case coming before the Court in 1987. The parallel analyses in contrasting cases like *Paradise* and *Johnson* underscore the Court's growing consensus on its analytical approach to employment discrimination cases. *Paradise* came to the Court involving constitutional issues stemming from a court order in response to intentional racial discrimination. The Court reviewed *Johnson* as a Title VII case involving voluntary affirmative action to overcome gender imbalances in "traditionally segregated job categories."

Paul Johnson applied for promotion to the position of road dispatcher with the Transportation Agency in Santa Clara County, California. Diane Joyce also applied for the job in which women were obviously underrepresented. The hiring authority determined both applicants to be qualified and eligible for the promotion. Under the county's affirmative action plan, Joyce was hired over Johnson who had received two more points than Joyce on the basis of an interview. Thus, the Court was faced with determining if an affirmative action plan which led to the hiring of a woman over a male violated Title VII.[22]

In a 6–3 judgment, the Court upheld the plan. Justice Brennan delivered the Court's opinion. The majority found the County's actions consistent with the provisions that the Court established in *Weber*. The County's plan was designed to break down traditionally segregated job categories. The plan established short-term goals which did not unnecessarily trammel the interests of nonminorities (males), did not require discharge of nonminorities (males) in favor of minorities (females), did not create an absolute bar to advancement of nonminorities (males), and were temporary in nature and not designed to maintain a racial (gender) balance but to eliminate an imbalance.[23]

In sum, while it is not always possible to predict the Court's decision, one can be increasingly confident that both majority and minority opinions will follow the same points of reasoning. In other words, the framework of analysis has become increasingly clear with the development of case law. The framework focuses on the justification for affirmation action and an examination to determine whether the means narrowly fit the scope of the problem. In assessing the consequences of affirmative action, the Court pays significant attention to the impact on nonminorities.

The Value Debate Within the Court

So far, this article has attempted to summarize the legal reasoning which underpins the Court's analysis in employment discrimination cases. But to understand more clearly the Court's direction, one must identify and examine the values debated within this analytical framework.

For 18 years the Court has debated the appropriate balance in employment discrimination cases between the competing values of individual rights, social equity, and efficiency in its effort to clarify the meaning of the law. This section views the Court's affirmative action decisions in terms of these values.

As a value, *individual rights* includes the expectations that employees and job applicants have of fair treatment and protection from arbitrary decisions, particularly in actions affecting job security and seniority. The Court's emphasis on "make-whole relief " to identifiable victims of discrimination reflects the value of individual rights. Similarly, its emphasis on protecting the interests of nonminorities grows out of its respect for individual rights. Thus, the key task of balancing the interests of minority victims and innocent nonminorities fundamentally revolves around questions of individual rights.

While the Court does not use the term *social equity,* its opinions nevertheless reflect this value which cannot be ignored in understanding human resources policy and administration. Another term for social equity might be "distributive justice." Adherence to the value of social equity results in fair treatment of people as members of a class rather than as individuals. Preference on the basis of race, gender, age, religion, or national origin reflects the value of social equity. Social equity is frequently expressed in compensatory terms where an action is taken to overcome some classwide past injustice or hardship. Social equity results in race-conscious affirmative action to nonvictim minorities as opposed to make-whole relief to identifiable victims of discrimination. One of the most common expressions of social equity, predating affirmative action by a century, is veterans preference awarded to individuals who have served in the armed forces and who may have lost a competitive position in the labor market.

Because the Court analyzes percentages of minorities to nonminorities in a work force to make inferences about underutilization and to assess progress in overcoming the effects of past discrimination, the value of social equity frequently is confused with a similar value, "representation." Clearly, moving towards a work force that is representative of the racial balance in a relevant labor pool demonstrates affirmative action progress. However, representativeness is used as a measure or instrument of this progress, not as an end value. The goal of eradicating past discrimination expresses the end value of social equity.[24]

Frequently people look upon social equity with suspicion. Among the reasons are: a preference in this culture to make awards based on variation in individual merit rather than either/or distinctions which erase individual differences. The value of social equity necessarily highlights differences due to race, gender, and national origin in a culture which largely seeks to downplay these differences.

Efficiency in the provision of public services is commonly measured with various input/output ratios. In personnel administration efficiency is advanced generally when personnel actions are taken on the basis of merit. Thus, efficiency is reflected in affirmative action with the concern for the qualifications (knowledge, skills, and abilities) of applicants.

The history of employment discrimination cases first focused on the values of individual rights and efficiency consistent with the assumption that violations of anti-discrimination law would consist of discreet incidents involving a victim and a person who had committed a discriminatory act. Victims would receive make-whole relief which would be balanced against the rights and interests of other victims and innocent nonminorities. The Court's unanimous opinion in *Griggs* emphasized that *individuals* should be subject to color blind criteria in employment decisions. Individual rights are expressed in the view that race-conscious relief should be confined to the identifiable victims of discrimination. This view is seen clearly in *Albemarle Paper Company* v. *Moody*[25] where the Court went to great lengths to specify how an employee could create the inference that he or she was a victim of discrimination, and in *Firefighters* v. *Stotts,*[26] where the Court implied a general policy limiting relief only to identifiable victims of discrimination.

Finally, a major expression of individual rights is the Court's concern that the burden that innocent nonminorities are called upon to bear in race-conscious relief will not cause them undue harm. This concern is expressed in all Court opinions where minority nonvictims benefit from race-conscious relief. It is even expressed where make-whole relief is involved, particularly when the job security of nonminorities might be affected. According to Justice Stewart, writing for the Court in *Teamsters*, "Especially when immediate implementation of an equitable remedy threatens to impinge upon the expectations of innocent parties, the courts must 'look to the practical realities and necessities inescapably involved in reconciling competing interests,' in order to determine the 'special blend of what is necessary, what is fair, and what is workable.' "[27]

In Justice Rehnquist's minority opinion in *Weber*, he expressed the unequivocal viewpoint that employment discrimination boils down to questions of individual rights: "I find a prohibition on all preferential treatment based on race as elementary and fundamental as the principle that "two wrongs do not make a right.""[28]

The problem with approaching employment discrimination from the perspective of individual rights alone is found in situations where systemic discrimination has created insidious barriers to fair treatment. For example, where blacks know it is a waste of time to apply for a job or a promotion, make-whole relief is very difficult to assign.[29] Further, to the extent that the Court has endorsed affirmative action to overcome race and gender imbalances in traditionally segregated job categories, as it did in *Weber* and *Johnson*, trying to limit relief to identifiable victims of discrimination is impractical.

Thus, in addition to individual rights, social equity has influenced the Court's decisions. These decisions invoke preferential treatment to minorities who may not have been victims of discrimination, with preference to them stemming from their minority status as opposed to characteristics which differentiate minority members one from the other or from nonminority employees or applicants. *Weber, Sheet Metal Workers, Firefighters, Paradise,* and *Johnson* (gender) all provide some kind of goal or quota with preference to minorities. Of course, in each of these cases, the Court makes a special effort to assess the impact of the goal or quota on the rights of nonminorities, recognizing that social equity can impinge upon individual rights and that the values require some balancing.

The strongest expressions of social equity go beyond establishment of goals and quotas to remedy employer discrimination. Justice Stevens has led the argument. In *Wygant*, he wrote in a dissenting opinion that the Court "should consider whether the public interest, and the manner in which it is pursued, justifies any adverse effects on the disadvantaged groups."[30] This "public interest" standard is distinguished from the stricter standards of "compelling" or even "important" government purposes, and it would open the door to broader justification for race-conscious personnel actions. More recently, in a concurring opinion in *Johnson*, where the Court supported the use of gender classification, Justice Stevens emphasized that "the opinion does not establish the permissible outer limits of voluntary programs undertaken by employers to benefit disadvantaged groups."[31] Further, he wrote: "Instead of retroactively scrutinizing his own or society's possible exclusions of minorities in the past to determine the outer limits of a valid affirmative-action program—or indeed, any particular affirmative-action decision—in many cases the employer will find it more appropriate to consider *other legitimate reasons to give preferences to members of under-represented groups*" [emphasis added].[32] These other reasons might include, "simply to eliminate from their operations all de facto embodiment of a system of racial caste."[33]

The sharper the emphasis on any particular value in a Justice's opinion, the more likely it is to be isolated and countered. Efficiency is one such counter concern, especially to be social equity arguments. But the efficiency argument itself had become muted over the years; in reality it moved to the background as social equity advanced. As an example in 1971 in *Griggs*, Chief Justice Burger delivered the Court's unanimous opinion endorsing a color blind interpretation of the law where job qualifications are the controlling factor in personnel decisions: "Congress has not commanded that the less qualified be preferred over the better qualified simply because of minority origins. Far from disparaging job qualifications as such, Congress has made such qualifications the controlling factor, so that race, religion, nationality, and sex become irrelevant.[34]

Sixteen years later in *Paradise,* the Court drew no distinction between "more or less qualified." The emphasis was solely on the "qualified," implying a dichotomy between "qualified" and "not qualified." In addition, instead of qualifications being the centerpiece as in *Griggs*, in *Paradise* they were used merely as one of several factors ameliorating the impact of a promotion quota—an expression of social equity. Delivering a plurality opinion for a 5–4 Court, Justice Brennam wrote that the promotion quota "may be waived if no qualified black candidates are available.[35]

Presently, the Court is attempting to balance the three values. This can be seen in the two most recent cases, *Paradise* and *Johnson*. In *Paradise*, a 5–4 Court supported an order for a promotion quota. But in justifying the remedy, which emphasized social equality, the Court acknowledged several qualifying conditions. Among those, in deference to the efficiency value it waived the quota in the absence of qualified minorities. In addition, the Court held that the quota would not trammel the individual rights of particular nonminorities because its impact was diffuse.

One finds similar compromises in *Johnson*. The hiring authority considered gender as a factor in the promotion decision, suggesting sensitivity to the social equity value.

With respect to Johnson's individual rights, the Court argued that he was not due a promotion, and denial in this particular case would not preclude a promotion in the future. As to the efficiency value, with both candidates being certified as well-qualified in a initial assessment, both the hiring authority and the Court— with a lively dissent—found negligible the two-point difference separating Johnson from Joyce on the basis of subsequent interview.

In sum, it is clear that those who favor class-conscious affirmative action place higher priority on social equity than those who favor individual rights. Practically speaking, while acknowledging the Court's rhetoric on efficiency, one may question the influence of this value in the Court's calculations. But regardless of the relative priorities, no decision of the Court in an employment discrimination case involving nonvictim beneficiaries is likely to occur in the near future without reflecting all three of these values.

The Future of Affirmative Action

As one speculates about the future of affirmative action and the relative priority of the values, one might consider three factors: the configuration of the U.S. Supreme Court, its respect for precedent, and the technical nature of personnel administration.[36]

Configuration of the Court

Justice Powell's retirement and Justice O'Connor's position seem critical in assessing the Court's future decisions on affirmative action. Justice Powell played a significant role in employment discrimination cases when he joined the Blackmun, Brennan, Marshall, and Stevens plurality to form a majority in *Sheet Metal Workers* and *Firefighters*. Justice O'Connor joined this new majority in *Johnson* and in *Firefighters*. Powell's move accompanied the plurality's adoption of his stricter standard of judicial review in *Sheet Metal Workers*. This is the present standard employed by the Court.

In similar fashion, it is not unreasonable to expect the plurality of Justices Blackmun, Brennan, Marshall, and Stevens to move closer to Justice O'Connor's more conservative position in order to maintain a majority. If so, despite Justice O'Connor's support in *Johnson*, the Court will place less emphasis on the value of social equity and more on individual rights. Justice O'Connor has shown no tolerance whatsoever for quotas or for quotas which purport to be goals.[37] Nonetheless, her support in *Johnson* separates her from Justices Scalia and White and from Chief Justice Rehnquist, who adhere to the view that affirmative action should focus on make-whole relief only.

Because *Johnson* involved affirmative action for women, some might argue that Justice O'Connor is more sympathetic to gender issues than to racial issues. Justice O'Connor has written opinions in several employment discrimination cases, however, and her arguments in *Johnson* appear entirely consistent with those she expressed in cases involving racial discrimination. Nothing exists in the Court's record to suggest that Justice O'Connor will show more sympathy towards affirmative action for women than for racial minorities.

If the plurality of Justices Blackmun, Brennan, Marshall, and Stevens are unable consistently to find areas of agreement with Justice O'Connor, Justice Kennedy's role in employment discrimination cases could become pivotal. Unfortunately, Justice Kennedy has not assembled a record comprehensive enough to permit an analysis.[38] However, it is anticipated generally that his support for affirmative action based on social equity will be modest.

Precedent

The future of affirmative action depends significantly on the respect that the newly configured Court shows for precedent, especially *University of California Regents* v. *Bakke*[39] and *Weber*. In those cases, the Court clearly ventured beyond the earlier statutory letter of the law, permitting use of race as one factor in admissions/selection decisions *(Bakke)*[40] and permitting voluntary affirmative action *(Weber)*. It was apparent at the time that with *Weber* the Court had expanded its interpretation of congressional intent in Title VII. Acknowledging the Court's new and broad interpretation of Title VII in *Weber.* Justice Blackmun invited Congress to act if it took issue with the Court's interpretation which permitted voluntary affirmative action.[41]

In *Johnson*, Justice Stevens acknowledged that the Court had gone beyond the letter of the statute in its interpretation of Title VII. He agreed with the dissent's position that if the Court adhered to Congress' "color blind" rhetoric and the Court's initial interpretation of Title VII, Paul Johnson would have prevailed in his claim. However, Justice Stevens reminded the Court that, "*Bakke* and *Weber* have been decided and are now an important part of the fabric of the law. This consideration is sufficiently compelling for me to adhere to the basic construction of this legislation that the Court adopted in *Bakke* and *Weber*."[42]

In Justice O'Connor's concurring opinion in *Johnson* she picked up Justice Stevens' theme that the Court had established a precedent in *Weber* warranting respect. Thus, with Justices Stevens and O'Connor joining Justices Blackmun, Brennan, and Marshall, it is highly unlikely that the present Court will undo *Bakke*—where the Court established that race could be used as one factor in affirmative action—and *Weber*—where the Court upheld voluntary affirmative action by private sector employers and set the stage for public employers as well.

Organizational and Technical Rationality

Speculation about the future of affirmative action must go beyond prognosis of the Court's configuration and estimation of its respect for precedent. Over an

18-year period, administrators have become sensitized to Court decisions expressing the value of social equity. It is unreasonable to anticipate sudden administrative reversal of these impacts now, regardless of Court action.

In the abstract, public organizations are value systems requiring legitimacy for survival. Currently, it is hard to conceive of a public organization claiming legitimacy if it does not recognize the value of social equity in its employment practices.

But tension remains in personnel practices largely because the Court has relegated the efficiency value to a backstage role while organizations cannot. The Court has demonstrated its legal predilection to view affirmative action originally and fundamentally as an individual rights issue regardless of whether Title VII or the Constitution is involved. The impact of social equity on the efficiency value is understated because of the judicial system's fundamental orientation which features individual rights. In addition, efficiency lost relevance in the debate once the Court adopted the "qualified/not qualified" notion of efficiency over a continuum of "more/less qualified."

While casting the debate as one juxtaposing social equity and individual rights serves a juridical perspective, the Court fails to acknowledge the organizational contexts within which affirmative action actually takes place, specifically within the context of "merit." In the day-to-day routine of personnel management based on merit, the debate over affirmative action is more likely to involve social equity and efficiency rather than social equity and individual rights—although clearly, in highly visible allocational decisions, this is not the case.

The values framework summarized in this article implies that any complex public personnel policy issue must involve debates of all salient values.[43] Failure in that regard results in the neglected value expressing itself in unintended ways. This very well may be the case with affirmative action. The common employee perception—whether accurate or not—that some minority employees have received unfair preferential treatment may be attributable to the relative neglect of efficiency as a value in the Court's deliberations when contrasted to its importance as an organizational value.[44]

The debate focusing on social equity and individual rights may prevail in the foreseeable future of affirmative action. But failure to pay more attention to the value of efficiency may erode its legitimacy further in organizational settings where affirmative action must be implemented.

Given the organizational—as opposed to judicial—emphasis on efficiency, one might confidently observe that those personnel practices reflecting social equity which coincide with rather than oppose practices consistent with individual rights and efficiency will endure. This means that, even without a hint of employment discrimination, at the minimum practices like targeted recruitment; job related tests, interviews, and performance appraisals; and merit pay based on job related factors are here to stay. They are now anchored in the core of public personnel practices. One would anticipate continuing organizational emphasis on social equity where inferences of discrimination can be drawn.

In summary, the U.S. Supreme Court assesses each case based on unique points of law and patterns of fact. On that basis, one might be reluctant to predict the Court's direction. However, drawing upon knowledge of the value base of personnel policy, one gains a broad interpretive tool. Putting together the present configuration of the Court, its respect for precedent, and the value patterns implied in past decisions, one could hardly conclude that affirmative action is dead, as some might believe. However, the emphasis on social equity is likely to shift somewhat in favor of a new balance—perhaps tempered by a renewed concern for organizational efficiency—based on complementary rather than opposing expressions of social equity and individual rights. Moreover, the legitimacy of affirmative action over the longer haul depends on incorporating the value of efficiency more consistently into formal channels of judicial review as well as public policy forums and organizational practices.

Notes

1. *Griggs* v. *Duke Power Company*, 401 U.S. 424 (1971).
2. In their dissent in *Teamsters* v. *United States*, 431 U.S. 324. p. 392 (1977), Justices Brennan and Marshall quoted the Congressional Record on this point, "in any areas where a specific contrary intention is not indicated, it was assumed that the present case law would continue to govern the applicability and construction of Title VII."
3. *Ibid.*, p. 383, fn 7.
4. *Steelworkers* v. *Weber*, 443 U.S. 193 (1979).
5. *Firefighters* v. *Cleveland*, 92 L Ed 2d 405, 437 (1986).
6. *Johnson* v. *Transportation Agency*, 94 L Ed 615 (1987).
7. *United States* v. *Paradise*, 94 L Ed 203 (1987).
8. *Wygant* v. *Jackson Board of Education*, 90 L Ed 2d 260. p. 269 (1985).
9. *Ibid.*, p. 276.
10. *Teamsters, supra.*, pp. 339, 358.
11. Consistent with *Teamsters*, a Title VII case, the various opinions in *Wygant, supra.*, pp. 270, 278, and 289, support this assertion with regard to constitutional review.
   More specifically, whenever a person or group can demonstrate an inference of employer discrimination—usually through a labor market demographic analysis—the burden shifts to the employer to show that the underutilization of minorities results from job related personnel practices or bona fide occupational qualifications.
12. See *Sheet Metal Workers* v. *EEOC*, 92 L Ed 2d 344 (1986) for the Court's parallel analysis of Title VII and Equal Protection Clause claims.
13. A variety of cases have reinforced this point since *Weber, supra.* Included most recently are: *Johnson, supra.; Paradise, supra.; Sheet Metal Workers, supra.;* and *Firefighters, supra.*
14. *Teamsters, supra.*, p. 372.
15. *Wygant, supra.*, pp. 272–275.
16. *Paradise, supra.*
17. *Ibid.*, p. 233.
18. *Ibid.*, p. 221.

19. *Sheet Metal Workers, supra.*

20. *Paradise, supra.*, p. 242.

21. *Johnson, supra.*

22. The hiring authority did not regard the difference in the interview scores between Joyce and Johnson as significant (*Ibid.*, p. 626). In their dissent, pp. 650–651. Justices Scalia and White and Chief Justice Rehnquist took issue with this claim.

23. *Ibid.*, p. 629.

24. Correspondence (June 1988) with David Rosenbloom assisted my exploration of the relationship between social equity and representativeness.

25. *Albemarle Paper Company* v. *Moody*, 422 U.S. 405 (1975).

26. *Firefighters* v. *Stotts*, 467 U.S. 561, pp. 579–580, 582–583 (1984).

27. *Teamsters, supra.*, p. 375.

28. *Weber, supra.*, p. 228, fn 10.

29. See *Teamsters, supra.*, pp. 365–368, and Justices Brennan, Blackmun, and Marshall's dissenting opinion in *Stotts, supra.*, pp. 612–613.

30. *Wygant, supra.*, pp. 293–294.

31. *Johnson, supra.*, p. 637.

32. *Ibid.*, p. 640.

33. *Idem.* Justice Stevens' advocacy of race consciousness extended to the value of effectiveness as well as social equity. In *Johnson, supra.*, p. 640. and in *Wygant, supra.*, pp. 294–295. Stevens cited examples where taking race into account in personnel actions can increase the effectiveness of a work force. One example was where a police force sought to integrate itself to enhance community relations. Thus, racially balancing a work force—that is, making it representative of a relevant labor pool or community—can impact effectiveness as well as social equity. However, the two goals may be pursued independently, and, in my observation, when the Court endorses racial preference, it does so primarily in pursuit of social equity—to eradicate the effects of past discrimination—not effectiveness.

34. *Griggs, supra.*

35. *Paradise. supra.*, p. 227.

36. Omitted in this general discussion are factors like the emphasis on civil rights enforcement of the President elected in 1988 and assignment power of the Chief Justice.

37. See her dissenting opinion in *Sheet Metal Workers, supra.*, and her concurring opinion in *Johnson, supra.*

38. I acknowledge Jan G. Levine's (People for the American Way) assistance in identifying related cases. In addition to case material, U.S. Senate, Committee on the Judiciary, *Nomination of Anthony M. Kennedy To Be An Associate Justice of the United States Supreme Court*, Executive Report 100-13 (February 1, 1988), similarly yielded little relevant information.

39. *University of California Regents* v. *Bakke*, 438 U.S. 265 (1978).

40. *Bakke* produced a split court with numerous opinions. However, it is clear that by joining Justice Powell's opinion with that of Justices Brennan, White, Marshall, and Blackmun, *ibid.*, pp. 320, 326, the Court did sanction the use of race as one factor in university admissions decisions where diversity within the student body is a stated goal. Further, in *Johnson, supra.*, pp. 634–635, the Court extended *Bakke* from the context of higher education to employment discrimination.

41. *Weber, supra.*, p. 216.

42. *Johnson, supra.*, p. 639.

43. For an elaboration of the framework, see Donald E. Klingner and John Nalbandian, *Public Personnel Management: Contexts and Strategies,* 2d ed. (Englewood Cliffs, NJ: Prentice-Hall, 1985) and John Nalbandian and Donald E. Klingner, "Conflict and Values in Public Personnel Administration," *Public Administration Quarterly,* vol. 11 (Spring 1987), pp. 17–33.

44. For example, according to the United States Office of Personnel Management, *Federal Employee Attitudes,* 1980, some 30 percent of the senior level federal employees surveyed in 1980–1981 indicated that they felt that minority employees were treated "better or much better" than nonminorities.

9

AFFIRMATIVE ACTION AND CITY MANAGERS

Attitudes Toward Recruitment of Women

James D. Slack

Historical and contemporary patterns of recruiting women into the management of the local public sector generally parallel the patterns of blacks and members of other minority groups. Recent advances in the recruitment of women can be attributed in part to the passage of the 1972 Equal Employment Opportunity (EEO) Act and its primary instrument of implementation, affirmative action. Equal employment opportunity means having a setting where discriminatory hiring practices are nonexistent. Affirmative action refers to special and exceptional efforts on the part of the public manager to rectify the results of current and previous discriminatory practices and, ultimately, to ensure equal employment opportunity. Since the 1972 enactment, affirmative action has been the primary mechanism for the development of a representative bureaucracy at the local level.

While change is evident, from seven female city managers in 1971 to over 100 in 1986, the absence of greater numbers of women in decision-making circles calls into question some underlying assumptions made in the area of public personnel administration. Specifically, this study examines the extent to which city managers support the use of affirmative action practices in the recruitment of women into managerial positions. Analysis also focuses on several exogenous factors that help to explain the level of support which city managers have to undertake special and exceptional efforts to recruit women.

Source: *Public Administration Review* 47 (March/April 1987): 199–206.

I. The Literature

A review of previous research underscores the fact that women are underrepresented *vis-a-vis* men in public sector management. At the federal level, white men are much more likely than women to have supervisory roles or to head projects and programs.[1] In state governments, women remain underrepresented because, in part, of the tradition of routinely selecting men for leadership positions.[2] Similarly, women have little opportunity in local government for entry into the managerial enclave[3] and are usually underrepresented in comparison to the overall female population within a metropolitan area.[4] In essence, occupational segregation by gender remains a fact of life in the management of human resources throughout all levels of government in the United States.[5]

Findings of previous studies show that some gains have been made by women and, furthermore, that these gains have not conflicted with similar advances made by minority groups.[6] Rather, the inroads made by women in state and local governments have been at the expense of positions formerly held by white males.[7] Previous results also indicate that minority women, in comparison to other disadvantaged groups, have made the greatest advances into the decision-making arena of the public sector.[8]

The delineation of exogenous factors, which determine the success or failure of affirmative action, remains a speculative and pretheoretical endeavor. Several variables, however, seem to be related to the acceptance of, or support for, affirmative action at the federal, state, and local levels. This list includes demographic factors,[9] the extent to which affirmative action groups are able to exert political influence,[10] ideological orientation,[11] education,[12] the history of affirmative action litigation,[13] and having a clear understanding of the meaning and purpose of affirmative action.[14]

While previous studies have generated much new and useful information about affirmative action, two gaps remain which this study helps to fill. First, analysis has neglected the smaller communities and "average" size cities, ranging from 2,500 to less than 100,000 in population. Indeed, previous research has focused generally on the larger cities nationally,[15] the larger cities in a single region,[16] the larger cities in a single state,[17] or individual case studies of larger cities.[18]

A second gap in the literature is the omission of city managers from analysis. Units of analysis generally consist of personnel directors, agency or department heads, public employees, or EEO-4 data for entire cities. The absence of city managers as the unit of analysis is significant, since over 2,500 communities have the council-manager form of government. In the larger municipalities, the city manager is in a position to influence and shape explicitly and directly the behavior and attitudes of the personnel director. In the smaller communities, the city manager quite often performs as the official personnel director. In both large cities and small towns, the city manager is ultimately responsible for the personnel function and, consequently, has the capacity to establish an implicit atmosphere about affirmative action throughout city government. Whether in addressing issues common to a civil service-based merit system or in negotiating with a local public union, the city manager can set the tone of discussion and action by being an advocate of representative bureaucracy. The particular nature of the city manager-generated atmosphere, therefore, can contribute significantly to the success or failure of affirmative action programs and policies.

II. Current Strategies in Affirmative Action

Both the public and private sectors are subject to federal equal employment opportunity/affirmative action regulations.[19] In a recent *PAR* article, Dometrius and Sigelman compare both sectors in terms of achieving representative recruitment patterns.[20] The findings suggest that, while women and minorities remain underrepresented in both sectors, affirmative action efforts have produced a greater level of utilization of protected groups in state and local governments than in the private sector. Furthermore, women and minorities experience less income disparity *vis-à-vis* white males at the state and local levels than they do in the private sector.

Figure 9.1 illustrates the components of affirmative action plans which are commonly used in the private and public sectors. Within organizations in either sector, aspects of the plans cause a certain degree of anxiety and discontent. Affirmative action plans generate a substantial amount of paperwork annually and consume a corresponding amount of staff time. Affirmative action considerations tend to take precedence over other important personnel factors, such as merit and seniority. Requirements to establish hiring goals and timetables also cause misunderstandings. Unlike quotas, which tend to be binding, court-ordered hiring ratios, hiring goals tend to be self-determined, noncontractual targets. That is, affirmative action goals are objectives which the organization strives to meet. Failure to do so does not necessarily result in the imposition of penalties. In essence, hiring goals or targets are intended to be a management tool and the concomitant timetables are meant to measure the progress made in reaching the target.

The federal government and professional organizations, such as the International City Management Association (ICMA), have assisted municipalities in their efforts to implement affirmative action. By providing funding for scholarships, the federal government has attempted to increase the pool of qualified affirmative action candidates for public management positions. The Department of Education has provided such scholarships to minority and female MPA students through its Education for Public Service (the Jacob Javits Fellowship) Program. Through various programs, such as the Comprehensive Planning Assistance Program, Minorities-In-Management Program, and the Community Development Work-Study Program, the Department of Housing and Urban Development has also encouraged growth in the numbers of affirmative action students entering public administration graduate programs.

FIGURE 9.1 Major Components/Steps in Affirmative Action Plans Public and Private Sectors

Public Sector[a]	Private Sector[b]
• Issue a written equal employment opportunity policy and affirmative action commitment.	• Establishment of quantitative (statistical) objectives for representation of women and minorities in all jobs, levels, and functions.
• Publicize the policy and commitment, both internally and externally.	• Inclusion of equal opportunity issues in regular management training.
• Appoint a top official to direct and implement the program.	• Specific training in equal opportunity, including:
• Survey the present work force to identify underutilization of female and minority employees by department and by major occupational classification.	(a) knowledge-focused training (i.e., legal issues, company policy benefits, changes).
• Develop and implement specific action plans to achieve equal employment opportunity.	(b) attitude-focused training.
• Establish a monitoring system to audit and evaluate progress for each aspect of the plan.	(c) behavior-focused training (i.e., training dealing with managerial expectations of behavior with an emphasis on behavior changes in recruiting, selecting, training, work assignment, and career development of employees).
• Develop supportive organizational and community programs.	
• Develop goals and timetables to increase the utilization of protected class members where underutilization has been identified.	

[a] SOURCE: Karen Ann Olsen, *Equal Employment Opportunity and Affirmative Action: A Guide for Mayors and Public Officials.* Prepared by Labor Management Relations Service (Washington, DC: U.S. Conference of Mayors, 1979).
[b] SOURCE: Daniel Quinn Mills, "Elements of a Typical Business Affirmative Action Plan," *Labor-Management Relations* (New York: McGraw-Hill, 1982), p. 50.

The ICMA has also attempted to improve the representativeness of municipal management through raising the salience of the issue within its membership.[21] For many years, it has sponsored a series of workshops and task forces on such topics as "Managing for Social and Economic Opportunity" (1968) and "Women in the Profession" (1972) and has encouraged its membership to participate in the work-study programs of the federal government. In 1973 the ICMA established the "Minority Executive Placement Program" (MEPP) to assist cities in tapping the expanding pool of qualified minority candidates. Eventually MEPP included a placement service for nonminority women and was expanded to state-level city management associations. Within its first five years of existence, MEPP was instrumental in placing over 700 affirmative action candidates in local public management positions.

Hence, the federal government and organizations like the ICMA have attempted to reduce the level of anxiety commonly associated with the hiring targets and timetables of affirmative action plans. Municipalities, however, have benefited from this type of support to a lesser extent in the 1980s than they did in the mid-to-late 1970s. Most of the federal scholarship programs have been eliminated or greatly reduced. Even the effectiveness of the ICMA affirmative action placement service has been hampered as a result of increasingly restrictive operating budgets. Nevertheless, the components of targets and timetables have remained critical ingredients in the pursuit of equal employment opportunity.

III. Research Design and Method

City manager support for the use of affirmative action in the recruitment of women is the dependent variable in this research. Based predominantly on previous research, five clusters of indicators are used as independent variables.[22] The clusters consist of: (1) community demographics, (2) city government demographics, (3) perceptions about the political clout of affirmative action groups in local politics, (4) the pattern of legal involvement with affirmative action, and (5) background characteristics of the city manager. Data are obtained through survey research and census material.

A 46-item questionnaire was constructed, using open-ended, forced-choice, and Likert scale formats. While some items were unique to this study, most were adapted from previously used questionnaires.[23] Two procedures were used to test the validity of each questionnaire item, as well as the survey instrument in total. First, a group of experts in the field examined the questionnaire and suggested several critical modifications. Afterwards, the questionnaire was pretested on 10 percent of the sample, which resulted in one additional change in format.[24] All suggestions for modification were incorporated into the final draft of the survey instrument.

A systematic, stratified random sampling technique was utilized to reflect the sample population, especially regarding community size and regional distribution. The sampling frame consisted of 2,520 cities with the council-manager form of government, as recognized in 1985 by the ICMA. Of the list, 504 cities (approximately 20 percent) were drawn for inclusion in this study. The distribution of respondents by state is shown in the appendix.

Each city manager in the sample received as many as three copies of the questionnaire, accompanied with a cover letter indicating the author's institutional affiliation. In addition, a postcard follow-up reminder was mailed prior to sending the second copy of the questionnaire. All mailings were sent with first-class postage. The third copy of the questionnaire, however, was mailed with first-class certified postage. The questionnaire was administered and returned during the summer months of 1985.

The dependent variable was measured through the construction of an additive index of eight questionnaire items. To test the unidimensionality of the index—hence, its utility as a dependent variable—an item analysis was conducted on its component parts. The analysis produced reliability coefficients of .70 (alpha) and .71 (standardized item alpha). A multiple regression equation was formulated to analyze the relationship between support for affirmative action and the independent variable clusters. The specific equation used the backward elimination/means-substitution procedures of *SPSS-X*.[25] Partial correlations were used as a measure of association and partial standardized regression coefficients (betas) were used to measure changes in the level of support attributable to changes in each indicator for the independent variables.

IV. Results

Two-hundred-ninety city managers returned usable questionnaires. The response rate, 58 percent, is acceptable in light of several factors which normally reduce the levels of response in any survey. The general issue of affirmative action, for example, is controversial in both the public and private sectors. The questionnaire was also mailed directly to the public office address, rather than to the private residence, and includes a temporary identification number. Overall, the 58 percent response rate is satisfactory, given that the returned sample includes more than one out of ten city managers in the United States.

The respondents and their respective communities reflect basic central tendencies which one would expect to find in the sample population. Community populations range from 2,500 to well over 600,000, with the average being about 19,500. The white population in these cities varies from five percent to 100 percent, with the mode and mean being 98 percent (n = 19) and 82 percent, respectively. Excluding nonrespondents, approximately 61 percent of the communities (n = 275) have affirmative action plans on-line.

The average city manager is white (94.9 percent), male (93 percent), and middle-aged (43.5 years old). He is in the sixth year of managing the city government and is a resident of 11 years in the community. Excluding nonrespondents, approximately 58 percent of the city managers (n = 267) have graduate-level education, of which 52 percent (n = 150) have degrees in public administration or a closely related area. The annual income distribution of the city managers is bi-modal (n = 81), $30–39,999 and $40–49,999, with the average being between the two salary categories.[26]

Table 9.1 shows the frequency distributions for the eight items comprising the dependent variable's additive index. City manager support for affirmative action toward women appears to follow two distinctive patterns. On the one hand, re-spondents demonstrate a substantial level of support for the principle of affirma-tive action. Over 55 percent believe that government should intervene on behalf of women (item 1) and over 60 percent agree that, when all factors are equal, hir-ing preference should be given to the female applicant to accomplish affirmative action (item 2). Furthermore, nearly 80 percent of the city managers oppose ex-pressions of sexism, such as off-colored jokes (item 3). Supportive attitudes to-ward the principle of affirmative action, however, are not universally shared. Ap-proximately 40 percent of the city managers either oppose, or are neutral toward, the use of affirmative action in support of women (items 1 and 2).

Table 9.1 also displays a second pattern in the attitudes of city managers. The level of support is substantially less for some specific mechanisms designed to im-plement the principle of affirmative action. Less than half of the respondents be-lieve that their respective city governments should make special recruitment ef-forts on behalf of women (item 4), while more than 65 percent believe that external groups and individuals from the community should not be involved in the local government hiring process (item 5). Furthermore, approximately 60 percent of the city managers oppose the use of hiring targets (item 6) and timeta-bles (item 7) in the recruitment of women. While approximately 20 percent are supportive, the majority of the respondents are opposed to the idea of hiring a fe-male applicant when a more competent male applicant is available (item 8).

Table 9.2 reports the results of regressing the dependent variable on the five in-dependent variable clusters. The regression equation generates a moderate level of association (multiple R = .54) and explains nearly 30 percent of the variance in affirmative action support levels. While the indicators for community demo-graphics (cluster I), city government demographics (cluster II), and city manager perceptions about local politics (cluster III) have minimal effects on the level of support for affirmative action, several indicators in the remaining two variable clusters appear to have important explanatory powers.

The fourth variable cluster taps the legal and formal dimensions of affirmative action. The beta (−.19) indicates that having an affirmative action plan in opera-tion has a negative effect on the level of support for affirmative action. This nega-tive relationship may simply reflect displeasure over what might be perceived as the voluminous annual paper work involved in complying with various affirma-tive action and civil rights regulations. This finding may also be indicative of dis-content over a perceived imposition of hiring targets and timetables.

The fifth variable cluster focuses on the background characteristics of city managers. Within this cluster, three indicators are important in predicting levels

TABLE 9.1 Support for Affirmative Action for Women by City Managers

Questionnaire Item	Percent Strongly Supportive of AA	Percent Supportive of AA	Percent Neutral	Percent Opposed to AA	Percent Strongly Opposed to AA	Percent Undecided
Item 1 If women are not getting fair treatment in jobs, government should see to it that they do. (n = 271)	22.5	34.3	19.6	15.5	8.1	—
Item 2 Where female and male applicants are of equal ability and women are underrepresented on the city's work force, the city's departments should give preference to female applicants. (n = 274)	18.2	44.9	17.2	12.0	7.7	—
Item 3 As long as they are told "privately" and "in fun," it is all right for members of my department to tell jokes at work about sex and women. (n = 285)	49.8	29.5	9.8	4.6	2.1	4.2
Item 4 The city should make a special effort to recruit women for positions in management and administration. (n = 279)	15.4	31.2	20.4	20.1	12.9	—
Item 5 Public agencies should set up committees of women civic leaders to make recommendations for improving hiring/promotion of women. (n = 271)	1.1	12.2	18.8	33.9	33.9	—
Item 6 The city should establish hiring targets for women. (n = 273)	7.0	16.9	16.1	35.2	24.9	—
Item 7 The city should establish timetables for reaching the hiring targets for women. (n = 272)	6.6	17.3	19.1	33.1	23.9	—
Item 8 The city's departments should not hire a female applicant if there is a more competent male applicant who wants the job. (n = 284)	20.8	9.5	11.6	33.5	20.8	3.9

For purposes of this table, the Lickert scale has been collapsed: 1 = strongly opposed, 2+3 = oppose, 4 = neutral, 5+6 = support, 7 = strongly support, 8 = undecided.

TABLE 9.2   Determinants of City Managers' Support of Affirmative Action for Women

Variable/Indicator	Partial Correlation	Beta	Significance T
I. Community Demographics			
1. Population size	.13	.14	.03
2. White population	*	*	—
II. City Government Demographics			
1. Number of employees supervised	.08	.07	**
2. Employees in administrative positions	.11	.10	**
3. Male administrators	.13	.11	.03
4. Black male administrators	*	*	—
5. Hispanic male administrators	*	*	—
6. Other minority male administrators	*	*	—
7. White male administrators	*	*	—
8. Black female administrators	.12	.12	.05
9. Hispanic female administrators	−.08	−.09	**
10. Other minority female administrators	*	*	—
11. White female administrators	*	*	—
III. Perceptions about Local Politics			
1. Minority group pressure for AA	*	*	—
2. Pressure by women for AA	*	*	—
3. Elected officials support for AA	.09	.08	**
IV. Legal Involvement with Affirmative Action			
1. Have adopted an AA plan	−.21	−.19	.00
2. Length of time AA plan in operation	*	*	—
3. AA plan court-ordered	*	*	—
4. Involved with AA litigation in present post	*	*	—
5. Involved with AA litigation during a previous post	−.06	−.05	**
V. City Manager Characteristic			
1. Age	−.20	−.19	.00
2. Sex	.07	.06	**
3. Education	*	*	—
4. Years held current post	.09	.09	**
5. Liberal-conservative orientation	−.20	−.18	.00
6. Clear understanding of the meaning/ purpose of AA	.27	.24	.00

Multiple R = .54; R^2 = .29; significance F ≤ .0000.

Adjusted R^2 (.26) used to determine when to discontinue removing variables from the regression equation.

  *Removed from regression equation.

**P > .05.

of support for affirmative action. First, older city managers express greater opposition toward affirmative action for women than do younger city managers. Similarly, those city managers who consider themselves to be politically conservative also oppose affirmative action. The final indicator in cluster V, however, has the greatest explanatory power. City managers express greater levels of support (beta = .24) when they believe that they have a clear understanding of the meaning and purpose of affirmative action.

V. Conclusions and Comment

In summary, the results of this study suggest that city managers support the principle of affirmative action but oppose some mechanisms to facilitate its implementation. The issues which generate the highest disagreement are (1) the use of local special interest groups composed of women, (2) the use of hiring targets, and (3) the use of timetables which impact the use of targets. Greatest levels of opposition are expressed by older, more conservative city managers who have had affirmative action plans in operation for a longer period of time. Greatest levels of support come from city managers who believe that they clearly understand the meaning and purpose of affirmative action. City manager perceptions about the local politics of affirmative action, as well as community demographics and the staffing configuration of city government, have either minimum or no effect on the level of support for affirmative action for women.

Based on the findings of this study, it appears that the federal government's strategy after 1972—oversight and compliance via the use of targets, timetables, and the concomitant paper work—may adversely affect the successful implementation of affirmative action. Indeed, many of the nation's strongest affirmative action proponents oppose the use of these mechanisms. Furthermore, city managers historically oppose the use of single-interest-group citizen committees in the in-house decision-making processes. In the long run, therefore, the nature of federal intervention may simply reinforce preexisting tendencies which are predicated on age and ideology.

The abrupt change in philosophy of the Reagan Administration, however, provides little evidence of solving the problem of underrepresentative bureaucracy. As Clynch and Gaudin point out, federal oversight capacity does facilitate the recruitment of members of disadvantaged groups into the workforce.[27] The rapid withdrawal of the Reagan Administration from the area of affirmative action results in an erosion of oversight capacity, especially that of the EEO Commission and the Justice Department.[28] Furthermore, the reduced amounts of funding available for affirmative action scholarships, coupled with the restricted placement capacity of professional organizations,[29] may lead to a corresponding reduction in the size of the pool of qualified affirmative action candidates for managerial positions.

TABLE 9.3   Distribution of Respondents by States

State	Number of City Managers in the Sample	Number of City Managers Responding to Questionnaire	State	Number of City Managers in the Sample	Number of City Managers Responding to Questionnaire
AK	3	1	MT	2	1
AL	1	0	NE	2	2
AZ	9	5	NV	1	0
AR	2	1	NH	3	2
CA	70	35	NJ	10	4
CO	11	6	NM	4	2
CT	7	6	NY	8	4
DE	2	2	NC	25	17
FL	30	20	OH	15	6
GA	12	4	OK	18	8
ID	1	0	OR	10	5
IL	17	14	PA	29	18
IN	1	0	RI	2	2
IA	7	3	SC	6	5
KS	11	4	SD	1	1
KY	2	1	TN	11	7
LA	1	1	TX	49	30
ME	18	8	UT	2	2
MD	3	2	VT	7	4
MA	3	1	VA	17	10
MI	34	22	WA	6	5
MN	11	5	WV	4	3
MS	1	0	WI	4	2
MO	9	7	WY	2	2
			Total	504	290

The findings of this study also suggest that, without some sort of federal presence in this policy area, the "new federalism" may turn into a "new feudalism." Equal employment opportunity may remain an integral component of public personnel administration and practice in many communities. Yet in other city governments, the rapid disappearance of federal involvement may alleviate the pressure and expectation to use distasteful mechanisms to implement affirmative action. Withdrawal of federal government support of affirmative action increases the importance of attitudes and actions of city managers. The climate, which is encouraged by city managers, will be extremely critical in determining the survival or decline of affirmative action objectives and practices in professionally-managed local governments.

Notes

I am indebted to several colleagues for assistance at various stages of this project: (1) the anonymous referees for extremely insightful comments and suggestions; (2) Janis Slack and Kris Hines, both of East Texas State University, and Kent Cagle, Texas Tech University, for assistance in data collection and coding; (3) Nelson C. Dometrius and Gerry Riposa, both of Texas Tech University, for assistance during the statistical analysis phase; (4) Don Borut and Dan Nissenbaum, both of ICMA, and Jewel D. Scott, City Manager of Delaware, Ohio, for providing unpublished information about ICMA activities; (5) Lana Wachniak of Georgia Southern College, N. Joseph Cayer of Arizona State University, Susan Welch of the University of Nebraska-Lincoln, Ronald Randall and Kari Vezner of the University of Toledo, and Nelson C. Dometrius of Texas Tech University for valuable comments about the design of the questionnaire.

1. Gregory B. Lewis, "Race, Sex, and Supervisory Authority in Federal White-Collar Employment," *Public Administration Review*, vol. 46 (January/February 1986), pp. 25–30.

2. Rita B. Bocher, "Does Tradition Affect Affirmative Action Results? How Pennsylvania Achieved Changes at the Middle Management Level," *Public Administration Review*, vol. 42 (September/October 1982), pp. 475–478; Steven M. Neuse, "Sex Employment Patterns in State Government," *State Government*, vol. 52 (1979), pp. 52–57.

3. Beryl A. Radin, "Leadership Training for Women in State and Local Government," *Public Personnel Management*, vol. 9 (March/April 1980), pp. 52–57.

4. John Tepper Marlin, "City Affirmative Action Efforts," *Public Administration Review*, vol. 37 (September/October 1977), pp. 508–510.

5. Patricia Huckle, "A Decade's Difference: Mid Level Managers and Affirmative Action," *Public Personnel Management*, vol. 12 (Fall 1983), pp. 249–257; Lee Sigelman, "The Curious Case of Women in State and Local Government," *Social Science Quarterly*, vol. 56 (March 1976), pp. 591–604.

6. Albert Karnig, *et al.*, "Employment of Women by Cities in the Southwest," *Social Science Journal*, vol. 21 (Fall 1984), pp. 41–48.

7. N. Joseph Cayer and Lee Sigelman, "Minorities and Women in State and Local Governments: 1973–1975." *Public Administration Review*, vol. 40 (September/October 1980), pp. 443–450.

8. Nelson C. Dometrius and Lee Sigelman, "Assessing Progress Toward Affirmative Action Goals in State and Local Government: A New Benchmark," *Public Administration Review*, vol. 44 (May/June 1984), pp. 241–246.

9. Peter K. Eisinger, "Black Employment in Municipal Jobs: The Impact of Black Political Power," *American Political Science Review*, vol. 76 (June 1982), pp. 380–392; Grace Hall and Alan Saltzstein, "Equal Employment Opportunity for Minorities in Municipal Government," *Social Science Quarterly*, vol. 58 (March 1977), pp. 864–872.

10. Thomas Dye and J. Renick, "Political Power and City Jobs: Determinants of Minority Employment," *Social Science Quarterly*, vol. 62 (September 1981), pp. 475–486.

11. Frank J. Thompson and Bonnie Browne, "Commitment to the Disadvantaged Among Urban Administrators," *Urban Affairs Quarterly*, vol. 13 (March 1978), pp. 355–378.

12. Peter K. Eisinger, *op. cit.;* N. Joseph Cayer and Roger C. Schaefer, "Affirmative Action and Municipal Employees," *Social Science Quarterly*, vol. 62 (September 1981), pp. 487–494.

13. Roi Diane Townsey, "Black Women in American Policing: An Advancement Display," *Journal of Criminal Justice,* vol. 10 (November/December 1982), pp. 455–468.

14. N. Joseph Cayer and Roger C. Schaefer, *op. cit.*

15. John Tepper Marlin, *op. cit.*

16. Susan Welch, *et al.,* "Correlates of Women's Employment in Local Governments," *Urban Affairs Quarterly,* vol. 18 (June 1983), pp. 551–564; Susan Welch, *et al.,* "Changes in Hispanic Local Public Employment in the Southwest," *Western Political Quarterly,* vol. 36 (December 1983), pp. 660–673.

17. Steven M. Neuse, "Professionalism and Authority: Women in Public Service," *Public Administration Review,* vol. 38 (September/October 1978), pp. 436–441; Grace Hall and Alan Saltzstein, *op. cit.*

18. Barbara A. Gutek and Bruce Morasch, "Sex-Ratios and Sex-Role Spillover, and Sexual Harassment of Women at Work," *Journal of Social Issues,* vol. 38 (Winter 1982), pp. 55–74; N. Joseph Cayer and Roger C. Schaefer. *op. cit.*

19. Public organizations which employ at least 15 people and private companies which employ at least 50 people and have at least $50,000 in federal contracts must comply with equal employment opportunity/affirmative action guidelines.

20. Nelson C. Dometrius and Lee Sigelman, *op. cit.*

21. Frank Wise, "The Quiet (R)evolution The History of Minority Involvement in ICMA," The International City Management Association (ICMA), unpublished document.

22. In all, 32 indicators for the independent variables were entered into the regression equations: city population, percent white population, percent population with high school degrees, percent population with college degrees, percent unemployed, percent under poverty line, sex of respondent, age of respondent, respondent's tenure of residence, respondent's tenure in position, education of respondent, respondent's political orientation, respondent's perception of minority group pressures on the city, respondent's understanding of affirmative action, respondent's perception of women putting pressure on the city, respondent's perception of support for affirmative action by elected officials, number of employees supervised, percent employees in management, percent male administrators, percent black male administrators, percent hispanic male administrators, percent other minority male administrators, percent white male administrators, percent black female administrators, percent hispanic female administrators, percent other minority female administrators, percent white female administrators, have an affirmative action plan, year affirmative action plan adopted, was affirmative action plan court-ordered, manager involved in litigation in present position, and manager involved in litigation in previous position.

23. Frank J. Thompson and Bonnie Browne, *op. cit.;* Frank J. Thompson, "Civil Servants and the Deprived: Socio-Political Occupational Explanations of Attitudes Toward Minority Hiring," *American Journal of Political Science,* vol. 22 (May 1978), pp. 325–347; Norman H. Nie, *et al., The Changing American Voter* (Cambridge, MA: Harvard University Press, 1976).

24. The pretest resulted in the splitting of one questionnaire item. The two items are not used in this study.

25. The following *SPSS-X* multiple regression procedures were also used on the data to compare with the results of the "backward/mean-substitution" procedure.

    1. Forward/pairwise: Multiple R = .53; R^2 = .28

    2. Stepwise/pairwise: Multiple R = .53; R^2 = .28

    3. Stepwise/meansubstitution: Multiple R = .50; R^2 = .25.

26. The annual income distribution for the city managers is as follows:

Value	Amount	Number	Percent
1	Under $10,000	1	0.3
2	$10–19,999	12	4.2
3	$20–29,999	57	20.1
4	$30–39,999	81	28.5
5	$40–49,999	81	28.5
6	$50–59,999	31	10.9
7	$60,000 and over	21	7.4

Missing values = 6
Mean = 4.43

27. Edward J. Clynch and Carol A. Gaudin, "Sex in the Shipyards: An Assessment of Affirmative Action Policy," *Public Administration Review*, vol. 42 (March/April 1982), pp. 114–120.

28. Frank J. Thompson, "Deregulation at the EEOC: Prospects and Implications," *Review of Public Personnel Administration*, vol. 4 (Summer 1984), pp. 41–56.

29. In January 1986, the ICMA established a "Talent Referral Service" to assist affirmative action candidates in finding public management positions. Local governments can subscribe to this service.

10

A Mini-Symposium

Affirmative Action in Public Employment

edited by Lloyd G. Nigro

Introduction

"Affirmative action" is a term deeply embedded in the language of today's public personnel administration. Nonetheless, its precise meaning for administrative thought and action is elusive. What is affirmative action? Does it mean doing something or not doing something? How does it relate to the functions of public agencies and to the role of government in our society?

Ambiguity can be useful. It allows room for maneuver and the flexibility needed to adapt and innovate in new or changing circumstances. However, it can also be counterproductive. Misunderstandings lead to unfulfilled expectations, mistrust, and conflict, The implementation of policies and programs can be blocked or sidetracked. Like the emotion-charged symbols of "pornography" and "national security," affirmative action has many meanings. It also shares their capacity to fragment and paralyze social systems.

Public administrators on all levels of government are at the centers of decision arenas wherein the *operational* definition of affirmative action is literally being created. They are participants in policy-making processes which set standards and structure rules and procedures. Perhaps most importantly, their day-to-day behavior is giving affirmative action its behavioral and, therefore, socially consequential meaning.

Yet, as a social group, public administrators are far from general agreement on what affirmative action is or should be. Witness these abstracts from an exchange

Source: *Public Administration Review* 34 (May/June 1974): 234–246.

between a U.S. Civil Service Commission regional director and a city director of personnel.

Director of Personnel

"The reason we apparently are not in compliance with U.S. Civil Service Commission standards is that we have been successful in hiring fully qualified minorities and women in various uniformed and civilian positions in our Fire Department, our Police Department, and several other departments through the use of our civil service rule permitting selective certification."

Regional Director

"For you to imply . . . that success in bringing about the employment of minorities and women in departments where they have been unrepresented or underrepresented does not comply with our Standards is thus a major misrepresentation of fact. What we have stated . . . is that certification or non-certification of eligibles solely on the basis of race or sex is discriminatory per se, and hence contrary to the merit principles embodied in the law and in our prescribed Standards for a merit system."

Director of Personnel

"During the past three years, I have been forced to conclude that the traditional ranking and certification process has an adverse effect that cannot be defended as valid in many competitive situations where there are large numbers of candidates and no prior knowledge or experience necessary for the relatively few vacant positions available. With this conclusion, the only ethical course of action open to me was to recommend the adoption of the selective certification rule to the Civil Service Board."

Regional Director

"We fully appreciate the aims of the Civil Service Board . . . in approving the selective certification rule. There can be no question that we are all working toward a public service in which all groups in our society are fairly represented. . . . No matter how laudatory the purpose, however, we cannot give our approval to a method which we find to be illegal, as well as contrary to the principles of merit service."

This exchange between sincere and well-meaning administrators serves as an illustration of the kinds of difficulties encountered when the concept of affirmative action in public employment must be broken down into specific criteria for evaluating personnel policies, programs, and procedures. If anything approaching a working consensus is to be established, viewpoints, information, and experiences must be shared. The process of communication should reach and actively involve as many of those concerned as possible.

This mini-symposium on affirmative action is intended to contribute in a modest way to this objective. Contributions were solicited with an eye toward presenting a variety of opinions and information. As anticipated, the participants have approached their topic from different but complementary perspectives.

Three Key Issues in Affirmative Action

As we attempt to implement affirmative action policies, three key issues always arise. *First*, the distinction between affirmative action and "non-discrimination"; *second*, why preferential hiring and the setting of target quotas are necessary to the affirmative action process; and *third*, why traditional standards of "quality" must be re-examined.

Until these issues are resolved, successful affirmative action programs cannot be implemented and substantial progress toward eliminating job discrimination will not be made. Their resolution will require fundamental shifts in individual values as well as changes in some of our collective norms.

Understanding the Difference Between Affirmative Action and Non-Discrimination

The distinction between affirmative action and non-discrimination is the difference between the *active* and the *passive* mode. It is illustrated by the difference between management by objectives and incrementalism. All of our public agencies have been "equal opportunity employers" operating under fair employment practices laws for nearly 30 years. What those laws require are policy statements against discrimination. The absence of overt discrimination has sufficed to meet this standard. Action is left to the individual applicant. Affirmative action in contrast, requires more than passive non-discrimination by the organization—it demands active programs of broadly applied preferential hiring systems. It requires definition of objectives for redressing employment imbalances and implementation of plans for reaching those objectives.

Setting operational goals, and developing criteria for measurement of progress toward these goals, is much talked about these days in management theory. Administrators, however, still more often than not observe such decision rules more in theory than in the doing, particularly in situations of strongly conflicting objectives and values. Yet, goal setting, action programs, and evaluation are the *modus operandi* of affirmative action. Affirmative action demands more from organizational leaders than lack of prejudice and belief in equal opportunity; operationalizing affirmative action requires leaders to take action stances in which priorities are reordered and time and energy is allocated to affirmative action *above other goals*.

There are many reasons why such a shift is extremely difficult even if the administrator is basically unprejudiced. Many see affirmative action as a diversion from "real" organizational goals. How do we answer the director of a city public works department who says, "My job is to repair roads and keep the storm drains operating. I need the best engineers I can get for that. My job isn't to solve social problems"?

Questions of this variety must be satisfactorily answered if affirmative action is to go forward. Public managers must be convinced to broaden their perspectives and to redefine their standards of performance if the values inherent in affirmative action are to be upgraded to an operational level. This will require new standards for evaluating what is important in public organizations and strategic revisions of reward systems to support new standards.

Why Is Preferential Hiring and the Setting of Targets and Quotas Absolutely Necessary to the Process?

Affirmative action guidelines require specified objectives, usually translated into numerical quotas, as minimum goals for the employment of minority individuals and women. Numerical objectives have emerged for the present as the only feasible mechanism for defining with any clarity the targets of action and the criteria for evaluation of progress toward achieving them within a given period of time. Thus, the courts have upheld the validity of goals and quotas in civil rights enforcement efforts and have stated that color-consciousness and sex-consciousness are both appropriate and necessary remedial postures.[1]

Nevertheless, the issue of preferential hiring has assumed the proportions of a major national controversy. The issue is partly one of varying definitions of the situation. Preference and compensation can be seen as words of positive connotation or as words of condescension and disparagement. Preference can be defined as choosing the more highly valued candidate at a given point in time and circumstance, and compensation can be defined as redress for past failures to reach the actual market of human resources available to our organizations. From a very different perspective, these words in combination may be defined as "reverse discrimination."

The characterization of preferential hiring and quotas as reverse discrimination provides a crutch for those who would avoid the changes in organizational behavior required by management by objectives. Obviously, to the extent that quotas as targets for progress become job "slots" and maximums rather than minimums, they perpetuate race and sex discriminations. Otherwise, the argument is diversionary and should be treated as such.

Until we are ready to recognize that years of experience with passive nondiscrimination in the public sector have not substantially changed its white, middleclass, male-dominated employment patterns and until we are ready to set objectives wherein results are what counts, it is unlikely that change will take place. Yet, when people with differing perspectives are asked to agree on concrete goals, and must attempt to reach collective agreement on priorities, conflict becomes inevitable.

However, we have learned to submerge conflict in organizations by avoiding explicit goal statements. We escape confrontations by letting statements of *intent* substitute for *action* plans in the most controversial areas. Conflict is also avoided by allowing sub-units to pursue their primary objectives with as little pressure as possible on them to agree on or produce on broader system goals. To the extent that affirmative action clashes with individual values or requires diversion of resources from each sub-unit's highly ranked goals it is met with avoidance or outright resistance. A serious affirmative action program, therefore, demands substantial departures from traditional policymaking practices and managerial styles.

Why Must Our Traditional Standards of "Quality" Be Reexamined?

Most attacks on preferential hiring programs are grounded in the assumption that the quality of performance and work standards will be severely diminished as a result of the systematic employment of minorities and women. They are also grounded in the assumption that few "qualified" Blacks, Chicanos, other minority individuals, and women are available. Both assumptions stand on the third assumption that present criteria of merit and procedures for their application can be accepted uncritically and have yielded the excellence intended. We have not asked ourselves why the use of certain standards has resulted in the virtual exclusion of women and minorities from many professional positions and almost all high-level positions. To the extent that the use of our present standards has resulted in this exclusion (or inclusion in only token proportions), our organizations have been denied access to important sources of intellectual and physical vitality. Thus, the logic of affirmative action says that where a particular criterion of merit, even while not discriminatory on its face or in its intent, operates to the disproportionate elimination of women and minority group individuals, the burden on the organization to defend it as an appropriate criterion rises in direct proportion to its exclusionary effect.

The problems raised by the quality issue are probably the most difficult of those faced in affirmative action. Questioning our accepted standards of quality strikes at tradition and destroys some of the most important groups of our individual self-definitions. The less secure the institution, occupational group, or individual concerned, the more threatening such examination becomes. Degrees and other labels provide a much more comforting definition of quality than does a continuing evaluation of job performance. The more the occupational group is involved in processes of professionalizing itself or is striving for higher status, the greater the tension between those processes and inclusionary requirements. All of these changes increase exclusivity. Attempts at implementation of affirmative action in police departments, for example, are running head on into the federally financed drive to "professionalize" according to traditional measures—particularly degree attainment.[2]

The case of several state colleges in California which are undergoing a change of status from colleges to "universities" provides us with another example. In this instance one of the main criteria for change of status is the number of PhD degree holders on the faculty. Teachers with master's degrees who had been receiving excellent evaluations from deans, peers, and students are suddenly being reevaluated according to a more "professional" standard, i.e., the PhD. Job performance is the same, but some are now being dismissed or not advanced because external criteria have changed. Any attempt to implement affirmative action programs in this atmosphere of degree consciousness is difficult. Suggestions that alternative standards of faculty quality be considered (for example a bachelor's or master's degree plus experience, cultural knowledge, ability to relate to students, ability to serve as a minority role model, and warmth, energy, and decency) are met with fears about lowering standards and allusions to the importance of "quality." We see here two conflicting sets of standards about what is important and what quality means.

Organizational leaders dedicated to pursuing inclusionary policies must be prepared to meet the "quality" issue head on. The development of alternative measures of accomplishment is essential to the success of affirmative action programs at this period in time. A complex of social factors has combined to exclude minorities and women from the higher levels of formal educational attainment, and great numbers have pursued avenues of development other than that of formal education. Yet, their experience paths prepare them to bring new perspectives, different values, and perhaps even equal or higher capabilities to many public jobs. If, as we say, our objective is the best person for the job, we are *committed* to affirmative action.

Finally, in the broadest sense, a public employee group representative of the differing values and various perspectives in our total society is essential to public accountability. Any procedures which exclude multiple experience paths and disparate values from organizations *will* in these terms *lower standards* of public accountability as well as organizational effectiveness.

Catherine Lovell, *University of California, Riverside* ∿

Affirmative Action Produces Equal Employment Opportunity for All

A program of equal employment opportunity which stops at merely eliminating overt discrimination in the competitive process may touch only superficially on many of the real issues involved in making equal opportunity a practical reality. Opening doors long closed is a necessary first step; making sure that those who were formerly locked out have a real opportunity to compete, not only to enter but also to move upward, is an essential follow-up. Affirmative action is the key to achieving equal employment opportunity for all. And only with equal employment opportunity for all can public jurisdictions conduct their personnel affairs in accordance with merit principles.

We need no longer theorize and speculate on this matter. We now know that equal employment opportunity can be significantly advanced by affirmative action directed against such practices as inadequate publicity about job openings, unrealistic job requirements, invalid selection instruments and procedures, and insufficient opportunity for upward mobility.

Meaningful response is now being made to the problems of those who have not participated in the competition for public employment, or who even now cannot do so successfully because the system may have been designed and operated without taking them into account. The response has taken a variety of approaches, depending on the nature of the problems of the work force and the needs of the employer. Generally, successful equal employment opportunity programs comprise a full range of affirmative actions. These actions are tailored to the problems of those who because of past discriminations are not competing successfully for entry into the system; or who, once on the rolls, are unable to realize their full potential because of gaps in education or skills, also often due to past discrimination. At the same time, the prudent manager makes certain that program activities are realistic in design and objective, so that they meet the needs of management for a work force which represents the best the market can produce in terms of the specific tasks to be performed.

In the past, persons qualified for employment often did not compete simply because they were members of societal groups not in the mainstream reached by the employer's recruiting activities. Recruiting efforts have now been redirected affirmatively to include these groups. Virtually every federal agency which sends recruiters to the campus to seek candidates for entry-level technical and professional jobs now makes special efforts to ensure that recruiting teams regularly visit schools with predominantly minority or female enrollment. This kind of effort has resulted in quickly discernible change in the racial, ethnic, and sex makeup of the work force. Further dividends have been produced as these employees advance through the ranks. Over time, significant changes will occur at the top because something affirmative was done at the entry level.

Even when recruiting programs did reach and attract people from all potential sources, some agencies found that candidates from certain groups frequently could not compete successfully. These agencies have taken a new look at how their work functions are divided into jobs and have designed new entry-level positions for which people not in the mainstream can qualify. This is more than equal opportunity; it is good management, because it helps assure that high-paid professionals and technicians are relieved of duties which do not call for their qualifications; and at the same time gives people who have not been able to qualify for the more demanding jobs a chance to enter the work force, get training and experience, and advance in accordance with their abilities. The employment system has undergone the necessary changes to assure that all this happens systematically and in full accord with merit employment principles.

On-board work forces represent a source of untapped talent. More recently, as part of their affirmative action programs, many federal managers have made an effort to use their internal resources. They have conducted surveys to inform themselves about any skills and abilities in the present work force which are not being utilized, so that employees whose talents have not been put to work can be reassigned to jobs in which their skills are needed. Broader programs of "upward mobility" have been designed to assure that workers who have the potential to perform more responsible duties, but need additional training and development in order to qualify for the higher-level jobs, have an opportunity to prepare themselves for advancement. As a result of this approach, thousands of federal employees who might otherwise have remained in "dead-end" positions or in occupations with limited potential for advancement have received the kind of training and education they need to pursue a rewarding and satisfying career. To correlate developmental training activities with placement opportunities, managers at all levels identify target positions and plot out career systems within or across organizational lines.

The manager and the first-line supervisor are really crucial to the success of an equal opportunity program in all its aspects. To assure their understanding and support, many federal agencies provide training on equal employment opportunity policy and practice, evaluate supervisory performance in this area, and use incentive systems to recognize achievements.

Top-level managers, moreover, have a particular responsibility to assure that affirmative action programs reflect the role of the employer in the total environment. No public employer can realistically confine equal opportunity activities to the worksite. The federal government has long recognized its responsibilities to the communities in which its facilities are located. Where discriminatory societal practices in housing, transportation, financing, etc., adversely affect the employability in federal agencies of some elements of the potential work force, federal managers actively support community efforts to eliminate these discriminatory practices.

An equal employment opportunity program must also include a means for employees or applicants to surface individual grievances related to equal opportunity and have them resolved quickly. In the federal government, nearly 27,000 applicants and employees consulted a governmentwide network of equal employment opportunity counselors regarding EEO-related problems and questions during Fiscal Year 1973 (July 1972 through June 1973). Counselors were able to resolve most issues informally at grass-roots levels, and less than ten percent of those counseled went on to file formal complaints. Formal discrimination complaint procedures are, of course, available to those whose problems cannot be resolved satisfactorily through informal counseling or conciliation.

These are the kinds of efforts which comprise an affirmative action program of equal employment opportunity. Specific activities in all of these areas are ordinarily documented in written plans, and this is a statutory requirement insofar as federal agencies are concerned. Actions are, of course, tailored wherever necessary to respond to the special employment problems of women and minority groups. Progress in carrying out an action plan must be evaluated periodically and systematically to assure the effectiveness of the program. The Civil Service Commission has published guidelines for use by agencies in evaluating their own equal employment opportunity programs, and also conducts on-site reviews of agency programs as part of the Commission's enforcement responsibility under the Equal Employment Opportunity Act of 1972.

The Civil Service Commission, as the central personnel agency of the federal government, reviews and monitors federal employment procedures, including tests and other selection devices, to help assure that they are job-related. The overall goal here is to eliminate any practices which in effect are barriers to the employment and advancement of members of any group.

A comparatively recent development, employment goals and timetables, can be a helpful management technique in dealing with some EEO problems. Experience has shown that such goals are rarely effective unless they are developed at the lowest practicable management level within the organization, where they can be arrived at after analysis of the skills and abilities available as they relate to employment opportunities projected for the time-table period. Goals must be realistic in these terms, and must be flexible indicators of what can reasonably be expected to result from a vigorously implemented affirmative action program, but goals should remain goals and should never be permitted to become mandatory quotas requiring selection on factors other than merit.

The effectiveness of a technique is, of course, ultimately measured in terms of its results. And positive results for the federal government's full-range affirmative action approach to equal employment opportunity are consistently reflected in the Commission's statistical data on minority employment. Negroes, Spanish-surnamed

Americans, American Indians, and Oriental Americans now account for a full 20 percent of the federal civilian work force, and minority employment has continued to rise in recent years despite declines in total federal employment. Between November 1971 and November 1972, ex., minority employment in federal agencies increased by 6,555 jobs, while total employment decreased by 31,703.

Even more significantly, the figures show all-time highs in the number of jobs held by minorities in the middle and upper grade and pay levels. Affirmative outreach recruiting programs and upward mobility efforts have helped boost minority employment in all grade groupings of the government's General Schedule or "white collar" occupations.

The Commission is now helping many state and local governments as they work toward equal employment opportunity in hiring and other elements of their personnel management. Experience to date provides convincing evidence that the principles and practices discussed earlier can be applied successfully in state and local governments.

Affirmative action is the logical extension of a nondiscrimination policy in employment. The United States Civil Service Commission does not think of equal employment opportunity as a separate program outside the mainstream of personnel management, nor does it administer it that way. Equal employment opportunity and employment based on merit principles are truly synonymous concepts. The Commission is committed to making these concepts come alive throughout government.

Bernard Rosen, *U.S. Civil Service Commission* ∾

Beyond the Sound and Fury of Quotas and Targets

Much of the rhetoric and conflict surrounding affirmative action programs focuses on the introduction and utilization of numerical quotas and target figures to increase minority group representation in public organizations. Despite criticism that they are moving too slowly, published statistics and casual observation reveal that many agencies have had considerable success at employing and promoting more members of minority groups than ever before. But, knowing that the number and percentage of employees from minority groups has increased and that more minority group employees are being promoted to higher grade tells us little about their work experiences and the extent to which racism and sexism persist in public manpower management systems.

As pressure has increased for agencies to incorporate larger numbers of minority employees at higher grades, a number of practices have evolved that have enabled agencies to cope with demands for affirmative action yet minimize the impact of minority employees on agency operations. These practices may be lumped together under the concept of "tokenism"—the assignment of minority employees to grades and positions normally associated with a certain level of authority and responsibility, while limiting the minority employees to minor roles and non-essential tasks. Tokenism is difficult to identify with currently used reporting devices that stress aggregate statistics because affirmative action reports rarely contain extensive or accurate job descriptions, and position classification systems are seldom very precise.

Since aggregate statistics rarely reveal patterns of differential incorporation or tokenism in bureaucracies, efforts to evaluate the impact of affirmative action programs must probe beyond statistics that report net changes in the number and percentage of minority employees in different agencies and grades. To combat tokenism, evaluations must focus on differences in patterns of mobility, leverage for investment in personal development, human resource investment, levels of authority and responsibility, organizational experiences, and policy impact between minority and white male employees. One might collect this type of information by administering a questionnaire to samples from both groups and comparing the distribution of responses to discover if significant differences exist. By further dividing respondents into categories by age, education, grade, agency, and specialization, problem areas can be more easily pinpointed.

A number of pertinent questions can be used to compare job contents and work experiences to discover patterns of discrimination. The following list is merely suggestive and hardly exhaustive, but if answers were obtained to questions like these and used for comparative purposes, we would know much more about the performance of an agency's affirmative action program than we are able to learn from most currently used reporting devices.

Mobility

Intra-agency Mobility

Are minority and white male employees experiencing similar rates and patterns of lateral and upward mobility within an agency? Are they being promoted into similar types of jobs with similar kinds of responsibilities? Are they leaving an agency for similar reasons?

Interorganizational Mobility

Are there similar rates and patterns of lateral and upward mobility between government agencies, jurisdictions, and private organizations?

Leverage for Investment in Personal Development

Educational Leverage

Are minorities and white males receiving equal status, pay, and responsibility for equivalent years and types of education?

Work Experience Leverage

Are there equal patterns of status, pay, and responsibility for equivalent years and types of work experience?

Human Resources Investment

Awards

Are minority and white male employees receiving distinguished service awards and other honors in similar rates for equivalent types of achievement?

Training and Career Development Opportunities

Are training experiences, including extended leaves for further study, being allocated between groups at similar rates and with similar selection criteria?

Authority and Responsibility

Authority

Do minority and white male employees holding equivalent grades have similar power and discretion over programs, budgets, manpower, planning, and policy?

Responsibility

Are there dissimilarities in the proportion of minority employees holding deputy, "assistant to," and staff positions? Are there dissimilarities in the number and composition of the subordinates supervised by minority and white male managers?

Extraorganizational Responsibilities

Are there differences in the kinds of extraorganizational activities to which minority and white male employees are assigned? Do executives of all groups represent their agency in similar roles at congressional hearings, OMB and GAO reviews?

Organizational Experience

Assignments

Do minority and white male employees cluster in different agencies, bureaus, field offices, functional specializations, programs, or work groups?

Perceptions

Do minority and white male employees see the goals and priorities of their agency alike? Do they see similar degrees of cooperation and conflict, ambiguity, formalization, in their agency? Do they see similar problems surrounding their authority, scope of responsibility, performance expectations, and prospects for advancement?

Perceptions of Discrimination

Are there similar perceptions of the degree of discriminatory behavior practiced by their agency and the government employment system? Do they similarly perceive patterns of discrimination against minority clients, job applicants, and contractors?

Job Satisfaction

Are there significant differences in the satisfaction expressed by minority and white male employees about their work assignments, relations with supervisors, pay, promotional opportunities, and relations with co-workers?

Policy Impact

Participation in Policy Making

Are there significant differences between minority and white male employees at similar grades in their participation in the agency's major policy-making activities? Are there differences in the extent to which they believe they can affect agency policy?

Charles H. Levine, *Syracuse University*

Affirmative Action in the Public Sector: Where Do We Stand Today?

Two black men were hired as firemen by the City of Sacramento in November 1971 for the first time in 12 years. Because black firemen *were* hired, federal civil defense funds to the City of Sacramento were cut off in December 1971 without notice, without hearing, and retroactively.

The hiring of minorities in the Fire Department (one Chicano and one Asian also were hired then) and the resulting cut-off of funds administered under the Intergovernmental Personnel Act by the U.S. Civil Service Commission precipitated a paradoxical confrontation. The issue was the city's deliberate use of selective certification to hire minorities in city occupations where minorities are under-represented.

The City of Sacramento has a minority population of about 30 percent. Selective certification may be used in occupations where minorities are less than 30 percent. In 1971, about two percent of firemen were minorities; about eight percent of sworn police positions were filled by minorities.

In October 1971, selective certification was first used to fill five of ten vacant police positions. No controversy ensued. The following month, seven fireman positions were filled, with four positions being filled through the use of selective certification.

The hiring of minorities in the fire service brought forth immediate, vigorous criticism from the president of the Support Your Local Police Committee, who was a Sacramento fire captain; a local American Legion chapter; and the U.S. Civil Service Commission. Litigation was threatened by an attorney for some white eligibles who ranked high on the firefighter list. The demand was made that the newly hired minority firemen be discharged and that the "better qualified" white candidates be hired. No litigation was filed, however.

For the past two years, the City of Sacramento has been hiring a minority in every other vacant position of fireman or police officer, provided, of course, that there are minorities on the eligible list to certify. No standards have been lowered. All persons on the eligible lists have passed all qualification tests. The city's policy goal is that the city's work force will approximate the city's population. Even hiring minorities at a rate of about 50 percent, it will require an estimated 14 years in the fire department, and eight years in the police department to reach the objective of 30 percent of policemen and firemen being from among the city's minority population. In October 1973, minority firemen had risen to seven percent; minority police to 14 percent.

In California, police officers and firemen usually make up 40 percent or more of city employees. Police and fire salaries often comprise half of the city salary budget. The employment of minorities in police and fire departments has been identified as a matter of critical importance by several presidential commissions as well as by state and local agencies. Yet relatively few minorities are employed as policemen or firemen, although the largest concentrations of minorities are in the cities.

As an example, the fire service in California cities employed about 7,500 firemen in 1947. Of these 7,500, 99 were black. By 1965, the number of firemen in California had doubled to 15,000, but the number of black firemen had actually declined to 86! Almost all of the firemen hired between 1947 and 1965 were hired through conventional civil service systems. In 1973, the number of fire jobs was about 16,500 in California, and the number of minority firemen almost certainly did not exceed three percent—although the state minority population was 26 percent, and the minority population within cities was undoubtedly higher than the state average. It is obvious that our merit systems collectively have operated to keep out almost all minorities.

Most selection procedures used by public personnel agencies have an adverse affect on minority applicants as compared to majority group applicants. However, one of the least recognized areas of adverse action against minority group persons is the ranking and certification process (especially using the "rule of three" or "rule of one"). Fire turnover is low, rarely exceeding five percent per year in most cities. The small number of vacancies, together with the use of the rule-of-three and intense competition from hundreds of candidates result in most minorities on the list never being certified for consideration for employment. Without the use of selective certification or other like techniques, I doubt that the goal of population parity will be achieved in the fire service in this millenium, or the next.

We use affirmative action recruiting, we attempt to validate our tests, we restructure jobs, and we use all the other methods which now prevail (and all of these are important), but the only thing that counts, ultimately, is who is hired. The achievement of goals and time tables requires accelerated hiring of minorities.

This brings us to the key affirmative action question at issue. The policy position of the U.S. Civil Service Commission is that any personnel system which deliberately considers race and ethnic origin cannot be a merit system. This policy position would deny any consideration of the use of such methods as selective certification, except when required by court order. An agency which acts affirmatively, *without waiting for a court order,* as the City of Sacramento has done, is not considered to be an approved merit system.

Selective certification is a "catch-up" device. It is to be used only until an occupation (such as police, fire, building inspection, etc.) becomes representative of the community's population. Without the use of such procedures, there can be no breakthrough, and any progress in integrating the city work force will be slow.

We have not only the problem of placing minorities, but also women, in the work force. The criteria for fair employment standards for women are not yet well defined. The City of Sacramento had used selective certification for women for a few occupations (parking lot attendant, fire dispatcher clerk) from which women had been arbitrarily excluded in the past.

The problems of achieving affirmative action results today are dynamic. In addition to the USCSC, several other regulatory agencies, federal, state, and local, are interested in affirmative action, as are representatives of recognized employee organizations.

Where do we stand today in regard to affirmative action in the public sector? If standing is the verb to use, it seems a bit like standing in a canoe while shooting the rapids. The course is swift. There are many unknowns. However, we are committed to finding ways of meeting the challenges of affirmative action within the limited time left to achieve meaningful results.

William F. Danielson ॐ

Civil Rights in Civil Service—The Winds of Change

"The essential point is not to find coal heavers who can scan Virgil correctly, but coal heavers who, being properly qualified for heaving coal, are their own masters . . . ," said the National Civil Service League in 1883.[3] "What Congress has commanded is that any test used must measure the person for the job and not the person in the abstract," said U.S. Supreme Court Justice Burger in a March 8, 1971, decision on—*coal handlers.*[4] Thus, almost a century after the National Civil Service League first expounded the idea of practical, job-related tests, the full power of the national government came down in favor of this fundamental merit principle.

In 1894, the League's Vice President, Theodore Roosevelt, said in support of League and government policy, ". . . it is now made a reproach to us that . . . honest and capable colored men are given an even chance with honest and capable white men. I esteem this reproach a high compliment."[5] Thus did Roosevelt uphold the second aspect of the merit principle on which the League was founded in 1881—the concept of nondiscrimination in public employment. "But it was in fiscal 1972 that the prohibition of discrimination on the basis of race, religion, national origin or sex in Federal employment was written into law for the first time," said the *Annual Report* of the U.S. Civil Service Commission for 1972 in noting the extension of the Civil Rights Act to government during that year.[6]

In the key area of equal employment opportunity, then, the League has led the way. Four League proposals are especially notable, having generated a degree of controversy. These are:

- League advocacy of special programs for minorities and women and "selective certification" for certain positions.
- League advocacy of rating tests on the basis of whole-group or "pass-fail" certification unless tests are fully validated.
- League support for quantifiable remedial action, or numerical goals and timetables, to achieve a representative workforce.
- League insistence upon a proven valid selection process.[7]

Special Programs and Selective Certification

The National Civil Service League Policy Statement says,

> It is clear from the Model Law [of 1970] that preferential treatment refers to programs of affirmative action, outreach recruitment, upward mobility and programs of training and education. The League advocates preference and attention to the employment problems of minorities because of a national history of discrimination. Minority group members, the disadvantaged, women, are a rich talent resource often discriminatorily barred from appropriate government employment. Full use of this resource would improve governmental efficiency while enhancing the merit principle of equal opportunity.[8]

The "Standards for a Merit System of Personnel Administration," administered by the U.S. Civil Service Commission, advocates absolute preference: "to facilitate employment of disadvantaged persons in aide or similar positions, competition *may be limited* to such individuals" (italics supplied).[9]

What of "selective certification"? It is a special form of job-related selection provided for in most civil services. The League has advocated its use "when there is a job-related factor that will improve the delivery of services, e.g., empathy with a client group as in the welfare field, female guards in women's prisons, young people to work with youth gangs."[10] We believe none of good faith would quarrel with this principle enshrined in the U.S. Civil Service System and every other level of government.

"The Rule of Three—It Troubles Me"

The second argument centers on the League's support in the 1970 NCSL Model Law for "administering culture-fair open evaluations to determine the relative fitness of applicants . . . and for certification . . . of persons who are categorized as qualified to fill a vacancy."[11]

It has been argued that grading and ranking of candidates on a 0 to 100 numerical scale is the only proper way to select employees. Yet as of late 1970, there was not a shred of evidence that the state of the civil service selection art has been developed to the point where this kind of finite ranking accurately measures ability to do the job. Therefore, the League's 1970 *Model Public Personnel Administration Law* advocated pass-fail certification of employees as a more desirable approach.

A 1970 survey of the state of the art of civil service showed that almost no civil services had ever validated *any* selection process to determine if, in fact, there was a direct relationship between test results and job performance. In spite of little proof of validity, the written test was the most relied-on selection test. Thirty-five percent of the governments required it even for *unskilled* jobs, 88 percent used it for entry office jobs, and 65 percent used it for professional and technical workers. In such circumstances, reliance on the "rule of one" or "rule of three" would seem sheer folly. And, in point of fact, NCSL found fully one-third of the nation's civil services now use "pass-fail" certification of employees (43 percent for unskilled workers, 32 percent for skilled workers, 26 percent for professional workers).[12] If one adds the field of education in which a teacher's pass-fail certificate suffices to qualify one for employment, over half of the public employees in the United States are selected on the basis of pass-fail.

The U.S. government fully accepts this position. The U.S. Civil Service Commission's guidelines for "Intergovernmental Cooperation in Recruiting and Examining" permit "qualifications appraisal and selection within broad quality categories rather than through the more precise ranking techniques." The Emergency Employment Act *Guidelines,* approved and administered by the Commission, also say, "Identification of the 'best qualified' may be by a score or by a grouping process."[13] Thus, NCSL views on equal opportunity, on special outreach programs and selective certification, and on "pass-fail" scoring have been adopted by or are in agreement with those of the federal government.

Numerical Goals and a Representative Public Service

The League's support for quantifiable remedial action in public service and its historic stand in favor of a representative public service have troubled some critics. The League recommends that affirmative action plans include: "use of employment goals, and in the case of unsupported disparity of treatment among races or sexes, quantifiable remedial action for those groups found to be suffering from the disparate treatment."[14]

U.S. Civil Service Commission Chairman Robert E. Hampton wrote the League on July 29, 1971,

> To be realistic and capable of achievement, employment goals and timetables cannot be based merely on population data but must rather be related to the potential supply of minority candidates in the workforce and in the recruiting area and to anticipated job opportunities. . . . To be most meaningful, goals and timetables should zero in on those organizations, localities, occupations, and grade levels where minor-

ity persons are under represented in relation to their skills rather than merely striving for across the board minority employment increases throughout an agency.

And Mr. Hampton said,

There is no question in our minds that goals and timetables are in harmony with the merit system. . . . The merit system provides the framework which permits goals and timetables to be an important management tool to assure equal employment opportunity.[15]

In 1972, the League supported the U.S. Court of Appeals' view that "we think some reasonable ratio for hiring minority persons who can qualify under the revised qualification standards is in order for a limited period of time, or until there is a fair approximation of minority representation consistent with the population mix in the area."[16]

Where Do We Go from Here?

For 93 years the citizens' National Civil Service League has fought for a public service which is open, representative, and non-discriminatory. And it has made progress. Though civil services are often exclusionary and discriminatory, they are better than much of private industry. Though unreal credentials, artificial barriers, and irrelevant tests have excluded many able people, governments are rapidly moving toward true merit principles.

As 1974 approaches, the federal government is about to adopt two landmark positions. The first calls for a *representative* public service. The second mandates *job-related selection*. Together, they apply to 12 million public employees.

The President's Advisory Council on Intergovernmental Personnel Management at its September 11 to 13, 1973, meeting tentatively adopted a unanimous policy statement which says,

Representativeness in the workforce is a desirable goal of public personnel policy which will be furthered by full application of affirmative action policy. . . . It is particularly important at this time in our history that women, persons of a minority race, and others who have not been adequately represented in government should be in the public service and hold high and responsible positions in it. A representative workforce would increase the credibility of government and the citizen's ability to identify with it.

In September 1973, the federal government issued draft guidelines setting forth required selection practices for all state and local government employers in the United States. They spell out in detail how all governments must follow the basic merit principle of job-related and valid selection systems. They state,

These guidelines are based on the belief that job-related and validated employee selection procedures can contribute significantly to: (1) sound personnel selection and placement systems on the basis of merit, and (2) the implementation of non-discriminatory personnel practices required by Federal law.[17]

Public personnel systems must now, as National Civil Service League President Curtis said in 1883, judge the ability of the worker in relation to his ability to perform the job at hand. One can ask no more or less of our civil services.

Jean J. Couturier, *Executive Director National Civil Service League* ᅟ

Some Concluding Observations

One of the most frequently heard criticisms of affirmative action is that it displaces the primary goal of public personnel administration—the staffing of public agencies with people who are best able to run these organizations effectively. Yet the message that unifies all of the statements on affirmative action in this symposium is that effective public administration in a democratic society relies heavily on the existence of genuinely representative bureaucracies. In other words, to be truly effective, our public organizations must be representative in the most positive and meaningful sense of the word.

Roughly defined, ". . . the term representative bureaucracy is meant to suggest a body of officials which is broadly representative of the society in which it functions, and which in social ideals is as close to the grass roots of the nation" or community it serves.[18]

At least in theory, representative bureaucracy performs two important functions for a democratic society. First, public personnel practices which establish and maintain truly open employment opportunity systems reinforce egalitarian norms relating to the value of the individual, open paths to socioeconomic mobility, and free competition for meaningful jobs on the basis of culturally accepted definitions of merit. Second, the existence of representative public organizations is more likely to assure high levels of responsiveness and responsibility than are external controls on administrative action. Representativeness is counted on to act as a sort of internal "thermostat" on administrative behavior, keeping it within the boundaries set by societal values and attitudes.[19] It is this concept which moved the U.S. Commission on Civil Rights to state that,

. . . the civil servant, in performing government's routine chores and housekeeping duties, makes many policy and administrative decisions which have a concrete and often immediate effect on the lives of the people living within the particular jurisdiction. If these decisions are to be responsive to the needs and desires of the people, then it is essential that those making them be truly representative of all segments of the population.[20]

Affirmative action in government, as a part of the total effort to develop a societywide structure of equal employment opportunity, is therefore a potentially valuable contributor to the social effectiveness of public administration on all levels of government. Through the concept of representative bureaucracy and its functions, there is a bridge between the policies and practices called "affirmative action" and the efforts to realize democratic values which have characterized the American experience.

A pervasive structure of equal opportunity employment is a prerequisite to a stable pattern of representative bureaucracy. Equal opportunity, as all of our symposium participants have emphasized, is a basic element of true merit systems. The "open door" is fundamental to the merit philosophy as it has evolved in the United States. That "door" must really be open to everybody, and the procedures and techniques used to select personnel have to be carefully evaluated and adapted to reflect new knowledge about their consequences for administrative effectiveness.

Experience tells us that simply opening the door is not enough to guarantee equal opportunity or representative public agencies. The public employer must move through the door into the environment, search out, attract, and *develop* a representative and competent manpower base for the public service. Representativeness and competence are not contradictory. They are mutually reinforcing and can be integrated if administrative resources, knowledge, and imagination are brought to bear on the task. In the final analysis, this challenge is the essence of affirmative action.

Lloyd G. Nigro, *Syracuse University* ∽

Notes

1. For a summary of court decisions regarding quotas, see Herbert Hill, "Preferential Hiring, Correcting the Demerit System," *Social Policy,* July–August 1973, pp. 96–102.

2. For further discussion of this problem as it relates to an actively professionalizing sheriff's department, see Catherine Lovell, "Accountability Patterns of the Los Angeles County Sheriff's Department," *Institute on Law and Urban Studies,* manuscript, November 1973.

3. Statement of League President George William Curtis, quoted in National Civil Service Reform League, *The Year's Work in Civil Service Reform* (New York: NCSRL, 1884), p. 16.

4. *Griggs v. Duke Power Co.,* 401 U.S. 424 (1971).

5. Quoted in William Dudley Foulke, *Roosevelt and the Spoilsmen* (New York: NCSRL, 1925), p. 41.

6. U.S. Civil Service Commission, *Mandate for Merit: 1972 Annual Report of the United States Civil Service Commission* (Washington, D.C.: U.S. Government Printing Office, 1973), p. 2.

7. *Policy Statement,* pp. 3–8.

8. *Ibid.,* pp. 4–5.

9. U.S. Departments of HEW, Labor, and Defense, *Standards for a Merit System of Personnel Administration* (Washington, D.C.: U.S. Government Printing Office, 1971), p. 4.

10. National Civil Service League, *A Model Public Personnel Administration Law* (Washington, D.C.: NCSL, 1970), pp. 6–7.

11. *Ibid.,* p. 7.

12. "Survey of Current Personnel Systems in State and Local Governments," *Good Government,* Vol. LXXXVII (Spring 1971), pp. 12–19.

13. U.S. Civil Service Commission, Bureau of Intergovernmental Personnel Programs, *Guidelines for Reevaluation of Employment Requirements and Practices Pursuant to Emergency Employment Act* (Washington, D.C.: U.S. Civil Service Commission, 1972), p. 11.

14. *Policy Statement,* p. 8.

15. Letter from Robert E. Hampton to the National Civil Service League, July 29, 1971.

16. *Carter v. Gallagher,* CA 8 (1971), quoted in *Policy Statement,* p. 5.

17. Equal Employment Opportunity Coordinating Council, "Uniform Guidelines on Employee Selection Procedures" (discussion draft), issued August 23, 1973, p. 1.

18. Paul P. Van Riper, *History of the U.S. Civil Service* (Evanston, Ill.: Row, Peterson and Co.), p. 552.

19. *Ibid.,* pp. 549–564.

20. Introduction, U.S. Commission on Civil Rights, *For All the People . . . By All the People,* Clearing House Publication No. 18, November 1969.

Part Three

Diversity

The lead article for this section identifies many of the challenges in the realm of civil rights, equal employment opportunity, affirmative action, and, more recently, valuing diversity. Broadnax attempts to focus attention on the need for society at large and managers individually to come to value differences—the fact that an employee is black, speaks another language as his or her first tongue, is female, or is older, should not immediately raise the specter that he or she is an outsider who generally does not belong. He believes that the objectives of the 1960s and 1970s are basically the objectives we are still groping to successfully realize and that the inclusion of differences as value added is essential to our success.

This chapter also includes articles originally published in 1974 as part of a symposium on minorities in public administration. These include an article that explores the status of Asian Americans in the public sector and an empirical study on the effects of race and sex on supervisory authority in federal white-collar employment. The symposium represents an effort to document the growth of minority public administrators and elected officials at all levels of government as well as to identify and comment on a number of significant challenges that have confronted minority groups. In his introductory piece, Adam Herbert summarizes four themes that emerge from the essays included in the 1974 symposium: (1) minority contributions to public service have not been adequately reflected in the theory, literature, or teaching of public administration; (2) before public agencies will become more responsive to their needs, minorities must become more active and visible in both administrative and elective government positions; (3) racial and cultural bias continues to limit hiring and advancement opportunities in government agencies; and (4) historically black colleges and universities must play a major role in the preparation of minorities who possess the skills necessary to research problems, analyze, advocate, and implement public policies that address the needs of low-income people.

163

The author of the first article makes the case for the importance of incorporating a black perspective in public administration. He argues that the black perspective ensures attention will be paid to what is happening—and has happened—to the collective. The group focus demands that attention be paid to such issues as the struggle to end slavery, establish full citizenship, outlaw Jim Crow, and attain equal employment opportunity—objectives to be realized alike by all blacks. Hunt also argues that greater inclusion and/or diversity within public administration might help facilitate a greater sense of community within the United States and reduce the distance between government and all its citizens. His strategy includes the suggestion that universities, professional organizations, and government agencies all find ways to incorporate the black perspective into course materials, exchanges between faculty, and professional journals. The Dobbins and Walker essay also focuses on the role of black institutions in public affairs education. They argue that black colleges should become part of the communities in which they exist and part of the problem-solving process for black Americans. The authors lay out how this role might be achieved, with an emphasis placed on improving the overall policy-making capacity of the institutions rather than one or two isolated policy outputs.

Nelson and Van Horne discuss tribulations commonly faced by black elected administrators. They point out that the goal of diversifying the government bureaucracy is particularly challenging for blacks because of the difficulties associated with attempting to change an entrenched institutional culture. Changing a system that was designed to keep blacks out—or even to ensure their failure—to a system that might allow for successful negotiation is a great deal to expect in a short time frame. As of 1974, when this article was published, the authors suggested multiple short-term solutions to the problems commonly experienced by black elected officials. The solutions proffered strongly suggested that blacks support and capitalize on civil rights, voting rights, and opportunities to create their own power bases, organizations, and institutions that promote and facilitate black progress.

Although not focused on a single minority group, the Robinson article complements the Nelson and Van Horne piece nicely because of the discussion about the impetus behind the birth of the Conference of Minority Public Administrators (COMPA). They tell us that the group was organized following the American Society for Public Administration's (ASPA) annual meeting in 1970 because minority administrators believed that ASPA was not measuring up to its responsibilities to promote an open, representative public system. Many of COMPA's objectives encompassed two broad areas of concern: (1) improvement of the quality of public services affecting the lives and well-being of minority citizens; and (2) expansion of opportunities for members of minority groups to assume leadership roles in public service. Robinson emphasized the importance of equal representation to a democratic society, and, similar to Nelson and Van Horne, she aimed to enhance black progress by making participation and representativeness a reality.

The Diaz de Krofcheck and Jackson article explores the underlying philosophic values and assumptions that are held by the majority culture and that are at the heart of perpetuating the exclusionary mechanism directed at Spanish-surnamed individuals. The authors begin their essay by illustrating that Chicanos are consistently underrepresented in federal employment and are often employed in lower job classifications. Diaz de Krofcheck and Jackson put forth a thesis that discrimination has been sustained because nativism has been institutionalized and is deeply rooted in the daily practices and operations of public institutions. They believe, as of 1974, that a greater understanding of nativism is necessary before any further remedial action is taken to alleviate discriminatory practices. Finally, the authors suggested actions to promote equal employment opportunities for Chicanos.

The editor concludes the symposium by offering an analysis of the minority experience in public administration. Herbert notes that despite EEO and affirmative action policies beginning in the 1960s, efforts to create a truly equitable system continued to be vigorously challenged in many circles. The author analyzes both 1973 state and local government employment rates by functional areas as well as federal government minority group employment rates to substantiate his point that most of the growth in numbers of minorities in government jobs were in token or lower level positions, not professional positions. Within the concluding section of the article, Herbert stresses—as did several of the authors included in the symposium—the importance of expanding opportunities for the inclusion of the perspectives of minority administrators. Furthermore, he suggested that there frequently exists a minority perspective on public problems that policy makers should understand if public programs are to be truly responsive and effective.

In their study on Asian Americans in public service, Kim and Lewis used a 1 percent sample of federal personnel records for 1978, 1985, and 1992 and multiple regression techniques to find that although grade and salary gaps between Asians and comparable whites are smaller than for any other minority group, many Asians do still face discriminatory practices. The authors suggest that Asian Americans have been favorably stereotyped as the "model minority" based partly on high family incomes, educational attainment, and occupational status. Although positive, the authors argue that this stereotype masks the very real social and economic problems faced by many segments of the Asian American population. Kim and Lewis determined that despite the progress experienced by Asian Americans, problems remain, especially for recent immigrants and for those without a college education.

Lewis's 1986 empirical analysis sums up the chapter on diversity nicely. His research indicates that white males are much more likely to supervise subordinates than are comparably qualified women and minorities. His findings also indicate that the gap between white men and others widens at the GS 12 level and above. As he does in several articles included in this volume, Lewis uses a multiple regression analysis while controlling for the effects of grade, education, age, and federal experience to determine the probability of being a supervisor or manager. Although his findings do not necessarily prove that discrimination causes so few women and minorities to achieve supervisory authority, Lewis concludes that there clearly seems to be a bias toward the selection of white men as supervisors and managers.

This chapter demonstrates how the discussion regarding equal employment opportunity has evolved. A conversation that began primarily focused on blacks and their desire for fairness and inclusion has evolved to include sex, race, ethnicity, and culture as part of the calculus of diversity.

11

RACE, SEX, AND SUPERVISORY AUTHORITY IN FEDERAL WHITE-COLLAR EMPLOYMENT

Gregory B. Lewis
University of Georgia

Are women and minorities as likely to supervise employees and to manage programs as are white males at the same levels in the federal bureaucracy? This study argues that they are not, based on analysis of a one percent sample of federal personnel records for 1982.

Samuel Krislov argues that in the late 1960s many top black bureaucrats in the federal government found more form than substance in their jobs, and that virtually all worried that they were filling the role of "Art Buchwald's Negro Ph.D. with an engineering background who speaks ten languages—to sit by the door to convince everyone of the egalitarian principle of the business office in which he is employed."[1] A great many black managers in the private sector seem to share this fear that they are "just being showcased."[2] Empirical research indicates that white males are much more likely to supervise subordinates than are women and minorities who appear to be similarly qualified.[3]

Affirmative action helps raise more women and minorities into upper level positions, but other forces may keep them out of the more powerful positions at those levels. Based on an intensive study of one corporation, Kanter argued that managers place a high premium on easy communication because they face great uncertainty in their work. They prefer peers very similar to themselves because it

Source: *Public Administration Review* 46 (January/February 1986): 25–30.

simplifies interaction. "Even people who looked different raised questions," she found, "because the difference in appearance might signify a different realm and range of meanings in communication." This made them especially reluctant to work with female and minority colleagues, whom they "decidedly placed in the category of the incomprehensible and unpredictable."[4] Some employees do succeed without fitting the social norm, she argues, but they rise primarily in staff rather than line positions and remain outside both the social mainstream and the main lines of power.[5]

Managers may hesitate to appoint female or minority supervisors because they fear resistance from subordinates. The federal government segregated black and white workers up into the 1950s, justifying the segregation as the only path for blacks to become bosses, since few considered the idea of assigning blacks to oversee whites.[6] A 1965 *Harvard Business Review* poll of 1,000 male and 900 female executives found that only 9 percent of the men and 15 percent of the women agreed that "men feel comfortable working for women."[7] In a survey of 30,000 federal civil service employees, nearly three-quarters said that men make better supervisors than women.[8]

Women and minorities may thus face even more obstacles in obtaining authority over fellow employees than they do in achieving high salaries in federal employment. Certainly, white males dominate the supervisory-managerial elite. Although they comprise only 41 percent of nonsupervisory white-collar employees, they make up 68 percent of the supervisors and 84 percent of the managers.[9] Even at the same grade levels, higher percentages of white men than of women and minorities supervise other employees. As seen in Table 11.1, the gap between

TABLE 11.1   Supervisory Status by Grade

| Grade Level | Percentage of Employees Who Are Supervisors or Managers: | | |
	White Males	*Others*	*Difference*
SES	92.3	86.7	5.6
GS15	70.9	62.5	8.4
GS14	45.6	38.0	7.6
GS13	33.4	29.6	3.8
GS12	19.1	16.6	2.5
GS11	15.9	16.8	−0.9
GS10	17.5	16.3	1.2
GS9	10.1	8.7	1.4
GS8	17.6	17.8	−0.2
GS7	7.5	8.2	−0.7
GS6	8.8	8.1	0.7
GS5	2.9	1.2	1.7

SOURCE: U.S. Office of Personnel Management, *Central Personnel Data File*, 1 percent sample, April 1982.

white men and others widens above GS-12, reaching a high of eight percentage points at GS-15.

This paper explores whether obvious differences in qualifications can explain this gap and whether the gap is equally wide for all race and sex groups. Specifically, it seeks to determine whether women and minorities are less likely to be supervisors or managers than are white males, even when they are at the same grade level and have the same educational level, major field of study in college, length of federal experience, and age.

Data

This study relies on a one percent random sample of 1982 data from the Central Personnel Data File (CPDF) for General Schedule, Merit Pay, and Senior Executive Service employees. The U.S. Office of Personnel Management (OPM) maintains the CPDF as the central personnel records of the federal government. Agencies submit background data on employees when they begin work and update their records when they change grade, occupation, supervisory status, or other conditions of employment. This study looks only at full-time employees with information on race, sex, age, educational level, federal experience, grade level, and supervisory status. The racial and other categories used in this article are those employed by OPM.

The CPDF classifies all employees as "managers," "supervisors," or "others." Managerial positions are those in which incumbents "(1) direct the work of an organization, (2) are held accountable for the success of specific line or staff programs, (3) monitor the progress of the organization toward goals and periodically evaluate and make appropriate adjustments," and perform a full range of additional duties, such as determining program goals, resource needs, and the need for organizational changes.[10] "Supervisors" have authority "to hire, direct, assign, promote, reward, transfer, furlough, layoff, recall, suspend, discipline, or remove employees."[11] They also "[p]lan, schedule, and coordinate work operations; [s]olve problems related to the work supervised; [and d]etermine material, equipment, and facilities needed." An employee must supervise at least three subordinates to qualify as a supervisor.[12]

A 1980 OPM study concluded that the CPDF is reasonably accurate.[13] Most data elements had error rates of 2.5 percent or less. The supervisory status measure had an error rate of 3.5 percent or less in 1980, and the report indicated that a concerted effort was made thereafter to improve the accuracy of this measure. Because agencies have little incentive to update files when employees receive additional education, the records tend to under-report educational levels, and the study finds an error rate that may be as high as 11.5 percent.

Methodology

Multiple regression analysis controls the effects of grade, education, age, and federal experience on the probability of being a supervisor or manager, in order to isolate differences in supervisory status by race and sex when employees are equal on the other measured characteristics. The dependent variable is dichotomous, coded 100 if the employee is a supervisor or manager and 0 otherwise. This represents either a 100 or a 0 percent chance that the person has supervisory authority. Coefficients therefore indicate the percentage point change in the probability of supervisory authority from a one-unit change in the independent variable. Since dichotomous dependent variables create heteroskedastic error terms, this necessitates the use of weighted least squares.[14]

Grade is strongly related to supervisory status, yet Table 11.1 indicates that the relationship is far from simple. For instance, higher percentages of employees are supervisors at GS-6, GS-8, and GS-10 than at GS-7, GS-9, and GS-11, because entry-level professionals and administrators hold positions only in the latter grades. To model this complex relationship, we enter grade into the regression equation through 12 dichotomous variables (coded 1 or 0), one for each GS-level where more than 1 percent of the employees are supervisors or managers. This allows the probability of being a supervisor to vary freely from grade to grade.

Education is measured both in years and, for employees with at least a bachelor's degree, through 24 dichotomous variables indicating the field of study in which the employee's highest degree was earned. The "years" variable implies an essentially linear relationship between education and job authority, which would be in line with most studies of the relationship between education and salary. The major field of study variables allows for two possibilities. First, there may be a "credentialing" effect from obtaining a college degree, which could substantially increase one's probability of being a supervisor. Since only employees with a degree have their major recorded, the credentialing effect would show up as positive coefficients on all the majors. Second, supervisors and managers may need specialized knowledge of technical fields. The probabilities of supervisory authority might differ substantially between, for instance, graduates with degrees in literature and engineering. The 24 field-of-study variables should capture most of that effect.

Federal experience and age are measured in both years and years squared. This allows for either a linear or smooth curvilinear relationship between authority and these characteristics.

Race and sex are included through nine dummy variables. (For instance, the "white female" variable is coded 1 for white females and 0 otherwise.) There is no separate variable for white males. Hence, the coefficient on any other race-sex variable indicates the expected difference in the probability of supervisory-managerial authority between a member of that group and a white male with the same education, experience, age, and grade. We expect all these coefficients to be negative.

Findings

Women and minority groups vary dramatically in the percentage of their members who are supervisors or managers. (See Table 11.2, column 1.) Nine times as

TABLE 11.2   Supervisory Authority by Race and Sex in 1982 Under Current and
Projected Conditions

	Percentage Who Are Supervisors or Managers[a]	Coefficients from Model I[b]	Predicted Percentage— Model I[b]	Coefficients from Model II[c]	Predicted Percentage— Model II[c]
White Males	20.9	—	20.9	—	20.9
Native American Males	27.2	6.1	21.1	9.2	18.0
Asian Males	17.1	−0.6	17.7	−3.4	20.5
Black Males	9.8	−2.1***	11.9	−5.6***	15.4
Hispanic Males	9.7	−2.2**	11.9	−6.4***	16.1
White Females	6.9	−1.5***	8.4	−5.4***	12.3
Asian Females	5.7	−2.2*	7.9	−6.3***	12.0
Native American Females	5.5	−1.7	7.2	−3.4***	8.9
Black Females	5.2	−1.5**	6.7	−5.7***	10.9
Hispanic Females	2.9	−2.4**	5.3	−6.8***	9.7

***Significant at .0001.
**Significant at .01.
*Significant at .05.

a Computed from U.S. Office of Personnel Management, *Central Personnel Data File*, April 1982, 1 percent sample.
b Model I includes years of education, 24 dummy variables indicating major field of study, age, age squared, federal experience, federal experience squared, and 12 dummy variables indicating GS level in 1982.
c Model II includes all variables from Model I *except* variables for GS level.

many native American males[15] as Hispanic females supervise other employees (27.2 vs. 2.9 percent). About 20 percent of white and Asian men supervise or manage, as opposed to only about 10 percent of the black and Hispanic males. Fewer than 7 percent of each female group supervise. These figures suggest a white male advantage over black and Hispanic men and especially over women. However, they do not show that white men are more likely to be supervisors than other equally qualified employees, because they do not control for the effects of education, experience, and other qualifications.

Column 2 reports the coefficients on the race and sex variables for the initial regression (Model I). (Results for the full model appear in Appendix Table 11.4.) Each represents the average percentage point difference in the probability of being a supervisor or manager between a member of that group and a white male, when both employees have the same grade, level of education, field of study, age, and length of federal service. For instance, a native American male appears to be 6.1 percentage points more likely than a white male to hold supervisory status, *all else equal, including grade.* However, neither this native American male advantage nor the small apparent disadvantage for Asian males (0.6 percentage point) nor the somewhat larger disadvantage for native American females (1.7 percentage points) is statistically significant at even the .10 level. Thus, we cannot conclude that their chances of having supervisory authority differ from those of white males at the same grade levels.

All other groups have a 1.5 to 2.5 percentage point worse chance than white males of supervising or managing—even at the same grade level. Differences in educational backgrounds, ages, and amounts of federal experience cannot explain this disadvantage. And there is little chance that this disadvantage exists only in this sample and not in the General Schedule as a whole—less than one chance in 100 for white women, blacks, and Hispanics and less than 1 in 20 for Asian females.

How much difference would it make if all employees were as likely to be supervisors as are white males at the same grade, holding constant age, education, and experience? We eliminate the disadvantages that can not be explained by these factors by subtracting the Model I coefficients from the current percentage in column 1. The results appear in column 3. In that scenario, there would be fewer native American male supervisors (21.1 vs. 27.2 percent) and only slightly more Asian male supervisors (17.7 vs. 17.1 percent). All other groups would show major increases. The number of black and Hispanic male supervisors would climb by one-fifth (from 10 to 12 percent). The number of Hispanic female supervisors would rise by 80 percent.

Many would argue that these results understate the differences because they only compare employees at the same grade level. Several studies have demonstrated that white males have higher salaries (and grades) than other employees with the same education, age, and experience.[16] By controlling for grade level, the model underestimates the obstacles that women and minorities face in obtaining supervisory authority since they must first reach the grade levels where that authority is possible.

How many women and minorities would be supervisors or managers if they were equally likely to attain that status as white males with equal educations, ages, and amounts of federal experience? To answer this question, the regression analysis was performed again using the same variables as in Model I, but all variables indicating grade level were dropped. Results for Model II appear in column 4. The coefficients are much larger than those of Model I. For blacks, Hispanics, and white and Asian females, the differences are in the 5.4 to 6.8 percentage point range, about three times larger than they were in Model I. All differences from white males are statistically significant at better than the .01 level, except for a 3.4 point disadvantage for Asian males and a 9.2 point advantage for native American males, both of which are significant at the .10 level. The final column presents the predicted percentage of employees in each group who would be supervisors if all employees were as likely to be supervisors as are white males with the same individual characteristics. Under those conditions, at least 15 percent of the men in each race would be supervisors, as would between 9 and 12 percent of the women. Compared to their current percentages in supervisory positions, this would represent a 50 percent increase for black and Hispanic males, a near doubling for most female groups, and a *tripling* for Hispanic females.

These results might reflect a personnel system slowly overcoming the effects of past discrimination. The number of female and minority supervisors could be rising slowly as the white males above them retire. Analysis of 1974 data provides little support for this hypothesis, however. Table 11.3 shows slightly higher percentages of white males supervising in 1982 than in 1974 (20.9 vs. 20.7 percent) but somewhat lower percentages of women and Asian and Hispanic men. The differences are all small and not statistically significant; they should not be taken too seriously. But they are definitely not the increases which one would expect if discrimination were decreasing.

The remainder of the table reports the results of performing regression analysis on the 1974 sample. Overall, the results strongly resemble those for 1982. Model II coefficients suggest somewhat narrower gaps between white males and other employees with similar individual characteristics. Model I coefficients, however, imply more "showcasing" in 1982 than in 1974—wider gaps between employees at the same grade levels. Again, the lack of statistical significance discourages

TABLE 11.3   Supervisory Authority by Race and Sex in 1974 Under Current and Projected Conditions

	Percentage Who Are Supervisors or Managers[a]	Coefficients from Model I[b]	Predicted Percentage—Model I[b]	Coefficients from Model II[c]	Predicted Percentage—Model II[c]
White Males	20.7	—	20.7	—	20.7
Native American Males	17.1	2.8	14.3	0.1	17.0
Asian Males	18.3	−0.2	18.5	−1.9	20.2
Black Males	10.1	−2.5**	12.6	−6.0***	16.1
Hispanic Males	7.5	−1.2	8.7	−6.0***	13.5
White Females	7.3	−1.3*	8.6	−5.8***	13.1
Asian Females	6.1	−3.7*	9.8	−9.3***	15.4
Native American Females	7.1	−0.8	7.9	−6.9**	14.0
Black Females	6.0	−0.8	6.8	−5.8***	11.8
Hispanic Females	3.0	−3.2**	6.2	−6.4***	9.4

***Significant at .0001.
**Significant at .01.
*Significant at .05.

[a] Computed from U.S. Office of Personnel Management, *Central Personnel Data File*, April 1982, 1 percent sample.
[b] Model I includes years of education, 24 dummy variables indicating major field of study, age, age squared, federal experience, federal experience squared, and 12 dummy variables indicating GS level in 1982.
[c] Model II includes all variables from Model I *except* variables for GS level.

confidence in these findings. However, regression analysis gives few reasons to feel comfortable about improvements over the past decade.

Conclusions

Do the findings necessarily mean that current discrimination causes so few women and minorities to achieve supervisory authority? No, a variety of other factors may be at work. Errors in measurement and the shortage of other measures of ability may overstate the differences. For instance, the model includes only the amount of federal experience but not the type. Women generally have less work experience than men of the same age. In addition, women and minorities may pass up opportunities to supervise other workers if they expect resistance from subordinates or, especially in the case of women, if they decide that the work will be too time-consuming and take them away from their families.[17]

The general pattern is discouraging, however. White males remain far more likely than women and minorities to supervise other employees. Differences in education, age, and federal experience cannot explain this fact. Neither can current grade levels. Supervisory and managerial authority are far from the only sources of power in the federal service. People in staff positions, for instance, may have substantial impacts on their agencies' policies. Still, if women and minorities are less likely to have control over subordinates and budgets even when they reach higher grade levels, they may be denied other aspects of power as well.

TABLE 11.4   Appendix

Independent Variables	Model I Coefficients	Model I Standard Errors	Model II Coefficients	Model II Standard Errors
White Female	−1.49***	0.39	−5.44***	0.59
Black Male	−2.07***	0.52	−5.57***	0.75
Black Female	−1.50**	0.45	−5.68***	0.64
Hispanic Male	−2.22**	0.87	−6.43***	1.07
Hispanic Female	−2.37**	0.67	−6.80***	0.87
Asian Male	−0.55	2.05	−3.43	2.07
Asian Female	−2.15*	1.09	−6.29***	1.34
Native American Male	6.08	3.82	9.20	5.53
Native American Female	−1.74	1.24	−3.35***	1.28
Federal Experience	0.015	0.061	0.635***	0.073
Federal Experience Squared	0.010***	0.002	0.004	0.003
Age	0.084	0.071	0.438***	0.084
Age Squared	−0.001	0.001	−0.005***	0.001
Years of Education	−0.144	0.107	0.474***	0.101

(continues)

TABLE 11.4 (*continued*)

Independent Variables	Model I		Model II	
	Coefficients	Standard Errors	Coefficients	Standard Errors
Major Field of Study				
Agriculture	10.89***	2.27	15.71***	2.75
Architecture	−0.50	2.72	5.00	6.84
Area Studies	4.09	7.39	16.31	9.32
Biological Sciences	−0.94	1.18	0.73	1.85
Business and Management	−1.43	0.80	5.75***	1.46
Communications	−1.12	2.39	3.00	5.57
Computers	2.96	4.26	15.39*	7.51
Education	1.24	1.28	5.84*	2.28
Engineering	−3.77***	0.85	2.94*	1.42
Fine and Applied Arts	8.26	6.00	12.48	6.97
Foreign Languages	−1.71	1.79	−0.41	2.56
Health Professions	2.86	2.33	9.05**	3.05
Home Economics	4.82	5.93	7.39	6.64
Law	−10.78***	1.19	8.97**	3.35
Letters	0.08	1.60	7.26*	3.71
Library Science	8.32	4.75	18.64*	8.35
Mathematics	−5.84***	1.12	−2.54	1.48
Military Science	−1.46	12.93	12.54	16.18
Physical Sciences	−8.11***	0.96	0.23	1.96
Psychology	−0.31	1.23	9.69***	2.18
Public Affairs and Services	−0.31	1.30	9.04**	3.42
Social Sciences	−2.01*	0.84	4.52**	1.71
Theology	8.22	9.98	9.44	10.82
Interdisciplinary Studies	−7.32**	2.15	−4.09	3.36
Grade in 1982				
GS-5	0.42	0.28	—	
GS-6	4.79***	0.93	—	
GS-7	4.75***	0.66	—	
GS-8	12.60***	7.27	—	
GS-9	6.21***	0.69	—	
GS-10	12.00***	1.82	—	
GS-11	9.83***	0.85	—	
GS-12	14.10***	0.95	—	
GS-13	28.59***	1.39	—	
GS-14	40.76***	1.96	—	
GS-15	67.01***	2.56	—	
SES	90.38***	1.86	—	
Intercept	1.73	1.83	−9.56***	2.01
R^2	.21		.11	

***Significant at .0001.
**Significant at .01.
*Significant at .05.

Notes

The author is grateful to Jerry Legge and Frank Thompson for helpful comments on earlier drafts of this article. Gratitude is also due to the U.S. Office of Personnel Management for providing access to statistical data from the Central Personnel Data File for this analysis. A previous version of this article was presented at the annual ASPA meeting in Indianapolis, March 1985.

1. Samuel Krislov, *The Negro in Federal Employment* (Minneapolis: University of Minnesota Press, 1967), p. 100.

2. John P. Fernandez, *Block Managers in White Corporations* (New York: John Wiley and Sons, 1975), p. 62.

3. James R. Kluegel, "The Causes and Cost of Racial Exclusion from Job Authority," *American Sociological Review*, vol. 43 (June 1978), pp. 285–301; Wendy C. Wolf and Neil D. Fligstein, "Sex and Authority in the Workplace: The Causes of Sexual Inequality," *American Sociological Review*, vol. 44 (April 1979), pp. 235–252; *idem.*, "Sexual Stratification: Differences in Power in the Work Setting," *Social Forces*, vol. 56 (September 1979), pp. 823–844.

4. Rosabeth Moss Kanter, *Men and Women of the Corporation* (New York: Basic Books, Inc., 1977), p. 58.

5. *Ibid.*, p. 55.

6. William Chapman Bradbury, Jr., "Racial Discrimination in the Federal-Service," Ph.D. dissertation, Columbia University, 1952; Krislov, *Negro in Federal Employment*.

7. "Are Women Executives People?" *Harvard Business Review*, vol. 43 (July/August 1965), p. 166.

8. "How Good Are Women Bosses?" *Changing Times* (April 1967), p. 16.

9. Based on 1 percent sample, U.S. Office of Personnel Management, *Central Personnel Data File*, 1982.

10. U.S. Civil Service Commission, *Supervisory Grade-Evaluation Guide and Qualification Standard* (1976), p. 3.

11. 5 U.S.C. 7103 (a)(10).

12. Civil Service Commission, *Supervisory Grade Guide*, p. 4.

13. Clifford W. Dyhouse and Sharrell L. Smoot, "CPDF/OPF Accuracy Survey Error Rates by Data Element," U.S. Office of Personnel Management, Quality Assurance Branch, Workforce Information Division, Agency Compliance and Evaluation (June 1980).

14. See John Neter and William Wasserman, *Applied Linear Statistical Models* (Homewood, Ill.: Richard D. Irwin, Inc., 1974), pp. 326–328.

15. Since 9 of 21 supervisory/managerial positions held by native Americans in this sample are in the Department of the Interior, their apparent advantage may be largely due to the Bureau of Indian Affairs.

16. Arthur J. Corazzini, "Equality of Employment Opportunity in the Federal White-Collar Civil Service," *Journal of Human Resources*, vol. 7 (Fall 1972), pp. 424–445; James E. Long, "Employment Discrimination in the Federal Sector," *Journal of Human Resources*, vol. 11 (Winter 1976), pp. 86–97; Sharon P. Smith, "Government Wage Differentials by Sex," *Journal of Human Resources*, vol. 11 (Spring 1976), pp. 185–199; Patricia A. Taylor, "Income Equality in the Federal Civilian Government," *American Sociological Review*, vol. 44 (June 1979), pp. 468–479; Burke D. Grandjean, "History and Career in a Bureaucratic

Labor Market," *American Journal of Sociology*, vol. 86 (March 1981), pp. 1057–1092; Gregory B. Lewis and Mark A. Emmert, "The Sexual Division of Labor in Federal Employment," *Social Science Quarterly* (forthcoming).

17. One study of a private corporation found that women were as likely to be offered promotions into supervisory positions as were men but were markedly more likely to turn them down, frequently citing family reasons. Carl Hoffman and John Shelton Reed, "Sex Discrimination?—The XYZ Affair," *Public Interest*, vol. 62 (Winter 1981), pp. 21–39.

12

ASIAN AMERICANS IN THE PUBLIC SERVICE

Success, Diversity, and Discrimination

Pan Suk Kim
Old Dominion University

Gregory B. Lewis
The American University

Does the experience of Asian Americans in the public service support their image as a "model minority?" The image of Asian Americans as a "model minority" conceals both their diversity and the discrimination they face. Although Asians are generally highly educated and well paid, Asian groups vary substantially in educational and earnings levels. Despite high average salaries, Asian federal employees earn less and wield less supervisory authority than comparably qualified nonminorities. For the men, the problem is not a "glass ceiling" that keeps highly educated and experienced Asians out of the top levels of the federal bureaucracy; instead, it is Asians without college degrees who receive worse treatment than comparable nonminorities. For the women, the pattern is more complex and more troubling.

Although high levels of schooling and occupational achievement suggest that Asian Americans have succeeded in American society (Taylor and Kim, 1980, p. 2), their image as a "model minority" conceals both their diversity and the discrimination they continue to face. In this article we investigate that diversity and

Source: *Public Administration Review* 54 (May/June 1994): 285–290.

179

discrimination and analyze the status of Asian Americans in the public sector, particularly the federal civil service. We begin with a general profile of Asian Americans in the United States, then narrow the focus to federal employees. We examine trends in employment and compensation of Asian Americans relative to nonminorities and question whether Asians face a "glass ceiling" that keeps them out of the top levels of the federal bureaucracy, perhaps by channeling them into professional occupations and away from supervisory authority.

General Profile of Asian Americans

The first Asians to arrive in the United States in large numbers were the Chinese who arrived as laborers in the mid-ninteenth century. The Chinese Exclusion Act of 1882 banned the immigration of Chinese laborers, but not merchants and students (Daniels, 1988). Shortly thereafter, large numbers of Japanese laborers immigrated and were followed by Filipinos and considerable numbers of Koreans, Indians, and other Asians. Restrictive immigration laws such as the Immigration Acts of 1917 and 1924 produced a 40-year break in Asian immigration starting in the 1920s (*Ozawa* v. *United States,* 260 U.S. 178, 1922; *Thind* v. *United States,* 261 U.S. 204, 1923). In 1965, when the United States lifted its anti-Asian immigration restrictions (by abandoning the national origins system of immigration), a new wave of immigration from Southeast Asia and other Asian countries began (U.S. Commission on Civil Rights, 1992; Takaki, 1989; U.S. Commission on Civil Rights, 1980).

By 1990, the U.S. Asian and Pacific Islander population was about 7.3 million, of whom 95 percent were Asian (U.S. Bureau of the Census, 1991). Asian Americans (hereinafter, the terms "Asians" and "Asian Americans" include Pacific Islanders) are the fastest growing minority group in the United States, primarily because of immigration, especially in the aftermath of the Vietnam War. Their numbers grew by 55 percent in the 1960s, by 141 percent in the 1970s, and by 76 percent in the 1980s (O'Hare and Felt, 1991). Asians nearly doubled their share of the U.S. population during the 1980s, increasing from 1.6 percent in 1980 to 2.9 percent of the population in 1990. The U.S. Census Bureau (1992a) projects that by 2020, Asians may comprise 7 percent of the U.S. population.

Although Asians have been classified as a single minority group in official U.S. statistics since 1976 (before that they were included in "other races"), they vary widely in culture, language, and recency of immigration. In 1980, nearly two-thirds of all Asian Americans (compared to only 6 percent of the U.S. population) were foreign-born, and one-quarter of Asian adults had immigrated in the previous five years, with considerable variation by national/ethnic origin (Table 12.1). Only about one-fourth of Japanese Americans were foreign born, compared to two-thirds of Chinese, Filipinos, and Indians, and 90 percent or more of Vietnamese, Cambodians, and Laotians.

TABLE 12.1   Characteristics of Asians by Nationality of Origin

National or Educated[b] Ethnic Origin	*Percentage of Asians*	*Percentage Foreign Born*	*Family Income[a]*	*High School Diploma (%)*	*College (%)*
Chinese	22	63	22,600	71	37
Filipino	21	65	23,700	74	37
Japanese	19	28	27,400	82	26
Indian	10	70	25,000	80	52
Korean	10	82	20,500	78	34
Vietnamese	7	90	12,800	62	13
Hawaiian	5	2	19,200	68	10
Laotian	1	94	5,200	31	6
Thai	1	82	19,400	72	32
Samoan	1	36	14,200	61	7
Guamanian	1	10	18,200	68	8
Cambodian	c	94	8,700	43	8
Pakistani	c	85	20,900	87	58
Indonesian	c	83	20,500	90	33
Tongan	c	75	16,700	66	13
Hmong	c	91	5,000	22	3
Other Asians[d]	1	n/a	n/a	n/a	n/a
All Asian Americans	100[e]	62	22,700	75	33
Total U.S. population	f	6	20,000	67	16

a Figures are based on 1979 income and rounded to the nearest 100.

b Percentage of all persons age 25 and over who have completed at least four years of college.

c Less than 1 percent.

d Includes other Pacific Islanders.

e Percents may not add to total due to rounding.

f Asian Americans, including Pacific Islander Americans, numbered 3.7 million or 1.6 percent of the U.S. population.

SOURCE: U.S. General Accounting Office, *Asian Americans: A Status Report.* Washington, DC: U.S. Government Printing Office, March 1990, pp. 13 and 26 (The 1990 GAO report is based on 1980 census data published in 1988 by the U.S. Bureau of the Census); and U.S. Bureau of the Census, *We, the Asian and Pacific Islander Americans.* Washington, DC: U.S.

Asian Americans are falsely perceived to be largely exempt from economic problems such as high unemployment or poverty (O'Hare and Felt, 1991). Their average family income exceeded the U.S. average by about 28 percent in 1985 primarily because Asian American households are generally larger; their per capita income was lower than the U.S. average and that of non-Hispanic whites (U.S. General Accounting Office, 1990). High family incomes also reflect the concentration of Asian Americans in high cost-of-living areas—94 percent lived in metropolitan areas in 1991, compared to only 77 percent of whites (U.S. Bureau of the Census, 1992b).

The high median family income of Asians as a group hides their diversity. According to 1980 census data (the most recent available by national origin), the median family income for Asian Americans was $2,700 higher than that for the U.S. population as a whole (Table 12.1). The Japanese median family income exceeded that of white non-Hispanics by 30 percent and the other populous Asian groups (Chinese, Filipinos, and Asian Indians) also fared better than white non-Hispanic families. Southeast Asian Americans (Cambodian, Laotian, and Hmong) had median family incomes far less than the national average in 1979 (U.S. Bureau of the Census, 1983, 1988). These groups were also the most likely to be foreign born, however, and were probably the most recent immigrants, so more recent data might reveal different patterns.

Educational achievements of Asian Americans are high: in 1991, similar percentages of Asians and whites age 25 or older had finished high school (82 percent and 80 percent, respectively), but Asians were almost twice as likely to have finished four years of college (39 percent compared to 22 percent) (Usdansky, 1992; U.S. Bureau of the Census, 1992b, p. 5). According to 1980 census data (the most recent available by national origin), educational attainment was lower in 1980 (only 75 percent instead of 82 percent of Asians had completed high school) and varied substantially by national origin. Over 80 percent of Japanese, Indonesians, Pakistanis, and Asian-Indians had completed high school, but the majority of Cambodian, Laotian, and Hmong had not (Table 12.1).

High educational attainment, however, does not prevent discrimination. Among male high school graduates in 1990, median earnings were only 79 percent as high for Asians as for whites. Asian male college graduates earned only 90 percent as much as white male college graduates. Asian females earned about 95 percent as much as comparable white females, both at high school and college levels of educators (U.S. Bureau of the Census, 1992b).

Asian Americans in the Public Service

Asian American employment has increased rapidly in all sectors of the U.S. economy: by 108 percent in the private sector between 1978 and 1990, by 82 percent in the state and local sector between 1980 and 1990, and by 46 percent in the federal sector between 1982 and 1990 (U.S. Equal Employment Opportunity Commission, 1991). No other group remotely approaches these rates of employment growth. Overall, Asian Americans comprise 2.6 percent of the civilian labor force. Oddly, they are overrepresented in the federal service (3.5 percent) and the U.S. Postal Service (4.3 percent) but underrepresented in the state and local sector (2.0 percent).

This pattern of underrepresentation holds for state, county, city, and town governments (though not for special districts). It also holds for positions in elementary and secondary education, where Asians made up only 0.7 percent of school teachers, principals, and assistant principals in the fiscal year 1990–91 (U.S. Equal Employment Opportunity Commission, 1991). Asian Americans are overrepresented among college and university faculty, however, while non-Asian minorities are underrepresented. In 1990, Asians comprised only 15 of 7,065 elected mayors/chairmen in municipal governments; only 8 of 5,056 chief appointed administrative officers (CAOs)/managers; and only 6 of 1,524 assistant managers or assistant CAOs. Overall, fewer than 1 percent of municipal officials are Asians (International City Management Association, 1991).

In federal white-collar employment, the mean annual salary of white non-Hispanics was $33,500 in 1990. On average, Asian Americans earned 97 percent as much, Hispanics 82 percent, African Americans 76 percent, and American Indians 74 percent as much. In the federal General Schedule and equivalent pay systems, the mean grade of Asian Americans (8.9) approached that of whites (9.3), while those of Hispanics (7.9), African Americans (7.2), and American Indians (7.1) lagged far behind (U.S. Office of Personnel Management, 1990, p. 44). Overall, Asians had a grade distribution much more like that of whites than of other minorities, but at the top levels, Asians were underrepresented. They held only 73 of 8,136 positions (0.9 percent) in the federal Senior Executive Service (SES), whereas white non-Hispanics held 92.0 percent of SES positions (U.S. Equal Employment Opportunity Commission, 1990).

Asian Americans in the Federal Service

The extensive literature on representation and employment discrimination in the federal bureaucracy has focused mostly on African Americans and women (e.g., Krislov, 1967, 1974; Meier, 1975, 1984; Kranz, 1976; Rosenbloom, 1977; Lewis, 1988; Kellough, 1990). It shows that women and minorities are concentrated at the lower job levels, hold less prestigious occupations in the federal bureaucracy, and earn substantially less than white males with similar qualifications. Only two studies (Taylor and Kim, 1980; Kim, 1993) focus on Asian Americans in the U.S. public service, although a few more general studies mention them in passing. They suggest that the situation for Asian Americans differs somewhat from that for other minority groups. Asian males tend to be concentrated in higher level occupations than other minorities (i.e., a higher proportion of Asians hold managerial and professional occupations) (U.S. Bureau of the Census, 1992b), and their salaries approach those of white males, but they still earn less than comparable white males. Asian females face double discrimination, but they seem to be held back more by their gender than their race.

We investigated several questions in this study. First, previous research (Taylor and Kim, 1980; Lewis, 1988) demonstrated that Asians were in lower grades and earned lower salaries than comparable white non-Hispanics, but the last detailed look at this issue (Taylor and Kim, 1980) used data that are now 15 years old. We examined whether grade gaps between comparable Asians and white non-Hispanics have widened or narrowed over time, and whether they were wider for men or women. We used a standard methodology in the economics of discrimination literature. Using multiple regression analysis, we controlled for a number of factors known to influence career success. We asked whether Asians earned less than white non-Hispanics with the same levels of education, experience, and age who were also comparable in veterans' preference and disability status. Because other factors also affect career success, the persistence of grade gaps after controlling for age, education, federal experience, veterans' preference, and disability status does not prove discrimination, but it does indicate problems that the government needs to investigate. Second, Asians are the group most similar to whites in grade, salary, and education, yet they remain underrepresented at grades 13 and above. Does this suggest that Asians face a glass ceiling, a general pattern of fair treatment until they reach the portals of power, at which point they find themselves restricted from top positions largely reserved for white males? Conversely, the rapid expansion of Asian American employment in the federal service may come largely from the newer immigrants, who may be less assimilated into American society. Is discrimination concentrated on this group? Third, Asians seem to choose or be directed to professional rather than administrative occupations in the federal government. Does this lead them to less supervisory and managerial power than comparably qualified white non-Hispanics?

We analyzed a 1 percent sample of federal personnel records for 1978, 1985, and 1992, taken from the *Central Personnel Data File* (CPDF). The CPDF, which is maintained by the U.S. Office of Personnel Management (OPM), is the best data set available for studying federal careers, but it classifies all Asians and Pacific Islanders as a single group. This makes it impossible to determine to what extent the expansion of Asian employment represents older, assimilated nationalities or newer immigrant groups. To simplify the analysis and isolate the impact of being Asian rather than nonminority, we eliminated all blacks, Hispanics, and Native Americans from the data set and analyzed men and women separately. Because the patterns for men and women differ so much, we discuss them separately below.

Asian and White Non-Hispanic Men

Consistent with previous studies, white men held a higher mean grade in federal jobs than Asian men in our sample (10.9 vs. 10.4) in 1992 (Table 12.2), and they were almost twice as likely as Asian men to be supervisors (27 percent vs. 15 percent). Both differences were significant at the .05 level or better, allowing us to conclude that the basic patterns held true for the entire federal work force. The supervisory situation was much worse for Asians in 1992 than in 1978, when Asian men had the edge in the sample (although the difference was not statistically significant). The gap between the mean grades of Asians and whites was

TABLE 12.2   Characteristics of Asians and White Non-Hispanics in Federal
Service, 1978, 1985, and 1992

Characteristic	Asian Females	White Females	Asian Males	White Males
Mean Grade				
1992	7.7	8.1	10.4	10.9*
1985	6.9	6.7	9.8	10.5**
1978	6.7	5.9*	9.8	10.2
Percentage with Supervisory Authority				
1992	7	12*	15	27**
1985	9	8	15	26***
1978	8	6	23	19
Mean Years of Education				
1992	14.4	13.7***	15.3	15.2
1985	14.1	13.3***	15.2	15.0
1978	13.6	12.9*	15.0	14.6
Mean Years of Federal Service				
1992	10.2	12.4***	11.6	14.1***
1985	9.5	11.0*	11.7	13.8**
1978	12.5	10.4*	12.9	13.2
Sample Size				
1992	203	4,436	209	5,569
1985	123	4,283	163	5,691
1978	76	3,883	110	5,965

*Asian-white difference significant at .05 level.
**Asian-white difference significant at .01 level.
***Asian-white difference significant at .0001 level.

SOURCE: U.S. Office of Personnel Management, *Central Personnel Data File,* 1 percent
sample, machine-readable data set.

slightly wider in 1992 (10.4 vs. 10.9) than in 1978 (9.8 vs. 10.2) but narrower than
in 1985 (9.8 vs. 10.5), suggesting no special trend.

Patterns for both education and federal experience suggest possible explanations for the worsening of the situation for Asians. Asians had more education
than whites in each year in our sample (though none of the differences were statistically significant), but whites gained steadily in years of service between 1978
and 1992. White men's mean length of federal service rose by 0.9 of a year between 1978 and 1992, but that of Asian men declined by 1.3 years. Because

experience influences grade levels, Asians' relative decline in seniority could have caused their grade levels to slip relative to that of whites.

Multiple regression supports that explanation (Table 12.3). In 1992, Asian men tended to be 0.3 of a grade lower than white men with the same amount of education, federal experience, and age who had the same handicap and veteran status. Earlier gaps between the grades of comparable Asians and white non-Hispanics had been wider (0.6 grade in 1978 and 0.5 grade in 1985). Thus, the gap tenta-

TABLE 12.3   Differences Between Expected Grades of Comparable Asians and Whites, 1978, 1985, and 1992

Characteristic	Women	Men
All Employees		
1992	0.6***	0.3*
1985	0.2	0.5**
1978	−0.0	0.6**
With High School or Less		
1992	1.6***	1.0*
1985	0.6	1.4*
1978	0.5	1.1
With Some College		
1992	0.1	1.0**
1985	0.0	1.1**
1978	−0.1	1.3**
With Bachelor's Degrees		
1992	0.1	−0.2
1985	0.4	−0.3
1978	−0.2	−0.2
With Graduate Degrees		
1992	1.9**	−0.2
1985	−0.8	0.5
1978	−0.4	0.9

*Coefficient significant at .05 level.
**Coefficient significant at .01 level.
***Coefficient significant at .0001 level.

NOTE: Numbers are unstandardized regression coefficients on the variable WHITE, which was coded 1 for whites and 0 for Asians. All regression models include years of education, years of service, years of service squared, age, age squared, and two dummy variables indicating whether the employee received veterans' preferences or was classified as disabled.

SOURCE: U.S. Office of Personnel Management, *Central Personnel Data File,* 1 percent sample, machine-readable data set.

tively attributed to discrimination rather than to the other factors in the model actually narrowed in the 1980s, despite the fact that the gap between the mean grades widened. In short, Asian men are in lower grades than comparable white men (consistent with an argument of discrimination), but the trend is toward greater equality.

Do the well-educated Asians nearing the glass ceiling feel the pinch of discrimination more than their less-educated brethren? For the men, the answer is a clear "no." In the 1992 sample, Asian men with bachelor's or graduate degrees had slightly higher grades than comparable white men (that is, white men of the same level of education, age, length of service, veteran status, and handicap status), but Asian men who had not gone beyond high school or who had started college but had not finished were one grade behind comparable white men. (The latter differences were statistically significant, while the former were not.) Trends over time suggest improvements in treatment for Asians with some college and, especially, for those with graduate degrees (where whites had a statistically significant 0.9 grade advantage in 1978 but had a statistically insignificant 0.2 grade disadvantage in 1992). Gaps held reasonably constant for those with college diplomas or with high school only.

In 1992, identical percentages of Asian and white men in the sample held professional or administrative positions. Much higher percentages of Asians than whites (50 and 34, respectively) held professional jobs, however, whereas much higher percentages of whites than Asians (39 and 23, respectively) filled administrative positions. Logit analysis confirms that Asians were more likely to be professionals than whites with the same years of education, federal experience, age, and with the same veteran and handicap status, while the opposite held true for administrative occupations.

Does this division of labor between professional and administrative occupations help explain why Asians attain less supervisory authority? No. Logit analysis confirms that Asian men are less likely to be supervisors than comparable white men. That difference remains virtually unchanged when controlling for occupational category in the logit analysis. Asian men are less likely than comparable white men to be administrators; they are also less likely to be supervisors; but there appears to be little connection between the two facts.

In sum, as a group, well-educated Asian men face little or no discrimination in achieving high grade positions and salaries, but they are less successful in attaining supervisory or managerial authority. Their choice of, or channeling into, professional rather than administrative occupations does not seem to explain this discrepancy. Less-educated Asian men face much greater obstacles to attaining the same grades as comparably educated and experienced white men. Asians without college diplomas were at least one grade behind comparable whites in all three years examined, although the gaps seemed to be narrowing somewhat. Asians' communication skills, especially less fluency in English, might account for some of the grade differences, if this group is made up largely of newer immigrants.

Asian and White Non-Hispanic Women

The story for Asian women is more complex and troubling. As shown in Table 12.2, the mean grades of Asian and white non-Hispanic women in our sample did not differ significantly in 1992 (7.7 vs. 8.1), although the mean grade of Asians had been significantly higher in 1978 (6.7 vs. 5.9). In 1992, 12 percent of the whites and only 7 percent of the Asians wielded supervisory authority (a difference significant at the .05 level), but in 1978 and 1985, Asian women in the sample had a (statistically insignificant) advantage over white women in supervisory authority.

The relative standing of Asian women in mean grades and supervisory status fell between 1978 and 1992, despite the fact that Asians had had significantly more education than whites in all three years and that the education gap did not shrink at all over the period. On the other hand, Asians had two more years of federal service than whites in 1978, but whites had two more years of federal service than Asians in 1992. The declining relative seniority of Asian women could be partially responsible for their declining status.

Multiple regression, however, shows that is not a complete explanation (Table 12.3). In 1978, white and Asian women with the same education, seniority, age, veteran status, and handicap status had nearly identical grades. By 1985, Asian women were a statistically insignificant 0.2 of a grade behind, and by 1992, that gap had widened to a statistically significant 0.6 of a grade. Thus, while the unexplained grade gap between Asians and whites was narrowing for the men, it was widening for the women.

Analysis by level of education suggests that the problem is primarily at the high school and graduate school level. White and Asian women with some college or a bachelor's degree held very similar grades in all three years, but Asians with high school only or with graduate degrees were 1.6 or 1.9 grades, respectively, below comparable whites in 1992. Both differences were clearly significant, and much larger than the gaps in 1978 and 1985. These findings provide marginal support for arguments of both the glass ceiling and discrimination against recent immigrants, but the evidence does not fall neatly into a coherent whole.

Similar percentages of Asian and white non-Hispanic women held professional or administrative positions in 1992 (47 percent vs. 45 percent). As with the men, however, the Asians were more likely than the whites to be in professional occupations (24 percent vs. 16 percent) and less likely to be in administrative occupations (23 percent vs. 29 percent). Logit analysis did not reveal significant differences between the two groups in choice of, or channeling into, professional or administrative occupations.

Logit analysis confirmed that in 1992 white women were significantly more likely to wield supervisory authority than comparably educated and experienced Asian women. Again, occupational differences between Asians and whites explained none of that difference in supervisory authority, although finer distinctions among occupations might reveal some effect.

Overall, Asian women fell in status relative to white women between 1978 and 1992. Asians and whites did not differ significantly in grades or supervisory authority in 1978, but by 1992 white women had a clear, statistically significant advantage on both measures. That advantage was apparent among both the most and least educated women (although not those in between), offering little insight into why the situation is worsening for Asian American women. This is especially surprising when the trend has been toward greater equality, not only for Asian men but for all minority and female groups. The most likely explanation is that white women are the group that has gained most from affirmative action in recent years (Lewis, 1988). Asian women have gained on white men, but not as rapidly as white women have, leading Asian women to fall behind relative to white women.

Conclusion

Asian Americans have often been stereotyped as the model minority (Taylor and Kim, 1980; Petersen, 1970), based partly on high family incomes, educational attainment, and occupational status (Hurh and Kim, 1989; Chun, 1980). As favorable as it might seem, this stereotype has damaging consequences. First, it masks the very real social and economic problems faced by many segments of the Asian American population and may result in the needs of poorer, less successful Asian Americans being overlooked. Second, emphasis on the model minority stereotype may also divert public attention from the existence of discrimination, even against more successful Asian Americans, in general employment practices and in discriminatory admissions policies in institutions of higher learning. Finally, the origin of this stereotype may be an effort to discredit other minorities by arguing that if Asian Americans can succeed, so can other minorities. Many Asian Americans resent being used in this fashion (Daniels, 1988; U.S. Commission on Civil Rights, 1992).

The Asian American community actually differs substantially from the myth of uniform success. The rapid expansion of the Asian population in the United States means that this population is changing more rapidly than others and that perceptions need to keep changing to keep up with the reality. The Japanese in this country have typically lived here for generations, speak English as their first language, are highly educated, and earn high salaries. The comparatively new Asian communities are composed primarily of recent immigrants who have learned or are learning English as a second language, have less education, and earn much less. If even the Japanese earn less than comparably educated and experienced whites, then newer Asian immigrants face much greater obstacles to success.

In the federal service, Asian Americans resemble white non-Hispanics in education, salary, grade, and supervisory authority more than they resemble other minority groups. Nonetheless, they continue to earn lower salaries, attain lower grades, and wield less supervisory authority than comparably educated and experienced whites. Among men, grade gaps between comparable Asians and whites have shrunk over the past decade and have essentially disappeared among the college educated. Sizable gaps remain, however, between Asian and white men who have not completed college. Among women, being Asian rather than white appeared to be no particular disadvantage in 1978, but the disadvantage has become apparent over the past 12 years, especially among the least- and best-educated women. These Asian women are still closing the gap relative to white men, but not as rapidly as white women. Being Asian has become a disadvantage for women more so than in the recent past.

The grade and salary gaps between Asians and comparable whites are smaller than for any other minority group, but even this model minority faces discrimination. Policy makers should not ignore this evidence and assume that the battle against discrimination has been won for Asian Americans. A problem remains, especially for those without a college education and probably for recent immigrants, although data currently available do not allow a clear test of the latter hypothesis. Diversity training needs to contain the truth about Asian Americans to battle false stereotypes and lessen discrimination. Recent immigrants from rural areas, where values and customs differ greatly from the predominant U.S. culture, may need special help to familiarize them with modern technology and American common culture. For a diverse group of Asian Americans, long-term recruitment and placement strategies, commitment to higher education funding, and transcultural programs that include job-related social services should be developed or expanded to attract them to the public service. Increasing the representation of Asian Americans in higher grade positions is a slow process. The Asian American national contingents still lack the numbers to mount a strong political influence by themselves, so pan-Asian efforts and pan-Asian organizations could promote opportunities for the establishment and expansion of Asian political and economic interests.

Notes

The authors are grateful to the U.S. Equal Employment Opportunity Commission, Public Programs Division, for sponsoring this research and for providing some of the data analysed; to the U.S. Office of Personnel Management, Division of Workforce Information, for providing the statistical sample of the *Central Personnel Data File* analysed in this article; and to The American University for funding purchase of these data.

References

Chun, Ki Taek, 1980. "The Myth of Asian American Success and Its Educational Ramifications." *IRCD Bulletin* 15 (Winter/Spring), pp. 1–12.
Daniels, Roger, 1988. *Asian America: Chinese and Japanese in the United States Since 1850.* Seattle: University of Washington Press.

Hurh, Won M. and Kwang C. Kim, 1989. "The Success Image of Asian Americans: Its Validity, and Its Practical and Theoretical Implications." *Ethnic and Racial Studies* 12 (October): 512–538.

International City Management Association, 1991. *The Municipal Year Book*. Washington, DC: International City Management Association.

Kellough, J. Edward, 1990. "Integration in the Public Workplace: Determinants of Minority and Female Employment in Federal Agencies." *Public Administration Review* 50 (September/October), pp. 557–564.

Kim, Pan Suk, 1993. "Racial Integration in the American Federal Government: With Special Reference to Asian Americans." *Review of Public Personnel Administration* 13 (Winter), pp. 52–66.

Kranz, Harry, 1976. *The Participatory Bureaucracy*. Lexington MA: Lexington.

Krislov, Samuel, 1967. *The Negro in Federal Employment*. Minneapolis: University of Minnesota Press.

_____, 1974. *Representative Bureaucracy*. Englewood Cliffs, NJ: Prentice-Hall.

Lewis, Gregory B, 1988. "Progress Toward Racial and Sexual Equality in the Federal Civil Service." *Public Administration Review* 50 (March/April), pp. 220–227.

Meier, Kenneth J, 1975. "Representative Bureaucracy: An Empirical Analysis." *American Political Science Review* 69 (June), pp. 526–542.

_____, 1984. "Teachers, Students and Discrimination: The Policy Impact of Black Representation." *Journal of Politics* 46 (February), pp. 252–263.

O'Hare, William P. and Judy C. Felt, 1991. *Asian Americans: America's Fastest Growing Minority Group*. Washington, DC: Population Reference Bureau.

Petersen, William, 1970. "Success Story, Japanese American Style." In *Minority Responses*, edited by Minako Kurokawa, pp. 169–178. New York: Random House.

Rosenbloom, David H., 1977. *Federal Equal Employment Opportunity*. New York: Praeger.

Taylor, Patricia A. and Sung-Soon Kim, 1980. "Asian-Americans in the Federal Civil Service in 1977." *California Sociologist* 3 (Winter), pp. 1–16.

Takaki, Ronald, 1989. *Strangers from a Different Shore: A History of Asian Americans*. Boston: Little Brown.

U.S. Bureau of the Census, 1983. *General Social Economic Characteristics of U.S. Summary, 1980 Census*. Washington, DC: U.S. Government Printing Office.

_____, 1988. *We, the Asian and Pacific Islander Americans*. Washington, DC: U.S. Government Printing Office.

_____, 1991. *Statistical Abstract of the United States 1990*. Washington, DC: U.S. Government Printing Office.

_____, 1992a. *Current Population Reports: Population Projections of the United States, by Age, Sex, Race, and Hispanic Origin, 1992 to 2050*. Washington, DC: U.S. Government Printing Office.

_____, 1992b. *Current Population Reports: The Asian and Pacific Islander Population in the United States, March 1991 and 1990*. Washington, DC: U.S. Government Printing Office.

U.S. Commission on Civil Rights, 1980. *Success of Asian Americans: Fact or Fiction?* Washington, DC: U.S. Government Printing Office.

_____, 1992. *Civil Rights Issues Facing Asian Americans in the 1990s*. Washington, DC: U.S. Government Printing Office.

Usdansky, Margaret L, 1992. "Report Spotlights Asian Diversity," *USA Today* (September 18), p. A10.

U.S. Department of Commerce, 1991. "Census Bureau Releases 1990 Census Counts on Specific Racial Groups." *U.S. Department Commerce News* (June 12).

U.S. Equal Employment Opportunity Commission, 1990. *Annual Report on the Employment of Minorities, Women and Handicapped Individuals in the Federal Government.* Washington, DC: U.S. Government Printing Office.

_____, 1991. *Indicators of Equal Employment Opportunity: Status and Trends.* Washington, DC: U.S. Government Printing Office.

U.S. General Accounting Office, 1990. *Asian Americans: A Status Report.* Washington, DC: U.S. General Accounting Office.

U.S. Office of Personnel Management, 1990. *Affirmative Employment Statistics.* Washington, DC: U.S. Office of Personnel Management.

13 _____

A Symposium

Minorities in Public Administration

edited by Adam W. Herbert

Introduction

Historically, few issues in America have generated such controversy as governmental requirements for "integration," "equal rights," "equal employment opportunity," and "affirmative action." While efforts to circumvent these obligations persist in a number of governmental jurisdictions and agencies, the list of minority public administrators and elected officials at all levels of government is growing at an impressive rate. With this growth have come a number of significant challenges for both minority administrators and public bureaucracies. This symposium represents an effort to document some of these challenges, particularly as they affect/have affected minority groups.

It is critical that the reader recognize that the views and perceptions of minority group peoples vary considerably relative to the good will of public administrators and the efforts of governmental agencies to address the broad social and economic needs of the American people. Any symposium of this type which fails to reflect cynicism and discontent on the one hand, and the pragmatic guarded optimism felt by others would be less than intellectually honest, or factually accurate. The articles in this symposium do reflect this range of views. They all are written, however, in the context of how the public affairs profession and educational institutions can be made more responsive to a set of established societal objectives and needs which have not been adequately understood or addressed. In this context, four themes seem to emerge from the essays included herein:

Source: *Public Administration Review* 34 (November/December 1974): 519–563.

1. The intellectual and operational contributions of minorities to the public service have not been accurately or adequately reflected in the theory, literature, or teaching of public administration.
2. Before public agencies will become more responsive to their needs, minority group people must become more active and visible in both administrative and elective governmental positions.
3. Racial and cultural biases continue to be major factors delimiting the opportunities of minority group people in many governmental agencies to be hired or to advance to professional or high-level administrative positions.
4. Universities, and particularly those with substantial minority group constituencies, have a major role to play in training more minority administrators who possess the skills necessary to research problems, analyze, advocate, and implement public policies which address the needs of low-income people.

In the first article, Deryl Hunt argues that public administration is experiencing an "identity crisis" which must be addressed by the profession. In this context, he suggests that particular attention should be given to the attitudes of administrators towards clients of their agencies. Central to this attitudinal change is a public policy and administrative emphasis on "collective" needs as opposed to "individual" aspirations or demands.

In the second article, on black elected administrators, William Nelson and Winston Van Home identify some of the most significant problems these officials have encountered, including a review of the strategies they have utilized to overcome the problems. Their analysis suggests that those problems confronting black elected administrators are not encountered by their white counterparts. The authors offer suggested improvements which might address the conditions about which they voice concern.

The third article, prepared by Maria Diaz deKrofcheck and Carlos Jackson, describes the forms of discrimination experienced by Chicanos—Spanish-surnamed Americans—in public personnel systems at all governmental levels. Their article suggests that "nativism" is frequently more subtle than racism, and calls for greater recognition of the causes and effects of this form of discrimination.

Cheryl Dobbins and Dollie Walker examine the role black colleges and universities can play both in training students and addressing problems facing low-income peoples. They point out the need for institutional cooperation, and suggest roles for NASPAA, ASPA, foundations, and predominately white academic institutions in the quest for public policies which are more responsive to the needs of "all" people.

Rose Robinson describes the conditions and perceptions which led to the creation of the Conference of Minority Public Administrators (COMPA). She refutes the arguments that COMPA is separatist in nature, and illustrates how it seeks to strengthen the public affairs profession.

The final essay, by the symposium editor, focuses on the roles and responsibilities of minority administrators. It identifies several of the pressures brought to bear on the minority administrator, and suggests the need for a new bureaucratic perspective with regard to role expectations of the minority professional. It presents the argument that minority administrators have a unique role in the formulation and implementation of public policies which they must assume in a more vigorous and effective manner, and which public bureaucracies should encourage.

The challenge of identifying a representative set of issues and perspectives related to minorities and public administration has been a major one. Added to this conceptual problem has been the length restrictions placed on *Public Administration Review* symposia. I do not believe that we have covered herein "all" of the significant issues or problems to be considered in this important subject area, and certainly not in the depth desired. This symposium, however, does constitute an important step in the effort to identify and place into a clearer perspective the contributions minority group people have made, and must continue to make to the public service.

The Black Perspective on Public Management

A review of public management theory since Woodrow Wilson reveals a number of what appear to be major changes.[1] During the 1870s reforms were introduced as a reaction to patronage.[2] About the turn of the century an interest in normative theory appeared.[3] The decade following World War I witnessed a shift to matters of process,[4] which after World War II gave way to management science and behavioralism.[5] Over this same period increased attention has been given to development administration.[6] The latest innovations stress public choice or matters of social equality.[7] This continuing ferment reveals an inability of public administration to work out a satisfactory disciplinary base. Can one not argue, then, that the first half of the last 100 years were spent trying to establish Public Administration as a field, and the second half in pointing out the futility of the previous efforts? If so, is it not understandable why Public Administration, as a field of study, is said to be in an "identity crisis?"[8]

During this same century, blacks have persistently sought from government solutions to the problems presented by their second-class status. While some significant gains were made, especially during the Civil Rights Movement of the late 1960s, the gains by and large have benefited only the black middle class.[9] For the masses of black Americans, "the dream" of Martin Luther King appears to be unattainable. Thus black frustration continues to mount.[10] The masses of blacks seem to be saying that fundamental, not incremental, changes are required,[11] and that at the heart of any such change is the recognition of blacks as active participants in the change process.

With all the changes and talk about changes in public administration during the past 100 years, one factor appears to have remained constant—the orientation towards clients and bureaucrats as individuals. This individualization of administrative practice presents major problems for blacks who project more of a collective orientation toward public action.[12] It may be that a reorientation of administrative practice to take more into account this collective perspective will produce a more viable public administration. It may also help hold in check the tendencies in public management toward organizational isolation from the people to be served and may ameliorate some of the arbitrary dimensions of what has been called the administrative state.

This article addresses the need for a modification of the practice of administration to better accommodate the perspective of black Americans. Its premise is that the failure of public administration theory to resolve its own state of crisis, coupled with a fundamental misunderstanding of black demands, has produced a condition of severe conflict.

The severity of this problem is heightened by increasing black assertions. Politically, economically, and socially, the black culture has emerged as a potent reality. While it has become fashionable to describe black "progress" in terms of the increased numbers of blacks entering the middle class, it would be a fatal mistake to assume that all is well. Indeed, the limited progress has been accompanied by a deepening sense of alienation and the rise of Black Nationalism.[13] At every level of government blacks are now struggling against public bureaucracy, against policies which are not responsive to the needs of blacks as a group. The black critique of failures in health care delivery, education, or public safety, for example, focuses on the unmet needs of the black community as an aggregate—even though individual blacks in increasing numbers may be working out satisfactory solutions. The crisis in governance is proposed precisely because blacks have both heightened frustration and increasing power.

This article then suggests the urgent need for changes in the public management field. Government must be made more responsive to the aspirations of blacks as a collective group. In order to direct attention to this need, it is important first to probe the black perspective on public management.[14] Thereafter, consideration will be paid to some avenues for channeling this "blackened" view of public practice into the training and retraining of public servants.

Black Perspective on Public Management

A perspective is a viewpoint or orientation: the way something is seen.[15] As I have suggested, conventional public administration tends to execute public policies as if the public clientele were composed of discrete individuals. In like manner, bureaucrats are also generally viewed in terms of their unique qualities. In contrast, the black perspective on public activity, while recognizing the need for treating clients and administrators as individuals, for some purposes, also demands that public action address blacks as a group both in the delivery and the consumption of public goods.

The individual perspective in conventional public administration can be illustrated in a number of ways. Most programs are set up for the individual or the family unit. We think of the individual taxpayer, the welfare family, or the student as a program participant. Similarly, we recruit administrators one at a time and through competitive examination. A public career is evaluated on the basis of personal merit and individual performance. There are exceptions: government does use categories such as the poor, the aged, or the military, but in the details of program implementation the practice of administration generally implies that one person is being considered at a time.

In contrast, the black perspective gives much more attention to what is happening to the group.[16] The struggles to end slavery, establish full citizenship, outlaw Jim Crow, or attain equal employment opportunity have all been objectives to be realized alike by all blacks. Suggestions by whites that some individual blacks have obtained good jobs, high incomes, status, or power have never been accepted as adequate responses to the masses of blacks. It is a common view in the black community that only if the lowliest among us has his or her full rights will any of the group really be free.[17] It is therefore not surprising that blacks have pushed group programs: public education, community development, citizen participation. Blacks give group survival a high place on their agenda.[18]

The group orientation of blacks is perhaps nowhere better exemplified than in the Negro spirituals and the blues. This music is about the struggle for black survival. It is the cultural expressions of a people. "Black music," as James H. Cone put it, "is unity music." It unites the joy and the sorrow, the love and the hate, the hope and the despair of black people; and it moves the people toward the direction of total liberation.[19] Much of the black perspective on administration is typified by black music with its moral tone, equality, high expectations; its improvisation and profound concern with releasing human potential.[20]

These contrasting perspectives highlight other profound divergences in black and white outlooks. Blacks, as many black writers have noted, tend to look to the group as a source of creative power and of normative value.[21] African survivals in the aesthetic expressions of American blacks are now fully accepted.[22] Could it be that the long history of the African tribe coupled with the American experience of caste has also conditioned a group orientation toward public programming?

DuBois in one of his most memorable passages called attention to the "twoness" in the black experience, being at once Euro-American and Afro-American. This "twoness," he said, had profound consequences for the views blacks have of American life in general.[23] This "twoness" cannot be ignored by the public sector; for blacks, clients and administrators are more than individuals, they are also bound up in mankind's struggles for freedom and fulfillment.

There is no sure way to project the future implications of these black attitudes toward government. What can be said is that a group orientation in government would be a beginning response to black demands as expressed in the past. Perhaps the field of Public Administration may be responsive because these changes might contribute to reducing the identity crisis in the field. Behind much of the call for a public choice, an equity ethic, or a developmental administration is the insistence that the outcome of government action be a fuller life experienced by people.[24] Enhancing the sense of community, registering gains in social indicators, reducing the distance between government and people—in short, achieving accountability, may all come closer by an approach to governance which keeps the collectivity in mind. Such an approach might return attention to what has been called the public interest or the commonwealth, even though they were so named, the terms did not include blacks as a group.[25] Acceding to black demands just could contribute to the attainment of America's historic ideals which are yet to be realized in practice.

The black perspective on public management brings out the need for making major changes in the way administrators are prepared for government service. If a republican crisis of severe dimensions is to be avoided, the public administration profession and the training institutions must become open to the legitimacy of the black perspective. Universities, government, and foundations have particularly critical roles to perform if these needed changes are to occur.

Increasing Black Inputs into Public Management

Though blacks and whites generally share the same values and attitudes toward issues and problems in the public sector, and granted the two carry out their responsibilities in like fashion, blacks do bring to public management a different perspective, one aimed at the welfare of the group. The call here is for public administration to open up to the perspective of black America. The first step in this journey is to come to the realization that blacks are a valuable resource: This, of course, dictates that whites change their attitudes with regard to training and retraining of public officials to accommodate the black perspective. The challenge is to devise some practical ways in which this accommodation may be brought about.

Universities

In the university the public manager learns by a combination of what he hears, sees, and experiences. If the student of public administration hears only the views of the dominant group, sees only the scholarly works of the dominant group, experiences only dominant group members in work places of influence, then the message to the black manager is that white determination to dominate is unrelenting.

To correct this interpretation, white institutions must find ways to accommodate the black perspective. Assuming that whites wish to accommodate the black perspective, at a minimum, cooperative programs with predominantly black institutions aimed at the exchange of faculty, students, and curriculum materials should be entered into.

Though this approach does not guarantee that the black perspective will be taught, it does increase the likelihood that whites will become more knowledgeable of black views.

Where it is not feasible to establish cooperative programs, white institutions may wish to systematically build into their curriculums courses dealing with the black perspective on public affairs. This may be done in any number of ways, one of which shall be discussed here.

Let us assume for the moment that whites wish to develop a model that provides for black inputs into the total educational program. Let us further assume that the program has an urban-problem focus on preparing students to work as public managers in urban centers (see Figure 13.1).

An urban problem-focused curriculum might provide general core courses which each student will be required to take. A course on The Black Perspectives on Public Affairs will have to be part of the general core. It might also allow students to major in a specific "cluster" area. By "cluster" is meant simply an area of concentration. As each "cluster" might contain four specialized courses and at least four elective courses, students will have a wide variety of courses to choose from as well as a large number of urban problems in which to specialize. An example of how this model works follows. Let us assume that the student chooses

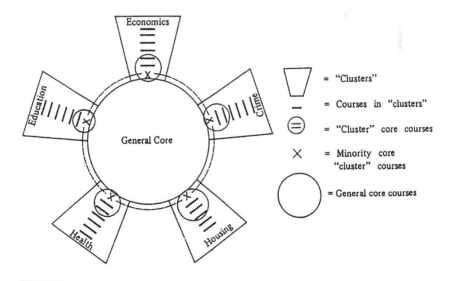

FIGURE 13.1   The Relationship Between Core Knowledge in General and Core Knowledge in Specific

housing as his "cluster" area. The student will be required to take his general core courses. In addition, he will take a minimum of four courses in the housing "cluster." From that point, he may generalize to other "cluster" areas for his remaining courses or he may continue to specialize in the housing area.

Since emphasis is upon building the collective perspective of blacks into the curriculum, one of the courses the student will take in housing is the Black Perspective on Housing Problems. If this same student desires, he may take additional courses in Black Perspective on Crime Problems, Black Perspective on Economic Problems, Black Perspective on Educational Problems, and Black Perspective on Health Problems.

Because it is possible to build a black perspective course into the specialized core of each "cluster," one of the noteworthy "sub-clusters" of this model is Black Perspective on Social Problems. This seems to be a unique feature of the model, and it is particularly important if the study of public administration is to reflect the black collective perspective.

Government Agencies

The influence of public managers in government agencies can be observed in every facet of public affairs. Because these agencies control vast resources in terms of financial support, they have an indirect, yet substantial, influence upon the development of public service programs. For this reason, I suggest that governmental agencies institute programs similar to the following:

1. Additional funds should be provided to schools of public affairs developing programs aimed at including the collective perspective of blacks into their curricular materials.
2. Increasing black involvement in public management should be established as a first level priority of governmental agencies.
3. Government agencies, including those charged with the responsibility of enforcing equal employment opportunity statutes, must cooperate with educational institutions in the training and retraining of both black and white public administrators such that the collective perspective of blacks is fully utilized in the development of public management theory.
4. Internal forces of the administrative system, i.e., recruitment, selection, screening, and promotion of personnel must be modified as to allow for increased black participation.

Professional Organizations

As it is important to provide a forum for blacks to share their views on important public policy issues, professional organizations like ASPA, COMPA, NASPAA, etc., may wish to influence the editors of their professional journal to provide systematic treatise of black views on public policy issues.

Local chapters of ASPA and COMPA may wish to develop special short-term training programs aimed at providing the black perspective on such issues as revenue sharing, unionization in the public service, regionalism, technological change, etc.

NASPAA may wish to reconfirm its commitment to increasing the number of blacks in public administration and systematically working to increase the number of black faculty members capable of teaching the black perspective in schools of public administration.

Foundations

Foundations in conjunction with senior educational institutions might establish non-degree granting institutes focusing on four major areas: continuing education, public affairs, research, and technical services.

In the area of continuing education, the institute could, either through the use of release time faculty or adjunct professionals, provide professional and technical training to career persons in:

The Black Perspective on Revenue Sharing

The Black Perspective on Comprehensive Planning and Its Impact on the Black Community

The Black Perspective on Bidding and Contract Compliance

The Black Perspective on Management by Objectives

In addition to a continuing education component, the institute might well establish a Bureau of Public Affairs which would (a) coordinate mini conferences, lecture series, and public citizens forum; and (b) publish and distribute a quarterly newsletter of information on pending state and federal legislation affecting black constituents.

The research arm of the institute might carry out public policy research. The results of the research should be widely disseminated in order to increase the probability that black views are considered in the formation of public policies (the black perspective on public administration would be very evident in this component).

Finally, a technical and support service unit might be established to provide professional consulting services, computer packaging, data preparation, and analysis as well as short-term released time assistance to black public administrators faced with limited resources.

Summary

This article is a reflection on the black perspective on public management. It began with the assertion that public administration is faced with an "identity crisis," which stems in no small part from the apparent inability of Public Administration to work out a satisfactory disciplinary base. It goes on to suggest that part of the problem may be related to the treatment of clients and bureaucrats as discrete individuals, and offers the black perspective, which focuses on the importance of the group as an alternative. It ends with specific suggestions as to the role universities, government agencies, professional organizations, and foundations might play in realizing the black perspective on public management.[26]

Deryl G. Hunt, *Southern Illinois University–Edwardsville* ✍

Black Elected Administrators: The Trials of Office

Few political movements in the history of the United States have emerged with more drama, emotion, and tension than the contemporary black upsurge in the electoral arena. Across the nation blacks are occupying public positions not held by members of their race since the end of the Civil War and the onset of the era of disfranchisement. To obtain these positions, blacks have marched, boycotted, picketed, and died. The psychological pain suffered by whites in the wake of black successes at the ballot box is reflected in the primitive response of the Wallace vote and the more sophisticated form of institutional hostility symbolized by Watergate.[27]

As the number of blacks elected to public office increases, serious questions arise concerning the implications of this trend for the black community. This article addresses some of those questions by analyzing a variety of problems faced by black elected administrators as they attempt to fulfill the black community's urgent desire for institutional reform and a radical shift in governmental priorities. The analysis will proceed as follows. First, an inventory will be made of the number of blacks elected to public office in recent years, and the kind of positions they have held. Second, the significant problems common to black elected administrators will be analyzed. Third, consideration will be given to the strategies adopted by black elected administrators to overcome these problems. Finally, comments will be made concerning the lessons that can be learned from the experiences of black elected officials.

Black Electoral Trends

One of the most important developments in contemporary American politics is the steady increase in the number of black elected administrators. Since the passage of the Voting Rights Act in 1965 the number of blacks holding elective office has increased five-fold. In 1967 only 475 blacks held public office throughout the country. By 1973 the number of black elected officials had climbed to 2,621.[28]

Before 1965, blacks were almost totally excluded from elective office in the South, and were grossly underrepresented in terms of the number of positions they held in the North. Today, blacks occupy public positions in every region of the country, and at most levels of the federal system. The last major strongholds of white resistance to black representation were Southern congressional seats. But those barriers were breached in 1972 with the election of Barbara C. Jordan (D, Tex.) and Andrew J. Young (D, Ga.) as the first blacks elected to Congress from the South since 1901. Their election, along with Mrs. Yvonne Brathwaite Burke (D, Cal.), brought the total number of blacks in Congress to 16, one in the Senate and 15 in the House of Representatives.

Blacks have displayed considerable strength in state legislative politics. In 1972, blacks held 238 legislative seats in 41 states.[29] Although among the lowest legislative representatives in terms of seniority, black state legislators have begun to wield significant influence in their respective chambers. In most states where they are in significant numbers, black state legislators have joined together to form political caucuses designed to increase their bargaining power *vis à vis* their white legislative colleagues. Demonstrating an affinity for hard work, they have begun to penetrate the leadership network of state legislatures. The highest ranking black state legislator is Howard Woodson, recently elected speaker of the New Jersey House of Representatives. Since 1969 F. Leroy Irvis has served as Democratic majority leader in the Pennsylvania State Legislature. Irvis demonstrated his political clout in 1971 when he successfully swung 12 crucial Republican votes behind a Democratic-sponsored state income tax bill. If the tax measure had failed, the State of Pennsylvania would not have been able to remain solvent.[30] In California, black State Assemblyman Willie Brown has advanced rapidly to become chairman of California Assembly's Ways and Means Committee. This committee monitors the appropriation of all state revenue except monies collected from the gas tax. Brown's impact on the budgetary process has made him one of the most powerful figures in California state politics.

Because of their heavy concentration in the cities, blacks have been able to make their most significant inroads in local politics. In 1973, blacks served in 211 county posts, an increase of 20 percent over the number of posts held in 1972.[31] The State of Michigan alone currently has more than 30 elected black county officials. Similar gains have been made by blacks at the city level, where they now hold more than 80 mayorships and 40 vice-mayorships. The recent election (1973) of blacks as mayors in Atlanta, Detroit, and Raleigh offers poignant testimony to the depth and force of black electoral strength in city politics. Further evidence can be gleaned from statistics regarding the election of blacks to city councils, school boards, judgeships, and other local offices. Black city councilmen increased from 780 in 1972 to 840 in 1973, an increase of 8 percent. During this same period the number of elected black law enforcement officials grew from 263 to 344, an increase of 27 percent.[32]

The key factor underlying this surge in the election of blacks to public office is the rising sense of black political consciousness produced by the civil rights movement. In the wake of heightened black political consciousness, an array of programs and institutions have been established to bring black political influence into greater balance with black political potential. Voter registration campaigns have been launched in the North and the South to locate and activate important segments of the black electorate. Permanent organizations have been formed to undertake the arduous tasks of mobilizing the black electorate in political campaigns. Southern electoral. efforts, for example, have been spearheaded by satellite black political organizations such as the Mississippi Freedom Democratic Party and the National Democratic Party of Alabama.[33] Utilizing techniques of grassroots mobilization, these organizations have succeeded in electing blacks to public offices in rural Southern counties where less than ten years ago they were uniformly denied the right to vote. Black politicians in the North have also used grassroots mobilization techniques to score critical political breakthroughs for the black community. The models for such mobilization efforts were fashioned in Gary, Indiana, and Cleveland, Ohio, in 1967. Running high-pitched emotional campaigns in the black community, Richard Hatcher in Gary and Carl Stokes in Cleveland successfully mobilized unprecedented numbers of black voters and became the first black mayors of major American cities.[34] Since 1967, similar mass mobilization campaigns have resulted in the election of blacks to major public offices throughout the North.

What difference has the election of these new black elected administrators made for the black community? What impact, if any, have they had on public polity? What problems have they faced? How have they attempted to overcome these problems? It is to these questions that we now turn our attention.

The Trials of Office

A careful inquiry into the political world of black elected administrators clearly indicates that the election of black public officials will not necessarily result in substantial improvements in the life situation of masses of black people. Black elected administrators face a range of problems which greatly diminish their impact on the policy-making process. Among the most critical of these problems is the factor of race. That race operates as a constraint on the policy-making capacity of black elected administrators is hardly surprising. Historically, black skin has been conjoined with the idea of inferiority in the minds of most white Americans. This is a socially significant fact and is a critical element in white resistance to blacks occupying official roles. White people, for the most part, do not perceive black people to possess the attributes which they conceive to be essential in individuals who fill certain roles in our society. And where black individuals demonstrate, without doubt, that they possess the attributes designated as essential in those who seek to fill certain roles, they are often denied the roles they seek on the grounds that appear to be reasonable, but are, in truth, quite specious.

When a black man is elected to public office he inherits all the problems of his race. The crucial foundation of these problems is the existence of a system of control which prescribes the continuing subordination and powerlessness of the black community. In the words of Harold Bacon, this system of control has been formalized into a web of institutional racism which "entraps black people much as the spider's net hold flies—they can wiggle but they cannot move very far."[35] A critical dilemma of the black elected administrator is the fact that he is expected to negotiate successfully a system which fosters black failure. Because of the negative images associated with blackness, the black community faces a "mobilization of bias"[36] in the political system, which imposes severe constraints on the exercise of effective power by blacks through ordinary channels. Thus, every black administrator—as representative of the black community—begins with the handicap of race. If he wishes to succeed, he must put forth extraordinary efforts for the sake of achieving modest results.

Although it is of major importance, race is not the only problem that confronts black elected administrators. The exclusion of blacks from significant positions in the governmental process has meant that most black elected officials have not been socialized into the principles, norms, customs, procedures, and routines of administrative and bureaucratic life. Due to this lack of administrative socialization, black elected administrators must learn in a narrower cross-section of time that which white counterparts learned over a greater cross-section of time. The necessity to learn quickly the complexities of administrative and bureaucratic life generates profound anxieties and insecurities in, and pressures upon, black elected administrators. Every black elected administrator feels that he must prove himself to white as well as black people. The imperative to prove himself, imposed from within as well as without, renders him vulnerable to the mistakes which are made invariably by those who are pressured by circumstances to learn and succeed quickly.

Problems of inexperience tend to especially frustrate the efforts of major black elected administrators such as congressmen and big-city mayors. Thus, for example, despite his good intentions, Mayor Hatcher in Gary found that for more than six months after his election he could accomplish little in the way of concrete policy initiatives because the bulk of his time—and that of his staff—had to be spent learning the procedures and routines of city administration. Ninety percent of the persons holding key positions on Hatcher's staff had no prior experience in government. Faced with the tremendous responsibilities produced by the demands of a complex city bureaucracy and an expectant public, members of the Hatcher administration gained most of the experience they needed to succeed in their roles through a frustrating process of trial and error.[37] While they experimented with various approaches to administration, city government teetered nervously on the brink of disaster.

Some white officials have attempted to exploit the unfamiliarity of blacks serving on multimember legislative and administrative bodies by denying them the basic information and appointments needed to operate effectively. Black police jurors in Louisiana, for example, have been deliberately excluded from key committees and kept totally in the dark on financial and budgetary matters.[38] One Louisiana city councilman was given the committee assignments he desired only after he presented documented evidence that his white predecessors had always served on the committees in question.[39]

The problem of inexperience tends to be compounded for black elected administrators by the attendant problem of institutional hostility. Bureaucracies are immanently conservative. Black elected administrators are expected to buck the bureaucracies in which they serve in order to change the priorities of government. However, when black elected administrators attempt to institute bureaucratic reform, they almost invariably encounter strong resistance from old-line bureaucrats who have a vested interest in the status quo. This is a natural response of bureaucratic conservers to those who are perceived as threats to the institution they man and the policies they espouse.

Black elected administrators who are willing to abide by the norms of bureaucratic routine are often warmly embraced and lavishly praised by their colleagues. When these same black administrators begin to promote causes which are not attuned to the intrinsic conservatism of the institutions of which they are a part, their relations with their white colleagues tend to become quite strained. Hostility and non-cooperation from bureaucratic associates is a principal source of frustration for activist oriented black elected officials. Their basic instincts tell them that they ought to be forthright in their advocacy of policies which shift power and benefits from whites to blacks. At the same time they are constantly aware of the fact that if they pursue such a course too vigorously they will generate bureaucratic resistance of such massive proportions that they will be unable to achieve even modest gains for their black constituents. Unable to accomplish their priority objectives, black elected administrators are forced to reorder their priorities—often to their chagrin—in order to perform more or less satisfactorily in their roles.

Examples of bureaucratic resistance to the programs and policies of black elected administrators are legion. Militant black congressmen such Adam Clayton Powell and Ronald Dellums have found themselves ostracized and labeled *personna non grata* by white congressional associates. When Richard Hatcher, while serving as a member of the Gary City Council, began pushing for the passage of open housing legislation, he was stripped of party patronage and treated as an outcast by both black and white councilmen. Resistance from members of the city bureaucracy has been one of the most serious problems faced by black mayors of major American cities. White bureaucrats fought the programs of the Stokes administration from the day Stokes stepped into office until the day he left. In Gary and Newark, members of the city hall work staff, protected by civil service, have openly defied Mayors Hatcher and Gibson; a number of these persons swore allegiance to the previous administration, and flagrantly disobeyed direct mayoral orders as they engaged in various forms of bureaucratic sabotage.[40]

Black elected administrators have been seriously handicapped by the lack of adequate political, economic, and technical resources to combat institutional hostility and other major administrative problems. Politically, the problem of scarce resources manifests itself in several ways. First, many black administrators are elected from all-black constituents whose collective influence in the political arena is so weak that the element of constituency pressure is neutralized as a bargaining resource in the decision-making process. As Jones has pointed out, the constituents of black elected administrators are likely to be badly disadvantaged in relation to other groups when it comes to backing demands made in formal political structures with socioeconomic muscle.[41] Second, many black administrators are elected to public office as token representatives on tickets sponsored by white-dominated party organizations. Here, relevant political resources are controlled by leaders of the party, making the black elected administrator a virtual captive of party preferences. Lacking an independent base of power, he must conform to the wishes of party leaders or face almost certain political defeat. Third, many black elected administrators are elected from at-large rather than district or ward political jurisdictions. At-large electoral arrangements artificially restrict the number of blacks that may be elected to public bodies and black administrators who are elected under such arrangements are constrained politically from forming black caucuses and voting blocs. The high degree to which black elected administrators are racially isolated is illuminated by Jones' survey of the status of black office holders in the South. He found that only 25 of 125 Southern city councils with black representation had more than one black councilman. Councils with more than two or three blacks were a rarity. Black representation of this sort was found mainly in small towns with predominantly black populations, or cities with exceptionally large councils.[42]

Economic and technical resource problems also greatly circumscribe the effective decision-making capabilities of black elected administrators. Technical assistance in the form of research assistants and administrative aides is generally not available to black officials. Most black office holders operate on very limited budgets which only permit the employment of a skeletal staff, or no staff at all. Limited to non-professional volunteer help, black elected administrators are forced to spend the bulk of their time attempting to keep up with the day-to-day housekeeping responsibilities of their office. Overburdened by "busy work," black elected administrators are unable to devote the time required for a thorough assessment of long-range goals and the planning of appropriate strategies. Administrative imperative such as the forging of key external contacts and the mobilization of economic resources to implement innovative programs often suffer due to other pressing demands and a paucity of technical assistance.

Problems of this sort have no geographic boundaries, but plague urban and rural black elected administrators alike. In the cities, blacks are only elected to public offices in appreciable numbers when the city is in economic decline because of the intense out-migration of middle and upper income whites. Property taxes and other funds raised from local revenues are inadequate to meet the demands for services within the cities. These factors have made the search for outside funds one of the most important and time-consuming functions of urban black elected officials. However, because of weak technical support, they frequently find themselves losing out to suburban officials whose quests for outside funds are usually buttressed with significant technical advice.

For rural black elected administrators, economic and technical problems are even more overwhelming. A recent report issued by the Joint Center for Political Studies on the administrations of Southern black mayors has documented the gravity of these problems. This report found that blacks in the South were primarily mayors of small poverty-stricken communities pervaded with immense social and economic problems, including high unemployment and underemployment, slum housing, and inadequate water and sewer facilities.[43] Community development programs in these communities were generally stifled by the fact that mayors worked only part time and operated with little or no staff. Although the mayors were extremely interested in obtaining federal assistance for their communities, most of them had no knowledge of available federal programs, and had no access to technical help in the preparation of proposals for federal grants. Consequently, despite their enormous needs, very little federal monies have been allocated to these communities in the area of social and economic redevelopment.

Underlying the problems we have discussed thus far is the general problem of demands and expectations. This problem stems mainly from the fact that the election of black elected administrators often requires that they make campaign promises which they have no hope of fulfilling. When they take public office, their black constituents expect and demand that they deliver certain goods and services. As we have seen, they are often unable to satisfy these expectations and demands because their roles usually lack the power and resources to do so. Moreover, the demands and expectations of their black constituents are often amorphous, incoherent, inarticulate, conflicting, and contradictory. Black elected administrators are therefore faced with the problem of rendering articulate the inarticulate interests of their constituents, and attuning the conflicting and contradictory expectations and demands made upon them. Since there are no universally agreed-upon criteria among black constituents for the attunement of conflicting and contradictory expectations and demands, there will always remain those who will be dissatisfied.

Though it is not logically impossible, it is empirically impossible for a black elected administrator to satisfy all of his black constituents on any matter. When there is significant dissatisfaction with his conduct among the politically relevant numbers of his black constituency, a black elected administrator often has to cope with the charge of having "sold out to the man." Though this charge may have its origins in the envies, jealousies, suspicions, and resentments of black individuals who wish him ill-success, it is nonetheless potentially damaging if those who support him, being unable to perceive clearly why he has taken a particular stand, begin to have doubts concerning his commitment to promote the interests of black people.

Black elected administrators are also pressured by the demands of the white electorate. For example, a black mayor, even in a predominantly black city, often faces demands and expectations of the white citizenry which are disharmonious with those of the black citizenry. Although he might have received his principal support from black citizens, he can neither ignore, be indifferent to, nor take lightly the demands and expectations of white citizens. Even in a predominantly black city, whites will probably be the major owners and controllers of the city's economic resources. Hence the success of a black mayor will turn in large measure on his ability to solicit the cooperation of economically powerful whites. Moreover, he must, as we have seen, look beyond the limits of the city to the state and federal government for assistance. At these levels, he deals almost exclusively with whites. A black mayor must, of necessity, become a skilled artist in walking a tightrope between the countervailing demands and expectations which emanate from the black and white citizens he serves.

Efforts to Overcome Constraints

Black elected administrators have attempted to come to grips with their problems primarily in two ways. First, they have practiced the politics of accommodation. This has required either the scaling down or abandoning of their programs of reform in exchange for white support for policies that would lead to a more equitable distribution of existing services and benefits to the black community. Many black elected administrators now perceive the striking of such bargains as the most *prudential* short-term option open to them. Operating in hostile white-dominated political arenas, they have found through bitter experience that while the championing of militant black causes is emotionally satisfying, this strategy does not add to their influence over policy making, but to the contrary, is sometimes extremely unproductive, and can, on occasion, be suicidal.[44] Given the political risks and liabilities of radical political activity, most black elected officials have concentrated on assiduously cultivating their images as public servants "quietly working with their colleagues to bring about desired changes."[45] Their impact on the decision-making process has reflected this posture. While they have been effective in obtaining a larger share of government resources for the black community, they have been notably ineffective in achieving systemic changes which would substantially alter prevailing power relationships between the black and white communities.

Second, they have practiced the politics of community resource mobilization. Black elected administrators have come to realize that the best hope for the future lies in the development of permanent bases of power in the black community.

Accordingly, they have been deeply involved in the process of building institutional structures which will assist in the realization of long-range black social, economic, and political objectives.

One aspect of this activity has been the formation of state, regional, and national organizations to provide technical, economic, and political support for the administrative responsibilities of black elected officials. In every state where a significant number of black elected administrators can be found, organizations of black elected officials have been established. These organizations display considerable structural variations. They range from groups organized from the congressional district down, such as the Twenty-first District Caucus in Cleveland, to state and local political assemblies and caucuses.

One of the most broadly organized statewide organizations is the Connecticut State Federation of Black Democratic Clubs. This organization has established branches (or clubs) in every major city in Connecticut. These local organizations meet once a month, and periodically send delegates to statewide conferences and conventions. Most of the state organizations are spearheaded by state legislators. Some involve participation by only elected officials, while others encourage the participation of persons drawn from the community at large. At the local level, a number of black elected administrators have successfully transformed their campaign organizations into permanent political groups. In Dayton, Ohio, State Representative C. J. McLin, chairman of The Black Elected Democrats of Ohio, heads a black citizens organization which seeks to promote the interests of the black community on a number of fronts. During election periods the organization is involved in the process of registration and turnout. In the interim between elections it serves as a major political pressure group to lobby for black causes in the councils of government.

The activities of these state and local organizations are bolstered by an array of regional and national organizations. The Black Congressional Caucus is composed of the 16 blacks currently holding seats in Congress. The Black Congressional Caucus has centered much of its activities around the dissemination of information about issues and events of vital importance to the black community. Caucus members have also attempted to dramatize special issues—such as the plight of returning black Vietnam veterans—by holding hearings and making special appeals to the President for action. Another prominent national organization is the National Black Assembly. This organization is an outgrowth of the National Black Political Convention held in Gary, Indiana, in 1972. Members of the Assembly meet approximately every two months to discuss issues affecting the black community, and propose policy stands which can be used to create a national black political agenda. The National Black Caucus of Local Elected Officials is a national black political organization sponsored by the Joint Center for Political Studies and the United States League of Cities. It brings together black elected officials from across the nation during the annual meeting of the League of Cities and Conference of Black Mayors to work on a range of problems of common concern. Regional organizations include the Southern Conference of Black Mayors and the Western Conference of Black Elected Officials. These organizations have periodically held workshops, conferences, and symposia designed to generate technical knowledge on problems affecting the administrative effectiveness of black elected officials.

The spiraling technical needs of black elected officials have fostered the creation of several organizations of national scope to service them. Under the leadership of Illinois State Senator Richard Newhouse, a clearing house for black state legislators has been established in Chicago. The objective of this organization is to provide a range of technical assistance—from the typing of bills to the undertaking of elaborate research projects—for black state legislators from across the country. In Washington, D.C., The Joint Center for Political Studies has been established as a research agency dedicated to providing black elected administrators with the information they need to meet the responsibilities of their positions. Since its founding in 1969, the Joint Center has been instrumental in the publication of numerous research reports on various aspects of black political life. Moreover, the Joint Center has conducted seminars and workshops on a range of topics and has made strenuous efforts to tie black elected officials to the appropriate agencies in Washington which might satisfy their needs for economic and technical assistance. The Joint Center also conducts an intern-fellowship program which provides stipends for students interested in political science and public affairs to work as interns for black elected administrators across the country.

The formation of broad networks of black political organizations and the parallel development of centers of technical assistance and research provide good grounds for the belief that the critical resource gap that has hampered the efforts of black elected administrators is beginning to close.

Evaluation of Needs

The experience of black elected administrators to date clearly establishes the fact that they can expect to face a host of problems not encountered by their white counterparts. At the same time, their stock of resources to cope with these problems will usually be extremely low. These factors point to the need for substantial improvements in several areas.

First, the number of black elected administrators must be increased. Despite the dramatic increase in the percentage of blacks holding public office, blacks are still grossly under-represented in all public offices. This reflects not so much black political apathy as the prevailing barriers to black political participation and success. These barriers take the form of archaic procedures for voter registration, gerrymandering, at-large election procedures, vote fraud, intimidation, and unethical, if not illegal, changes in voting and candidacy requirements. A concerted campaign needs to be waged to attain electoral reform in all of these areas. The desired goal is to obtain black representation in public offices which truly reflects the black percentage of the population. Realization of this goal would permit the formation of black voting blocs in some arenas, and the complete takeover of governmental units in others. This, in turn, would markedly reduce the need for black elected administrators to attune their policy proposals to the preferences of their white political adversaries.

Second, black elected administrators will continue to need access to a variety of economic and technical assistance. Given the range and complexity of black problems, it is no doubt true that in the immediate future the bulk of the resources needed to cope with them will have to come from the federal government and private foundations. Dependence on these sources of support will require that black elected administrators be sufficiently informed, organized, and unified to strike the most rewarding bargains possible when such resources are negotiated. Federal and foundation funds are never gifts; they are always accompanied by specifications and limitations. Black elected administrators must always seek to discern what price they are paying in terms of autonomous decision-making capabilities and future strategies when they agree to accept federal and private assistance.[46]

Third, it is axiomatic that the success of black elected administrators requires a high degree of black unity and trust. If black elected administrators are to wield significant political clout, they must be able to count on the solid support of their black constituents. In part, this means that their performance must be of a kind which engenders trust and confidence in them by their constituents. It also means that special interests in the black community will have to set aside their individualistic concerns for the sake of achieving larger community goals. Conflict and tension within the black community invariably undermines the bargaining capabilities of the community's elected representatives. When proposals dealing with widespread community interests are introduced into the political process by elected black administrators, it is imperative that all major community interest groups coalesce behind them in order to maximize their chances of success.

Black electoral politics cannot be the exclusive preoccupation of elected black officials; the most crucial resource that can be brought to bear is broadscale community support behind specific policies. It is in pursuit of this goal that much of the energy and imagination of black political leaders must be expended in the years ahead.

Finally, there is a critical need for a careful assessment of the limitation of electoral politics. Some of these limitations have been cogently summarized by James Q. Wilson:

> Where Negroes can and do vote, they have it in their power to end the indifference or hostility of their elected representatives, but the representatives do not have it in their power to alter fundamentally the lot of the Negro. The vote is a legally important, morally essential weapon for the protection and advancement of individual and group interests but it cannot protect or advance all the relevant interests. It can force the passage of laws, the ending of obvious forms of state-sanctioned discrimination, and the removal from office of race-baiters and avowed segregationists. It can only

marginally affect the income, housing, occupation or life chances of Negro electorates.[47]

Wilson's remarks underscore the fact that much of the power exercised in America is not public but private. Black powerlessness is promoted not only through the actions and inactions of governmental officials, but through the policies of myriad private institutions—not the least of which are large corporations. Given the corporate dominated structure of American society, it would be foolish indeed for blacks to limit their political activities to electoral politics. Black electoral victories which do not lead to a restructuring of the institutional framework and economic resource distribution of American society will, at best, replace colonialists with neo-colonialists. If black political and economic liberation are to be achieved, electoral politics can only be viewed as one facet of a larger political struggle.

William E. Nelson Jr. and Winston Van Horne, *The Ohio State University* ◯◡

The Chicano Experience with Nativism in Public Administration

Under provisions of the 1964 Civil Rights Act, various programs to improve the socioeconomic status of minorities have been implemented over the past decade. In the public sector, the legitimacy and effectiveness of these programs have been seriously questioned by minority communities, as well as by civil rights leaders. This concern has been reinforced by government publications studying these quality of life and related administrative issues. In reviewing state and local government programs generally, the Equal Employment Opportunities Commission in 1969 concluded that:

> Minority group members are excluded almost entirely from decision making positions, and even in those instances where they hold jobs carrying higher status, these jobs usually involve work only with the problems of minority groups and largely tend to limit contact to . . . minority group members. . . .[48]

The problem of excluding minorities from "responsible government jobs" and from participating in the policy-making process is far from being resolved, especially

---

The authors wish to express their appreciation to Silas Abrego and his staff at the Central Chicano, University of Southern California, for their encouragement and support.

as it affects the Chicanos.[49] The Spanish-surname minority group is the second largest minority in the U.S., but has been perceived by some as a non-minority, or as an "invisible minority."[50] Within the Spanish-surnamed population there is a growing number of people who adhere to a position of self-determination and regard themselves as Chicanos. The federal government employment statistics support the position that the Spanish-surnamed is excluded from federal employment, as can be seen in the data contained in Tables 13.1 and 13.2. Table 13.1 shows a percentage of minority employees in federal government for the years 1966–1972. Table 13.2 represents a further breakdown of the percentage of Spanish-surnamed and black employees (the two largest minorities) in federal government for the years 1966–1972.

Tables 13.1 and 13.2 demonstrate that the Spanish-surnamed Americans are consistently under-represented in federal employment. During the period between 1966 and 1972 there has been only a .5 percent increase of Spanish-surnamed federal employees, as compared with 10.3 percent increase in the total federal work force. In, 1972 the Spanish-surnamed federal employees represented only 3.1 percent, which is disproportionate when compared with their national population percentage of 5.8 percent.[51] Also, the minority employees during 1972 were still employed in lower job classifications.[52]

The statistics used to show the exclusion of Spanish surnamed from federal employment raise a further problem for the Chicano. In employment reports the Chicano is identified and included within the category comprising all Spanish surnames, thus making it extremely difficult to report the exact figures of the number of Chicano employees. This fact fails to distinguish the Chicano's unique commitment to the concept of self-determination. Federal employment reports

TABLE 13.1   Federal Employees

Year	Total Employees	Total Minority Employees (Blacks, Spanish-Surnamed, Orientals, and Native Americans)	Percent
1966	2,303,906	442,374	19.2 (91% of employees identified)
1967	2,621,939	• 496,672	18.9
1968*	2,621,939	496,672	18.9
1969	2,601,611	501,397	19.3
1970	2,571,504	505,035	19.6
1971	2,573,770	502,752	19.5
1972	2,542,067	509,307	20.0

SOURCES: U.S. Civil Service Commission, Reports 1962–1972.
      *U.S. Civil Service Commission, *Challenge and Change*, Annual Report, 1968.

TABLE 13.2   Spanish-Surnamed and Black Federal Employees

Year	Spanish Surnamed	Percent	Blacks	Percent
1966	59,853	2.6	320,136	13.9
1967	68,945	2.6	390,842	14.9
1968*	68,945	2.6	390,842	14.9
1969	73,591	2.8	389,251	15.0
1970	74,449	2.9	391,173	15.2
1971	75,717	2.9	386,812	15.0
1972	77,577	3.1	389,936	15.3

SOURCES: U.S. Civil Service Commission, Reports 1962–1972.
*U.S. Civil Service Commission, *Challenge and Change*, Annual Report, 1968.

prepared by the U.S. Civil Rights Commission document the fact that the federal government, which is the largest employer in the nation, is guilty of job discrimination as a result of maintaining discriminatory policies. It is our position that this discriminatory practice is partially a result of an exclusionary process perpetuated by the dominant society.[53] Consequently, as the Chicano strives towards self-determination, the dominant Anglo culture continues to negate his identity. In the remainder of our article, it will be our purpose to establish this position, especially as it relates to the area of the Chicano in public employment.

This article identifies certain underlying mechanisms existing in public institutions which selectively exclude Chicanos from participating in policy making and rendering services to the public. The consequence of this exclusion will also be discussed as is exemplified by the Kerner Commission's findings of a polarized society leading ". . . ultimately, [to] the destruction of basic democratic values."[54] From our perspective we will explore underlying philosophic values and assumptions which are held by the majority culture and which are at the heart of perpetuating the exclusionary mechanism directed at Chicanos.

Such philosophic values are crystallized in the concept of *nativism* as distinct from that of *racism*. The latter is an ideological doctrine which asserts the superiority of one race over another based on assumed rather than scientifically verified racial attributes and limitations, and seeks to maintain the supposed purity of a race. Nativism, on the other hand, is a fear of non-Anglo foreigners, or as John Higham identifies, "the anti-foreign spirit."[55] Nativism in the U.S. seized upon the 19th century Darwinism which helped to encourage interest in heredity and, therefore, racial determinants.

The concepts of "survival of the fittest" and the process of natural selection confirmed the American spirit of rugged individualism, thereby strengthening the ideas of a select group and nationality in this country. With the influx of immigrants, there was a manifestation of prejudice towards Catholics, foreign radicals, and immigrants of different culture and race by Americans who considered themselves as the select and superior group. The combinations of ethnocentrism and xenophobia resulted in the nativistic response which led to immediate legislation that protected the socioeconomic interest of the select Anglo group.

The anti-foreign spirit is not exclusive to the Anglo culture. It applies to all groups, including minorities, as is evident in the history of the Southwest when various ethnic groups fought against each other in their struggles to survive against "manifest destiny."[56] The concept of nativism has seldom been related to the process of discrimination, especially against minorities, until this time. Usually discrimination has been seen as having roots in racism, a phenomenon which "White Americans have never fully understood . . . although . . . White institutions created it, White institutions maintain it, and White society condones it."[57] It is nativism, however, which perennialized the discrimination toward the Chicano. On this point, David F. Gomez states:

> . . . that Mexicans are [considered] inferior because of their values, traditions, culture, et cetera. This runs deeply within general society's bias against anything or anyone foreign or colored. It [is] not difficult for people with such biases to seize upon a particular explanation that emphasizes the inferiority of Mexican culture as compared with Anglo culture. It reinforces all that they had been taught to believe: the basic superiority of Anglo-White culture and the deprivation of anyone not in that select category.[58]

Higham, whose 1956 work appears to be the most in-depth study of nativism to date, traces this concept to the early 1820s, when there was increased immigration to this country. Immigrants were considered racially inferior to native stock. Intolerance towards these "strangers" led to the formulation of severe restrictions, including more stringent immigration laws. Higham also found that recurring nativist cycles coincided with periods of social tension such as those brought on by the rapidly industrializing urban society and the conquering efforts that occurred during the Westward Movement.[59]

Returning to our particular perspective, our main theme places nativism at the foundation of this exclusionary process for Chicanos. Our thesis is that this discrimination has been sustained because nativism has been institutionalized and is deeply imbedded in the common and daily practices and operations of public institutions. In short, we see the assumptions and values of nativism as perpetuating racism. For the Chicano, these pejorative attitudes are illustrated through stereotypic concepts depicting him/her as "lazy," "dirty," "greaser," and/or other degrading characteristics. These stereotypic attitudes associated with nativism are directed against the Chicanos because of the differences and conflicts that have existed between the Anglo-Saxon culture and the Mexican heritage.[60]

While a Chicano is not a foreigner in his own land, the Anglo Saxon has historically viewed him as a foreigner from Mexico or other Latin American countries. The Anglo's suspicion of foreigners in general and of the Chicano in particular has been heightened due to the differences in skin pigmentation, culture, language, and the Catholic heritage surrounding the Mexican culture.

The concept of Anglo nativism is also inherent in the continued conflicts that have occurred throughout American history between the two cultures. The Anglo's fear of the Mexican in the 1840s and now towards Chicanos has not disappeared. The Treaty of Guadalupe Hidalgo, the massive repatriation of Chicanos during the 1920s and 1950s, and the zoot suit riots during the 1940s are some of the incidents which highlight the numerous conflicts between the two cultures. That the concept of nativism persists is evident as one reads of the massive repatriation of "illegal aliens" in Los Angeles by the U.S. Immigration Service. Other current examples of nativism include: (1) the continuation of placing the non-English-speaking Chicano students into the elementary "educably mentally retarded" classes;[61] (2) the mistreatment of Chicanos in the Southwest by law enforcement agencies;[62] and (3) the lack of Chicano teachers, social workers, and other public employees in all levels of government in areas where there is a heavy concentration of Chicanos.[63] Such examples of nativism are highlighted in Judge Chargin's commentary about Chicanos as he sentenced a 13-year-old youth who had committed incest:

> We ought to send you back to Mexico . . . You ought to commit suicide! Maybe Hitler was right. The animals in our society probably ought to be destroyed because they have no right to live among human beings. If you refuse to act like a human being, then you don't belong among the society of human beings.[64]

Institutional Nativism Exemplified

The values and assumptions implicit in Anglo nativism as has been previously discussed, have given rise to stereotypic attitudes of the Chicano. Covert and overt racist actions are subsequent manifestations of Anglo nativism. Overt racist practices were highly visible at the turn of the 20th century when Chicanos were specifically discriminated against in certain public restaurants, public bathrooms, and in public schools.[65] Continued practice at the present time has become highly obscured and covert in nature. As a result of nativism being institutionalized, it has become more difficult for the Anglo to see its reality and impact on Chicanos.

Recurring litigations alleging discrimination in public agencies reinforce our point of view that nativism has been institutionalized. Recently a U.S. District Judge ordered the Department of Labor:

> To end all discrimination against migratory and seasonal farm workers who had been denied benefits from federally funded State Employment Offices . . . [as] it was illegally supporting State rural employment agencies that "subjected minority farm-workers to racial, national origin, sex, and age discrimination in recruiting and referring applicants" for employment.[66]

Fire departments in a number of cities have also been accused of "outrageous racial discrimination." A spokesman of a Presidential Commission on Fire Problems has stated that "both the number of Blacks, Spanish Americans and American Indians in our fire departments and the number of group fire chiefs is so small that our record in this area is the disgrace of the nation."[67]

In a speech on "Noble Efforts on Behalf of America's Second Largest and Most Ignored Minority," Senator Tunney confirmed our position as he stated:

> ... today, in California, there are 3,101,000 Spanish Americans ... the largest minority in the Southwest according to the U.S. Census Bureau. Employment statistics at both private and government agencies indicate that Chicanos are also the group that are least likely to be hired, and most likely to be fired ... [that] less than 5 percent of all employees in the top 100 corporations headquartered in California are Spanish surnamed, that less than 5 percent of California State government employees are Spanish surnamed, and less than 6 percent of the Federal government's employees are Spanish surnamed.[68]

Importance of Personnel Practices and Processes

The underlying values of nativism have also permeated all aspects of public administration such as in policy making, finance, personnel, and behavior in organizations. Our area of emphasis, however, will concentrate on personnel practices and processes because we believe that this is the area in which employment discrimination is most visible. The importance of this emphasis is reinforced by the need for equal employment legislation (1964 and 1972) and Executive Orders which mandated that both the public and private sectors take affirmative actions aimed at alleviating discrimination.

As previously stated, employment discrimination has been recognized as a form of institutional oppression; therefore, personnel practices and processes are important in the evaluation and analysis of Chicano participation in public institutions. Included within the personnel practices and processes are criteria used for recruitment, screening, selection, specialization, staffing, training, and fringe benefits.

In our framework, the internal forces constitute the life space of public institutions. These include the employee's individual differences such as skills and ability, level of work expertise, and role prescriptions. Role prescriptions are identified as the things that people who work for the institutions are expected to do. The intent is to develop such prescriptions which will contribute most effectively to the goals of the institution. Once the role prescriptions are established, they impose limitations on personnel procedures. The life space of institutions is influenced by nativistic values and assumptions. Chicanos are excluded from prestigious positions due to personal appearance, language accent, and other characteristics dissimilar from the Anglo's accepted social norms.

Recruitment as the first aspect of the pre-employment phase looks at the pool of prospective candidates. This is followed by screening which involves obtaining information on candidates through various techniques such as personal applications and interviews, reference checks, and other requirements. The last component of this phase involves the selection of candidates who have the potential to contribute to the institution. The recruitment of Chicanos in public institutions has been easy in one respect, and extremely difficult in another. Chicanos are easily found for menial task jobs. In fact, the majority of Chicano workers are still employed in the lowest paying jobs, which obviously reinforces nativistic values. The employment statistics of the federal government support this comment.[69] Subsequently, Chicanos are either qualified for the less significant jobs, or they are systematically excluded from the selection process.

Many public employers have come to the conclusion that if they concentrate their efforts on "recruiting minorities," this qualifies them as "equal opportunity employers." If more minorities applied for jobs, they feel that the number of minority employees would automatically increase. But this is not true because many of the minority people are rejected from the beginning due to the qualifications imposed on the jobs by the employers, without considering whether the qualifications are discriminatory. This was and still is the most common way Chicanos have been excluded from the work force.

Testing as part of the selection process has been challenged on the grounds of racial, ethnic, and class bias. As Knowles and Prewitt express: "Often . . . written tests are used to assist in rating applicants. These tests are almost always designed to test ability in the context of White society"[70] The area of testing has been revolutionized by the United States Supreme Court's decision on *Duke Power v. Griggs* in 1971. In this case, a black employee challenged the validity of the company's test he took for a position, and the court consequently ruled that job tests such as the one in question have the effect of screening out blacks and other minorities; thus, non-job-related testing is illegal under Title VII.[71]

If the selection process purportedly searches for the "right kind" of "Mexican American," these assimilated individuals are most often sought because they have adopted the Anglo values and would, therefore, easily meet the preconceived image that departments have of "desired" minorities.

The structural and functional facilitators include task specialization and staffing which assist in the establishment of role prescriptions. The functional facilitators involve in-service training and development programs, and employee wages and benefits. In-service training programs for Chicanos have suffered from a lack of administrative support as evidenced by limited financing, staffing, facilities, and program provisions. In a report of the Governor's Task Force on Equal Rights in Pennsylvania, it was stated that "In practice, [the] training emphasis has been directed toward training the White male. As a result, the system has encouraged the pursuit of higher degrees by the 'favored few professionals'."[72]

Once individuals enter the institutions, they will be effective and successful as long as their behavior is consistent and correlates with the respective role prescriptions. For the Chicanos, however, to be effective and successful is fraught with obstacles due to nativism which has historically caused them to suppress their cultural identity. With the 1970s, Chicano public employee organizations are emerging to provide an essential base for cultural expression as well as to alleviate discrimination within the institutions.

Performance Evaluation

Techniques used to provide an evaluation of the performance which occurs between the role behavior and role prescription are affected by nativism through attitudes and criteria underlining job performance and appraisal of promotability. This is one of the reasons why Chicanos are relegated to low-paying positions and classifications. As the Commission on Civil Rights has found, "the subjective nature of most performance evaluation allows for discrimination" and is one of the major barriers to equal opportunity.[73]

Summary and Recommendations

The concept of nativism has been identified as the underlying concept existing in public institutions which excludes Chicanos in contemporary society. The major areas of this article included, wherever possible, examples of how nativism has been institutionalized in the personnel process, especially as it relates to the Chicano experience. It is our point of view that until the dominant society addresses itself to the nativism which manifests itself in pejorative stereotypic attitudes, the issue of racism will prevail as a form of institutional oppression. Current token remedies to alleviate discriminatory practices will only serve to reify the concepts of "democracy" as providing equal opportunities to all its citizens.

A critical analysis must be made of nativism before any further remedial action is taken to alleviate discriminatory practices. Some of the actions which would promote equal employment opportunities for Chicanos are: (1) re-evaluation of Civil Service job requirements at the entry and promotion levels; (2) increase of the proportional distribution of Chicano employees throughout public organizations; (3) utilization of the experience and ability of minority administrators in areas other than minority-related programs.

The American Society for Public Administration can contribute to the eradication of nativism by encouraging its membership and schools and programs in public administration to insure that the concept of nativism be taught in such institutions as the basis of institutional racism, especially in the Southwest; that the concept of Chicano be taught and clearly identified with U.S. citizens and residents of Mexican ancestry who adhere to political, social, and economic self-determination and *not* with stereotypic nativistic response associated with pejorative racist attitudes; that ASPA recognize the Chicano Association of Public Administrators (CAPA) as a formal subgroup and support the efforts of its membership; and that the enrollment of Chicano students within these schools and programs of public administration correspond to the population base in which they are located.

Maria Dolores Diaz de Krofcheck and Carlos Jackson,
School of Public Administration, University of Southern California ∾

The Role of Black Colleges in Public Affairs Education

Many voices are proclaiming that all institutions of higher learning must face boldly the challenge that they become public service agencies capable of providing leadership in a troubled society. There is, however, no unanimity in this proclamation. Some see it as being inconsistent with the university and/or college's role—that of teaching, research, discovery, and transmission of knowledge. Others feel that the college has an obligation not only to recognize urban and rural social problems but to be aggressive in their prevention and in their ultimate elimination.

For the authors the answer lies somewhere between the two; and we would agree with those who view the college, black or white, as a public service institution. Its primary and most important function is to feed into the life stream a new generation of highly motivated, enlightened, and responsible citizens, entrepreneurs, and specialists capable of facing the personal and social problems of their age with resolution, judgment, and vision.[74]

This is a tough assignment and sometimes risky, especially for black institutions of higher learning. But there is an undisputed fact that black colleges can and must rise to the challenge. That is what this article is about. In approaching this topic the authors will discuss: (1) the organizational structure—the explicit role of black colleges in public affairs education present and future; (2) how the role can be implemented; (3) the obstacles to fulfilling this role and responsibility; and (4) recommendations.

Organization and Structure

Perhaps the myriad of bad conditions facing urban and rural minorities proliferates until it curdles the initiative of black colleges. These conditions include: (a) hungry children; (b) economic exploitation, underemployment, unemployment, and employment under intolerable circumstances; (c) genocide education; (d) inadequate health and welfare services; (e) lack of recreational facilities and activities; (f) inequities in law enforcement; (g) unjust treatment by communications media; (h) poor or no transportation; (i) absentee and/or, if available, hostile landlords; (j) rodent-infested neighborhoods; (k) few human services; (l) urban decay; (m) energy conservation; (n) sociological conflicts; (o) pollution; and (p) disparities in municipal services in urban sectors and poor rural areas compared with other sections of the community. The implications are many, for business, welfare services, industry, government, and, above all, education.

It is an unrealistic assumption to expect the historically black college with its traditional and narrowly defined role, focus, and organizational structure to impact positively on such far-reaching and deep-seeded needs. It is time to clear up the axiom that the college has always responded to social needs unless it be clearly recognized that this response has traditionally been made by and large in terms of the indirect effect of scholarly productivity and the augmentations of academic programs to serve new manpower needs.

People have lost faith in their government and their colleges, too. There is a harshness in the tones of the populace who declare that the institutions of higher learning cannot afford the luxury of the ivory or ebony tower image and must become sophisticated, systematized, and apply taxonomy creatively and wisely to the resolution of society's problems.

The extent to which a college may successfully cope with complex problems depends to a large degree on the efficacy of a college's courage and educational endeavor to set up a public affairs education program. There has been a mushrooming of urban studies centers and a sprinkling of urban planning programs on black college campuses (see Table 13.3). The burning question at this juncture is to what extent these programs have actually impacted upon the local planning process in, for example, low-income housing or mass transit facilities which more often than not go unbuilt.

If the planners are doing busy work and the municipal leaders absorbed in bureaucratic minuets, black colleges can ill afford to turn their backs in disgust and indignation, for they may be the only force left in the community which can press for its ultimate rehabilitation. The writers, rather than being disparaging of their efforts, are pinpointing the need for black colleges to be responsible for the improvement and rehabilitation of *all* the people and their *total* environs. They must be just as responsible for providing technical expertise in developing policy, feasibility, marketing site location, layout, auxiliary services, and amendatories for an Early Childhood Development Center as they are in staffing such a facility. They must assure that what is on the public planner's drawing board reflects the most viable alternatives synthesized from a divergence of viewpoints.

Currently, however, few black colleges have themselves been given to planning in order to analyze the manner in which *they* make decisions, arrive at organizational structures, provide finances for and reflect people's views and needs in the formulation of public policy in behalf of education.

TABLE 13.3 Public Affairs, Planning, and Administration Course Offerings at Historically Black Colleges and Universities*

	Admin. of Justice	Criminal Justice	Finance	Hospital Facilities Mgmt.	Industrial Admin.	Mgmt.	Office Admin.	Police Science	Public Admin.	Urban Affairs	Urban Regional Planning	Urban Mgmt.	Urban Community Development
1. Alabama A&M													
2. Alabama State						●				●			
3. Atlanta University									○ ⊙				
4. Bishop						●				●			
5. Bishop State							●						
6. Bowie						●			☆				
7. Central State			●							●			
8. Clark			●		●								
9. Coppin								●					
10. Delaware State						●	●		●	●			
11. Federal City			●			●			★	★	☆		
12. Fisk												●	
13. Florida A&M			●		●	●							
14. Florida Memorial		●											
15. Grambling						●				●			
16. Hampton			⊗			●							
17. Howard			●	☆		★			☆	☆	☆		
18. Kentucky State									☆	☆			
19. Langston						●							
20. Malcolm X				●						●			

(continues)

TABLE 13.3 *(continued)*

	Admin. of Justice	Criminal Justice	Finance	Hospital Facilities Mgmt.	Industrial Admin.	Mgmt.	Office Admin.	Police Science	Public Admin.	Urban Affairs	Urban Regional Planning	Urban Mgmt.	Urban Community Development
21. Morgan						★				★	☆	★	
22. Norfolk State			●		●								
23. North Carolina Central								●					
24. Paine			●		●								
25. Prairie View		●	●										
26. Rust					●								
27. Savannah State		●	●			★	●						
28. Shaw						●			●	●			
29. Southern Baton Rouge						●							
30. Southern New Orleans													
31. Tennessee State		●				●	●			●			
32. Texas Southern	⊗					★	●		⊙	★	⊙		□
33. Virginia Union										●			
34. West Virginia State		●	☆			●							
35. Wilberforce						●							
36. Xavier							●						

*Derived from the *Moton Guide to American Colleges with a Black Heritage*, published by the Moton Consortium on Admissions and Financial Aid, 2001 S. St., N.W., Washington, D.C. 20009, and the TACTICS Black Colleges and Community Development Program Conference Evaluation, June, 1973.

Code:

○   Graduate program leading to MA with concentration including internship

●   Undergraduate major

☆   Graduate

□   Two-year program with internship; offered as sociology option

★   Graduate and undergraduate

⊙ or ⊗   Anticipated start-up September 1974

White and black educational institutions in this country evolved over a long period of history without wide consideration of alternatives, and without the application of systematic and logical reasoning to the method and manner in which policy is made, revenue is sought, and programs implemented to carry out the many operations of our complex system—including setting up schools of public affairs and/or public administration.

The word structure as applied to a college or to public service usually connotes the arrangement of parts of a body. It may also encompass the interrelation of discrete parts as dominated by the general character of the whole. The rationale applied to black colleges would necessitate a careful analysis of the purposes of each of the major portions of the institutional system followed by a method of determining the relationship of any one portion of the system—here the public affairs education department—to any other part of the college.

The explicit role of the black college is that it should not only serve as a center of black culture, but should as well provide education and training generic to the solution of society's problems. It should offer its students options. This in itself is difficult, because for so long blacks have had so few options available to them.

Black colleges and universities must act and function as integral parts of the communities where they are located. Historically, some of these institutions have insulated themselves socially, economically, and politically from neighboring communities and so called "ghettos." Black colleges must lose their preoccupation with their historical status and accept themselves in their current roles as temporary, solution-oriented, inter-institutional structures.

One way to remain viable in the highly competitive business of higher education is for black colleges to organize on either a state or regional basis to specialize in particular areas and facets of program/policy emphasis. Models are presently being set up on longitudinal bases subject to testing (see Figure 13.2).

In the area of housing and community development, for example, the network would be comprised of between four (regional) and 22 (state-by-state) institutions. The number of members would vary dependent upon whether the program area was of such significance as to warrant more than sub-state regional consideration. It should be noted that multi-state regional organizations offer the most latitude by limiting the probability of conflict and drain on the same resources, as well as by increasing the possibility for impact and exposure of the college as a "special purpose" policy science institution. The basis of statewide organization would be such that each of the special policy interests of a particular state could be addressed by one of the state's public or private institutions.

The coordination of this network would be provided by a "center" located at a sponsoring college with established resources and capabilities in the particular program/policy area. The function of that "center" would be to identify critical program/policy issues, distribute program/policy information to member institutions, disseminate research findings of member colleges, provide linkage between the colleges and national program-related organizations and offices, and lend technical assistance in conducting research and demonstration projects.

226

Region I
Delaware
District of Columbia
Illinois
Maryland
Michigan
Ohio
Pennsylvania
Virginia
West Virginia

MICHIGAN
SHAW COLLEGE
AT DETROIT

PENNSYLVANIA

OHIO
CENTRAL STATE
UNIVERSITY
WILBERFORCE
UNIVERSITY

LINCOLN UNIVERSITY
CHEYNEY STATE
COLLEGE
MD.
DEL.
DELAWARE STATE
COLLEGE

MALCOLM X
COLLEGE
WEST VIRGINIA
BOWIE STATE
COLLEGE
DISTRICT OF
COLUMBIA
BALTIMORE
MORGAN STATE COLLEGE
COPPIN STATE COLLEGE

ILLINOIS
WEST VIRGINIA
STATE COLLEGE
HOWARD UNIVERSITY
FEDERAL CITY
COLLEGE
MARYLAND STATE
COLLEGE

VIRGINIA
BLUEFIELD STATE
COLLEGE
ST. PAUL'S
COLLEGE
HAMPTON INSTITUTE
VIRGINIA STATE
COLLEGE

RICHMOND
VIRGINIA UNION
UNIVERSITY
NORFOLK STATE
COLLEGE

Region II
Kentucky
North Carolina
South Carolina
Tennessee

NORTH CAROLINA A&T
STATE UNIVERSITY

KENTUCKY STATE
COLLEGE
NORTH CAROLINA
COLLEGE
RALEIGH
ST. AUGUSTINE'S
COLLEGE
SHAW UNIVERSITY

KENTUCKY
WINSTON-SALEM
WINSTON-SALEM STATE
ELIAZBETH CITY
STATE UNIVERSITY

LANE COLLEGE
KNOXVILLE COLLEGE
MORRISTOWN
COLLEGE
LIVINGSTONE
NORTH CAROLINA
CENTRAL UNIVERSITY
GREENSBORO
BENNETT COLLEGE
A&I COLLEGE

LE MOYNE-OWEN
COLLEGE
TENNESSEE
BARBER-SCOTIA
NORTH CAROLINA

FRIENDSHIP
JR. COLLEGE
SOUTH CAROLINA
FAYETTEVILLE STATE

NASHVILLE
FISK UNIVERSITY
CHARLOTTE
JOHNSON C. SMITH

TENNESSEE A&I
UNIVERSITY
CLAFLIN
COLLEGE
MORRIS
COLLEGE

MEHARRY MEDICAL
COLLEGE
VOORHEES
COLLEGE

TENNESSEE STATE
UNIVERSITY
COLUMBIA
ALLEN UNIVERSITY
BENEDICT COLLEGE

SOUTH CAROLINA
STATE COLLEGE

FIGURE 13.2   Regional Clustering of Black Colleges

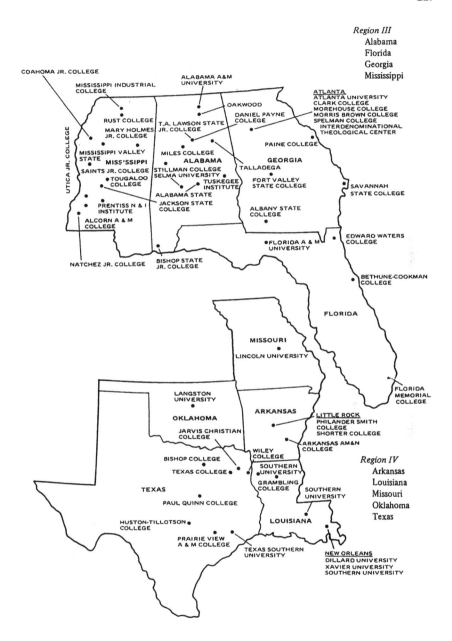

Region III
Alabama
Florida
Georgia
Mississippi

COAHOMA JR. COLLEGE

MISSISSIPPI INDUSTRIAL
COLLEGE

ALABAMA A&M
UNIVERSITY

OAKWOOD

DANIEL PAYNE
COLLEGE

ATLANTA
ATLANTA UNIVERSITY
CLARK COLLEGE
MOREHOUSE COLLEGE
MORRIS BROWN COLLEGE
SPELMAN COLLEGE
INTERDENOMINATIONAL
THEOLOGICAL CENTER

RUST COLLEGE

T.A. LAWSON STATE
JR. COLLEGE

MARY HOLMES
JR. COLLEGE

UTICA JR. COLLEGE

MISSISSIPPI VALLEY
STATE

MISS'SSIPPI

MILES COLLEGE

PAINE COLLEGE

ALABAMA

GEORGIA

SAINTS JR. COLLEGE

TOUGALOO
COLLEGE

STILLMAN COLLEGE
SELMA UNIVERSITY

TALLADEGA

TUSKEGEE
INSTITUTE

FORT VALLEY
STATE COLLEGE

SAVANNAH
STATE COLLEGE

PRENTISS N & I
INSTITUTE

ALABAMA STATE

JACKSON STATE
COLLEGE

ALBANY STATE
COLLEGE

ALCORN A & M
COLLEGE

EDWARD WATERS
COLLEGE

FLORIDA A & M
UNIVERSITY

NATCHEZ JR. COLLEGE

BISHOP STATE
JR. COLLEGE

BETHUNE-COOKMAN
COLLEGE

FLORIDA

MISSOURI

LINCOLN UNIVERSITY

FLORIDA
MEMORIAL
COLLEGE

LANGSTON
UNIVERSITY

ARKANSAS

OKLAHOMA

LITTLE ROCK
PHILANDER SMITH
COLLEGE
SHORTER COLLEGE

JARVIS CHRISTIAN
COLLEGE

ARKANSAS AM&N
COLLEGE

WILEY
COLLEGE

BISHOP COLLEGE

SOUTHERN
UNIVERSITY

Region IV
Arkansas
Louisiana
Missouri
Oklahoma
Texas

TEXAS COLLEGE

GRAMBLING
COLLEGE

TEXAS

SOUTHERN
UNIVERSITY

PAUL QUINN COLLEGE

HUSTON-TILLOTSON
COLLEGE

LOUISIANA

PRAIRIE VIEW
A & M COLLEGE

TEXAS SOUTHERN
UNIVERSITY

NEW ORLEANS
DILLARD UNIVERSITY
XAVIER UNIVERSITY
SOUTHERN UNIVERSITY

Winston-Salem State University, for example, has completed developmental research for the establishment of a Center for Housing and Community Development. Although its focus will initially be directed toward the development of a housing and community development curriculum with emphasis on certification for housing managers, inter-institutional linkages are considered with Temple University, which is investigating the management and structural consideration of housing for the elderly and handicapped; Texas Southern University, which is spearheading university acquisition of the management of the CUNEY Homes, a public housing project adjacent to the campus; Bishop College, whose focus is planning, design, and management of "New Town" community development, using Flower Mound as its laboratory; Southern University, Baton Rouge, which is developing para-professional training modules in housing; and Shaw College of Detroit, whose programmatic focus is the development of municipal acquisition and disposition alternatives for HUD-owned properties (Figure 13.3).

The decision on the part of Winston-Salem State University (WSSU) to pursue the development of a Housing and Community Development Center was made

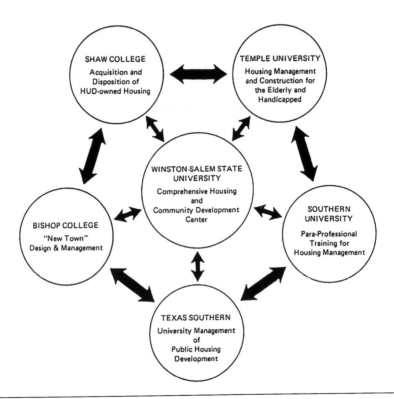

FIGURE 13.3   Winston-Salem State University Housing and Community
Development Center Possible Inter-Institutional Linkages

in light of extensive surveys of curricula offerings and demonstration projects of other universities within the North Carolina State University system; statewide and regional commitment of resources to the support of such a center from public, private, and non-profit housing interests; and the determination of the efficacy of such a center in light of national and regional HUD policy.

To date, WSSU has received monies from the Office of Housing Management, Department of Housing and Urban Development, and the Ford Foundation for the planning and execution of its initial course in "Housing Management," as well as the subsequent planning of the entire curriculum. That survey developed for WSSU a programmatic agenda which inter- and co-related with the other universities within the system, as well as identified a distinctly unique focus for the institution's developmental planning. Such a commitment from HUD and the Ford Foundation was based on their willingness to assist the college in the development of feasible and viable institutional goals which also address national policy issues of vested interest to each. Figure 13.3 also points up how important technology transfer between institutions can be. Once each institution engages in its own distinctive endeavor, its findings in overlapping program concerns will be of secondary and in some cases primary value to the other cooperating institutions.

But, let us not digress too much from the explanation of the model. The special interest or special purpose status of the college would be based on the determination of areas of interest and priority for that given geographical location. Its designation, resulting from an extensive community needs assessment and strategic forecasting conducted by each college, should neither restrict nor be viewed as a restrictive mechanism which limits the college and its focus.

Rather, it should be viewed as a vehicle by which an entire process may be taught; a concept to be expanded upon later. Taking Texas Southern University, for example, its determination as a "Special Interest University for Urban Programming" by the State of Texas is broad enough to enable its venturing into a host of public policy/service areas. From this identification of objectives, prospective students, faculty, and staff; interested foundations; corporations; federal, state, and local governmental departments; alumni; and national and local agencies and organizations would be better able to determine the institutional direction of the college or university.

This fact has great significance for staffing patterns and funding strategies. In each case, the efforts at interface would by necessity have to be more directed and specific, Resultingly, faculty, organizations, and governments that share a common program/policy area interest will gravitate toward a particular college by virtue of the nature and quality of the course offerings and data generated.

Such a mechanism would also serve to attract students interested in particular areas of programming. This, conceivably, would add elasticity to the educational services being provided by Winston-Salem State University, for example, and enable it to draw students from a wider population base, i.e., individuals interested in housing and community development, code enforcement, regional and metropolitan planning, etc., as well as service delivery and administrative practitioners within the present housing and community development system who desire career up-grading.

Carrying the illustration further, such a specification would require a reorientation of trustees, administrators, faculty, and students alike. Rather than continuing as a strict "arts and letters" institution providing a broad-brush orientation through a host of core courses and areas of emphasis, a college may wish to continue to be termed a liberal arts university, but develop a program/policy emphasis in housing and community development. As such an institution, it would engage in research and development directed toward the generation of information and data of significance to the housing and community development policy sciences, locally as well as nationally. It would be a function of the "Center" to urge a comprehensiveness of program/policy focus among its network members. As Tansik and Radnor suggest:

> We must develop an organizational policy which recognizes the autonomy and singularity of each of our institutions in terms of their goals and their capacities, and that which gauges their worth on how effective they are.[75]

How the Role Can Be Carried Out

Several black colleges have assumed a leadership role in an enlarged program of community development, urban affairs, and rural programming. Texas Southern University, for example, speaks of setting up a School of Communication and Human Understanding.[76] A major program unit is also to be established—School of Public Affairs and an outreach internship program—for preparation of urban professionals for entry at key points in the university itself, and in local, state, and national decision-making agencies—governmental, corporate, and others. This is a comprehensive program with all facets of the institution embracing some aspect of the increasing urban needs brought in by the rapid growth of technology.

Within the College

When one considers that education is not for education's sake alone, and that upon completion of a prescribed curriculum at any university most individuals expect to engage in either governmental, industrial, or private enterprise, it becomes necessary for colleges to assume the responsibility of providing students an understanding of the interplay between these three spheres. This understanding is even more critical for black students whose experiential base generally does not naturally afford them such an orientation. What follows is the component of the design which makes understandable the "system," provides for the development of leadership, generates needed information and orientations to program/policy-related matters, and provides a resource base that can be utilized by governments, businesses, community organizations, and ordinary citizens.

Creating the Atmosphere

Prior to any institution's determination to become an agent of the development of policy sciences, it must first of all look at itself as a policy-making system. "Innovative policy recommendations stand very small chances of being carefully considered, adopted, implemented, and revised unless the policy-making system develops new capacities for creativity, consideration, implementation, and feedback."[77] New patterns of decision making are called for. In those instances where only a few have traditionally had the responsibility and authority to make decisions, that power will have to be shared. Just as the power is shared, so too are the liabilities and the shortcomings of the decisions. This new pattern of decision making will identify institutional needs and requirements that will warrant changes in many of the elements of the policy-making system. As has been experienced by Shaw University and Texas Southern University, these changes have meant new configurations in personnel, structure, "rules of the game," equipment, and, perhaps most important of all, "policy-making culture."

Thorough internal analysis has revealed for these and several other schools that changes in institutional output with respect to their being able to effect a meaningful number of policy decisions—which might relate to innovative and non-traditional education, urban planning, housing, etc.—could only be achieved through changes in the performance of the whole institution as a policy-making system. Therefore priority was placed on improving the overall policy-making capacity of the institution rather than on one or two isolated policy outputs.

Curriculum

Because most black colleges are undergraduate institutions, the focus of the design is toward undergraduate education. The logical linkage to development on the graduate level will become evident, shortly.

Freshman and sophomore curricula offerings could remain essentially the same with minor adaptive changes in the manner in which core information is taught. For example, grammar would be taught while utilizing and reinforcing the basic tenets of set theory. Composition courses would be based on writing requirements from other departments (banking, sociology, biology). Research courses would be designed around pragmatic and utilitarian concerns of local and national policy significance such as the identification of local ramifications of a national land-use policy, the cost-benefit analysis of curbside as opposed to alley pick-up of refuse, the feasibility of the installation of a multi-county water and sewer project as opposed to an independent system installation.

The thrust of the curriculum design after that period would lie in teaching the "planning-implementation-evaluation" process. This process would be provided using the program/policy area as a vehicle. Thus, as is the case with Winston-Salem State University, third- and fourth-year curricula would be planned which reinforced the development and dissemination of information in the area of housing and community development.

Regular course offerings would be developed which provide students a sound theoretical undergirding in the program area of interest. In addition, seminar series, internship programs, demonstration projects, and applied research would be built into the fabric of the entire accredited program of that institution.

Because resources are to be drawn, for example, from the various components of the institution, community, and housing industry, it is not difficult to decide upon that activity or set of activities which meets both the informational needs of the jurisdiction and the capability of the institution. Such an interchange provides students positive role models, direction, and actual experience in decision making and policy analysis, formulation, etc. From such a well-integrated developmental team, direction and monitor is provided the programs and the students; this becomes the basis for realistically expecting students to assume a responsible role in the planning, implementation, and evaluation of each activity engaged in by the institution.

Other Structural Changes

The structure of many black colleges calls for radical changes to encompass viable programs for training careers in public affairs. Special institutes are planned for public officials who need to be provided information to impact upon and alter chronic or festering rural and urban problems. Improved training programs for local government leaders and workers such as clerks, planning board members, city councils, etc., too, are advocated. Many of them are not equipped to handle the multiplicity of complex problems they now must face; so the universities must find ways to serve the varied needs of these public servants.

University without walls; week-end colleges; continuing education for para-professionals, the veteran, and other adults are all a part of a vigorous public administration program. Para-professionals are often dealing with problems of day care, social disorganization in the inner cities, meeting minimum national needs in rural areas, etc. Black colleges would do well to focus the training for this group on the particular content of their jobs, but at the same time provide a broad educational component which could lead to upward mobility of the non-professional.

The recent Carnegie Commission report supports the enhancement of other channels, including on-the-job training, proprietary schools, education by off-campus extension courses, and national service opportunities.[78]

Black colleges in developing mentalities for thoughtful, thorough public affairs programs should delve deeply into operations research. They should develop mechanisms to concert community organizations and professional planning bodies, pre-professionals, academic researchers, and practitioners from other disciplines to design and implement new innovative projects aimed toward social change. Such activities could serve as a base for sound policy analysis, determination of the use of time and monies, etc.

Recommendations

A variety of new academic ventures and models are necessary to train a cadre of people to perform well and comfortably the public affairs educational functions.

1. *It is recommended that a human services curriculum be included in this effort, as public administration has important contributions to make in human services; such a curriculum is well within the focus in public administration on planning and policy making in complex systems.*

Since human service is a new field or a new approach which relies firmly on (but in no way duplicates) other fields or other services, considerable care must be taken to fashion training which incorporates specialized knowledge and problem solving, but within an integrated framework. Somehow the academic "pie" will have to be fashioned differently to include a holistic human service training approach. Such a curriculum could include specialized training in:

1. Politics, power structures, and policies in human service policy processes and networks;
2. The methods, procedures, and processes of planning and policy making in human service systems, including regional planning for individual services and integration of services;
3. Management of the human service enterprise, including examination of the changing role of individualized service in integrated human service programs and strategies and methods of organizational change which accompany new modes of delivery;
4. Interagency relationships in multi-service delivery programs and in networks of independent agencies; and
5. Models of delivery in human services programming and alternative delivery system for the human service.[79]

2. *Consistent with the paradigm of human resource development and human services, it is further recommended that such curricula provide a vehicle that enables students to receive experience in alternative modes of communication.*

Activities must be developed which create real learning situations in which the student can confidently make the conversion from being "managed" to considering himself a "manager;" from being planned "for or against" to being a "planner." Such a status entails a facility in varying modes of written and verbal communications; proficiency in managing people, minorities as well as non-minorities; and technical competence.

These situations would provide the opportunity for the natural, generally untapped, leadership ability of the students not only to be identified, but also nurtured and enhanced. What the students choose to do with that information would be their own business. What the college would have provided is a real situation from which students could discover their own competencies. The choice after that point would be personal.

Following our example further, at WSSU, situations and activities would be designed in which students would have to write and speak about housing and community development. Arrangements would be made for students to make formal presentations of feasibility studies, research findings, etc., to regional planning boards, housing authorities, community organizations. Education and engineering majors would develop simulations that varied in complexity from those that elementary school-aged children could learn from to those that could be used to bring understanding between two local and regional planning groups. Thus, communication would not be only about the hypothetical, but also about abstractions and pragmatic which have specificity in the real world. Versatility, creativity, innovation, and responsibility would be key because the situations would preclude that to be the case.

Carrying the illustration further, rather than dispensing with the "down-home" or "ghetto" dialects most blacks come to college with, students would start to identify for themselves the situations when those modes of conversing are not only useful but necessary in order to derive the data which must be translated into "proper" English for broader impact, consumption, and effectiveness. As well, they would discover that the reverse of that process is just as essential in getting the legislative and program-related information out to the "people."

Moreover, these new learning situations would avail the student the opportunity to identify for himself the aspect(s) of the delivery system for which his personality and host of skills are best suited. Skill development would be based on the task or function the student would be expected to perform in a given activity. This non-threatening situation would provide an added incentive for achievement and excellence. The responsibility for the success or failure of a project or venture would be tied not only to the team's (practitioner, student, academic, citizen) effectiveness in executing its task, but more importantly to those students' effectiveness in learning to manage that entire system, which enabled them to complete their task.

3. *Intern programs, demonstration projects, and applied research must be tied one to another and integrally with priority program/policy needs of the attendant jurisdictional community.*

Consequently, the findings, outcomes, accomplishments, and information would have utility not only to the college but also to the local, regional, and state governments; businesses, civic organizations, etc. It is here that actual participation by the American Society for Public Administration is sought to assist in identifying local and jurisdictional needs as well as resources that may be called upon to assist in execution of these projects.

4. *In order to accomplish the above, it is recommended that alternative reward systems be developed by educational institutions which positively sanction active leadership on the part of faculty.*

Faculty, too, would be expected to engage in comprehensive planning, identify problems and resources, direct solution approaches, and monitor research, internship, and demonstration procedures. These activities would logically become the basis of innovation and creativity and provide situations in which academicians, practitioners, and students begin to collectively program toward the solution of common problems. Through it, the dynamics of a reciprocal system of responsibility become not only theorized but practiced.

The permanence of the black college enables the process to continue. Students will come and go, but the process, *the teaching mode,* remains as the college assembles a wealth of pragmatic and functional information. Such activities would open communication and develop viable working relationships between entities whose lines of contact have in some instances been strained, such as between professor and student, between the college and government, between the college and the community and—most importantly—between the government and the community.

The thrust of research and demonstration projects would, by its nature, assist municipal governments in identifying community needs, problems, and the resources with which to address both. Services provided may range from transportation feasibility studies to the development and sponsorship of weekend training workshops for local, county, state, or regional municipal workers, to programming consumer information "spots" for broadcast on public service TV.

A logical outgrowth of such a process is that students, upon graduation, will have a clearer understanding of the system within which they find themselves operating. The type of graduate program to be pursued from that point would be based more definitively on their assessed strengths and competencies. Such an undergraduate mode would also offer black undergraduate schools an acknowledged basis from which to develop graduate programming that is distinctive from course offerings elsewhere.

5. *Prior to the establishment of new schools, programs, and degree offerings, existing programs should be closely examined as to the efficacy of their conversion.*

The previous chart indicates that a sound basis for education in public affairs, planning, and administration is already existent on more than a third of all black college campuses. It would be wise to test the utility of each or combinations thereof in order to determine how best to respond to specific and local resource demands. Such an analysis would allow the school adequate time to develop program linkages, overcome political hurdles, and assure the legal integrity of their planned endeavors. Such a redeployment of personnel and financial resources would also appreciably decrease the cost and increase the effectiveness of the planning phase.

6. It is recommended that the National Association of Schools of Public Affairs and Administration (NASPAA) take the initiative to assist black colleges and universities in the design and redesign of public affairs programs.

With the number of black elected officials in the United States having more than doubled in the last four years from 1,185 in 1969 to 2,621 in April 1973,[80] there is developing a "corresponding increase in the demand for professionally trained minority group members at all levels of municipal government."[81] Located in urban and rural sectors from which many of the black elected officials derive their support, the movement of black colleges into public affairs, planning, and administration education seems more than adequately justified and supportable. If that trend continues augmented by the realization in responsible local governments that there is need for minority perspectives and racial balance in municipal governmental decision making, the demand for skilled and experienced minority participation will become increasingly more crucial.

This is particularly significant because in recent years will over 70 percent of all black college graduates receiving undergraduate degrees did so from historically black colleges and universities. If there is any truth to the thought that minorities entering undergraduate or graduate programs in public affairs and administration come with inadequate skill bases with which to handle course offerings, then that issue presently demands to be faced squarely as it receives policy consideration by NASPAA.

7. It is further recommended that existing Conferences of Minority Public Administrators (COMPAs) in conjunction with local ASPA chapters urge their membership to actively support:

A.   ASPA-sponsored seminars and regular local meetings on black college campuses,
B.   student ASPA chapters on black college campuses,
C.   recruitment of ASPA members from black college campuses,
D.   identification of related professional and special interest organizations as part of the on-going planning, implementation, and evaluation process,
E.   exploration of state and local officials taking the initiative in involving more educational institutions, both black and white, in local community decision making, and
F.   utilization of ASPA members on both a full- and part-time basis to expand public affairs programs at black colleges and universities.

Conclusion

Black colleges and universities, in seeing themselves as resources, are intent on becoming forums which bring together community people, who are both fearful and distrustful of local government, with public administrators and planners who tend to be the source of such feelings. Provided, as a result, will be equalitarian systems of information exchange which hopefully will form the basis of enlightened and responsible policy formulation.

Moreover, the methodologies would be provided by which black colleges would be given the entree to furnish their students the exposure to facets of the system which have generally been categorically denied them. This would further serve to proselytize the broader educational community to the merits of meaningful integrated planning.

It is to be noted that these recommendations deal not only with the symptoms of problems expressed by students, institutions, and governments alike; but they also focus on possible root causes of limited exposure of blacks to the operational bases of the "system" and likewise those operational bases to blacks. Such a relationship might well mark the beginning of a new educative process, not only for blacks, but for the entire public affairs community. Clearly much of the foregoing may seem like a tall order; but while there is a void, there is movement.

Cheryl Dobbins and Dollie R. Walker

Conference of Minority Public Administrators

The Conference of Minority Public Administrators (COMPA) is an affiliate of the American Society for Public Administration. Organized following the 1970 annual ASPA meeting, COMPA has identified organizational objectives which encompass two broad areas of concern. The first of these is improvement of the quality of public services affecting the lives and well-being of minority citizens. The second is expansion of opportunities for members of minority groups to assume leadership roles in public service. Program activities which have been undertaken by COMPA have fallen within these broad areas.

For example, as one of its regular activities, a COMPA chapter conducts workshops involving minority administrators in federal, state, and local governments; academicians; students; and other interested persons. These workshops are providing opportunities for fruitful dialogue among the participants, addressing some of the unique problems confronting minority administrators, as well as strategies for extending spheres of influence, for institutionalizing minority perspectives in the conduct of government, and for sensitizing policy makers to the differential impact of certain policy decisions on minority citizens. As an added feature of the most recent workshop, representatives of public agencies and universities were invited to conduct interviews with participants interested in employment. Based on initial response to it, this feature will probably be retained and expanded. Examples of other COMPA activities related to its over-all objectives appear elsewhere in this discussion.

COMPA to some extent regards its second objective as further articulation of the first. This is because it firmly believes the quality of public services to any population is affected by the representativeness of the delivery systems of the perspectives and concerns of that population. The public service delivery systems in this country—federal, state, and local—have never reflected this kind of representativeness, nor will they be able to as long as there are barriers denying access of minorities to the levels of government at which substantive planning and decision making occur.

COMPA is in its fourth year. In a number of ways it is a considerably more viable organization than it was as recently as one year ago. At the same time, it has not been completely successful in putting to rest the question, ". . . but what is COMPA doing?" Whether or not it ever will remains to be seen, since the question, itself, is more a function of the knowledge and expectations of the asker than it is of what COMPA actually is or is not doing. In any case, it would probably be agreed even by members of COMPA that, while it has made significant progress, its accomplishments to date have not been a full reflection of its potential for developing and conducting coordinated, output-oriented programs in pursuit of the above-stated objectives.

This discussion will consider briefly some of the factors which, in the opinion of the author, have slowed COMPA's realization of its potential, how these are being overcome, some of its accomplishments and, finally, what appear to be its prospects for the future. An initial comment, however, on COMPA's governance and membership seems appropriate.

Governance and Membership

COMPA is governed by a national executive board which has responsibilities for implementation of national COMPA programs and for providing guidance to and coordination of local efforts through regional coordinators in each of six regions. Additionally, the executive board represents the official liaison with ASPA. The national chairman of COMPA is a member of the ASPA National Council, and one member of the ASPA Council sits on the COMPA Executive Board.

Local chapters have been organized and are operative in several cities, including Washington, Los Angeles, New York, Detroit, Cincinnati, Kansas City, and Atlanta. Among cities in which chapters are expected to begin functioning in the very near future are Boston and Richmond, Virginia.

Full membership privileges are extended to all persons who support the goals and programs of the organization and who are members of ASPA. At the present time, COMPA has 245 active members, including a large number of persons who have joined over the past few months. This trend is expected to continue, as

COMPA simultaneously develops its program capability and recruits new members, both inside and outside ASPA.

Development of the Organization

The normal problems faced by new organizations with limited resources were aggravated for COMPA by the climate in which it was conceived. COMPA emerged out of the frustrations of a small group of minority members of ASPA who perceived a reluctance on the part of the larger organization to direct its attention in any meaningful way to the special needs and concerns of minorities as administrators, as potential administrators, and as consumers of public services. It was felt that, as a professional organization in the field, ASPA was not measuring up to its responsibilities to promote an open, representative public service system.

At the outset there was, perhaps, greater consensus among COMPA's founders on what it believed ASPA was not doing than there was on what COMPA should do. A considerable amount of time was spent resolving these and other philosophical differences, not the least of which was whether or not COMPA should be part of ASPA at all. Concurrently with internal efforts to define the organization, there were outside challenges to its legitimacy. Among members of ASPA, both minority and non-minority, establishment of COMPA was criticized as being a separatist move. Some critics labelled COMPA "self-serving," while others regarded it as providing ASPA a "cop-out" from its expressed commitments to promote recruitment and upward mobility of minorities in the public service. Some minority members of ASPA chose not to have any association with COMPA.

In this climate, it appears, the sense of urgency to *do,* i.e., to act to alter the status quo for minorities, overshadowed the need for facing several important realities, a more thorough consideration of which might have led to more effective action plans. First, COMPA, even with unlimited resources, could not provide a cure-all for the effects of generations of social inequity. Second, COMPA did not have at its disposal unlimited resources to develop programs. Third, questions raised concerning COMPA's legitimacy would, no doubt, lead to pressures to show quick results, even beyond what had been expected of ASPA, a firmly established organization. Fourth, given the first three, it would be necessary to identify those available assets from which COMPA could draw in establishing program priorities and determining feasible courses of action. The next step would have been to select and implement the project(s), which would: (1) be manageable in light of available resources, (2) contribute to accomplishment of a broader objective, and (3) offer the greatest investment return in terms of generating additional resources (money, expertise, legitimacy, etc.) for increasingly more substantial programs.

What seems to have happened, instead, is that the value of rapidly increasing membership was overrated as a key to program development. In fact, however, there is strong interdependence of the two, particularly in organizations which rely heavily on membership fees to support programs. Money and manpower assets emanating from memberships contribute to development and implementation of programs. At the same time, however, without active programs with which potential members can identify, the problem of attracting those very assets becomes much more difficult. An organization which does not successfully balance allocation of its existing resources to the two efforts threatens itself with paralysis.

A second problem related to disproportionate attention to growth in membership was that the organization had not developed internal mechanisms for processing applications, communicating with members, and tying them into program development. As a result, COMPA was unable to fully utilize the resources it was attempting to attract. Further, it seemed for a while that increasing membership was on the way to becoming an end in itself. Fortunately, this did not occur, as it would have lent substance to earlier allegations that COMPA was "self-serving" (beyond the extent to which any professional association is self-serving).

COMPA is now experiencing increasing success in breaking into the potentially crippling cycle generated by the interdependence of programs and resources. One of the factors to which this success may be attributed is the availability of staff support made possible through use of funds provided by ASPA. Last year, for the first time, COMPA had the services of a part-time national coordinator, who helped strengthen its communication capability and who gave support to the Executive Board.

Also significant is what appears to be growing awareness among members of COMPA that irrespective of the extent of agreement among current or prospective minority administrators with the stated objectives of COMPA, this agreement, alone, does not ensure their support. Rather, it is recognized that membership appeals must be based on positive programs and proposals for addressing those problems which contribute to suffering, despair, alienation, and waste of human talent, which take their greatest tolls on members of minority groups. As the level of meaningful COMPA program activity in this direction increases, some of the membership and other organizational maintenance problems are beginning to dissipate.

Accomplishments

The purpose of the foregoing discussion has been to point to some of the obstacles which have blocked more rapid development of the organization and a more coordinated approach to pursuit of its objectives. In spite of these obstacles, through the persistence of a small but growing nucleus of very capable, dedicated persons, COMPA has been able to sponsor a variety of activities in furtherance of its objectives, which have included:

- Workshops on the roles, dilemmas, constraints, and opportunities of minority administrators;
- Small group meetings with public officials, focusing on issues and programs having significant implications for large numbers of minority

citizens, such as the future of low-income housing, home rule (for the District of Columbia) and health care administration;

- Presentation of awards for outstanding contributions of minority administrators;
- Employment fairs and position referral services;
- Peer counseling for career development;
- A panel discussion addressing career development of minority mid-level public service careerists, from the perspectives of anticipated manpower requirements, expectations of potential employers of minority administrators, and individual self-assessment and goal-setting;
- Conduct of survey of ASPA chapters for programs planned or underway to increase minority participation in ASPA and to promote upward mobility of minorities in public service;
- Publication of "Urban Administration from a Minority Perspective," published jointly with an ASPA chapter; and
- Presentation to ASPA of a position paper on social equity for minorities, calling attention to six specific areas of concern, including ASPA's lack of an affirmative action plan.

Additionally, COMPA continues to encourage its members to participate actively in COMPA and ASPA programs, thereby simultaneously contributing to the organizations and extending their individual professional experiences. It also encourages its members to regularly create and/or take advantage of opportunities to provide role models for potential minority entrants to the field of public administration.

Some of the pay-offs of COMPA's efforts are becoming apparent. For example:

- Whereas in the past, most COMPA memberships were solicited, more and more, individuals are inquiring as to how they might join the organization, and are volunteering for service on committees. (There is also greater organizational capacity for handling a larger membership.)
- More minorities are volunteering for service on ASPA committees, and are being elected in greater numbers to local ASPA councils. At present, there are three minority persons on the council of the ASPA National Capital Area Chapter, two of whom were elected this past spring.
- Several ASPA chapters have indicated plans for strengthening or initiating programs directed toward minorities, based on recommendations from COMPA.
- There have recently been more indications of support from senior minority administrators, to whom COMPA previously has had very limited appeal.
- As a result of the social equity paper presented at the annual ASPA meeting, a committee has been formed and charged by ASPA with responsibility for drafting an affirmative action plan.

- It has been possible to identify from local COMPA projects some which can and should be expanded to regional or national scale.

These represent examples of some of the small gains which make COMPA optimistic about its future.

What Lies Ahead?

One of the most immediate tasks facing COMPA, which has been discussed as a possibility for the coming year, is that of identifying existing resources among minority administrators in federal, state, and local governments. Both from the perspectives of internal management and effective program development, COMPA has been somewhat constrained by insufficient knowledge of the diversity of experiences, skills, interests, etc., in its active membership and in the larger population of minority administrators. As envisioned, this project would, in some ways, be an extension and refinement of an earlier effort to establish a skills data bank. It would serve a variety of purposes, enabling COMPA to:

- Strengthen its internal management capabilities;
- Mobilize the combinations of expertise needed for planning, implementation, and assessment of specific projects;
- Expand and systematize the job referral services begun locally, to operate on either a regional or nationwide basis;
- Provide various forms of technical assistance to minority organizations and other organizations with large minority clienteles;
- Recognize outstanding contributions of minority administrators to resolution of problems affecting minorities in particular, and contributions to the field of public administration in general.

Also in the short-run, COMPA plans to assume a more active role in encouraging students to prepare for careers in the public service. This is to be accomplished through services to guidance personnel in colleges and public schools having sizable minority populations and to minority students, themselves. Such services might take the form of:

- Information dissemination on the wide range of career opportunities in public service;
- Provision of speakers and other participants in career development programs at educational institutions;
- Identification of opportunities for work-trial and other direct pre-career exposure to public agencies and their management; and
- Provision of incentives to students to explore and write on topics related to public policy.

A third possibility for a short-run project is a follow-up study of members of minority groups who have participated in public management and executive development programs. The study, if carried out, will utilize and supplement available data to determine where minority graduates of these programs are, what they are doing, and how participation in the program has impacted on their career development. Hopefully, the study would suggest ways of optimizing the various program benefits to reduce the barriers to upward mobility of minority public service careerists.

COMPA still has much work to do to define and plan for accomplishment of its immediate and longer-range goals. Relative to where it started, however, it has come a long way. If the momentum achieved over the past year can be sustained, COMPA has promising prospects for becoming a viable force for increasing the representativeness of ASPA and the field of public administration, and for improving public service delivery to members of minority groups.

It must be remembered, however, that as COMPA attempts to stimulate change in these areas, its primary targets are program administrators and managers, directors of personnel, equal employment opportunity officers, and university administrators and faculties. These are the persons who, to varying degrees, regularly influence political and administrative processes throughout the country. These are also the persons who comprise the bulk of ASPA's membership and who profess belief in "participation" and "representativeness" as important values in a democratic society. It must follow, then, that COMPA's success is linked closely to the willingness of these persons to acknowledge and carry out their responsibilities—both individually and collectively, as members of ASPA— for bringing about needed change.

Rose M. Robinson, *U.S. Civil Service Commission* ⌒

The Minority Administrator:
Problems, Prospects, and Challenges

The first National Conference on the Role of Minorities in Urban Management and Related Fields was held in Washington, D.C., on June 10 and 11, 1973. The significance of this conference was three-fold: (1) it was the first organized national meeting of non-elected minority public administrators and educators held to discuss the problems, education, responsibilities, and needs of minority public sector professionals; (2) it represented a symbolic acknowledgement that the quest of minority groups for more responsive government must, and does now include a sophisticated concentration on the political and administrative affairs of government; and (3) its theme suggested, quite appropriately, that minority administrators do have an important and unique role to play in the public management field, which they must accept if the plight of minority (if not all) people in America is to be improved.

Since this Conference, a number of major developments around the country suggest that minority administrators, however small in number, are increasingly gaining positions from which they can respond to the universal cry for more responsive government. Five cities as diverse as Compton, California, and East Lansing, Michigan, have selected black city managers to administer their governments. Black elected administrators are leading 108 cities in all regions of the nation, including Los Angeles, Atlanta, Raleigh, and Detroit. Another 62 serve as vice mayors.[82] Data from the 1973 State and Local Information Survey (EEO-4) reveal that 18.2 percent of the total labor force in state and local governments represent minority groups (Blacks, Spanish-Surnamed Americans, Asian, American Indian, and Other). While only 6.8 percent of this group is labeled "Professional," on the surface these figures do suggest growing influence on local government policy implementation and formulation.[83]

Recent federal employment data as reflected in Table 13.4 reveal that despite the continued decline in total federal employment, minority employment has continued to increase. Total minority employment (20.4 percent of the federal work force) expanded 1.9 percent for the period May 1972–May 1973.[84] While the increase in the number of GS 14–15, and supergrade administrators is not significant current hiring practices will result in greater opportunities for minorities to make inputs into agency decision-making and policy execution.

Although there has been a conscious movement toward equal employment opportunity and affirmative action in the field of public administration since the late '60s, the nature of these public sector efforts continues to be questioned in many circles. Indeed a major finding of the aforementioned Conference was that:

> Minority persons are still skeptical about the willingness of governmental systems to accept them as trained professionals with the knowledge and ability to perform in administrative positions of increasing responsibility and authority.[85]

This finding appears to coincide with several conclusions reached by the Civil Rights Commission in its 1969 survey of cities in seven SMSAs. While employment rates have improved for minority group administrators since this 1969 survey, some of the Commission's conclusions are worth mentioning, particularly in light of the skepticism felt by many minority group members relative to the good will of government agencies. The Commission found that:

> Minority group members are denied equal access to State and local government jobs.
>
> A. Negroes, in general, have better success in obtaining jobs with central city governments than they do in State, county, or suburban jurisdictions and are more successful in obtaining jobs in the North than in the South.

TABLE 13.4 Net Change in Employment Under the General Schedule and Similar Pay Plan (By Grade Grouping from May 31, 1972–May 31, 1973)

Grade Grouping	Total Employment Change	Minority Group Employment Change					
		Total Minority	Negro	Spanish Surnamed	American Indian	Oriental	All Other
Total, General Schedule or Similar	−173	+11,210	+8,756	+1,913	+200	+341	−11,383
GS-1–4	+9,159	+3,704	+2,797	+869	−45	+83	+5,455
GS-5–8	−6,906	+3,952	+3,538	+348	+48	+18	−10,858
GS-9–11	−4,298	+2,169	+1,518	+434	+130	+87	−6,467
GS-12–13	+1,133	+961	+697	+173	+45	+46	+172
GS-14–15	+805	+416	+199	+84	+24	+109	+389
GS-16–18	−66	+8	+7	+5	−2	−2	−74

SOURCE: U.S. Civil Service Commission, *Minority Groups Employment in the Federal Government* (Washington, D.C.: U.S. Government Printing Office, 1973).

B. Negroes are noticeably absent from managerial and professional jobs even in those jurisdictions where they are substantially employed in the aggregate. In only two central cities, out of a total of eight surveyed, did the overall number of black employees in white-collar jobs reflect the population patterns of the cities.

C. Access to white collar jobs in some departments is more readily available to minority group members than in others. Negroes are most likely to hold professional, managerial, and clerical jobs in health and welfare and least likely to hold these jobs in financial administration and general control.

D. Negroes hold the large majority of laborer and general service worker jobs—jobs which are characterized by few entry skills, relatively low pay, and limited opportunity for advancement.[86]

Related to these conclusions (particularly point "C") are data from the aforementioned EEO-4 survey which indicate that while minorities do hold a number of administrative positions outside *social* agencies, most continue to work in these areas. Table 13.5 provides a summary of current local government hiring practices by functional areas. As the Civil Rights Commission indicated in 1969, minorities continued in 1973 to be assigned primarily to departments that have a "social" orientation. It is particularly significant to note that police and fire departments continue to employ significantly lower percentages of minority group people than do other governmental agencies. Financial administration also continues to be an area in which minority people have been unable to make significant inroads, although employment rates in this area are higher than in police and fire departments. It is also important to note that with the exception of housing, the percentage of professionals and officials/administrators (white collar jobs) continues to be low in all functional areas.

At the federal level, a similar pattern of minorities being hired by some agencies at much higher rates than others is evident, as reflected in Table 13.6. Three distinguishable groups of agencies seem to be evident with reference to the percentage of minority group members employed. The first group contains four agencies, three of which—Action, OEO, and Labor—might be labeled as "traditional." The presence of the State Department in this first group reflects a deviation from the usual governmental pattern related to minority employment. The Office of Economic Opportunity and ACTION stand out above all other federal agencies as the employers of both the greatest percentage of minority professionals at the GS 9 levels or above, and the greatest percentage of supergrade administrators. The Departments of State and Labor also have relatively high rates of minority employment overall, and particularly at the GS9–11 levels. At the super grade levels, however, both departments have much lower minority employment rates.

The second cluster of agencies contains three departments, two of which might be labeled as "social" or "traditional" in the sense referred to by the Civil Rights Commission—Health, Education, and Welfare; and Housing and Urban Development. To some observers it may be surprising to note the presence of the

TABLE 13.5 State/Local Government Employment Rates by Functional Areas (1973)

Group		Percent Non-White Employment	Officials/ Administrators	Professionals
I	Sanitation and Sewage	38.8	12.4	8.9
	Housing	34.6	20.7	24.2
	Hospitals and Sanitariums	30.4	9.1	18.6
II	Public Welfare	23.6	11.0	15.4
	Utilities and Transport	22.7	9.4	10.6
	Other	18.9	7.9	10.0
	Employment Security	18.7	8.2	13.5
	Corrections	18.7	9.8	14.7
	Health	17.8	3.2	11.6
	Natural Resources	15.9	6.2	8.9
	Community Development	15.1	7.9	13.2
III	Streets and Highways	11.8	3.8	6.0
	Financial Administration	11.4	5.3	7.9
IV	Police	9.3	4.4	5.5
	Fire	5.0	2.2	2.8

SOURCE: Compiled from data cited in the Equal Employment Opportunity Commission, *State and Local Government Information, EEO-4, National Statistical Summaries* (Washington, D.C.: EEOC, Office of Research, 1974).

TABLE 13.6 Federal Government Minority Group Employment Rates, 1972–1973

Agencies	Total Employment Rates of Agency GS 9–18	Total Minority Employment of Agency GS 9–18	Percent of Total GS 9–18	Percent of Total GS 9–11	Percentage Minority Employment	
					Percent of GS 12–15	Percent of GS 16–18
OEO	1234	385	31.2	46.3	26.6	40.9
ACTION	946	220	23.3	30.3	19.6	18.8
State	2491	456	18.3	32.2	8.5	2.5
Labor	7568	1336	17.6	27.3	14.3	6.8
HEW	40178	5796	14.4	18.0	10.9	9.3
HUD	9912	1304	13.2	15.9	11.0	9.4
OMB	383	47	12.3	22.1	10.0	9.0
Interior	27883	2646	9.5	12.7	5.9	3.2
Commerce	16108	1434	8.9	11.7	7.3	2.3
Treasury	45133	3004	6.7	8.3	5.0	2.1
Defense	262726	16797	6.4	8.2	4.2	1.1
Transportation	46337	2578	5.6	7.9	4.3	7.0
Justice	20041	1109	5.5	7.4	3.6	3.3
Agriculture	41725	2110	5.1	6.2	3.3	2.4

SOURCE: Compiled from data cited in the U.S. Civil Service Commission, *Minority Group Employment in the Federal Government* (Washington, D.C.: U.S. Government Printing Office, March 1974).

Office of Management and Budget in this second group. The OMB employment figures are especially significant because of that agency's overall importance in the governmental process.

The third cluster of agencies includes Interior, Commerce, Treasury, Defense, Transportation, Justice, and Agriculture. None of these agencies are usually regarded as being social service agencies; as a consequence, the lack of substantial minority employees is not surprising. It is significant that at the federal level, as in the case of state and local governments, the percentage of minority employees decreases rapidly as decision-making responsibility (GS level) increases. The one exception to this trend is the Office of Economic Opportunity, where the percentage of supergrade administrators (40.9 percent) is at a level comparable to those at the GS 9–11 levels (46.3 percent) within that agency.

Although we in the public affairs field have given little attention in our literature to these data and the resulting debate, it is important to recognize that, as the number of minority professionals and administrators at all levels of government increases, the expectations of minority people for more responsive government will probably expand simultaneously. As will be argued later, the powers possessed by minorities employed in the public sector in most cases seldom are adequate to meet these expectations. As a consequence, short of a commitment on the part of administrators generally (white and non-white) to become responsive to the needs of "all" citizens, governmental agencies will continue to address on a priority basis the demands of the more powerful and affluent in our society. Where public agencies do not manifest a change in programmatic efforts which might be interpreted by minority communities as being more responsive to their needs, the tasks of minority administrators within those agencies, particularly at the local level, will become increasingly more difficult.

These difficulties will arise, in part, because of the collective perception that minority administrators understand the nature and magnitude of the problems confronting those from lower socioeconomic backgrounds. Indeed, whether one is black, brown, or red, the visible presence of an administrator with whom he/she can identify causes at least greater initial security that someone is listening who can understand the needs, realities, and perceptions being described, and who will help if at all possible.

Another factor creating the expectation among minority groups that the system will change as a result of greater "integration" of public agencies is the belief that many of these positions were made possible through community efforts. It is expected, therefore, that minority administrators and professionals will be spokesmen for other minorities out of an inherent *obligation* to speak out in their best group interest.

Perhaps the most critical factor, however, relates to bureaucratic promises made as the number of minority group members working for an agency or jurisdiction increases. In far too many cases, hiring practices are utilized to demonstrate efforts to be responsive to minority community needs. Because many agencies or governmental jurisdictions equate programmatic commitment or effort with the employment of a larger number of minorities, governmental employees from those groups can become convenient targets of protest when expectations and/or promises to the community groups are unfulfilled.

These and many other related demands and expectations create a number of major dilemmas for minority administrators to which most agencies are insensitive. In some respects many of the dilemmas and forces mentioned in this article confront all administrators, but the minority administrator seems to be subject to their weight more than most. For ultimately, every minority administrator and professional must consciously or otherwise respond to two basic and difficult questions: (1) "What responsibility do I have to minority group peoples?" (2) "What role should I attempt to play in making government more responsive to the needs of all people?"

Role Determinants

In addressing these questions, it is useful to consider six forces which confront the minority administrator, and which influence significantly his/her potential effectiveness and perhaps perceptions of responsibility to both the governmental agency and minority peoples more generally. Graphically these forces might be viewed as indicated in Figure 13.4.

A. *System Demands.* The first force, "system demands," refers to those expectations of public employees that a governmental system reinforces through a range

FIGURE 13.4 Role Demands on Minority Administrators

of sanctions and rewards. Bureaucratic systems are perpetuated because they demand and receive obedience to orders. The traditional model of hierarchy as described by Weber suggests that decisions are made at the top and implemented by those at lower levels within the organization. For political appointees, a failure to respond to demands made by those at the top may mean harassment, dismissal, and embarrassment. Similarly, in a civil service system, pressures are applied "to do as ordered." In cases where the civil servant "bucks" authority, intensive pressures and/or sanctions are applied (e.g., the Fitzgerald vs. Department of Defense case, as well as political pressures recently applied on the IRS, CIA, and FBI).

With regard to blacks, the system has successfully enforced its demands through a careful "weeding out" process. Only the "very best" minority group members could advance as illustrated in Sam Greenlee's novel. *The Spook Who Sat by the Door.* The techniques utilized by agencies to assure the hiring and advancement of these "outstanding" and, as Greenlee suggests, "safe" minority group members include: high education requirement, experience, oral examinations, performance tests, arrest records, probationary periods, general requirements related to residency, etc. Again, if the minority administrator is able to meet these requirements, the ongoing test that remains is that of the willingness to respond to the demands of higher-ups *without question.* Because of their historical difficulties in obtaining employment, some minority public administrators placed job security over program content or impact, and thus have become impediments to efforts to address the needs of their communities.

B. "Traditional" Role Expectations. A conventional wisdom in public administration has been that certain people do particular kinds of jobs well. Tables I and II, as well as the aforementioned Civil Rights Commission report, revealed that a large percentage of minority administrators work in specialized areas. The Civil Rights Commission noted that:

> Access to white-collar jobs in some departments is more readily available to minority group members than in others. Among the seven metropolitan areas studied, the same general pattern of employment in white-collar jobs was discernible in both the North and the South. Negroes were most likely to hold jobs in health and welfare and least likely to hold them in financial administration and general control.[87]

The Commission went on to point out that:

> In addition to the "old traditional jobs" for Black Americans, "new traditional jobs" appear to be emerging. These are usually jobs as staff members of human relations councils, civil rights commissions, or assistants to ranking administrators. They are status jobs carrying major responsibilities and usually bring excellent salaries. But they remain almost exclusively related to minority group problems.[88]

Many of the jobs given minority administrators at both the federal and local levels have been "flak-catching" positions. As Tom Wolfe has indicated in *Radical Chic and Mau-Mauing the Flak Catcher,* during the 1960s in particular, black and brown administrators were often placed in their positions only to become sacrificial lambs in the face of community unrest.

With regard to the future, it is important that minority group members not be herded into "traditional" departments only, nor should they blindly allow themselves to be so directed. Important decisions which affect minority people are made in agencies throughout a governmental jurisdiction or agency. Minority group participation and contributions in all these decision-making processes are becoming increasingly more critical.

C. Colleague Pressures. One of the greatest dangers to the quest for governmental responsiveness remains the pressures imposed by one's peers. Peter Maas recent book and the adopted movie, *Serpico,* clearly document the pressures which can and frequently are brought to bear on public administrators. The pressures on minority group members take many forms:

1. The minority group policeman who wants to be accepted by his peers may be forced to "bust heads" to gain acceptance, and promotions;
2. The minority welfare worker may be forced to "get tough" with welfare recipients to be regarded as a competent professional;
3. The minority school teacher is placed in the position of "blaming the victims" of the educational process to retain a place of acceptance among his/her colleagues. It is not allowed that these professionals begin to question the quality of the educational experiences of the children supposedly being served, or the unions which represent them in the quest for working conditions which may not be in the best interest of the children.

As social animals, we desire to be accepted as peers by our colleagues. It is difficult, therefore, to ward off these peer pressures. Clearly the task for the minority administrator is that of placing such collegial pressures into a perspective that does not allow them to overshadow broader program objectives and community needs.

D. Community Accountability. In recent years we have heard growing demands for greater community control, coupled with a cry for more minority group professionals who will be responsive to the needs of their people.[89] The problem historically confronting black communities in this latter regard is well described by Piven and Cloward:

> Much Negro leadership exists largely by the grace of white institutions: white political parties and government agencies, white unions and businesses and professions, even white civil-rights organizations. Everything in the environment of the Negro politician, civil servant, or professional makes him attentive to white interests and perspectives.[90]

The demand is clear. Minority people want and need administrators who will listen to them, who can communicate with them, who care about them. If this is not manifested, community control becomes the ultimate demand, and perhaps a necessity.

E. Personal Commitment to Community. Of critical importance in this context is personal commitment to the community. The degree to which the administrator feels that there are obligations to fulfill and a role to be played which only he/she can fulfill can make a critical difference in public policy discussions, decisions, and ultimately, service output. It is my belief that as the number of minority administrators increases, commitment to addressing community needs will increase if only because there is more security in numbers. Equally important is the fact that a growing number of committed young minority administrators are gradually assuming more responsible positions in public agencies. They appear able to address the difficulties of balancing agency objectives with client expectations and their own personal ambitions far better than many of those who have preceded them.

F. Personal Ambition. People want to advance their careers. It is my belief that all administrators weigh important decisions not only in terms of possible programmatic consequences, but also with regard to implications for their own careers. As employment opportunities for minority group people have expanded, personal ambitions among this group have also increased. Until the early 1960s, the bureaucratic system was very effective in minimizing this desire for advancement, basically because it was clear that few opportunities for promotions into professional positions existed. As positions became more available in the 1960s, the initial result was greater competition for an apparently large but actually limited number of high-level appointments. Although employment opportunities have expanded, as mentioned above, it is still argued by some that most agencies do place limits on the numbers of minorities who will fill these positions. The challenge to minority administrators is that of seeking personal security, while simultaneously manifesting a commitment to urge greater efforts to meet governmental responsibilities more effectively.

Dilemmas of the Minority Administrator

In light of the above discussion, several dilemmas stand out as being of particular significance for the minority administrator. The effective minority administrator will be one who can respond to the challenges of leadership in the quest for more responsive government in light/in spite of these obstacles:

- Governmental role expectations of minority administrators do not necessarily coincide with the minority administrator's own perceptions, goals, or expectations;
- Unresponsive public policies put minority administrators in extremely tenuous positions *vis-à-vis* the agency, himself/herself, and the community of which he/she is a part;
- Frequently the minority administrator is put into flak-catching positions without the capacity to make meaningful decisions, but is expected to accept the responsibilities of programmatic failures and "keep the natives calm."

- Advancement within the governmental system is generally a function of adherence to established organizational norms; one of these norms historically has been that one need not be concerned about the needs or priorities of minority communities.
- Informal pay and promotional quotas still seem to exist for minority administrators; moreover, it is assumed that they can only fill certain types of positions, usually related to social service delivery or to communication with other minority group members.
- Minority communities sometimes expect much more of the minority administrator than he/she can provide; and in most cases demand a far faster response to their demands than these administrators have developed the capacity to deliver.
- Agencies seem to search for the "super" minority administrator; and even these are frequently hired as show pieces. In other cases there has been evidence of agencies hiring individuals who clearly would be unable to do a job with the intent of showing that an effort was made but "they just can't do this kind of work."

While other dilemmas might be identified, this brief listing seems to reinforce the argument that the task of being a minority administrator within public agencies is not an easy one. Moreover, in the short run the challenges reflected in these dilemmas may become greater in magnitude as governments at all levels fail to address in a meaningful fashion such quality of life problems as hunger, health, housing, etc.

Conclusion

For almost two centuries, minority groups have been systematically excluded from making inputs into the administrative processes of government as both decision makers and policy implementors. In the final analysis, it is now the responsibility of governmental leaders generally to expand opportunities for the perspectives of minority administrators to be articulated and acted upon. This responsibility derives not only from executive orders and congressional mandates, but also from the reality that there frequently is a minority perspective on public problems which policy makers should understand if public programs are to be truly responsive and effective.

Schools of public affairs also have a major charge to educate more minority administrators to assume these critical positions. The frequently criticized decrease in foundation monies previously utilized to provide financial assistance to these students must not be utilized as a cop-out to explain away lack of effort in this regard. The minority academic also has a role to play in supporting these efforts to provide the kind of professional training essential to the development of the number and caliber of top-flight minority administrators so critically needed in public agencies. They must also begin to work more closely with both minority elected officials and administrators in continuing education, and in policy research and analysis if some of the major problems facing minority group communities are to be effectively described, understood, and attacked.

Finally, to the minority administrator goes the challenge of accepting the obligation of working for the development and operation of public programs which more effectively meet the needs of *all* people. In some cases this may require an advocacy position. It may demand that the minority group perspective on public policy questions be researched, developed, and articulated. It will frequently demand the capacity and willingness to discuss policy options, directions, and needs with those who have expressed a lack of faith in the governmental process. It will demand a rejection of the argument that administrators are/must be value free and completely neutral in implementing policy decisions. Simultaneously, however, there exists the reality that public employees do work within a bureaucratic context with established procedures, job requirements, and program objectives. These neither can, nor should be ignored. Nor should minority public administrators be *expected* to present minority views, or be given positions solely because they are black, red, or brown. Public agencies, however, must begin to recognize and accept the reality that, in light of the problems confronting our society, it is in the public interest that minority administrators not forget who they are, or from whence they have come.

Adam W. Herbert, *Virginia Polytechnic Institute and State University* ∿

Notes

1. The importance of focusing attention on Public Management since Woodrow Wilson is related to the fact that modern inquiry in American Public Administration is often identified with Woodrow Wilson's essay on "The Study of Administration," published in 1887.

2. See *Politics and Patronage in the Gilded Age,* James D. Norris and Arthur H. Shaffer (eds.) (Madison: State Historical Society of Wisconsin, 1970).

3. For a detailed discussion on normative theory see Stephen K. Bailey, "Objectives of the Theory of Public Administration," in James C. Charlesworth (ed.), *Theory and Practice of Public Administration: Scope, Objectives and Methods* (Philadelphia: The American Academy of Political and Social Science, 1968).

4. Luther Gulick, "Notes on the Theory of Organization," in Luther Gulick and L. Urwich (eds.), *Papers on the Science of Administration* (Columbia University: Institute of Public Administration, 1937).

5. Elton Mayo, *The Human Problems of an Individual Civilization* (New York: The Macmillan Company, 1933).

6. See for example, Milton J. Esman and John D. Montgomery, "System Approaches to Technical Cooperation: The Role of Development Administration," *Public Administration Review,* Vol. 29 (September/October 1969).

7. The proponents of the New Public Administration typify this position. See *Toward a New Public Administration: The Minnowbrook Perspective,* Frank Marini (ed.) (Scranton: Chandler Publishing Corp., 1971), or *Public Administration in a Time of Turbulence,* Dwight Waldo (ed.) (Scranton: Chandler Publishing Corp., 1971). One might also view the "Symposium on Social Equity and Public Administration," *Public Administration Review,* Vol. 34 (January/February 1974).

8. The concept "identity crisis" was borrowed from Psychology and applied to the field of Public Administration. Its meaning varies but by and large it refers to the enormous expansion of the periphery of Public Administration without retaining or creating a unifying center.

9. See "After Twenty Years: New Turn In Black Revolution," *U.S. News and World Report,* May 20, 1974, pp. 24–26.

10. See Lawrence C. Howard, "The Black Praxis as a Perspective on Administration," unpublished paper, University of Pittsburgh, 1974.

11. See Stokely Carmichael and Charles V. Hamilton, *Black Power: The Polities of Liberation in America* (New York: Vintage Books, 1967).

12. This point needs little documentation as long-established organizations such as the NAACP, and Urban League, and newly formed organizations such as NWRD have consistently pushed for the welfare of all people.

13. See Sterling Stuckey, *The Ideological Origins of Black Nationalism* (Boston: Beacon Press, 1972).

14. For further discussion on this matter see Howard, *op. cit.,* pp. 1–2.

15. On the one hand, perspective may be defined as a viewpoint which an individual holds toward a set of objects, events, or people. On the other hand, it may be defined as a viewpoint which a group/society holds toward a set of objects, events, or people. Thus every group/society holds a collective viewpoint. Although each person is not the exact replica of another member, all members share similar feelings, attitudes, values, and beliefs. As a result, a collective perspective is formed. The collective perspective may be age specific, sex specific, fraternity specific, or race specific. The writer's concern here is with the race specific perspective of blacks as it relates to public management.

16. See "Newark and We" by Kenneth A. Gibson in *What Black Politicians Are Saying,* Nathan Wright, Jr. (ed.) (New York: Hawthorn Books, Inc., 1972), pp. 121–125.

17. *Ibid.,* pp. 124–125.

18. *Ibid.,* p. 123.

19. Howard, *op. cit.,* p. 30.

20. *Ibid.,* p. 30.

21. See "A Black Value System" by Imamu Baraka in *Contemporary Black Thought,* Robert Chrisman and Nathan Hare (eds.) (New York: The Bobbs-Merrill Company, Inc., 1973), pp. 71–79.

22. See "The West African Roots of Afro-American Music" by Ralph H. Metcalfe, Jr., *ibid.,* pp. 26–40.

23. W. E. Burghardt DuBois, *Dusk of Dawn* (New York, 1968), pp. 114–116.

24. See David K. Hart, "Social Equity, Justice, and the Equitable Administrator," *Public Administration Review,* Vol. 34, No. 1 (January/February 1974), pp. 3–17.

25. Howard, *op. cit.,* p. 5.

26. For a detailed discussion of how this model works, see Clyde O. McDaniel and Deryl Hunt, "Toward a Revision of the Curriculum for Masters Level Education in Urban Schools of Social Work," *The Indian Journal of Social Work* (October 1973).

27. On the implications of Watergate for the black community see William Strickland, "Watergate: Its Meaning for Black America," *Black World* (December 1973).

28. For a listing of blacks who have served in public office since 1969 see *National Roster of Black Elected Officials* (Washington, D.C.: Joint Center for Political Studies), Vols. 1, 2, and 3. The data for 1967 was supplied by John Dean, consultant, Joint Center for Political Studies.

29. *National Roster of Black Elected Officials* (Washington, D.C.: Joint Center for Political Studies, 1973), Vol. 3, p. ix.

30. Alex Poinsett "Black Power in State Government," *Ebony* (April 1972), pp. 94–95.

31. *National Roster of Black Elected Officials, op. cit.,* p. x.

32. *Ibid.*

33. For a comprehensive analysis of these black political movements see Hanes Walton, Jr., *Black Political Parties: A Historical and Political Analysis* (New York: The Free Press, 1972).

34. On the Hatcher and Stokes election see Philip J. Meranto and William E. Nelson, Jr., *Electing Black Mayors: Political Action in the Black Community* (Columbus, Ohio: Charles Merrill Publishing Company, forthcoming, 1974).

35. Harold M. Baron, "The Web of Urban Racism," in Louis L. Knowles and Kenneth Prewitt (eds.), *Institutional Racism in America* (Englewood Cliffs, N.J.: Prentice-Hall, Inc., 1969), p. 144.

36. For a cogent discussion of this concept in the context of political decision making see Peter Bachrach and Morton s. Baratz, *Power and Poverty: Theory and Practice* (New York: Oxford University Press, 1970).

37. Edward Greer, "The Liberation of Gary, Indiana," in Alan Shank (ed.), *Political Power and the Urban Crisis* (Boston: Holbrook Press, Inc., 1973), pp. 327–328.

38. Mack H. Jones, "Black Officeholders in Local Governments of the South: An Overview," unpublished paper delivered at the annual meeting of The American Political Science Association, Los Angeles, California, 1970, p. 29.

39. *Ibid,* p. 28.

40. Problems encountered by Stokes and Hatcher with the city bureaucracy are discussed in Meranto and Nelson, *op. cit.,* For a discussion of Gibson's problems with the bureaucracy in Newark see Robert Curvin, "Black Power in Newark: Kenneth Gibson's First Year," unpublished paper delivered at the annual meeting of the American Political Science Association, Chicago, Illinois, 1971.

41. Jones, *op. cit.,* p. 32.

42. *Ibid.,* p. 15.

43. See Kenneth S. Colburn, *Southern Black Mayors: Local Problems and Federal Response* (Washington, D.C.: Joint Center for Political Studies, 1973).

44. Recently Berkeley, California, City Councilman D'Army Baily was recalled because he pushed too aggressively for policies which sought to upset the balance of power between the black and white communities. Robert Blackwell, black mayor of Highland Park, Michigan, recently beat back a recall petition on similar grounds.

45. Jones, *op. cit.,* pp. 36–37.

46. The ultimate goal ought to be the establishment of independent bases of funding and technical support for black programs. This means that in future years the black community itself will have to assume a greater share of these responsibilities. Black dependence breeds black subordination. The sinews of colonialism will only be snapped when the black community has become heavily self-reliant.

47. James Q. Wilson, "The Negro in American Politics: The Present," in John P. Davis (ed.), *The American Negro Reference Book* (Englewood Cliffs, N.J.: Prentice-Hall, Inc., 1966), p. 456.

48. "For all the People . . . by all the People," *A Report of Equal Opportunity in State and Local Government Employment,* Clearinghouse Publication, No. 18, November 1969.

49. The term Chicano in this article refers to U.S. citizens and residents of Mexican ancestry who adhere to political, social, and economic self-determination.

50. Leo Grebler, Joan Moore, and Ralph Guzman, *The Mexican American People* (New York: Free Press, 1970).

51. U.S. Cabinet Committee of Opportunities for Spanish Surnamed People, Clearinghouse Publication, 1971. These statistics have been contested by major Chicano organizations (Mexican American Legal Defense and Education Fund) and leading Spanish-surnamed politicians (Senator Montoya, and Congressmen Roybal and Badillo) that the 1970 Census constituted an undercount of Spanish surnamed of as much as 20 to 50 percent. President Nixon's Cabinet Committee for the Spanish Speaking reported to the *Washington Star* (November 6, 1970) that the number of Spanish surnamed is 17 percent.

52. U.S. Civil Service Commission. *Study of Minority Group Employment in the Federal Government,* Clearinghouse Publication, SM 70-70B, 1970.

53. For further information on the concept of institutional racism, see Lewis Knowles, *Institutional Racism in America,* (New York: Englewood, 1969); Stokeley Carmichael and Charles V. Hamilton, *Black Power: Politics of Liberation in America,* (New York: Vintage, 1967); Melvin Sabshin, *Dimension of Institutional Racism in Psychiatry,* (Chicago: University of Illinois, 1970), and Paul Jacobs, *Prelude to Riot: A View of Urban America from the Bottom* (New York: Random House, 1967).

54. *Report of the National Advisory Commission on Civil Disorders* (New York: Bantam Books, 1968), p. 1.

55. John Higham, *Strangers in the Land* (New York: Atheneum, 1965).

56. See Leonard Pitt, "The Beginnings of Nativism in California," *Pacific Historical Review,* Vol. XXX, No. 1 (February 1961), pp. 23–38, as an example of nativist account during the Westward Movement.

57. *Report of the National Advisory Commission on Civil Disorders, op. cit.,* p. 2.

58. David F. Gomez. *Somos Chicanos: Strangers in Our Own Land* (Toronto: Beacon Press, 1973), p. 88.

59. John Higham, *op. cit.*

60. For further information, see Cecil Robinson, *With the Ears of Strangers* (Tucson, Ariz.: University of Arizona Press, 1963); and Armando Rendon, *Chicano Manifesto* (New York: Macmillan, 1971).

61. Henry Sioux Johnson and William J. Hernandez (eds.), *Educating the Mexican American* (Valley Forge: Jodson Press, 1970).

62. U.S. Civil Rights Commission, *Mexican Americans and The Administration of Justice in the Southwest* (Clearinghouse, March 1970).

63. Armando Morales, *Ando Sangrando* (La Puente, Calf.: Perspectiva Publications, 1972).

64. Honorable Gerald S. Chargin, Judge, Court Transcript, Superior Court of State of California in and for the County of Santa Clara, Juvenile Division, September 2, 1969.

65. For additional information, see Carey McWilliams, *North From Mexico* (New York: Greenwood Press, Publishers, 1968); Grebler, Moore, and Guzman, *The Mexican American People, op. cit.*

66. *Los Angeles Times,* June 2, 1973, Part 1, p. 23.

67. *Los Angeles Times,* June 3, 1973, Part 1, p. 4.

68. *Congressional Record,* 92nd Congress, Second Session, Vol. 18, No. 61B, April 19, 1972.

69. See the U.S. Civil Service Commissioner's Study of *Minority Group Employment in the Federal Government, op. cit.*

70. Knowles, *Institutional Racism, op. cit.,* p. 21.

71. 400 U.S. 424 (1971).

72. Governor's Task Force on Equal Rights, *Discrimination, Racism, and Sexism, in State Employment and Recommendation for Change,* Technical Standards Unit, Commonwealth of Pennsylvania, March 1972, p. 45.

73. "For all the People ... by all the People," *op. cit.,* p. 10.

74. Paul R. Anderson, "The University in an Urban Society," an inaugural address given by the president of Temple University, May 1, 1968.

75. David A. Tansik and Michael Radnor, "An Organization Theory Perspective on the Development of New Organizational Functions, *Public Administration Review,* Vol. 31, No. 6 (November/December 1971), p. 644.

76. G.M. Sawyer, "The Urban University: Toward Harmony or Hiatus?" paper presented at a Regional Conference on the Urban Involvement of Higher Education, April 5, 1974, Braniff Place, New Orleans, pp. 16 and 18.

77. Yehezkel Dror, *Design for Policy Sciences* (New York: American Elsevier Publishing Co., Inc., 1971), p. 74.

78. *Priorities for Action, Final Report of the Carnegie Commission on Higher Education* (New York: McGraw-Hill Book Company, 1973).

79. Robert Agranoff, "Human Service Administration: Service Delivery, Service Integration, and Training," in *Human Services Integration,* special publication of the American Society for Public Administration, March 1974, p. 50.

80. *National Register of Black Elected Officials* (Washington, D.C.: Joint Center for Political Studies, May 1973), p. 8.

81. National Conference on the Role of Minorities in Urban Management and Related Fields, *Proceedings of First National Conference* (Washington, D.C., 1973), p. 14.

82. Joint Center for Political Studies, *National Roster of Black Elected Officials* (Washington, D.C.: The Joint Center, April 1974).

83. Equal Employment Opportunity Commission, *State and Local Government Information, EEO-4 National Statistical Summaries* (Washington, D.C.: Office of Research, 1974).

84. U.S. Civil Service Commission, *Minority Group Employment in the Federal Government* (Washington, D.C.: U.S. Government Printing Office, March 1974), pp. i, ii.

85. *Summary of the First National Conference on the Role of Minorities in Urban Management and Related Fields* (Washington, D.C.: Metropolitan Washington Council of Governments, 1973), p. 19.

86. U.S. Commission on Civil Rights, *For All The People ... By All The People* (Washington, D.C.: U.S. Government Printing Office, 1969), p. 118.

87. *Ibid.,* p. 2.

88. *Ibid.,* p. 3.

89. For a representative sample of the literature describing these attitudes, see: Alan Altshular, *Community Control* (New York: Pegasus, 1970); Charles E. Wilson, "Year One at I.S. 201," *Social Policy* (May/June 1970), pp. 10–17; Sherry R. Arnstein, "Maximum Feasible Manipulation," *Public Administration Review,* Vol. XXXII (September/October 1972), pp. 377–390; and Mario Fantiri and Marilyn Gittell, *Decentralization: Achieving Reform* (New York, Praeger, 1973).

90. Francis Fox Piven and Richard A. Cloward, "Black Control of Cities," in Edward S. Greenburg, et al. (eds), *Black Politics* (New York: Holt, Rinehart and Winston, Inc., 1971), pp. 128–129.

Part Four

Gender

Women became a protected class as a part of the Equal Employment Opportunity Act of 1972. Since that time, the concerns of women as related to equal employment opportunity and affirmative action have increasingly found their way to center stage. Although, as this collection of essays indicates, many of the issues and challenges faced in 1972 are still there to be dealt with in 1999. However, as we move into the twenty-first century, there is reason for optimism: Women have made significant strides toward their goals of equity and parity in the work place. Yet as these articles clearly indicate, there is much still that remains to be done.

Bullard and Wright's findings, based on data gleaned from the American State Administration Project's 1984 and 1988 surveys, demonstrate that women have made noteworthy progress in securing top administrative posts in state governments. At the time the surveys were completed, women filled approximately 20 percent of the top administrative positions in state agencies. This represents a higher percentage than can be found in most other executive sectors, including private (corporate) and other public sectors. Despite the increased presence of women in top state-level jobs, the numbers still fall far short of equity with men. Additionally, women still tend to direct particular types of agencies, including: aging, library, personnel, and social services. Along the same lines, women were also distinctively represented in some of the agencies (arts, community affairs, consumer protection, human resources, and Medicaid) that were newly created during the 1960s and 1970s. In fact, these agencies have provided women with a chance to circumvent the glass ceiling that has been present in many of the older, more traditional state agencies.

The next author believes that despite large strides forward, as of 1996 women continued in their struggle to establish credibility in the workplace. In an attempt to identify behavioral patterns, Rusaw examines the accounts of fourteen women managers in five federal agencies. Based on her findings, she determined that

261

women in public sector agency settings continue to face significant obstacles to achieving credibility as leaders. The article highlights several key obstacles, including: technical bias, promotion bias, little managerial encouragement, no margin for error, and zero-sum games. Rusaw then focuses on the development of a critical set of leadership skills. The following skill sets were thought to empower respondents to overcome obstacles and achieve credibility as leaders: consistency, visibility, earned positive regard, earned legitimacy, and verisimilitude. Earning the trust of followers, colleagues, and superiors requires developing and using task and relationship skills and enacting them within the context of organizational norms. The author reminds the reader that in spite of their advanced educational credentials, certificates of specialized training and in some instances, high occupational ranks prior to entering the government, women often face significant gender-related hurdles to advancement.

The equity issue is revisited by Guy as she examines two decades of affirmative action initiatives as they pertain to women. Her findings indicate the number of women in decision-making positions is disproportionately low when compared to their numbers in the public workforce. Comparing the status of women to that of men in career public management positions, Guy argues that women have a long way to go before they reach parity. In the introductory section, the article points out that in legislative chambers and top-level career posts, women's voices are still mostly heard indirectly through the mouths of their husbands, fathers, brothers, and sons. The article then outlines the pattern of women's integration into public management and characterizes it as being not unlike that of women's integration into society at large—"three steps forward, two steps backward." The overriding message is that women have a long way to go before they will hold management positions proportional to their numbers in the workforce.

The editor of the symposium on women in public administration, Nesta Gallas, included articles on a broad spectrum of topics. Topics covered in the symposium are wide ranging and move from historical perspectives to profiles of successful professional women, then to barriers to high level public sector positions, and finally to current (as of 1976) feminist theories and case studies. Two of the authors trace the women's movement. They first highlight key details of the women's movement beginning with the Seneca Falls Convention in 1848. Then the women's liberation movement is discussed, and the essay wraps up by covering the birth and development of the women's movement within the American Society for Public Administration (ASPA). The second author discusses how the 1972 Equal Employment Opportunity Act extended the Civil Rights Act to include women as a "protected class." In her discussion of affirmative action goals in the employment context, Newgarden recommends the use of what she identifies as *utilization analysis* to determine if goals and timetables are appropriate in the employment arena. Newgarden also reviews the four federal agencies responsible for Equal Employment Opportunity and uses census data to demonstrate

Sacramento, California's well-known efforts to realize a truly nondiscriminatory personnel system.

Another of the authors included in the symposium (Lepper) refutes several of the reasons frequently put forth by society to account for women's lack of progress in the workplace. She accomplishes this by arguing that the most common explanations, such as discontinuous occupational careers, relative lack of spatial mobility, and women's lack of interest in working for other women, are patently false and cannot be empirically validated. Her concluding section makes the point that any progress made tends to result from women overexcelling in order to compete with men in the marketplace, not from government programs. Yet another author (Stewart) bases her article on the assumption that the expansion of employment opportunity for women in American society calls for a focus not on jobs per se, but rather on job stratification. The 1976 national occupational data used by Stewart revealed that small numbers of women had gained acceptance to the most prestigious occupations. At the time the article was written, for example, women comprised only 9.8 percent of all physicians, 7.0 percent of lawyers and judges, 9.4 percent of full professors, and 2.3 percent of GS 16–18 level federal civil service positions. After presenting these statistics, the author details three theories that have been enlisted to explain why so few women made it into highly regarded professions as of 1976. The author suggests that the three theories or explanations most commonly put forth are political, biological, and sociological.

Another important contribution to the symposium, the Hooyman and Kaplan article discusses the significant barriers to high-level positions within human services organizations. The authors include suggestions about what types of training and skill sets might help women overcome persistent interpersonal, internal, and structural barriers to their professional success, even in the realm of human services organizations.

14

Circumventing the Glass Ceiling

Women Executives in American State Governments

Angela M. Bullard
University of North Carolina–Chapel Hill

Deil S. Wright
University of North Carolina–Chapel Hill

Are women executives in state governments confronted with the "glass ceiling"? Using data from the American State Administration Project's 1984 and 1988 surveys, Angela M. Bullard and Deil S. Wright answer that and related questions. They find that women have made considerable inroads in securing top administrative posts, especially in certain types of agencies and newly created organizations. However, much of their progress has been accomplished by circumventing or avoiding rather than "breaking" the glass ceiling. The data also indicate female and male executives are becoming more similar in terms of educational levels, types of graduate degrees, hours worked per week, the mix of administrative and policy functions, and salary levels. Differences in factors such as party affiliation, age, interagency mobility, career progress, and dependence on gubernatorial appointment remain noticeable.

Source: *Public Administration Review* 53 (May/June 1993): 189–202. Special thanks are expressed to the Earhart Foundation of Ann Arbor, MI for assistance in collecting some of the data on which this article is based.

265

Gender issues are now and probably will remain for the foreseeable future highly significant aspects of both the theory and the practice of public administration (Hale and Kelly, 1989; Guy, 1992). One issue, equal female representation, has been particularly prominent in organizational studies in both the public and the private sectors. This article addresses gender representation at the top levels of administration in American state governments. Our focus on women agency heads in state governments, however, extends beyond mere representative proportions. We also explore (with survey data) several common and not-so-common characteristics of women and men who head the thousands of administrative agencies, large and small, of the 50 states.

From a representational standpoint, the presence of a glass ceiling is a prominent issue in American organizational culture. We define a glass ceiling as the actual or perceived barrier or cap beyond which few women (or other previously excluded minorities) in public and private organizational structures are able to move. For example, many women may have obtained the position of corporate vice-president, but for some reason cannot achieve the top position of chief executive officer despite their qualifications and efforts. In this respect, the glass ceiling is roughly comparable to a pay cap for women.

The glass ceiling operates in both the public and the private sectors. A report by the U.S. Department of Labor in 1991 was widely recognized as confirming the presence of a glass ceiling in corporate America (Desky, 1991). One columnist (Rivers, 1991) noted that, "Now even a conservative administration has certified that the glass ceiling is as real as steel." Conservative pundit J. J. Kilpatrick (1991) weighed in with a strong critical commentary on Labor Department and other studies about restricted prospects for women. "American employers, for the most part, are overlooking a resource that could make a tremendous difference over the next 40 years. They are ignoring women. This is, when you think about it, a thoroughly dumb thing to do."

Somewhat lost in the commentary was a stark statistic: only 6.6 percent of the corporate executives were women. Less than three weeks after the Labor Department study, another report released by the Feminist Majority Foundation disclosed that only 2.6 percent of 6,500 corporate officers in the *Fortune* 500 companies were women. Whether the percentages are 2–3 or 7 seems inconsequential in relation to the larger questions of individual, organizational, policy, and political significance surrounding the access of women (and other minorities) to top-level executive positions.

We will explore a few findings that are somewhat more encouraging with regard to executive career prospects for women. Our focus is on the public sector. More specifically, we examine gender patterns at the peak administrative levels across the 50 American state governments.

Female State Administrators

Research on women as public executives, managers, and administrators (we use the three terms interchangeably) has received relatively limited attention. A 1984

BOX 14.1　Major Features of the American State Administration Project (ASAP) Surveys

The ASAP surveys (and resulting data sets) are recurrent mail questionnaire studies that have been conducted twice in each of three decades—1964, 1968, 1974, 1978, 1984, 1988. The ASAP respondents are the administrative heads of the various and numerous "agencies" in the 50 state governments. The names (and addresses) of the agency heads were obtained from *The Book of the States*, Supplement II, *State Administrative Officials by Function*. This biennial publication lists the administrative heads by type of agency (function) on a biennial basis. The listing of agency heads (ranging from 2,000 to 4,000 individuals) was current as of 1 July in the year prior to the one in which the survey was conducted. (It takes several months to compile and publish each list.)

During the 1960s, 2,000–2,500 names were compiled for 40–50 different types of agencies. For the two surveys conducted in the 1960s, the designated heads of 30–35 different types of agencies constituted the universe (of 1,400–1,600) that received questionnaires. The numbers of respondents to the 1964 and 1968 surveys were 925 and 989, respectively, for response rates of 71 and 64 percent. Beginning with the 1974 survey, the number of agencies (and heads) was expanded significantly to accommodate the rapidly increasing number of new types of agencies created in state governments across the country during the late 1960s and 1970s. (See Jenks and Wright, 1993, for documentation of "agency activism" in the states across the decades from the 1950s through the 1980s.)

The number of agencies, universe (possible respondents), number of respondents, and response rates for the four surveys in the 1970s and 1980s are indicated in the following tabulation:

Year	Number of Agencies	Universe (Possible Respondents)	Actual Respondents	Response Rate(%)
1974	68	2,909	1,580	54
1978	76	2,985	1,393	47
1984	74	2,963	1,120	38
1988	80	3,115	1,453	47

The scope, content, and length of the ASAP questionnaires has varied across the three decades. In the 1960s, the survey instrument contained only 80–100 data elements. In addition to fairly standard personal attributes and characteristics of administrators, the instrument covered selected agency-descriptive and administrator-attitude items.

(continues)

BOX 14.1   (*continued*)

Data collection instruments in the 1970s were expanded considerably to encompass approximately 200 data elements. The three major areas of expanded coverage were agency head policy relationships, educational and professional attributes and activities, and intergovernmental perspectives and preferences.

An effort to continue in 1984 with the scope and length of the 1970s survey instruments produced a significantly reduced response rate—from around 50 percent in the 1970s to under 40 percent in 1984. To compensate for survey-saturation problems, we reduced the scope of the 1988 instrument from nearly over 200 data elements to around 160 (from 11 pages to 7 pages). This change, plus other operational enhancements, raised the response rate to nearly 50 percent in 1988.

The coding, check-coding, data-entry, and other mechanics of the data gathering and processing followed as closely as possible the recommended standard survey techniques. It is impossible to acknowledge here the numerous graduate assistants, faculty colleagues, and others who have made significant contributions to the ASAP surveys, analyses, papers, and publications. Four sources of financial assistance and operational support can and should be briefly noted. University-based sources include the University of Iowa (Graduate Research Council) and the University of North Carolina (the University Research Council), and particularly the Institute for Research in Social Science at the latter institution. Also, significant assistance in connection with the 1974 ASAP survey was provided by the National Science Foundation, Research Applied to National Needs Program. A fourth and most significant source of support of the ASAP surveys (in the 1970s and 1980s) has been the Earhart Foundation of Ann Arbor, Michigan.

---

study revealed that women administrators were significantly better represented in state-local governments than in the private sector (Dometrius and Sigelman, 1984). A study in California of top-level career executives found women better represented than in the federal senior executive service. It also disclosed that women shared a "management ideology" and other attitudinal and demographic characteristics that were quite similar to their male counterparts (Rehfuss, 1986).

More recently, a six-state study found that "state-level governmental positions may be more likely to reward women than federal positions," and that "women are promoted at younger ages with less time in rank than men are" (Kelly, Guy, *et al.*, 1991, p. 411). The study concluded, however, that "Nonetheless, little evidence exists that more than minimal level and type of equality have taken place." This was based on the persistent lagging percentages of women in supervisory and managerial posts. The focus of our research likewise involves gender representation as well as the comparability of various personal, professional, and role attributes of women and men who head state administrative agencies. The primary database for this analysis came from successive mall questionnaire surveys of the official heads of state government administrative agencies in all 50 states. Agency heads were surveyed regardless of the method of appointment/approval process by which they gained office (popularly elected, politically appointed, or merit and professional selection). The primary survey years were 1984 and 1988, but these constituted only two in a series of six surveys of the same populations conducted by the senior author in comparable years of the 1960s and 1970s. For reference purposes, these are termed ASAP (American State Administration Project) surveys.

Only data for the decade of the 1980s are analyzed in depth here, although comparable figures from all six ASAP surveys are mentioned for longer-term trend purposes.

Female Representation Among State Agency Heads

Particularly pertinent to this study is the proportion of state administrative heads who are women. The percentages for each ASAP survey were:

1964: 2	1974: 4	1984: 11
1968: 5	1978: 7	1988: 18

The three-decade upward trend and the 1988 figure of 18 percent make the exploration of these data especially interesting, and they also raise significant questions. Do state governments show more than a slight crack in the glass ceiling? Are state administrative establishments conducive to women "circumventing" rather than "breaking" the ceiling? By circumventing, we mean moving to the top by going around or outside the glass ceiling through routes such as new agencies or gubernatorial appointment. By breaking, we refer to large numbers of women taking the conventional path of working their way diligently, perhaps patiently, and effectively to the top.

Before we analyze the 1980's ASAP survey data in greater depth, we will supplement these findings and confirm the ASAP survey results through an independent method. The Council of State Governments (CSG) publishes sources that include the given names (as well as surnames) of all state agency heads. We counted the number of clear (or probable) female names appearing among the three to four thousand names listed. We did this for each of the years of the ASAP surveys, as well as for the most recent (1990) list. For the six ASAP-related lists, we also tallied female-designated names by type of agency. For the 1990 list, we identified women agency heads both by agency type and by state. This process produced the following results:

Year	Number of Female Names	Approximate Number of Agencies	Percent
1964	116	3,000	4
1968	139	3,000	5
1974	188	3,500	5
1978	251	3,500	7
1984	489	4,000	12
1988	658	4,000	16
1990	770	4,000	19

In each instance, this approach produced results comparable within 2 percentage points of the ASAP figures for each survey year. Although the exact proportion of women agency heads remains elusive, the ASAP survey results combined with the name-counting procedure give us reasonable confidence that by the end of the 1980s women held nearly 20 percent of the top administrative (agency head) posts in state governments.

Although this figure remains far short of equality, it represents one of the highest proportions identified among almost any broad-based administrative or political cohort that we have encountered. It is a long distance ahead of the 5 percent of all city managers who are women (Renner, 1990). It evidently exceeds the 16 percent of all state legislators who are women (Carroll, 1991).

If women have gained notably greater access past the ceiling in state administrative establishments, we need to seek explanations for this encouraging and significant phenomenon. Our first step in exploring the increase in the number of women executives relied on the name-counting process. We report below the frequencies of women executives by type of agency and also by state in order to determine where the glass ceiling has been broken or circumvented.

Agency (Stereo)Typing

The idea of gender typing, as well as stereotyping, is one of the more pervasive concepts in the literature on female socialization generally, and on organizational roletyping in particular. Individual-level socialization analysis has its organizational-level counterpart, namely, the likelihood of gender-linked/typed administrative agencies (Powell, 1988). This line of thinking prompted us to look at state agencies from a gender-based perspective. That is, in some agencies it might be highly unlikely that females could achieve the top post despite aspirations and qualifications for the position. Two illustrative agencies in this group might be the national guard (headed by the adjutant general) and forestry. However, some administrative agencies are characteristically more open and accessible to women, for example, library and welfare.

Although these examples are oversimplified and extreme, they offer a starting point for classifying agencies by degree of female access to top-level state administrative posts. Using the gender-identifiable given names from the CSG lists (by type of agency), we constructed the following classifications of 52 agencies that existed in both 1964 and 1988.

1. Male exclusive: no female executives in 1964; none in 1988.
2. Male dominant: 0–2 female executives in 1964; 1–5 in 1988.
3. Modified male dominant: 0–2 female executives in 1964; 6 or more in 1988.
4. Modest female presence: 3–9 female executives in 1964; 10 or more in 1988.
5. Significant female presence: 10 or more female executives in 1964; 20 or more in 1988.

The product of our analysis according to these numerical criteria appears below.

Gender Group	Number of Agencies	Illustrative Agency Titles
Male exclusive	6	Adjutant General, Agriculture, Corrections, Fishery, Forestry, State Police
Male dominant	18	Aeronautics, Budget, Highway, Parks, Parole, Water Pollution
Modified male dominant	19	Banking, Comptroller, Education, Health, Securities, Purchasing
Modest female presence	5	Employment Security, Mental Health, Personnel, Secretary of State, Social Services
Significant female presence	4	Aging, Library, Public Assistance, Treasurer

(The full listing of all 52 agencies by each gender grouping appears in Table 14.6.)

The frequencies of agencies appearing in the male-exclusive and male-dominant categories are not surprising given the continued preponderance (about 80 percent) of males as executives in state governments. Nor do the types of agencies remaining the primary preserve of men offer any surprises; they are agencies with tasks and career paths that women have not been encouraged to pursue.

The substantial number of agencies (19) in the modified male dominant category presents an interesting and perhaps transitional group. Recall that these are agencies with 2 or fewer female executives in 1964 but 6 or more (several had 10–15) women in 1988. In terms of numbers and variety, this grouping of agencies probably offered important arenas or avenues of opportunity for women to reach state agency top administrative posts. The names of these agencies, from administration and finance through workers compensation, suggests that women gaining these leadership posts represented breaks or at least cracks in the glass ceiling.

In a few state agencies, even as early as 1964, women had already achieved a modest or significant presence. These types of agencies are listed (in full) for the two groups above (also in Table 14.6). These nine agency types also offered major increased opportunities for women to achieve positions at the top of state government agencies.

Perhaps a more significant avenue to the top of state agencies is the access by women to the executive posts in newly created state agencies. We call this the ceiling-circumvention strategy because women need not work their way up the ladder and through the ceiling of an established agency's power structure to attain the top leadership post. To grasp the significance of this concept, it is necessary to mention briefly the "agency activism" occurring in state governments during the 1960s and 1970s (Wright, Hebert, Brudney, 1991; Jenks and Wright, 1993).

Agencies in existence in 38 or more of the 50 states at the end of four recent decades are listed in appendix 2. In 1959, 51 types of agencies were present in 38 or more states. By 1989, the number had nearly doubled, to 99. In short, a tremendous surge of administrative activity occurred in state governments from the 1960s through the 1980s, with almost 50 new types of agencies appearing on the administrative scene. The crest of this activity came during the 1970s (Table 14.7). That decade was also one of emergent and strengthened activism on the part of women in several social, economic, and political-administrative arenas.

The last component in Table 14.6 is an alternate way of showing the expanded opportunity structure in state government available to women. Listed there are 19 agency types that came into being after 1964. The parenthetical frequencies indicate the number of states in which women headed those agencies in 1989. The number of female executives is nearly 200. This is roughly 5 percent of all state agency heads and is also nearly one-fourth of all female state executives.

The convergence of women's activism and state administrative activism may have been fortuitous; on the other hand, the two developments may have been linked in some way. Whatever the case, from the 1960s through the 1980s, somewhere in the vicinity of 1,500 new and/or formally identified state administrative agencies came into existence. It seems evident that these entities constituted an opportunity that was accessed by significant numbers of women. Instead of needing to crack or break the glass ceiling, these agencies permitted avoidance or circumvention. These new agencies reduced women's need to wait their turn (if it ever came) or to "pay their dues" (to whom?). The new agencies may also have modified the pressures to break the glass ceiling in older, more established agencies.

Administrative activism in the states, it seems to us, offered women an extension ladder to climb to the top of state agency "roofs." This external ladder reduced the need for aspiring female administrators to pursue the long, slow stair climbing from within administrative structures.

We have examined in the aggregate the increased representation of women in state administration. What about individual states? We again used the gender-name process from published sources to identify those states with the highest and lowest numbers of women executives. Not every state has identical or even the same total number of administrative agencies, so it is not possible to specify percentages of female administrators for each of the 50 states. Therefore, only simple frequencies of female agency heads are reported below. These results reflect the different political, administrative, and organizational conditions across the states confronted by women seeking executive positions.

Number of Female State Administrators (Agency Heads) by State 1989

Highest	Lowest
Minnesota (24)	Texas (4)
Vermont (23)	Georgia (5)
Ohio (21)	South Carolina (6)
Nebraska (19)	Kentucky (6)
Washington (19)	Alabama (7)
Virginia (18)	Missouri (7)
New Mexico (17)	Delaware (7)
Nevada (17)	New Hampshire (7)
Illinois (17)	North Dakota (8)
Utah (17)	North Carolina (9)
South Dakota (9)	
Maine (9)	

Displaying these state-specific figures is a reminder of the obvious: the 50 states are separate, distinctive, relatively autonomous, political-administrative systems. Any breakthroughs or circumventions by women must occur within these state-specific systems. Already, for example, the 1990 election of a woman governor in Texas has transformed the character and composition of that state's administrative arrangements (Maraniss, 1991). Organizational ceilings, ladders, and roofs do not exist in aggregate, metaphorical, or abstract forms. Rather, they are clearly present (or absent) around the state capitol, the governor's mansion, and in the executive offices of state agencies. Progress toward greater and equal representation by women occurs in state-specific, agency-specific, and individual-specific instances.

Executive Attributes and Backgrounds

In this section we compare the personal, social background, and educational attributes of female and male executives using data chiefly from the 1984 and 1988 ASAP surveys. Three common personal attributes—age, education, and party identification—are discussed.

Age

Consistent with findings from other research on public executives, we found that female state executives are younger than their male counterparts (Kelly, Guy, *et al.*, 1991). Furthermore, even in the short span between the two ASAP surveys a notable drop in age occurred for women as well as for men. In 1984, roughly 40 percent of the women executives were under 45, but by 1988, the proportion was well above 50 percent. The comparable percentages for men were 29 and 39, respectively (Figure 14.1).

Why are women executives younger? Is the age difference linked to less experience? To faster career tracks? To greater educational and other competencies? The difference, which is substantial, prompts more questions than we can address from either descriptive, policy, or theoretical standpoints. We can, however, address the factor of education.

Education

The findings by level of education reveal no consequential or prominent contrasts in the educational achievements of female and male state executives (Figure 14.2). Slightly less than 10 percent of both groups in both survey years had less than a bachelor degree. At the other end of the spectrum, around 60 percent of both groups held graduate degrees in 1984 and 1988. The level of education shows little difference as a distinctive variable in demonstrating gender contrasts among state agency heads.

What about the type of educational experience obtained by female and male executives? Is there a difference in educational preparation? Tables 14.1 and 14.2 provide data, by type of degrees and by major fields, that enable us to address these questions.

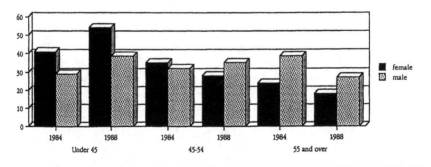

FIGURE 14.1   Age of Female and Male Agency Heads, 1984 and 1988
                      (in percent)

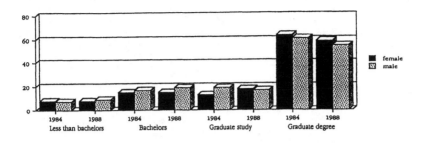

FIGURE 14.2   Education of Female and Male Agency Heads, 1984 and 1988
(in percent)

Some differences existed in the content of the educational experiences of
women and men executives in state governments. Women were far more likely to
hold bachelor of arts degrees. In contrast, men held their first degree(s) more in
engineering and business than women. Although some differences are pronounced, they are by no means extreme or polarized. In the science field, for example, the percentages were roughly comparable.

An exploration of the second (or master) degrees held by state executives suggests some attenuation of the differences present at the bachelor level. A slightly
higher proportion of women held MA degrees in 1984, but this margin virtually
disappeared by 1988. Likewise, the MS degree margin favoring men in 1984 declined in 1988.

The comparability of professional degrees in law and public administration between women and men is striking. Both sexes appear to have responded, consciously or not, to the call for nonspecialists in the management of state agencies.
For both groups and for both years, 25 to 30 percent of the agency heads held law
or public administration degrees.

Two specialty degree categories reveal some gender differences, but the contrasts are anything but dramatic. Higher proportions of men than women in both
survey years held master's degrees in engineering or business. In the health and library science fields, the reverse was true. The 1988 figures show the largest contrasts, with differences of 9 percentage points. These deserve mention mainly because of the *absence* of large and consistent differences.

The lack of dramatic differences in educational preparation and experience is
borne out by the data in Table 14.2. These tabulations are slightly more refined
versions of those in Table 14.1. They enable us to identify the specific field in
which the bachelor and master degrees were conferred. At the bachelor level, the
gender differences are evident in three field clusters. (1) Higher proportions of
women than men held degrees in education, behavioral science, and journalism;
(2) higher proportions of men than women held degrees in the natural/life

TABLE 14.1   Education of State Agency Heads: Type of Degree by Gender, 1984 and 1988 (as percentages)*

	1984		1988	
	Female	*Male*	*Female*	*Male*
Type of First Degree				
Bachelor of Arts	64	37	44	25
Bachelor of Science	23	25	18	25
Engineering, or Business	2	23	9	25
Other, not ascertained	11	14	30	25
Total	100	100	100	100
Number of Cases	*120*	*884*	*220*	*1,069*
Type of Second Degree				
Masters (Arts)	25	18	11	12
Masters (Science)	15	24	7	12
Law	13	15	14	17
Pub. Admin./Planning	14	15	13	17
Engineering, or Business	5	8	5	14
Health, Library Science	10	4	15	6
Other, not ascertained	18	22	35	26
Total	100	100	100	100
Number of Cases	*80*	*548*	*144*	*641*

*Percentages may not total 100 because of rounding error.

sciences; and (3) men have had significantly more exposure to engineering, business, and mathematics.

When we examine gender differences involving second-level degrees, however, the bachelor-level results are substantially modified. Almost without exception, the female-male percentage-point differences are notably reduced. What appears to happen is that the few gender differences that seem somewhat sharp at the first-degree level are noticeably reduced by predominantly professional second degrees. Recall, of course, that about 60 percent of all the executives hold graduate degrees. We should also note that nearly 75 percent of those with baccalaureate degrees also have obtained master's degrees.

Political Party

Another important personal attribute to consider when comparing male and female state agency heads is their political party preference. One major barrier facing women in both politics and administration is active and open recruitment. Both the Democratic and Republican parties have been slow in accepting women

TABLE 14.2   Education of State Agency Heads: Major Field by Degree Level and
Gender, 1984 and 1988 (as percentages)*

	1984		1988	
	Female	Male	Female	Male
Major/Field—First Degree				
Behavioral science, education, humanities, journalism, library science	44	19	31	16
Natural and life science, natural and agri. resources	6	17	7	14
Criminal justice, social work, public administration/management/policy	1	3	5	5
Social sciences	34	29	31	24
Engineering, business, math	12	30	13	28
Other, not ascertained	2	1	13	13
Total	100	100	100	100
Number of cases	108	764	219	1,065
Major/Field—Second Degree				
Behav. sci., educ., humanities, journalism, library science	30	22	37	16
Natural and life science, natural and agri. resources	5	9	3	8
Criminal justice, social work, public administration/management/policy	25	26	26	21
Social sciences	11	10	6	10
Law	14	16	15	17
Engineering, business, math	8	17	6	16
Other, not ascertained	6	0	7	13
Total	100	100	100	100
Number of cases	79	562	149	669

*Percentages may not total 100 because of rounding error.

as equals, in giving them important roles in party management, and in encouraging and supporting them as candidates for public office (Githens and Prestage, 1977). As Stanwick phrases this dilemma, "Women will run in spite of the party, not because of the party" (Stanwick, 1983, p. 4).

Although both parties have lagged in recruiting females for top leadership and campaign positions, they do not seem to provide equal amounts of openness and support. Currently, Democratic women feel more positive about party participation

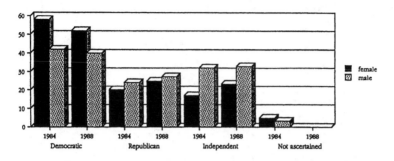

FIGURE 14.3   Political Party Identification of Female and Male Agency Heads,
             1984 and 1988 (in percent)

than do Republican women. Overall, many politically active females feel the terms "feminism" and "Republicanism" contradict each other. Although some female Republicans are choosing to remain with their party in a attempt to change this situation, other women advocate crossing party lines to increase female political participation and election (Stanwick, 1983).

As a result of this partisan difference in political support for females, presumably at all levels of government, one might expect that a majority of female state agency heads would identify with the more supportive Democratic party. Analysis of the ASAP data shows this to be the case (Figure 14.3). In both 1984 and 1988, a majority (58 and 52 percent) of women classified themselves as Democrats. By way of contrast, only 20–25 percent identified themselves as Republicans. Independents were roughly 20 percent of the female respondents.

One difficulty with this Democratic dominance thesis for women is that the partisan configuration of many/most top-level state agency posts can be and regularly is strongly affected by the partisan character of the gubernatorial office. In fact, 35 of the states had incumbent Democratic governors in 1984 and 30 in 1988. We are, therefore, not surprised to see a majority of female state executives expressing Democratic party allegiance.

What is somewhat surprising, however, is the significantly lower proportion of men who are Democratic identifiers. Roughly 40 percent of the men put themselves in this category. Where are the non-Democratic male identifiers? Not in the Republican column in any appreciable number, but rather in the independent category. Thus, there is a political gender gap among state executives but it is asymmetric. It exists chiefly on the Democratic side of the political fence. Neither the origins nor the dynamics of these results can be examined further here.

Social Backgrounds

When considering state executives' personal attributes, it is important to remember family background factors. Parental influence on children is obviously great.

Children are usually more similar to than different from their parents. Since state agency heads overall have achieved a high level of education, it seems quite likely that they were encouraged toward educational achievements by parental educational attainment.

The ASAP data on the education of state executives' parents demonstrate that overall, state administrators come from high-achieving backgrounds. Roughly 20–40 percent of the executives' parents held college degrees. (Recall that the parents of the average-age state administrator would have attended college prior to World War II.) The main question, however, is whether women achievers in the administrative arena come from backgrounds that are more highly educated. Our analysis of the ASAP data tend to confirm this. Higher proportions of both the mothers and fathers of female executives held college degrees than was the case for male executives (Table 14.3). The percentage-point differences are slightly larger between the women and men when the father's education is examined. The consistent differences with regard to maternal educational achievement, however, should not be discounted.

Education, of course, can be a powerful socializing force, regardless of gender. Another significant orienting and socializing factor can be parental involvement in the public service, in either elected or appointed posts. To explore the presence and potential influence of parental participation in public affairs, we asked the ASAP respondents to indicate maternal and paternal involvement in public life. Only about 5 percent of all respondents' mothers had held some public office, but 15–20 percent of respondents' fathers had been in public affairs.

Was parental public affairs participation greater among the parents of female executives than among the parents of men? The answer is a firm but cautious, yes. It is firm because the proportions are consistently higher, for both mother and father, for women executives and cautious because the differences, while consistent, are very modest, only 2 to 5 percentage points. Here, too, the percentage-point separations are larger among the fathers of women executives than among the mothers.

Although the results bear further analysis and reflection, it is evident that social background factors exert consistent and perhaps important influences on the prospects for women attaining posts in state government. It is of little consolation, of course, to admonish aspiring females to "choose your parents carefully." However, if the current real, artificial, and arbitrary barriers to female entry into top posts are removed, then past legacies, such as family background, may disappear as a distinctive factor in the social origins of women executives.

Career Paths

Our attention now shifts to the paths or routes by which female and male executives reach the prime position in their agencies. How do executives reach the top in state administrative agencies? How long does it take? How long do they stay?

TABLE 14.3   Parental Education and Public Service of State Agency Heads by Gender, 1984 and 1988 (as percentages)*

	1984		1988	
	Female	*Male*	*Female*	*Male*
Education of Mother				
Less than a bachelor's degree	68	79	74	81
Bachelors–graduate degree	27	17	26	19
Not ascertained	5	5	0	0
Total	100	100	100	100
Number of cases	132	958	233	1,123
Education of Father				
Less than a bachelor's degree	61	77	65	77
Bachelors–graduate degree	33	19	35	23
Not ascertained	5	5	0	0
Total	100	100	100	100
Number of cases	132	958	240	1,125
Mother in Government Office				
Yes	5	4	7	4
No	93	94	93	96
Not ascertained	2	2	0	0
Total	100	100	100	100
Number of cases	132	958	240	1,175
Father in Government Office				
Yes	20	15	21	16
No	79	83	79	84
Not ascertained	2	2	0	0
Total	100	100	100	100
Number of cases	132	958	241	1,177

*Percentages may not total 100 because of rounding error.

What types of mobility have they had? And most important for our purposes, are there significant differences between women and men in their respective routes to the top? We focus on these questions exclusively from the standpoint of gender similarities and contrasts.

Mobility Track to the Top

How did female and male executives enter the top posts in their agencies and what was the nature of the positions they held immediately prior to assuming direction of the agency? Perhaps the dominant image of a track to the top of an

TABLE 14.4   Career Paths of State Agency Heads by Gender, 1984 and 1988
(as percentages)*

	1984		1988	
	Female	*Male*	*Female*	*Male*
Age at Entrance into State Government				
25 and under	27	33	33	33
26–30	25	25	16	25
31–40	30	23	28	23
41–and over	18	19	23	19
Total	100	100	100	100
Number of cases	*132*	*958*	*241*	*1,170*
Mean age	*33*	*32*	*33*	*32*
Median age	*30*	*29*	*32*	*29*
Number of Other State Agencies Have Served				
No other	40	50	45	49
1	28	25	26	25
2	20	14	15	15
3 or more	12	11	13	11
Total	100	100	100	100
Number of cases	*132*	*929*	*238*	*1,174*
Service in Another State's Government				
Yes	8	16	14	14
No	92	81	86	86
Not ascertained	0	3	0	0
Total	100	100	100	100
Number of cases	*132*	*929*	*236*	*1,175*
Previous Position or Post				
Subordinate position	29	40	34	40
Another agency	35	20	22	19
Agency in another state	2	8	5	5
Local, state, or fed. legislation	14	12	18	12
Private, self, military, other	21	20	21	23
Total	100	100	100	100
Number of cases	*115*	*820*	*231*	*1,122*

*Percentages may not total 100 because of rounding error.

agency is spending many years laboring in the agency trenches and expecting a gradual but progressive rise to the top post. This pattern, however, for both women and men is the exception rather than the rule in state administrative agencies.

For men in both 1984 and 1988, only 40 percent succeeded to the top post from a subordinate position in the agency. For women executives, the proportions are somewhat less—roughly one-third. In short, more women than men come in as agency outsiders to head state administrative units (Table 14.4).

A substantial component of women move into top posts from other agencies within the same state. Over one-third followed this route in 1984, while in 1988 the proportion dropped below one-fourth. Only 20 percent of the men took over agencies through this type of lateral move.

Another type of lateral movement is from an agency in another state. This interstate geographic mobility is a sparse recruiting strategy for agency heads; only about 5 percent follow that route. A small difference was evident between women and men along this exceptional path in 1984, but the difference disappeared in 1988.

Other sources for recruiting state agency heads are several and substantial. Roughly 10–15 percent come to the top posts from local or national positions, or from the state legislature. Around 20 percent come directly from the private sector. For none of these categories, however, are there large and consistent differences between women and men. In sum, the path to the top in terms of penultimate positions is not greatly different between women and men, apart from a somewhat smaller proportion of women coming from a subordinate post within the agency. The overriding feature seems to be that, regardless of gender, numerous and varied roads are traveled by persons who succeed to state agency top positions.

How disparate is the mobility of state executives in terms of interagency movement? In how many different agencies (in the same state) have the executives served? About half of the men have worked in only one agency while somewhat smaller percentages (40–45 percent) of the women have had only single-agency experiences (Table 14.4). Here, too, the gender differences are minimal, although they tend to be consistent. The women who have attained the top posts in state agencies have slightly more interagency mobility than men. This pattern fits the circumvention theme developed earlier; female executives make more lateral moves among agencies to attain a top post. The empirical evidence for this pattern is suggestive but it falls far short of solid confirmation.

The slightly greater agency mobility and outsider patterns involving females' routes to the top is supported by another tabulation in Table 14.4. This is the age at which female and male executives entered state government. The mean and median figures show that females are slightly *older* than males when they first held a state position, but the differences are very small and not statistically significant. Nevertheless, the entry age differences and the younger current age of women agency heads compared to men hints at more rapid upward mobility for females. The next section addresses this question directly.

Career Progress

Temporal aspects of executives' careers reveal both consistent and sharp gender contrasts—in terms of years in state government, years in agency, and years in current position. The percentage distributions as well as the means and medians for women and men are reported in Table 14.5. The general thrust of the findings

TABLE 14.5   Career Progress Rates of State Agency Heads by Gender, 1984 and 1988 (as percentage)*

	1984		1988	
	Female	*Male*	*Female*	*Male*
Number of Years in State Government				
Under 5	32	20	28	22
5–9	30	21	25	16
10–14	21	24	25	19
15 and over	17	35	22	44
Total	100	100	100	100
Number of cases	132	939	239	1,166
Mean years	8.9	13.2	10.1	13.8
Median years	7	11	9	13
Number of Years In Current Agency				
Under 5	61	37	50	37
5–9	27	24	27	20
10–14	8	16	11	16
15 and over	5	23	11	28
Total	100	100	100	100
Number of cases	130	936	237	1,155
Mean years	5.4	9.9	6.9	10.7
Median years	4	7	5	8
Number of Years In Current Position				
1–2	58	36	55	39
3–4	22	23	23	22
5–9	18	26	19	33
10 and over	3	16	4	17
Total	100	100	100	100
Number of cases	130	932	231	1,158
Mean years	3.3	5.3	3.4	5.4
Median years	2	4	2	4

*Percentages may not total 100 because of rounding error.

is to confirm that women have shorter tenure than men (a) in their current posts, (b) in the agency they head, and (c) in state government.

The mean length of time worked in state government by women was, for 1984 and 1988, roughly 9 and 10 years. The comparable figures for men were 13 and 14. The median measures reflect the similar and significant differences, roughly four years shorter service for women.

The consistency of the previous findings is borne out in the statistics for tenure in the agency that they head. The means are about four years shorter for women than men. The medians show women averaging three years less in the agency than men—four compared to seven in 1984; five compared to eight in 1988. Finally, in terms of current executive positions, women have served, on average, two years less than men.

While women move to the top more rapidly than men, they also have been at the top for notably shorter periods of time. These findings offer further support for the thesis that in recent years women have experienced greater success in circumventing rather than breaking the glass ceiling.

Aggregate Issues and Further Findings

Our research results lead to an important question. Are state governments different? If state administration is distinctive, then how and why? We have addressed in an aggregate way the degree of openness of executive posts in state governments to women. Are state administrative agencies, with their accompanying gender similarities and differences, exceptions to the patterns present at other levels of government? Are there other small niches or larger opportunity structures where women have made advances that are comparable to those made in the states? Further research is needed to identify such niches or structures, in particular states and/or in other jurisdictions.

Appointment/Approval Process

Also at the aggregate level is the question of *administrative* as contrasted to *political* executives. Early gender-focused research examined varieties of political participation and access to political office—commonly defined as elected public office. More recent research efforts have examined female access to and careers, styles, and effectiveness in public administrative posts (Kelly, Guy, *et al.*, 1991; Guy, 1992; and references cited therein).

A small percentage of the administrative posts falling within the purview of the ASAP surveys were elected positions. The proportions of all respondents who were elected officials in 1984 and 1988 were 4 and 5 percent, respectively. There were no differences in these percentages by gender (Figure 14.4).

The small percentage of elected state agency heads and the general absence of sharp gender differences emphasize the role and significance of appointed ad-

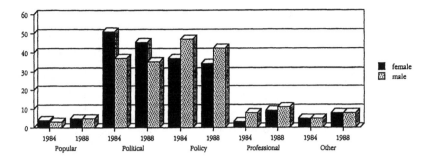

FIGURE 14.4   Method of Appointment/Approval of Agency Heads, 1984 and
1988 (in percent)

ministrators. From an explanatory standpoint, does open politics in a state promote an administrative climate more open to females? Some research (Saltzstein,
1986; Astin and Leland, 1991; Carroll, 1991) suggests that the symbolism, leadership, and influence of elected women make an impact on administrative personnel and policies. Whether such relationships can be confirmed at the state level or
elsewhere depends on further research and analyses.

Of course, the vast majority of state administrative posts are political, either in
an open partisan sense or in a policy/program advocacy sense. This is evident from
the fact that roughly half of all the agency head posts are filled through direct or indirect appointment by the governor. Examination of appointment methods by
gender disclosed two noteworthy differences (Figure 14.4). First, in both 1984 and
1988, significantly higher proportions of the female executives were governor appointed. (The percentage-point differences between women and men were in the
10–15 range.) Second, higher proportions of men than women were appointed
through an independent board or commission or through civil service processes.
These are designated as "policy" and "professional" appointments, respectively, in
Figure 14.4.

Time Allocation

There were virtually no differences in how female and male executives allocated
their time on the job between internal management, policy development, and
building public support (the most openly "political" activity). The percentages
were consistently similar not only across gender but also across ASAP surveys. In
both 1984 and 1988, women and men executives spent their time, on average, as
follows: internal management, 51 percent; policy development, 25 percent; public
support, 24 percent. These findings are consistent with a substantial body of research which, on balance, shows that the similarities between women and men in
management style and behavior outweigh the differences (Brown, 1979; Donnell
and Hall, 1980; Statham, 1987; Powell, 1988).

Hours Worked and Salaries

On two additional features of the executives' jobs, only modest differences were apparent. These involved hours worked (per week) and salaries. In 1984, women executives worked, on average, 3–4 hours more per week. The 1988 survey found virtually no differences in hours worked (Figure 14.5). The mean for female executives was slightly above 53 hours per week while it was slightly below 53 for males. The median hours worked per week by both men and women executives in 1988 was 50.

Slightly surprising were the results of reported salaries (in thousands of dollars) for female and male state executives in the two surveys.

Survey Year	Mean		Median	
	Female	Male	Female	Male
1984	45.8	47.1	44	46
1988	52.3	57.4	52	55

The salary findings are noteworthy because of their rough similarity (Figure 14.6). Salaries of female executives averaged around 95 percent of the average paid to male executives. A salary ratio this close to parity seems exceptional given the extensive findings on the great divergence between the average wages of women and men generally. A recent study reported on 1987 wage disparities between women and men in administrative and professional occupations in state and local governments. The difference was approximately 20 percentage points, or women in these positions earned about 80 percent of male salaries (Lewis and Nice, 1991).

The ASAP results suggest that as the upper ranks of state government have become, on a comparative basis, more open to women, the women who reach the

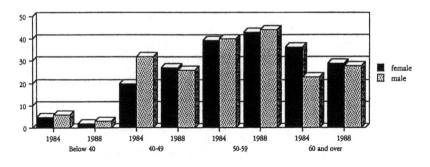

FIGURE 14.5   Hours Worked per Week by Female and Male Agency Heads, 1984 and 1988 (in percent)

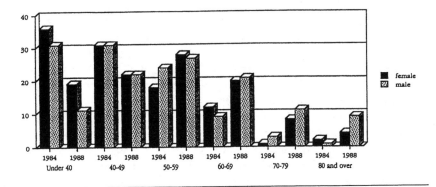

FIGURE 14.6   Salary of Agency Heads, 1984 and 1988 (in percent)

top appear to be treated more as equals from a salary standpoint. As the bulk of the reported data indicate, female and male administrators are more similar than different, and their salaries come closer to reflecting this fact. Of course, we cannot argue the fact that equality will only come when no gender-created salary disparity exists between male and female state agency heads.

Concluding Observations

This exploration of the executive opportunities for and the experience of women in state governments has disclosed several significant findings and has identified areas worthy of further research.

Major Findings

Women have made noteworthy progress in securing top administrative posts in state governments. While the proportion of agency heads who are women (about 20 percent) is higher than in most other executive sectors, including private (corporate) and other public sectors, the female component in state governments still falls far short of equality.

Despite their increased presence as executives in state government, women still tend to direct particular types of agencies. Examples include aging, library, personnel, and social services. Although shrinking in number, a few types of state agencies (e.g., adjutant general, corrections, forestry) remain headed exclusively by men.

A different "type" of state agency in which women are distinctively represented is the newly created agency. Large numbers of new agencies were created in the 50 states, especially during the 1960s and 1970s. These agencies have provided women with a chance to circumvent the glass ceiling that has been present in the older, more traditional state agencies, and women have taken advantage of this in considerable numbers. Examples of the newer agencies include: arts, community affairs, consumer protection, human resources, and medicaid.

Data from surveys of state agency heads in both 1984 and 1988 enable us to compare several attributes and activities of female and male executives. We find that gender similarities are greater than the differences, but the gender differences which do exist are noteworthy.

Among the general similarities are (1) level of education, (2) types of graduate degrees, (3) hours worked (per week), (4) allocation of time between management and policy activities, and (5) salary levels.

Among the differences between female and male state executives the following are most prominent: (1) political party identification, (2) age, (3) interagency mobility, (4) rates of progress to attain executive positions, and (5) appointment by the governor. The nature and direction of these differences can be briefly stated. Female agency heads, in contrast to males, (1) are more Democratic in party identification, (2) are younger, (3) have greater interagency mobility, (4) move to executive posts at a more rapid rate, and (5) secure their posts more through gubernatorial appointment than through standard professional career paths.

Evidence from multiple sources suggest that significant numbers of women have gained access to top state administrative posts by circumventing rather than breaking the glass ceiling. While there is evidence of movement by some women through traditional barriers, a major component of female access to executive posts in state governments has been the bypassing or circumvention route. These alternative avenues to the top for women have been identified as (1) access to new agencies, (2) appointment by the governor, and (3) interagency mobility. For women, these routes result in shorter periods of service in state government and in the agency they head.

Further Research

Our research, like research in general, raises as many or more questions than we have answered. We identify only a few of the paths deserving further investigation.

First, has female access to top posts in state governments continued to increase in the 1990s? If it has, what is the character, type, and extent of the increase? If gender (and other) diversity at the top has stabilized, what accounts for the stasis?

Second, is gender segregation by type of agency decreasing in the 1990s? In other words, is the glass ceiling being cracked or broken more than circumvented (as indicated by our analyses of the 1980s)?

Third, what changes, if any, are occurring in the gender similarities and differences among female and male agency heads? We might expect that the well-established similarities in attributes, achievements, and activities would continue. Have the gender differences in partisanship, age, mobility, career advancement rates, and routes to the top diminished?

TABLE 14.6 Types of State Administrative Agencies by Gender Presence/Dominance, 1964 and 1988

Male Exclusive (6)
(No females in 1964; none in 1988)

Adjutant General
Agriculture
Corrections
Fishery
Forestry
Law Enforcement (State Police)

Male Dominant (18)
(0–2 females in 1964; 5 or less in 1988)

Aeronautics
Attorney General
Budget
Commerce
Economic Development
Emergency Management
Geology
Highway
Labor
Liquor Control
Natural Resources
Oil and Gas
Parks and Recreation
Parole
Post-Audit
Soil Conservation
Water Pollution
Water Resources Management

Modest Female Presence (5)
(3–9 females in 1964; 10 or more in 1988)

Employment Security
Mental Health
Personnel
Secretary of State
Social Services

Modified Male Dominant (19)
(0–2 females in 1964; 6 or more in 1988)

Administration and Finance
Pollution
Banking
Comptroller
Education
Food Inspection
Health
Higher Education
Insurance
Labor Arbitration
Motor Vehicles
Planning
Public Utilities
Purchasing
Revenue Collection
Securities
Tourism
Vocational Education
Workers' Compensation

Significant Female Presence (4)
(10 or more females in 1964; 20 or more in 1988)

Aging
Library
Pubic Assistance (Welfare)
Treasurer

Agencies Created After 1964 (19)
(Number of female executives' names in 1988 in parentheses)

Arts (24)
Community Affairs (18)
Consumer Protection (10)
Criminal Justice Planning (4)
Drug Abuse (13)
Environment (7)
Federal-State Relations (16)
Highway Safety (8)
Housing Finance (4)
Human Relations (15)
Human Resources (18)
Juvenile Delinquency (9)
Licensing (9)
Manpower (18)
Mass Transit (6)
Medicaid (13)
Occupational Health (3)
State-Local Relations (15)
Vocational Rehabilitation (9)

TABLE 14.7 The Presence and Proliferation of State Administrative Agencies: 1959, 1969, 1979, 1989

A. Traditional or first-generation agencies (agencies present in 38 or more states consistently from 1959) –

1. Adjutant General
2. Aeronautics
3. Aging
4. Agriculture
5. Alcoholic Beverage Control
6. Attorney General
7. Banking
8. Budgeting
9. Child Welfare
10. Corrections
11. Education
12. Emergency Management (Civil Defense)
13. Employment Services
14. Fire Marshall
15. Fish and Game
16. Food (inspection/purity)

37. Purchasing
38. Revenue
39. Secretary of State
40. Securities (regulation)
41. Soil Conservation
42. Solid Waste (Sanitation)
43. Tourism (Advertising)
44. Treasurer
45. Unemployment Insurance
46. Veterans Affairs
47. Vocational Education
48. Water Quality
49. Water Resources
50. Welfare
51. Workers' Compensation

B. Second-generation agencies—1960s (additional agencies present in 38 or more states since 1969)

4. Child Abuse
5. Civil Rights
6. Consumer Affairs (Consumer Protection)
7. Energy
8. Environment
9. Ethics
10. Exceptional Children
11. Finance
12. Historic Preservation
13. Housing Finance
14. Human Resources
15. International Trade
16. Manpower
17. Mass Transit
18. Medicaid
19. Occupational Health Safety
20. Public Lands
21. Railroad
22. Savings & Loan

17. Forestry
18. Geology
19. Health
20. Higher Education
21. Highways
22. Insurance
23. Labor
24. Labor Arbitration & Mediation
25. Law Enforcement
26. Library
27. Mining
28. Mental Health
29. Motor Vehicles
30. Oil & Gas
31. Parks & Recreation
32. Parole
33. Personnel
34. Planning
35. Post Audit
36. Public Utility Regulation

1. Administration
2. Air Quality
3. Commerce
4. Community Affairs
5. Comptroller
6. Court Administration
7. Criminal Justice Planning
8. Economic Development
9. Federal-State Relations
10. Highway Safety
11. Juvenile Rehabilitation
12. Natural Resources

C. Third-generation agencies—1970s (additional agencies present in 38 or more states since 1979):

1. Alcohol and Drug Abuse
2. Archives
3. Arts Council(s)

23. Social Services
24. State-Local Relations
25. Telecommunication
26. Transportation
27. Veterinarian
28. Vocational Rehabilitation
29. Women's Commission(s)

D. Fourth-generation agencies—1980s (additional agencies present in 38 or more states in 1989)

1. Emergency Medical Services
2. Equal Employment Opportunity
3. Ground Water Management
4. Hazardous Waste
5. Small and Minority Business
6. Training & Development
7. Underground Storage Tanks
8. Horse Racing

SOURCE: Based on listing(s) found in *Book of the States*, Supplement II, *State Administrative Officials Classified by Functions*, Council of State Governments, Lexington, KY: 1959, 1969, 1979, 1989. Special thanks are due Deirdre Chernomas and Gordon Wright for their assistance in the development of this table.

Fourth, beyond the arena of state government rests an array of questions about which our research encourages exploration. What are the access patterns and opportunities for women executives in national and local governments? Are the access avenues or barriers to executive posts similar or different from those we have found in state government? Even more broadly and equally applicable to further state government research is the politics-administration question. Does greater access to *administrative* posts by women precede or follow the increased presence of women in *elected* political posts?

We interpret our research results as sending several messages. To the women who have attained top-level state positions, the message is one of commendation for achievements in finding avenues and access points that enabled them to circumvent significant barriers. To that same group, the message is one of esteem gained by serving as role models for other women who aspire to similar executive positions.

For any women who have an interest in public service, there is also a message. It is a positive one about the prospects for equity and advancement to key administrative posts, especially in state governments. Educational requirements are high, varied experience is common, and some type of state-level political participation is likely to be important.

Another message we draw from our findings is targeted to state government policy makers. Women executives have become, in our estimation, a critical component of the governance and administrative processes of the states. Barriers that encouraged or required women to circumvent glass ceilings in state agencies should no longer be tolerated. Good governance as well as equity argue that those obstacles shall not stand.

References

Astin, Helen S. and Carole Leland, 1991. *Women of Influence, Women of Vision.* San Francisco: Jossey-Bass.

Brown, Stephen M., 1979. "Male Versus Female Leaders: A Comparison of Empirical Studies." *Sex Roles: A Journal of Research,* vol. 5, pp. 595–611.

Carroll, Susan J., 1991. "Taking the Lead." *Journal of State Government.* vol. 64 (April–June), pp. 43–47.

Desky, Joanne, 1991. "Lower Level Managers Hit Glass Celling." PA TIMES, vol. 14 (November), p. 1.

Dometrius, Nelson C. and Lee Sigelman, 1984. "Assessing Progress Toward Affirmative Action Goals in State and Local Government: A New Benchmark." *Public Administration Review,* vol. 44 (May/June), pp. 241–246.

Donnell, S.M. and J. Hall, 1980. "Men and Women as Managers: A Significant Case of No Significant Difference." *Organizational Dynamics,* vol. 8, pp. 60–77.

Duerst-Lahti, Georgia, 1990. "But Women Can Play the Game Too: Communication Control and Influence in Administrative Decision-Making." *Administration and Society,* vol. 22 (August), pp. 182–205.

Githens, Marianne and Jewel L. Prestage, eds., 1977. *A Portrait of Marginality: The Political Behavior of the American Woman.* New York: Longman.

Guy, Mary E, ed, 1992. *Women and Men of the States: Public Administrators at the State Level.* Armonk, NY: M. E. Sharpe.

Hale, Mary M. and Rita Mae Kelly, eds., 1989. *Gender, Bureaucracy, and Democracy.* Westport, CT: Greenwood Press.

Jenks, Stephen S. and Dell S. Wright, 1993. "An Agency-Level Approach to Changes in Administrative Functions of American State Governments." *State and Local Government Review,* vol. 25 (forthcoming).

Kelly, Rita Mae and Mary E. Guy, *et al.,* 1991. "Public Managers in the States: A Comparison of Career Advancement by Sex." *Public Administration Review,* vol. 51 (September/October), pp. 402–412.

Kilpatrick, James J., 1991. "Where the Good Ol' Boys Are Is Still Off-Limits." *News and Observer.* Raleigh, NC, 17 September, p. 9A.

Lewis, Gregory B. and David Nice, 1991. "Interstate Differences in Racial and Sexual Segregation of Occupation by State and Local Governments: Causes and Consequences." Paper presented at the annual meeting of the American Political Science Association, Washington, DC: 28 August–1 September, 27 pp.

Maraniss, David, 1991. "What's Texas Without All Those, Good Old Boys?" *Washington Post National Weekly Edition,* January 21–27, p. 14.

Powell, Gary N., 1988. *Women and Men in Management.* Beverly Hills, CA: Sage Publications.

Rehfuss, John A., 1986. "A Representative Bureaucracy? Women and Minority Executives in California Career Service." *Public Administration Review,* vol. 46 (September/October), pp. 454–460.

Renner, Tari, 1990. "Appointed Local Government Managers: Stability and Change." *The Municipal Year Book 1990.* Washington, DC: International City Management Association, pp. 41–52.

Rivers, Caryl, 1991. "Glass Ceiling and Limits on Leadership." *News and Observer.* Raleigh, NC, 25 August, p. 31.

Salzstein, Grace Hall, 1986. "Female Mayors and Women in Municipal Jobs." *American Journal of Political Science,* vol. 30 (February), pp. 140–164.

Stanwick, Kathy A., 1983. *Political Women Tell What It Takes.* New Brunswick, NJ: Center for the American Woman and Politics.

Statham, Anne, 1987. "The Gender Model Revisited: Differences in Management Styles of Men and Women." *Sex Roles: A Journal of Research,* vol. 16, pp. 409–429.

Wright, Deil S., F. Ted Hebert, and Jeffrey L. Brudney, 1991. "Administrative Activism in the American States: Three Decades of Aggregate, Agency, and Administrator Actions and Activities." Paper presented at the annual meeting of the American Political Science Association, Washington, DC, 28 August–1 September, 38 pp.

Wright, Deil S., Jae-Won Yoo, and Jennifer Cohen, 1991. "The Evolving Profile of State Administrators." *Journal of State Government,* vol. 64 (January–March 1991): pp. 30–38.

15

ACHIEVING CREDIBILITY

An Analysis of Women's Experience

A. Carol Rusaw

Credibility, the essence of trust, is critical to the development of leadership skills among women managers in male-dominant organizations. This article describes credibility as an emergent theme in the accounts of fourteen women managers in five federal agencies. Women who established follower credibility exhibited three key behavioral patterns: (a) building a track record of success; (b) displaying technical competence; and (c) demonstrating a service ethic. The article discusses organizational obstacles encountered by women, effective strategies used, and derives implications for public personnel management.

Building trust is an essential leadership skill for managers. Trust enables followers to accept leader power and influence strategies (Kanter, 1983), to develop commitment to tasks and organizational purposes (Kouzes and Posner, 1987), and to create possibilities for future productivity (Pfeffer, 1981). Developing trust or credibility, however, is problematic. Not only must leaders have thorough knowledge of task requirements, resources, and contexts in which jobs are performed, they must also have an intuitive understanding of organizational power coalitions, strategies, and tactics for supporting efforts. Such understanding often comes after prolonged exposure to and reflection upon task organization, coordination, and implementation within political settings.

Developing relationships of trust in organizational settings, which is essential for successful and effective task completion, is often difficult for women man-

Source: *Review of Public Personnel Administration* (Winter 1996): 19–30.

agers in male-dominant hierarchies. Because women managers are distinctive minorities in such organizations, they are excluded frequently from developing a tacit understanding of organizational dynamics (Kanter, 1977). Having little direct, face-to-face experience working with women managers, male managers typically rely on stereotypes (Symonds, 1986; Bayes and Newton, 1978; Frank and Katcher, 1977; and Kruse and Wintermantel, 1986). The lack of information and direct experience frequently leads to suspicion. When commonly-held stereotypes of women managers' effectiveness are not reinforced, for example, the cognitive dissonance may be assuaged through rationalization rather than through the collection of more facts (Festinger, 1957).

Credibility—involving task competency, sense of personal confidence, and supportive interpersonal relationships—is largely heuristic; its meaning is subjectively defined and validated among participants in an interactive social setting. Credibility may be defined as a negotiated process of actor intentionality and observer reactions. As managers of meaning, leaders create linkages between desired or symbolic states and behavioral outcomes (Smirchich and Morgan, 1982). For women managers in male-dominant organizations, the task is to re-define behavioral roles apart from existing stereotypical definitions. This requires an understanding of self—characteristics, feedback from the context, and development of valid criteria for assessment and consequent actions. If behaviors occur in potentially-biased contexts, how do women managers create an accurate and consistent framework for eliciting credibility?

To answer this question an "account analysis" of critical incidents was used with women managers. A type of qualitative research methodology, account analysis enables the researcher to understand the construction of meaning as it has been described and analyzed by those participating in significant events (Harre and Secord, 1973). Participants analyze the meaning of prior experiences, internal states of feeling and cognition, contextual variables, follower reactions, and assessment of outcomes. By observing common patterns in the account analyses, researchers identify any patterns of intentions, perceptions, and behaviors emerging from the accounts collected.

Method

Analyzing credibility from the leader's viewpoint occurred through investigating a data subset of a previous study of career advancement among a sample of fourteen federal women managers in the Washington, D.C. area (Rusaw, 1989). Women ranged from GS-12 to Senior Executive Service managers in five agencies of varying sizes, programs, and missions. Each was nominated by a top-level manager on the basis of centrality in the organization, use of formal and informal learning activities, and demonstrated effectiveness in task and interpersonal relations skills. Data were obtained and analyzed simultaneously in two iterations of a semistructured interview schedule, office observations of manager-staff interactions, and analysis of agency documents pertaining to mission, recent hiring, promotion, and training statistics.

Thematic Components of Credibility

In the analysis, credibility emerged as a central theme. Three common behavioral patterns were identified as instrumental in developing credibility: (a) building a track record of success; (b) displaying technical competence; and (c) demonstrating a service ethic. A discussion of each behavior pattern follows.

Building a Track Record of Success

Reputation, appearing as a highly important component of credibility in each woman's account, involves gaining acknowledgement of one's skills and abilities. Demonstrated achievement, as observed and interpreted usually by men, creates the reputation. Once a woman's reputation is developed, upward mobility is expedited. For example, a woman who had developed a reputation for expert technical assistance in personnel management issues was invited to apply when a vacancy for a temporary director occurred. She was selected, and eventually she was named permanent director. One black manager described many supportive people at high levels who recognized her competence and provided opportunities for her to participate in departmental deliberations over strategic planning. Another executive reflected that

> . . . the network has served me well. I know who my connections are. People I've known for ten years have made positive comments on my behalf to various officials at the department level, and that can't help but improve the situation.

Displaying Technical Competence

In the respondents' agencies, the elite occupations were technical professions traditionally filled by men, such as engineering, policy analysis, law, and military procurement. As leaders, women recounted particular difficulties in breaking through gender bias in occupational status and in gaining legitimacy. One cited an example of being made an "acting" director of a program for which she had little specialized expertise:

> The program was difficult to put together. I didn't have an engineering or a physicist's background. So I hired some great, young, excellent staff. This program was a major event in my career. A major improvement in a product came about, and its results can be seen today in the industry.

Women overcame bias as well as gained leader acceptance by working to achieve recognition for their competence and visibility within their organizations.

This occurred in a variety of ways. One was through forming mentorships with individuals. In their descriptions of mentors, the women depicted individuals who exhibited energy, trust, a sincere willingness to share information, and novel ways of solving difficult organizational problems. In modeling these behaviors within their agencies, the women gained an organization-wide reputation for both task and interpersonal competencies. Based on this reputation, observers recommended the women for promotion into highly visible positions. Ms. Murphy, a lawyer, recalled how her "wheeler-dealer" boss would send her on errands to "deliver packages so I would be seen by other people."

At other times, women developed competency during organizational transitions. Reorganizations, abrupt top-level manager vacancies, and reductions-in-force, for instance, created opportunities for women to develop a broader understanding of technical and managerial functions and interrelationships. One woman, for instance, encountered increased workloads and fewer resources as an acting director of a new departmental program. Before her promotion as permanent director, however, she had shared the position with a peer and with her second-level manager. "We were colleagues and bosses," she observed. "We became closer and saw each other's work in different ways."

Demonstrating a Service Ethic

Women managers described performing their jobs effectively in terms of balancing hard work, loyalty to an organization, and attention to detail. Ms. Rogers, a personnel manager, noted that

> I was driven enough and attentive enough to details that I was able to teach myself what I needed to know. I also had the attitude that I have a job to do. It's important to be responsive. I have a service outlook and was able to survive. I had a management orientation. That was my key to advancement.

In some instances, women volunteered their expertise to their male managers when they experienced problems in such areas as budgeting, procurement, and technical manual editing. Ms. Pierce, who worked in a defense agency, recalled that she had gained her manager's respect by applying zero-based budgeting techniques she had learned on her own:

> He liked the fact that I brought problems and solutions to him. 'That's how a manager thinks,' he'd say. He was a personable man for whom I had a great deal of respect. But he could be hardnosed as well. I had to convince him of my recommendations. But he treated me fairly.

Obstacles to Achieving Credibility

In their accounts, women managers described issues that called for reflection and reassessment of their intentions and actions. These involved: (a) norms governing the organizational culture and climate; (b) personnel management policies and procedures that constrained career advancement; and (c) gamesmanship among politically-appointed superiors.

Cultural Norms

Technical Bias. In several accounts, women described strong agency norms for both technical knowledge and practical experience. Having academic training alone was insufficient for gaining leadership legitimacy, regardless of gender. But some women who had technical skills and experience and advanced educational credentials still were not recognized as powerful. Ms. Pierce, a military procurement manager, observed that male managers did not want female managers in their units, ostensibly because they believed women lacked practical experience with equipment. Having such women in their units would make them "look bad"; to protect themselves, she noted, men would "make sure she doesn't do her job well."

The technical bias, with bias against women as a subtext, showed up in selections and promotions. Those with appointing authority, who were most often men, favored candidates who demonstrated knowledge from practical experience. Yet, women who had this experience in addition to advanced educational certificates were often not selected. One woman remarked that such women "went down just as fast as women without."

No Margin for Error. Managers in the federal agencies who made noteworthy errors lost credibility. Mistakes in practicing a technical skill, in judgement, and in understanding and complying with informal standards were costly. One woman noted that "in this agency, everything is so visible that even a small mistake, if you are in a highly visible job, will just finish you off."

Respondents expressed considerable confusion, frustration, and anxiety resulting from their experiences with biased norms and practices. Some typical responses to the stresses included over-preparing for tasks and "working harder" to "prove" their competencies. Ms. Henry, an equal employment opportunity officer, pointed out that

> If you're challenged, you should be prepared; if you're prepared, they will never challenge you because they don't want to challenge a person who knows more than they know.

Ms. Pierce, describing her frustration, also revealed that she reduced the pressure by reflecting on her work perspective and adapting her expectations to the prevailing male-defined norms:

> I'd knock myself out and do a lot more than expected. . . . I always take deadlines to be life or death. . . . When they say something is due on such and such a date, a lot of my male counterparts would do a sloppy job and hand something in; but I would take it as though I would not be getting an extension. . . . This caused me some problems

because I'd meet the deadlines on time and the others wouldn't. 'She's just trying to show us up,' they'd say. . . . Now. that's one of the things I've had to learn politically. 'Don't take some of these deadlines too seriously because you may come up with an answer that maybe your boss doesn't want you to come up with.'

Women learned the norms and behaviors incidentally. One woman used organizational "barometers"—people role-played potentially precarious encounters with her and provided feedback before she met with male managers; another used "allies and protectors" who helped out when men attacked her in meetings. All fourteen women described male and female mentors and role models who helped them analyze discursive situations and provided helpful skills for gaining acceptance.

Zero-Sum Games.   The women described conflict management in their agencies as win/lose affairs. One woman characterized them as "playing hard-ball politics":

> Men in this agency are not sophisticated at all or subtle in their dealings with each other from a human relations stance. I think there's a lot of pretty latent, aggressive conversation. I think it's because of the environment. It's easy to become a victim because people just blow up at you and come on very strong.

Women would be put into what Ms. Pierce described as "sink or swim" situations. Men as supervisors, she stated, would give women nearly impossible tasks, few resources with which to accomplish them, and expect them to fail. In her experiences, Ms. Pierce recalled being sent to a high-level procurement briefing with only one week's notice. She spent most of her time trying to be as familiar as possible with the parts and the inventory system. The morning of her presentation, she learned that her supervisor's commanding officer would be attending. When her boss received the commander's call two weeks later extolling Ms. Pierce's presentation, the boss called Ms. Pierce into his office and said he would have made the presentation if he'd known the commander was going to be there.

Personnel Management Obstacles

Limited Job Potential.   Two women noted that they had entered government service from clerical orientations and had eventually moved into journeyman (GS-9 to GS-12) positions. Mobility beyond that, however, peaked. Agencies offered little formal training for women to qualify for supervisory positions. If women wished to become managers and move off the professional career plateaus, they largely obtained necessary training and education at their own initiative.

Little Managerial Encouragement.   Lack of supervisory support hampered promotion opportunities. One recreation management specialist was not recommended for a promotion because her male manager did not think it appropriate for her to inspect men's locker rooms. A lawyer who had been a successful partner in private practice before entering government handled only one grievance case when she was hired as a personnel management specialist in government. Another woman said that her supervisor hid bulletins announcing agency-sponsored training activities and that, on another occasion, she learned a slot she had applied for in a specialized management development program was given to a man.

Promotion Bias.   Seeking redress for complaints often ended fruitlessly. When a woman who had been interviewed by a promotion panel questioned the panel spokesperson about her non-selection, the panelist remarked, "You know the way things are around here." Another noted that a selecting official whom she had queried stated that he "hadn't thought of choosing a woman" for the managerial vacancy. Last, one woman complained to personnel officials that she had applied but been rejected for a vacant director's position three times, and that each time, a less-qualified male had been chosen. Although her complaint was resolved nearly two years later in her favor, she indicated the incident had placed in jeopardy her "reputation for competence."

Political Gamesmanship.   In three case histories women reported that learning to work with political officials created dilemmas. One noted that officials tend to have a clear-cut list of things they wish to accomplish. They know they have perhaps two years or less in which to do so, she added, and this put pressure on her. She described an incident in which, as a manager for a women's interest program, she sought to involve all stakeholders in a particular decision. When she did not disproportionately weight the views of a particular group favored by her politically-appointed supervisor, however, her supervisor gave her a "non-assignment"—that is, a program that had "no funding and was of minor political importance." That, she added, was a major consideration when she turned down an executive level position. Two other women described feeling pressured to speak on their managers' behalf, giving only favorable examples of the political appointee's performance.

Constructing Shared Meaning Through Relationship Building

Displaying technical competence, providing expertise in managing difficult, complex organizational programs and changes, and providing information as liaisons with organizational stakeholders facilitated follower acceptance or legitimacy. Women earned respect, however, through developing interpersonal relations skills as leaders. In particular, the accounts revealed five central competencies: (a) self-and-other assessment; (b) negotiation in conflict resolution; (c) coalition building; (d) participatory decision making; and (e) coaching and counseling.

Self-and-Other Assessment

The accounts indicated frequent introspection into motives, interests, behaviors, and feelings in interpersonal encounters. Women reflected on their own as well as others' actions and used the information to improve, modify, or re-construct their relationships. To Ms. Henry, a personnel management executive, credibility was

> ... perhaps two kinds of things. One is how others perceive you. Do you seem to others to be correct? Able? Certain? Informed? And that's only the perception. How do others view you? Maybe you're a phoney. ... Sometimes, that person may not be perceived to have credibility because they do not know it all, not be able to articulate well or do not look the part.

Ms. Henry pointed out that in presenting themselves to others, women need to analyze the dominant norms operating in the encounter; they should follow them only so far, however, she added. Women should assert their views, but in ways that such actions facilitate listener respect. For instance, she noted that it is important for women to select their mode of dress carefully. Appropriate clothing facilitates men's acceptance of her, she reported, and the likelihood that they would pay more attention to what she has to say.

Negotiation as a Conflict Resolution Skill

Negotiation promoted respect and enhanced trust. Ms. Thompson, as a newly-appointed director of a national program, cited difficulties her staff experienced working with a "difficult" woman editor. She met with her staff as well as with the editor, encouraging them to share their perceptions and feelings about the conflicts with her. After that, she facilitated joint problem-solving meetings.

Dealing with discrimination issues, particularly that which involved superiors, was problematic. The women indicated that they used negotiation strategies and informal routes. Ms. Henry, for instance, brought her complaint at first to her commanding officer's secretary, who she knew to be "enormously powerful and who could grease it for me." The secretary used her influence and Ms. Henry, in turn, stated her case matter-of-factly. "If I had gone in alone and said, 'Hey! I think I'm not getting a fair shake here!' he would have been taken aback."

She added that she had learned the strategy from a friend, a psychologist, who gave her advice on managing human relationships:

> As women are emerging, men are saying. ... 'Where do I as a man fit in their social phenomena?' Men are changing. They are not going to tell you what's troubling them. What you must do is constantly work toward negotiation; work toward effective change with them, as opposed to beating them to a pulp.

Women consciously avoided over-reacting to conflict, as they believed women were stereotypically expected to react. One noted that she responds to management's "ranting and raving" by adopting a more controlled, reasoned approach. Another noted that she dealt with a male subordinate which got his kicks out of making life miserable for me." But, she added, she tries to figure out "why he does obstructive things":

> I realize there's a lot of jealousy with competitive situations. But this person will eventually self-destruct. He's plain dirty. Some battles aren't worth fighting.

Creating Supportive Networks

The fourteen women involved in this study became influential in key agency networks through a variety of means. Often, having access to a powerful person in the agency provided legitimacy. One such person who served as a role model for a senior executive was a female political appointee who was "in a powerful position and could demonstrate the skills needed to get the job done." Women noted that developing support bases was a careful process of deciding which people were "worth cultivating" and which were of little advantage in terms of helpfulness. All women were members of multiple networks of professionals and managers, both within their organizations as well as externally. Personal relationships with Congressional staff members, special interest groups, and professional association membership were key to gaining many supporters. In addition, some women continued affiliations with their pre-government professional contacts who on occasion provided them advice, encouragement, and creative ideas.

Inviting Participation

Women revealed that sharing information in solving problems and making decisions were critical to being accepted by staff as well as superiors. This was crucial not only in resolving conflicts, as indicated, but in managing a diverse staff. Ms. Garret, a special education professional before entering government, noted that she coped with being thrust into an acting director's position by: (a) appointing a veteran manager, a male, to run the day-to-day programs; (b) holding frequent meetings with her superior and the superior's experienced deputy; and (c) meeting often with her staff to work on program priorities, workloads, and individual development planning.

Coaching and Counseling

Occasionally, women would gain the trust of male superiors not only by helping them solve work-related problems, but also by giving advice on managing human relations issues. Ms. Garret noticed that her supervisor, Dr. Overby, used a controlling managerial style that elicited hostile staff reactions; she decided to help him facilitate more staff involvement and satisfaction.

> I suggested that he work with the problem staff one-on-one rather than in group situations. When he did so, I would give him feedback and encouragement. He did respond to my suggestions, but his style nevertheless remained fixed. Staff relationships however, were much better.

Ms. Lindstrom, a lawyer, worked with a staff member whom colleagues labeled as "tough, remote, and having few friends." Ms. Lindstrom, however, provided advice on how to win several cases the staff member was managing. "We had fun talking about legal issues," she recalled, "and out of that interaction, we developed mutual respect and eventually trust."

Discussion

This analysis, in which credibility emerged as a major theme in the career histories of fourteen women managers in the federal government, provides a glimpse into the development of a critical set of leadership skills. Earning the trust of followers, colleagues, and superiors requires developing and using task and relationship skills and enacting them within the context of organizational norms. The ecology of task and relationship enactment was saturated with biases about women. In spite of their advanced educational credentials, certificates of specialized training, and, in some instances, high occupational ranks prior to entering government, women often faced significant gender-related hurdles to advancement. The blockages appeared particularly in the concretized ideologies that permeated personnel management policies and practices.

Their credibility evolved through verbal as well as non-verbal behaviors, receiving and acting on feedback, and taking action. While the respondents confronted practices that inhibited their career mobility, they also constructed a set of beliefs, attitudes, and values through their experiences. By inviting openness about feelings and perceptions, the women took the initiative in creating opportunities for changing biased frameworks of meaning. This also occurred in behaviors in which they purposefully failed to perform stereotypical roles. Assuming risk, showing a willingness to believe conditions and people could change, taking action, and engaging in periodic self-assessments and reflections on interactions were integral to the credibility building process.

A Foundation for Credibility Achievement

The respondents achieved credibility as leaders by employing six traits that build a foundation for professional advancement in the executive ranks. They are consistency, visibility, verisimilitude, mutuality, earned positive regard, and earned legitimacy.

Consistency. Consistency appeared as observable linkages between attitudes and behaviors. Women produced exemplary results whenever they were given a particularly difficult or technically complex project. They characterized their efforts as reflecting a service ethic. This entailed building loyalty to the organization and staff through finding a way to balance competing priorities from technological demands, bureaucratic policies and practices, and individual needs and interests.

Visibility. Women as leaders established a presence among followers through participation in multiple internal and external networks. By virtue of these networks, they could connect themselves, their staff, their superiors, and their peers with each other, with other units, and with the external political environment. Their network activities had the side effect of enhancing their reputations for achievement and strong interpersonal relationships, and contributed significantly to their career mobility.

Verisimilitude. Verisimilitude involved creating an image or reputation for effectiveness in informal relationships and organizational practices in spite of gender bias. In constructing the image, the women first identified stereotypical attitudes and actions. They then de-constructed the biased assumptions by behaving in unexpected ways. When followers became aware of the biases that interfered with the relationship, the women as leaders initiated new norms and behaviors characterized by trust, openness, and cooperation.

Mutuality. The successful women managers showed a strong tendency to involve followers in problem solving and decision making, constructing meaning through consensus. They also sought to understand the motives, interpersonal behaviors, and interests of others in social relationships. Women used feminist relational strategies with followers, such as counseling, coaching, negotiation, and mediation (Ferguson, 1984). The favorable outcomes in terms of greater individual and group productivity for a diverse set of followers earned the esteem of both men and women.

Earned Positive Regard

In demonstrating effective leader-follower relationships and task outcomes, the women developed particular skills—tools gained formally as well as incidentally. These tools included participatory decision making and problem solving, mediation, counseling and coaching, oral and nonverbal communications skills, and self-and-other assessment techniques. Women may have had both technical and academic credentials necessary to perform their managerial and professional roles in the organizations, but how they used them through day-to-day interpersonal relationships provided a foundation for esteem-building among internal as well as external constituencies.

Earned Legitimacy

The women studied here encountered numerous obstacles in the process of obtaining acceptance. Norms and practices, reflected in personnel management decisions, were particularly troublesome. Positional power was limited because of the women's status in non-technical, support or clerical positions. This was compounded by the fact that few women were promoted into top management positions in their agencies. Even when women had credentials as well as practical experience to qualify for such positions, they were not selected. The women used a great deal of socialized power, incorporating human relations skills into their job functions. They also obtained informational influence through such means as attending training on their own, joining professional associations, and forming networks with organizational stakeholders. Through their power and influence bases, the women were able to demonstrate that they had the technical competency to design and carry out highly-specialized and complex organizational projects. Ultimately, their display of such skills helped them overcome gender bias and gain management posts.

Credibility Deterrents

Figure 15.1 represents a summary chart of obstacles to developing credibility as observed in these fourteen accounts. Under the guise of neutrality, personnel management practices often reflect biased standards. Agencies continue to select, promote, and train too few women as managers and leaders; their merit often has to be proved through flawless performance under difficult circumstances before they are granted the legitimacy they merit. Beyond acceptance of their credentials, women as leaders face continuing challenges to acquire the skills necessary to influence a wide array of followers in various social circumstances.

Implications

Developing credibility is important to women's leadership, for without the trust of followers, attempts to influence and exercise power are thwarted. When the productivity potential of women managers is limited, lowered performance leads to lowered motivation and output among followers. Hence, it is vital that organizations take action to enhance the credibility of women managers, particularly in male-dominant organizations. The account analysis described in this research suggests several possible strategies:

FIGURE 15.1 Credibility Blocks

Organization Culture	Organization Climate	Organization Structure	Organization Processes
*Zero-sum political games	*Fear of failure	*Women clustered in low status support jobs	*Select and/or promote less qualified male job candidates
*Gender-based stereotypes	*Lack of supervisory support	*Few numbers of women in high-level managerial positions	*Inadequate management training
*Insistence upon hands-on experience in "men's" jobs	*Fear of making others look bad by succeeding *Anxiety from frequent changes	*Limited openings in upper level jobs	*Use of informal norms vs. merit in personnel decisions

Examine Biases.   Personnel management officials should analyze both policies and taken-for-granted assumptions in practice, especially as they affect the selection and promotion of women into managerial positions.

Create Opportunities.   Women managers should be encouraged to participate in highly-visible task forces, special assignments, and discussions of the details of agency strategies and tactics in dealing with their political commitment. These should be with managers who themselves have a reputation for being trustworthy, open to change, supportive of innovation, participative, and skilled in counseling and coaching.

Provide Training.   Training programs should be developed for managers to enhance their sensitivity to gender bias. The training should provide a safe forum for discussion, critical reflection, and skill building. Especially helpful would be strategies to expose "theories-in-use" (Argyris and Schon, 1978) and tactics for learning new responses based on erroneously-framed and defined constructs about women managers.

Future Inquiry

Developing managerial credibility is important to individual and organizational productivity. It rests on the construction of meaning through critical and creative reflection and the willingness to engage in dialogue. A question that arises from this study is the degree to which obstacles to building credibility, particularly in personnel management decisions, differ for women as compared to men of similar positional status and academic credentials. It is hoped that future inquiry will address this question.

References

Argyris, C. and D.A. Schon (1978). *Organization Learning: A Theory of Action Perspective.* Reading, MA: Addison-Wesley Publishing Company.

Bayes, M. and P.M. Newton (1978). "Women in Authority: A Sociopsychological Analysis." *Journal of Applied Behavioral Science* 14, 7–20.

Ferguson, K.E. (1984). *The Feminist Case Against Bureaucracy.* Philadelphia, PA: Temple University Press.

Festinger, L. (1957). *A Theory of Cognitive Dissonance.* Stanford, CA: Stanford University Press.

Frank, H.H. and A.H. Katcher (1977). "The Qualities of Leadership: How Male Medical Students Evaluate Their Female Peers." *Human Relations* 30: 405–416.

Harre, M. and P.F. Second (1973). *The Explanation of Social Behavior.* Totowa, NJ: Littlefield, Adams.

Hosking, D.M. and J. Morley (1988). "The Skills of Leadership," pp. 80–106 in J.G. Hunt, R.R. Baliga, H.P. Dachler, and C.A. Schriesheim (eds.) *Emerging Leadership Vistas,* Boston, MA: Lexington.

Kanter, R.M. (1977). "Women in Organizations: Sex Roles, Group Dynamics, and Change Strategies," pp. 371–386 in A.G. Sargent (ed.) *Beyond Sex Roles*. St. Paul, MN: West Publishing.

Kanter, R.M. (1983). *The Change Masters*. NY: Simon and Schuster.

Kouzes, J.M. and B.Z. Posner (1987). *The Leadership Challenge: How to Get Extraordinary Things Done in Organizations*. San Francisco: Jossey-Bass.

Kruse, L. and M. Wintermantel (1986). "Leadership MsQualified I: The Gender Bias in Everyday and Scientific Thinking," pp. 171–197 in C.F. Graumann and S. Moscovicl (eds.) *Changing Conceptions of Leadership*. NY: Springer-Verlag.

Pfeffer, L. (1981). *Power in Organizations*, Marshfield, MA: Pittman.

Rusaw, A.C. (1989). *The Relationship of Training and Development to the Career Histories of Federal Women Managers in Selected Agencies*. Unpublished Ph.D. Dissertation. Blacksburg, VA: Virginia Polytachnic Institute and State University.

Smirchich, L. and G. Morgan (1982). "Leadership: The Management of Meaning." *Journal of Applied Behavioral Science* 18: 257–273.

Symonds, S.M. (1986). "Coping With the Corporate Tribe: How Women in Different Cultures Experience the Managerial Role." *Journal of Management* 12: 420–431.

16

THREE STEPS FORWARD, TWO STEPS BACKWARD

The Status of Women's Integration into Public Management

Mary E. Guy
University of Alabama at Birmingham

Is there symmetry between women and men in public management in terms of opportunity, power, and numbers? Mary Guy examines two decades of affirmative action initiatives. She finds the number of women in decision-making positions disproportionately low when compared to their numbers in the public work force. Women's integration into the fabric of American governance has been marked by surges of progress followed by periods of quiescence. Her article compares the status of women to that of men in career public management positions and argues that women have a long way to go before they will reach parity.

Today, as in the past, women must convince men that their demands for governmental action are legitimate before their desires are transformed into policies, programs, and services. This is because men hold the vast majority of decision-making positions in government. In legislative chambers and top-level career

Source: *Public Administration Review* 53 (July/August 1993): 285–292. Portions of this article are excerpted from the author's following works: Guy 1992a and 1992b.

An earlier version of this article won a Lilly Award for Outstanding Research at the 1992 Annual Meeting of the American Society for Public Administration.

311

posts, women's voices are still mostly heard indirectly through the mouths of their husbands, fathers, brothers, and sons. When Abigail Adams reminded her husband to "remember the ladies" as a new nation was being founded, he responded in jest to her. The thought of treating women as full-fledged citizens was considered frivolous. Two hundred years later, women's political status has improved, but women remain largely dependent on the goodwill of the men around them. This is true in policy implementation and program management as well as in the political arena.

In this article, I outline the pattern of women's integration into public management. I characterize the pattern as being not unlike that of women's integration into society at large—"three steps forward, two steps backward." Each series of advances toward equality for women is followed by a backlash of restraint and a yearning for a social order that lurks in archetypes from an era long gone.

Challenges to Contemporary Public Administration

To borrow from Paul Appleby's (1949) argument, public administration is the enterprise of making a mesh of things. In today's world, "to make a mesh of things" means integrating the strengths that diverse interests and forces bring to governing. If the differentness of women and men makes a difference in the workplace, then those strengths that are attributed to women, such as mediating, facilitating, and consensus building are too valuable to ignore. The fact that women pay attention to the human dimension is exactly the reason they should have a place on center stage as this nation grapples with a changing work force, the transition from an industrial economy to a service economy, a troubled educational system, an inadequate health care system, an unsettled Eastern Europe, a changing international economy, and a world in which environmental hazards threaten not just the nation but the planet. If ever there were a need for building bridges, it is now. If ever there were a need to build on the skills that women have always been characterized as bringing to management, it is now.

Why, then, are women still on the outside looking in, when it comes to managing government's interests? Government, in combination with economic forces, is the train that engineers social change. In the case of women entering managerial levels in the public service, the train forces change, and accommodation to it, by treating jobs as resources and redistributing them. This, in turn, creates changes in behavior and changes in attitudes coincident with the behavioral changes. No organizations, least of all public agencies, operate in a vacuum devoid of the pushes and pulls that societal values exert.

As much as diversity is the wave of the future, a backlash of reaction against it occurs periodically (Faludi, 1991). Images of the past creep into the national consciousness and promote a yearning for lifestyles of the past. As recently as the 1992 Republican Convention, platform speeches were still encouraging the outmoded Norman Rockwell image of the traditional family, including a husband who is the breadwinner for the family, a wife who is a contented mother and happy housewife, and healthy children who are well dressed and well adjusted. The fact is that too much has changed in American society to turn the clock back. By 1986, the so-called "typical" American family of husband earner, wife home-maker, and two children accounted for only 3.7 percent of all the nation's fami-lies (U.S. Dept of Labor, 1987; Kosterlitz, 1988).

Women's Entry into the Work Force

A thumbnail sketch can describe women's entry into the world of work and into public administration: By the mid-1800s, it had become acceptable for women to fill clerical positions in the public service (Van Riper, 1976). Women stenogra-phers were described as especially capable because of their ability to radiate sym-pathetic interest, agreeableness, and courtesy in the office (Kanter, 1977). The growth of administration brought women into numerical dominance in the of-fice, placing them in clerical but not managerial positions. Prior to World War II, women left the work force when they became pregnant, not to return. The period between the end of World War II and the mid-1960s were watershed years, how-ever, for they heralded what has come to be the norm. Women entered the work force upon completion of their formal education and stayed in the work force, with only brief absences associated with childcare responsibilities. Economic and social pressures had combined in such a way that women started to climb the ca-reer ladder and knock on doors for higher level jobs.

By the mid-1960s, the nation started paying attention to this phenomenon. In 1963, an article in the *Wall Street Journal* argued that it was advantageous to have women in management positions because they were "good listeners" and "sym-pathetic in nature" and thereby brought a "humanizing" influence to managerial ranks. Just as with secretarial positions, women were credited with humanizing organizations. But convincing employers that women were capable of effective performance in more powerful positions has been, and continues to be, a difficult process. Legislation has helped. The Civil Rights Act of 1964 provided a milestone for women's employment in the federal government by prohibiting job discrimi-nation on the basis of sex. The Equal Employment Opportunity Act of 1972 amended the Civil Rights Act of 1964 by bringing state and local governments, governmental agencies, political subdivisions, and any governmental industry, business, or activity within its coverage (Grossman, 1973). Rapid spurts soon in-creased the proportion of women in the public service, especially in the higher grades.

In 1972, another *Wall Street Journal* article declared that employers were com-ing to grips with demands for women's equality on the job. The article closed with a quote that "You might as well face it—women aren't going to go away" (Mor-genthaler, 1972, p. 17). That was in 1972. Over 20 years have passed and it will still be many years before the number of women in management is proportionate to the number of women in the workplace. The workplace is marked by vertical sex segregation. Women are able to make much greater inroads into lower paid positions than into higher paid male-dominated ranks. In fact, if progress toward integrating women into top management continues at the pace set by the first six years following passage of the Equal Employment Opportunity Act of 1972, *it will take until the year 2040* for women to gain perfect representation among career agency leaders (Dometrius, 1984).

Moreover, sex segregation has been a remarkably stable feature of the American workplace during the 20th century both in the private sector and in the public sector (Lewis and Emmett, 1986; Powell, 1988). In 1900, 67 percent of the total work force would have had to change jobs for sex segregation to be eliminated. By now, about 60 percent of the work force, both public and private, would have to switch jobs for sex segregation to be eliminated (Lewis and Emmett, 1986; Powell, 1988). Although the proportion of women and men employed in professional and technical jobs is roughly the same for both sexes, women are more likely to be employed in traditional female jobs such as health, human services, and education (Diamond, 1987). For instance, as of 1986 women were two-thirds of the employees in the U.S. Department of Health and Human Services (Kaplan, 1987).

Regardless of whether or not the work force of an agency is majority female, the top ranks are invariably filled with men. When tracing women's integration into public management, we see a pattern of rapid progress in the middle and late 1970s, followed by a period of quiescence in the mid-1980s. The late 1980s and early 1990s, however, are showing enhanced progress once again. Thus, women's integration into the public service is marked by spurts of progress followed by periods of redefinition, a sequence that is best described by the expression "three steps forward and two steps backward."

Three Steps Forward

Projections show that women will continue their climb into decision-making posts. For example, between 1976 and 1986 the number of women in federal General Schedule (GS) jobs at grades 13 through 15 doubled from 5 percent to 12 percent of the total workers in those grades (Barnes, 1988). And between 1976 and 1986, the female share of new entrants to the federal work force who were under the age of 35 tripled to 27 percent. In 1970, women made up only 1.4 percent of all federal employees in the top grades (GS 16–18). By 1985, women composed 6.1 percent (Fox, 1987). Table 16.1 shows the impact of equal opportunity initiatives which, when combined with underlying social forces (or vice versa), significantly affected the composition of the federal work force. In 1960, for example, only 1 percent of the women in the federal work force were in grades 9 or above. By 1987, this proportion had increased to 28 percent.

Windows of opportunity open in ironic ways. Between 1976 and 1986 the increase in General Schedule jobs held by women increased by 6.5 percent while the

TABLE 16.1   Percentage of Women in the Federal Work Force and in Federal GS Grades, Selected Years, 1910–1987

Federal Work Force

Year	Percent	Year	Percent
1910	10	1960	25
1939	19	1968	34
1945	37	1978	37
1947	24	1987	48

Federal GS Grades

Year	GS 8 or below	GS 9 or above
1960	99	1
1987	72	28

SOURCE: Guy, 1992a.

white male share of these jobs decreased from 50.2 percent to 41.8 percent (Lewis, 1988). These were the years in which candidates for President campaigned for office by railing about the inadequacies of the federal bureaucracy. They were years of low morale and declines in real pay. Thus, it appears that societal biases against government provided an opportunity for women to make greater than usual inroads into the public service.

The gradual integration of women into federal managerial levels is mirrored at the state and local levels. The information in Tables 16.2, 16.3, and 16.4, which is drawn from data provided by the U.S. Equal Employment Opportunity Commission (1982, 1985, 1990), provides a look at new hires and salaries across all levels by gender. Table 16.2 shows that women are now entering the public work force in greater numbers than men.

In a spot check of states, these same trends are represented in different regions of the United States. Table 16.3 shows new hires in states in the southeast, southwest, west, and upper midwest.

TABLE 16.2   New Hires in State and Local Government, 1980, 1985, and 1989 (in Percent)

Year	Women	Men	Difference
1980	50.5	49.5	+1.0
1985	49.0	51.0	−2.0
1989	51.4	48.6	+2.8

SOURCE: U.S. Equal Employment Opportunity Commission, 1982, 1985, 1990.

TABLE 16.3   Percentage of New Hires in Six State Governments, 1980, 1985, 1989

	Women	*Men*	*Difference*
Alabama			
1980	49.1	50.9	−1.8
1985	44.5	55.5	−11.0
1989	54.6	45.4	9.2
Arizona			
1980	48.2	51.8	−3.6
1985	47.8	52.2	−4.4
1989	52.3	47.7	4.6
California			
1980	52.5	47.5	5.0
1985	54.1	45.9	8.2
1989	54.5	45.5	9.0
Texas			
1980	47.8	52.2	−4.4
1985	47.1	52.9	−5.8
1989	53.1	46.9	6.2
Utah			
1980	48.4	51.6	−3.2
1985	46.3	53.7	−7.4
1989	47.6	52.4	−4.8
Wisconsin			
1980	48.9	51.1	−2.2
1985	49.1	50.9	−1.8
1989	56.7	43.3	13.4

SOURCE: U.S. Equal Employment Opportunity Commission, 1982, 1985, 1990.

Data in Tables 16.2 and 16.3 show that women have made the greatest strides in gaining employment in state and local government toward the end of the 1980s. In all the states shown except Utah, more women than men were hired in 1989. The increase is anything but steady throughout the decade, however. In 1980, the only state shown in which there were more women than men hired was California. In 1985, the gap continued in most states, and grew wider in many. By 1989, though, the numbers show a turnaround. More women than men were hired in Alabama, Arizona, California, Texas, and Wisconsin. If the past informs the future, then it is obvious that the rate by which women will move into key posts will be anything but steady.

Two Steps Backward

By the beginning of the 1960s, it had become socially acceptable to question the wage disparities between women's and men's earnings. It was in 1963 that Congress passed the Equal Pay Act requiring that women receive equal pay for equal work. Despite legislation, sexual inequality in earnings has remained a telltale sign of the status of women in the workplace (Cooney, Clague, and Salvo, 1980; National Committee on Pay Equity, 1989; Smith and Ward, 1984). Fully employed women high school graduates with no college had less income in 1979, on the average, than fully employed men who had not completed elementary school. And in that same year, women with four years of college had less income than men with only an eighth grade education. By the latter 1980s, the inequity had not changed substantially and the wage gap persisted, with women earning $.65 for every $1.00 that men earned.

In fact, since 1955 the female-male average annual earnings gap of full-time, year-round workers in the United States has hovered around 60 percent. It has been as low as 57 percent in 1973 and 1974 and as high as 65 percent in 1987 (National Committee on Pay Equity, 1989). Administrative positions in state and local government have done a little better than this (Table 16.4). According to data gathered by the U.S. Equal Opportunity Commission (1982, 1985, 1990), in 1980 the median salary for men who held administrative positions in state and local government was $23,150; for women it was $17,493, leaving women's average earnings at just 75 percent of men' average earnings. Ten years later, the median salary for men in the same type of positions was $40,469; for women it was $32,686, a gap of $7,783. This represents a narrowing of the wage gap to 81 percent. If salary is a windsock for indicating progress, then only a slight breeze is blowing. Salary figures reflect not only the lack of pay equity between the sexes but also the fact that women are often relegated to working in lesser valued missions that pay lower wages. In fact, Lewis and Emmett (1986) report that one-third of the male-female earnings gap is attributable to occupational sex segregation.

The fact that societal pushes and pulls result in women's gaining entrance to administrative positions while the wage gap continues reveals the relationship between gender and salary (Ahn and Saint-Germain, 1988; Welch, Karnig, and Eribes, 1983). One scenario goes like this: As government employment is maligned by elected officials and public opinion, those nearing retirement (men) remain at higher wages, while those newly hired (women) are paid less for they have fewer years' experience. Although this is plausible, it risks oversimplifying the facts of the matter. The systemic causes of this phenomenon are better explained by the differential effect of opportunity, power, and numbers.

TABLE 16.4 Full-Time Median Salary for Officials/Administrators in State and Local Government, 1980, 1985, 1989

Year	Women	Men	Difference	Wage Gap (percent)
1980	$17,493	$23,150	−$5,657	75
1985	$26,440	$33,370	−$6,930	79
1989	$32,686	$40,469	−$7,783	81

SOURCE: U.S. Equal Employment Opportunity Commission, 1982, 1985, 1990.

Opportunity, Power, and Numbers

Opportunity, power, and numbers are three significant features that differentiate men from women in the workplace. The consequences of high or low opportunity, high or low power, and high or low numerical representation affect public administration and program implementation. Rosabeth Moss Kanter (1977) generated a rich set of hypotheses related to these structural determinants of behavior in organizations. These factors also help to reveal and explain women's status in public administration. For example, Kanter hypothesized that people low in career opportunity behave differently than people high in career opportunity. Opportunity relates to expectations and future prospects for mobility and growth. Those with high opportunity have high aspirations, are more attracted to high-power people, are competitive, and are more committed to the organization and to their careers. They value their competence, and become impatient or disaffected if they do not keep moving. On the other hand, those in low opportunity positions limit their aspirations, seek satisfaction in activities outside of work, and have a horizontal orientation rather than a vertical orientation. They find ways to create a sense of efficacy and worth through personal relationships, they resign themselves to staying put; and they are concerned with basic survival and extrinsic rewards.

Kanter also developed notions about power, which she defined as the capacity to mobilize resources. People low in organizational power tend to foster lower group morale, behave in more authoritarian ways, and use coercive rather than persuasive power. They are more controlling and more critical. People high in organizational power foster higher group morale, behave in less rigid ways, and delegate more control. They allow subordinates more latitude and discretion and are more often seen as helping rather than hindering.

Kanter called a third characteristic "proportions." This concept relates to the composition of people in approximately the same situation. It is a numerical matter of how many people of a kind are present, so that differentness is, or is not, noticeable. People whose type is represented in very small proportion tend to be more visible, that is, they are "on display." They feel more pressure to conform and to make fewer mistakes, they find it harder to gain credibility, they are more isolated and peripheral, and they are more likely to be excluded from informal peer networks. Thus, they are limited in their source of power-through-alliance. Furthermore, they are stereotyped and placed in role traps that limit effectiveness. People whose type is represented in very high proportion tend to "fit in" and find it easier to gain credibility in positions beset by high uncertainty. They are more likely to be accepted into the informal network, to form peer alliances and to learn the ropes from peers. They are also more likely to be sponsored by higher status organization members and to acquire mentors easily.

These three possessions, opportunity, power, and numbers, combine to produce self-perpetuating cycles. Thus, those with high opportunity behave in ways that generate more opportunity, which in turn produces further inducement for the behavior. High opportunity is accompanied by more power. Both opportunity and power coincide with being a member of a group that constitutes a large enough proportion of the work force so that any one member of the group is not immediately noticeable as "different." The confluence of opportunity, power, and proportion, then, produces upward cycles of advantage or downward cycles of disadvantage. The cycle of high opportunity, power, and numbers makes it very difficult for newcomers (such as women) to break into the managerial work force. The cycle of low opportunity, powerlessness, and tokenism is also difficult to break because of its self-perpetuating nature.

The glass ceiling that prevents women from reaching top positions is partially explained by the combined effects of tokenism and sex-role expectations. When Frances Perkins, the first woman to be appointed to a cabinet post, was named Secretary of Labor in 1933, she was wary of being identified as a special champion of women. She felt everyone was watching her to see if she appointed too many women. Consequently, she went to great lengths to quell such fears by not catering to concerns of women in the department's Women's Bureau (Sealander, 1983). Such is the dilemma of tokens. If they respond too directly to the expectations of the group that they represent, they lose credibility in the eyes of the dominant group. If they ignore the expectations of their own group, they are accused of being mere tokens. If women are too assertive, they are castigated as being too aggressive and "unfeminine," making them unworthy representatives of their gender. If they are too cooperative and conciliatory, they are seen as being too weak to be an effective representative of their gender.

The Gendered Workplace

Gender infuses organizational processes and shapes our interpretations of behaviors and events (Kelly, 1991). Although we take it for granted, it is important to understand that policy implementation is conducted by gendered instruments, women and men. The reason women are so few in top levels of state administrative positions flows from the innumerable small influences that shape the way we organize, along with who decides how we do it. To aid our understanding of this, career managers in state agencies have been surveyed in seven states: Alabama, Arizona, California, Texas, Utah, and Wisconsin (Guy, 1992b; Kelly, Guy, *et al.*, 1991) and Florida (Newman, 1992). These surveys provide a systematic comparison across organizational and political units. The results show that gender is more predominant than geographic boundaries or political traditions when it comes to affecting one's status in public management.

Although the cultural foundation upon which women's and men's experiences are based is generally the same, it is the differences that are most visible. Thus, even though differences show up as only one point, or a fraction of a point on a Likert scale, the direction of the differences persists across the states. The patterns are inescapable and haunting. They appear in regard to career advancement, personal background, family obligations, access to mentors, exposure to sexual harassment, fitting into the organizational culture, management style, and policy preferences. The differences between the sexes are the visible part of women and men in public management. The invisible part is the commonality that arises from being socialized in the same culture, living in the same communities, working in similar surroundings, and sharing the same overriding views about American government and democracy in general. Thus what women and men have in common is much greater than what they do not have in common. This is why the differences that occur are so remarkable.

Even with all the homogenizing influences of television public education, and cultural and workplace socialization, a consistent pattern of differences shows up in all the states surveyed over most of the issues included in the questionnaire. Job titles provide an example. For instance, the survey results show that people hold jobs in their agencies in sexually coded positions and locations. Power titles, such as "administrator," "chief," and "director" are dominated by men, even in agencies that address traditional women's issues, such as health and human services. This holds true even when states differ politically, culturally, and economically (Guy and Duerst-Lahti, 1992). Patterns such as these prevail in all the states studied. A brief review of findings related to career advancement, workplace policies, personal background, family obligations, and mentoring, uncovers the components that influence gender roles in the managerial workplace.

Career Development

The career paths of women and men are different. The pattern in the states is that women tend to move into management at a younger age than their male counterparts. The women who make it are promoted from one position to another in less time than men are (Kelly, Guy, *et al.*, 1991; Bullard and Wright, 1991). Thus, for the very small portion of women in the public work force who break into the high opportunity cycle, they break into it early. Women managers however, receive lower pay than men in each state surveyed, are under-represented in traditionally "male" occupations, and are over-represented in public welfare, health care, and employment security agencies.

Workplace Policies

Policies affecting workplace reform, such as affirmative action programs, prohibitions against discrimination and harassment, and moves toward pay equity and childcare, affect women and men differently. Changes in these policies alter the workplace and level the playing field for women and men in public administration. As one might expect, workplace policies that treat all workers as if they were men get the most support from men. Policies that favor advancing women's interests received the most support from women. Women express a greater preference for workplace reforms related to proportionate representation of women and for issues related to childcare and pay equity.

Women and men disagree over whether or not there is equal opportunity for both sexes. While men believe that discrimination against women is diminishing, women believe that it is increasing. In fact, Simon and Landis (1989) report a study that asked about employment discrimination in general. They conclude from their findings that the percentage of women perceiving discrimination against them has increased from 46 percent to 56 percent between 1975 and 1987; but the percentage of men perceiving discrimination against women decreased from 50 percent to 46 percent.

Personal Background

The positions that public managers achieve are influenced by their background. Women and men who have attained equally high positions in state government differ in their educational achievement and socioeconomic status. The similarity between the effects of gender across the states cannot be overstated. Regardless of political traditions, economic differences, systemic differences, and geographic differences, the same patterns prevail. Women who make it to the top managerial ranks in state agencies tend to come from more advantaged backgrounds than do the men who make it into those ranks. In the states surveyed, as many as 58 percent of the male managers held an advanced degree beyond the bachelor's degree, while as many as 76 percent of the women held such degrees. As many as 28 percent of the women managers had mothers who held professional or managerial jobs, whereas only as many as 13 percent of male managers' mothers had such a work history. As many as 44 percent of female managers' fathers held professional or managerial jobs, while only as many as 32 percent of the male managers' fathers held such jobs. While as many as 29 percent of the female managers reported that they had grown up in an upper-middle or upper class setting, only as many as 11 percent of the men reported such a background. Finally, as many as 32 percent of female managers said they had grown up in a lower-middle or lower class background, whereas as many as 59 percent of male managers reported such a background.

What does this information tell us? It says that while the average man is able to climb the bureaucratic ladder, the average woman is shut out. She needs to be above average in order to make it. The networks provided by one's socioeconomic status, family connections, and education, apparently help women to crack the barriers that they meet and gain a toehold where those without such networks are more likely to fail.

Family Obligations

Public work and private lives intersect in the careers of top level public servants. The personal is political because conventional career patterns assume a particular relationship to family/private life obligations that pose problems for women who pursue careers. The fact is that men in top-level positions tend to live traditional family lives, while women disproportionately live nontraditional lives. Women who lead traditional lives carry an extra burden of family obligations and are less likely to be promoted into management ranks. Women who do not lead traditional lives carry an extra burden of being "different" from most women. As many as 71 percent of female managers reported they had no dependents while only as many as 48 percent of male managers reported this. About 50 percent of the women managers were married, while over 80 percent of the men were married. Women are caught in a Catch-22: a woman's power is diminished by being "different" once she arrives in a management post. On the other hand, if she is not different, then she will have family obligations that are likely to prevent her from being promoted to management.

Mentoring

Because there are so few women in top posts, women who aspire to such posts find few mentors to turn to for advice. Although as many as 57 percent of men in management positions in state agencies reported having a male mentor at the agency director level; only as many as 35 percent of the women reported having a woman mentor at that level. There are so few women who hold management positions that senior women mentors are hard to find. Although women benefit from having male mentors, they also need mentors who have successfully forded the barriers that confront women but which men may not even be aware exist.

Conclusion

Regardless of whether one evaluates the status of women in public administration from a political, psychological, or sociological paradigm, the realities are clear (Stewart, 1990). We know that women are making advances into management posts. But there is a long way to go before women will hold management positions proportional to their representation in the work force, let alone their representation in the population. We know that women in management in state and local government earn only 80 percent to 90 percent of what men earn. We know that women who live traditional lives are not nearly as likely to progress up the career ladder as are nontraditional women. We know that both women and men rely on mentors to assist their advancement, but that women have few senior women to look to for mentoring. We know that the higher a woman goes in the organization, the more likely it is that she has not only heard about sexual harassment happening to those around her but that she has actually experienced it. In terms of management style, we know that sex role stereotypes seem to sculpt what are thought to be appropriate styles for women and men. When we closely examine styles, however, we see that what is thought to be real often fades into fantasy. We know that women in management ranks are concentrated in only a few agencies. In sum, the structure of the workplace militates against women having opportunities equal to those of men. But these structures are not immutable and it is within our reach to adjust these structures to accommodate the needs of the changing work force and to breathe life into the ideal of a representative bureaucracy.

It is time to think "out of the box" about new leadership styles and new structures for classifying positions. We need to rest our career structures on assumptions that go beyond simple gender dualisms. What levers would have to be pulled to correct the differences between the sexes that disadvantage women? Three come readily to mind. They pertain to loosening rigid position classifications to accommodate women's career paths, encouraging agencies to be representative bureaucracies vertically as well as horizontally, and to promote affirmative action in deed as well as in word.

Systems that use broad-band classifications to signify skill levels without the lock step progression that inheres in more rigid systems provide at least some degree of flexibility toward this end (National Academy of Public Administration, 1991; *PA Times*, 1991). The incorporation of flexitime and job sharing opportunities also expand opportunities for women to continue working and accruing experience when their family obligations cannot accommodate a standard 40-hours per week work schedule. A theory of career development, Larwood and Gutek (1987) remind us, needs to be "roomy" enough to allow for breaks in service for women to accommodate childcare responsibilities. By facilitating childcare and parental leave, employers remove a major obstacle for employees whose family obligations interfere with their promotion potential.

Vertical representation is currently missing. Women occupy the lower rungs on the agency ladders and men occupy the upper rungs. Although giving the appearance of being representative in terms of sheer numbers, most agencies are anything but representative in their decision-making processes. While the number of state agencies with a significant number of women in the upper grade levels is increasing, many agencies and departments still have no women in these top grades. The promise, as yet unrealized, of the notion of representative bureaucracy is that policy implementation should be directed by women and men, not just men.

Practicing affirmative action means much more than merely adhering to the letter of the law in terms of considering applicants for promotion. It means *affirmatively* reinforcing equal opportunity in the workplace by actions as well as words. It means promoting qualified women into positions even though there may never have been a woman who held that position before. It means making reasonable accommodations to the workplace so that women who are qualified for promotion are not penalized for being female. Only when such measures are taken can an unfair system be altered so that women are treated as equals when they compete for management positions. It means setting the stage for women to enter the high opportunity cycle, rather than the low opportunity cycle.

The legitimacy of governmental action depends upon broadening the scope of vision in order to understand confluence of opportunity, power, and numbers. Integrating women into public administration requires reweaving the fabric of societal expectations about the rightful place of women. The 200-year record of the women's movement for equal rights and opportunities in the United States tells us that initiatives that seem eminently reasonable to women have only been secured by persistent, patient pushing. History tells us that the path of change is marked by three steps forward and two steps backward.

References

Ahn, Kenneth K. and Michelle A. Saint-Germain, 1988. "Public Administration Education and the Status of Women." *American Review of Public Administration,* vol. 18 (3), pp. 297–307.

Appleby, Paul H., 1949. *Policy and Administration.* Tuscaloosa, AL: University of Alabama Press.

Barnes, Lesley, 1988. "The Work Force of the Future." *Government Executive,* November, pp. 56–57.

Bullard, A. and D. Wright, 1991. "Circumventing the Glass Celling? Women Executives in American State Government(s)." Paper presented at the Southeastern Conference on Public Administration, Charlotte, NC.

Cooney, Rosemary S., Alice S. Clague, and Joseph J. Salvo, 1980. "Multiple Dimensions of Sexual Inequality in the Labor Force: 1970–1977." *Review of Public Data Use,* vol. 8, (October), pp. 279–293.

Diamond, E. E., 1987. "Theories of Career Development." In B. A. Gutek and L. Larwood, eds., *Women's Career Development.* Newbury Park, CA: Sage, pp. 15–27.

Dometrius, N. C., 1984. "Minorities and Women Among State Agency Leaders." *Social Science Quarterly,* vol. 65, pp. 127–137.

Faludi, Susan, 1991. *Backlash: The Undeclared War Against American Women.* New York: Crown Publishers.

Fox, S. F., 1987. "Rights and Obligations: Critical Feminist Theory, the Public Bureaucracy, and Policies for Mother-Only Families." *Public Administration Review,* vol. 47 (5), pp. 436–440.

Grossman, Harry, 1973. "The Equal Employment Opportunity Act of 1972, Its Implications for the State and Local Government Manager." *Public Personnel Management,* vol. 2 (5), pp. 370–379.

Guy, Mary E. 1992a. "The Feminization of Public Administration: Today's Reality and Tomorrow's Promise." In Mary T. Bailey and R. Mayer, eds., *Public Administration in an Interconnected World: Essays in the Minnowbrook Tradition.* Westport, CT: Greenwood Press, pp. 91–115.

Guy, Mary E., ed., 1992b. *Women and Men of the States: Public Administrators at the State Level.* Armonk, NY: M.E. Sharpe.

Guy, Mary E. and Georgia Duerst-Lahti, 1992. "Agency Culture and Its Effect on Managers." In Mary E. Guy, ed., 1992b, *Women and Men of the States: Public Administrators at the State Level.* Armonk, NY: M.E. Sharpe, pp. 157–188.

Kanter, Rosabeth Moss, 1977. *Men and Women of the Corporation.* New York: Basic Books.

Kaplan, Paul A., 1987. "Affirmative Employment Statistics for Executive Branch (Non-Postal) Agencies as of September 30, 1986." *Employment and Trends as of . . .* , May, pp. 69–75, available from U.S. Office of Personnel Management.

Kelly, Rita M., 1991. *The Gendered Economy.* Newbury Park, CA: Sage Publications.

Kelly, Rita M. and Mary E. Guy with J. Bayes, G. Duerst-Lahti, L. Duke, M. Hale, C. Johnson, A. Kawar, and J. Stanley, 1991. "Public Managers in the States: A Comparison of Career Advancement by Sex." *Public Administration Review,* vol. 51(5), pp. 402–412.

Kosterlitz, Julie, 1988. "Family Cries." *National Journal,* vol. 20(16), pp. 994–999.

Larwood, L. and B. A. Gutek, 1987. "Toward a Theory of Women's Career Development." In B.A. Gutek and L. Larwood, eds., *Women's Career Development.* Newbury Park, CA: Sage, pp. 170–183.

Lewis, Gregory B., 1988. "Progress Toward Racial and Sexual Equality in the Federal Civil Service?" *Public Administration Review,* vol. 48 (3), pp. 700–707.

Lewis, Gregory B. and Mark A. Emmert, 1996. "The Sexual Division of Labor in Federal Employment." *Social Science Quarterly,* vol. 67 (1), pp. 143–155.

Morgenthaler, Eric, 1972. "Under Pressure, Firms Try Upgrade Status of Women Employees." *Wall Street Journal,* March 20, pp. 1, 17.

National Academy of Public Administration, 1991. *Modernizing Federal Classifications: An Opportunity for Excellence.* Available from NAPA, 1120 G St., NW, Washington, DC 20005.

National Committee on Pay Equity, 1989. Briefing Paper no. 1: *The Wage Gap.* 1201 Sixteenth St., NW, Suite 420, Washington, DC 20036.

Newman, Meredith, 1992. "Career Advancement: Does Gender Make a Difference?" Paper Presented at the Annual Meeting of the American Political Science Association, Chicago, IL.

P A Times, 1991. "Report Calls for New Federal Classification." September 1, p. 15.

Powell, G.N., 1988. *Women and Men in Management.* Newbury Park, CA: Sage.

Sealander, Judith, 1983. *As Minority Becomes Majority.* Westport, CT: Greenwood Press.

Simon, R. J. and J. M. Landis, 1989. "Women's and Men's Attitudes About a Woman's Place and Role." *Public Opinion Quarterly,* vol. 53 (2), pp. 265–276.

Smith, James P., and Michael P. Ward, 1984. *Women's Wages and Worth in the Twentieth Century.* Santa Monica, CA: The Rand Corp., R-3119-NICHD.

Stewart, Debra W., 1990. "Women in Public Administration." In Naomi B. Lynn and Aaron Wildavsky eds., *Public Administration: The State of the Discipline.* Chatham, NJ: Chatham House Publishers, pp. 203–227.

U.S. Department of Labor, 1987 "Over Half of Mothers with Children One Year Old or Under in Labor Force in March 1987." Press Release, August 12, USDL 87-345.

U.S. Equal Employment Opportunity Commission, 1982. *Job Patterns for Minorities and Women in State and Local Government, 1980.* Washington, DC: Government Printing Office.

_____, 1985. *Job Patterns for Minorities and Women in State and Local Government, 1985.* Washington, DC: Government Printing Office.

_____, 1990. *Job Patterns for Minorities and Women in State and Local Government, 1989.* Washington, DC: Government Printing Office.

Van Riper, Paul P., 1976. *History of the United States Civil Service.* Westport, CT: Greenwood Press.

Wall Street Journal, 1963. "More Women Conquer Business World's Bias, Fill Management Jobs." February 25, pp. 1, 16.

Welch, Susan, Albert K. Kamig, and Richard A. Eribes, 1983. "Correlates of Women's Employment in Local Governments." *Urban Affairs Quarterly,* vol. 18 (4), pp. 551–564.

17

A Symposium

Women in Public Administration

edited by Nesta M. Gallas

Introductory Comments

Nesta M. Gallas, *John Jay College of Criminal Justice, City University of New York*

When asked to serve as editor of this symposium, I accepted with alacrity. My enthusiasm for the project was shared by members of ASPA's Committee on Women in Public Administration, with whom plans for the symposium were discussed. My condition soon turned to alarm as I read my mail following a *P.A. News and Views* announcement of symposium plans. I had not anticipated the volume of suggestions (and prescriptions) both in number and intensity—nor the sharp differences of opinion as to appropriate coverage.

Women in public administration became an elusive subject compounded by the uniqueness and individuality of the women in public administration who contacted me—practitioners, academics, students, and combinations of each.

An attempt to synthesize suggestions (and prescriptions) was abandoned in favor of finding a focus that permeated divergencies. Three were found: There has been and is discrimination against, underrepresentation of, and underutilization of women in public administration. Despite the foci identified, pandemonium prevailed as I sorted and resorted the materials submitted for consideration. Analyses of why conditions of discrimination, underrepresentation, and underutilization exist and remedies for their removal covered the spectrum of beliefs and concerns.

Source: *Public Administration Review* 36 (July/August 1976): 347–389.

The manuscripts selected for inclusion only sample the complexities of the subject, the diversities, and the heterogeneity of those having an interest in and a commitment to advancing the cause of women in public administration. All, however, project a positive stance rather than negative rhetoric.

The restrictions of available space resulted in the exclusion of several articles that hopefully may be published at a later date. Criteria for selection became one of balance in presentation and the extent to which each complemented the substance or significance of the others. If both conflict and consensus—hidden or exposed—are seen by PAR readers, it will be par for the course this symposium has traveled.

The articles included are placed against two backdrops. The first is an article on the women's movement in ASPA by Joan Bishop, a pioneer activist in this effort. The second is a selected profile of women in public administration by Andrea Stoloff, my research assistant, who has worked with me on affirmative actions.

These are followed by four articles that explore discrimination, underrepresentation, and underutilization and their removal from varied vantage points—both general and specific.

Debra Stewart focuses on the dilemma of why so few women have been able to move into top jobs. Three theses are advanced for analyzing the blockages to female entry into high level decisional posts: The political, biological, and sociological. Some directions for federal leadership in removing existing barriers are suggested.

Mary Lepper presents a timely overview on the status of women in the United States and their search for justice and equity. Affirmative action processes are weighed against other means of ending the unequal position of women in employment.

Peggy Newgarden describes and critiques the federally recommended process for determining affirmative action goals and suggests a more workable set of criteria for reaching measurable goals. The application of these criteria to a local government setting is provided, based on work done in Sacramento, California.

Nancy R. Hooyman and Judith Kaplan concentrate on a specific occupational area in which women predominate but have little visibility and exert little influence as administrators in the human services profession. The focus here is on how women can enhance their influence by removing internal, interpersonal, and structural obstacles. A training model for modifying barriers to career advancement and effective performance is presented.

The next two articles turn to women and women's groups as the vehicle for exploring behavior in complex organizations. The first of these, by Robert B. Denhardt and Jan Perkins, relates concepts of administrative man to alternative theories of organization emerging from the women's movement—both women's rights groups and radical feminists. This "women's way" analysis may seem to some to be blatantly sexist. That women have been able to form effective work groups, however, is evidenced by the strength and number of the divers pieces that are labeled the women's movement.

The final article by Jennifer Dorn Oldfield presents a case study of women as the makers of policy and designers of programs dealing with women's rights. Connecticut's Permanent Commission on the Status of Women is the focus of the study. An issue raised is whether the "status of women" provides a unified goal for organizing a government program. A second issue is whether an advocacy role can be performed by a government agency.

Lurking throughout each of these articles is the specter of sexism in traditional strongholds, i.e., everywhere, at high levels and in the processes designed to combat it. In these times of transition in public administration generally and for women in public administration specifically, a variety of options are open to women for surfacing and confronting sexism—whether overt or covert. Through litigation, negotiation, socialization, enthusiasm, commitment, and competence in their public service roles, the imbalances and plateaus are being challenged.

This symposium sets forth some selected stances for scrutinizing women in public administration. If you wish to read more, Joan Bishop (and I) suggest the following references.

References

Amundsen, Kirsten, *The Silenced Majority: Women and American Democracy* (Englewood Cliffs, N.J.: Prentice-Hall, 1971).

Andreas, Carol, *Sex and Caste in America* (Englewood Cliffs, N.J.: Prentice-Hall, 1971).

Babox, Deborah, and Madeline Belkin (eds.), *Liberation Now: Writings from the Women's Liberation Movement* (New York: Laurel, 1971).

Bernard, Jessie, *Women and the Public Interest: An Essay on Policy and Protest* (Chicago & New York: Aldine-Atherton, 1971).

Bird, Caroline, and Sara Welles Briller, *Born Female: The High Cost of Keeping Women Down,* Rev. Ed. (New York: David McKay Co., Inc., 1974).

Bullough, Vern L., and Bonnie Bullough, *The Subordinate Sex: A History of Attitudes Toward Women* (Urbana: University of Illinois Press, 1973).

Carden, Maren Lockwood, *The New Feminist Movement* (New York: Russell Sage Foundation, 1974).

Catt, Carrie Chapman, and Nettie Rogers Shuler, *Woman Suffrage and Politics, the Inner Story of the Suffrage Movement* (Seattle: University of Washington, 1970).

Cafe, William Henry, *The American Woman: Her Changing Social, Economic and Political Roles, 1920–1970* (New York: Oxford University, 1972).

Chesler, Phyllis, *Women and Madness* (New York: Doubleday, 1972).

_____, and Emily Jane Goodman, *Women, Money and Power* (New York: William Morrow & Co., Inc., 1976).

Cudlipp, Edythe, *Understanding Women's Liberation* (New York: Paperback Library, 1971).

Epstein, Cynthia Fuchs, *Woman's Place: Options and Limits in Professional Careers* (Berkeley: University of California, 1971).

Ferris, Abbott L., *Indicators of Trends in the Status of American Women* (New York: Russel Sage, 1971).

Firestone, Shulamith, *The Dialectic of Sex: The Case for Feminist Revolution* (New York: Bantam Books, 1970).

Flexner, Eleanor, *Century of Struggle: The Women's Rights Movement in the United States* (New York: Atheneum, 1970).

Freeman, Jo, *New Thoughts on Women* (Berkeley: National, 1974).

_____, *The Politics of Women's Liberation: A Case Study of an Emerging Social Movement and Its Relation to the Policy Process* (New York: David McKay Co., Inc., 1974).

Friedan, Betty, *The Feminine Mystique* (New York: Dell, 1963).

Githers, Marianne, and Jewel L. Prestage (eds.), *A Portrait of Marginality: The Political Behavior of the American Woman* (New York: David McKay Co., Inc., 1976).

Gornick, Vivian, and Barbara K. Morgan (eds.), *Women in Sexist Society: Studies in Power and Powerlessness* (New York: Basic Books, Inc., 1971).

Holt, Judith, and E. Levine, *The Rebirth of Feminism* (New York: Quadrangle, 1971).

Huber, Joan (ed.), *Changing Women in a Changing Society* (Chicago: University of Chicago, 1973).

Jacquette, Jane E. (ed.), *Women in Politics* (New York: Wiley, 1974).

Kanowitz, Leo, *Women and the Law, The Unfinished Revolution* (Albuquerque: University of New Mexico, 1969).

Klein, Viola, *The Feminine Character: History of an Ideology* (Urbana: University of Illinois, 1971).

Kraditor, Aileen S., *The Ideas of the Woman Suffrage Movement, 1890–1920* (Garden City, N.Y.: Doubleday, 1971).

_____ (ed.), *Up from the Pedestal: Selected Writings in the History of Feminism* (Chicago: Quadrangle, 1970).

Kreps, Juanita, *Sex in the Market Place: American Women at Work* (Baltimore and London: Johns Hopkins Press, 1971).

Lifton, Robert Jay (ed.), *The Women in America* (Boston: Beacon, 1967).

Mead, Margaret, *Male and Female: A Study of the Sexes in a Changing World* (New York: Dell, 1949).

Millett, Kate, *Sexual Politics* (Garden City, N.Y.: Doubleday and Company, Inc., 1970).

Mitchell, Juliet, *Woman's Estate* (New York: Pantheon Books, 1971).

Morgan, David, *Suffragists and Democrats: The Politics of Woman Suffrage in America* (East Lansing, Mich.: Michigan State, 1972).

Morgan, Robin (ed.), *Sisterhood Is Powerful* (New York: Vintage, 1970).

Myrdal, Alva, and Viola Klein, *Women's Two Roles: At Home and Work* (New York: Humanities, 1968).

Murphy, Irene L., *Public Policy on the Status of Women: Agenda and Strategy for the 70s* (Lexington, Mass.: Lexington Books, 1973).

Oltman, Ruth M., *Campus 1970: Where Do Women Stand* (Washington, D.C.: American Association of University Women, December 1970).

O'Neill, William L., *Everyone Was Brave: A History of Feminism in America* (Chicago: Quadrangle, 1969).

_____ (ed.), *The Women's Movement: Feminism in the United States and England* (Chicago: Quadrangle, 1971).

Perrucci, Carolyn C., and Dena B. Targ (eds.), *Marriage and the Family: A Critical Analysis and Proposals for Change* (New York: David McKay Co., Inc., 1974).

Rapoport, Rhona, and Robert Rapoport, *Dual-Career Families* (New York: Penguin, 1972).

Reeves, Nancy, *Womankind: Beyond the Stereotypes* (Chicago: Aldine-Atherton, 1971).

Riegel, Robert E., *American Women: A Story of Social Change* (Cranbury, N.J.: Fairleigh Dickinson University, 1970).

Roberts, Joan I. (ed.), *Beyond Intellectual Sexism: A New Woman, A New Reality* (New York: David McKay Co., 1976).

Rossi, Alice S., and Ann Calderwood (eds.), *Academic Women on the Move* (New York: Russell Sage, 1973).

Samuels, Catherine, *The Forgotten Five Million: Women in Public Employment* (New York: Women's Action Alliance Inc., 1975).

Sargent, Alice G. (ed.), *Beyond Sex Roles* (St. Paul, Minn.: West Publishing Co., 1975).

Schneir, Miriam (ed.), *Feminism: The Essential Historical Writings* (New York: Vintage, 1972).

Scott, Ann Firor (ed.), *The American Woman: Who Was She?* (Englewood Cliffs, N.J.: Prentice-Hall, 1971).

_____, and Andrew M. Scott, *One Half the People: The Fight for Woman Suffrage* (Philadelphia: J.B. Lippincott Co., 1975).

Sochen, June (ed.), *The New Feminism in Twentieth-Century America:* (Lexington, Mass.: D.C. Heath, 1971).

Sullerot, Evelyn, *Women, Society and Change* (New York: McGraw-Hill, 1971).

Tanner, Leslie B. (ed.), *Voices from Women's Liberation* (New York: New American Library, 1970).

Theodore, Athena, "The Professional Woman: Trends and Prospects," in *The Professional Woman*, Athena Theodore (ed.), (Cambridge, Mass.: Schenkman, 1971), pp. 1–35.

The Women's Movement in ASPA

The establishment in 1971 of the ASPA Task Force on Women in Public Administration took place during the period when task forces or committees for women were bursting forth in a wide range of professional organizations. Its activities and progress exemplified efforts made by many professional associations to address the serious issues that existed in relation to women in the respective professions. These developments must also be viewed within the context of the Women's Movement which had arisen in all sectors of society and the economy.

Legal Precursors

Looking back, one finds the first organized beginning of the current Women's Liberation Movement in the Women's Suffrage Movement. The Seneca Falls Convention in 1848 is considered a first milestone in organization in the United States. The purpose of the Women's Suffrage Movement, to gain for women the right to vote, was achieved 72 years later with the passage of the 19th Amendment in 1920 and its ratification by the states. Following this, a notable pioneering organization of women for women, the League of Women Voters, was established. Its mission was to enable newly enfranchised women to become informed and effective voters. Its focus was the education of women in political issues, government processes, and the complex questions facing the nation's electorate at both local and national levels. The strong and successful League continues to make significant contributions to many facets of the Women's Movement today.

Decades after the passage of the 19th Amendment, the Civil Rights Act of 1964 and later amendments provided legal foundation for wider application of women's right to equality. Next came the Equal Rights Amendment: "Equality under the law shall not be denied or abridged because of sex, race, color, creed or national origin." This was passed by the Congress in 1970, 47 years after it was first proposed in 1923. The struggle for its ratification by the states is still under way.

Rise of Women's Liberation Movement

While this progress was being made on the legal front, the Women's Liberation Movement developed in many sectors. It coincided with the rise of other movements to effect change, such as the civil rights thrust for minorities, protest against the Vietnam War, and students' action to move into the power structures.

The Feminine Mystique by Betty Friedan, published in 1963, was a strong catalyst, bringing rapid growth in the '60s to the Women's Liberation Movement. The National Organization of Women, established in 1966, became a strong action arm of the movement and grew into the largest organization of women working for equality of opportunity in a diversity of areas.

Coincident with the publication of the Friedan book was the issuance of the Report of the President's Commission on the Status of Women. Eleanor Roosevelt was its first chairperson, appointed by John F. Kennedy. This report led to the establishment of Commissions on the Status of Women in most states, some cities and territories, and later to a number of federal task forces.

By 1970 the Women's Liberation Movement was waxing strong. The general objective was equality. Within that framework came the shattering of stereotypes and widening of options to choose the kinds of lives women wished to lead. Many specific goals emerged: equal pay for equal work, elimination of sex as a qualification for employment, revision of abortion laws, child care provisions, equality of educational opportunity, elimination of alimony for divorcees able to work, election of women to political office, and many others. Organized groups open to all women evolved, such as the Women's Equity Action League and the National Women's Political Caucus. There were also groups of women opposed to what had become known as Women's Lib, believing this a threat to the position and protection they had and preferred to keep. In the words of the Pussycat League,

"One of North America's most precious natural resources is being greatly threatened—American women's femininity is being eroded."

Techniques of the different groups to achieve their goals varied dramatically. Fierce confrontation and demonstrations were early attention-getting devices employed, for example, by the Red Stockings, who designated themselves as radical feminists, and the Women's International Terrorist Conspiracy from Hell (WITCH). As the movement grew, however, more reasoned voices prevailed, and the issues were taken out of the streets and into the councils and programs of many organizations, to conferences, to elections, and to the courts.

Development of Committees for Women's Professional Organizations

In professional organizations task forces or committees for women had begun to appear by 1970. The ASPA Task Force was among the early ones. Their number is now legion. The initial exchanges of information among the first committees established were on an informal basis. The chairpersons came to know each other and to compare notes. As the committees proliferated, the need for an organized vehicle for exchange and a center and clearing house for information became apparent. The Federation of Organizations for Professional Women was established. Headquarters are now maintained both in Washington, D.C., and at Cheever House, the Center for Research on Women in Higher Education and the Professions, in Wellesley, Massachusetts, in conjunction with Wellesley College.

Birth of the Women's Movement in ASPA

At the ASPA annual conference in Denver in April 1971, evidence of the women's movement in the Society surfaced. Twenty-eight women gathered informally as the Women's Caucus. The sessions were stormy. Differences of opinion as to how to proceed were evident in this group, as had been true in the Women's Movement in general. These were resolved. Joan Fiss Bishop, then the only woman on the National Council and a participant in the Women's Caucus, was asked to present the following report to the National Council:

Resolutions of the Women's Caucus

The Women's Caucus, composed of interested women, ASPA members and non-members, in attendance at this conference, has met to discuss the serious issues that exist in relation to the role of women in the field of public administration, both as practitioners and as academicians. We recognize the need for ASPA, as THE professional organization for public administrators, to assume its leadership role in attacking institutional discrimination against women. We therefore present the following resolutions to the ASPA Council and to this membership body for adoption. We urge adoption of similar resolutions and activities at the regional and chapter levels of ASPA.

We strongly urge:

1. national ASPA and the individual chapters to support and help implement affirmative action programs for the hiring and the promotion of women in public service and in public service education. We recommend also that ASPA actively support the full participation of women in all areas of government.
2. that a committee of women chosen by the Women's Caucus be designated to organize a series of panels for next year's national conference on the role of women in public administration, that such panels include participation of both men and women, and that the program committee insure that women are invited to participate and chair regular substantive panels. We further recommend that the ASPA Council encourage regional councils to include similar panels at regional conferences.
3. that there be appropriate representation of women on all ASPA committees and the editorial board of *Public Administration Review.*
4. that a task force be formed on the status of women in public administration and in education for public administration, that the task force include a significant number of women, and that women be chosen as Chairman and Executive Secretary.
5. that in organizing, sponsoring, and participating in educational programs at the undergraduate, graduate, mid-career, and faculty levels ASPA assume a leadership role to assure the equal participation of women in these educational programs.
6. that the national ASPA membership drive give special emphasis to the need to increase the participation of women in ASPA. We pledge our support to this total membership recruitment effort.

These resolutions received the strong approval of President Walter Mode and the National Council; and the report was accepted at the annual business meeting.

Initial Task Force for Women

At the next meeting of the National Council in June 1971, Joan Fiss Bishop was appointed chairperson of the Task Force on Women in Public Administration. The scope and objectives of the Task Force were then defined at a meeting of a steering committee which met in Washington on September 10, 1971. On this committee were representatives of diverse organizations and agencies which had a strong interest in women in the public sector. Members of this steering committee provided perspective and gave focus to the programs proposed for the fledgling ASPA Task Force.

There was consensus among all groups involved in the establishment of the Task Force (the Women's Caucus, the National Council, ASPA headquarters staff, the steering committee) that priority must be given to a survey of women members of ASPA. From the membership printout, approximately 1,026, one-tenth of the membership, were identified by name as women. A questionnaire was sent to each in November 1971. The purpose was to learn the current status of these women in public administration, their qualifications, and needs that ASPA might serve. A statistical compilation was made and an analysis of the survey followed.

Meanwhile, a four-point action program was developed. Task Force members were appointed to carry through the program. Responsibility for each project was assigned to a chairperson and his/her sub-committee. The studies were made during the ensuing months and the results presented at the annual ASPA conference in New York in March 1972. The four areas addressed were:

1. Practices and policies of schools of public administration and related professional programs to encourage women to enter and later have opportunities for future development in public service. What should be done further? *Chairperson:* William M. Capron, associate dean, John Fitzgerald Kennedy School of Government, Harvard University.

2. Identification of opportunities in current shortage fields in public administration and methods to stimulate applications from well-qualified people for specific needs. *Chairperson:* Esther C. Lawton, assistant director of personnel, U.S. Treasury Department.

3. Report on Women's Rights and employment policies in the public sector. *Chairperson:* James A. Norton, president, Greater Cleveland Associated Foundation.

4. Compilation of information about accomplishments and interests of individual women members of ASPA and statistical profiles of these women. *Chairperson:* June Martin, director, Standing Committee Central Staff, New York State Assembly.

Since no ASPA funds were available, all projects undertaken by the Task Force and its sub-committees were labors of love. The one exception was the mailing of the questionnaire from ASPA headquarters to women members.

The reports, presented at a well-attended morning session at the New York ASPA Conference in 1972, provided information and background needed for future plans of the Task Force, as well as education in the issues for the ASPA membership at large.

During 1971–1972 the chairperson of the Task Force had coordinated plans and communications among the four members of the first Task Force who served as chairpersons for the projects and their respective sub-committees. She had also provided suggestions, from information in some 400 returned questionnaires, of well-qualified women for membership on various ASPA committees, and as speakers for ASPA programs, both national and regional. An additional use of the questionnaires was to identify women as possible candidates for positions. By this time affirmative action had prompted many organizations, not previously so inclined, to seek qualified women. The first chairperson of the Task Force provided a placement service from her office. The number of referrals mounted, during her period as chairperson from 1971–1973, to several hundred. For the New York conference important responsibilities were to identify qualified women as speakers and also to insure provision of topics related to women's issues. A new feature was a specialized service embodied in the job referral center for women members of ASPA and for employers who were seeking well-qualified women.

During 1971–1972 the emerging Task Force had the enthusiastic interest and cooperation of John Garvey, executive director. Barbara Byers provided articles about the Task Force regularly in *News and Views* to keep the membership informed.

The Second Task Force

The strong support of President Walter Mode and the 1971–72 National Council was equally evident in 1972–73, when President John Ryan and the Council members of that year endorsed with confidence the work of the Task Force. Cooperation continued from Seymour Berlin, the new executive director, and the ASPA headquarters staff. Joan Fiss Bishop was reappointed chairperson to develop action programs for 1972–1973 which had been identified for priority.

One was the establishment of a joint NASPAA/ASPA committee to address itself to affirmative action needs in schools of public administration for women students, alumnae, faculty, and professional personnel. Co-chairpersons for this project were Morris W. H. Collins Jr., president of NASPAA, and Joan Bishop, chairperson of the ASPA Task Force. The report concerning this survey of 66 programs for public administration was presented in 1973 at both the NASPAA national conference in San Diego and the ASPA conference in Los Angeles. That survey highlighted, among other things, the small number of women in each category covered. Significant, also were the paucity of senior faculty who were women and the growing number of women appointed as junior faculty in 1971 and 1972.

A second action program of the Task Force was to identify at local, state, and regional levels the affirmative action programs relevant to the interests of ASPA women. It had become clear to the 1971–1972 Task Force that such information was spotty and difficult to track down. June Martin, a continuing member of the Task Force, was appointed chairperson for this project. Through the cooperation of local ASPA chapter presidents, 36 chapter liaison representatives from the various regions were appointed to her committee to secure information about affirmative action programs in their areas and their effectiveness, and to initiate action wherever possible. The report of this committee was presented in the program at the 1973 ASPA national conference.

Impact of the Task Forces

The initial period of the Task Forces, 1971–1973, had been a productive one for ASPA. The surveys undertaken and the results publicized had turned a spotlight on the current status of women in ASPA, had heightened awareness that there were able women in all sectors, and thus facilitated their inclusion in offices, committees, and programs. In addition, the Task Force on Women in Public Administration was well publicized beyond ASPA in the general press and in meetings and publications of a number of other professional associations. The chairperson of the Task Force attended and spoke at meetings concerned with equal status for women at universities, government commissions on the status of women, and women's action groups of great variety. Women's student groups, college librarians, directors of women's programs, and other individuals and organizations throughout the country wrote by the hundreds for information. Because the ASPA Task Force was among the first in professional associations it had high visibility and introduced ASPA to a wide and diverse public.

Committee on Women in Public Administration 1973–1974

In May 1973 the Task Force became the Standing Committee on Women in Public Administration of ASPA. June Martin, who had served as a member of the Task Force in the preceding two years, was appointed chairperson. The charge from President Frank Sherwood and the National Council to the committee stated: "The purpose of this committee is to promote equal employment and educational opportunities for women in the public service, with particular emphasis on developing programs for women in ASPA."

During 1973–1974 there were 40 chapter liaison representatives working with June Martin and the 23 committee members. Through the chapter liaison persons, local action could be instigated. The importance of this was clear to members of the National Women's Committee. For the May 1974 ASPA conference in Syracuse, a comprehensive report was prepared and presented. This covered employment problems and status of women in federal, state, and local government. Also presented was a summary of extensive proposals for improving the quality of educational programs in public administration. The need for feed-back systems through Civil Service, ASPA, and NASPAA was emphasized. A number of recommendations concerning all of these were stated. It was also pointed out that the information concerning women members secured in 1971 by the Task Force was now out of date and a current questionnaire was proposed.

Committee on Women in Public Administration 1974–1975

Beverly Hawkins was appointed chairperson of the Committee on Women in ASPA by President Philip Rutledge in June 1974, with Ruth Ann Barrett as vice-chairperson. As had been the case with the preceding Task Force and Committee, the difficulties of communication and planning through correspondence were equally clear. The 25 committee members were widely scattered geographically and no funds were available for meetings. Therefore, it was decided to hold simultaneous committee meetings on January 25, 1975, in San Francisco and Washington, communicating with each other through telephone amplification equipment. This communications experiment was an attempt to partially solve problems created by the geographically dispersed committee.

At the 1975 ASPA National Conference in Chicago the Women's Committee again scheduled a Women's Caucus open to all interested ASPA members, a no-host reception in honor of women conference participants, and a panel cosponsored with the Conference of Minority Public Administrators (COMPA) on "Black Women and Professionalism." A child care service was offered for the first time. Other activities of the Women's Committee included the establishment of an internship for a woman MPA student at ASPA headquarters, publication of a brochure explaining the purpose and programs of the Women's Committee, and the recommendation that a single issue of PAR be concerned with women's issues.

Committee on Women in Public Administration 1975–1976

Ruth Ann Barrett, who had been actively interested in and involved with the activities of the Women's Caucus, Task Force, and Women's Committee, became chairperson for 1975–1976, appointed in April 1975 by President Randy Hamilton. Gill Robinson was named vice-chairperson. With 36 committee members from all over the country, the expedient of simultaneous committee meetings on the East and West Coast was again employed on January 10, 1976. The agenda included two subcommittee reports. The one on Chapter Development and Membership reported that 14 chapters had established a committee on women. The report from Education and Continuing Development of Women described a project planned with the Los Angeles Social Systems Research Center to initiate 120 minority women to the field of public administration through a two-day work-shop. A Policy Statement on Equal Employment of Women in the Public Service was reviewed and a later revision submitted to the committee members. Guidelines for non-sexist terminology were to be widely distributed throughout ASPA, as well as a brochure on the Committee on Women. The development of a directory of women in ASPA was discussed. The Committee members considered recommendations for the 1976–1977 program of activities and funds needed to carry them out, as well as procedures for the appointment of Committee members.

In the fall of 1975, the ASPA Committee on Women in Public Administration became a member of the Federation of Organizations for Professional Women. The appointed ASPA representative to the Federation was Joan Fiss Bishop, who had from the beginning of both the ASPA Task Force and the Federation served an informal liaison function between the ASPA group and chairpersons of a number of women's committees of other professional organizations now members of the Federation.

Progress of Women in Public Administration

This synopsis of the history of the ASPA Task Force on Women in Public Administration and its successor, the Standing Committee on Women in Public Administration, reveals steps taken for the introduction of women into the mainstream of ASPA. The goals of the first Task Force continue to be those of its successors. Some techniques to achieve these remain the same; new ones have been added. The work of the hundreds of women and men on the ASPA Task Forces and Committees, with wide support from the membership, officers, and headquarters staff, has brought notable improvement in the status of women in ASPA. For example, in 1970–1971 there was one woman on the 26-member National Council; in 1975–1976, four on a Council of 36 members; and in 1976–1977 eight on a 46-member Council. Nesta Gallas, ASPA's current president, is the first woman to hold the position. Comparable increases in leadership roles at regional and local levels are evident. Representation on programs, sparse in 1970, has increased markedly. Of the 28 current members of the PAR Editorial Board, five are women, as contrasted with one in 1970–1971. Women are achieving visibility and a voice in policy and programs. An interesting speculation concerns the percentage of woman members in ASPA. In 1971, in the membership of 10,000, 10 percent were identified as women. From the 1975 questionnaire sent to 15,000 members, 50 percent responding showed 20 percent were women. Unknown is the percentage in the 50 percent who did not respond.

Other indications of progress are apparent in areas closely related to ASPA concerns. Schools of public administration have addressed themselves to a better balance in the student body and in faculty appointments. An increase in appointments of women to top level positions in government and improved mobility from lower and middle rungs are evident. The numbers of women elected to school boards, city and town councils, and mayoralties mounted noticeably, as did those on county boards. In 1975 at the state levels there were 610 women out of 7,561 state representatives, 11 secretaries of state, three lieutenant governors, and one woman governor. In the U.S. House of Representatives were 19 women, but none in the U.S. Senate.

International Women's Year officially ended on December 31, 1975. Its impact in bringing attention to the status of women throughout the world will now be translated into action during International Women's Decade 1975–1985: A United Nations proclamation officially calls it the Decade for Women: Equality, Development and Peace.

The ASPA Committee on Women in Public Administration will continue its vigorous program. With the action in the last five years as encouragement, the Decade of Women 1975–1985 beckons now to ASPA for achievement of the ultimate goals of equality.

Joan Fiss Bishop, *Harvard Graduate School of Design* ∽

Women at the Top: Selected Profiles

In November 1975, ASPA's new Membership Information System yielded the first profile of ASPA membership, published in *P.A. News and Views*. Compiled by Sally Greenberg, the analysis was based on a 50 percent response to the MIS questionnaire, a return representative enough to form the framework for the profile. Ms. Greenberg's ASPA Profile, as well as a variety of other "raw data" sources, have been drawn on in the preparation of the "Selected Profiles" that follow.

As a totality, women in ASPA have been described (based on MIS data) in a pamphlet distributed by ASPA's Committee on Women in Public Administration. The profile shows that ASPA women comprise 21 percent of the organization; 34 percent of the women are under 30; 24 percent are students, while 42 percent have obtained a bachelor's degree. They are found in a wide variety of occupations, with specialties in the policy and program planning, general administration, fiscal and budget, personnel, and academic areas.

This study describes two selected groups of women in public administration: those in ASPA earning over $30,000 and the female membership of the National Academy of Public Administration. The group portrait of these women "at the top" is limited and select, based, as it is, on available data. However, the study suggests several interesting characteristics common to top level women in public administration. Even in its limited scope, therefore, its implications may be valuable for the vast majority of women striving to achieve similar goals and, in the process, to eliminate discrimination in the field.

ASPA Women Earning over $30,000

The ASPA woman earning over $30,000 typically is Caucasian, 51 years old, possesses a master's degree, and works on the East Coast. She holds a high level position with the federal government and considers herself a specialist in "general" administration. She is a rare phenomenon.

About one-fifth of the 15,542 members of the American Society for Public Administration are women. Only two per cent of these women earn over $30,000 each year (while, of the men, 18 percent are in this high salary bracket). The available data have been assembled so as to present a portrait of this unique group of 47 women in top management positions.

Age

The group ranges in age from 35 to 66; the median age is 51. Eight (18 percent) of the women are over 60, as compared with six (12 percent) who are under 40. The median age of ASPA members is 39.

Race

The vast majority (38, or 83 percent) of these women are Caucasian, compared to 92 per cent of ASPA members who report that they are Caucasian. Black women number seven (15 percent) of the 47 women earning over $30,000, but, significantly, the black women are representative of the larger group in terms of age, educational background, employment sector, and occupational speciality. The overall ASPA figure for black (the largest racial minority group in the organization) membership is 5 percent of the total.

Education

The top level ASPA women are well educated. Twenty-six (73 percent) of them possess at least the master's degree and eight (17 percent) the doctorate. Compared with the rest of the organization (60 percent of the non-student membership with at least the master's), the women show a broader level of educational attainment.

Geographic Analysis

Clustered primarily in the eastern, mid-Atlantic portion of the nation, these women are rather representative of the overall ASPA membership in their geographic distribution. For example, 17 of the women live in New York State (and about half of these in New York City). Ten are located in Washington, D.C. The mid-Atlantic region, which includes Pennsylvania, Maryland, and Virginia, accounts for a similar number. An exception to the national figures is found in the California region, in which two women (4 percent) are located, compared with the national 15 percent representation.

Employment

Thirty (64 percent) of the 47 women in ASPA who earn over $30,000 per year do so by working in government, at the federal, state, county, and local levels. By far, the largest number are federal employees—20 women; state employees number six. The national ASPA figure for employment with the federal government is, by contrast, only 20 percent of the membership. Five of the women are involved in academic work. Four are in consulting or business, and the same number are in non-foundation, nonprofit work.

Occupational Specialties

Reflecting the national ASPA tendencies, 13 (28 per cent) of the high-salaried women report their occupational specialty as general administration, compared to 22 percent of all ASPA members, 24 percent of all male members, and 14 percent of all female members. Nine women (20 percent) report public administration as their primary occupational specialty, compared to 17 percent generally. Policy and program planning and the field of management analysis interest five (11 percent), each, of the women. Three (6 percent) of the women are concerned with civil rights and equal opportunity. However, there is no significant interest in this area on a national level. Three women (6 percent) name personnel administration as their primary occupational specialty, a figure again reflective of the national ASPA figure of 8 percent, but less than the 11 percent of female ASPA members generally.

Among the 30 (64 percent) women working in government, nine are found to be specialists in general administration. Six of these government employees are declared specialists in public administration; this group represents two-thirds of the public administration specialists.

The federal level of government claims the services of the largest number, 6 out of 13, of the general administration specialists working in government, four out of the nine public administration specialists, and three of the five, each, of those specializing in management analysis and the field of policy and program planning. All three civil rights/equal opportunity specialists work for the federal government.

The public administration specialty (second most popular among these women) is most often represented in the federal sector (four women out of nine) and, to a lesser degree, in academia (two of the nine).

Academics, themselves, who total five (11 percent) of the 47 women, report themselves as equally involved in general administration, personnel administration, and policy and program planning, but with twice as many in public administration as in the other areas.

Remarks

The data show that women in this rare group at the top do have much in common with the national ASPA membership. The most striking disparity, of course, is the low number of women in high-salary positions, and the even lower proportion of minority group women in these ranks.

National Academy of Public Administration: Its Female Membership

Six percent of the membership of the National Academy of Public Administration are women. Of the 13 women who have been elected to the National Academy, five are ASPA members, three of whom earn over $30,000 each year.

The National Academy women show distinction in their professional achievements and in the range of their educational experience. Nine women have earned the doctoral degree, while three have the master's. Thus, almost all of these women possess at least the master's degree. (These proportions, incidentally, are reversed for the ASPA women earning over $30,000.) The median age for National Academy women is 52.5, slightly higher than that of ASPA women in top positions (51).

Six of the National Academy women are academics, three of whom also serve as deans or directors; five are with state or federal government agencies; two work in leadership capacities in non-foundation, nonprofit organizations. Here, again, the comparison with high-salaried ASPA women yields an interesting contrast: the ASPA women are primarily employed in government (64 percent), while a high percentage of National Academy women work in academic settings. The federal government employs, in both cases, the greatest proportion of the women working in government.

Almost all Academy women have published in conjunction with their professional work, and achievements in both areas combine to show a wide variety of interests and accomplishments. Academy women include, in their distinguished ranks, the director general of the Foreign Service, the chairman of the National Endowment for the Arts, the president of the League of Women Voters, the director of the Center for Computer Sciences and Technology of the National Bureau of Standards, and the secretary general of the International Planned Parenthood Federation.

Andrea Stoloff,
John Jay College of Criminal Justice,
The City University of New York ⌒

Women in Top Jobs:
An Opportunity for Federal Leadership

The year 1976 finds American women firmly entrenched in the country's labor force. With nine out of ten women having worked during their lifetime and 46 percent of all American women currently engaged in salaried employment, the female worker is no longer a deviant case.[1] This trend toward large-scale participation is mirrored in the public sector. There females constitute some 41.7 percent of the white collar work force and, in certain cases, occupy up to 63 percent of all agency slots.[2] Accordingly, policy objectives, congruent with emerging national needs in this sphere, relate less to mere participation of women in the labor force and more to the character of that participation. Focusing specifically on government as employer, the issue becomes not how many women will be employed in the public service of the future, but rather in what capacity they will be employed.

This article is grounded in the assumption that expansion of employment opportunity for women in American society calls for a focus, not on jobs per se, but rather on job stratification. National occupational data reveals small numbers of women have indeed gained acceptance in the most prestigious occupations: 9.8 percent of the physicians, 7 percent of the lawyers and judges, 9.4 percent of the full professors, and 2.3 percent of highest level (GS16–18) federal civil servants.[3] Yet the pattern of mobility parallels that recently identified in Great Britain. There women's entry into top slots has gone from breakthrough in earlier decades to acceptance, but now remains fixed on a plateau.[4] The public policy question is simply: "how might these percentages be increased?" Through an analysis of obstacles to full participation in the upper echelons of private and public bureaucracy, this article aims to bring change direction into sharp relief and, in the process, to illuminate the special leadership role for the federal public service.

Obstacles to Change

In the plethora of recent works on women in American society three broad explanations for the blockage of female entry into high-level decision-making positions are found: the political, the biological, and the sociological.[5] Each type of explanation contains elements of the others, the sociological in particular having pronounced biological and political dimensions. Nevertheless, these labels do function to locate the core of each explanation as well as to allow for some demarcation of boundary lines. Critical examination of each explanatory model, and its implications, in conjunction with data on public and private sector employment patterns serves to highlight that set of factors best explaining the barrier to movement beyond the current threshold. Only through such isolation of the "problem," will the solution in the form of a change strategy emerge.

The Political Thesis

In the most extreme form the political thesis posits that men constitute the ruling class of the world and are determined to stay in power. In the words of one author, male-female relations reflect " . . . the oldest, most rigid class/caste system in existence, the class system based on sex—a system consolidated over thousands of years, lending the archetypal male and female roles an undeserved legitimacy and seeming permanence."[6] This analysis points out that characteristically "feminine" traits are nothing more than the traits of any oppressed class. While emphasizing the historical similarity between the condition of women as an oppressed class in American society and the condition of blacks, this mode of analysis stresses the ubiquitous character of the sexual class system.

To the extent that this thesis is correct, only a rigorously enforced quota system would facilitate the movement of significant numbers of women into top jobs in American society. And yet, if this analysis does capture reality, the possibility of gaining the political clout to make such a quota system effective, even in government employment, is highly problematic. But, before subscribing to an analysis which yields only the alternatives of subjection or revolution, elements of federal service experience, challenging the political thesis, should be brought forward.

While at one level the class/power explanation fits with the picture of women clustering in the low pay and low status jobs, it is contradicted by formal government action endorsing EEO for women, as well as by the pattern of employment variation across agencies within the federal government. With respect to the formal endorsement of EEO, which may go as far as requiring affirmative action, one could simply respond that this is just a move in the symbolic politics game. Such moves are necessary to feign compliance with the formal American "equality of opportunity" ideology. Indeed we know from cross-national studies that formal ideology may account for little in explaining the position of women in modern society.[7] The debate on formal vs. real opportunity is not easily resolved, for it gets into the motivations of EEO rule makers. Fortunately, we need not await such resolution before pronouncing judgment on the political thesis.

The pattern of employment within and across government agencies clearly flies in the face of this class/power analysis. If, in fact, there were a conscious male conspiracy, bent on keeping women in low status jobs, then one would expect to find little variation in opportunity for distaff advancement across agencies. This expectation is, however, not borne out by the data. On the contrary one is struck by the apparent variation in opportunity across agencies. Table 17.1 illustrates this point.[8]

These agencies are selected for examination because they exhibit substantial variation. While the percentage of women in GS grades 1–6 ranges from an ade-

TABLE 17.1   Women as Percent of Total Employed by Grade, Within Selected
             Federal Agencies, 1974

Grade(s)	HEW	HUD	Agriculture	NASA	Transportation
1–6	81.0%	84.1%	54.1%	77.9%	77.5%
	(49,447)*	(4,417)	(14,776)	(3,928)	(7,438)
7–12	55.6%	29.6%	9.8%	14.2%	9.4%
	(24,212)	(2,311)	(4,628)	(1,314)	(3,084)
13	18.3%	10.4%	3.9%	1.8%	1.3%
	(1,227)	(177)	(212)	(98)	(169)
14	14.3%	6.1%	3%	.8%	1.1%
	(641)	(66)	(72)	(25)	(53)
15	9.2%	5.2%	1.1%	.5%	.7%
	(268)	(31)	(13)	(9)	(13)
16	8%	1.4%	1.7%	0%	2.1%
	(22)	(1)	(3)	(0)	(4)
17	5.5%	0%	0%	**	1.2%
	(5)	(0)	(0)		(1)
18	3.8%	0%	0%	0%	0%
	(1)	(0)	(0)		(0)

*N = (49,447)
**NASA shows no personnel in 17 and 18 grades in the GS equivalent pay plan.

quate 54.1 percent in Agriculture, to an expansive 84.1 percent in HUD, variation in the percentage employed in GS grades 7–12, and 13+ is truly striking. In the middle-range grades, GS 7–12, women account for a high 55.6 percent in HEW, and a low 9.4 percent of the total in Transportation. Differences become even more pronounced in grades GS 13 through GS 18. Here, if figures reflect real opportunity, HEW stands out as the agency where women have made greatest strides, with the percentages in grades 14–15–16 appearing as 14.3, 9.2, and 8 respectively. While admittedly there remains room for opportunity expansion in HEW, these percentages seem quite favorable when juxtaposed to the NASA figures of 8 percent (GS 14), .5 percent (GS 15), and 0 percent (GS 16). The point verified by even a cursory glance at Table 17.1 is that advancement for women has varied by agency. Since men have traditionally been the guardians of the gates in all agencies, the variation calls into question the political thesis itself.

The Biological Thesis

As distinct from the political thesis, which blames men, the biological thesis blames evolution for the dearth of women in positions of power. The thrust of the "biology is destiny" argument is not simply that certain mental or behavior traits may be sex linked and hence physiologically determined, but that presence of some traits and absence of others act directly on the fitness of women for high-level decision-making positions. One variation of this argument fixes on the concept of leadership. Leadership, seen here as the major activity of the high-level decision makers, is not merely associated with an official position, but must be granted to a would-be leader by a follower. Yet, as Lionel Tiger, the major proponent of this position, would argue, it is just this trait, the capacity to compel followership, that women do not have and, furthermore, can not have because of their physiological makeup.[9] Adapting such an argument to organizational life, one would say that underlying regularities in the species explain the paucity of women in top jobs. Women have not laid claim to leadership roles in the bureaucracy chiefly because they are women, and not because of limited opportunity. Should an aggressively enforced affirmative action program put a woman into formal leadership position, male colleagues will, on any issue of great significance, be strongly disposed to form an all-male group and accordingly to exclude the interloper from decision making on that issue.

A second variation of the "biology is destiny" thesis attributes the sparseness of women in positions of power to the functioning female sex hormones. The very facts of menstrual cycle and menopause limit a woman's capacity for leadership because these biological conditions lead inevitably to periodically impaired judgment. Put most practically by Dr. Edgar Berman, physician and advisor to former Vice-President Hubert Humphrey, "If you had an investment in a bank, you wouldn't want the president of your bank making a loan under these raging [female] hormonal influences at that particular period."[10]

To the extent that the "biology destiny" thesis is correct, we may simply be wrong headed in trying to move women up into high-level decision-making positions in American society. Whether the explanation is rooted in an inability to command followership or to control raging hormones, the public policy implication is obvious. No realistic conception of the "public interest" could be served by moving boldly against "nature."

The popular appeal of this kind of argument is unquestionably limited, since it goes against the grain of a fundamentally egalitarian ethos in U.S. political culture. One can as well question the character of research that supports these conclusions.[11] For our purposes, however, it is sufficient to examine this explanation in light of both our own national experience and empirical data on trends in female employment.

As was suggested at the very beginning of this article, the fact that some women have made it into top jobs is indisputable. They are found, albeit in small number, in the most prestigious of occupations. Particularly in the Executive Branch of government where merit weighs heavier toward promotion than family relationships[12] numerous women have held top positions and have unquestionably "commanded" followership.[13] At one level this may constitute prima facie evidence of the fatuousness of the "biology is destiny" explanation. If biological considerations set the limits of possible achievement, how does one explain these loophole women?

Furthermore, to the extent that biological considerations hold sway, one would expect little variation in the general pattern of labor force participation over time. We would expect the life-cycle pattern, conventionally identified with the female labor force, to remain constant, i.e., "taking a job when first out of school, withdrawing from the labor force for marriage and motherhood, and returning to paid work in later years when children are in school or on their own."[14] Yet Labor Department statistics suggest that a dramatic shift has occurred in participation rates among women in the 25 to 34 age bracket. Participation rates of this cohort, traditionally thought most intensely constrained by their biological stage of life, jumped from 34 percent in 1950 to 52 percent by 1974.[15] While such a pattern does not directly refute the biological determinant thesis, as far as top jobs are concerned, it does make one skeptical of broad generalizations rooted in biological makeup.

The Sociological Thesis

From a sociological perspective, the concept of role differentiation holds the key to the difficulties faced by women when entering high-level positions in the organizational world. As formally defined, the term role refers to "a position in a social structure, involving a pattern of specific expectations, privileges, responsibilities, including attitudes and behaviors, and codified to some recognizable degree by norms, values, and sanctions."[16]

Using this framework, the thesis holds that while for men role differentiation within the family complements occupational role achievement, it frustrates such "outside" role achievement for women. The role conflict phenomenon is highlighted in discussion of both the functions of the women in the family and the personal qualities deemed necessary for adequate performance.

Motherhood, as distinct from fatherhood, has traditionally been viewed as a full-time job. Women report spending 60 hours a week in their housewife role; even when employed outside the home, women tend to remain responsible for both the mothering and general housekeeping functions.[17] These essentially caring and cleaning functions are best carried out by one who exhibits conventional female traits of understanding, helpfulness, solicitousness, and passivity.

Obviously, the role conflict stems from the fact that top jobs in government and elsewhere demand both a full-time commitment, irrespective of family obligations, and a strength in personality traits diametrically opposed to those cultivated by the mother role. For women, goals set by the occupational role and the family role are at worst mutually exclusive and at best only partially reconcilable. As stated in an earlier study of role contradiction: "the full realization of one role threatens defeat in the other."[18] In short, the major obstacle to enlarging the percentage of women in top government jobs is that society is organized so as to discourage larger numbers of female contestants for those jobs.[19]

Having said all this, one might still raise the question: why must this be? What is it that in fact sustains a pattern of action which results in differential access to top jobs based on sex? Role differentiation, it can be argued, is rooted in gender differentiation which encompasses dimensions of both the political and biological theses elaborated above. It is from the biological fact of sex that gender differences are inferred. To view the woman as passive, solicitous, understanding, and nonachievement oriented is to say nothing of her biology and everything about her gender. Gender as a cultural phenomenon reinforces family and occupational role choices insofar as it sanctions those choices. The political dimension of gender differentiation intrudes with the realization that those attributes commonly associated with the "feminine" are also the attributes generally associated with ruled classes.[20]

Hence, while neither the biological nor political thesis stands on its own, dimensions of each fit when viewed in conjunction with the gender-based analysis of role differentiation. In a recent work, Kenneth Boulding effectively weaves these competing explanations together in the concept of role prejudice.[21] Role prejudice is viewed as a product of a false social learning process by which certain biological or genetic characteristics of individuals come to be associated with certain roles. According to Boulding role prejudice develops when there are genetic differences in the human population which are visible, but not significant for role performance. The political implication is that such role prejudice translates into discrimination against individuals who strive to achieve outside of their socially defined role set. It is this "role prejudice," a prejudice shared by women and men alike, that accounts for the political reality of few top spots for women.

If the analysis is correct, the question then becomes how to dissolve role prejudice. Is it possible, given the grounding of role prejudice in the psychocultural phenomenon of gender differentiation, that women as a percentage of top job holders in the federal service or elsewhere will ever surpass the single digit mark? In order to answer this question one must probe the attitudinal and the structural supports for role prejudice.

The Response of the Private Sector: Role Prejudice as Attitude

At first glance the term role prejudice suggests a problem of individual attitude. In conventional usage, prejudice suggests an inner tendency to respond unfavorably to persons on the basis of their group membership.[22] This inner tendency is essentially a problem of attitude and hence is susceptible to modification through innovative techniques of organizational development. Accordingly, the response of private industry to the role prejudice phenomenon has been to employ various kinds of awareness training programs in the service of an "integration" objective. Recognizing that career advancement for women is blocked by organizational "scripts" that discourage women from aiming high, concerned private firms are trying to develop new scripts that facilitate female adaptation to the existing career system.[23]

To be sure, this direction promises to improve the organizational climate for women already competing for top slots in American industry. Just as federal equal opportunity legislation mandated the elimination of formal barriers to advancement for women, awareness training programs undermine those informal obstacles to change that stem from individually held sex role stereotypes. Still, given this thrust, the question from an analytical perspective remains: will this combination of legal and organizational development measures facilitate substantial movement beyond current threshold?

Admittedly the data is not yet in to answer this question definitively. Still, there is reason to believe the answer to the question will be no. That negative response emerges from a more probing consideration of the role prejudice concept, a consideration stressing the structural dimension of the role prejudice phenomenon.

From decades of research in the field of social psychology we know that individual attitudes can in fact be modified. Yet role prejudice as it resides in the very structure of the career system may account to a far greater degree for the dearth of women at the top. I would argue that this is indeed the situation we now face in the consideration of equal opportunity for women. Through understanding the symbiotic relationship between gender differentiation and career systems the road for public service action is illuminated.

The Nature of Career Systems

In advanced industrial societies the career system is biased in favor of the "two-person, single career."[24] This two-person, single career option is played out through an organization which places a combination of formal and informal demands on both members of a married couple, while formally employing only the man. To insure success in this single endeavor the wife role requires meeting fully the stereotype definition of "feminine," e.g., to be the supporter, the comforter, the child rearer, the housekeeper, and the entertainer.[25] Her achievement is vicarious; achievement needs are met either completely or predominantly in her husband's accomplishments.[26]

The two-person, single career pattern that has received the most popular attention is that associated with corporate executives,[27] but the analysis applies equally well to any high-level organizational decision-making position. Since reputation in high-level executive careers is measured against time, and recognition for achievement is frequently a function of age, the supportive role played by the wife is a key element in success.[28] A recent analysis of career executive marriages stresses the importance of this supportive female role by pointing out that the substantially lower divorce rate among executives could be attributed to the dampening effect such separation would have upon a man's career.[29] This two-person, single career route to success has become so institutionalized that even those observers concerned with the potentially dehumanizing aspects of contemporary bureaucracy eulogize the traditional wife for her shelter-giving qualities.[30]

Those women who do try to achieve nonvicariously within the modern career system tend to start later and may proceed more slowly in large part because they are acting out a single-person, rather than two-person career. Most succinctly summed up in a recent study by Hochschild (1975) the essential problem with the career systems of the modern world is that their guiding rules are made to suit men. The traditional family functions as the service agency supporting the organization in which the male career is conducted.[31] Role prejudice resides thus in the very structure of modern careers systems, not merely in the attitudes of individuals towards members of the opposite sex.

If this analysis of role prejudice as inherent in the structure of modern career systems is correct, it casts serious doubt on the feasibility of private industry's integration strategy. The burgeoning literature on private sector opportunity expansion glorifies the aspiring female executive in terms of the extent to which she magnifies her male counterpart.[32] Debate centers largely on the effectiveness of alternative mechanisms for integrating females into the male career system. One analyst assures us that although a time lag is inevitable until women change individual role expectations, amalgamation is clearly down the road.[33] Little attention is paid to the less tractable obstacles blocking the way.

Yet if the analysis presented above accurately describes the bias in modern career systems, "making it" within that system is simply not feasible for most women. Only women who enjoy the services of a full-time house-husband will start out in the race on equal footing with their male colleagues. Even with all other things being equal, structural factors will assign women to a competitive disadvantage in the push for top jobs. Nothing in the career histories of top executives in the United States suggests that the structural characteristics of the modern career system will change in a more favorable direction. On the contrary, if any change has occurred in recent years it has been in the direction of intensification.[34] Hence we must challenge the feasibility of this method for moving beyond the current level of accomplishment. We can as well question on normative grounds the desirability of a change strategy which accepts as given a requirement that women desirous of "public" success give up family life while men continue to enjoy the family life option. This seems to be the practical outcome of the private sector approach.

It is against this backdrop that a new direction for public sector equal opportunity can be set and strategies for implementation considered. The time has come for the public service to bring a new orientation to the very concept of career and accordingly to go beyond the now traditional "modern" career system.

A Leadership Role for the Federal Service

The federal service historically has taken the initiative in removing formal barriers to female participation in the labor market.[35] Nonetheless, it is now time to probe deeper into the barriers to further advancement. To the extent that the career system blocks further advancement, it is necessary to attack that system directly. Quite naturally questions arise as to the shape of an alternative career system. Here only in broad strokes can the vital dimensions of this ideal be sketched.

The hallmark of a career system free of role prejudice is formal recognition of employees as whole people. In terms of the shape of the alternative career system this suggests that organizations themselves must assume the responsibility for meeting many needs now met by the family-*qua* service agency. Further, it implies that we must develop and institutionalize new models for measuring achievement. Such models should take into account success in broad life experience as well as in "service to the agency" as narrowly defined. Finally, we must cultivate an organizational ethos that balances the conventional "male" value of competition with the traditional "female" value of cooperation.[36]

Today the federal service could move toward this ideal by acting on any or all of the following: the further development of flexible work schedules and the institutionalization of permanent, part-time, promotion track slots for men and women; the de-emphasis of "freedom of movement" as a criterion for advancement; the exploration of job splitting possibilities for husbands and wives, and the conscious development of career tracks for such couples; the establishment of government career counseling, advertising, and legitimizing these options; and finally, the securing of government support for comprehensive quality child care.

In reaction to this alternative future for the public organization, one might protest that such "reform" strikes at values close to the heart of modern public management—the values of excellence and of productivity.

To recommend the transformation of the modern career system is not to gainsay the importance of excellence, but rather to recognize that excellence as a concept relates to the quality of personnel and not to the organization of work itself. With attention focused on people and the quality of their contribution, one might stress that excellence in this sphere resides neither in numbers of hours worked, nor in the distribution of those hours. Indeed, research suggests that excellence can be achieved under varying conditions.[37] For those who cling to measuring performance by the totality of commitment to a job, it need be stressed that individuals choosing to define personal achievement in that way would remain free to make that choice, just as many ambitious women have done, per force, under today's rules of the game. What this new vision of the public service promises is simply multiple career routes to excellence, within the organizational structure, including one which views the human being as a multifaceted creature.

But what of the more pressing issue of productivity? Few would deny that productivity is on the mind of most public managers today. Improved productivity management means simply getting more out of all available resources. Thus, on one level at least, little conflict is generated when productivity needs are juxtaposed to important dimensions of the alternative career structure. Some advocates of the alternative career model might even argue that the part-time employment strategy would yield a dividend in enhanced productivity per employee.[38] The least that can be said is that there is no compelling reason for believing in an inverse relationship between productivity and the modification of the work environment suggested above.

Conclusion

This article began with the posing of a dilemma. Why, when women constitute nearly 40 per cent of America's labor force, have so few women made it to the top? While the political and biological explanations both hold some appeal, the sociological explanation casts the most revealing light on this phenomenon. Specifically, it has been argued that the concept of role prejudice, as it resides not merely in attitudes, but more significantly in the structure of contemporary career systems, holds the key to understanding the dearth of women at the top. To the extent that this analysis is correct, success via the concerned private sector's "integration" approach becomes problematic, while a new direction for public service leadership emerges. That direction implies movement toward the alternative career system ideal, and preliminary steps along that road have been suggested.

Since the federal government has long set the tone for employment practice in the equal opportunity area, the impact of its response to the current dilemma will resonate far beyond the immediate federal employee population.[39] Presently, the impulse for expansion of opportunity for women at the top of government service is strong. This thrust need not flounder on the shoals of organizational myopia. If the history of federal service leadership in an earlier era holds a vision of the future, we might rest confident that it will not.

Debra W. Stewart, *North Carolina State University* ∿

The Status of Women in the United States, 1976: Still Looking for Justice and Equity

American womanhood has never worn iron shoes, burned on the funeral pile (sic), or skulked behind a mask in a harem yet though cradled in Liberty, with the same keen sense of justice and quality that man has, she is still bound by law in the swaddling bands of an old barbarism.[40]

As the United States celebrates its bicentennial, it is appropriate that we ask— What is the status of women in this nation dedicated to equality, for didn't Abigail Adams remind her husband during the writing of the Constitution to put "something in for the ladies"? And a hundred years later we read the following from a congressional debate:

This government owes it to the women of the country . . . that they shall no longer be held in a subordinate position and treated as inferiors: that it shall say to them there shall be hereinafter no position under this Government for which they are fitted which shall not be open to them equal (sic) with men.[41]

Yet of all the forms of discrimination in American life today, none remains more pervasive or more invidious than that directed against women. Despite the increased representation of women in the labor force, there is strong evidence to suggest that women are not entering male-dominated fields and that sexual segregation in the American occupational structure is as strong today as it was in 1900.

Present Employment Status

In addition to the failure to ratify the Equal Rights Amendment, the employment situation is woeful. In government, industry, and academia, women, by and large, are excluded from positions of power, as defined by salary, prestige, and decision-making authority. The percentage of women in managerial and professional positions has gone up less than one per cent in the last five years. Taking academe as an example, let's examine the statistics of women's participation: in 1879, 40 per cent of faculties in higher education were women; in 1939, 30 percent were women; in 1964 this figure had dropped to 22 percent; there was a slight increase in 1974, bringing the total to 24 percent. The picture is more disturbing when one looks at the distribution—nearly 90 percent of full professors are male. One-fourth of the female faculty members in colleges and universities are instructors, compared to 6.3 percent of the males at this rank.[42]

If one accepts that a snail's pace is better than none, then the situation is somewhat better in government.

Social science, psychology	29.1%
Personnel management	53.3
General administration	68.0
Accounting and budget	46.8
Medicine, dentistry, pharmacy	57.8
Legal and kindred	48.7
Information and arts	30.7
Library and archives	62.4
Mathematics and statistics	36.6
Education	38.2
Supply	41.4[43]

It is interesting to note in which occupational groups women constitute more than 25 percent of federal government employment:

The five largest professional groupings of women in all employment are: nursing, 96.3 percent; education and vocational training, 49.1 percent; librarians, 68.3 percent; medical technologist, 70.6 percent; and accounting, 7.5 percent. These highly female populated occupations do not reflect and substantiate change in recent years. It takes longer than six or seven years to undo what society, plus schools, plus mothers/fathers have been doing for centuries.

Comments on Being Female

There is much ambivalence within society as to the proper role for women. Much of our attitudes toward objects is learned behavior based upon the opinion of the learned in our society. Here are a few examples of this thinking.

Aristotle:	"Female nature is afflicted with a natural defectiveness."
St. Thomas:	"A female is something deficient."
Nietzsche:	"God's second mistake."
Shakespeare:	"Frailty is thy name."
Rousseau:	"Women was made to yield to man and put up with injustice."
S. Johnson:	"A man is better pleased with a good dinner on the table than when she speaks good."
Freud:	"Make it very clear that we wanted his fiance docile and ignorant so that she wouldn't compete with him."[44]

The congressional clergy of Massachusetts stated the opinion of our founding fathers with the following: "The power of a woman is in her dependence flowing from the consciousness of that weakness which God has given her for her protection." In Henrik Ibsen's play *A Doll's House,* published in 1879, a furor was raised when the heroine, Nora, gave her reasons for leaving to her husband:

> Nora: . . . I believe that before all else, I am a reasonable human being, just as you are—or at all events that I must try and become one. I know quite well, Torvald, that most people would think you are right, and that views of that kind are to be found in books; But I can no longer content myself with what most people say, or with what is found in books. I must think over things for myself and get to understand them.[45]

Nora was describing the position of many middle-class Victorian women, a condition that has not changed appreciably in the past 100 years. One social critic, H.L. Mencken, felt that the nonparticipation by women in male-dominated fields was an indication of the superiority of women.[46] Despite Mr. Mencken's view of the advantages of being a woman, I suspect that most women would like the opportunity to decide for themselves what participation in the work world of society they would like. As Bernice Sandler, director of the Project on the Status of

Women, succinctly put it, "We would like to see whether the Peter Principle is applicable to women."

Why the Lack of Progress

Impeding the progress of women in competing for professional positions are a number of stereotypes or myths. Among the most often cited are the following:

1. Women generally have discontinuous occupational careers, interrupted by marriage, childbirth, child-care problems, etc.
2. Women are generally secondary wage earners, supplementing rather then generating family income.
3. Women tend to be less spatially mobile. Women are, thus, more limited in accepting employment or moving than men are.
4. Women are controlled by sex-specific employment laws. Although these laws may exist under the guise of protecting women, they are also used to reduce the effectiveness of women as competitors for men's jobs.
5. Women won't work for other women.
6. Women are afraid to travel.
7. Women do not possess administrative skills.

Most of the above statements are patently false and none of them can be empirically validated. Nonetheless, they serve as effective barriers to keep women out of the better paying, more prestigious positions.

There are two schools of thought as to why women are not advancing at a pace commensurate with their abilities and skills: (1) women are different physiologically and temperamentally from men, and (2) women are essentially no different from men but are victims of a discriminatory sex-based socialization process. In recent years there has been a steady decline in the emphasis on anatomical differences. Major attention has been given to differences which are the product of socialization. Even female researchers have concluded that girls are socialized to be neater, more restrained, more emotionally demonstrative, less analytic, and more dependent than boys.

Today, the feminists are saying that we have to break down the psychological barriers that prevent women from being full people in society, and not only end explicit discrimination, but build new institutions. Women are beginning to read a good deal about their own place in history; as a consequence, the hierarchy is being told to change both its habits and its definitions, its understanding of how the world is put together; and making these demands are the untenured, the uncredentialed, the unfrocked women whom it can only regard with emotions that it would be too kind to call mixed. Kenneth Boulding, the economist, has noted:

It is well recognized that discrimination among existing members of the labor force is only a special case of a much larger process of role learning and role acceptance, which begins almost from the moment of birth. It is not merely that differences in skills are learned, as in Adam Smith's famous passage about the porter and philosopher, but images of possible roles on the part of both the role occupants and the role demanders are likewise learned in the long process of socialization. . . .[47]

Certainly the increasing number of women on a professional level of equality with men forces a rethinking of one's opinions on sex roles and functions, and these tend to run fairly deep. As a result, the attitudes are highly resistant to change.

Justice, Equity, and Affirmative Action

One approach to overcoming the centuries of past discrimination has been to urge that affirmative action be taken to move women into positions from which they were previously excluded by virtue of their sex. The establishing of a process to recruit more women and minorities and the establishing of numerical goals and timetables in this regard has met with violent rejection by many political theorists and philosophers as well as the citizenry in general. They argue that affirmative action sets up a group preferential system and disregards principles of individualism and merit. As one critic has noted:

> The specific conceptual and moral conflict . . . is the displacement in law of individual justice, wherein a designated person is held responsible for wrongs which can be laid to him, by the introduction of its opposite: collective edicts wherein an entire group is held corporately and legally responsible for past wrongs (or for current unwanted social effects) impossible to lay to any determinate individuals.[48]

Other eminent scholars who take a like stand in opposing affirmative action principles and particularly reject numerical goals and timetables are Daniel Bell, Sidney Hook, and Daniel Boorstin.[49]

Without a doubt, the debate raises fundamental questions about the nature of society regarding what is just and unjust. Few critics of affirmative action justify their objections with clear concepts of what social justice requires of the system. Most do not even allow that society has indeed set up a condition whereby some are not sharing in the benefits of society due to circumstances of discrimination or that a group has no moral obligation to overcome unjust treatment regardless of whether each individual in the group has been guilty of discrimination. At the same time, these critics of affirmative action argue that compensatory justice can only apply to individuals, not groups. This appears to be a "straw man" argument, since almost all the members of those groups labeled "minorities" or "women" have been sufficiently disadvantaged as to require that restitution will have to be made for all in order to overcome the past inequities.

Affirmative Action and the Future

The two positions—the difficulty of overcoming role socialization and the question of what constitutes justice—laid a foundation for the development of affirmative action programs guaranteeing equality in employment opportunities. There will be some inequities in such programs, but they will not be of the magnitude of the present unjust system. Women, in particular, have been depending upon government regulation to attain the desired goal of overcoming past discrimination in employment. At present these programs are less than successful. There is little reason to believe that they will materially improve in the next few years. Those changes that are being made are more a result of court actions than the actions of either the Office for Civil Rights in the U.S. Department of Health, Education, and Welfare or the Equal Employment Opportunity Commission. A state in civil rights enforcement has been reached where the issues are more narrowly focused and refined, resulting in a clash of interests, with those previously deeply committed to civil rights questioning current policies and practices.

The depressed economic situation has exacerbated the tension. In a stable-state marketplace, the hiring of one person is going to mean that another with the necessary qualifications will not be hired. This means that a government that is truly responsive to public sentiment may not always be the most efficient arbiter when substantial blocks of opinion in the community are unwilling or unable to present a *modus vivendi* of fundamental points. In fact, the ability to perceive the true public interest in the midst of controversy and competing claims is becoming more and more elusive and less conducive to quick and ready answers.

The recent attempt to change the employment birth—being born black and/or female.

It is helpful to examine Professor John Rawls' treatise for a succinct definition of justice.

> A conception of social justice, then, is to be regarded as providing, in the first instance, a standard whereby the distributive aspects of society are to be assessed. . . .[50]

For Rawls, justice is fairness and the foundation of fairness rests initially on two principles:

> First, each person is to have an equal right to the most extensive basic liberty compatible with similar liberty for others.
> Second, social and economic inequalities are to be arranged so that both (a) reasonably expected to be to everyone's advantage, and (b) attached to positions and office open to all.[51]

While scholars, citizens, and government officials may have differing views of what constitutes justice, there can be no doubt that present conditions in our society fail to meet Rawls' second principle as far as women and minorities are concerned. For as Rawls points out, within institutions of society which favor certain starting places over others are especially deep inequalities. "Not only are they pervasive, but they affect men's initial chances in life. . . ."[52] He points out that if one has a *just* society, then it is only necessary to "police" it, but if one starts with an unjust society, then there is an obligation to eliminate the institutional causes of injustice. If ours is a just society, all that would be needed is to insure that individual cases of discrimination are not taking place. If, however, ours is an unjust society, it will be necessary to eliminate the causes of inequalities. Since present conditions in our society do not meet Rawls' second premise of what constitutes justice, we are left with an unjust society. Thus, is raised the notion of compensatory justice to overcome those inequalities which individuals have met with as part of a group rather than as a product of their own efforts.

Affirmative action is one way to overcome the existing allocations of benefits in a society whereby some have been disadvantaged as a result of "natural chance or the contingency of social circumstances."[53] Rawls' argument is complex, yet it is lucid. However, no moral position is ever clear-cut; certainly not one posing the difficult distinction between equality of opportunity versus equality of results. If, indeed, those who are perpetuating the present system of unequal benefits could be presumed to be "behind a veil of ignorance,"[54] then and only then could one accept their argument that there can be no group picture in higher education is particularly relevant in this regard. In no other sector of employment has the controversy been as virulent as it has in higher education.

If the two problems cited earlier are accurate, then it appears that higher education should have been more amenable to change. A case could be made that higher education carries a greater obligation than other sectors of employment, for surely the mission of education should include the raising of social consciousness and the implementation of justice, both by teaching and by example. Unfortunately, higher education appears to have been unable to perform this social function if we use as a standard the number of complaints that have been filed against institutions of higher education alleging sex discrimination in employment practices.

It appears fairly certain that the unequal position in which women find themselves in employment will continue for the next decade. The progress that is made will be due more to the continued striving of women to over-excel in order that they may compete with men in the marketplace, rather than a product of government action or of a general recognition by society that women are entitled to justice and equity in practice as well as theory.

Mary M. Lepper, *University of North Carolina* ∽

Establishing Affirmative Action Goals for Women

Federal policies concerning equal opportunity employment encourage—and sometimes mandate—organizations to adopt affirmative action programs. The 1972 Equal Employment Opportunity Act extended the Civil Rights Act to include women as a "protected class" and to remove the exempt status held by local governments and educational institutions. The policy has the strength of national law and has been both upheld and strengthened by the courts. The trend is clear, few employers will be exempted from affirmative action requirements. The enforcement of anti-discrimination legislation has opened up a whole new arena for community/organization/employee dialogue.

Women are the most recent category of people covered under the act. National guidelines for the development of affirmative action programs for women have followed, almost point by point, the precedents established by the guidelines developed for other protected groups. An important area in which precedent is not followed is in the process required for establishing numerical goals.

Goals provide a numerical objective which the organization is to realize within a given time through the implementation of affirmative actions—actions which the organization has designed to enhance the representation of "labor force minorities" in their work force to accord with the law. Goals provide a measurable purpose to equal employment opportunity efforts and help to move an organization from the level of "intention" to "action."

Although the extension of the general concept of human rights to include women is well known, the identification of specific numerical objectives and timetables for the economic enrichment of women's lives has been slow in development. Few jurisdictions have actually established measurable goals for women and, of those which have, most are dissatisfied and confused with the basis by which their goals were established.[55] It was not uncommon to hear the process by which their goals were created likened to the random process of "picking names out of a hat." Such an approach is dysfunctional and unsatisfactory for both management and women.

This article examines the federally recommended process for determining affirmative action goals and then suggests a more workable set of criteria for arriving at measurable affirmative action goals for women. The discussion seeks to provide first a history of affirmative action goals; second, the criteria for establishing affirmative action objectives for women compared to the criteria used to develop objectives for other labor force minorities; and finally, the article presents a set of common denominators which can be used for developing reasonable affirmative action goals for women.

Affirmative Action Goals

A quota system, applied in the employment context, would impose a fixed number or percentage which must be attained, or which could not be exceeded; the crucial consideration would be whether the mandatory numbers of persons have been hired or promoted. Under such a quota system, that number would be fixed to reflect the population in the area, or some other numerical base, regardless of the number of applicants who meet necessary qualifications. If the employer failed, he would be subject to sanction. . . .[56]

During the early '70s, the news media depicted a strong sentiment in favor of abolishing quotas on the grounds that they were an arbitrary, unjust measure for hiring or evaluating equal employment efforts. Quotas were considered arbitrary in that they failed to allow for the diversity which emerged when particular organizations and particular geographic areas were considered, diversity which had to be accommodated to develop workable equal opportunity employment efforts. In this context, quotas were correctly criticized as being an arbitrary, inflexible, and oversimplified measure for determining progress in remedying discrimination. The process of establishing quotas to actualize equal employment opportunity created a conflict between social justice and organizational justice. Organizationally, quotas were unjust in that they contradicted traditional employment practices supposedly established on the principle of merit. Race or ethnic identity, rather than ability, became the primary criterion for hiring one individual over another, a practice which, if maintained as permissable, could destroy merit principles as the crux of an organization's system of justice. Quotas represented a direct attack on the organization's established system of justice and led to a reevaluation of how merit is and is not determined.

The 1972 amendment to the Civil Rights Act requiring the inclusion of women as a "protected class" further stressed the need to abolish quotas as the basis for federal enforcement. The use of population quotas for women was highly impracticable. Fifty-one percent of the population is female. The potential application of general population quotas to govern employment practices related to women accentuated the difficulties generated by the application of a single criterion measurement technique to complex problems.

The use of quotas was a major domestic campaign issue in the 1972 presidential election. Richard Nixon promised to ban the arbitrary quota system and create a more flexible, reasonable mechanism for evaluating employers' efforts to move from a discriminatory to a nondiscriminatory personnel system. This was a campaign promise which Nixon kept. Quotas were declared impermissible and goals were introduced in their place.

A goal . . . is a numerical objective, fixed realistically in terms of the number of vacancies expected, and the number of qualified applicants available in the relevant job market. Thus, if through no fault of the employer he has fewer vacancies than expected, he is not subject to sanction, because he is not expected to displace existing employees or to hire unneeded employees to meet his goals. Similarly, if he has demonstrated every good faith effort to include persons from the group which was the object of discrimination into the group being considered for selection, but has been unable to do so in sufficient numbers to meet his goals, he is not subject to sanction.[57]

It was determined that quotas which focused on categorical population figures were inconsistent with the principles of merit hiring. Goals, which focused on organization needs and geographic characteristics and which maintained the merit principle as the *primary* criteria for personnel practices, became the accepted basis for evaluating an organization's progress in achieving equal opportunity employment practices. This change of focus from demographic to geographic, from the general to the particular, had interesting implications for the process by which numerical objectives for women were to be developed.

A Utilization Analysis

The four federal agencies responsible for equal employment opportunity issued a memo addressing goals and timetables in March 1973.[58] In this joint memo, the Civil Service Commission, the Equal Employment Opportunity Commission, the Justice Department, and the Office of Federal Contract Compliance recognized that goals and timetables are appropriate as a device to help measure progress in remedying employment discrimination. A labor market analysis or utilization analysis is required to determine if in fact goals are necessary. Labor market analysis, based on population and/or work force statistics, determines whether protected classes are being underutilized. "Underutilization is defined as having fewer minorities and/or women in a particular job classification than would be reasonably expected by their availability."[59] This analysis, combined with the organization's turnover and growth trends, provides the basis for evaluating equal employment efforts and for developing goals and timetables.

It is through the use of a utilization analysis that the responsible federal agencies make their decisions relative to the existence of discriminatory practices within a particular organization. If discriminatory practices are encountered, then the courts can impose goals and timetables on the offending agency. A utilization analysis also provides management with the necessary data for determining whether or not it would be prudent for them to take the initiative to develop their own goals and timetables. Thus the utilization analysis and the criteria for its development are very important to the achievement of nondiscriminating personnel systems. The criteria used in conducting a utilization analysis become the essential components for determining the necessity of goals and timetables for a specific protected class.

The criteria used for establishing goals for minorities differ in one important way from the criteria used for establishing goals for women.

Comparing Criteria for Goals

A utilization analysis is the crux of affirmative action programs. Federally admissible criteria for analysis of a particular labor market can determine whether or not goals need to be implemented for a particular agency or jurisdiction. The guidelines set forth by the member agencies of the Equal Employment Opportunity Commission call for the use of different criteria to establish appropriate utilization levels for women as compared to minorities. For minorities, population statistics are admissible. For women they are excluded. The pamphlet, *Guidelines for the Development of an Affirmative Action Plan* (1975), developed by the U.S. Civil Service Commission's Bureau of Intergovernmental Personnel Programs, illustrates this difference. It provides a suggested list of factors to consider in an analysis of the labor market to determine the presence of underutilization in an organization. The first three factors illustrate the differences:

1. *Minority population* of the area surrounding the workplace;
2. Availability of *women* seeking employment in the labor or recruitment area of the employer;
3. Size of the *minority/female* unemployment force in the labor area surrounding the workplace (emphasis added).[60]

The base criterion used for minorities is area population figures which are then balanced by other statistics relative to the area work force. The first criterion for establishing women's goals is "the availability of women seeking employment in the labor or recruitment area of the employer." Functionally, what does this criterion mean? Is this factor really different from the third factor, "size of the minority/women unemployment force in the area surrounding the work place"? Operationally, the meaning of this criterion and the difference between it and general population figures becomes very significant. Comparing work force figures to population statistics is much simpler and more easily understood than the matching of work force figures to the ambiguous criterion, "availability of women seeking employment in the labor or recruitment area of the employer."

The guidelines state that numerical goals *should be* established in relation to availability studies based on skills in the labor force rather than the proportional representation of the male/female and minority/majority composition of the population. However, a survey of those public agencies *with* measurable goals will reveal that a preponderance of those goals have been based almost solely on population figures. A complete availability analysis is both difficult and costly.

Much data on various minorities and females in the population and work force of relevant labor areas and their general or specific skills can be obtained. . . . *However, excessive data collection is not necessary if your own employment survey reveals absence or serious underrepresentation of any group.* Affirmative efforts to locate and/or train females and minorities for jobs where they are not represented will be more productive than intensive effort to locate data justifying their utilization (emphasis added).[61]

Figures on availability must necessarily vary among job classification, and are in no way interchangeable with general population statistics provided by the Census Bureau. Despite this, one staff member of the Civil Rights Commission, who asked not to be identified, said that most federal agencies rely on general population statistics if the contractor has not done a complete availability analysis.[62]

The preceding passages suggest that rather than going to the expense of detailed utilization analysis, many agencies can evaluate the meaningfulness of their equal opportunity employment efforts by conducting a less formal work force analysis. The best and most obvious criterion for such analysis is general population statistics. In fact, in the case of minorities, population is a legitimate variable to be used in the determination of availability. This makes good sense, when one considers the problems associated with labor statistics and the quagmire in which personnel managers find themselves relative to the validity of selection procedures and recruitment requirements.

Sacramento, California, is well known for its efforts to realize a truly nondiscriminatory personnel system. Among its efforts toward this end, the City Council approved a five-year plan for minority hiring using population as its base criterion:

It is recommended that the overall goal that the City of Sacramento should strive to attain would be 31% career minority employment during the next five years. . . . At the present time, it is estimated that the minority population of the City of Sacramento is 31.4% (Black, 10.7%; Spanish Speaking/Surname 12.9%; Asian, 6.6%; Filipino, Native American, and other minorities, 1.2%). While the overall goal of 31% minority employment can be reached in five years, it will not be possible to reach 31% in each City occupation within that period of time. . . .[63]

Similar to a city budget, this overall goal provides a context within which each department can develop its own goals. It provides a general figure for evaluating success or for determining the specific barriers to success. It is not a rigid quota but a guide. The ideal goal as well as the goal in practice is designed to be flexible. It can be modified based on general labor force statistics or labor force statistics specific to one department or occupational category. A goal is always modifiable based on organizational turnover or growth rates. The use of population statistics as a general guide does not do a disservice to the concept of goals. It does provide a common denominator by which measurable, meaningful goals can be determined.

Unlike the criteria for minorities, the complexity and ambiguity of the federally recommended criteria for determining measurable goals for women lead to inertia. The public administrator committed to making equal employment opportunity a reality is typically stymied by the lack of a logical common denominator of developing goals and timetables for women. For most public agencies, the obvious criterion, proportional population, represents too great a number to develop achievable goals within a five or ten-year time frame and is, therefore, politically unacceptable. However, given the reality of the underutilization of women in most occupational categories, it seems reasonable and is possible to approach the establishment of measurable affirmative action goals for women based on *levels* of utilization. Population figures, available through the U.S. Census, offer the necessary data for determining measurable goals for women.

Numerical Goals for Women

In addition to overall population figures for a city or standard metropolitan area, the U.S. Census provides a detailed statistical breakdown of female characteristics. To exemplify, it is helpful to look again at Sacramento. Table 17.2 provides significant census information about the female population of Sacramento. The U.S. Census includes labor force information as well as marital status and head-

TABLE 17.2   Female Census Data: Sacramento, California

General Characteristics

Total Population	254,613	
Males—all ages	121,523	48%
Females—all ages	133,090	52%
Females—all ages	133,090	
Females—18-64 yrs.	82,033	32.34%
Females—16-17 yrs.	4,557	1.79%
Females—16-64 yrs.	86,590	34.03%

Social and Economic Characteristics

Total Families	65,930	
Families with female heads	9,357	14.19%
Total Females—14 yrs. and over	102,193	
Single Females—14 yrs. and over	20,794	20.34%

Employment Status—16 Years and Over

	Potential Labor Force in City	Active in Labor Force	
Total	182,197	103,715	
Female	97,627	41,888	40.38%
Male	84,570	61,827	59.62%

of-household percentages. Such characteristics that go beyond mere population ratios can be and have been utilized to develop reasonable goals for women.

The City of Sacramento has assumed a leadership role in respect to establishing measurable and understandable goals for women. The City Council voted to approve affirmative action goals for women based on the percentage of single women residing in the city.

> The subject of affirmative action goals for the employment of women is very new. I have been able to find only one other city which has established specific goals for the employment of women. . . .
>
> As of June 30, 1974, the City of Sacramento employed 360 women in career, full-time positions out of 2,662 positions, which is equal to 13.52% of the City's work force. It is recommended that the City establish as a goal that the City should strive to employ women in at least 20% of the career positions in the City's work force over the period of the next five years.
>
> At this time, single women comprise 20.34% of the labor force in our area. This criterion is recommended as the best potentially achievable goal in the near future, with due consideration that most jobs within the City's employment are positions requiring heavy labor.
>
> Attachment "A" Table 17.2 shows the most recent available information taken from the 1970 census data concerning women in the Sacramento work force. The table shows that women of all ages comprise 52% of the population of the City of Sacramento; however, women in the work force comprise 40.38% . . . Attachment "B" shows that 82.5% (264 of 360) of women City employees are working in clerical and kindred positions. In order to achieve an employment goal of 20% of the work force being women, it would be necessary to increase the number of women employees from 360 to 593, using the same City employment base of 2,662 positions. This requires a net increase of 173 positions to be filled by women. This can only be achieved by increasing significantly the number of women who would serve as police officers, firefighters, maintenance workers, building trades workers, plant operators, refuse collectors, etc.
>
> Prior to 1972, almost all of these positions were forbidden to women because of the state "protective" laws which prevented employers from placing women in positions that required heavy lifting. These laws were struck down in 1972. . . .
>
> It is not known whether it will be possible to achieve a goal of 20% of the City's work force being women within five years. If the City of Sacramento can continue the net annual increase in employment of women which took place between 1973 and 1974, the goal is feasible.[64]

The logic of Sacramento's approach was both politically and administratively rational. It is a safe assumption that the percentage of single women represents the *minimum* percentage of self-supporting females for a given geographic area; a goal based on this percentage is morally defensible and politically acceptable. Administratively, Sacramento determined that it would be possible to achieve a five-year goal based on this criterion through the use of affirmative recruitment, selection, and retention procedures.

A question often raised in relation to this approach has been: What about married women? Goals do not select the individual for the job, they provide a numerical objective so that an agency can evaluate its progress in providing more equitable employment opportunities to a given category of people. By design, affirmative action goals are not static. In Sacramento, 13.5 percent of the city's work force was female; it was reasonable for that city to choose the single women population (20.3 percent) as its goal for the next five-year period. If the city's female employees had comprised a different percentage of the work force, the city might have used a different census category as its common denominator.

It is hard to imagine the realization of a full employment economy for women within the next 50 years. However, it does seem reasonable to expect employers to hire an increasing number of women in all occupational classifications within the next ten years. Based on U.S. Census data, the percentage of single women or families with female heads within a given geographic area will generally provide enough information for an agency to establish a measurable affirmative action goal which everyone can understand. Whereas the use of total population statistics or female labor force statistics may be impolitic, it seems reasonable to expect jurisdictions to consider the percentage of single females as a practical and rational guide for establishing a general goal; and if a jurisdiction has a history of high underutilization, a five-year goal might be appropriately based on the percentage of families with female heads. Thus we have four different, yet easily accessible, general population statistics for conducting a less formal utilization analysis of women in an organization's work force:

Female population	=	optimal criterion[65]
Females in the labor force	=	significant criterion
Single females	=	acceptable criterion
Families with female heads	=	minimal criterion

It is reasonable to expect that all public agencies are able to introduce recruitment, selection, and retention practices that will enable them to meet ten-year goals based on the population statistics for single women or families with female heads. With these goals accomplished, governments will be able to demonstrate how a model affirmative action program for women really works.

Summary

The intent of this article has been to suggest that women, as well as other labor force minorities, can benefit from the use of demographic data for the establishment of an agency's affirmative action goals. The need for both politically and administratively reasonable criteria for determining such goals has been recognized. Population statistics provide a meaningful and reasonable common denominator from which both general and particular goals can be established. The approach used by the City of Sacramento has been described to illustrate how such statistics have been used to develop goals for both women and minorities.

The article suggests that general goals for women be developed on an incremental basis utilizing U.S. Census data for base criteria. An informal utilization analysis can be conducted by comparing an organization's percentage of female employees with the following census categories: female population (optimal utilization), female labor force (significant utilization), single females (acceptable utilization), or families with female heads (minimal utilization). Significant underutilization would be revealed by a female work force representing less than the percentage of single women in the geographic area. In such cases, the organization's recources would most productively be spent on affirmative efforts to locate and/or train women for jobs where they are not represented, rather than a more extensive utilization analysis.

Peggy Newgarden, *Texas Christian University* ∿

New Roles for Professional Women: Skills for Change

There's this clever maneuver you have to watch for. At the beginning of a meeting, men will hug and kiss you hello. Then they greet each other with a handshake. The kiss means 'Hiya Honey.' The handshake means "Let's get down to business.' There's nothing particularly friendly about those business meetings and that kiss never has had any real personal feeling. It diminishes a woman.

Governor's Staff Assistant[66]

In meetings, I noticed that my voice was a problem. Men just didn't tune into my higher pitched voice. I had to compensate by coming on stronger and talking faster.

Lawyer[67]

It's lonely being the only woman planner. The secretaries are uncomfortable, the men are uncomfortable.

Human Services Planner

Introduction

Everyday, in both informal and formal ways, women's influence within the human service professions is minimized. This article describes the concentration of women in lower-level positions and suggests changes necessary to enable women to assume higher-level administrative or planning jobs. It is assumed that even if—and when—systemic changes provide full opportunity for women to advance, internal and interpersonal barriers that derive primarily from women's socialization can prevent them from fully utilizing such opportunities. In other words, even when women occupy a formal authority position, they may face internal, interpersonal, and structural obstacles to exerting influence.

The authors have implemented a training program as one means to begin to remove such barriers to women's participation in upper-echelon decisionmaking processes. The training model deals with values, skills, and knowledge within internal, interpersonal, and organizational contexts. While it focuses upon women in the human services, the model is relevant to women attempting to increase their power in a variety of professions.

History of the Problem

Human service professions, such as teaching, nursing, and social work, have generally been defined as appropriate for women because they involve expressive, person-oriented tasks and require the skills of helping, nurturing, and empathizing.[68] Women, however, did not enter human services simply because they had the unique skills or desire to do so; until recently, that was one of the few areas open to women in any large numbers.

Sex stratification has, in turn, occurred within such professions.[69] While women predominate in lower-level positions, changes in the human services have increased the number of positions in management, administration, research, policy, and planning that have attracted men. Many of the recent job openings are assumed to require qualities traditionally associated with men, such as detachment, analytic objectivity, and the effective exercise of power—qualities which women often lack because of their socialization not to be ambitious or aggressive.[70]

When the administrative component of a female profession expands, the increasing demand for administrators enhances the tendency of men to move relatively quickly into authority positions.[71] In social work, for example, men form a higher percentage of administrators, researchers, consultants, and university teachers than women do.[72] Men are thus concentrated at the top of human service organizations, implementing plans, administering programs, and contributing to the profession's knowledge development through publications and presentations at professional conferences.[73]

Admittedly, structural changes regarding admissions to professional schools and promotion and hiring for women have occurred. While necessary, these changes are not sufficient as strategies to maximize women's influence within the human services. Any strategy must take account of women's values, self-concepts, and attitudes, as well as the institutional factors that have minimized their influence. For example, women are socialized to believe that they do not belong among those who make important decisions[74]; such beliefs constitute a strong internal barrier to entering or to being effective after attaining a higher-level position of responsibility. Women's power in the past has generally been confined to their private lives and their ability to please men.[75] Women have not been socialized to be comfortable with exerting the authority of upper echelon positions that can involve substantial resources or have negative repercussions on others.[76]

Women's lack of confidence, fear of acting aggressively, and desire to smooth away difficulties and to meet others' needs are societally taught norms. Once internalized, these become formidable psychological obstacles buttressing structural barriers. Therefore, both subtle, built-in psychological resistances and social-structural conditions within agencies and professional schools need to be altered.

A Training Model

The authors have developed a training program as one means of modifying such barriers. The model focuses upon training women for upper-level positions in planning, administration/management, and policy formulation. These positions require the abilities to set long-range goals and develop the plans to attain them, to make and implement significant decisions that affect others, to negotiate and resolve conflict, to develop proposals and grants, to influence and mobilize others, to form coalitions, and to run meetings efficiently. The authors have identified internal, interpersonal, and structural barriers to women's acquiring these skills.

Internal Barriers to High-Level Positions

Internal barriers, or the forces originating from within women, may be the most difficult to change because of the years devoted to learning them. Women are socialized to perform a "stroking" function which disqualifies them from competitive, challenging jobs and deflects them from their highest potential achievement.[77] Horner's study of women's fear of succeeding suggests strong internal barriers.[78] Socialized to meet others' needs, women generally are not taught intellectual aggression or problem-solving abilities. Women grow up thinking of a career as a contingency plan; until recently, many women entered a profession idiosyncratically rather than as a result of deliberate planning.[79] Women who are promoted to high-level administrative positions often experience ambivalence and inner conflict with their role of mother and wife.[80] One way to resolve such conflicts is to leave an upper-level position in order to return home or to a lower-level position that requires nurturing qualities more consistent with the role of wife and mother. Another means of resolution is to attempt to become a "superwoman" to perform both roles more adequately than is expected of either a male administrator or a full-time housewife.

Interpersonal Barriers to High-Level Positions

Such role relationship barriers refer to the manner in which women are defined—or not defined—by others in their interactions. Women who enter upper echelon jobs or administration/planning sequences in professional schools do not have many other women with whom to identify, either as successful role models or as support systems. For the woman administrator, the loneliness of being a "pioneer" can often interfere with her competency.

Women face the added burden of not being able to garner respect as competent decision makers from most other women. This lack of respect stems from being socialized to define their lives in terms of being the "other half" of a man, to compete with other women for men, and to use power covertly. Those who have "made it" in male-dominated functions such as administration may mistrust and exclude other women. Women need to develop the skills for working effectively and supportively with each other.

Men's attitudes and behaviors toward women administrators or planners are another interpersonal barrier. Women's appearance in collegial networks as co-professionals often confuses men, because these women no longer fit their role definitions as being sweet, pretty, passive, and nurturing. Past standards for interaction are no longer appropriate or are ambiguous. In meetings, attention often becomes focused on the uneasiness which everyone feels and on the need to define new ground rules for the situation rather than on carrying out the business at hand. Men frequently resort to humor as one way to deal with their uneasiness. Unable to engage in a collegial relationship with women, men may fall back on the traditional norms of male-female interactions or attempt to compensate by being overly solicitous, congenial, underdemanding, or overdemanding. Thus, men may respond to a woman agency director as a woman and secondly as director. Women are then confronted with the dilemma of how to respond to male colleagues in a way that will preserve their dignity and influence.

Structural Barriers to High-Level Positions

Structural barriers refer to organizational patterns and practices; these include discrimination in hiring and promotion, nepotism, full-time work requirements, lack of child care facilities, and maternity-paternity leaves. While federal laws and administrative rules have brought about organizational changes that benefit women, relationships and opportunities have been formally and informally structured to minimize women's influence after they enter such organizations.

Sexism is manifested in the organizational atmosphere primarily through informal interactions, unstated norms, and casual exchanges. Clubs, cliques, the "culture" of a profession, even the golf game and handball courts for men are structured to exclude women.[81] A woman in a position of formal power may often be denied the informal signs of belonging and recognition, such as having lunch with the other agency directors, stopping for a drink after work with her male colleagues, or being able to share in "locker room talk." Use of titles, especially in an academic setting, becomes a way of bestowing—or withholding—recognition and thereby power; for example, a male administrator may use all the appropriate titles when referring to other men, but call a woman Mrs. or Miss rather than Doctor. Men can diminish a woman's influence by referring to her as a girl or gal, particularly if she is the one female member in an agency or committee. Secretaries, socialized to defer to men, may fail to inform women of meetings, phone calls, or appointments. In addition to the debilitating effects such experiences have upon professional women day after day, they deny women access to information and other kinds of resources essential for effective decision making. Without such resources, women's power may be marginal at best.

Another effect of these structural barriers is that women have to invest considerable time, energy, and skills in changing their organization and in gaining access to informal channels of influence. Yet their resources could be put to better use in planning and administering programs. In addition, such demands of fighting organizational constraints can simply wear a person out. In fact, women may oftentimes choose to leave an organization rather than attempt to join the "old boys club." Thus, women need the organizational, analytical, and research skills to understand and to change their organizational settings from within.

The Training Program

The training model deals with the three areas both sequentially and simultaneously. The initial training stage focuses on the individual woman's values, goals, and attitudes. This component leads into the interpersonal sphere in which role relations are explored in terms of communication, assertion, problem-solving skills, and team development. In the organizational stage, the awareness and skill attainment resulting from the previous components form the basis for developing techniques of conflict resolution, coalition formation, and mobilizing others. The authors have found the greatest success conducting a one-day session to provide an overview and then having women complete the process described below for one evening a week for five or six weeks. This extended time period enables women to approach each skill exercise in depth.

Internal Skills

Women need to increase their own personal power to be most effective in higher-level positions. A series of tools are used for this purpose. Life scripting aids women in understanding the effects of their upbringing on their current decisions.[82] Through an internal dialogue exercise, women can focus on their strengths, weaknesses, fears, and hopes about exercising responsibility. Life planning and skills assessment exercises enable women to explore a range of career possibilities and examine them in relation to a detailed inventory.[83]

Interpersonal Skills

Learning how to develop effective working relationships with both men and other women is the focus of the model's second stage. Early in the program, women are asked to find a partner with whom they feel comfortable sharing their thoughts and ideas. From working in pairs, they move into small groups. Such small group interaction begins to build some of the necessary interpersonal skills in communication, problem solving, and decision making. Techniques such as values clarification and assertion training help individuals develop a well-thought-out set of value concepts consistent with their own needs and then to express those needs (along with their feelings) comfortably and honestly.[84] Videotaped case situations allow women to practice interpersonal skills.

Organizational Skills

To overcome some of the structural obstacles facing them, women need skills in conflict resolution, organizing others, and leading groups. They must be able to increase their own effectiveness by learning when, where, and how to intervene in organizations. Simulations, role plays, and games are used to learn skills of lobbying, grant-writing, coalition formation, and planning.[85] Videotaped role plays and trigger films of conflict situations and of how to be effective as the "token" woman are also included.

Women need to expand their knowledge base in order to be well prepared when they appear at legislative hearings, in committee meetings, or on the media. They need a firm grasp of substantive areas such as the law, computer terminology, research, management information systems, and political processes. Women need to know where to attain information and how to use it. Through lectures and mimeo handouts, women are informed of the availability of abstracts and directories for such purposes. Likewise, lectures and tapes are used to transfer information about how to write a grant, read legislation, or write reports.

Much of the knowledge base cannot be communicated in a short-term training program, but is best developed through professional education. In other words, formal education provides a woman with the credentials required to enter an institution; the training program can help her develop additional skills required to function as effectively as possible, despite the constraints of existing institutional sexism. A woman formally trained in administration still needs to learn to be comfortable with conflict among her staff, to make decisions when the proverbial buck stops at her desk, to deal with being a token, or to fire someone when it becomes necessary. Her socialization, even her formal education, may not have adequately prepared her for such daily experiences.

Conclusion

The training program is adaptable to formats such as seminars, workshops, regularized small group meetings, and continuing education and extension programs. Ideally, the authors would like to see such training built into staff development programs within human service agencies and the curriculum of professional schools. The provision of this training will be a social change in and of itself, which will lead to further social change initiated by women who have the necessary decision-making, reinforcement, and implementation power to bring about changes from within.

Nancy R. Hooyman and Judith S. Kaplan, *University of Minnesota* ∽

The Coming Death of Administrative Man

Contemporary theories of organization are largely theories about men in organizations, by men, and for men. For this reason, it should not be surprising (nor considered coincidental) that the key paradigmatic commitment of organizational analysis is expressed by the concept of administrative *man*. Nor should it be surprising that the behavior of most organizational practitioners is well characterized by this idea. Administrative *man* provides not only a starting point from which all major components of the rational model of organization flow, but also a model for the culturally dominant version of how people in organizations should act.

In marked contrast to this view of organizational life, some feminist theorists are developing alternative models of organization, based primarily on their experience in the women's movement. Both women's rights groups and radical feminists are experimenting with new patterns of group activity which substantially depart from the rational model of administration. In this article, we will ask how these new patterns may affect the way individuals think about and consequently behave in complex organizations. After describing the concept of administrative *man,* we will focus on alternative theories of organization developed in the women's movement. We will then consider the implications of these ideas for the future of organizations.

Concept of Administrative Man

The concept of administrative *man* can be traced to a series of writings appearing in the late '40s and early '50s, involving most prominently the organization theorist, Herbert Simon. In his now classic work, *Administrative Behavior,* Simon suggests that "the theory of administration is con-concerned with how an organization should be constructed and operated in order to accomplish its work efficiently."[86] Since the skills, values, and knowledge of the individual organizational member are limited, these attributes become the scarce means which must be maximized to attain organizational ends. When this occurs, the "bounded rationality" of the single organizational member is transcended by the rationality involved in the efficient utilization of organizational resources. "The 'administrative man' takes his place alongside the classical 'economic man'."[87]

In the organization's pursuit of rationality, administrative *man* is hardly an active participant. By accepting the goals of the organization as his own, administrative *man* loses his distinctiveness and becomes an instrument to be used in the pursuit of organizational rationality. In a passage from *Public Administration,* Simon et al. describe administrative *man* in terms more reminiscent of organization man:

> Administrative man accepts the organization goals as the value premises of his decisions, is particularly sensitive and reactive to the influences upon him of the other members of his organization, forms stable expectations regarding his own role in relation to others and the roles of others in relation to him, and has high morale in regard to the organization's goals. What is perhaps most remarkable and unique about administrative man is that the organizational influences do not merely cause him to do certain specific things (e.g., putting out a forest fire, if that is his job), but induce in him a habit pattern of doing *whatever* things are appropriate to carry out in cooperation with others the organization goals. *He develops habits of cooperative behavior* (emphasis added).[88]

Indeed, such patterns of behavior are absolutely essential in order for rationality to be achieved by social institutions. "Since these institutions largely determine the mental sets of the participants, they largely set the conditions for the exercise of docility, and hence of rationality in human society."[89]

Having chosen to emphasize the rational achievement of purpose, Simon is led inevitably to an instrumental view of the organizational member. As Dahl and Lindblom point out,

> A bias in favor of a deliberate adaptation of organizational means to ends requires that human relationships be viewed as instrumental means to the prescribed goals of organization not as sources of direct prime goal achievement. Joy, love, friendship, pity, and affection must all be curbed—unless they happen to foster the prescribed goals of the organization.[90]

As we will see, this depersonalization of the organizational member is in considerable contrast to much contemporary feminist thought.

The means-end dilemma faced by administrative *man* suggests another component of the rational view of organization, the inevitability of hierarchy. As

Simon points out, "Ends themselves, however, are often merely instrumental to more final objectives."[91] These intermediate levels become ends with reference to levels below, but means with reference to levels above. Following this chain, one is forced to conclude that the only sensible way of ordering the complex process of achieving goals is through a hierarchical structure in which various sub-units contribute their limited goals as means toward the ultimate goal of the total organization. As Vincent Ostrom notes in *The Intellectual Crisis in Public Administration*, Simon chose to confine his analysis to organizations in action rather than to develop a broader theory of rational choice. In doing so, he was forced to focus primarily on institutions "characterized by hierarchical ordering."[92]

From the top of the resulting organizational hierarchy flow the directives that govern the behavior of administrative *man*. Simply put, "the values and objectives that guide individual decisions . . . are usually imposed in the individual by the exercise of authority."[93] Authority is basically a relationship between a superior and a subordinate in which it is expected that the superior will issue directives which will be followed by the subordinate under normal circumstances. In Simon's formulation, orders are accepted only when they fall within the individual's "zone of acceptance." However, when one recalls that administrative *man* develops "habits of cooperative behavior," which greatly expand the zone, this hardly presents a serious problem.

The rational organization requires that individuals accept (1) a view of organization as a method or instrument for achieving rational efficiency, and (2) patterns of superior domination through hierarchical patterns of authority. In the world of administrative *man*, these elements have assumed the proportions of "cultural traits," adopted through a process of social learning at an early age.[94] Indeed, the pressure to conform to the standards of the rational model is so strong that the concept of administrative *man* is no longer an abstraction helpful in developing a theory of rational choice, but is now a model for the behavior of people in complex organizations. We are all socialized to adopt the character of administrative *man*, efficient but also joyless.

More Hopeful Alternatives

In contrast to the dismal picture of administrative *man* drawn by the rational theory of organization, certain elements of the current women's movement are developing more hopeful alternatives. While differences are apparent in the way in which divergent feminist groups conceptualize the primary problem confronting women, there are developing similarities in approaches to organization. In this section, we will discuss the emerging organizational concerns of two types of feminist groups, women's rights feminists and radical feminists. Women's rights feminists, probably comprising a majority of women in the movement, are those seeking expansion of women's rights within the existing social structure. Radical feminists, on the other hand, see the social structure itself as the problem and thus are seeking radical alteration of the system.

National *women's rights* organizations with local chapters such as the National Organization for Women, National Women's Political Caucus, and Women's Equity Action League accept "the basic structure of the society and social relationships, but (seek) to improve the status of women through legal, economic, and political means."[95] For example, NOW has as its original and stated goal to "take action to bring women into full participation in the mainstream of American society *now*, exercising all the privileges and responsibilities thereof in truly equal partnership with men."[96] Accordingly, little is considered wrong with current institutions beyond the fact that women are excluded from them.

The formal structure of NOW consists of a well-defined hierarchy of authority, with a national board at the top and statewide organizations serving as bridges from the national level to the local chapters. National NOW has written rules, by-laws, procedures, and membership dues requirements which are to be followed by all state and local NOW organizations. On the local level, like the national, a complex division of labor with specified job assignments is found; for instance, most local chapters have the positions of president, membership chairperson, treasurer, fund-raiser, and anywhere from one to 15 task force chairpersons.

Although the formal structure is fairly traditional, increasingly the top leadership and local chapters are informally adopting an anti-authoritarian stance, with aspirations of a participatory ideal. The developing ideal is that

> "all participants should be able to express their personal needs and to develop their individual talents in a sympathetic social environment. . . . Implicitly and explicitly such members adopt a consensus model of decision-making in contrast to the adversary model of the 'male world'."[97]

In this view, leaders are considered facilitators, persons with special talents in helping the group reach decisions. All members have the responsibility to fully participate in the process and let the leader know their feelings. Conversely, the officers must "learn to grasp the sense of a meeting and to present this in a way that emphasizes everyone's responsibility."[98] NOW has adopted consciousness raising as a means to bring its members into active participation of the organization.

The *radical feminist* branch of the women's movement consists of local or regional feminist groups, such as Female Liberation in Boston, the N.Y. Radical Feminists, Redstockings, and WITCH. Radical feminists see their mission as going to the root of social phenomena to criticize and to seek changes in power relationships and social institutions. Radical feminists may agree to the need for some reforms sought by women's rights groups, but reforms are not considered the ultimate solution. Indeed, some feel that to accept reform constitutes the greatest danger for the feminist movement, for to engage in reform is to accept the present structure, and risk being co-opted by it, thereby preventing in the future fundamental change in the structure.[99] Furthermore, by accepting reform and thus an immediate increase in opportunities for participation in economic and political institutions, many radical feminists fear that women end up trading off positive aspects of the traditional female role for less attractive aspects of the male role.[100]

Female Liberation of Boston, a radical feminist group, has articulated its struggle with these issues in its quarterly, *The Second Wave*. In one issue of the magazine its members discussed the organization's split into two groups: socialist feminists and radical feminists. The root difference was the socialist emphasis upon end product as opposed to the radical insistence on the "importance of process-consciousness."[101] The socialists contended that so-called personal change must wait until "after the revolution"; the other group argued that if feminists are not developing new ways of relating to each other and the world around them along the way then there will be no revolution.

> If we have not developed new forms, the same types of structure will supplant the old with only a change in content. That is no revolution. Power must be shared, not controlled by a few at the top of the pyramid.[102]

Female Liberation began to understand that work on interpersonal relations and projects go together, with one enhancing the other, and that women "have been conditioned to be receptive to each others' needs and feelings, and we must *not* lose this quality."[103] The group felt that a major difficulty in its organization was equalizing the desire to be a supportive group for its members, with the goal of bringing about social change in the environment. "We recognize that the integration of internal and external, or personal and political, is a classic problem in our schizoid society and that the attempt itself is revolutionary."[104] Indeed the foundation of their feminism has been the integration of "male and female" principles: female-principle qualities of inner growth and nurturing and male-principle qualities of action and outreach (not to be confused with women and men).[105]

In their third year, Female Liberation found that the division of labor issue was central, so they set out to (1) uncover the covert informal structure and examine its destructive effects, (2) discover why they had drifted into that structure, and (3) develop an alternative structure and the means to get there.[106] They found that although they held the ideal of collective effort, their process was in fact not collective. Secondly, the process was found to be physically and emotionally oppressive to the person in charge, while the interrelationships of the staff were not enhanced. They felt that because they had all been socialized to operate in hierarchical structures they naturally fell into that pattern. Consequently, the organization periodically consciously evaluated its efforts in light of its ideology and goals.

Basis for Challenge

The organizational challenges posed by the women's groups described in the preceding section go to the heart of the rational theory of organization—the concept of administrative *man*. Specifically, parts of the women's movement extol alternative values which contrast sharply with the traditional concerns for (1) organization as a method for achieving rational efficiency, and (2) superior domination through hierarchical patterns of authority. In this section, we will examine the basis for this challenge, suggesting that these alternatives may eventually help change the way we think about organizations and the way we behave as members of organizations.

As noted earlier, the traditional view of organization as a method for achieving rational efficiency leads directly to an instrumental conception of the organizational member. To the extent that the organization is conceived as devoted to the efficient utilization of resources, including human resources, the individual organizational member is simply a tool in the organizational process, not a part of the process itself. The focus of administrative *man* is on the completion of tasks (e.g., putting out the forest fire); therefore, he needs little involvement in the process of determining organizational operations.

A significant challenge to this view is coming from radical feminists in their insistence upon fluid, temporary structures in which process is as important as tasks. Emphasis in these groups is upon consensual decision making for the purpose of enhancing both creativity and group solidarity.[107] Personal development of members' skills and insights is aided by the flexible structure of feminist groups. This concept of self-realization, developing full human potential both intellectually and emotionally,[108] is clearly inconsistent with the bureaucratic emphasis upon task efficiency. Radical feminists believe that it is only after members feel they have had an opportunity to develop their personal ideology and understand the views of others that they can effectively work towards common goals. Indeed, once a goal is formulated, tasks are then divided upon the basis of skill and interest in the particular situation.

The rational view of organization suggests that it is only through his participation in organized endeavor that administrative *man* can approximate full rationality. "The rational individual is, and must be, an organized and institutionalized individual."[109] The rationality of the organizational member is not defined in terms of the full range of the individual's interests, but only in terms of a contribution to the accomplishment of organizational purpose. The notion of rationality does not extend to the individual's life-work outside the organization. The direction for administrative *man* is clear—full rationality requires complete commitment to the pursuit of organizational goals.

This degree of commitment is unacceptable to feminists who wish to balance various life interests. Women participating in the workforce are more conscious of the competing demands of marriage and family than previously had been the case among male workers.[110] Traditionally career success for men has meant that if conflict arose between work and family roles, the conflict would be resolved in favor of work.[111] Career in this sense connotes a demanding, pre-ordained life pattern, to which everything else is subordinated. Success for men has been traditionally measured in terms of upward mobility, status, and monetary rewards; there have been no predetermined standards against which to measure "success" for women if one removes marriage and motherhood as role indicators. A number of new strategies are aimed at developing a new concept of increased occupational flexibility, through part-time work, flexible work hours, longer leaves of absence without pay, educational leaves, and alternative retirement options.[112]

The feminist challenge to the second major theme suggested by administrative *man* is even more explicit; it argues that superior domination through hierarchical patterns of authority is not essential to the achievement of important goals but in fact is restrictive of the growth of the group and its individual members. All feminists agree that women should have the right to control their own lives, which necessarily precludes continued male domination. The issue is carried further by radical feminists in their stance that domination by males should not simply be replaced by domination by leaders. Where women's rights feminists largely operate within formal hierarchical organizations, some (e.g., NOW) have recently adopted more flexible and egalitarian forms at the local level. All along most radical feminist groups have sought equality of members within an anti-elitist structure.

As the notion of superior domination relates to the more general issue of power, feminists are struggling with what they see as the root of their oppression. Women's rights feminists feel that if they are given a significant amount of power, particularly in economic and political institutions, then the essential problems facing women will generally be solved. Radical feminists too realize that feminist visions can only be obtained if women gain some control or power in society. The problem as they see it is to redefine power so that there is not simply a substitution of a female elite for the present male elite, a situation which would still maintain the oppression of men and most women. Such a redefinition of power would include such questions as the following:

> What kind of organizations must [feminists] develop to support a different kind of power and decision making? Must women dominate or might it be possible to share power with men once [women] have obtained it? Will a feminist society have leaders at all? If so, how will they be chosen? Is it possible to envision a society in which there is not power, where there are no leaders? Are women ready to work collectively? With men?[113]

One response is the belief that it is impossible to significantly develop one's own ideology and personhood if one accepts the authority of leaders and thereby abdicates personal responsibility. Operationalization of this strategy has sometimes led to "structureless" and "leaderless" groups, with structurelessness "a natural reaction against the overstructured society" in which feminists find themselves.[114] Others have found that the informal structure allows formation of elites, who have, in effect, control over the group and exclude other members from participation in decision making.[115] However, effectiveness in achieving group goals is undermined where there is no structure within which expectations can become explicit and egalitarian decisions can be made.

This is not to say that traditional organizational forms are being adopted by radical feminist groups. Indeed these groups are finding that "temporary" structures are often best suited to their needs. These structures usually last "only as long as the activity and then dissolve, leaving no permanent leaders or organizational apparatus."[116] Another form of structuring to accomplish goals is through focusing of certain groups on particular problems.[117] For example, there may be one group conducting classes on women's history and another one teaching self-defense within one particular region or locality. Similarly, other groups (such as the Michigan Women's Liberation Coalition) are experimenting with the use of coalitions which serve to provide flexible coordination of groups and activities while preserving the autonomy of members. The structure is nonhierarchical—one of diffused leadership and responsibility.[118]

Potential Impact

The feminist challenge to the concept of administrative *man* has not yet been fully articulated; however, the basic elements of that challenge are clear. In contrast to the dependence of administrative *man* on a view of organization as a method for achieving rational efficiency, a growing number of feminists view group activity as also valuable in terms of personal growth and are therefore interested in *both* task and process. In such a view, the inevitable passivity and impersonality of administrative *man* is replaced by activity and self-disclosure on the part of the organizational member. In contrast to the traditional domination of administrative *man* through hierarchical systems of authority, feminists are experimenting with alternative forms of organizational structure and alternative patterns of leadership. The emphasis in such experiments is on the development of individual capacities as well as feminist ideology in a more open and supportive environment.

We can anticipate that feminist theories of organization will continue to be refined and more clearly articulated, especially as they are consistent with and encouraged by other organizational humanists.[119] However, it remains an open question as to whether such theories will have any major impact on the structure of public and private organizations in the future. Increasing numbers of women will be entering such organizations in the coming years; however, larger numbers of women in these organizations will not in itself bring about the demise of administrative *man*. As noted earlier, there are powerful social forces which act to maintain the existing model of organization. Women entering traditionally structured organizations will be subject to substantial pressures to adopt the model of administrative *man;* they may be socialized into traditional patterns of behavior.

In order for alternative beliefs to develop in traditional organizations, it will be necessary for feminists to counter the pressures to conform. For those feminists who are willing to undertake this task, several activities may be useful. Among these, feminists must develop appropriate systems of support among others in the organization for the purpose of sharing information, mutually resolving emerging difficulties, and aiding one another in resisting the forces of socialization. A related activity is the formation of consciousness-raising groups, which encourage independent thinking concerning the central issues of feminist thought. Consciousness-raising activities may bring about changes in the way women view themselves, developing new images which may deviate from the traditional view of organizational life. Such groups could develop a close connection between personal development and organizational change.

The key to the potential impact of feminist thinking on organizations of the future may finally come in the radical feminist rejection of the notion of superior domination—either by men or other elites—and their adoption of the concept of the authority of personal experience.[120] Rejecting the traditional acceptance of "expert" opinions, ideology, or structure, radical feminists believe they must develop an ideology and a structure from their experience of being female in a male-dominated society. They are therefore unwilling to give up personal responsibility for their own actions by submitting to the authority of some accepted theory or structure. To the extent that individuals follow this admonition and accept personal responsibility for their actions, even in the face of powerful pressures to conform to the model of administrative *man,* we may expect more and more people to become aware of the values of a feminist and ultimately humanist organization. And we may expect the coming death of administrative *man.*

Robert B. Denhardt and Jan Perkins, *University of Kansas* ❧

A Case Study on the Impact of Public Policy Affecting Women

Lost in government's preoccupation with organization is perhaps the most fundamental problem in its dealings with women's rights: Does the "status of women" provide a unified goal around which one can organize a government

The author wishes to thank Harold Seidman for reading and commenting upon an earlier draft of this article.

program? Or is the concept just another form of sexism, assuming the presence of a coherent group that, in fact, does not exist?

Connecticut's Permanent Commission on the Status of Women underscores the significance of this issue. While its legislative mandate assumes a unified goal for women, its actual operation casts serious doubt on such unity. The following case study explores the implications of this diversity as they affect the policy development of a legislative commission for women.

From its inception, the commission has been unable to come to agreement on its mission. This basic disagreement has manifested itself in three areas critical to the fulfillment of its mandate: (1) in the commission's composition, (2) in its operating style, and (3) in the issues it chooses to confront.

The study also points up a second issue: Can the advocacy role be performed by a government agency?

Creation and Climate

Connecticut's Permanent Commission on the Status of Women (PCSW) was established in 1973. It was an idea whose time had come.[121] In fact, its time had nearly come and passed. Almost 12 years had elapsed since John F. Kennedy created the national Commission on the Status of Women, and by 1972, 48 states had functioning groups of their own.

Many members of the Connecticut General Assembly believed the function of such a commission superfluous, but may have felt a subtle pressure to keep up with their colleague states and establish a government body to deal with the concerns of women.[122]

The pressure of a powerful coalition of women's groups was not nearly so subtle. Legislators could not underestimate the influence of a lobby which had, during the previous year, skillfully rallied the votes for passage of the State Equal Rights Amendment, and now urged the creation of an advocate group for women.

While the legislative support was at least passive, the governor had to be coaxed into not opposing the bill. In spite of this half-hearted acceptance of a commission for women, the PCSW was given a broad charter to combat sex discrimination.

The commission was directed to:

- Review the general statutes with regard to sex discrimination and recommend legislative revisions to the General Assembly.
- Inform the community—including business, education, state and local governments—of sex discrimination practices and enlist its support to change such practices.
- Serve as a liaison between government and private interest groups concerned with services for women.
- Promote consideration of qualified women for all levels of government positions.

- Oversee coordination, and assess programs and practices in all state agencies as they affect women.

The PCSW was to be directed by a body of 17 commissioners, five of whom were appointed by the governor, four by the speaker of the house, and four by the president pro-tempore of the senate. Its membership also included the co-chairman of the joint standing committee on human rights and opportunities, and the ranking minority representative and senator of this committee.

The commission was authorized to hire an executive director and staff (although its initial budget was just $30,000), and to perform a variety of quasi-judicial functions. These included the right to hold fact-finding hearings, with the mandate to subpoena witnesses and records, to receive and refer complaints of sex discrimination to the State Commission on Human Rights and Opportunities; to recommend policies to state agencies, to promulgate such regulations, and, finally, to request and receive from all state agencies "such information and assistance as the commission may require."

Problems of Definition

In the last few years, women's liberation has become a household word.[123] But in every household, it generates a different word. To some, perhaps the minority, women's liberation is an unnecessary and negative concept. To others, it is an issue of equal rights only, rights which are to be achieved quietly, through legislation. To still others, it is an issue of women's liberation in the full sense, requiring a transformation of roles in society, by more activist "radical" methods.

Connecticut's Commission on the Status of Women was a microcosm of this diversity.[124]

Yet the assumption in the legislative mandate was a common agreement on goals. That agreement, whether in concept or technique, was rare in the PCSW.[125] When agreement did occur, it was with the most non-controversial issues. Indeed, that magic spiritual bond which has been said to unite all women in a crusade for justice,[126] was mere fantasy. Each of the commissioners had a personal philosophy and a private agenda for the commission, and pulling together as a team was difficult.

Said a former staff member:

> The commission could never seem to come to a consensus about its mission. As a result, its projects tended to ricochet from one enthusiastic idea to another.

The group was constantly shifting its emphasis or response to a situation. Often, issues would be brought before the commissioners for reconsideration, after a decision had been made. This resulted in confusion and a great deal of inactivity.

> From month to month, the commission would change its policy or decisions . . . As a group, it would make a decision, and then individually, members would come in and

whack away at it, giving other directions to the executive director. And then they would criticize her for whatever she had done.

Commission Composition

Philosophical and practical disagreements on the issues were reinforced by the type of appointments made to the commission.

Some have suggested that the governor, who opposed the establishment of the PCSW, deliberately appointed persons who would not be as effective as others, in order to reduce the commission's ability to perform.[127]

Said one former PCSW staff member:

Many well-known feminists in the state had looked forward to serving on the commission, and then the appointments seemed to be political favors, to women who had no experience, and frankly, no interest in feminist things.

The significance of such political appointments to the commission lies with the priority given the women's issue by some of these members.

According to one commissioner:

Originally, there were three people who had been working in the feminist fields on the commission. The rest were political appointments. . . . Those people have problems because they have allegiances to their respective parties, which come first. . . . All commissioners who are beholden to the Democratic party or to the Republican party will unite against a feminist who is not beholden to either party. . . . I think the Democrats and the Republicans are feminists as long as it is okay with the party. And it is okay with the party as long as it doesn't make too many waves.

Party allegiance provided just one more methodological difference among an already diverse body. Those without party allegiance and not accustomed to using the political ropes believed in a different approach to problem solving. In the view of the same commissioner:

The political appointees were generally more conservative. They moved slowly, doing what the appropriations committee told them, trying to get along by personal interview . . . "Joe, or whomever, on the appropriations committee is a friend of mine, and I'll call him up and ask him what we should do about our budget". . . . That kind of thing is really difficult for a feminist to handle.

The party-feminist conflict provided another cross division of commissioners. It was not only Democrat versus Republican, but also old hands versus idealists.[128]

According to one commissioner, the "old political hands" were dealing in old ways:

The activists are the effective new politicians. After all, we (the activists) got the commission established. The old political hands had nothing to do with it. . . . It is my view that the activists would never have been so shoved around by the legislature if they had run this commission, and the PCSW role would be entirely different today.

Compounding the problems of party allegiance and political-feminist backgrounds, was the fact that several of the appointees were relatively unaware of the problems of women. Before the PCSW could even begin to discuss its mission, it had to help educate and raise the consciousness of its own members. This resulted in a slowdown on the commission's action front.

The diversity of group affiliation within the commission was also bound to produce a wide range of views. Organizations as dissimilar in membership, purpose, and technique as the National Organization for Women, the League of Women Voters, the Women's Political Caucus, and the Business and Professional Women's Club, were represented on the commission.

And, like many other commissions, the Connecticut body was composed of a group of strong and dominant personalities, most of whom had been "kingpins" in their own organizations. While cooperative action under these circumstances is difficult, it was magnified in the PCSW by the multiplicity of goals and strategies which emerged from those group loyalties.

Operating Style

The disagreement on objectives and approach was reflected in the PCSW's operating style. "Delegation" was not in the commission's vocabulary. A group can only delegate responsibilities with confidence if all are agreed as to what should be done. Since indeed they were not, the strategy was high participation by all commissioners.

Said one:

> We take on a lot of the work ourselves. We want to become involved in the work of the agency. We've fought for the idea that individual commissioners' talents and ideas should be used where it is appropriate, and that has happened purely because of the force of the personalities of the various commissioners.

However, that "force of personalities" often overstepped its function of policy making and became involved in the minutiae of day-to-day operations. Duplication of effort with the staff often resulted in confusion and embarrassment. At one point, the executive director found that she was five minutes behind a commissioner in making technical arrangements for the publication of an ERA brochure—an obvious function of the staff.

A commitment to high participation was one of the organizing principles of the commission. Early in its existence, the commissioners voted against the formation of an executive committee, because they wanted all to participate in decisions.[129] And although they did elect a chairperson, she served as a mere figurehead, as many commissioners would often speak and act on behalf of the group.

Ironically, while the commissioners accepted this "leaderless" group concept as appropriate to their own operation, they could not accept the same style of management for the staff.

The former executive director was a "team" person, one who did not believe in hierarchy, operating in perhaps the most hierarchical of structures—a government agency. She espoused what she called the "feminist way," where the five-member staff was not on different levels, but worked together.

However, some commissioners believed strongly in the need for a hierarchical staff structure:

> The "feminist process," in which there is an attempt to achieve some level of equality among members of the organization, has become confused with getting a job done. That requires a tough executive director, who is capable of establishing stations, of giving orders.

This conflict in style, led to a complete changeover in the five-member staff in just two years.[130]

In some respects, the former executive director may have been "an idea whose time had not yet come." She was a strong director acting firmly on what she saw as direction from the commission, in a time when the commission's directions were often contradictory. As she noted, "the telephone was always ringing with controversial directions from individual commissioners," telling her how to move from point A to point B, or suggesting that she not move in that direction at all, despite a recent vote by the commission.

The leaderless style of operation could not be supported by a mandate so broad, or a group so diverse.

Issue Avoidance

The disagreement on PCSW objectives also caused it to concentrate basically on procedural issues and non-controversial matters. The body was indeed a firm subscriber to Seidman's Law: Controversial decisions which can be deferred, are deferred.[131]

In its first year of operation, the commission took very few policy stands, concentrating instead on the so-called "safe" issues.[132] Its stance has moved only moderately from that point in its second year. Certainly, the commission has not tapped the extensive power given in its mandate, and has rather focused on its research and education functions.

The sensibility of such an approach is dubious to the "activists" on the commission. One commissioner said cynically: "The commission wants to study whether or not discrimination exists when everyone knows it exists."

But another staunchly defends that approach:

> If we wanted to play it a certain way as a commission we could come up with all kinds of information in the area of discrimination against women . . . and publish it right away and create an absolute hailstorm. But that's not a good way of handling it, particularly when a lot of men don't understand that women are discriminated against at all. . . . It is better to do an education program first and save these kinds of rockets for some other time when you feel the legislature is thoroughly informed and thoroughly educated.

The "political realists" believed that if they took on controversial topics too soon they might jeopardize the commission and its development.[133] The opposing faction felt that the commission was there to serve the women of the state and it should deal with all areas—including difficult issues like abortion. Staff members, as well as some commissioners, regretted that the commission seemed reluctant to take stands on this, as well as other issues such as the problems of welfare women, and the sex discrimination case of waitress Judith Quist, who was fired because she refused to shave her legs.

Government Agency as Advocate

When the commission did unite in project and approach, it soon discovered its own limitations. Serving at once as an advocate, and as a state agency, became a difficult balancing act.

> There was always the overriding . . . problem that we had as a state agency, in terms of the political realities: We had to make sure we didn't step on people's toes. When working in a political situation, we obviously have to consider the point of view of the administration on an issue, and the point of view of the various people on committees who are going to say "yes" or "no" to our budget, and the things we want to do.

For example, the PCSW has had a stormy history with the Committee on Legislative Management, the powerful group charged with reviewing all commission expenditures over $250. It has often said "no" to the things the commission has wanted to do. In one instance, the committee refused to allow the PCSW to spend $1,000 on pamphlets supporting the passage of the Equal Rights Amendment, in spite of two state attorney generals' rulings that it was within the commission's mandate to do so. The legislative group would approve the expenditure only if the publication was revised into simply an informative, rather than an endorsement piece.

Its status as a legislative commission has cast severe limitations on its impact on other state agencies, as well.

Of course, if a state agency is not fulfilling its responsibility in the area of equal rights, said one commissioner, "we must make a stink about it. But what kind of a stink can a state agency make about another state agency?"

The commission has instead chosen a more delicate approach to the problem, relying on the cooperation/education technique with the establishment of formal interagency committees.

Sensitive to its structure as a tax-supported agency, the PCSW takes a hard line on its non-alignment strategy with other women's groups. This, too, is a subject for conflict within the commission:

> What the commission could have been was a focal point in the state for all those groups—NOW, the Women's Political Caucus, the League of Women Voters, etc.— but what it tried to do was get away from these groups. They did not want to be like them, and they would become nervous. . . . That's crazy. They have all those women out there who are dying to help, but they (the commissioners) didn't want to be contaminated, or be confused with these groups which they thought were too radical, or too vocal.

As an agency dealing with a broad constituency and a controversial, sensitive issue, the commission's interest groups were many and diverse. To represent and serve as an advocate for *all* women in the state was an incredible mandate—a mandate impossible to carry out to the satisfaction of even a small number of organized women's groups. Methodologies, ideologies, and opinions of the PCSW were all over the map, from "too conservative" or "too radical" to "we don't need an advocate for women" or "we need a more active group to be our ombudsperson."

However, it has been the active women's groups who have been the most critical of the PCSW's mild approach to the problems of women in the state. While the commission has been sensitive to this, its organizational maintenance (perhaps the only basis for agreement among commissioners) has received top priority. The PCSW's survival is dependent on legislative good will. And many commissioners feel the only way to maintain that passive support is with a "tiptoe" approach to the problem of sex discrimination.

A Concluding Note

Does the "status of women" provide a unified goal around which one can organize a government program? In the case of the Connecticut Commission, the answer is clearly no. Indeed, the existence of a commission assumes the presence of a coherent group that does not exist.

However, given the present scope of the problem of sex discrimination, and the pressure to formulate such public advocate agencies, government may not have the luxury of choice. Certainly, Connecticut government was not accustomed to having an advocate within its own ranks, and many within the commission, as well, found themselves uncomfortably bound in a public agency.

The basic challenge for government, then, is to recognize this diversity and its ramifications for a public agency, and to attempt to organize within and around it. Connecticut's commission was unable to do that. For its diversity was emphasized and magnified by other forces.

Changes in the structure, the scope of the mandate, and the composition of such a body may serve to accommodate such diversity. These are surely issues which government must examine. In the end, however, it is the women themselves who must develop an acceptable operating style and approach, within the confines of a public agency, if they are to help unite this broad-based group in a modified "crusade for justice."

Jennifer Dorn Oldfield, *University of Connecticut* ⌒

Notes

1. "International Women's Year . . . More Women Focus on a Career," *Monthly Labor Review,* Vol. 98, No. 11 (November 1975), p. 2; and U.S. Department of Labor, Women's Bureau, "Facts on Women Workers" (February 1973).

2. U.S. Civil Service Commission, *Study of Employment of Women in the Federal Government, 1974,* GS and Equivalent Pay Plan. Women occupy 63 percent of all full-time slots in the Department of HEW.

3. Stuart H. Garfinkle, "Occupations of Women and Black Workers, 1962–74, *Monthly Labor Review,* Vol. 98, No. 11 (November 1975), p. 28; for university professors see "Making Affirmative Action Work in Higher Education," Carnegie Council on Policy Studies in Higher Education (July 1975), p. 26; for federal civil servants, GS 16–18, see U.S. Civil Service Commission, *op. cit.*

4. Michael P. Fogarty, R. Rapoport, and R.N. Rapoport, *Sex, Career, and Family* (Beverly Hills: Sage, 1971), p. 20. Also see Elizabeth Waldman and Beverly J. McEaddy, "Where Women Work—An Analysis by Industry and Occupation," *Monthly Labor Review,* Vol. 97, No. 5 (May 1974), p. 3.

5. For an analysis of similar constraints on women in state legislative politics see Jean J. Kirkpatrick, *Political Women* (New York: Basic Books, 1974), ch. 1.

6. Shulamith Firestone, *The Dialectic of Sex* (New York: William Morrow, 1970), p. 19. Also reflecting this perspective are: Gunnar Myrdal, "A Parallel to the Negro Problem," in *An American Dilemma* (New York: Harper and Row, 1962), Appendix 5; Helen Hacker, "Women are a Minority Group," *Social Forces,* Vol. 30, No. 1 (October 1959), pp. 60–68; Kirsten Amundsen, *The Silenced Majority* (Englewood Cliffs, N.J.: Prentice-Hall, 1971).

7. Elena Haavio-Mannela and Veronica Stolte-Heiskanen, "The Position of Women in Society: Formal Ideology vs. Everyday Ethic," *Social Science Information,* Vol. VI (December 1967), p. 171.

8. U.S. Civil Service Commission, *op. cit.*

9. Lionel Tiger, *Men in Groups* (New York: Random House, 1969), ch. 4.

10. Nancy L. Ross, *Washington Post,* July 29, 1970, cited by Judith Hole and Ellen Levine, *Rebirth of Feminism* (New York: Quadrangle Books, 1971), p. 174.

11. *Ibid.,* pp. 172–174.

12. Martin Gruberg reports that family relationship has been traditionally a major access route to elected political office for women. Martin Gruberg, *Women In American Politics* (Oshkosh, Wis.: Academia Press, 1968), p. 121.

13. For an abbreviated review of such women see *Ibid.*, pp. 134–144.

14. U.S. Department of Labor, Women's Bureau, *Handbook of Women Workers* (Washington, D.C.: U.S. Government Printing Office, 1969), p. 18.

15. Deborah Pisetizner Klein, "Women in the Labor Force: The Middle Years," *Monthly Labor Review*, Vol. 98, No. 11 (November 1975), p. 11.

16. Jean Lipman-Blumen, "Role De-Differentiation as a System Response to Crisis," *Sociological Inquiry*, Vol. 43, No. 2, p. 106.

17. Kenneth M. Davidson, Ruth Bader Binsburg, and Herma Kay Hill, "Marriage and Family Life," in *Sex-Based Discrimination: Text, Cases and Materials* (St. Paul, Minn.: West Publishing Company, 1974), p. 188. See also Janice Neepert Hedges and Jeanne K. Barnett, "Working Woman and the Division of Household Tasks," *Monthly Labor Review*, Vol. 95, No. 4 (April 1972), pp. 9–14, which reports results of one study indicating that wives, employed more than 30 hours a week, spend an average of 34 hours a week on household tasks. Women not employed report spending 57 hours a week on household tasks. Husbands' contribution to household jobs averaged to 1.6 hours a day, whether or not their wives worked.

18. Mirra Komarovsky, "Cultural Contradictions in Sex Role," *American Journal of Sociology*, Vol. 52, No. 3 (November 1946), p. 184.

19. Recent research suggests that the domestic role differentiation phenomenon is reified in the response of managers to employees. Managers expect male employees to give top priority to jobs when career demands and family obligations conflict; yet they expect female employees to sacrifice their careers to family responsibilities. See Benson Rosen and Thomas H. Jerdee, "Sex Stereotyping in the Executive Suite," *Harvard Business Review*, Vol. 52, No. 2 (March/April 1974), p. 47.

20. Hacker, *op. cit.*

21. Kenneth Boulding, "Role Prejudice as an Economic Problem," *Monthly Labor Review*, Vol. 97, No. 5 (May 1974), p. 40.

22. See Milton Yinger, "Prejudice," *International Encyclopedia of the Social Sciences* (New York: Macmillan Company, 1968), p. 449.

23. For a discussion of the need for and operation of such programs, see Rosalind Loring and Theodora Wells, *Breakthrough: Women into Management* (New York: Van Nostrand Reinhold, 1972), pp. 57–64; and Dorothy Jongeward and Dru Scott, *Affirmative Action for Women: A Practical Guide* (Reading, Mass.: Addison-Wesley, 1973), ch. 7–10.

24. Hanna Papanek, "Men, Women, and Work: Reflections on the Two-Person Career," *American Journal of Sociology*, Vol. 78, No. 4 (January 1973), pp. 852–872. The term "two-person, single career" was coined by Papanek, whose work informed this analysis. The concept of "two-person, single career" needs to be distinguished from the "dual career" in which the husband and wife are each gainfully employed in their own individual careers.

25. *Ibid.*, pp. 856–864.

26. For a recent study of the correlates of vicarious achievement orientations, see Jean Lipman-Blumen, "How Ideology Shapes Women's Lives," *Scientific American*, Vol. 226, No. 1 (January 1972).

27. William H. Whyte (tr.), *The Organization Man* (New York: Anchor Books, 1957), pp. 286–291.

28. For analysis of the same phenomenon in the academic world, see Arlie R. Hochschild, "Inside the Clockwork of Male Careers," in Florence Howe (ed.), *Women and the Power to Change* (New York: McGraw-Hill, 1975), pp. 47–80.

29. Signs by the early 1970s that even the executive divorce rate is on the rise have generated substantial concern among personnal specialists in the private sector. See "The High Cost of Executive Divorce," *Duns Review*, Vol. 98 (October 1971), pp. 52–54.

30. Warren Bennis warns the aspiring executive that ". . . living in temporary systems . . . [of the future organization] . . . augur[s] social strains and tensions. . . . To be a good wife in this era will be to undertake the profession of providing stability and continuity," "Changing Organizations" in William Scott (ed.), *Organizational Concepts and Analysis* (Belmont, Calif.: Dickenson Publishing Co., 1969), p. 154.

31. Hochschild, *op. cit.,* p. 59.

32. This point is well illustrated in recent issues of the *MBA* magazine. See "The Woman MBA," *MBA*, Vol. 9, No. 2 (February 1975), pp. 25–41; and "The Struggle for Status," *MBA*, Vol. 10, No. 2 (February 1976), pp. 25–40.

33. Victor Fuchs, "Women's Earnings: Recent Trends and Long-Run Prospects," *Monthly Labor Review*, Vol. 97, No. 5 (May 1974), pp. 23–26.

34. "The New Youth Movement," *Dun's Review*, Vol. 98 (August 1971), p. 47. This article reports a trend toward putting younger men in top slots of old line as well as new companies and predicts "In five years or so you will find the top men in business are going to be in their forties."

35. For discussion of specific measures taken, see Samuel Krislov, *Representative Bureaucracy* (Englewood Cliffs, N.J.: Prentice-Hall, 1974), p. 114.

36. Hochschild, *op. cit.,* p. 28.

37. *Exploitation From 9 to 5: Report of the Twentieth Century Fund Task Force On Women and Employment* (Lexington, Mass.: D.C. Heath and Company, 1975), p. 80.

38. *Ibid.,* p. 79.

39. *Ibid.,* p. 72.

40. E.C. Stanton, Susan B. Anthony, and M.J. Gage, *History of Woman Suffrage* (Rochester: Susan B. Anthony, 1877) vol. 2, p. 510.

41. Congressional Globe, 41st Congress, 2d Session, Vol. XCII, Part V, p. 4354, 1870.

42. National Center for Educational Statistics, U.S. Department of Health, Education, and Welfare, *The Condition of Education—A Statistical Report on the Condition of American Education, 1975.* (Washington, D.C.: U.S. Government Printing Office, 1975) (NCES 75-412).

43. U.S. Civil Service Commission news release, October 6, 1975. The 1974 figures are not absolutely compatible with the '67 and '72 ones, as the 1974 figures do not include the Postal Service.

44. As quoted in Marie Rosenberg and Len V. Bergstrom, *Women and Society: A Critical Review of the Literature with Selected Annotated Bibliography,* (Beverly Hills: Sage Publishing Company, 1975).

45. Henrik Ibsen, *A Doll's House, The Wild Duck, The Lady from the Sea*, Everyman's Library Edition (New York: E.P. Dutton, 1958), p. 68.

46. H.L. Mencken, *In Defense of Women* (New York: Alfred A. Knopf, 1924), pp. 9–10.

47. American Economic Association Committee on the Status of Women, "Combatting

Role Prejudice and Sex Discrimination," by Kenneth Boulding and Barbara B. Reagan, *The American Economic Review,* Vol. 63, No. 5 (December 1973), pp. 1049–1061.

48. Virginia Black, "The Erosion of Legal Principles in the Creation of Legal Policies," *Ethics,* Vol. 84, No. 2 (January 1974), p. 93.

49. For a good discussion of the opposition to affirmative action, see Daniel Bell "On Meritocracy and Equality," *The Public Interest,* Vol. 29 (Fall 1972), pp. 29–68.

50. John Rawls, *A Theory of Justice* (Cambridge: Harvard University Press, 1971), p. 9.

51. *Ibid.,* pp. 14–15.

52. *Ibid.,* p. 7.

53. *Ibid.,* p. 12.

54. *Ibid.*

55. This conclusion resulted from an informal survey conducted for the City of Sacramento while in the process of determining appropriate criteria for that jurisdiction to use in the development of its goals for women.

56. Robert Hampton, Chairman, U.S. Civil Service Commission; Stanley Pottinger, Assistant Attorney General; William Brown, Chairman, Equal Employment Opportunity Commission; and Philip Davis, Acting Director, Office of Federal Contract Compliance, *Memorandum—Permissible Goals and Timetables in State and Local Government* (March 23, 1973), p. 3.

57. *Ibid.,* p. 3.

58. *Ibid.*

59. Bureau of Intergovernmental Personnel Programs, U.S. Civil Service Commission, *Guidelines for the Development of an Affirmative Action Plan* (Washington, D.C.: U.S. Government Printing Office, 1975).

60. *Ibid.*

61. *Ibid.*

62. Michael J. Malbin, "Employment Report/Agency differences persist over goals and timetables in nondiscrimination plans," *National Journal Reports* (September 22, 1973), p. 1402.

63. William F. Danielson, director of personnel, City of Sacramento, *Memorandum to Honorable City Council Regarding City Employment Goals and Timetables* (October 18, 1973), p. 2.

64. William F. Danielson, director of personnel, City of Sacramento, *Letter to Honorable Robert T. Matsui, Chairman, Employee Relations Committee—City of Sacramento* (February 21, 1975), p. 1.

65. The decision to view total female population as an optimal common denominator for purposes of conducting a utilization analysis assumed the desirability of a full-employment economy for women. Support for this position can be found in the HEW Task Force Report, *Work in America* (Cambridge, Mass.: M.I.T. Press, 1973), pp. 56–66, which recommends that *"housewife" be considered a legitimate occupational choice for which financial remuneration should be provided.* Among other things, such a decision would increase our present labor force and more accurately represent the percentage of employed females.

66. Letty Cottin Pogrebin, "The Intimate Politics of Working with Men," *Ms.,* Vol. 4 (October 1975), pp. 48–52.

67. *Ibid.*

68. Margaret Adams, "The Compassion Trap," in Vivian Gornick and Barbara Moran (eds.), *Women in Sexist Society* (New York: Basic Books, 1971), p. 404.

69. C. Bernard Scotch, "Sex Status in Social Work: Grist for Women's Liberation," *Social Work*, Vol. 16 (July 1971), pp. 5–12; Martha Williams, Liz Ho, and Lucy Felder, "Career Patterns: More Grist for Women's Liberation," *Social Work*, Vol. 19 (July 1974), pp. 463–467; Janet Saltzmen Chafetz, "Women in Social Work," *Social Work*, Vol. 17 (September 1972), pp. 12–19; Jessie Barnard, *Women and the Public Interest* (Chicago: Aldine-Atherton, 1971); Florence Howe, "Women and the Power to Change," in Florence Howe (ed.), *Women and the Power to Change* (New York: McGraw-Hill Book Co., 1975), pp. 166; and Cynthia F. Epstein, "Encountering the Male Establishment: Sex—Status Limits on Women's Careers in the Professions," in Athena Theodore (ed.), *The Professional Woman* (Boston: The Schenkman Publishing Company, Inc., 1971), p. 52.

70. Winifred Bolen, *Feminism, Reform and Social Services: A History of Women in Social Work* (The Minnesota Resource Center for Social Work Education, July 1973); p. 18; Edward Gross, "Plus Ca Change? . . . The Sexual Structure of Occupations over Time," in Athena Theodore (ed.), *The Professional Woman, op. cit.,* p. 49; and Aaron Rosenblatt, Eileen Turner, Adalene Peterson, and Clare Rollesson, "Predominance of Male Authors in Social Work Publications," in Athena Theodore, (ed.), *The Professional Woman, op. cit.,* pp. 103–115.

71. James W. Grimm and Robert N. Stern, "Sex Roles and Internal Labor Market Structures: The Female Semi Professions," *Social Problems*, Vol. 21, No. 5 (June 1974), p. 702.

72. *Ibid.,* p. 703.

73. Bolen, *op. cit.,* p. 18.

74. Pamela Roby, "Structural and Internalized Barriers to Women in Higher Education," in Jo Freeman (ed.), *Women: A Feminist Perspective* (New York: Mayfield Publishing Co., 1970), p. 178; and Sandra L. Bem and Daryl J. Bem, "Training the Woman to Know Her Place: The Power of a Nonconscious Ideology," in *Women's Role in Contemporary Society* (Avon Books, 1972), pp. 101–115.

75. Howe, *op. cit.,* p. 134.

76. Adams, *op. cit.,* p. 404.

77. Bernard, *op. cit.,* pp. 88, 126.

78. Matina Horner, "Fail Bright Women," in Athena Theodore (ed.), *The Professional Woman, op. cit.,* pp. 252–260.

79. Cynthia Epstein, *Woman's Place* (Berkeley: University of California Press, 1971), p. 29.

80. *Ibid.,* p. 20.

81. Epstein, "Encountering the Male Establishment," *op. cit.,* p. 55.

82. Claude M. Steiner, *Scripts People Live* (New York: Grove Press, 1974).

83. George A. Ford and Gordon L. Lippitt, *A Life Planning Workbook* (Rosslyn, Va.: NTL Learning Resource Corporation, 1972).

84. Sidney Simon, et al., *Values Clarification* (New York: Hart Publishing Company, 1971); Robert E. Alberti and Michael L. Emmons, *Your Perfect Right* (Impact, 1970).

85. Armand Lauffer at the University of Michigan has produced *Lobbying, Compacts, and Shoot for Marbles* for practicing skills necessary for higher-level positions.

86. Herbert A. Simon, *Administrative Behavior* (New York: The Free Press, 2nd ed.; 1966), p. 38.

87. *Ibid.,* p. 39.

88. Herbert A. Simon, Donald W. Smithburg, and Victor A. Thompson, *Public Administration* (New York: Alfred A. Knopf, 1950), p. 82.

89. Simon, *op. cit.,* p. 104.

90. *Ibid.,* p. 252.

91. *Ibid.,* p. 62.

92. Vincent Ostrom, *The Intellectual Crisis in American Public Administration* (Tuscaloosa, Ala.: University of Alabama Press, 1974), p. 46.

93. Simon, *Administrative Behavior, op. cit.,* p. 198.

94. See Herbert G. Wilcox, "The Cultural Trait of Hierarchy in Middle Class Children," *Public Administration Review,* Vol. 28 (May/June 1968), pp. 222–235; and Robert B. Denhardt, "Bureaucratic Socialization and Organizational Accommodation," *Administrative Science Quarterly,* Vol. 13 (December 1968), pp. 441–450.

95. Barbara Bovee Polk, "Women's Liberation: Movement for Equality," in Constantine Safilios-Rothschild (ed.), *Toward a Sociology of Women* (Xerox Corp., 1972), p. 321.

96. Nancy Reeves, *Womankind* (Chicago: Aldine Publishing Co., 1973), p. 119.

97. Maren Lockwood Carden, *The New Feminist Movement* (New York: Russell Sage Foundation, 1974), p. 128.

98. *Ibid.,* p. 129.

99. Jo Freeman, *The Politics of Women's Liberation* (New York: David McKay Co., 1975), p. 241.

100. See Jessie Bernard, *Women and the Public Interest* (Chicago: Aldine Publishing Co., 1971), p. 41; and Caroline Bird's "old feminists," in *Born Female* (New York: McKay, 1970), p. 161.

101. "From Us," *The Second Wave,* Vol. 2, No. 2, p. 2.

102. *Ibid.*

103. *Ibid.*

104. "From Us," *The Second Wave,* Vol. 2, No. 4, p. 2.

105. Linda Thurston, "On Male and Female Principle," *The Second Wave,* Vol. 1, No. 2.

106. "From Us," *The Second Wave,* Vol. 3, No. 1, p. 2.

107. See Reeves, *op. cit.,* p. 182; and Alice Rossi, "Sex Equality: The Beginnings of Ideology," in Safilios-Rothschild, *op. cit.,* p. 352.

108. Carden, *op. cit.,* p. 86.

109. Simon, *Administrative Behavior, op. cit.,* p. 102.

110. See Rhona Rapoport and Robert N. Rapoport, "The Dual-Career Family: A Variant Pattern and Social Change," in Safilios-Rothschild, *op. cit.,* p. 236.

111. Bernard, *op. cit.,* p. 192; also see Philip Slater, *The Pursuit of Loneliness* (Boston: Beacon Press, 1971), p. 73.

112. Constantina Safilios-Rothschild, *Women and Social Policy* (Englewood Cliffs, N.J.: Prentice-Hall, Inc., 1974), p. 73.

113. Jane Dolkart and Nancy Hartsock, "Feminist Visions of the Future," *Quest,* Vol. II, No. 1 (Summer 1975), p. 6.

114. Joreen (Jo Freeman), "The Tyranny of Structurelessness," in Anne Kordt, Ellen Levine, and Anita Rapone (eds.), *Radical Feminism* (New York: New York Times Book Co., 1973), p. 285.

115. *Ibid.*

116. Polk, *op. cit.,* p. 329.

117. Carden, *op. cit.,* p. 73.

118. Polk, *op. cit.,* p. 326.

119. Wendell L. French and Cecil H. Bell, *Organization Development* (Englewood Cliffs, N.J.: Prentice-Hall, Inc., 1973), pp. 65–66.

120. Carden, *op. cit.,* p. 86.

121. Harold Scidman, "Decisional Strategies in Public Administration," lecture (University of Connecticut, October 1975).

122. Personal interview with PCSW commissioner (October 1975).

123. J. Freeman, "The Women's Liberation Movement: Its Origins, Structures, Impact and Ideas," in J. Freeman (ed.), *Women: A Feminist Perspective* (New York. Mayfield Publishing Co., 1975), p. 451.

124. Personal interview with PCSW commissioner.

125. Even the publication of a pre-Equal Rights Amendment brochure for Connecticut voters was disputed by some commissioners. And even the vote in support of the Supreme Court decision allowing abortion, an issue that many consider to be a basic female right, was split eight to four.

126. Freeman, *op. cit.*

127. Personal interview with PCSW staff member (October 1975).

128. Personal interview with PCSW commissioner (October 1975).

129. *Ibid.*

130. According to the commission's former executive director, this situation was not unique to other commissions on the status of women, which have also had a high turnover rate in staff.

131. Scidman, *op. cit.*

132. The commission was reluctant to tackle controversial issues. Said the former executive director: "One of the first things the commissioners were interested in was child care. Some of the less sophisticated members felt somehow this would be a safe issue. . . ." One commissioner admitted that the PCSW had saved perhaps the most explosive issue for last, family law: "I think the reason the commission has delayed on the family law is because this is the reach crunch. . . . Women's existence in the home and the marriage is going to be the hardest thing of all to change, and we all know that. It's going to cause a revolution for these middle-aged men."

133. Personal interview with PCSW's former executive director (October 1975).

Part Five

Aging and Disabilities

Aging and disability policies and practices represent the most recent set of concerns to receive widespread attention within the context of equal employment opportunity and affirmative action. Without a doubt these matters deserve careful and thoughtful attention, as do the other items of concern here; however, it is fair to suggest that the fractiousness of the debate does not reach the levels experienced when addressing equity and fairness as related to race or gender. Possibly the lowered voices and reduced emotion may be attributable to the fact that age and disability cut across all races, ethnicities, and sex.

The essay "Greying at the Temples" is an empirical study using workforce data that were collected from personnel records (1984–1985) in seven local governments. The authors use the data to examine aging and its impact on local social service agencies. The article explores some of the effects of the aging phenomenon, including plateauing, organizational dynamics created by the baby boom generation, and promotional opportunities. In addition to explaining the problems inherent to an aging workforce, the authors also address affirmative action and entry-level shortages in local welfare agencies. They put forth two strategies to address the issue of an aging workforce: management strategies and individual strategies. Management strategies include job rotation, sabbaticals, and opportunities for professional development outside the job, as well as membership on special task forces and groups. Some of the individual strategies include learning how to remain useful to the organization, learning how to live with the reality of plateauing, and adopting realistic expectations of management.

This chapter also includes a mini-symposium published in 1984 entitled, "New Roles for Older Workers: The Neglected Option." The first author, Jarold Kieffer, provides an historical context for our country's ongoing struggle to develop appropriate policies for dealing with an aging workforce. The strategy of encouraging the retirement of older workers was initiated because of a post–World War II concern that the economy would not be strong enough to provide adequate jobs for both younger and older workers. Unfortunately, the policy that demanded the removal of masses of older workers has produced major unanticipated problems for the nation, such as the anticipated insolvency of the Social Security system. Attitudes are beginning to shift, however, and the lure of early retirement does not appear to be as strong as it once was. People are no longer convinced that on account of age alone, they have somehow slipped to low levels of competence and productivity. In addition, longer work lives are simply becoming a necessity as increasing numbers of people continue to work to gain necessary income and to establish qualifications for meaningful Social Security benefits, pensions, and health insurance benefits. Kieffer also offers some provocative ideas about how the nation might adopt creative policies that would encourage and enable large numbers of able older people to voluntarily lengthen their work lives and thereby help to ease the retirement income demands being faced by the Social Security system and many private pension programs too. The author promotes the idea that this country should adopt a vigorous job expansion strategy for older workers and points out that older people have been prematurely written off as a productive resource in this society, with potentially adverse consequences.

Two of the other articles in the mini-symposium focus on strategies aimed at increasing the economic self-sufficiency of older Americans. The article by Whitman and her colleagues suggests that social policies regarding older persons must be reconsidered and recast. They believe that existing strategies, institutional and political, have inadvertently precluded the economic self-sufficiency of those dependent persons who wish to work. The article then offers several strategies aimed at reducing dependency. The Lynch article is similar in that it also focuses on the intrinsic value of hiring older workers. It also offers several strategies for identifying job opportunities and preparing older Americans to take advantage of existing job opportunities.

The Lewis and Allee article investigates the status and progress of disabled federal employees in the late 1970s and 1980s. The authors determined that many previous studies suffered from definitional problems and from self-reporting errors due in large part to the absence of a broadly accepted definition of disability. The essay employs regression analysis to control for most of the factors thought to be important determinants of federal salaries and grade levels. Based on the analysis presented, it appears that the disabled have not yet achieved equality in the federal civil service. Interestingly, nonsevere disabilities appeared to have less impact on federal careers than did sex or minority status. For example, even severely disabled white males typically had higher grades than comparably educated and experienced but nondisabled females. The study also found that the grade gap at entry was smaller between comparable disabled and nondisabled employees than between women or most minority males and nonminority males. Yet, the disabled experienced greater disadvantages in promotions. Although the authors do not directly state that the disabled–nondisabled career difference gaps are the result of discrimination, they do establish that they were not due to disparities in education, age, federal experience, race, sex, or veteran status. Finally, Lewis and Allee argue that despite the Rehabilitation Act of 1973, disabled employees have made few gains in the federal workplace except in their overall numbers.

18

Greying at the Temples

Demographics of a Public Service Occupation

James F. Wolf
Virginia Polytechnic Institute and State University

Carole M. Neves
National Academy of Public Administration

Richard T. Greenough
National Academy of Public Administration

Bill B. Benton
Maximus, Inc.

Societal, agency, and program demographic trends are leading to career plateauing and aging of the workforce. This article presents the results of an empirical study of the effects of demographic trends on a local government occupational group—local public welfare workers. It considers the effects of these trends on managers' abilities to foster new ideas and developments, to achieve affirmative action goals, and to ensure employee motivation, performance, and productivity. It concludes with a discussion of diverse strategies for human resource management.

Changing societal, occupational, and organizational trends are powerful pressures affecting public sector management. This article explores the effects of these trends, particularly the demographic composition of the workplace, through a study of a

Source: *Public Administration Review* 47 (March/April 1987): 190–198.

local government occupation—public welfare agency workers. Workforce trends of seven local welfare agencies are presented along with the significance of these findings for local governments, welfare administrators, and personnel managers. The picture is one of a relatively stable workforce with some disturbing underlying forces. This paper begins with an overview of the age profile of the agencies and follows with a closer look at the side effects of these trends: plateauing, organizational dynamics created by the baby boom generation, and promotional opportunities. Although the study focuses on public welfare agencies, the problem goes beyond human services and affects many other local, state, and national agencies.

Social and Occupational Forces

Social service agencies, like most public organizations, are faced with continuing problems and challenges created from several closely related social and demographic factors:

- Of particular importance is the overall *slowing of organizational growth* in the public sector since the late seventies and the reduction of career opportunities for professionals in all sectors.[1] The number of middle level positions in private and public sectors, in particular, has declined.
- The *baby boom generation* is getting attention as the leading edge of this group turns 40. Twenty million more babies were born between 1946 and 1965 than the cohorts on either side of this group.[2] More aspirants are seeking middle and senior level positions.
- *New, and* to some extent *conflicting, career values* are emerging. On one side is the belief in the right to have meaningful work and successful careers. While this view persists, new perspectives are developing.[3] In response to diminished opportunities, employees in their twenties and thirties are seeking self-fulfillment outside their jobs and regard employment as a means to engage in other rewarding endeavors.

Although some of these factors seem beyond the control of local government, they nonetheless directly bear upon employees who will work in the agencies for the next several decades. Further, they affect the ability of public managers to foster new ideas and developments; to achieve hiring goals that emanate from affirmative action programs; to ensure employee motivation, performance, and productivity; and to achieve a more dynamic view of the workplace. Over the long run, these factors are transforming the management of human resources.

Methodology

Research for this study was sponsored by the U.S. Office of Human Development Services (HDS) under the Small Business Innovation Research (SBIR) program.[4]

Workforce data were collected from 1984–1985 personnel records in seven local governments. Sample sizes varied between 100 and 400 full-time employees in each organization ranging from direct service workers to agency directors. Sample sizes were sufficient to permit statistical analysis of significance at the .95 level. Principal variables included employee age, sex, and race; dates hired by agency; length of time in current position; grade level; and program areas.

General Description of Agencies

The following agencies opened their personnel files: Alexandria, Virginia; Baltimore County, Maryland; Jefferson County, Colorado; Monroe County, New York; Prince William County, Virginia; Ramsey County, Minnesota; and Wake County, North Carolina. These agencies were chosen because of their comparability of functions, organizational size, and structure.

Each jurisdiction is located in a state where major public welfare services are delivered by local governments rather than by state agencies. The seven agencies match several general demographic characteristics of the workforce of local public welfare agencies. The labor forces are predominately female (82.8 percent) and white (82.7 percent). All seven agencies have primary responsibility for administering both social services and income maintenance programs. The number of personnel for services and income maintenance program areas is almost evenly divided in each jurisdiction. Each represents about 40 percent of the organization. The remaining 20 percent consists of administrative personnel, including the director's office and financial, personnel, legal, and shared clerical services.

The Public Welfare Worker: Slightly Greying at the Temples

The employees in this sample of local welfare agencies are best characterized as "slightly greying at the temples." Clearly they are not geriatric workers, but they are not young either. As shown in Figure 18.1, the median age of the workforce across all seven agencies is 40.2 years. The age profile of the agencies becomes more significant as the median age of the different levels of the hierarchies is examined.

To explore this phenomenon, the sample was divided into ten groups (deciles) according to grade levels shown in Table 18.1. The similarity of median age at each grade level is noteworthy. With the exception of the top levels and bottom two deciles, variations in the median ages are less than +/− two years. The standard deviation for each grade level is approximately ten years. What does it mean to have similar age distributions at different organizational levels? To answer this question it is necessary to examine the baby boom's role, career plateauing, program expansion and decline, and the importance of an aging workforce.

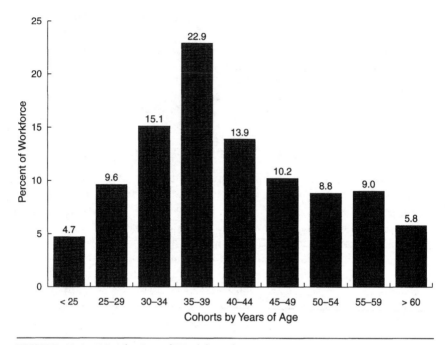

FIGURE 18.1   Distribution of Workforce by Age

TABLE 18.1   Median Age at Different Grade Levels

Grade Level Decile	Median Age	Difference from Overall Median
Top 10% Grade Levels	48 Years	+8 Years
10–20%	42 Years	+2 Years
20–30%	39 Years	−1 Year
30–40%	38 Years	−2 Years
40–50%	38 Years	−2 Years
50–60%	42 Years	+2 Years
60–70%	39 Years	−1 Year
70–80%	39 Years	−1 Year
80–90%	43 Years	+3 Years
Lowest 90–100% Grade Levels	36 Years	−4 Years
All Grade Levels	40 Years	

Baby Boomers

The conspicuous presence of the baby boom cohort in American society is a well known fact. This group is now exerting a strong influence in organizations, and the workforce of the public welfare agencies is no exception. Figure 18.2 illustrates this point. In the local social welfare agencies examined, the age group between 35–39 is prominent. This cohort occupies nearly 23 percent of all positions in the agencies. The age group between 30–39 years comprises over 38 percent of the workforce compared to 24 percent of the age group between 40–49 and to nearly 14 percent of the age group between 20–29. These data suggest that the baby boomers are firmly in place and are likely to remain so for another 25 years.

The baby boomers are a large, diverse group, and some of its members have fared far better than others. The group born between 1946 and 1956 and between 30 to 40 years of age, has done well. This group represents 38 percent of the workforce and 43 percent of the top 40 percent of the grades. Fourteen percent more workers are in the leading edge group than in the 40–50 age group, and 23 percent more workers than in the 20–30 age group.

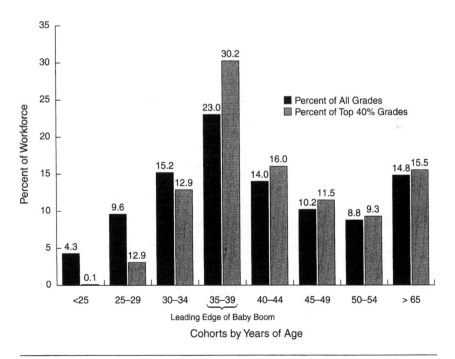

FIGURE 18.2   Level of Grade Attainment by Age Groups

Program Booms and Busts

The growth and decline of programs are also important forces. A second reason that the 35–40 age group is so prominent is that this group entered the profession from the late 1960s to the mid-1970s. This period coincides with the addition and expansion of many programs that local social welfare agencies now administer. The contraction in professional opportunities, beginning in 1978, is also evident from the data. The numbers of representatives from younger cohorts are less than the group that succeeded during the halcyon days of social service program growth.

Career Plateauing

Plateauing does not yet seem to be a critical issue in the agencies examined. However, it will be during the next decade. Figure 18.3 provides a breakdown of employees who have been in their current positions for at least five years. For purposes of this analysis, an employee working in the same position for at least five years is used as an indicator of plateauing. Plateauing is not severe at this time as only 31 percent of the agency staff have been in the same position for at least five years. However, a closer look indicates that plateauing is an emerging problem at higher levels of the agency, especially within social service programs. Nearly half of the social service staff have been in the same positions for five years or longer, and 40 percent of all staff have been in the top half of the grades. Plateauing is most severe for the top 10 percent of the grades. At the top, 57 percent of the staff have been in their current positions for five years.

Plateauing will worsen in the years to come. Most of the staff is relatively young. For example, only 21 percent of those in the highest 10 percent of grade levels are over age 55 (see Figure 18.4). Consequently, a large portion of the staff will be staying with the agency for the next 15 to 25 years. With the exception of a few retirements at the top level, in the next ten years, little upward movement can be anticipated.

The plateauing problem can be further understood by reviewing the age demographics along with turnover rates within the agencies. In general, the picture is one of a great deal of mobility where it is least needed, *not* enough where it would relieve the plateauing pressures. Only 11 percent of those in the top 20 percent of grade levels were hired during the 12 months prior to this study, while 47 percent of those in the lowest 20 percent of the grade levels were hired during the same period. Nothing in the data suggests that retirements will occur at a faster rate during the next decade. Because the majority of employees are under 40 years of age, and because expansion in the size of social welfare agencies is unlikely, the outlook for relief from plateauing pressures is not bright.

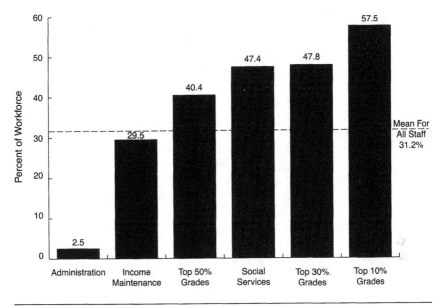

FIGURE 18.3   Percent of Employees in Current Position at Least Five Years

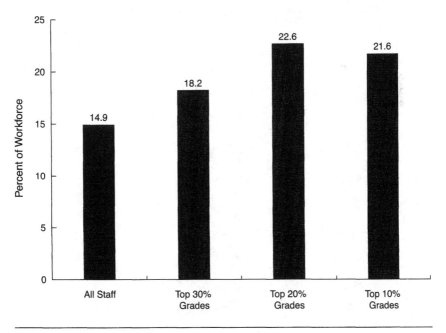

FIGURE 18.4   Percent of Employees over 55 Years of Age

Significance for Affirmative Action Programs

Affirmative action programs for women and minorities will be heavily affected by promotion slowdowns. Despite intensive efforts by local agencies to increase the numbers of women and minorities in top management positions, a large gap exists between the actual and expected numbers of women and minorities in senior posts. The overall slowdown in mobility will make it more difficult to reach affirmative action goals. Figure 18.5 presents the current status of women and minorities in senior programs.

Both minorities and women are underrepresented at the supervisory and senior management levels. At the highest levels each group is underrepresented by nearly 50 percent. The top level of the human service agencies is disproportionately white male. Virtually no age difference exists between the men and women at the top level; 50 percent of each group is over 45.

These data suggest that it takes longer for minorities to move into senior posts than for their white counterparts. The white supervisory staff is younger. Only 28 percent of black supervisors and top managers are under 45 years of age while 52.5 percent of whites in such positions are under 45 years of age.

Fewer opportunities will exist to recruit and promote women and minorities over the next decade. The agencies are not expanding, and few positions will open. Goals and strategies of affirmative action programs will have to be reexamined.

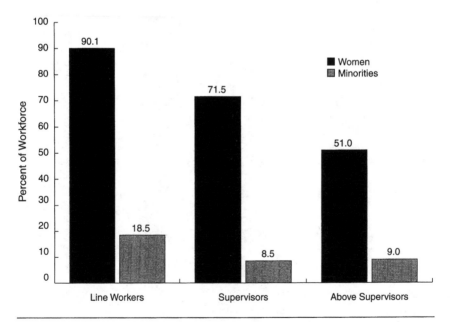

FIGURE 18.5   Representation of Women and Minorities

Shortages and Surpluses

Beyond the problems of aging, plateauing, and affirmative action, the demographic trends of social service agencies suggest problems which are associated with shortages and surpluses within the workforce. While the discussion thus far has been about an aging and plateaued bureaucracy, there is an associated problem of eventual workforce shortages. Since the workforce at middle and upper levels is stable and aging, little movement into the middle and upper ranks will occur in the near future. What is missing is a young generation of social welfare workers who will carry on the organizational memory and collective capacity. In fact, young workers are turning over at an alarming rate. For example, less than half of the employees in the bottom 40 percent of grades have been with the agency for more than four years. With limited opportunities for career advancement, it is reasonable to expect that agency ability to retain newer workers may be more difficult.

This would not be so bad if the agencies could be assured of a continued supply of entry level workers. Unfortunately, this is not the case. The baby boom generation is followed by a baby bust group, and opportunities for recruiting new social service workers as earlier cohorts retire will diminish. There simply will not be a continued supply of trained workers. Further, the diminished attractiveness of social service has already reduced the pool for the public social service occupations. In addition, there is increased competition for service workers from the private sector for a shrinking supply of new career entrants. For example, state human service departments are having trouble attracting MSW graduates because many are entering private practices.[5]

Strategies and Alternatives

What can be done about an aging workforce, projected plateauing, and entry level shortages in local welfare agencies? At some level, all occupations are subject to the demographic trends of the labor market. The middle aging of the worker population is occurring in practically all sectors. It is exacerbated in the public sector because of an employment bust and a decline in the attractiveness of working for public agencies. Consequently, strategies are required to insure public sector output and enhance individual workers' productivity and satisfaction.

Preliminary data show that the age of the workforce and the phenomenon of career plateauing influence agency performance. Although these data are inconclusive, worker satisfaction appears to be positively correlated with age. Apparently, people enjoy their jobs more as they get older.[6] However, older workers derive satisfaction from different factors than do their younger co-workers. For the young worker, the potential for career advancement and salary increases as well as the job itself are most important. In contrast, for the older worker, the quality of relationships with co-workers is most important.[7] Given the aging workforce this places a burden on supervisors to ensure that working relationships are effective.

Insuring effective relationships assumes more significance when the reality of an aging workforce is set in the context of limited promotional opportunities and increased career plateauing. During the decade, career plateauing has been given increased attention. Plateauing results from many of the factors described in the introduction—the decline in the size of middle levels of organizations, the baby boom cohort, technological change, and financial cutbacks for human service programs. Each limits opportunities for employees and appears also to be contributing to an erosion of quality in human service delivery. While the consequences of plateauing on individual and agency performance are still unclear, there are reasons for concern.

At the organizational level, the plateauing of a particular cohort can jeopardize organizational effectiveness. The danger exists if a cohort develops a generational viewpoint or collective blindspot. Cohorts of employees that come into an organization at the same period tend to share views about agency problems and solutions. As a result of this shared history they are more likely to pay attention to similar things in their environment. They may also have the same blinders that screen out awareness of new problems and opportunities. A large cohort of the human service workers in this study, for example, came into their agencies in the late sixties and early seventies when the programs were growing. There are also fewer representatives from younger groups. As it becomes increasingly difficult to get new perspectives into an agency, the possibility of a common mindset increases unless measures are taken to bring in new ways of looking at the agency's world.

Research on the effect of plateauing on individual employee job satisfaction and performance is mixed.[8] First, not all people are affected by plateauing in the same way. It depends on the individual's background, expectations for career success, stage of career, and personal factors outside the career. However, managers can begin to take advantage of some of this preliminary research on career plateauing.

Katz examined whether job satisfaction was influenced by the length of time in a particular job. The study focused on state and local government workers. He found that the factors which influenced satisfaction for new workers were different from those for workers who had longer tenure in the same job. Factors that are usually associated with job enrichment programs, for example, seem to be less important as one spends more time in the same job. Katz speculates that people who spend more time on a job may look less for job challenge and more for other organizational features such as tangible rewards and good interpersonal and supervisory relationships.[9]

Bateman and Organ examined the effects of aging and plateauing on performance.[10] They were uncomfortable with findings that seemed to suggest no real slackening of performance with plateauing. They concluded that these studies occurred over too short a time span and looked at performance of tasks that were too specific. They employed the construct of "solid citizen" to more fully capture the relationship between plateauing and performance. Included in this concept are: (1) a willingness to take on duties that cannot be prescribed in advance; (2) a toleration of temporary impositions; (3) a "stewardship" view of protecting and conserving organizational resources; (4) an enhancement of organizational effectiveness; and (5) a need to act in a responsible manner when tasks are not explicit. Its success depends on the willingness of employees to go above and beyond specific task assignments. Bateman and Organ found that these behaviors are dependent on a positive attitude toward the job, and citizenship behavior decreases with plateauing.

Management Strategies

Clearly, the plateaued worker presents special challenges for supervisors. The quality of relationships among co-workers and supervisors appears to be a significant factor for the plateaued employee. The physical working environment and tangible rewards also seem important. Unfortunately, these motivating factors are the most difficult to offer in public service agencies.

Often the physical conditions are poor, and the extras that make work pleasant such as training and development, job restructuring, and team efforts, are the first to be cut.

What can managers of local agencies do? The literature on plateauing suggests the use of a variety of strategies including job rotation, sabbaticals, opportunities for professional development outside the job, and membership on special task groups.[11] These techniques attempt to make jobs more interesting and appeal to the individual's need for growth. One strategy for helping a plateaued group might be to redesign middle-level positions by holding a "change desks" exercise. This can inject some vitality into a static career structure.

Other strategies attend to the supervisory skills in the agency. Since the quality of the relationship with coworkers is essential for workers who stay in positions for long periods of time, the capacity of supervisors to relate effectively with these workers becomes critical. Immediate supervisors are the key links for ensuring the performance levels of plateaued workers. Additional training of supervisors will be needed.

At a minimum, agency managers can spend more effort examining the agency's demographics and making the best of any windows of opportunity that may emerge. For example, a local welfare department discovered that two-thirds of its top managers will retire in the next five years. After that, retirements will slow appreciably for the next 15 years until the leading edge of the baby boom becomes eligible. Replacement slots will become very scarce, and opportunities for promotion during this five-year retirement bulge will pass quickly. As a result of this analysis, the department is more acutely aware of the importance of careful succession planning during the next few years.

Individual Strategies

Plateauing is more than a managerial problem. If individual workers are to remain effective on the job, they will have to work at remaining solid citizens, learn how to live with the reality of plateauing, adopt realistic expectations of management, recycle effective experiences, do a fair day's work for a fair day's pay, and, if possible, make the institutional environment work for them.[12] Accordingly, they can seek additional developmental experiences in and outside their organizational lives and develop themselves in avocations. Further, they can learn to redefine success as something other than moving up the hierarchy; horizontal movement can be as rewarding and interesting as vertical movement. Similarly, they can improve the quality of work by improving communications and by building a participatory environment in which they utilize judgment, maturity, and experience to address clients' problems. Should their situations prove unbearable, they may have to consider career switches.

Another way exists. Most strategies assume that the worker must be motivated. This implies that organizations have a responsibility to motivate workers or they will leave or quit on the job. Of course, it is important to provide an exciting and satisfying environment for agency workers. However, the vocational dimensions of the public service profession are also critical. Through vocations, public servants obtain meaning and fulfillment by developing a connectedness with a broader community rather than from career success or on-the-job satisfiers alone. Knowledge that they have vocations and that they are part of a community effort provides energy. While this is admittedly difficult in today's bureaucracy, there is perhaps no greater opportunity to develop this sense of vocation and service than in the local social services agencies where direct contacts with clients are critical. This vocational perspective encourages human service workers to: (1) recommit themselves to the vocation; (2) understand that positive worth does not only come from being motivated, but also from being given the opportunity to serve the community; and, (3) resurrect a system of professional values such as the notion that all citizens are entitled to a decent standard of living and that community service is dignified.

Conclusion

If these agencies are visited a decade from now, many of the same people who are working in them today will be on the job. They will only be greyer and more experienced. Their contributions to their agencies during the intervening period will depend to a great extent on how managers, personnel specialists, and the workers themselves respond to the constraints and opportunities presented by a plateaued and aging workforce.

From a wider perspective, the issues presented in this paper are not only of concern to the public welfare occupations. While little hard data are available about the demographics of local, state and national public agencies, indications are strong that a similar problem exists throughout the public sector workforce.

Notes

1. A. Patton, "The Coming Promotion Slowdown," *The Harvard Business Review,* vol. 59 (March/April 1981), pp. 46–52.

2. C. Wright, "The Pig in the Python: The Baby Boomers Get a Job," in R. Salinger, ed., *The Pig in the Python and Other Tales* (Washington: American Society for Training and Development, 1981), pp. 1–28.

3. D. Yankelovich, *New Rules, Searching for Self-Fulfillment in a World Turned Upside Down* (New York: Random House, 1981).

4. This study was part of a more comprehensive project performed by Urban Systems Research and Engineering, Inc., to develop a system of management indicators by which managers of local human service agencies could monitor agency performance and identify areas for cost effective improvement.

5. Reported by University of Maryland School of Social Work (May 1986).

6. Martin D. Hanlan, "Age and Commitment to Work: A Literature Review and Multivariate Analysis," *Research on Aging,* vol. 8 (June 1986), pp. 289–316; Susan R. Rhodes, "Age Related Differences in Work Attitudes and Behavior: A Review and Conceptual Analysis," *Psychological Bulletin,* vol. 93 (No. 2, 1983), pp. 328–367; Special Committee on Aging, U.S. Senate, *The Costs of Employing Older Workers* (Washington: U.S. Government Printing Office, 1984), S.PRT.98-229.

7. J. Gibson and S. Klein, "Employee Attitudes as a Function of Age and Length of Service: A Reconceptualization," *The Academy of Management Journal,* vol. 13 (December 1970), pp. 411–426.

8. J. Carnazza, A. Korman, T. Ference, and J. Stoner, "Plateaued and Plan Plateaued Managers: Factors in Job Satisfaction," *Journal of Management,* vol. 7 (July 1981), pp. 7–25; J. Near, "Work and Nonwork Correlates of the Career Plateau," in K. Chung, ed., *Academy of Management Proceedings '83* (New York: Academy of Management, 1983), pp. 380–384; R. D. Sylvia and K. Sylvia, "An Empirical Investigation of the Impacts of Career Plateauing," *International Review of Public Administration,* vol. 8 (No. 3, 1986), pp. 227–243. Carnazza, *et al.,* and Near found that plateauing did affect satisfaction with performance. Sylvia and Sylvia reported no significant relationship.

9. R. Katz, "Job Longevity as a Situational Factor in Job Satisfaction," *Administrative Science Quarterly,* vol. 23 (June 1978), pp. 204–223.

10. T. Bateman and D. Organ, "Job Satisfaction and the Good Soldier: The Relationship Between Affect and Employee Citizenship," *Academy of Management Journal,* vol. 26 (December 1983), pp. 587–595.

11. D. Hall and J. Goodale, *Human Resource Management: Strategy Design and Implementation* (Glenview, IL: Scott, Foresman, 1986); B. Kaye, *Up Is Not the Only Way* (Englewood Cliffs, NJ: Prentice-Hall, 1982).

12. J. Wolf, "Career Plateauing in the Public Service: Baby Boom and Employee Bust," *Public Administration Review,* vol. 43 (March/April 1983), pp. 160–165.

19

THE IMPACT OF DISABILITIES ON FEDERAL CAREER SUCCESS

Gregory B. Lewis
The American University

Cheryl Lynn Allee
The American University

What impact has anti-discrimination legislation had on the careers of disabled federal employees? Gregory B. Lewis and Cheryl Lynn Allee ask that question in light of the recent passage of the Americans with Disabilities Act (1990). Disabled federal employees have had such protection since passage of the 1973 Rehabilitation Act. Using an annual sample drawn from OPM's Central Personnel Data File between 1977 and 1989, the authors focused their analysis on hiring patterns, grade level assignments, and promotions. Lewis and Allee found that disabled federal employees "made few gains in the federal work force except in their numbers." While cautious in attributing these findings to discriminatory practices, the study's authors suggest that greater attention be paid to what happens to the career paths of disabled Americans.

Recent passage of the Americans with Disabilities Act of 1990 has highlighted both the progress that disabled people have made toward equality over the past

Source: *Public Administration Review* 52 (July/August 1992): 389–397.

The authors are grateful to the U.S. Equal Employment Opportunity Commission, Public Programs Division, for sponsoring this research and for providing some of the data analyzed; to the U.S. Office of Personnel Management, Division of Workforce Information, for providing the statistical sample of the Central Personnel Data File analyzed in this article; and to The American University for funding purchase of these data. We wish to thank Harry Redd, Rom Finnell, Philip Schneider, and several anonymous reviewers for their constructive comments.

two decades and the distance they have yet to go. The most important civil rights act passed by Congress in the past decade, the act addresses the elimination of discrimination in all aspects of day-to-day life and gives special attention to the areas of employment, public services and transportation, public accommodations, and telecommunication services. The act applies to state and local governments and most large private employers. The federal government, however, has long been prohibited from discriminating against disabled people by amendments to the 1973 Rehabilitation Act (P.L. 93-112). Federal experience with nondiscrimination policy may reveal not merely how effective it has been in improving the status of federal employees with disabilities; it may also offer insights into the potential and limitations of more general legislation on prohibiting barriers to the disabled.

This article investigates the status and progress of disabled federal employees in the late 1970s and the 1980s. It begins with a brief review of previous studies of the disabled in the federal service and in the general economy. Using a 1 percent sample of federal personnel records, it then examines the impact of disability status on grade level, entry level, and promotion probabilities for 1977 through 1989.

Previous Research

People with disabilities and scholars writing about them have frequently contended that, because the disabled are limited from fully participating in the society, they should be viewed as a social minority (Bowe, 1978, 1980; Gliedman and Roth, 1980; Zimmer, 1981). Erekson and Rotatori (1986, p. 3), for instance, saw limitation of the disabled's participation in employment and other activities as a characteristic violation of the civil rights of social minorities. Levitan and Taggart (1977), Grossman (1980), Zimmer (1981), and Wielkiewicz and Calvert (1989) have attempted to elevate disabled persons from the second-class citizenship implied by minority status by suggesting ways of improving the lives of disabled people both in and out of the workplace.

Mithang (1979) found that employers had negative attitudes toward hiring persons with disabilities, although his small sample size limits the generalizability of his findings. Levitan and Taggart (1977, pp. 8–10, 97) reported that employers preferred nondisabled workers, even if socioeconomically disadvantaged, over disabled workers. Schechter (1981, p. 267), however, discovered that employers appeared reluctant to hire disabled persons but willing to retain workers who became disabled on the job.

A variety of multivariate statistical analyses have shown earnings disparities between disabled and nondisabled workers in the U.S. economy. Davis (1972) found that the presence of a disability adversely affected the number of hours worked and hourly earnings of men aged 45 to 52. Davis (1973) determined that earnings did not increase steadily with additional education for disabled men as was the case for nondisabled men. Luft (1975) concluded that health problems lowered earnings even more for black women (38 percent) and black men (45 percent) than for white men (36 percent). According to Johnson and Lambrinos (1985), discrimination based on health status accounted for almost one-third of the wage differential between disabled and nondisabled men and one-half of the differential between disabled and nondisabled women. Craft *et al.* (1980) found wage differences among disabled persons to vary by degree of disability severity.

All of these studies suffered somewhat from definitional problems and from self-reporting of handicaps. No perfect definition of "disability" exists, as the concept is subject to social interpretation and people may be legally disabled in some jurisdictions but not in others. (This has frustrated both national [Zola and Kirchner, 1990] and international [Rouault, 1978; Haveman *et al.* 1984] comparisons.) Studies which rely on health status to define disability face even bigger problems, because people with recognized disabilities may be otherwise healthy and people in poor health may not meet the definition of disability for employment or other purposes.

There are several weaknesses with self-reporting of disabilities, as shown by Stem (1989), although he also found little over- or underreporting of disabilities for either economic or psychological reasons. This argument contradicts the view that employees fear that reporting disabilities to employers will impede their careers and that the "information will be adversely interpreted when promotion time comes up" (Ellner and Bender, 1980; p. 37).

Federal Studies

Table 19.1 presents the federal government's list of "the physical or mental disabilities, or history of such disabilities, that are likely to cause individuals to experience difficulty in obtaining, maintaining, or advancing in employment" (OPM FPM Supplement 292-1). Those that the U.S. Equal Employment Opportunity Commission (EEOC) categorizes as "serious" or "targeted" disabilities are marked with an asterisk.

Self-reporting has been a problem because substantial percentages of federal employees failed to identify themselves as either disabled or nondisabled, although this tendency has declined over time. In the sample described below, the percentage of nonreporters dropped rapidly from 34 percent in 1977 to 19 percent in 1978, then more gradually to 7 percent in 1989.

Both the EEOC and the U.S. Office of Personnel Management (OPM) report regularly on the status of disabled federal employees, but differences between these reports and changes over time in the types of employees who are included and in the questions that are covered in the reports make comparisons and trend analysis difficult. According to EEOC (1988), the percentage of federal employees with disabilities rose every year from 1982 (5.0 percent) to 1988 (6.0 percent)—a 21 percent increase in their share of federal employment. OPM (1990), on the

TABLE 19.1   Medical Disabilities

Speech and Hearing Impairments
    Severe speech malfunction or inability to speak
    Hard of hearing
    Total deafness in both ears (with or without understandable speech)*

Vision Impairments
    Ability to read ordinary size print with glasses but with loss of peripheral vision
    Inability to read ordinary size print, not correctable by glasses*
    Blind in one eye
    Blind in both eyes*

Loss of Function in Extremities
    Missing one or more hand, arm, foot, or leg*
    Nonparalytic orthopedic impairments (chronic pain, stiffness, or weakness) in
        one or more hand, foot, or leg, or in hip, pelvis, or back
    Partial paralysis of one hand, arm, or leg
    Partial paralysis of both hands, arms, or legs or of one side of body or of three
        or more major parts of the body*
    Complete paralysis of one hand
    Complete paralysis of both hands or of one or both arms or legs*

Other Impairments
    Heart disease, with or without limitations on activity
    Convulsive disorders*
    Blood diseases
    Diabetes, under control or with limitation on activity
    Pulmonary or respiratory disorders
    Kidney disfunctioning
    Cancer, including a history of cancer with complete recovery
    Mental retardation*
    Mental or emotional illness*
    Severe distortion of limbs and/or spine*
    Disfigurement of face, hands, or feet

---

*Classified as "severe" disabilities by the EEOC.

SOURCE: U.S. Office of Personnel Management, Central Personnel Data File (CPDF) Data Elements and Representations (FPM Supplement 292-1)

other hand, reported that the number of disabled employees rose 6 percent over this period (from 124,381 to 132,317), but that because total federal employment was rising even faster, the disabled's share of federal nonpostal employment dropped from 6.9 percent to 6.6 percent. The percentage of federal employees with more serious, targeted disabilities rose steadily, from 0.8 percent in 1982 to 1.1 percent in 1988 according to EEOC (1988) and from 1.0 to 1.2 percent according to OPM (1990).

Disabled employees clearly hold lower-status positions in the federal hierarchy. EEOC (1988) reported the mean grade level in 1988 to be General Schedule (GS) grade 8.5 for nondisabled employees, GS 7.8 for disabled employees, and GS 6.6 for those with targeted disabilities. Among the nondisabled, 42 percent held professional or administrative positions, compared to 33 percent of the disabled and 24 percent of those with targeted disabilities. (OPM [1990] reported slightly higher percentages for all groups but with the same pattern.)

EEOC figures (1988) showed federal employees with disabilities to be losing ground to the total work force in terms of grades and occupations. While the percentage of the federal work force in grades below GS9 dropped from 53 to 50 percent between 1982 and 1988, the percentage of disabled employees in those grades rose slightly (from 53 to 54 percent). Over the same period, the percentage of disabled workers who were professionals or administrators rose by 2 percent, while the comparable rise for the entire federal work force was 4 percent. Figures for 1988, 1980, 1979, and 1978 all show that the disabled had below-average promotion rates. In 1988, for instance, those rates were 11.2 percent for the total work force but only 9.2 percent for disabled employees.

In short, by 1988, disabled employees had lower grades, salaries, and promotion rates; were less likely to be in professional and administrative positions; and had been losing ground to nondisabled employees for a decade. They were steadily increasing their numbers in federal employment, but whether their share of employment was rising or falling is controversial.

The position of the disabled contrasts in some respects with the situation for women and minorities in the civil service, who also have below-average grades and occupational levels but have shown slow, steady progress in their shares of federal employment (Hellriegel and Short, 1972; Gibson and Yeager, 1975; Kranz, 1977; Rose and Chia, 1978; Guyot, 1979; Rosenbloom, 1980; Lewis, 1988) and in salary gains relative to white males (Lewis, 1988). Kellough and Kay (1986) showed that federal civil rights legislation may have had some positive impact on overall employment and on employment at higher grade levels for women and blacks. One might have expected that disabled employees would have experienced similar progress.

A substantial body of research has examined factors influencing individuals' pay in the federal service (e.g., Corazzini, 1972; Eccles, 1976; Rodgers, 1977; Taylor, 1979; Borjas, 1982, 1983; Lewis, 1986, 1988). Education, length of federal service, sex, and ethnicity appear to have the greatest impact on pay. Most of these studies, however, have ignored the issue of physical disabilities or have touched on their effect only in passing. Borjas (1982), for instance, included a physical disability variable in his model but did not discuss it, and Taylor (1979) addressed disability only from the standpoint of disabled veterans relative to nondisabled veterans. In both cases, the results indicated that the disabled earned less. Smith (1976) found that disabilities had a less severe impact on pay in the federal service than in the private sector, a pattern confirmed by Johnson and Lambrinos (1985).

OPM (1981) presented the grade distributions of disabled and nondisabled federal workers at each educational level. At most levels, the disabled had similar or higher grades than the nondisabled. This might suggest the absence of discrimination, except that the disabled were also older, more experienced, and more likely to be white males. All these factors would tend to raise the grades of disabled relative to nondisabled employees.

The basic structure for studying federal pay is well established, but little has been done to investigate the particular effects of disabilities. This article attempts to fill that gap.

Basic Patterns

Analyses were performed on a 1 percent sample (see grey box of the Central Personnel Data File (CPDF) for 1977 through 1989. Table 19.2 shows the average characteristics of disabled and nondisabled employees in the sample in both years

TABLE 19.2   Characteristics of Disabled and Nondisabled Employees, 1978 and 1988

	1978		1988	
	Nondisabled	Disabled	Nondisabled	Disabled
Grade (mean)	8.17	8.28	8.90	8.18***
Salary (mean)	17,596	18,327*	29,256	27,258***
Supervisor or manager (percent)	14.0	19.1**	15.1	14.0
Promoted by next March (percent)	19.8	11.6***	22.5	17.7**
Schooling	13.7	13.6	14.2	14.0**
Years of service	12.9	16.5***	13.4	13.9
Age	41.0	47.4***	42.3	45.8***
Male (percent)	56.3	68.4***	52.9	60.4***
Nonminority (percent)	79.6	85.6***	75.5	81.9***
Nonminority male (percent)	48.1	60.3***	43.5	51.0***
Veterans' preference (percent)	39.8	54.8***	30.2	40.9***
Severely handicapped (percent)	N.A.	12.8	N.A.	21.0

*Disabled-nondisabled difference significant at .05 level.
**Disabled-nondisabled difference significant at .01 level.
***Disabled-nondisabled difference significant at .0001 level.
SOURCE: U.S. Office of Personnel Management, Central Personnel Data File, 1 percent sample.

(see grey box). The two groups had similar mean grades in 1978, but the disabled had higher average salaries and were more likely to be supervisors or managers while the nondisabled were more likely to receive promotions. Educational levels of the groups were similar in 1978, but the disabled were older, more experienced, and more likely to be males, nonminorities, and veterans. Age and experience differences partly explain differences in promotion rates, and that, plus sex and minority status, help explain the disabled's advantage in supervisory authority.

By 1988, that advantage had disappeared, and the disabled earned significantly less than the nondisabled (about $2,000 less in the sample) and had lower mean grades (by 0.6 of a grade). Differences between the disabled and nondisabled in education, sex, and minority status were about the same in 1978 and 1988. However, the disabled were six years older than the nondisabled in 1978 but only three and one-half years older in 1988, and their additional three and one-half years of service in 1978 had shrunk to a statistically insignificant half year in 1988. The severity of disabilities had also increased. In 1988, 21 percent of the disabled in the sample had targeted disabilities, compared to only 13 percent in 1978. Thus, preliminary examination suggested that increases in the severity of disabilities and a decline in the level of federal experience among the disabled seemed the most likely explanations for their relative decline in grade and salary, although changes in levels of discrimination could also have played a role.

The Impact of Disabilities on Grade Levels

This study used a regression model that controlled for most of the factors found to be important determinants of federal salaries and grade levels in previous studies of this variety. Grade was the dependent variable, and separate regressions were run for each year's data from 1977 through 1989. Education was measured as years of schooling. Length of federal service and age were measured in years and years squared to account for the fact that grade increases are more common among younger and less experienced employees. Nine dummy variables accounted for sex and minority group membership, and a tenth variable indicated which employees received veterans' preference.

Disability status was measured in a variety of ways. First, a dummy variable was coded one if an employee reported any disability and zero otherwise. If that disability was classified by the EEOC as severe, a second dummy variable was also coded one; otherwise, for both the nondisabled and the less seriously disabled, that variable was coded zero.

The effect of handicap type was also tested. Disabilities were divided into four types: hearing and speech impairments, vision impairments, loss of function in extremities, and other impairments. However, addition into the regression model of three dummy variables based on these categories did not lead to statistically significant improvements on simpler models, so these results are not reported. Also not reported are analyses including a dummy variable distinguishing between employees who indicated they had no physical disabilities and those who

Box 19.1   Data

The Central Personnel Data File is an automated database compiled by OPM from agency submissions on employee and personnel actions. The CPDF covers over 90 percent of federal nonpostal civilian employment. The sample was restricted to permanent, full-time, white-collar employees covered by the General Schedule or a similar pay system. Under the GS, each position is assigned to one of 18 grades based on the difficulty and responsibility of the work performed. In our study, members of the Senior Executive Service (SES) were treated as being at grade 16. Employees' grade level and step (essentially, time in grade) almost wholly determine their salary levels. This simplified the analysis of both pay trends and promotions. Because salary rates tend to rise every year due to inflation while grades are supposed to have unvarying meanings over time, grades offered a more constant measure of the relative standing of disabled and nondisabled employees. (However, grades have inflated unevenly across agencies and regions over time, and this "grade creep" makes grades a less-than-perfect measure.) Second, because a rise in grade represents both greater responsibility and higher pay, grade increases could be clearly identified as promotions.

This 1 percent sample was drawn annually in March, based on the final three digits of employees' Social Security numbers. Because the digits remained the same from year to year, employees in the sample one year were in the sample for all other years in which they worked for the federal government. Promotions were identified by raises in grade from one March to the next. Because only about 10 percent of the data set turned over each year, patterns found in this data set would tend to be more stable over time than if the samples were independent. The sample included between 13,000 and 15,000 cases each year.

Employees were classified as "disabled" or "severely disabled" if they reported an appropriate medical condition on their personnel records (see Table 19.1). All other employees were treated as nondisabled. As noted earlier, however, a large number of civil servants, especially in the late 1970s, neither identified a medical disability nor checked off that they had no handicap. In addition, employees who became disabled after joining the civil service may not have updated their personnel files; they would have been treated as nondisabled in this study.

As some disabled workers were classified as nondisabled, because of these or other problems, our findings may understate the career disadvantage of disabilities if the disabled who are treated as nondisabled in this study lowered the average grade of nondisabled workers. It might exaggerate the disadvantage, however, if the disabled who "passed" for nondisabled had above-average grades for disabled employees. In fact, in this sample, those who did not report their disability status had slightly higher grades, on average, than similar nondisabled employees. Dropping the nonreporters from the data set or treating them as a separate group (through the use of a dummy variable in the regressions) had a negligible effect on the findings. This suggests that these errors did not substantially bias the results.

did not report their disability status; inclusion of that variable did not markedly influence the findings.

Findings

Table 19.3 shows the regression results for the earliest and latest years of data. As expected, the more educated had higher average grades (a year of schooling was worth 0.7 of a grade in 1989), and grade levels rose faster with experience and age early rather than late in the career (as shown by the positive coefficients on years of experience and age and the negative coefficients on years squared).

White, nonminority males had significantly higher grades than comparable female or minority employees. The expected grades of black males were 1.3 grades below those of comparably educated and experienced white males in 1989, the largest grade differential for any male group in that year. Females were expected to be 1.8 to 2.8 grades below comparably educated and experienced white males. However, expected grade differentials shrank for all groups except Native American

TABLE 19.3   Regression Results of Grade Level, 1977 and 1989

	1977	1989
Handicap	−.51***	−.53***
Severe handicap	−1.02***	−.92***
Years of education	.64***	.70***
Years of service	.24***	.24***
Years of service squared	−.004***	−.003***
Age	.24***	.15***
Age squared	−.003***	−.002***
Asian female	−3.26***	−2.31***
Asian male	−.51*	−.29
Black female	−2.91***	−2.46***
Black male	−1.76***	−1.27***
Hispanic female	−2.86***	−2.21***
Hispanic male	−1.51***	−.84***
Native American female	−3.50***	−2.82***
Native American male	−1.17**	−1.32***
Nonminority female	−2.63***	−1.81***
Veterans' preference	.07	−.02
Intercept	−6.15***	−5.21***
Adjusted R²	.60	.55
N	13,150	14,302

  *Coefficient significant at .05 level.
  **Coefficient significant at .01
  ***Coefficient significant at .0001 level.

males between 1977 and 1989, by at least one-half grade in most cases, suggesting some progress toward equality.

In 1977, the nonseverely disabled had expected grades .51 below those of nondisabled employees of the same level of education, experience and age, and of the same sex and minority group. Thus, having a nonsevere disability had somewhat less expected impact on grade than having one less year of education. In addition, the nonseverely disabled were about as far below comparably educated and experienced nondisabled employees of the same sex and minority status as Asian males were below nonminority males of comparable education, experience, and disability status.

The impact of severe disabilities was determined by adding the coefficient on Severely Disabled (-1.02) to the coefficient on Disabled ($-.51$), for a total effect of an expected grade 1.53 below that of comparable nondisabled employees. This gap was about the same size as the gap between comparable Hispanic and nonminority males. Both coefficients were highly significant for 1977.

We cannot attribute these grade gaps wholly to illegal discrimination, since physical and mental disabilities can impair employees' capacity to perform a task successfully. In addition, the disabled may choose to apply for less demanding, and less high-paying, positions. Thus, part of this "unexplained" grade gap may have been due to individual choices or real differences in productivity.

However, if part of the grade gap in the late 1970s was due to discrimination and if that discrimination lessened during the 1980s, we would expect to see the coefficients on Disabled and Severely Disabled shrink between 1977 and 1989. The coefficients on the sex and minority group variables did shrink, suggesting progress toward sexual and racial equality. However, the grade disadvantage to being nonseverely or severely disabled rather than nondisabled was essentially the same in both years.

Table 19.4 presents the disability coefficients for two sets of regressions for 1977 through 1989. The first regression includes both Disabled and Severely Disabled, and the second eliminates Severely Disabled from the model. With Severely Disabled included in the model, the coefficient on Disabled shows the average grade difference between nonseverely disabled and nondisabled employees with the same education, age, experience, sex, and minority status. With Severely Disabled excluded, it shows the average grade difference between comparable disabled (severely or nonseverely) and nondisabled employees.

The expected grade gap between comparable nondisabled and nonseverely disabled employees dropped in the late 1970s, then rose slowly for most of the 1980s, suggesting that the situation deteriorated slightly for the nonseverely disabled in the 1980s. The gap between the nonseverely and the severely disabled (the coefficient on Severely Disabled) showed greater fluctuation, with a slight downward trend, suggesting that there was somewhat less difference between the disabled and the severely disabled in the late 1980s than in the late 1970s.

TABLE 19.4   Impact of Disability on Grade and Promotion, by Year, 1977–89

| Year | Coefficients for Grade Regressions | | | Promotion Logits |
	Disabled	Severely Disabled	Disabled Only	Disabled
1977	−.51***	−1.02***	−.66***	−.28*
1978	−.45***	−1.06***	−.59***	−.41**
1979	−.39***	−.81**	−.50***	−.26*
1980	−.38**	−.89***	−.52***	−.26*
1981	−.43***	−.77**	−.56***	−.19
1982	−.42**	−.73**	−.54***	−.49**
1983	−.47***	−.79***	−.60***	−.20
1984	−.49***	−.76**	−.62***	−.23*
1985	−.58***	−.51**	−.67***	−.26*
1986	−.70***	−.48**	−.79***	−.18
1987	−.61***	−.76***	−.77***	−.31**
1988	−.52***	−.87***	−.70***	−.31**
1989	−.53***	−.92***	−.73***	N.A.

*Coefficient significant at .05 level.
**Coefficient significant at .01 level.
***Coefficient significant at .0001 level.

SOURCE: U.S. Office of Personnel Management, Central Personnel Data File, 1 percent sample.

Potentially, the rise in the Disabled coefficient could have resulted from the decline in the Severely Disabled coefficient. In fact, even with Severely Disabled excluded from the regression, the coefficient on Disabled followed the same pattern (see the third column of Table 19.4). Overall, the grade gap between comparable disabled and nondisabled federal employees widened during the 1980s. This result does not necessarily mean that discrimination worsened, but it does not provide any evidence that discrimination against the disabled declined in the 1980s—nor any evidence that the federal antidiscrimination policy worked.

The Impact of Disabilities on Entry Grades

The disabled may have had lower grades than comparable nondisabled employees because of lower starting points, slower advancement, or a combination of the two. We examine here the factors influencing employees' grades during their first year of federal service. (Federal employees are generally not eligible for promotion until they have completed one year of employment.) Because new employees comprised less than 10 percent of the work force each year and the disabled made up about 5 percent of new employees, small sample sizes for single-year regressions would lead to excessive fluctuations in coefficients from year to year and less accurate estimates of the impact of disabilities on entry levels. Therefore, data on employees with less than one year's service were divided into three periods (1977–1980, 1981–1984, and 1985–1989), and regressions were run separately for each period. This approach provided reasonably small standard errors and allowed some trend analysis. The model was identical to that used for the civil service as a whole, except that years of service was naturally dropped from a model concerned only with new employees.

Findings

Over these periods, the mean entry grade of new employees in the sample rose from GS 5.4 to GS 5.7 to GS 6.0. The average age rose from 30 to 31 to 32 and years of education, from 13.6 to 13.8 to 14.0. The entry grade regression model was nearly as strong as the more general model, explaining nearly half of the variation in entry grades in each period (Table 19.5). Age, education, and the minority-sex variables had the same signs and similar magnitudes as in the more general model, but veterans appeared to begin their careers at higher grades than comparable nonveterans. Although the impact of an additional year of age on grade was reasonably steady over the decade, education played an increasingly important role in entry levels. The expected impact of an additional year of education on entry level rose from .44 to .59 to .71 of a grade during the three periods studied.

Each of the race-sex coefficients was a little smaller than in the general model, indicating that both entry grade and advancement played roles in the below-average grades of women and minorities. Many groups seemed to lose ground to white males between 1977–1980 and 1981–1984. Although all gained on nonminority males in 1985–1989, only half the groups had better relative positions in 1985–1989 than in 1977–1980. The entry disadvantage to being female or minority showed no overall decline in the 1980s.

In general, nonseverely disabled employees entered federal service more than half a grade below nondisabled employees of the same age, education, sex, and minority status. Severely disabled employees were a further half-grade below. The grade gaps between nonseverely disabled and nondisabled employees in 1985–1989 were of the same general magnitude as the gaps between nonminority males and comparable Asian, Hispanic, and Native American men.

The coefficients on Disabled were somewhat larger in the entry regressions than in the more general model for most years. This might mean that the disabled's grade disadvantage held fairly constant over their careers, meaning that their advancement rates were about average. Alternatively, disabled individuals entering the federal service during the past decade may have faced greater obstacles than those entering earlier. Or those who were already disabled when they

TABLE 19.5   Entry Grade Levels, 1977–80, 1981–84, and 1985–89

	1977–80	1981–84	1985–89
Disabled	−1.07***	−.71**	−.35**
Severely disabled	.58	−.57	−.61**
Years of education	.44***	.59***	.71***
Age	.25***	.20***	.20***
Age squared	−.003***	−.002***	−.002***
Asian female	−1.24**	−1.66***	−1.17***
Asian male	−.04	−.31	−.21
Black female	−1.74***	−1.86***	−1.42***
Black male	−.90***	−1.18***	−1.14***
Hispanic female	−1.72***	−1.93***	−1.44***
Hispanic male	−.75*	−.53	−.46**
Native American female	−.90*	−1.67***	−1.30***
Native American male	−.01	−1.31	−.53
Nonminority female	−1.55***	−1.43***	−1.14***
Veterans' preference	.24	.22	.71***
Intercept	−4.34	−5.50	−7.24
Adjusted R^2	.44	.53	.54
N	3,580	3,299	5,771

*Coefficient significant at .05 level.
**Coefficient significant at .01 level.
***Coefficient significant at .0001 level.

SOURCE: U.S. Office of Personnel Management, Central Personnel Data File, 1 percent sample.

entered federal service may have been more seriously handicapped or faced greater discrimination than employees who became disabled on the job.

The trend in entry grade for handicapped employees was positive. The coefficient on Disabled dropped from −1.07 in 1977–1980, to −.71 in 1981–1984, to −.35 in 1985–1989, suggesting that nonsevere disabilities made less difference in the late than in the early 1980s. However, the coefficient on Severely Disabled was a positive half-grade in the first period and a negative half-grade in the latter two. As most of these coefficients were not statistically significant and as the severely disabled comprised one-fourth to one-third of all disabled new hires, dropping this variable from the model might give a clearer picture of the impact of disabilities. Even with Severely Disabled out of the model, the trend was positive (if weaker). The coefficient on Disabled was −.86 in 1977–1980 and −.85 in 1981–1984, then fell to −.51 in 1985–1989.

In short, the disabled entered federal service at lower grades than did comparable nondisabled new hires, but there was some evidence that the disadvantage they face at entry has shrunk. Federal antidiscrimination policy may have had some effect. (There was no evidence of comparable narrowing of the gap for women and minorities.)

The Impact of Disabilities on Promotions

Once disabled employees have entered the civil service, how do their career prospects differ from those of the nondisabled? To explore advancement potential, we investigated the probability of obtaining a promotion between one March and the next. As this dependent variable was dichotomous (the employee either was or was not promoted), logit rather than regression analysis was necessary. To simplify the model, we replaced the nine minority-sex variables with two dummy variables, one for sex and one for minority-nonminority status, and the veterans' preference variable was dropped. To account for the fact that promotion is easier from the lower than the higher grades, we added four dummy variables to indicate hierarchical status. With Severely Disabled in the model, the coefficient on Disabled showed the effect of a nonsevere disability; when it was dropped from the model, the coefficient showed the average effect of a severe or nonsevere disability.

Findings

As expected with a dichotomous dependent variable, these models explained much less of the variation in promotions than did the grade level models. Still, most of the variables had the expected signs and were statistically significant. In general, the higher one's grade, the less likely one was to be promoted, all else equal. Among employees at the same grade level, promotions were more likely for those with more education. The probability of promotion fell as length of service and age increased.

Nonminorities were significantly more likely than comparable minorities to be promoted in both years, with little change over the period studied. Somewhat surprisingly, given previous research (Lewis, 1986), men were significantly more likely than comparable women to be promoted in 1977–1978, but that male advantage was statistically insignificant in the following year and disappeared the next. Throughout the 1980s, the logits suggested that women's promotion probabilities were about as good as, perhaps better than, those of comparable men (the coefficients on sex were statistically insignificant in most years).

The coefficient on Disabled, however, was larger than that on sex or minority status in both 1977–1978 ($-.28$) and 1988–1989 ($-.31$). Examination of the coefficients on Disabled in the logit analyses for the 12 years (last column of Table 19.4) showed a general stability in the coefficient over the period, fluctuating between a low of $-.18$ and a high of $-.49$, with half of the coefficients between $-.26$ and $-.31$. There was no obvious downward trend. Thus, the disabled were consistently less likely to be promoted, after accounting for their concentration in the lower grades, where promotions are more common. Given the starting grade,

TABLE 19.6   Logit Results for Promotions, 1977–78 and 1988–89

	1977–78	*1988–89*
Handicap	−.280*	−.308**
Years of education	.037**	.057***
Years of service	−.129***	−.109***
Years of service squared	.0026***	.0024***
Age	−.012*	−.004
Age squared	−.0002	−.0004
Male	.173**	−.041
Nonminority	.210**	.183***
GS1–GS3	2.034***	1.827***
GS4–GS6	1.180***	1.212***
GS7–GS9	1.491***	1.479***
GS10–GS12	.729***	.643***
Intercept	−1.547**	−1.456**

　*Coefficient significant at .05 level.
　**Coefficient significant at .01 level.
　***Coefficient significant at .0001 level.

SOURCE: U.S. Office of Personnel Management, Central Personnel Data File, 1 percent sample.

being disabled appeared to be a greater obstacle to promotion than being a woman or racial/ethnic minority.

Addition of Severely Disabled to the model had an erratic effect. Its coefficient was actually positive in three years (suggesting that the severely disabled were more likely to be promoted than the nonseverely disabled), and the expected negative impact was statistically significant in only three years. In addition, the coefficient on Disabled lost statistical significance in about half the years, and the size of the coefficient fluctuated more than without Severely Disabled in the model.

The bulk of the evidence indicated that the disabled were less likely to be promoted than similar nondisabled employees at the same grade levels, and that the severely disabled faced even greater obstacles to promotion. There was no obvious evidence of progress toward equality in promotion chances.

Conclusion

The disabled have not achieved equality in the federal civil service, but nonsevere disabilities appeared to have less impact on federal careers than did sex or minority status. Even severely disabled white males typically had higher grades than comparably educated and experienced, but nondisabled, females. The disabled faced obstacles in both entry and advancement; they entered federal service at lower levels and were promoted at slower rates than nondisabled employees of the same education, age, experience, sex, and minority status. The grade gap at entry was smaller between comparable disabled and nondisabled employees than between women or most minority males and nonminority males, but the disabled experienced greater disadvantages in promotions. At least relative to women and minorities, then, disabled employees faced their most formidable obstacles in advancement.

Did these disabled-nondisabled career difference gaps result from discrimination? The method used can only establish that they were not due to disparities in education, age, federal experience, race, sex, or veteran status. Differences in other unmeasured characteristics, including real differences in ability to perform the work, might explain the lower grade levels and promotion rates.

Most people would assume that discrimination was at least part of the reasons for the lower grades and salaries of disabled workers. One would expect, therefore, that, if legal and administrative changes have lessened discrimination against the disabled, then the gaps between disabled and nondisabled workers should have narrowed over the past decade. Instead, the disabled have seen their grades, salaries, and likelihood of being supervisors fall relative to those of the nondisabled.

This drop was partly due to the changing characteristics of disabled and nondisabled employees, but disabled workers barely held their own relative to comparable nondisabled workers in grade levels and promotion rates. They appeared to have made gains in entry levels, however. The nondisabled's advantage over the disabled thus remained stable for a dozen years while white males' advantage over women and minorities was shrinking.

Despite the Rehabilitation Act of 1973, this study found that disabled employees have made few gains in the federal workplace except in their numbers. Has federal disability policy enhanced the ability of these persons to participate more fully in the society at large? Since disabled employees tend to be among the super-qualified or less-severely disabled, federal policy may not be directed toward those disabled persons most in need of employment assistance. Disabled persons who do work may tend to become pigeon-holed into the jobs where they were originally employed. Disability policy in employment should continually be examined, beginning with the selection stage at which many disabled individuals may be screened out of the employment process. Attention to what happens to disabled individuals during employment is also needed, however, in order to ensure that disabled employees who have an opportunity to work have an opportunity to grow and advance in their work as well.

References

Borjas, George J., 1982. "The Politics of Employment Discrimination in the Federal Bureaucracy." *Journal of Law and Economics,* vol. 25, pp. 271–299.

———, 1983. "The Measurement of Race and Gender Wage Differentials: Evidence from the Public Sector." *Industrial and Labor Relations Review,* vol. 25, pp. 79–91.

Bowe, Frank, 1978. *Handicapping America: Barriers to Disabled People.* New York: Harper & Row, Publishers, Inc.

_____, 1980. *Rehabilitating America: Toward Independence for Disabled and Elderly People.* New York: Harper & Row, Publishers.

Corazzini, Arthur J., 1972. "Equality of Employment Opportunity in the Federal White-Collar Civil Service." *Journal of Human Resources,* vol. 7, pp. 424–445.

Craft, James A., Thomas J. Benecki, and Yitzchak M. Shkop, 1980. "Who Hires the Seriously Handicapped?" *Industrial Relations,* vol. 19, pp. 94–99.

Davis, Joseph M., 1972. "Impact of Health on Earnings and Labor Market Activity." *Monthly Labor Review,* vol. 95, pp. 46–49.

_____, 1973. "Health and the Education-Earnings Relationship." *Monthly Labor Review,* vol. 96, pp. 61–63.

Eccles, Mary Eisner, 1976. "Race, Sex, and Government Jobs: A Study of Affirmative Action Programs in Federal Agencies." Unpublished Ph.D. dissertation, Harvard University.

Ellner, Jack R. and Henry E. Bender, 1980. *Hiring the Handicapped.* New York: AMACOM.

Erekson, Thomas L. and Anthony F. Rotatori, 1986. *Accessibility to Employment Training for the Physically Handicapped.* Springfield, IL: Charles C. Thunen, Publisher.

Gibson, Frank K. and Samuel Yeager. 1975. "Treads in the Federal Employment of Blacks." *Public Personnel Management,* vol. 4, pp. 189–195.

Gliedman, John and William Both, 1980. *The Unexpected Minority: Handicapped Children in America.* New York: Harcourt, Brace, and Jovanovich.

Grossman, Vigdor, 1980. *Employing Handicapped Persons: Meeting EEO Objectives.* Washington, DC: Bureau of National Affairs.

Guyot, James E., 1979. "Arithmetic and Inference in Ethnic Analysis: EEO in the Federal Service." *Public Administration Review,* vol. 39, pp. 194–197.

Haveman, Robert H., Victor Halberstach, and Richard A. Burkhouser, 1984. *Public Policy Toward Disabled Workers: Cross-National Analyses of Economic Impacts.* Ithaca, NY: Cornell University Press.

Hellriegel, Don and Larry Short, 1972. "EEO in the Federal Government: A Comparative Analysis." *Public Administration Review,* vol. 32, pp. 851–858.

Johnson, William G. and James Lambrinos, 1985. "Wage Discrimination Against Handicapped Men and Women" *Journal of Human Resources,* vol. 20, pp. 264–277.

Kellough, James E. and Susan Ann Kay, 1986. "Affirmative Action in the Federal Bureaucracy: An Impact Analysis." *Review of Public Personnel Administration,* vol. 6, pp. 1–13.

Kranz, Harry, 1973. "How Representative Is the Federal Service?" *Public Personnel Management,* vol. 1, pp. 242–255.

Lambrinos, James, 1981. "Health: A Source of Bias in Labor Supply Models." *Review of Economics and Statistics,* vol. 60, pp. 206–212.

Levitan, Sar A. and Robert Taggart, 1977. *Jobs for the Disabled.* Baltimore, MD: Johns Hopkins University Press.

Lewis, Gregory B., 1986. "Gender and Promotions: Promotion Chances of White Men and Women in Federal White-Collar Employment." *Journal of Human Resources,* vol. 21, pp. 406–419.

_____, 1988. "Progress Toward Racial and Sexual Equality in the Federal Civil Service." *Public Administration Review,* vol. 48, pp. 700–707.

Luft, Harold S., 1975. "The Impact of Poor Health on Earnings," *Review of Economics and Statistics,* vol. 57, pp. 43–57.

Mithang, Dennis E., 1979. "Negative Employer Attitudes Toward Hiring the Handicapped: Fact or Fiction." *Journal of Contemporary Business,* vol. 8, pp. 19–26.

Rodgers, Charles S., 1977. "The Internal Allocation of Labor in a Federal Agency." Unpublished Ph.D. dissertation, Brandeis University.

Rose, Winfield H. and Tiang Ping Chia, 1978. "Impact of the Equal Employment Opportunity Act of 1972 on Black Employment in the Federal Service: A Preliminary Analysis." *Public Administration Review,* vol. 38, pp. 245–251.

Rosenbloom, David H., 1980. "The Federal Affirmative Action Policy." In David Nachmias, ed., *The Practices of Policy Evaluation.* New York: St. Martin's Press.

Rouault, Georges Y., 1978. *The Handicapped and Their Employment: A Statistical Study of the Situation in the Member States of the European Community.* Luxembourg: Statistical Office of the European Community.

Schechter, Eva S., 1988. "Employment and Work Adjustments of the Disabled." In Donald T. Ferran, complier, *Disability Survey '72: Disabled and Nondisabled Adults,* Research Report No. 56, 55A Publication No. 13-11812. Washington, DC; U.S. Department of Health and Human Services, Social Security Administration.

Smith, Sharon P., 1976, "Pay Differences between Federal Government and Private Sector Workers." *Industrial and Labor Relations Review,* vol. 29, pp. 176–197.

Stern, Steven, 1989, "Measuring the Effect of Disability on Labor Force Participation." *Journal of Human Resources,* vol. 24, pp. 361–395.

Taylor, Patricia A., 1979. "Income Inequality in the Federal Civilian Government." *American Sociological Review,* vol. 44, pp. 468–479.

U.S. Equal Employment Opportunity Commission, 1988. *Annual Report on the Employment of Minorities, Women, and Persons with Disabilities in the Federal Government, Fiscal Year 1988.* Washington, DC: Government Printing Office.

_____, 1987. *Employment of Individuals with Disabilities in the Federal Government, FY2982–FY2987.* Washington, DC: Government Printing Office.

U.S. Office of Personnel Management, 1981. *Statistical Profile of Handicapped Federal Civilian Employees,* OPM Doc 128-06-6. Washington, DC: Government Printing Office.

Wielkiewicz, Richard M. and Christine R. X. Calvert, 1989. *Training and Habilitating Developmentally Disabled People: An Introduction.* Newbury Park, CA: Sage Publications.

Zimmer, Arne B., 1981. *Employing the Handicapped: A Practical Compliance Manual.* New York: AMACOM.

Zola, Irving Kenneth and Corrine Kirchner, eds., 1990. *Disability Studies Quarterly,* vol. 10, pp. 1–25.

20

Mini-Symposium on New Roles for Older Workers

The Neglected Option

edited by Jarold A. Kieffer

Since the end of World War II, the United States has followed and continuously strengthened retirement strategies that induced most older workers to leave the work force at or before age 65. Such strategies were designed to keep open hiring and promotion channels for younger workers in a work force commonly judged to be too large for meeting the nation's production and service requirements. The sought for reduction in the numbers of older workers also was rationalized as necessary for improving productivity and lowering labor and other costs. To these ends, older workers were presumed to have declining physical and mental capacities and, therefore, to be less productive than younger workers. Broad assumptions developed that older workers really were not interested in longer worklives, that they were resistant to learning new things, that they were troublesome and difficult to have around, and that they tended to look backward rather than forward.

The whole notion that most older workers could leave the work force and be supported in retirement by the work and contributions of younger workers also rested upon certain assumptions and presumptions, namely that adequate retirement income and other benefits and services for such retirees could be provided, that a growing productivity of the younger work force would help pay the costs of the retirement strategy, but that on account of the short life expectancies then

Source: *Public Administration Review* 44 (September/October 1984): 433–452.

prevalent, the retirement periods for most older people would not be too long anyway.

Over the past several years, the economic and social underpinning for the retirement strategy has been dissolving. Twice in less than five years, the solvency of the Social Security system has been the subject of major remedial efforts. Growing numbers of private pension systems are in trouble, and major questions are being raised about the resources available to meet the commitments projected for many public pension systems. Then, too, the economy has proved to be troubleprone and undependable in its capacity to take on greater public spending loads, productivity growth has proved to be uncertain, younger workers are increasingly restive about the growing burden of Social Security taxation, retirement periods have lengthened dramatically as older people have gained in life expectancy, and lastly, increasing numbers of able older people are resisting the stereotype that they are decrepit, unable to learn, and non-productive.

Five practitioners, with wide experience in one or more levels of government and other sectors have developed accounts of efforts they have been making to shape and/or administer activities that seek to reverse pro-retirement policies. These activities all stem from the belief that the growing older population has large numbers of able, experienced people in its make-up and that they can and should remain valuable to employers and our communities.

Jarold Kieffer, now a consultant and writer living in Fairfax, Virginia, addresses, in the lead article of a series of four, the broad issue context of the nation's pro-retirement policies and outlines why these policies need to be changed.

Gloria Whitman, associate director for human resources of the Council of State Planning Agencies, Roger Vaughan, an economics consultant, and Arthur Boyd, a management and training consultant, describe an innovative, federally-funded national demonstration project in the field of older worker employment. The Council of State Planning Agencies, an affiliate of the National Governors Association, has been given funds by the U.S. Office of Aging to conduct a pilot project to encourage and assist state economic development planning and action to help older people gain effective employment and, thereby, to reduce their need for public assistance and other dependency services. The initial activity will focus on five states.

Terri Lynch, director of the Arlington County (Virginia) Area Agency on Aging, describes the leadership and coordinating activities of the National Association of Older Worker Employment Services (NAOWES), a constituent unit of the National Council on the Aging, Inc.

The final article was written by Barbara Plimpton, career development coordinator for the Department of Personnel of the State of Colorado. She details how the state government addresses the further employment interests and capacities of its age 50–64 employees.

Longer Worklives:
A Strategic Policy Reversal Needed

Our society is developing an increasingly unmanageable contradiction. Over the past several generations, we have been evolving a population over age 55 that is unprecedented in its health and educational status and life expectancy. Yet, ironically, since the end of World War II, the nation has been systematically writing off the productive capacities of this remarkable group. Most employers and many younger workers perceive that older workers have declining work capacities and little or no interest in working longer. Most employers prefer not to hire older workers. If on the job, workers over age 55 only rarely are given opportunities for further training that could extend or increase their productive value. Then, too, most workers who stay on the job after age 65 do not get credit for longer service in determining their future starting pension benefits.

With few inducements to stay at work and many financial and other inducements to retire, it is not surprising that older workers have been retiring as soon as they have become eligible to do so. The workplace atmosphere in most places of employment, public and private, is pro-retirement, and the assumption that older workers will soon retire or, indeed, are expected to retire, is pervasive. To close this loop, this expectancy then confirms the view of employers that their investment in the further training and development of older workers is not cost-effective.

The Success of the Retirement Strategy

The strategy of encouraging the retirement of older workers started from a post–World War II concern that the economy would not be strong enough to provide adequate jobs for both younger and older workers. The feasibility of this strategy depended upon the presumption that technological advances and a younger work force would bring higher productivity. Also, it was presumed that the growing Social Security system and expanded memberships in pension systems would provide adequate retirement income, and that most workers would not live too long after retirement anyway.

In the 1950s and 1960s, when productivity grew rapidly and inflation rates were low for long periods, the retirement strategy seemed not only to be feasible, but, indeed, probably could be widened to include the retirement of many workers below the age of 65. Implemented by many compulsions, inducements, and social reinforcements, the strategy has worked. At this time, only about 16 percent of the men and 7 percent of the women over age 65 are still in the work force. Now also, only 68 percent of the men and 42 percent of the women in the ages 55–64 are still counted as members of the work force. Most workers applying for starting retirement benefits under Social Security are under age 65. In private pension systems, the average retirement age is about 62–63. In public systems, it is about 61–62 (61 in the federal government). Once they quit, most retirees do not work again in any substantial way.

Disastrous Success

The removal of masses of older workers from the work force is producing major unresolved problems for the nation. Productivity growth slowed badly in the 1970s and looks only marginally better more recently because the recession forced massive lay-offs of workers and closed down many marginal plants and operations. Record high inflation rates, only recently slowed by the recession, compelled large cost-of-living adjustments to be made in Social Security and some pension benefits, thereby drastically increasing the future outlays that these systems must make. Then too, the economy was not strengthened by the removal of older workers, and its performance is hardly easing the task of supporting their retirement. It has become wobbly and unpredictable, and its future is threatened by unprecedented competition from abroad. High levels of unemployment over long periods have reduced the payroll tax revenues needed to bolster the Social Security Retirement and Survivors Insurance Trust Fund reserves.

Finally, the underpinnings of the retirement strategy are being dissolved further by the unexpectedly large gains in the size and life expectancy of the older population. From John Kennedy's election in 1960 to the federal census of 1980, the number of people over age 55 jumped from 32 million to nearly 47.5 million. By the year 2000, the total will be nearly 59 million. By 2010, it will be 74 million and by 2020—91.7 million. The numbers of the oldest of these people are expanding the fastest. In 1960, the people over age 75 totaled 5.6 million. In 1980, they numbered 10 million—almost double. By 2000, they will have increased to 16.9 million, and by 2020 to 21.5 million.

In policy terms, these huge increases in the numbers of older people have another critical dimension. The periods when they will be getting retirement benefits are projected to get longer and longer. The current policy of encouraging early retirement takes on special significance as yet a further contributing factor in the lengthening of benefit payout periods. In 1900, a man who had reached age 60 could expect to live another 14.2 years. A woman of the same age could expect to live another 15 years. In 1983, men and women at age 60 could expect to live another 17.8 and 22.7 years, respectively. By the year 2020, these further life expectancy figures are projected to be 20 and 25.7 years, respectively. Some demographers think these official Census Bureau figures may be too conservative.

These developments already have foreshadowed the need of the nation to move away from the retirement strategy, but no clear line of action has evolved. Twice in less than five years, the integrity of the Social Security system came into serious question, compelling loans, benefit reductions for future retirees, and earlier than scheduled increases in the taxes workers and employers pay for Social Security. The political struggles that produced such remedial actions had the unfortunate result of enlarging the fears of many current younger workers about the vulnerabilities of the system in the likely event that the country experiences a return of higher inflation and unemployment rates. They sense that policy-makers will be compelled to make further benefit reductions and require even higher taxes on their earnings to meet the growing payout demands upon the system.

The prospect of younger workers that they will be paying more during their worklives for smaller benefits when they retire has major implications for their future support of the Social Security system. From its beginning, the system has depended upon maintaining a strong intergenerational consensus relating to its objectives and means of support. Most younger workers have understood that they are being taxed during their work years to support those already retired and that when they, in turn, reach retirement their retirement benefits will be financed, in part, from the payroll taxes paid by the younger workers of that day. The growing concern of younger workers that they will have paid more but not have adequate retirement benefits could weaken that consensus, and such a process could have disastrous consequences for Social Security, which is the foundation of retirement income planning for most older people today and in the future.

The great tragedy in these negative prospects is that they are based upon a widely held view among policy-makers that the further reduction of benefits (and perhaps even some limitation of eligibility for them) and increased taxation options for maintaining the integrity of the Social Security system are the only options that may still be open to them or their successors. Indeed, the president and the congress already have resorted to options that used to be considered as last ditch measures. In 1983, they eliminated the federal worker exemption and closed down the discretionary option of state and local governments and non-profit organizations to exempt their employees. They also instituted taxation of a portion of the benefits of current and future beneficiaries. Another option, namely, the idea of tapping a portion of the cigarette tax or other nonpayroll tax revenues seems not to have gained political momentum.

The Neglected Option

An option not seriously considered yet is the adoption of creative policies that would encourage and enable large numbers of able older people voluntarily to lengthen their worklives and thereby help to ease the retirement income demands facing the Social Security and many pension systems. The fact that this option has been neglected reflects how far older people have been written off as a productive resource in our society. We have yet to grasp the fact that their continued productivity and the delay in the time they start drawing retirement benefits could be of help in reducing the scale of our present and future retirement income predicament to more economically, socially, and politically manageable levels. Viewed within this context, some fundamental questions need to be explored.

- Why is this seemingly attractive option neglected at a time when the other options appear to be generationally divisive, economically counterproductive, and politically hazardous?
- Why is it that neither public nor private sector employers are making a serious effort to enhance the further employability and productivity of able older workers or to attract able retired people back into the work force?
- Why is it that only a few employers have issued policy statements encouraging their older workers to stay on, with full benefits and pension accruals intact?
- Why is it that public training programs allocate only tiny fractions of their resources for helping older people to stay productive?
- Why are employers, both public and private, still making wide use of early retirement to ease lay-off problems for younger workers?

One reason is that we have not perceived the rapid expansion of the older population and longer life as constructive developments. Instead of rejoicing about these phenomena as the result of major gains in public health, improved medical care and diets, and biomedical knowledge, we are, for the most part, preoccupied with their growing cost and problem aspects. Indeed, these cost and problem aspects are serious, but they should not continue to blind us to the central and most encouraging fact about the older population. It is of great policy significance to recognize that it is not monolithic. Rather, it is quite diverse in its make-up. In its oldest component we find millions of people who are survivors of the generations that experienced the Depression, long periods of unemployment or low earnings, racial and sex discrimination and other denials of educational and work opportunity. Most had jobs that involved heavy manual labor in factories or on farms. The women in this group mostly were housewives who had limited, if any, periods of paid employment, usually at low wages. Large numbers of this group are now disabled or retired early, either by choice or compulsion. Large numbers of them live in poverty or just above it. While they, too, are living longer, they tend to have small Social Security and health insurance benefits, and most have little, if any, income from pensions or savings. When asked, few of these people evidence interest in working again, and most assume that employers would not hire them anyway because of their age, lack of skills, and/or poor physical condition.

However, as the over 55 population has been evolving, over two-thirds of its members are in good to excellent health and physical condition—a situation that appears to be still improving. Moreover, many of this group are highly skilled, and, year by year, the workers passing their 55th birthdays have higher and higher levels of educational experience. Most have had fairly steady employment in their worklives, have earned middle to high level retirement income and other benefits, and have some savings and other assets. An exception within this category are large numbers of minority males and women from all groups. Here we find good to excellent physical condition but employment gaps, low earnings records, lesser skills, late employment starts, and poor to modest retirement benefit eligibilities.

New Interest in Longer Worklives

For the factors noted earlier, large numbers of people in the age 55 and over population are already retired or soon will be on account of the nation's pro-retirement policies. However, attitudes are beginning to shift for various reasons. Among the younger people in this age category, the lure of early retirement does not appear to be as strong as it used to be. Many regard themselves more fit and better educated than their parents were at the same ages. They have a new, non-biological view of increasing life expectancy. They simply expect more of life and resent the notion that they should have to quit work and drop to lower income levels because of outmoded, impersonal standards about how long worklives should be. They are not convinced that, just on account of age, they have somehow slipped to low levels of competence and productivity. We can expect that more of these people will decide to stay in place or at least not volunteer to retire prematurely.

Other workers, especially many middle-age and older women who started working or rejoined the work force late in their lives, are gaining a clearer view that the statistics of poverty are dominated by old, single women living alone. Many are well aware that on account of inflation older couples increasingly need two incomes just to get by. Moreover, they appreciate that very large numbers of women will wind up unmarried, separated, divorced, or widowed. Consequently, they are beginning to understand more clearly that longer worklives may be a simple necessity for them, both to gain necessary income and to establish qualifications for meaningful Social Security, pension, and health insurance benefits.

Still other older workers equate work with social worth. Whether or not they prefer to work, they feel that they should not be denied the opportunity to continue working either full-time or part-time. Finally, as more older workers perceive themselves as still sound in mind and body, they fear retirement and the idleness they assume it will bring. They may not necessarily wish to stay in the same job, but they would like to be engaged in some kind of meaningful work role considered useful in society and rewarding to themselves. People of such motives have always existed. Now, however, the current and projected numbers of them can be counted in the millions. Now, also, they cannot be forced to retire before age 70 for age reasons alone in most classes of employment. Against this backdrop of changing demographics and perceptions, two factors stand out in clearer relief as reasons why longer worklives remains a neglected option, namely, the issue of where the needed jobs would come from and the attitudes of policy-makers.

In our society a general presumption exists that if older people are encouraged to work longer, then the job and promotion prospects of younger workers would be impaired. Such a view assumes that the stock of jobs is somehow fixed in number. However, we have seen recently that the job situation, indeed, is a fluid and complicated affair. Even when the nation still has unemployment over 7 percent, the total number of people holding jobs has been climbing to historic highs. In other words, the competitive economy, even though uneven and stressed in many of its sectors and geographic areas, still seems to be creating more and more jobs. This picture may even look better next year, if the economy continues to recover at a sound pace. Also, more public and private sector employers are becoming painfully aware of the projected pension and health care insurance costs and Social Security payroll taxes needed to support early and longer living retirees and their surviving spouses. Some of these employers are beginning to calculate that it may well be less expensive to invest in retraining, working out interesting new assignments for, or keeping older employees on the active payroll longer than it would be to retire them early and support them longer in non-productive ways. Such workers could be kept productive in activities that strengthen the competitiveness of their companies, e.g., improved quality and cost control, new product development and evaluation, new market development, and better training of new workers or workers experiencing shifts in functions or work processes and equipment. Already, some employers recognize that when they hire and train able older workers they are finding them to be reliable and highly motivated and that they have lower turnover rates than younger workers.

Expanded Community Jobs Strategy

For further job expansion purposes, the nation could adopt a vigorous job expansion strategy that would put more people to work in expanded community services and problem solving efforts. Such a course would not be inflationary, because it would not create a scarcity of labor or, in the long run, add to budget deficits. It would draw in people from the ranks of the unemployed, the retired, or the otherwise about to be retired or unemployed. Specifically, throughout the nation, many critical needs of individuals and communities are poorly served or neglected. Leaving such needs unmet does not really help balance the budgets of the nation or its communities. On the contrary, problems poorly met or neglected usually come back into budgets at much higher figures over the long term and create heavier burdens for taxpayers. These neglected needs come back to the communities in the form of crime, drug addiction, unsafe streets and fear, failed educational opportunities, underemployment and unemployment, community tensions, lost property values, lower tax revenues, and lost business and other investments and opportunities. Thus, they hurt both on the revenue and cost sides of budgets.

Already, some employers understand well how they suffer from such conditions. They have a practice of loaning or detailing employees and providing supplies or other kinds of help to community service and problem-solving efforts. What is needed now is an expansion in both the number of employers who do this and the whole scale of such efforts. If more employers are helped to understand the alternatives to and possibilities from expanded loan and detail practices, more will participate. They would see that loans or details of able older workers would facilitate longer worklives and thereby help defer and reduce the costs of carrying them as retired, non-productive benefit receivers. Employers also would be helped, because the loaned or detailed workers would contribute to strengthening the quality of community life and make their communities better places for businesses to operate. Finally, loans and details of employees to such community efforts would likely strengthen employer-community relationships. Beyond contributing the services of their employees, employers could help by carrying the salaries/wages and benefit costs of loaned or detailed employees, or they might join with other employers, public agencies, local foundations, and churches in creating pools to support these costs.

Large numbers of people, older and younger alike, could be employed in highly cost effective ways of coping with unmet individual and community needs in such areas as home health care and services, daycare and respite services in connection with children and others, including older people who need supervised attention, exercise, recreation, and meals. Further major need areas include remedial education and tutoring programs, crime and drug prevention and law enforcement efforts, job finding, counseling, and training initiatives, and efforts to encourage stronger community participation by individuals and families and strengthening of cultural and recreational opportunities. In meeting these needs more adequately, the job holders would help people of all ages to improve their existence and, in many cases, their life prospects. To the extent that such workers accomplish these results, they would be helping to reduce or eliminate many types of budget costs that are a growing burden on taxpayers. They also would be helping to produce more effective and viable communities and thereby strengthen property and business values.

Lastly, and of critical importance to the longer worklives option, an expanded community jobs strategy would help remove the argument that this option is not feasible because not enough jobs exist to employ both the younger and older workers. An effective community jobs strategy would enable both younger and older workers, including the retired, the near-retired, and people interested in career changes or further careers to consider preparing for and taking jobs in this area. As additional ranges of these jobs become available, both the younger and older people would see that both groups have new opportunities. An older worker leaving a company to take one of these jobs may leave a vacancy for a younger worker to fill or vice versa. Also, of great importance, the new strategy would help assure both middle age and older people, who may be retired or thinking of retirement, that if they take the time to train or otherwise prepare for new or further careers, there really are stable and socially useful jobs out there for them to seek and hold. The lack of such a real prospect, or the widely based perception of it among these people has been a major difficulty in retraining programs and employment programs focused upon the older worker. Obviously, it has been a critical impediment to policy-makers in their consideration of the longer worklife option.

The short-term costs of a community jobs strategy may also be a problem for policy-makers. However, if large numbers of able older workers were encouraged and enabled to work longer, they would be reducing the time and probably the degree to which they are on the cost side of our budget ledgers. To the extent that they are employed in community problem-solving efforts, they not only would be contributing to reducing costly problems, but in the meantime, they would continue to pay income and Social Security taxes, and some would be contributing to pension and health care insurance programs. In time, effective implementation of the longer worklife option would bring social and economic savings and open up new opportunities for all age groups well beyond any of the costs and problems that it might generate.

The longer worklife option also would create whole new demands upon, and markets for educational and training institutions, because middle age and older workers would see that the pursuit of new or further careers in the additional work time they could have in front of them would require new skills, skill refreshment from time to time, and career and job counseling. An effective institutional response to these new demands would help strengthen these institutions as much as it would help the workers involved. They would demonstrate their capacities to respond to new demands and they would gain new insights on the teaching/learning process.

These constructive and hopeful possibilities, when contrasted with the negative, costly and unhopeful consequences of present pro-retirement policies, suggest strongly that the need for imaginative change is both compelling and urgent. Maintenance of the intergenerational consensus that has undergirded the Social Security system is critical to its future. Preserving it, however, will require that our society evolve new models and roles for older people. Increasingly, they have been stereotyped as an idle, benefit-receiving class, supported at greater and greater cost by younger workers. The longer worklife option can be the way to enable younger people to have daily evidence of large numbers of able older people who do not fit that stereotype. Instead, they would appear in voluntarily active roles, as productive workers, students preparing for further careers, contributors to the nation's tax resources, and community problem-solvers. In addition, such a different view of older people would open up for younger people a whole new prospect of what longer worklives could mean in their own career planning and help them to prepare to deal effectively with such prospects.

It seems clear that unless our public- and private-sector policy-makers act quickly and imaginatively to gain the financial and social dividends that can accrue from longer worklives, our country, by default, will find itself preoccupied over the next 30 years with the unnecessarily high costs of supporting its longer living and rapidly expanding older population, many of whose still able members have been idled by premature retirement.

Jarold A. Kieffer ∾

Creating Opportunity: Strategies for Increasing Economic Self-Sufficiency of Older Americans

The nation's income maintenance and retirement policies trap increasing numbers of older Americans who are able and willing to work. States will play a central role in shaping job-related strategies to move older people from maintenance programs to the revenue-producing side of the national economy.

Challenges of Today and Tomorrow

"We are paying a national fortune for not grappling with the problem of older workers," says Pat Choate, senior policy analyst at TRW, Inc. "Today's workers are tomorrow's workers," Choate notes, estimating that 75 percent of today's labor force will still be working at the end of the century. "A lot of people may not like what they see, but America is aging. Older people are the fastest growing cohort in our society. What that means is, in a tumultuous time of change, how well we harness the productivity of older workers will in large measure determine how well we rebuild this economy."

Yet increasingly, older persons are at the margin or excluded from the economy. Millions of older people depend on social welfare and retirement benefits as their primary source of income. And in spite of attempts to reduce the trend, says Hugh O'Neill, senior policy advisor to New York Governor Mario Cuomo, the incidence of older persons experiencing financial hardship is growing, their dependence on income maintenance programs and retirement benefits is increasing, and resulting costs to taxpayers, government, and business are rising.

For most older persons, according to O'Neill, the problem of dependency will not disappear with the restoration of a healthy economy, by expanding present social welfare programs, or by tinkering with the system. "To reduce dependence, social policies and the policy development process must be radically reconsidered and recast. Instead of attempting to reduce dependency by changing eligibility requirements, benefit formulas or administrative procedures, O'Neill advocates use of proven economic development policies to create opportunities for increased economic self-sufficiency of older persons. "The best alternative to public and third-party support of older persons who are able and wish to work," says O'Neill, "is a well-paid job."

Strategizing by States Underway

The Council of State Planning Agencies, membership organization of senior policy advisors to the nation's governors, recognizes that states must play a central role in this transition. To help in this process the council has embarked on a national demonstration, State Leadership for Older Worker Employment, to assist five states in extending the earning power of thousands of older Americans.

With the council's guidance, teams of gubernatorial policy aides from the five states will collaborate on strategies for their own states which create economic opportunity for persons 55 years and older. While it is difficult to predict how the participating states may shape their initiatives, the policies will, at a minimum, result in programs which: leverage existing resources to improve local arrangements for older worker employment; encourage more older people to work longer and postpone the time when they must rely on public support for income; and create meaningful roles to which older people, working or retired, can realistically aspire.

Supported by the Administration on Aging in the Office of Human Development Services, U.S. Department of Health and Human Services, the 13-month venture was begun in July 1984. The project was in response to a departmental objective to encourage social and economic development as a means of reducing dependency in certain populations, such as: the elderly, the developmentally disabled, disadvantaged youth, Native Americans and women with dependent children.

In consultation with AoA, the council is presently selecting states for direct participation from among those states whose governor or his/her senior policy advisor has expressed interest in the joint venture. Among those states who may participate are: Colorado, Ohio, Montana, Illinois, Pennsylvania, New Hampshire, Florida, Arizona, Nebraska and Utah.

Prior Research Helpful

The new project grows out of an extensive series of CSPA research and policy development efforts to create new economic opportunities for welfare recipients, the elderly, and those without jobs. The effort drew on the resources of its members, the Corporation for Enterprise Development, and the National Congress for Community Economic Development. The full results of these studies, to be used by participants in the State Leadership for Older Worker Employment project, are available as CSPA publications.

Barriers to Increased Self-Sufficiency of Older Persons

If states in the council's national demonstration project are to create new job opportunities for older persons, argues Jim Souby, the council's executive director, they must integrate the objective of economic self-sufficiency of older persons into their development programs. He indicates that project states will have to overcome two types of difficulties: first, the economic and social problems that lead to dependence; and, second, the institutional and political forces that have, inadvertently, precluded the successful use of economic development initiatives to help dependent persons who wish to work.

Solving the first set of problems requires changes in either the economic and social environments confronting older persons or in their ability to deal with that environment. The second obstacle that must be addressed, according to Souby, is the way social and economic policies are developed and managed.

The Trap of Dependence

Older people come to depend on social welfare and pensions as their primary source of income for many different reasons. Some do not want to work longer at a tiresome old job. Some want to retire. Some are victims of negative generalizations and myths about retirement, age, senility, and work capacity. Some are unable to find work in their communities. Some lack the basic skills needed to secure and hold jobs. Others lack the capital to start the small businesses of their dreams or to invest in retraining to begin new careers. Still others cannot land jobs after their employers close down, or do not want to relocate where jobs can be found.

Once they have left the workforce through layoff or retirement, older people face further obstacles to getting a job. The loss of social welfare benefits and perhaps eligibility that results from accepting a job attach a large financial risk to the already hazardous task of finding work. Special public training programs may stigmatize the participant in the eyes of potential employers or may impart nonmarketable skills. Moving to a more promising labor market may trigger loss of local or state supported program benefits. A successful state strategy must be versatile enough to deal with all of these obstacles.

Policy Failure

The reasons why states have been unable to mount effective campaigns to reduce dependency among the elderly vary. First, there is a long established tradition of treating dependency on public support among older persons exclusively with income transfers and categorical aid programs. These programs are seen as temporary expenditures needed to sustain the poor through a period of financial adversity. They are not intended to be "investments" to enhance the employability of the recipients. In part, this is because of unquestioning acceptance of the myth that older workers want to retire. In addition, the programs have been particularly vulnerable to drastic cuts during periods of tight state budgets, which have prevented long-term planning and management that program innovation requires.

Second, state governments separate the design and management of social programs and economic development programs. There is rarely any regular contact between the heads of the commerce and social service departments, or any interaction among policy people responsible for social programs and those responsible for economic development. Often, this separation is reinforced by the belief that the objectives of economic development are inimical to the objectives of social programs. The result is that neither side understands the goals or the programs of the other. This problem can only be overcome with the direct involvement of the governor and the executive staff in developing and implementing policies that span both agencies.

Third, the massive federal presence in the social welfare system poses a large obstacle to state initiative. Federal social programs have been developed in a haphazard fashion with inadequate attention paid to state and local administrative needs or to potentially harmful interactions among programs. Strong, centralized control by the federal government has discouraged state initiative.

States Are Pivotal

States cannot afford the economic costs of foregone output of millions of older Americans, the fiscal costs of income maintenance programs, and the social costs of long-term dependency of the elderly on public support. Moreover, they have the power and resources to link older worker employment to job creation strategies. They wield extensive taxing, regulatory, and spending powers that shape local patterns of economic development. They exercise broad fiscal and administrative responsibilities over social welfare and other income support programs for older persons. And state governments as employers can set model retirement, fringe-benefit, flexible work arrangement, and other personnel policies for other employers to follow.

The federal government cannot exercise direct leadership in creating economic opportunity for older persons. There are too few federal economic development programs to command the resources required to create widespread opportunities. Successful economic programs must be developed at the local level using the extensive powers of the state and targeted at the specific economic and social needs of older workers and employers. Local governments find it difficult to take the initiative because their role in most social welfare programs is primarily administrative. They do not exercise sufficient discretionary power over the design and implementation of these programs.

Although the state will be primarily responsible for developing the strategy, it must maintain strong contacts with federal and local agencies. There is some discretionary flexibility in federal programs that can be exploited effectively in developing a comprehensive strategy. Because they will be primarily responsible for administering the new policies and determining its success, state and local government should cooperate at all stages of development.

Massive state and federal spending is not needed to create economic opportunity for older Americans, according to Tom Berkshire, policy advisor to Illinois

Governor Jim Thompson and current president of the Council of State Planning Agencies. "In fact," he says, "successful programs can be mounted by states to save money." Berkshire suggests that it does require states to specify, carefully and precisely, the anticipated results of many different programs that have not been successfully coordinated before, and to deploy resources that are spread across many agencies, levels of government, and sectors of the economy. "These changes are not easy," he notes, "but they are not impossible."

Building an Effective Strategy

There is no simple solution to the problem of reducing dependency among older Americans and creating economic opportunity to extend the earning power of older workers. Years of disappointing demonstration projects and programs attest to how difficult it is in the absence of a carefully designed and comprehensive strategy. In formulating strategies, the demonstration project states will therefore consider certain basic principles.

First, the states will treat budget allocations—including those for social services—as investments that are part of a broader state strategy to strengthen its economy and to remove the barriers to economic development. Such a broad strategy requires an unprecedented level of cooperation between government agencies, education and training institutions, business, labor, and government—interest groups which usually pursue narrower goals that serve their own particular constituencies. Cooperation requires strategic thinking and reform of the policy making and bureaucratic apparatus.

Second, the states will design their economic policies to remove the barriers to effective public and private investments in ideas, enterprise, infrastructure, natural resources, and—most importantly—people. The most effective way to expand economic opportunity is to remove the impediments to growth and development, and to create an environment that rewards individual initiative.

Third, a broad-based strategy will be employed. The many reasons for economic dependency among the elderly and the complexity of the labor market barriers to them preclude a simple solution. Instead, states should develop a strategy that is build around five components:

- *Reducing the barriers to older worker labor market participation* created by the rules and regulations that govern social welfare programs, through using transfer payments to create private sector employment opportunities for recipients, job clubs, supported work, sheltered contracts, and other reinvestment mechanisms.
- *Improving the ability of older people to get jobs* by helping them finance training or retraining to acquire the knowledge and skills needed for employment. Among the policy options states would consider are tax-supported training, entrepreneurship training, incentive financing for

education and training institutions, and extending student loan programs for older worker non-degreed training and remedial education.

- *Making low income neighborhoods with elderly residents more attractive as places to conduct business and employ residents through investments in needed public works,* by building local capacity of neighborhood organizations to strengthen the business climate, zoning and land use regulation reform, licensing regulation reform, and enterprise zoning.
- *Encouraging entrepreneurship among older persons* through changes in state tax policy, venture capital formation, deregulation of financial institutions in risk taking, small business investment corporations.
- *Assuring the adequacy of local arrangements* for matching job opportunities and older workers through systematized networking, counseling, information dissemination, and job-seeking assistance.

Most of the above policy options to be considered by the demonstration states have been successfully applied by at least one state or city. However, that does not mean that they can be adopted elsewhere with equal success. The effectiveness of the states' strategies will depend not only on their design but the skill of their managers and the political and institutional conditions of each state.

Making It Happen

The changes necessary to reform the design and management of social and economic policy cannot be brought about overnight. In the project states, habits of many years must be overcome, "turf " issues must be disputed and resolved, and new institutional structures must be built. But the project states can take the national lead to move toward a more integrated approach to policy making without harming their economic development objectives, their ability to manage social policies, or their relationships with various constituencies.

The degree of the states' successes will depend, to a large extent, upon the personalities involved, upon the way in which the governor's office is organized, upon the particular governance structures of the relevant state agencies, and the relationships built with localities. But the chances will be improved by following some basic principles built into the demonstration project design.

First, and most important, initiative will come from the chief executive. Bringing together department heads, and their staffs, from agencies that have little experience of working together can only be done to good effect by the governor.

Second, department heads will be encouraged to negotiate the allocation of responsibilities for certain issues. There will be many areas of potential conflict: departments of labor and social services have overlapping jurisdictions for job placement and training. Departments of education and labor are both responsible for certain education and training programs. Economic development departments often offer targeted training programs that duplicate what can be offered by the labor and education departments. It is neither necessary nor desirable to eliminate all areas where responsibilities overlap—competition can sometimes spur greater efforts. The goal is to develop a *modus operandi* in all those areas where departments will potentially be in conflict—over budgets, staffing, and access to certain state resources.

Third, the objectives of the older worker policy will be made very explicit. The objectives define how success is measured and, therefore, how the different agencies will be monitored. Is the goal to create jobs? Place X hundred people from a particular social program in jobs? Reduce the caseload by Y percent? Provide services to at least Z percent of older persons able and willing to work? Nothing guarantees failure more assuredly than the failure to specify what is intended. Goals should be achievable and cumulative. The ideal is to start with modest interaction among the agencies on a specific issue and to increase the level of interaction slowly as initial goals are met.

Fourth, the governor's office staff will play a central role in the process. Agency staff are familiar with how programs are administered, and this expertise will have to be used. But their loyalty is to their department and they may be less able to see how the state's objectives may be better served by bringing in another agency or changing the department's procedures. Developing the expertise to be able to discuss details of program design and management with agency staff requires a great deal of effort, but it is essential if program areas are to be successfully integrated.

Project Design and Anticipated Results

Through the project, CSPA intends to help states redefine the state role, orchestrated by the governor, to support local action for increasing the economic self-sufficiency of older Americans.

Results of previous CSPA research show that this purpose can best be served by people from different states working together, assisted by CSPA and its resources, in a program of multi-state shared policy development. The assistance program, using the strategic planning academies, has been field tested and proven effective.

CSPA will work with the five participating states identified jointly by their governors, AoA and CSPA, from among those states who have expressed an interest and a willingness to cooperate in the development and implementation of state strategies to prompt local action—states that are ready to make major commitments in order to do it.

The selected states will redefine the role of state government and develop state strategies which advance older worker employment linked to job-creation strategies. To this end, each state will appoint an executive team, representing relevant state agencies (including the state unit on aging) whose activities affect economic opportunity for older citizens, and whose task it is to develop a recommended older worker employment strategy for the governor. Of these team members, three or four persons, headed by a person from the governor's own staff and including a person who can speak for local jurisdictions within the state, will be designated to participate directly in the multi-state policy-shaping work sessions. It will be the responsibility of this core academy team to provide direction and guidance to the larger state policy development team, and to lead the governor's action plan for putting the policy into place.

To facilitate this collaborative strategic planning, CSPA's role will be to: adapt the already-tested academy process to the more sharply-defined purpose of this effort; arrange for the services of resource persons as needed by the state teams; conduct three multi-state academy work sessions; provide—before, between, and after the academy work sessions—on-site and other assistance to the state teams as necessary; and document results of the project.

At the first of three academies, in early September 1984, state teams will identify the issues involved, define their policy objectives, and sketch out their strategy outline and direction. Between the first and second academies, state teams will utilize their internal state policy development processes to develop the strategy for their governors. Once the governor's final approval is obtained, the team will move into implementation planning.

The second academy, in December 1984, will focus on reviewing and refining the state policies as the governors have acted on them, and begin planning the specifics of putting these policies in place. Between the second and third academies, CSPA will draft the project report, reflecting the information available up to that point, and provide copies to all participants for review and comment at the third academy.

At the third academy, in May 1985, participants will: assess progress made by the state teams; further strengthen their implementation plans; refine the draft report on *State Leadership for Older Worker Employment*, and evaluate the utility of the project process and products.

This collaborative effort will result in at least five state initiatives which advance older worker employment; a cadre of state practitioners who have had the experience of developing cross-cutting state strategies to create economic opportunity for older people, and who can thus be helpful to other states; and a CSPA publication useful to state officials and others who want to capitalize on the lessons learned by the lead states. This publication will be disseminated nationally by the Council, with the active cooperation of governors and key officials in the lead states.

Gloria Whitman, Roger Vaughan, and Arthur Boyd ∼

Additional Sources

"Creating Opportunity: Strategies for Reducing Poverty Through Economic Development," by Hugh O'Neill, provides an overview of the barriers confronting dependent people, the elderly, poor, and disadvantaged, as they attempt to find and keep jobs, and a description of the types of programs that states can undertake to overcome these barriers. (Washington, D.C.: Council of State Planning Agencies, 1984).

"The Safety Net as Ladder," by Stephen Quick and Robert Friedman, discusses the ways in which income maintenance programs unintentionally create hurdles to job seeking and increase the financial risks for recipients, including older persons. The final chapter describes how states can reduce these hurdles and increase the incentives to recipients and employers for job seekers and job creation. (Washington, D.C.: Council of State Planning Agencies, 1984).

"The Human Services Industry," by Thomas Rodenbaugh, describes the rapidly growing for-profit and not-for-profit industry that has grown up around the provision of health and social services, and suggests ways that this growth can be harnessed to provide employment and entrepreneurial opportunities for older persons and other dependent populations. (Washington, D.C.: Council of State Planning Agencies, 1984).

"Escape from Dependency: A New Approach to Social Policy Development," by Susan E. Foster, summarizes how the states of Illinois, Ohio, Mississippi, New Hampshire, North Carolina and Utah used peer assistance to broaden the policy formulation process in each state, and design innovative programs to reduce dependence around gubernatorial priorities. Two of the states' initiatives dealt with increasing self-sufficiency of older citizens. (Washington, D.C.: Council of State Planning Agencies, 1984).

"Policy Development Academy: Guidebook," by Gloria Whitman and Arthur Boyd, describes how the same six states participated in the shared policy development process. It also analyzes what was learned that can be applied to development of related policy in human services. (Washington, D.C.: Council of State Planning Agencies, 1984).

The National Association of Older Worker Employment Services: Activities and Policies

The challenge of assisting older workers to obtain suitable employment opportunities is being met nation-wide by a variety of organizations. Over 60 of these organizations have combined to create the National Association of Older Worker Employment Services (NAOWES), a constituent unit of the National Council on the Aging. The NAOWES membership varies in organizational structure and funding source, but each agency carries out similar functions. This paper is

The National Council on the Aging (NCOA) is a private non-profit organization serving practitioners in the field of aging. NCOA maintains a broad focus, encompassing programs to support healthy active older people retain their involvement in the mainstream of American life to programs devoted to improving the long-term care delivery system for frail, vulnerable, and dependent older adults.

devoted to describing the work of NAOWES and its members, outlining the members' varied organizational sponsors and funding sources, detailing the functions carried out by each older worker employment service, and describing the activities, goals, and policies of the association.

Organizational Structure and Funding Sources

NAOWES members are composed of local, free standing, private, non-profit agencies with Boards of Directors, units of local or state government, and local chapters of national organizations. The private, nonprofit agencies themselves are of three types: (1) exclusively devoted to older worker employment issues, (2) devoted to aging issues, of which employment is one component, and (3) devoted to employment concerns, older workers forming only one group for which assistance is provided. The units of local and state government which are represented include aging departments, aging units of umbrella human services departments, women's bureaus, mental health departments, and rehabilitation agencies. The local chapters of national organizations are typified by organizations such as the Salvation Army and the American Association of Retired Persons (AARP).

The array of funding sources used by all these organizations is worth a study in itself because in many cases it drives the decision about the demographic characteristics of the population which will be served. As basic a decision as how old a person must be to be considered an older worker and, therefore, eligible for services is often dictated by funding source. The most common funding sources used by the employment services are federal funds (including the Job Training Partnership Act (JTPA), and Titles III and V of the Older Americans Act), state and local revenue, private charitable donations from organizations such as the United Way, and modest fees for service.

Local Older Worker Employment Service Functions

Irrespective of the organizational sponsor or funding sources, each local program carries out similar functions. These functions are all geared toward enabling older workers to enter/re-enter the labor force, and they focus on two major areas: (1) direct assistance to the job seeker, and (2) job development with local employers. These two major areas are broken down into specific components which are described in the following section.

Direct Assistance to Older Workers

Job Interest and Skill Assessment.   The first step in assisting anyone to find employment is identifying the type of employment for which the job seeker is suitable. Some agencies utilize extensive testing procedures including interest inventories, personality tests, and/or skill testing. Most agencies, however, use a much more casual approach. Job counseling staff review the applicant's work history and discuss the basic question of whether the applicant wishes to remain in the same field or seek a different type of employment. This phase of the program can take from as little as 30 minutes to as long as several weeks during which time the applicant decides future employment goals. Discussion then centers on the work, volunteer, or other experience which makes the applicant a suitable choice for a prospective employer. Especially when dealing with older workers, it is valuable to consider non-work experience at this stage of job counseling process. A retired foreign service employee knew only that he wanted to work again, but he had no idea of what kind of employment to seek. The job counselor elicited the fact that this individual had enjoyed picture framing as a hobby for years, and that for him a job in this field would be ideal. However, picture framing had always been a hobby and he never considered it as an avenue for employment. Three weeks later he was happily employed in a small art gallery.

Application or Resume Counseling. After identifying the appropriate employment field, the work shifts to ensuring that the older worker knows how to describe the relevant experience on a job application or resume. After 30–40 years of adult life, each applicant has extensive experience and older workers often find it difficult to distill their experience into a concise format. Most job counselors for older workers can recall at least one older job seeker whose resume exceeded ten pages. Job seekers always seem to feel that they owe the prospective employer their entire work history. It is never easy to assist the job seeker in distilling only the relevant and most important parts of the resume. Frequently job applicants are counseled to prepare two or more different resumes if their experience covers very different fields.

Job Seeking Skills Counseling. Job seekers initially arrive at the employment service program with the expectations that they will describe their interests and experience to the job counselor and that then the responsibility is the job counselor's to get them the job. Most older workers are also very pessimistic about the likelihood of their finding a job. One older worker's comments are typical. She said to the job counselor, "I came to you because who is going to hire an old lady like me,"—and she was only 59. While employment services provide numerous referrals to specific vacancies, job counselors begin by pointing out that only the job seeker can find and get the right job. Most older workers have stayed with the same employer for their entire work life. They are not familiar with the frequent job, and even career, changing pattern which has become so common during the last 20 years. Their job hunting experience is 30 or 40 years old. Helping an older worker find a job is a combination of providing concrete advice and esteem building.

Job counselors assist job seekers to develop a personalized job hunting strategy. If the goal is to find a job within walking distance of home, the technique may be to inventory all the employment possibilities within the appropriate radius, identify the types of jobs which are most appealing, and then visit those specific employers. If the goal is to find a job related to the former career, a workable technique may include notifying former colleagues that the job applicant is seeking employment. Although both techniques can lead to success, the job counselor may encounter initial resistance to these suggestions. In the first example, applicants may feel that it is silly to talk with an employer when there is no actual job vacancy, not realizing that for jobs with a moderate turnover that is the very time to apply. In the second example, many older job seekers initially feel that it is not right to ask "favors" of former colleagues, although they recognize that employed people are the ones who know where the job vacancies are located. Other individualized strategies include studying local labor market reference material found in many libraries or local economic development offices. The appropriate individual strategy depends on the job seeker's educational and employment background, level of self-confidence, and the type of job sought.

Many older worker employment services have organized "job clubs." Job clubs are groupings of job seekers who come together on a regular basis in order to offer each other mutual support and share information. Under the leadership of a job counselor, the older workers assess their interests and skills, learn job hunting skills, role play job interviews, investigate the local labor market, contact employers to develop job leads, and bring information back to the group. This technique has been successful because of the mutual support the job club members offer each other during a stressful period.

Referral to Jobs and Follow-up.   All older worker employment services are contacted by local employers who list specific job vacancies. The job counselors review their file of registered applicants and refer older workers who are interested in and have the necessary qualifications for the type of job offered. Before making the referral, the job counselors also check items such as transportation and/or parking availability, work schedule, salary, and benefits. At this point, job counselors can also "sell" their client to the employer, by pointing out the strengths that a particular applicant will bring to the job. Because the counselors know the applicants well, the counselors often suggest minor modifications in the job requirements that will improve the fit between employer and employee.

After the interview between employer and applicant, the job counselor follows up with both parties. In addition to finding out whether the applicant got the job, the purpose of follow-up is to get more information about the applicant's interviewing skills and the actual working conditions offered by the employer. When an applicant performs badly during an interview, the employer is usually willing to share that information with the job counselor who can pass along the information in a supportive manner to the job applicant. Thus, the interview, although not resulting in a placement, can be used as an effective learning device. Feedback from the applicant provides general information about the workplace and more details about the specific job. This information is used to refine decisions about appropriate future referrals.

Job Development and Employer Awareness

Job development activity has two distinct purposes: identifying specific job vacancies for the service's clients, and, more broadly, making employers aware of the advantages of hiring older workers. These two purposes are generally carried out in tandem. With varying degrees of sophistication all older worker employment services seek to dispel the myths that persist about older workers. The focus is simply a marketing strategy—older workers are a valuable resource, and are "sold" as such. Recent research has demonstrated that older workers have lower absenteeism and tardiness rates, fewer workplace accidents, equal levels of productivity and interest in training opportunities as younger workers. However, most employers still are not aware of these facts, and believe that older people are, first of all, not really interested in working, and that when interested, make less desirable employees.

Older worker employment services devote considerable efforts, employing a variety of strategies, to marketing older workers. Methods include speaking with employers at meetings of organizations such as the Chamber of Commerce, paying individual calls on people who make hiring decisions, and working with local economic development offices and small business associations. As part of the presentation, employers are told about the work of the local employment service and its frequent ability to refer qualified older workers for specific vacancies. Older worker employment service staff take care never to oversell their product, the older worker, and never oversell their own ability to function as a referral source. Just as older workers, themselves, must be told that they should not totally rely on the job counselor to find a job, employers are told that there will be times when no suitable job applicants will be available through the older worker employment service. Each program anticipates and works to avoid any employer reaction that they have been sold something that does not exist, that is, older people who are looking for work. It remains a careful balancing act to locate job vacancies for the applicants who are registered at any given time.

NAOWES Network

Older worker employment issues are only now beginning to receive some of the national attention they deserve. NAOWES was founded in 1979; it was created so that small, isolated agencies could pool information, share experiences, and learn from each other. The agency representatives who came together in 1979 felt as though each had invented the wheel. There was nothing in writing about developing and administering an employment service for older workers. Almost no agency was within 50 miles of a similar organization. Each agency had simply begun its program in the best way it could. Everyone felt all alone, and everyone was delighted to find other practitioners with whom they could share experiences.

All of NAOWES' work is centered around improving employment opportunities for older workers and improving the capacity of the member organizations to serve their constituents. Improving organizational capacity is still accomplished by sharing the innovations of the past year. At the 1984 annual meeting, one member from Memphis described her successful efforts in job creation. Memphis, like many other localities, has a significant shortage of infant care centers. Using federally funded job slots, free space, and a one-year local start-up grant, the director of the Memphis older worker employment service opened "Gramma's," an infant day care program employing low-income older workers. The fees were set at the market rate, and as the income from the parents grew, this funding source began to be used to pay employee salaries. This transition in employee funding source also met one of the goals of the Title V program, placing enrolees in private sector jobs. After this creative program had been described, several other NAOWES members decided to find out whether a similar program would be useful in their own communities.

A Chicago project, Operation ABLE, has specialized in marketing older workers. This project has concentrated on educating employers about the generally high quality of the mature worker. Operation ABLE put together a sophisticated slide and tape show, along with a "how to" kit which they are marketing to other older worker employment services.

Within the past several years, there have been a few innovations among private sector companies. One insurance company modified its retirement policy and now allows its own annuitants to return on a part-time basis without a reduction in the annuity. The advantage to the company is the ability to hire already trained personnel for peak period work. One high-tech firm went into business hiring only workers age 55 or over. The firm conducted its recruitment campaign through the newspaper classified sections in several large cities. The ad promised six weeks of computer training for applicants who passed a math ability test. The flood of older worker respondents demonstrated that, contrary to general belief, large numbers of older workers are eager for training in new fields.

It is at the NAOWES annual meeting and through the NAOWES quarterly newsletter that practitioners learn what is going on in the older worker employment field. Experienced staff share effective innovations and provide training and stimulus to practitioners who are new to the field. New programs for older workers are being started throughout the country and the new staff is starved for "how-to" information.

National Policies

NAOWES members recognize that the best job they could do would be to put themselves out of business. The change that would have to occur before that would be possible would be a major shift in public attitude toward older worker employment. The Social Security retirement test still forces beneficiaries age 65–69 who earn over $6,960 to return $1.00 to the social security system for every $2.00 earned. Because earnings are subject to federal and state income taxes as well as the FICA (social security) tax itself, these earnings are taxed at a rate well over 50 percent. The vast majority of social security recipients pay no taxes on their benefits, so there is little financial gain from employment for these workers. There is no comparable tax on Social Security beneficiaries whose income comes from any other source.

Older workers are also particularly interested in part-time employment. Part-time workers are still regarded as somehow less professional and less committed to their jobs than full-time workers. This attitude persists in the face of evidence that employees who work part-time schedules are more productive, have lower rates of absenteeism, tardiness, and turnover, and exhibit fewer signs of burn-out than full-time workers.

Among the current proposals of ways to deal with the Medicare financing problems, is a proposal to make age 67 the age for Medicare eligibility. The effect of that proposal would be to persuade employees with employer-provided health insurance benefits to remain in the workforce.

NAOWES has developed a public policy statement which promotes older worker employment issues. The statement follows:

It is the guiding principle of the National Association of Older Worker Employment Services (NAOWES) that people should have the right to be included in the nation's work force regardless of age. Chronological age is not an appropriate criterion for any employment decision. The appropriate criteria for employment selection, retention, promotion, retraining are based on the individual's knowledge, skills and abilities. Furthermore, NAOWES believes that maintaining older workers in the work place does not necessarily "freeze out" younger workers; an expanding economy requires the participation of all who desire to do so.

NAOWES recognizes and respects the desire of many Americans to retire at relatively early ages but also recognizes the emotional, health, social and economic importance of work for many middle-aged and older persons. We, therefore, recommend that the following actions be undertaken by both the public and private sectors to provide continued employment or easy and equal access to the job market for all who are willing and able to work, regardless of age:

- Elimination of all mandatory retirement legislation.
- Elimination of age-related restrictions on access to training, retraining and apprenticeships.
- Elimination of provisions in public and private pension plans that discourage working.
- Recognition of part-time employment as equally valid as full-time employment by ending legislative and regulatory impediments to part-time work, including:

    elimination of full-time requirement for eligibility for unemployment benefits;

provision of prorated benefits for part-time employees consonant with benefits paid to full-time employees.

- Vigorous enforcement of the Age Discrimination in Employment Act.
- Continuation of the Older Americans Act Title V program as an employment, not social services, program.
- Support for private and public sector organizations that work to dispel myths about older workers.
- Provision of incentives to employers for hiring older workers.

Attention should also be addressed to the following:

- Continuation of worker benefits to older workers who have fulfilled company established criteria for benefit eligibility (e.g., TEFRA, Tax Equity and Fiscal Responsibility Act, negatively impacts on the older worker). Employers have to pay a larger percentage of health care costs for older employees due to higher actuarial rates. In short, they are less likely to employ, or continue employing older workers because of the employer's added expense of health care coverage.
- Using Job Training Partnership Act (JTPA) Title II-A funds to provide employment and training services for older individuals above and beyond those already provided by other sections of the act and available in communities, e.g., 3 percent monies for older workers.
- JTPA state and local Private Industry Councils (PICs) should have committees on aging mandated to recommend policy and monitor programs.
- There should be more uniform state divorce laws. In the present system, women are usually denied a share in any part of a pension plan, which negatively impacts on the older woman, who often has worked but is not covered by any pension except the husband's.
- Spouses should have equal access to the marital partner's pension plan. Access could be dependent on the length of marriage and the length of time in the pension plan. The ratio would be dependent on the years marriage and pension coincide. Perhaps a minimum number of years of marriage could be maintained, such as 10-plus.

Terri Lynch, Director,
Arlington County (Virginia) Area Agency on Aging ∾

Senior Careerists: Strategies for Using Their Skills

"She's too old to send to training."
"He's retired on the job."
"Poor Henry, that's as far as he'll go—he's peaked out."
"It's too bad for John but, as they say, you can't teach an older dog new tricks!"
"I didn't get the promotion. After all I've done for this place!"

Sound familiar? Unfortunately, too many of us too often hear similar statements. This article will share some of the concerns and issues related to an aging work force and what we in Colorado state government are doing about the people who are part of it.

The discussion will focus on the career problems of the currently employed senior careerist (aged 50–64) and what can be done effectively to utilize and retain these employees.

Part of the "problems" we encounter in managing today's changing work force result from outdated ways of thinking. In the areas of mandatory retirement, our slavish insistence on a 40-hour work week for all employees, and our boxed-in lives, we insist on an artificial world. When older employees question this model, we label them "problems." The folly of mandatory retirement is discussed elsewhere in this series and work hours will be discussed later in this article. For now, consider Richard Bolles' challenge to us as stated in *The Three Boxes of Life*. Bolles writes that we have placed unnecessary stress and limitations on ourselves by compartmentalizing our lives in three boxes: education (for the first 20 years), work (for the following 40 years), and leisure (for the years after work). In order to live effectively, we need to break down the boxes and combine education in our working years and work in the years typically designated for leisure and education. It makes a lot of sense, doesn't it? The problem is, we don't do it. And when employees ask for opportunities that would allow them to get out of the boxes, we again label them as "problems."

Other "problems" we encounter are based on ignorance about the aging process and the capabilities of older people. Although many Americans believe that most old people live in institutions, the fact is a little less than 4 percent of all persons over age 65 are institutionalized. Still another common belief is that after age 65, the human body steadily deteriorates. Actual studies detect no deterioration in physical condition because of age. Results suggest that any observable decline is due to boredom, inertia, and the awareness that infirm behavior is expected.

Of all the myths that color our view of older workers, those concerning mental abilities and learning capacity are probably the most dangerous to the worker. Many people accept the belief that as we age our mental capacities diminish. But studies tell us that there is very little mental decline. Speed of response may decline slightly but there is no change in intelligence and little in memory. Why is it, then, that many older people seem frightened to learn a new skill? Why do so many seem to fit that stereotype so well? Research findings indicate that these behaviors result from the negative expectations we may have of older people.

In addition to general attitudes, we need to consider those circumstances that affect the work environment in which workers perform. Briefly, there are a number of changes and conditions that have an impact on career management today.

- There is a growing need for knowledge workers. Occupations requiring skills and knowledge are increasing and physically demanding or hazardous jobs are decreasing. This shift increases the likelihood of older workers remaining in the workforce.

- Organizational growth is slowing or, in some cases, at a standstill. With organizational structures becoming flatter and trimmer, the race up the pyramid to fill decreasing numbers of higher-level positions is more competitive than in the past.

- Equal employment opportunity pressures will not only focus on hiring practices affecting underutilized groups but will include the developmental and advancement needs of these groups. The pressure to develop and promote group members comes at a time when promotional opportunities are limited and might be used as a reason to retire older employees.

- If changes in retirement policies and legislation do come about, competition for desirable jobs will be intense.

- The composition of the workforce has changed to include large numbers of mature workers. The first contingent of well-educated "baby-boomers" has reached midcareer. One of the most significant characteristics of these midcareerists is their attitude of *entitlement*— their belief that they are owed the very best and on their terms. The high aspirations of the "baby-boomers" will conflict with the needs of other segments of the population.

- Two-career families are prevalent and values they hold reflect different views from the traditional attitudes toward geographical mobility. With two-income and two-career roles to juggle, this group often holds different views on how much time and energy they are willing to devote to following organizational rules or policies.

- Over the years there has been a change in employee's attitudes toward loyalty to the organization. Employee level of commitment has shifted to devotion to the craft rather than to the organization. Thus, an employee may view himself or herself as a programmer rather than a member of X organization. Because of this self-image, employees are more willing to change employers if they perceive thwarted career ambitions.

- Increasing numbers of employees are considering personal values when making career decisions. A greater emphasis is placed on career development, freedom, leisure time, and quality of work life issues.

In Colorado state government, as we deal with midcareerists (those about 35–49 years old) and senior careerists (employees approximately age 50 and over), we realize that some special needs will have to be met. Mid-life transition presents many challenges, and we find that many senior careerists have not reached closure on these issues. Consequently, a number of life tasks associated with "mid-life transition" need attention from senior careerists. In addition to this "unfinished business," senior careerists need to resolve developmental issues associated with their age group, some of which are related to and aggravated by the present changes and conditions of the work force.

Based on adult development research and our experience, we note the following issues facing senior careerists:

- From midcareer to senior career, employees take more responsibility for the direction of their careers, especially in light of decreasing promotional opportunities.
- Interpersonal relationships at all levels present challenges in communication and identification of roles.
- Problems stemming from overspecialization, burnout, and skewed work/life activities need attention to insure maximum productivity.

The challenges facing managers of the present workforce are not so much caused by an "aging workforce" as much as they are caused by the combination of large numbers of senior careerists facing volatile career issues at the same time organizations are dealing with difficult external and internal conditions often in conflict with each other.

As managers how can we translate these findings to our immediate work situations? How can we better utilize the skills of older workers aged 55 and up currently in the workforce? With the present Social Security provisions, attitudes toward retirement, current social conditions, current disincentives to remain in the workforce, what can we do to utilize better the senior careerist in the workforce?

Based on the preceding information, we have restructured the career planning workshops which are open to all employees who wish to attend. The workshops are based on a self-directed approach to career planning which recognizes that employees have a responsibility and a desire to plan their careers. Each workshop is composed of four, two-hour group sessions, individual counselings, and written exercises completed outside of the group sessions. Because the content and exercises of the workshop closely link with human development, specific tasks at life stages are stressed. Therefore, all participants may use a core of exercises, but supplementary materials, additional readings, and individual career counseling sessions focus on the tasks unique to specific life stages.

Career counseling and planning for senior careerists assists them in identifying and resolving these issues especially pertinent to them:

- Realization of the aging process.
- Consequences of past actions.
- Analyzing perceptions and expectations.
- Resolving problems in relationships.
- Identifying and dealing with feelings.
- Defining career goals.

Senior careerists are very aware of the aging process. Many of the messages they hear from our youth-oriented society are negative. In part, these negative messages can be combated by presenting factual information about aging. In career planning and the preretirement planning workshops we discuss disincentives to remaining in the workforce: Social Security eligibility test and retirement delay penalties, pension rules and policies, and age discrimination. Our presentations make no effort to advocate that all workers should continue working nor do we suggest that failure to disengage oneself from working is a personal denial of the aging process. We do not believe that "disengagement" is an appropriate life task for all workers. It is irrational to encourage or compel all employees to retire at ages 60–65.

In addition to realizing that the time remaining is not unlimited, senior careerists realize that the present is the result of decisions and choices made in the past. As with most life/work transitions being experienced by the older worker, self-image and sense of achievement color how transitions are handled. If the senior employee has a sense of successful achievement and a positive sense of self, consequences of past choices are accepted more readily. In general, this employee has accepted ownership of his/her decisions and their consequences. However, if the senior careerist possesses low self-esteem and a negative self-image, past accomplishments may be seen in terms of failure. Closure on issues typically accomplished at midcareer may still need to be resolved. Often these employees project their personal lack of achievement, perceived or real, onto the organization, superiors, or family members. Written workshop exercises particularly geared to clarifying values, listing accomplishments up to this point in life, reevaluating work priorities and feedback on skills and abilities have proved helpful in dealing with these problems.

Although senior participants enter the career planning workshop eager to plan their careers, set goals, and determine timetables for the achievement of these goals, perceptions of "work" often impede accomplishment. For employees who remember Depression days, holding a job is of great importance. How "career" is defined is also important. Faced with changes in their personal lives and in their work, all too often senior careerists adopt an "only 15 more years to retirement" attitude. They view their careers as plateauing or descending, their work stagnant, their competence threatened, their futures without hope. Personal growth and career growth become inextricably bound, often resulting in hopelessness, overemphasis on career goals to the exclusion of personal priorities, and the perception that no matter how dreary, the only hope of fulfilling aspirations comes through career opportunities. Added to these perceptions is the attitude that no matter how outrageous and unrealistic their career plans may be, people close to them will support the plans.

Exploration of these perceptions is one of the most difficult challenges in counseling senior careerists. In the workshop two major means of addressing these areas are reality feedback and discussion of the concept of career.

When asked what a career is, many senior careerists respond, "my life," "a series of jobs over the years," and "work I get paid for." We discuss E. C. Hughes' definitions of objective and subjective careers. In thinking about the *objective career* as a series of positions people hold throughout time, senior careerists trace their lives in terms of position titles and organizational affiliations. But charting the *subjective career* is more difficult because they have rarely viewed their careers as a series of experiences, hopes, satisfactions, and periods of growth. Exploring the subjective career through timelines and other exercises enables them to see accomplishments, fulfillments, and expectations that have been met. Viewing careers this way allows participants to see the possibilities for challenge and growth in the subjective career, while these opportunities may be limited in the objective career.

From this retrospective and two-dimensional look at their careers, workshop participants plan balanced career goals for the next 12 months. Topics that are emphasized are time management; balancing leisure, family, and work requirements; developing support systems; and monitoring stress and burnout. Each participant shares his/her immediate (next 12 months) goals with another workshop participant. Reality testing of goals and peer feedback is essential for senior careerists. At this point in their lives, senior careerists have rich life experiences which they bring to such a critiquing session. They are able to see another's burnout, another's fear of change, and another's inability to set realistic goals. But, it is difficult for senior careerists to accept their own limitations and see their own weaknesses. Peer feedback and reality testing assist in performing this function.

Another special problem senior careerists experience is difficulty in their relationships with others. For senior careerists, relationships become extremely complex. With the American belief that upward movement is the only sign of growth at the same time that the top of the organizational pyramid is narrowing, senior careerists see themselves engaged in a last-chance effort to "go for it." At the same time they feel prodded by younger midcareerists to "get out of the way and make room for others." Tense and fierce competition arises among senior careerists. Instead of the cooperation needed for organizational productivity, feelings of envy, rivalry, resentment, and isolation are likely to occur among peers. This environment increases the sense of isolation and doubts about self-competence that many senior careerists already have. With subordinates and younger workers, senior careerists may again feel their competence threatened and their value to the organization called into question. Again, this is why a thoughtful process of career planning coupled with the interventions mentioned below is so needed.

In addition to career planning workshops, there are a number of interventions managers can use which address the needs of senior careerists and retirees who may wish to reenter the workforce.

1. *Develop career counseling services.* Focus on two points when providing these services for senior careerists.

- Stress the transferability of skills. Skills fall in three categories: work content, functional, and adaptive/personal management. A work content skill may involve operating equipment or interpreting requests according to rules unique to the organization. As such, work content skills are job specific and have low transferability. But senior careerists possess a host of other skills. Examples of functional skills include decision-making, planning, and interpersonal communication. Adaptive skills are more personalized and include such tasks as time management, building a healthy self-image, and coping with stress. Skills in the last two categories transfer readily to a variety of environments and occupations. Acknowledging and assessing the degree of strength to which these skills are possessed will enable senior careerists to see that options and work alternatives are available to them.
- Train in subject areas where career development barriers are most significant. These areas include: recognizing conflicting roles; assessing personal career success; decision-making techniques; developing alternative strategies; developing support systems and networks; realistic goal setting, and accepting limitations while emphasizing strengths.

In addition, provide career counseling training to managers and supervisors to equip them to help senior careerists. In turn, senior workers will be able to counsel subordinates. The organization is able to tap, formally and informally, the wealth of knowledge possessed by senior staff and allow them an opportunity for self-affirmation.

2. *Offer experience-based training opportunities.* Job enrichment, training, and revitalization will be provided to senior careerists as well as to younger workers. Experience-based training involves learning through doing. Two types of experienced-based training particularly appropriate are:
   - *On-the-job training (OJT).* An extensively used technique, OJT can be used to make maximum use of a senior careerist's knowledge and coaching skills. Under the tutelage of an experienced senior careerist, younger workers can learn work content skills as well as the culture of the organization. Because it is a highly individualized method of training, it is an excellent method of training experienced senior workers also. OJT provides the personalized, self-paced, supportive and actively participative environment in which older workers learn best.
   - *Mentoring.* Using this method, an organization not only prepares individuals for new responsibilities but gives senior careerists an opportunity to affirm their competence and worth. As mentioned earlier, one of the critical life tasks senior careerists have to accomplish (if not done

earlier) is accepting the end of upward mobility and yet creatively engaging their energies in activities which benefit themselves and the organization. Mentoring allows the passing on of wisdom, coaching younger workers in the behaviors and skills that will aid their career development, and the sharing of unique expertise.

3. *Offer lateral moves.* Moves involving a change in responsibilities and functions can also provide a growth experience although not changing pay or status in the organization. In the past, such movement was a way to "shuffle" unwanted employees. Now, these moves are being handled more carefully. The method offers new challenges in a work environment where upward mobility is not possible. It also provides the senior careerist an opportunity to transfer skills to a new area and avoid becoming stagnant. Lateral movement benefits both employee and organization with minimum disruption.

4. *Job Redesign.* For many years, job enrichment was talked about but not used to full advantage. Senior careerists have enough pressure so, when designing jobs, care should be taken not to enlarge them but to enrich them. Job enrichment is particularly apt for senior careerists because it provides challenge at a time when careers may be plateauing. It also provides recognition of strengths and skills when self-doubt and questions of competence may arise, and offers a developmental opportunity on the current job. This intervention does not require using the same skills more often (job enlargement) but involves expanding the scope and learning potential of the job. Studies show that adults reach their intellectual peak at about age 60 and experience only slight decline thereafter. Job enrichment, especially for knowledge workers, is one of the most effective means of capitalizing on this period of peak performance.

5. *Education and Training.* Often, experience-based training is not cost-effective nor appropriate. Senior careerists should not be denied classroom training because of the misconception that they are a poor return on investment. Because of their low turnover rates, they will remain with the organization longer after training.

6. *Alternative Work Schedules.* Numerous studies, national surveys, and testimony before Congress affirm that senior careerists and many retirees want to continue working in some capacity after age 65. One stumbling block seems to be inflexible work schedules. Shorter work weeks, work at home, job-sharing, and permanent part-time agreements are among the variety of alternatives which would allow more creative management of the workforce.

There are a number of other changes we can make that will enable us to retain older workers and ensure maximum use of their skills. Some involve adapting existing mechanisms and programs. Some involve policy changes. Some of the areas needing our attention are:

- Classification systems which are not structured to promote lateral entry into classified positions at middle and upper career levels. This makes it difficult to hire into the system inexperienced older workers whose skills fit, but for whom no entry mechanism exists. This also acts as a barrier for older workers wishing to change career fields.
- Civil service examinations which emphasize abstract knowledge and therefore favor younger job applicants with more recent academic experience.
- Retirement systems which provide inducements for employees to leave and penalties for continued service.
- Examination procedures which do not allow credit for experience to substitute for college degree requirements.

By making actions to change these systems and policies part of our future agenda, we will alleviate many of the tensions and inefficiencies we experience today. Additionally, we will recognize the riches of a vast, untapped resource—the competencies of the older worker.

Barbara W. Plimpton, Colorado State Department of Personnel ∿

Index